To our families

Lisa, Justin, Caitlin, Benjamin, William, and Isaiah Archer
Isabel, Chris, and Daniel Gibbins
Robin, Kyle, and Joel Knopff
Mary, Matthew, Michael, and Meredith Pal

CONTENTS

LIST OF FIGURES

LIST OF TABLES

LIST OF DOSSIERS

PREFACE

The central public questions confronting Canadians as the second edition of *Parameters of Power* goes to press have not changed much since the first edition was published in 1995—and many of these questions are institutional in nature. From the Meech Lake to the Charlettown accords, from the 1995 Quebec independence referendum to the 1998 Quebec election, from the Calgary declaration of 1997 to the so-called "social union" initiatives of late 1998, the "national unity" question has dominated the political agenda. The question has been how to address not only the nationalist demands of Quebeckers but also the regionalist demands of other parts of the country, especially the West. The nationalist and regionalist strands in Canadian politics—sometimes overlapping, often pulling against each other—have tied a constitutional Gordian knot that we have not yet managed to cut or untangle. This is institutional politics of the highest and most difficult kind.

Reflecting Canada's constitutional impasse, the federal party system continues in the fragmented pattern established in the 1993 election. Five long-term constituencies in Canadian federal politics—Liberals, Tories, social democrats (NDP), right-wing western populists, and Quebec nationalists—now all have their own party vehicles in the House of Commons, each with its own distinct regional power base. The last two of these constituencies, western populists and Quebec nationalists, have in the past moved in and out of the Liberal and Conservative parties, and may do so again. In any case, efforts are currently underway to establish some kind of "united alternative" capable of unseating the Liberal government. Here, too, we find institutional politics at the top of the public agenda.

Underlying the obviously institutional politics of party building is the deeper institutional influence of the electoral system. Canada's electoral system makes it easier to build regional rather than national parties. It thus contributes to the problem and makes it more difficult to solve. Accordingly, electoral reform is a perennial, if muted, issue on Canada's overflowing agenda of institutional politics. (The issue is "muted" because the party in power, which has by definition benefited from the existing electoral system, is naturally loathe to change it.)

The examples could be multiplied—and they will be in the rest of the book—but for now the point is clear enough. We remain as convinced as when we originally conceived this book that Canadian politics is as much *about* institutions as it is channeled and shaped *by* them. Then as now, an educated citizen, one who wishes to participate meaningfully in Canadian public affairs, must have some understanding of the country's political institutions, its "parameters of power." We hope this book contributes to that understanding.

Parameters of Power, second edition, is a collegial work, involving the collaboration of four authors. But the colleagueship supporting the book extends well beyond the four of us. Any textbook builds upon—perhaps "scavenges" would be the better word—the work of countless scholars. The Canadian political science community is a vibrant one, and its collective works make possible textbooks such as this. Our bibliographic references cannot do justice to the extent of our debt.

Colleagues in the Department of Political Science at the University of Calgary have had a special influence on our work. One of us no longer inhabits the department, but all of us are stimulated and influenced by the ongoing conversation about Canadian politics conducted, both publicly and privately, by University of Calgary political scientists. In this respect, Barry Cooper, Tom Flanagan, Ted Morton, Anthony Perl, Anthony Sayers, and Lisa Young deserve special mention, though we are also grateful to the department as a whole for providing a remarkable environment for engaged and productive scholarship. Tom Flanagan's work with and on the Reform Party, and his and Stephen Harper's thinking about the party system more generally, were particularly valuable as we substantially revised our discussion of political parties in Chapter 10.

We are similarly grateful to colleagues elsewhere who have used the book and have taken the trouble to suggest improvements. Special thanks are owed to the following for reviewing this second edition: Chaldeans Mensah, Grant MacEwan Community College; Judith Oakes, Wilfrid Laurier University; Heather MacIvor, University of Windsor; Marlene Hancock, Douglas College; Michael Lusztig, University of Western Ontario; Raymond Bazowski, York University; Jeffery L. Braun-Jackson, Memorial University of Newfoundland; Donald E. Blake, University of British Columbia; Brenda O'Neill, University of Manitoba; and Ian Brodie, University of Western Ontario. We should mention that Brodie team-taught the first edition of the book with two of the authors while he was a doctoral student at the University of Calgary, and has influenced our thinking in many ways over the years.

Undergraduate students, both past and present, have also played a significant role in the evolution of the book. Undergraduates are, of course, the book's primary audience, and our own students have not been shy in bringing to our attention problems, errors, and infelicities in the first edition. One undergraduate, Chris O'Neill, was a valuable research assistant for the second edition.

This edition of the book has benefited as well from the indispensable research assistance of two graduate students: Jennifer Stewart (who also worked on the first edition) and Kelly Morrison. Jennifer Stewart played an especially important role in the extensive revisions to Chapter 7. Without the indefatigable work of these two students, we never would have met those *final* deadlines set by our increasingly desperate publisher.

Which brings us to Nicole Gnutzman, Jenny Anttila, and Rosalyn Steiner of ITP Nelson, who gently but firmly, and with good grace and humour, nudged and cajoled us into finishing our work. We could not have wished for better editors!

INTRODUCTION

The first edition of this book appeared in 1995, when a combination of constitutional, political, and economic upheavals persuaded us that the "Canadian political system has been challenged to reinvent itself." The scope and pace of change has outstripped anything even we could imagine, and Canada stands on the cusp of the new millennium as a country transformed. In 1995 the annual federal deficit hovered at $40 billion; in 1998 the federal department of Finance predicted surpluses. In 1995 the federal government looked like a typical welfare state and played much the same role in Canadian society and the economy as it had since the 1960s; by the fall of 1997 its dimensions had been scaled back to those of the 1950s. Between 1995 and 1998 the federal civil service cut 50,000 positions. Everything from food inspection to air navigation has been reexamined and often either substantially downsized or turned over completely to the private sector.

Canadian federalism has also been transformed in this period. Ottawa has willingly granted more discretion in program spending to the provinces, as well as greater powers in key policy areas such as immigration, labour market development, and taxation. Quebec's distinctiveness has been recognized in federal legislation, while the constitution itself has been amended twice to deal with religious education in Quebec and Newfoundland. The Territory of Nunavut, with a population of approximately 22,000 and covering almost 2 million square kilometres (five times the size of Germany) will be officially established on April 1, 1999. Canada has formally apologized to its native peoples for their treatment in the last century, and agreed to deal with Aboriginals on a government-to-government basis. Louis Riel, hanged for treason in 1885, was touted as a Father of Confederation in 1998.

Even that hardy perennial of Canadian politics, the question of Quebec sovereignty and separation, has been transformed since 1995. In the Quebec independence referendum of October 1995, the No side won by a hair (50.6 percent). While we can debate the clarity of the question or whether some Quebeckers actually knew what they were voting for, the paper-thin margin of victory came as a profound shock and disappointment to many Canadians. Ottawa's strategy until then had largely been to accommodate Quebec's desire for more autonomy by decentralizing powers to all provinces in an effort to show how flexible Canadian federalism could be. This approach—Plan A, as it came to be known—quickly gave way to Plan B, a sort of constitutional tough-love approach that permitted federal politicians to debate something they had steadfastly refused to discuss in the past: the terms and conditions of separation. In a move that would have been unthinkable in 1994, Ottawa submitted a reference to the Supreme Court of Canada on the question of whether Quebec had the legal right to unilaterally leave Confederation. While support for separation had declined by 1998, the popularity of Premier Lucien Bouchard and the Parti Québécois remained high as they positioned themselves for both a provincial election and another referendum.

Canada is not alone in debating these issues and transforming its political system. In 1997 the newly elected British Labour government campaigned successfully in referendums for devolution in Scotland and Wales. New Zealand changed its electoral system and came to a new settlement with its aboriginal peoples, the Maori. The United States completely redesigned its welfare system. The European Union moved steadily toward a single currency and admitted Poland, Hungary, and the Czech Republic. Throughout the Organization for Economic Cooperation and Development (comprising 29 industrially developed states around the world), the public sector was being changed in a myriad of important ways, often resulting in completely new institutional arrangements.

Understanding the Canadian political system at the end of the 1990s, therefore, is perhaps more challenging than at any other time in our postwar history. Imagine someone in 1950 with a good grasp of the Canadian political system of that time. If that person were to be magically transported to 1960, he would see differences, of course, but the fundamental dimensions—or parameters—of governance would seem quite familiar. The same would be true in 1970 and even in 1980. The familiar ingredients would be there: a fairly prominent federal government and subordinate provinces, welfare state expansion and growing spending commitments in health, education, and social assistance, a Westminster-style system of parliamentary government, a weak Quebec separatist movement, an international system defined by the bipolar tensions of the United States versus the USSR, nationalist trade and economic policies designed to protect and project Canadian industry vis-à-vis the United States, and a largely invisible and anemic Aboriginal community. Our same observer moved forward to 1998 might well look around in bewilderment at a country he once knew. Though the size of the federal government would seem familiar, its posture of retreat and spending cuts would seem bizarre, especially in contrast with more assertive provinces that increasingly see Ottawa as an inconvenience. The Westminster system has been dramatically altered with the addition of a Charter of Rights and Freedoms and new powers for the courts to essentially make law and instruct legislatures on policy. The international system is completely transformed with the collapse of communism, and former east bloc countries are invited to join NATO, the old defence alliance *against* the USSR. Nationalist trade and economic policy has been replaced by the North American Free Trade Agreement between Canada, the United States, and Mexico, and Aboriginal peoples have become both more assertive and more confident of their rights.

It would be wonderful if a single book could meet the challenge of understanding political institutions by providing detailed backdrops of Canadian history, geography, society, and economics. No book can do everything, of course, and authors have to make choices. We have chosen to focus on the institutions themselves, their historical development and the underlying logic of institutional change. We do not ignore the rest of the political process, but institutions form the lens through which we view that process. We take this approach in part because of our own theoretical inclinations as scholars, but also because we are convinced that an understanding of institutions is one of the key obligations of citizenship. On an issue such as Quebec separatism, much of the debate quite properly centres on emotions, a sense of country, and historical ties. But the core of that debate is the same for this question as it is for any other fundamental issue of contemporary governance: What are the rules? Who are the legitimate players? What is forbidden and what is permitted? What are we trying to achieve? And what is the connection between our proposals and our objectives? Institutions, in short, are the parameters of political power.

FOCUS ON INSTITUTIONS

Institutions consist of systems of rules that define the roles that people play as parts of those institutions. The patterned sets of roles are related to an overriding set of purposes or tasks performed by the institution. Institutions set the parameters of political power by (1) determining the legitimate participants and their rights and obligations, (2) structuring the interactions of those participants, (3) shaping interests, and (4) influencing ends. Canadian government, as an example of an institution, is a specific mixture of federalism (a division of powers between central and provincial governments) and a parliamentary system of the Westminster type. This particular combination of rules helps explain a great deal about first ministers' conferences, intergovernmental competition, and complaints that the system is dominated by governmental (i.e., jurisdictional) interests. The United States too is a federal system, but governance there is vastly different from governance in Canada because the U.S. executive and legislature are organized along presidential and congressional lines.

It is important to keep several things in mind about institutions. First, while institutions structure politics—indeed, they *are* the structure of politics inasmuch as they set the rules of the game—they are also themselves influenced by other forces. Economic forces, for example, can literally demolish entire political systems. In late 1997 and early 1998, the Asian economies experienced turbulence so severe that it threatened the stability of several countries in the region. A global trading system makes governments in some instances *less* powerful and corporations *more* so. Demographic forces are also important. The aging of the Canadian population is having huge impacts on pensions and health-care systems. Even personality has an influence on institutions. The role and powers of the prime minister, for example, are the same for every occupant of the office, but Prime Minister Jean Chrétien's hands-off, managerial style is very different from Brian Mulroney's style or Pierre Trudeau's.

Second, institutions are not static. They change, evolve, expand, develop, and sometimes collapse. A prime example of this is the role of courts in the Canadian constitutional system since the adoption of the Charter of Rights and Freedoms in 1982.

Courts used to have a limited role in striking down law and virtually no role in actually *making* law. The Charter has changed that. It has encouraged the courts to evolve into something closer to a third branch of government.

Third, while institutions are obviously fluid and dynamic to some degree, they nevertheless contain a solid core of principles. In common usage, after all, the term "institution" conveys a sense of permanence, stability, and solidity. Understanding an institution means understanding its "code" or its core of rules. Once this is grasped, it is easier to discern when and how an institution changes and whether that change is fundamental or trivial.

Fourth, institutions are often contested and challenged. This is a paradox of politics: institutions (in the sense of rules) are indispensable in setting boundaries and informing expectations, but they can do this only by imposing constraints. An institution in which "everything goes" is, like a game without rules, a contradiction in terms. Even when they are conspicuously fair in their own terms, institutions create winners and losers, and the losers may eventually attack the institutions themselves. For example, political parties that are disadvantaged by a first-past-the-post or plurality voting system are great supporters of proportional representation.

There is some irony in a book that focuses on political institutions at a time when the size and role of government in Canada seems to be diminishing. Expenditure cuts, privatization, contracting out, and deregulation have been pursued by all governments, regardless of political stripe. For many observers, the result has been a withering of the Canadian state. While there is certainly some validity to this diagnosis, several broader points have to be kept in mind. The Canadian state, while retrenching in some ways, remains robust and important. Consider recent court decisions on gay rights, or Ottawa's role in the public pension system, or the importance of public authorities in dealing with the great ice storm of January 1998, and it is immediately clear that the state remains a visible and even indispensable part of our everyday lives. Moreover, many of the initiatives to downsize government actually involve profound questions of institutional design and simply cannot be accomplished well without a solid grasp of institutional principles. When, for example, should alternative dispute-resolution mechanisms be used instead of traditional litigation? How are "special operating agencies" to be accountable to taxpayers if they are at arm's length from government agencies?

Finally, understanding institutions helps us understand the limits to institutional change. No limits are impermeable to political will—if Canadians want an elected Senate or a different electoral system badly enough, they can have it. But changes of this magnitude in one institutional arena will often conflict with underlying principles in other arenas, and at minimum create tensions or inconsistencies as these institutions connect in the political process. A classic case of this is the push to make the appointment of judges more publicly accountable. Since the adoption, in 1982, of the Charter of Rights and Freedoms, Canadian judges have increasingly been attracted to the notion that the judiciary can and should pronounce on policy and legislative issues. As their influence and impact grows, however, it should not be surprising that publicly impermeable judicial appointments are challenged on the grounds that judges must be accountable to the electorate whose lives they now affect so dramatically.

THE APPROACH IN THIS BOOK

This book explains and analyzes Canada's key political institutions, showing the ways in which institutional arrangements have structured political behaviour and debate. The explanation and analysis differ, however, from those in traditional texts with a similar focus. Our approach tries to capture the underlying logic or architecture of Canada's main political institutions, and tries to make sense of issues as they move dynamically from one institutional arena to the next. We also place greater emphasis on contestation, on the *debates* over proper institutional forms. Canadian institutions have changed rapidly in recent years, so understanding the competing visions of what these institutions are designed to accomplish becomes increasingly important.

By linking institutions to political practice and contemporary political issues, we show how an understanding of discussions of democratic participation, Senate reform, or Aboriginal government demands a solid grasp of constitutional theory, law, and philosophical principles. These factors together constitute the matrix of rules at the core of any political institution. We emphasize detail, in short, because a clear understanding of rules depends on knowing precisely what those rules are and how they interact. Our description of these details, however, is consistently placed within the broader context of the core principles that define that institution.

Parameters of Power is designed, as much as a textbook can be, to facilitate contextual learning of principles and concepts. This book is about Canadian political institutions, but each chapter tries to set those institutions against a backdrop of comparative examples drawn from the United States, Europe, and other regimes. In addition to the usual illustrations and tables, *Parameters of Power* relies on several techniques to both enliven the text and assist students. The *Dossiers* contain additional information, background, or opinion pertinent to important topics. *Key Terms* appear in boldface when introduced in the text and are grouped at the end of each chapter for easy reference and review. Following this grouping are *Discussion Questions* that apply and extend concepts and arguments developed in the chapter. The *Appendix* at the end of the book contains a full text of the Canadian Constitution. In addition, students may benefit from ITP Nelson's Canadian politics Web site, http://polisci.nelson.com, which has links to a wide variety of sources on Canadian politics and institutions.

INSTITUTIONS AND POLITICS

1

Without institutions there is no society, only a bunch of strangers milling around on top of the ground sharing propinquity.[1]

Political life cannot be understood without reference to political institutions. The force of political charisma and statesmanship are important, political strategy cannot be ignored, and in a democracy the significance of public opinion and its determinants cannot be underestimated. But political institutions provide the indispensable backdrop to all of these political phenomena and more. Institutions are the "rules of the game," the channels in which political forces flow. The exercise of statesmanship requires the political stage provided by public office. Political strategists manoeuvre against the backdrop of institutional structures. And public opinion is filtered and organized by institutional rules and procedures. Because they shape political outcomes, moreover, institutions are much more than the background for the thrust and parry of political life; more often than not, institutions are the very things at stake in politics, institutional change the central goal of political striving. Institutional politics has characterized Canadian public life and has become even more central in the age of globalization.

■ ■ ■

The main theme of this book is that political processes are fundamentally shaped by political institutions, and that an increasing amount of our political debate concerns the design of appropriate institutions of governance. What people do in a political system is powerfully affected by the "rules of the game": the institutional structures that channel conflict and apportion resources. We often forget how much of politics is about what the rules say, who has the right to take certain actions, and which mechanisms should be used to resolve disagreements. We also sometimes forget how much of our political debate concerns the appropriate design of institutions and decision-making processes, from bureaucratic reform to new electoral systems. When we see individual politicians wield power, we sometimes ignore the institutional sources of that power, and instead ascribe their influence to sheer charisma or personality. And yet we instinctively understand that the failure of individuals to meet their obligations—whether as presidents, priests, politicians, professors, or physicians—often brings into disrepute the institutions with which they are associated.

There is more to politics, of course, than institutions. Demographic forces, underlying economic factors, interests, culture, and personalities all have an impact. Our point is simply that institutions are like the channels along which these forces flow. The way in which those channels are designed—the depth and direction of the grooves—makes a difference to the way in which political issues are addressed and resolved. Consider four examples.

The Reform Party and Parliament: At its inception, the Reform Party wanted to bring a different tone to parliamentary debate. The party felt that Question Period, with its raucous shouting matches and "I gotcha" tactics, was undignified. Reform MPs, rather than pounding their desks to show approval, would clap instead. What Reform had not counted on was the interplay between parliamentary tactics and media attention. By the time the party won official Opposition status in the 1997 election, it had adopted an entirely new approach. Rookie MPs were urged to "think Hollywood" when preparing for Question Period. They were coached in asking questions that were more dramatic, combative, and performance-oriented. Preston Manning, the Reform leader, was quoted as saying that Question Period had to be accepted for what it was—pure political theatre. "There are different forums for being critical and different forums for putting forward constructive alternatives in the parliamentary system," Mr. Manning said. "Question Period is not conducive to putting forward constructive alternatives. It's essentially the place where you can hold the government accountable for its own failures."[2] In a related development, Manning reversed an earlier promise not to take up residence in Stornoway, the residence of the leader of the official Opposition. Why? In part because simply occupying that role in the institutional matrix of Parliament made it seem logical to have a residence of this type—one in which to receive foreign visitors and to reflect the dignity of the office.

The Reform Party's experiences were not unique. Every protest party in Canadian history has had to confront the sheer gravitational pull of our political institutions. The Progressives in the 1920s (another Western Canada–based protest movement) were within a decade absorbed in what would soon be called (illogically) the Progressive Conservative Party. The Co-operative Commonwealth Federation, Social Credit, the New Democratic Party—while their electoral fortunes varied, all were slowly absorbed into the institutional processes of government and found their original radicalism blunted and tamed until gradually they came to resemble the politicians they had come to replace. One of the most comical examples of this, not just in Canadian but parliamentary history, was the spectacle of the Bloc Québécois as official Opposition between 1993 and 1997. The party is dedicated to Quebec separation and sovereignty, but because of the high concentration of its supporters in one seat-rich province, it found itself playing the role of Her Majesty's "Loyal" Opposition. So, while it did all it could to further its separatist agenda, it simultaneously had to speak for all Canadians. It often succeeded in doing this, but the fact that it felt obligated to do so was an artefact of institutional context.

Canadian Abortion Policy: Though few Canadians realize it, Canada has one of the world's most relaxed legal regimes governing abortion.[3] Aside from some court decisions and some regulations governing medical practices, no federal or provincial law specifies the circumstances under which abortion should be permitted or prohibited. Perhaps just as surprising, these circumstances have never been addressed in an election or determined through legislation. Current policy, such as it is, is almost completely the result of accident, and accident that is largely rooted in institutional factors. Legislation in 1969 prohibited abortion except in special circumstances (primarily if the pregnancy posed a threat to the mother's health), and was challenged in the courts in the 1970s by Dr. Henry Morgentaler. While he consistently won, he did so on the fairly narrow legal grounds permitted in the Criminal Code. By the 1980s, however, with the adoption of the Charter of Rights and Freedoms, new constitutional arguments were available to those who wanted greater access to abortion. The Charter had changed the policy terrain significantly, not only because one could now argue policy in terms of entrenched rights (something that had not been possible before 1982) but because the courts—in making judgments on the Charter—were a new arena for putting these arguments forward.[4] In 1988 the Supreme Court of Canada struck down the existing abortion legislation. Courts also played an important role in preventing various provinces from trying to pass restrictive laws. Parliament then tried twice to pass new abortion legislation. In both cases, despite a desire by the government to create a new legal regime, voting rules in the House of Commons and the Senate prevented the passage of legislation (Bill C-43, for example, received a tie vote in the Senate, which under that chamber's rules counts as a defeat).[5]

Abortion is a controversial issue, and groups on different sides lobbied and mobilized in an almost supercharged atmosphere.[6] It would be foolish to ignore the nature of this atmosphere, or the fact that foes and supporters of legislation were fairly evenly split. However, no matter how charged the issue or what the array of coalitions, the antagonists still had to pursue their policy agendas through political and judicial institutions, in the context of a Charter of Rights and Freedoms. Understanding *abortion* requires substantial background in sociology and philosophy; understanding *abortion policy* requires a grasp of the institutional context and how it affected the issue's evolution.

The Federal Deficit: In 1993 the federal government was running an annual deficit of approximately $40 billion. This was about the same as the deficit almost ten years earlier, when the Conservatives were in power and vowed to deal with overspending. By 1998 the federal deficit had been eliminated, and Canada's books were balanced for the first time since the 1970s. Surprisingly, this was achieved by two successive Liberal governments, a party that had not previously been associated with a hard line on government spending. What happened?[7]

Personalities mattered, of course. Paul Martin, the federal minister of Finance, was convinced on entering office that the deficit was a problem, but initially he thought it could be dealt with through modest cuts and increased economic growth. His officials convinced him that the problem was more severe and that in order to meet the government's promised target of a deficit/gross domestic product (GDP) ratio of 3 percent, he would have to make drastic changes to the government's finances. Once convinced, Martin succeeded in getting the prime minister's support, and at a crucial cabinet meeting in June 1995 Chrétien used his authority to beat back increased spending requests from various ministers.

However, personalities and ideological commitments cannot be the whole story. Canada has been trying to get its finances under control for almost a quarter century.[8] Personalities in the past have been as strong and as committed, ideologies equally if not more devoted to spending reductions, and circumstances about as favourable. Arguably, some accidental factors helped the process. For example, the Liberal government was extraordinarily lucky to have lower-than-forecast interest rates and higher-than-forecast revenues. But two of the keys were institutional. One was the willingness of Jean Chrétien to use his prime ministerial power strategically to support a difficult policy decision taken by his minister of Finance. The second was the establishment in 1995 of a new Expenditure Management System (EMS) that worked with explicit targets for each department and blocked any attempt at end runs that would secure more funding outside of the established envelopes. This system bound politicians to spending controls in a way that previous systems had been unable to do. The new EMS had firm short-term fiscal targets so that departments could not postpone their spending cuts. The system also did away with the idea of reserves—pots of federal money that could be accessed by departments with bright new spending ideas. Any department that wanted to mount a new program would have to do so from its existing (and usually shrinking) budget—i.e., something else would have to be cut.

Aboriginal Governance: The Royal Commission on Aboriginal Peoples, established in 1991, was the most expensive inquiry of its type in Canadian history. Its 1996 report filled five volumes, 3500 pages, and made 440 recommendations.[9] It dealt with every conceivable issue in the relationship between Canada and Aboriginal peoples. One of its key recommendations, however, was a change in the relationship—by that it meant in large part the political and governance relationship—between Aboriginals and the governments of Canada. On January 7, 1998, Jane Stewart, the federal minister of Indian Affairs and Northern Development, released the government's formal response to the royal commission. At the centre of her statement and the plan, entitled *Gathering Strength: Canada's Aboriginal Action Plan,* was a redesign of institutions and the relationships they create. This redesign can be seen in the four broad initiatives for renewal:

First, we will renew the partnership to engage all possible partners and resources so the relationship will be a catalyst to better the lives of Aboriginal people in Canada.

Second, we will strengthen Aboriginal governance so that communities have the tools to guide their own destiny and to exercise their inherent right of self-government.

Third, we will design a new fiscal relationship that provides a stable flow of funds in support of transparent and accountable community development.

Fourth, we will sustain the growth of strong, healthy Aboriginal communities, fuelled by economic development and supported by a solid, basic infrastructure of institutions and services.[10]

For the first time, the federal government implied that it would treat Aboriginal governments as equal partners and, more importantly, that it would treat them as *governments*. The minister's statement included a promise to create "an Aboriginal governments recognition instrument to guide jurisdictional and intergovernmental relations," and it spoke of the need to make Aboriginal governments more self-reliant. Just words? Perhaps, and certainly Canadian history is full of political promises that never bore fruit. But consider the nature of this political initiative. First, while it is certainly about relationships, it recognizes that those relationships are channelled through institutions. If the relationships are to change, the institutions must be redesigned. Second, the statement links words to those relationships. To speak, as the minister did, of partnership is one thing. To speak of "intergovernmental relations" with Aboriginal peoples means something quite different. Words have meaning because of institutional relationships they imply. Third, the renewal initiative recognizes that stable solutions to political and social problems require institutional responses—not simply the provision of money, for example, but the transfer of skills so that revenue can be properly managed.

These examples illustrate the importance of institutions. Later chapters in this book deal in detail with, among other things, the long-term impact of decisions made at Confederation about the structure and powers of the Senate, the effect of the electoral system on party competition and representation, the nature of the built-in adversarial nature of the House of Commons, the almost invisible but extraordinary influence of monarchy on the prerogatives and powers of Cabinet, the rules that underpin judicial decision making, and the character of intergovernmental bargaining in the context of the institutional arrangements of the Canadian federal system. The chapters also address the extraordinary debates over and reforms to many of these institutions in recent years. As we will briefly discuss at the end of this chapter, the context for Canadian governance has been changing rapidly, bringing predictable pressures for institutional change.

THE INSTITUTIONAL APPROACH

Dictionary definitions of the term **institution** stress the idea of *established* practice. Indeed, that is all that political institutions are: complex sets of established practices, or "rules of the game," that enable us to accomplish collective ends. All institutions consist of two key elements: (1) an overriding set of purposes or tasks[11] and (2) a patterned set of roles connected to those purposes. We begin to make sense of an institution in terms of its central tasks, which are often defined in relation to, or in contrast with, the tasks of other institutions. Courts and legislatures, for example, are designed to do different things in the political system. The judiciary is "perceived as being essentially technical and non-political"[12] because the courts are expected to undertake the impartial adjudication of disputes. Partisanship in a legislative assembly, on the other hand, is normal, since a legislature exists to represent political interests. In the real world the lines between governmental institutions are often blurred, and their tasks and behaviours overlap. But we could never make sense of the blurring and overlap without first having some idea of formal institutional tasks. The second element is just as important. Every institution consists of a patterned set of roles. Entering new institutions, or playing new roles in old ones, often demands a nuanced understanding of the patterns of roles, rights, and responsibilities.

The institutional approach adopted in this book builds on these two key elements of institutions, and consists of four interrelated questions or issues.

1. *What is the institution's "logic"?* As argued earlier, every institution has an overriding set of tasks that makes sense of its activities. In some cases, an institution is designed with clear ends: a hospital gives medical care, for example, and a university provides education. The **state,** in general terms, maintains social order and is a mechanism for collective decision making that affects the entire society. The state itself, however, is an amalgam of distinct institutions, such as the legislature, the executive, the judiciary, and agencies and bodies attached to these branches. Each of these institutions is understood to have a discernible role within the state system. For example, the primary role of the executive branch is to propose legislation and administer laws and programs; the primary role of the legislature is to represent the public in the consideration of proposed legislation; the primary goal of the judicial branch is to decide on legal disputes. Interest groups and political parties operate within these institutions and have their own rules and structures. Institutional analysis tries to understand the **logic of an institution**—that is, the principles that make it tick and give a sense of order and purpose to the actors within it. Another way to understand the logic of an institution is to grasp its set of underlying rules. To take a non-political example, the institution of the traditional family can be understood in terms of the rules defining the roles and expectations of parents, children, and relatives.

2. *Are there inconsistent "logics" or principles, and are they contested?* All institutions have some discernible logic that helps makes sense of the behaviour of actors within them, but most institutions (and certainly most political ones) reflect more than a

single set of principles. The executive in modern political systems, for example, both administers laws approved by the legislature and proposes legislation for passage. One role is subordinate to the legislature, the other is dominant. Administrative departments of government are expected to implement public policy impartially, but implementation without some policymaking discretion is impossible.[13] Even a text like the Charter of Rights and Freedoms has conflicting principles and clauses. Consider the provisions of section 15 of the Charter. Subsection 1 prohibits discrimination on any grounds, in particular those of "race, national or ethnic origin, colour, religion, sex, age or mental or physical disability." But subsection 2 allows discrimination in favour of the same groups if that discrimination "has as its object the amelioration of conditions of disadvantaged individuals or groups."

These conflicting logics at the heart of institutions are far from invisible or unknown to actors. Indeed, institutional reform is often designed to try to reduce institutional dissonance to some more consistent pattern. The debate over Senate reform, for instance, has been concerned with the contradiction between the Senate's role in providing regional representation and the federal government's practice of making Senate appointments as partisan rewards. The inconsistent behaviour of political actors may be the result of following different institutional rules at different times.

Because the principles at the heart of an institution are often inconsistent or at least in tension with one another, most institutions are beset with some measure of conflict or, at the very least, some measure of disagreement or misunderstanding about the rules that constitute them. All institutions are therefore in varying degrees of self-discovery and self-definition as actors strive to understand both what they should be doing within the institution and what the institution as a whole should be doing.

Rules are always indeterminate to some extent and can thus be pushed and pulled in different directions, to different degrees, by different occupants of the offices they establish. Intrainstitutional politics is the result of conflicts among actors in an institution about the best (or correct) interpretation of its defining rules. As in any political process, there are always (provisional) winners and losers in such intrainstitutional struggles, so institutions change shape over time. Canadian federalism is a good example of this phenomenon. In formal terms, federalism means a distribution of powers between two orders of government—in Canada's case, between the federal and provincial governments. But are the provinces equal in power and status with one another and with Ottawa? Should the federation be decentralized or centralized? Should special circumstances across provinces be accommodated constitutionally (e.g., the French language in Quebec, the importance of natural resources to the West)? These are among the perennial questions of Canadian constitutional politics. They were at the heart of constitutional controversy during Canada's founding period and remain there today. The answers to these questions have changed over time, however, leading to swings between the poles of centralization and decentralization.

As understandings of federalism change, so too do the powers of the provinces and Ottawa.

In workable institutions, however, there appear to be limits to this process of internal self-transformation. While the defining rules can be pushed, pulled, and bent, they retain some integrity. They are not generally so deformed that they become unrecognizable, as if the institution had transformed itself from one species into another. For example, federalism requires at least two levels of government, each effective in its own sphere. The balance of power in federal systems can and does change over time, but some balance must remain if we are to speak of a real federal system rather than a form of government in which the preponderance of powers is wielded at only one level.

Workable institutions therefore always have a balance between solidity and flux and between acceptance and contestation. Sensitive institutional analysis should pay attention to the defining core of principles as well as to the alternate visions, the different definitions, the contested alternatives that are posed both within and without the institution. These provide clues not only to institutional resilience but also to the potential trajectories of institutional change.

3. *How are institutional logics connected to specific systems of rules and roles?* Understanding politics and government is ultimately about understanding why people in government and politics do what they do. Answers to questions 1 and 2 provide the tools for grasping the most fundamental context within which political actors manoeuvre. Answering question 3 ensures that we go further and analyze each role, with its bundle of rights and responsibilities, and the relationships that these roles have with others within an institution.

Consider the prime ministership. As subsequent chapters show in detail, the Canadian prime minister must first be understood in terms of parliamentary practice. An elementary but telling observation is that the prime minister operates in a political system in which the executive and legislature are integrated, and in which the role of the head of state is performed by the Crown or its representative. The result is that the prime minister serves both as a legislative representative and as head of the sovereign's advisory council or cabinet. The American system, by contrast, is designed to separate the executive from the legislative branch, and cabinet ministers do not participate directly in congressional debates.

A complete grasp of the prime minister's role would depend, however, on close study of a host of finer rules and conventional practices. In Canada, for example, federal party leaders are selected at delegate conventions. The leader of a party that happens to win an election becomes the prime minister but has a separate power base in the party as a whole. The prime minister enjoys numerous prerogatives, such as making Senate and cabinet appointments as well as hundreds of other appointments to government boards, agencies, and courts. Each prime minister, moreover, will structure the cabinet system to suit personal style and preferences, and this in turn will lead to different relations with ministers and officials.[14] Some of these rules are clear and established, others are a matter of convention or individual preference in the interpretation of prerogative and obligation. Together they provide powerful insight into why political actors act as they do and some sense of the constraints on their actions. As noted above, however, although institutional rules shape action, they do not determine every detail.

4. *What is the interaction among institutions in a given system?* The state is a good example of a complex combination of distinct institutions that are more or less coordinated toward the end of societal governance. Good institutional analysis requires a knowledge of the principles that make sense of the entire system (e.g., parliamentary or presidential) as well as of the rules and roles within each of the distinct components of that system. But the components interact with one another in patterned ways. It is this interaction of institutional rules and actors that is usually referred to as the "political process." An institutional analysis of this process focuses on the fact that each arena differs in fundamental respects from the others. The legislative arena, for example, is powerfully shaped by the imperatives of democratic representation. In framing laws, MPs and parties in the House of Commons inevitably look to popularity, reelection, compromise, and feasibility. The rules of parliamentary procedure usually ensure that a wide array of groups and individuals appear before committees to submit their views. Judicial decision making, on the other hand, is much less affected by the dynamics of electoral representation. The courts are expected to be neutral and above politics, and to make decisions based almost exclusively on legal reasoning. If the decision proves to be unpopular, so be it.[15]

An important fact about the political process is that many issues cross from one **institutional arena** to the next, and in so doing are often "processed" according to different sets of rules. An increasingly visible example of this is legislation that gets appealed to the courts. In a variety of "hot-button" issues like abortion, sexual orientation, the definition of the family, or gender roles, governments often legislate (or refuse to legislate) based on a political calculus that weighs the preferences of the majority, or at least tries to minimize controversy. Affected groups, especially in the era of the Charter and various human rights codes, go to the courts with the hope that judges will give greater weight to the rights of minorities. Another well-known example concerns the fate of issues and political promises between the time that parties fight elections and win them.[16] In the heat of political competition in an election campaign, parties are ready to promise almost anything that they think will be popular and garner votes. Once in power, however, the institutional context changes and the governing party has to deal with the bureaucracy, the Opposition, and provincial and foreign governments. Promises sometimes have to be trimmed or broken.[17] Another example comes from Canadian foreign and trade policy. In the negotiations leading up to the 1988 Free Trade Agreement, Canadian strategy was based on the view that as long as trade issues were processed in the Congress, American policy toward Canada would be erratic and often punitive. One Canadian goal was to establish a system of tribunals consisting of appointed experts who would handle trade disputes in a more dispassionate manner. These examples illustrate why political

DOSSIER 1.1 INSTITUTIONAL CONTESTATION

In February 1998 the Supreme Court of Canada heard arguments on a reference from the federal government on the constitutional legality of Quebec secession. As the following excerpt from the department of Justice's rationale for the case illustrates, the case hinged on how we understand political institutions. (The Supreme Court decided the case in August 1998; for further discussion, see Chapter 3.)

The Government of Canada submitted the Reference to the Supreme Court of Canada as a direct result of the position repeatedly taken by the current Quebec Government—that it has a right to take Quebec out of Canada unilaterally, that international law sanctions such a process, and that Canadian laws and courts have no role to play in the process. The Government of Canada believes that there is no basis in Canadian or international law for this claim of the Government of Quebec.

Any attempt at unilateral secession by Quebec's governing institutions would have grave consequences for all Canadians, with particular serious consequences for Quebeckers. It would create the greatest uncertainty for the average citizen, business, or institution in Quebec. Individual Quebeckers would be uncertain about what laws applied and who would guarantee their rights. Since such an action—by its nature—would be done without the consent of the Government of Canada, Quebec would likely find itself without recognition by all or most of the international community, and unable to manage its relations with sovereign states....

THE CONSTITUTION OF CANADA AND THE SECESSION OF A PROVINCE

Unilateral secession involves the breaking away of part of an existing state in an attempt to form a new state. This necessarily occurs at the expense of the territorial integrity and political unity of the existing state. Secession is destabilizing, disruptive, and, in most cases, fundamentally opposed to the goals of the existing state, whether unitary or federal. It is, by its very nature, extraordinary. Only a very few countries' constitutions recognize secession as possible and then only if certain conditions are met.

As in the case for most countries, the Canadian Constitution neither prohibits secession nor provides for it. The Government of Canada believes that the Constitution is capable of accommodating any change to the federation or its institutional structures, including even such an extraordinary change as the secession of a province.

The Canadian Constitution specifies the procedures necessary to make constitutional amendments and sets out a number of amending formulas that apply in different circumstances. There is only one procedure that permits amendments by a province acting alone and it applies only to matters internal to the province and its institutions.

The secession of a province from Canada clearly involves more than a mere change in matters internal to a province and its institutions and would by its very nature affect the Canadian federation as a whole. Since there is no other mechanism for unilateral constitutional amendments by a province, it follows that there is no right of Quebec's governing institutions to effect unilaterally the secession of Quebec from Canada under the Canadian Constitution.

Reference to the Supreme Court of Canada, *Summary of the Government of Canada's Position: General Context.* Available at http://canada.justice.gc.ca/News/Communiques/1997/fact_en.html.

disputes are often won or lost early through the determination of where and how an issue is to be addressed. Institutional arenas matter.

These four basic questions—What is an institution's logic? Is it consistent or contested? How are logics connected to rules and roles? How do institutions interact in the policy process?—underpin the analysis and discussion in the rest of this book. The objectives of this analysis should be clear: to determine how the machinery of Canadian government works, to identify the underlying principles and the debates surrounding those principles, and to determine what difference those debates make to the ways in which political objectives are pursued.

INSTITUTIONAL CONTESTATION AND THE CANADIAN NATION-STATE

The previous section outlined some key theoretical points to consider in coming to grips with political institutions. But there are two major practical reasons for a focus on institutions as we have defined the term. One is that Canada, despite its stable and continuous political history as a unified state over 130 years (one of the longest such histories in the world), has been preoccupied with issues of institutional design. The other is that around the world countries are suddenly reforming and redesigning their institutions quite radically. Understanding both Canadian and world politics increasingly depends on a solid grasp of institutional principles and debates concerning the nature of the modern nation-state.

Canada and Institutional Contestation

Canada's history is one of contested visions, and the degree of contestation has risen so dramatically in the last 10 years that bookshelves groan with the accumulated wisdom of would-be lawgivers who think nothing of starting Canada from scratch. International newspapers joke about the Canadian obsession with constitutional politics, an obsession all the more perplexing in a country with one of the highest standards of living in the world and an enviable history of social peace—twice voted the best country in which to live by the United Nations.[18]

A key theme of this book is that Canada's constitutional and political debate, the range of its contestation over first principles, is institutional in character. It may even be institutionally caused, in the sense that we have never succeeded in designing sufficiently flexible or legitimate political institutions. The degree of **institutional contestation** over principle is so great that it amounts to what Carolyn Tuohy has called **institutionalized ambivalence,** or disagreement over "the very legitimacy of the state itself and to the identity of political community."[19] This ambivalence or contestation is institutionalized because it is built into the very structures of the state.

> *First, the system legitimizes competing principles: It combines an unwritten with a written constitution, a Westminster model of centralized cabinet government with a decentralized federation and, since 1982, parliamentary supremacy with a constitutional charter of rights. Second, it allows these principles to co-exist in a context of constitutional and institutional ambiguity.*[20]

Our political mythology holds that Canada is a "peaceable kingdom" where compromise is a national talent. But events like the failed Meech Lake Accord in 1990, the failed Charlottetown Accord and the national referendum in 1992, the October 1995 Quebec referendum, and the constitutional reference case of 1998 reveal widely divergent visions of the country. The very foundations of the Canadian state have become an obsession and an irritant. Institutions matter here because they have been taken so seriously, disputed so tirelessly, and redesigned so zealously in the last decade. Many Canadians are tired of the debate. They want the country to address pressing social and economic issues, real as opposed to chimerical problems. Others have responded by arguing that a country that has not resolved fundamental questions of representation, democracy, and the distribution of political power is unlikely to build the stable political structures it needs to address substantive policy challenges.

No state, no matter how stable, is immune to contestation over institutional principles, but Canadian political history has often been preoccupied with the search for suitable forms of governance and unresolved conflicts over what those forms should be—particularly since the early 1960s. The surprising strength of the Bloc Québécois and the Reform Party in the October 1993 election reflected just this sort of debate about the Canadian federal state and about key policies, such as bilingualism, multiculturalism, and universal social programs, that have defined the state profile for decades. The 1997 federal election results, where the five parties ended up representing distinct regions of the country (NDP and Tories in Atlantic Canada, Bloc Québécois in Quebec, Liberals in Ontario, and Reform in the West) showed a dangerous regionalization of political support. Aboriginal self-government poses a fundamental challenge to traditional concepts of sovereignty and the nation-state. How can Aboriginals form "governments" of nations within another nation-state? Conflicting interpretations of the Charter of Rights and Freedoms are heard daily in virtually every courtroom and tribunal across the country, and even the "definitive" interpretations of the Supreme Court of Canada yield ambiguities and uncertainty. The most striking example of this, one that threatened to bring the court itself into disrepute in the eyes of many, was the federal government reference in 1998 on the question of the constitutional legality of Quebec's proposed separation. Policy questions such as employment training or income security eligibility get transposed into institutional issues: Which level of government should be responsible? Which constitutional powers should apply? Which sections of the constitution should be invoked? No citizen can comprehend Canadian politics without a firm grasp of institutional principles.

Ambivalence and contestation can be seen in virtually every arena of Canadian politics. The Senate, for example, has been a lightning rod for contestation over the nature of the parliamentary system, federalism, and political parties. The fact that senators were appointed by the federal government quickly turned the Senate—originally intended to provide regional representation—into a patronage chamber. The Canadian parliamentary system encourages disciplined political parties, since staying in power depends on controlling votes in the legislature, and that too tended to stifle regional voices in Canada's central institutions. In the last round of constitutional design, the Charlottetown Accord offered a model of a new Senate that would be elected by popular vote, have equal representation from each province, and hold powers roughly equal to those of the House of Commons. Some critics of the Charlottetown Senate proposal thought that it did not go far enough in ensuring strong regional representation. Other critics felt that it went too far and would undermine a key feature of parliamentary democracy: the responsibility of the cabinet to the House of Commons.

All of Canada's other core political institutions have been the subject of similar contestation and ambivalence. As a parliamentary system Canada traditionally relied on the British practice of embedding individual rights in law and in convention, while at the same time vesting extensive powers in the elected legislature. In 1982, however, with the adoption of a written Charter of Rights and Freedoms, government powers were constrained in favour of individual rights. The Charter has a unique feature whereby governments may override some Charter freedoms; it thereby tries to combine a new supremacy of individual rights with the traditional powers of a parliamentary regime. Similar ambivalence and contestation can be seen in the evolution of Canadian federalism and in the development of the judicial system, political parties, and the bureaucracy.

The Nation-State and Globalization

The intensity of Canada's obsession with constitutional issues may be unique, but countries all across the world are struggling with fundamental challenges to traditional political regimes. The collapse of the Soviet Union unleashed ethnic tensions both within its old borders and throughout erstwhile Soviet satellite states such as the former Yugoslavia. More recently, the NATO alliance voted to admit three former "enemies" (Poland, Hungary, and the Czech Republic), while the European Community is launched on expansion as well.[21] In early 1998 the Australians convened a constituent assembly to recommend whether the country should replace the queen as head of state and become a republic. New Zealand adopted a new electoral system based on proportional representation. The United Kingdom held referendums on devolution of powers to Wales and Scotland and in 1998 was preparing to give Scotland what Canadians would call "quasi-provincial" powers. In Asia the slump in financial markets forced political reform in South Korea, Thailand, and Japan, and had the International Monetary Fund deeply involved in domestic economic policy through loans. At the Kyoto Conference on Climate Change, in December 1997, states wrestled with the adoption of global emission standards and targets that would previously have been considered matters of domestic policy.[22]

This turbulence and increased pace of institutional reform around the world reflects fundamental changes in the nature of the **nation-state,** the preeminent form of political organization in the last 200 years. The nation-state was defined as having, ideally, an integrated public administration wielding ultimate authority and power over a clearly defined territory and a broadly homogenous population.[23] The state was the jurisdictional component, the nation was the cultural or ethnic component, and the two were welded together to form an imposing instrument of political will. The international system consisted, by definition, of interacting nation-states. Obviously, this "ideal" was rarely achieved in practice, and in reality the world system comprised various hybrid political forms. France is typically considered one of the best examples of the nation-state in this ideal definition; Japan is another. But most states had several ethnic and cultural groups in their populations, and many large nationalities (e.g., Germans) were represented by several states. Overlaying these states were the great empires of the past, such as the British, Dutch, and French.

Despite these often wide variations, the central idea of the nation-state was that it had both legal and effective sovereignty within its territory, that it could manage the affairs of its people on its own terms. This level of autonomy implies a degree of insulation from outside forces. Again, it is important not to exaggerate: obviously international trade and far-flung networks of communication, transportation, and exchange existed in the last 200 years. Canada owes its existence to these networks. But the important fact remained that until the early 1970s most nation-states could claim effective control over the fundamental levers of public policy: they could tax, spend, and regulate as they saw fit, and maintain control over their populations and their economies. The modern welfare state, with its agencies and departments and programs, is a consequence of this capacity. Take away the capacity, and the nature of the state itself is called into question.

That is precisely what has happened in the last 25 years with the increasing pace and intensity of globalization. **Globalization** is "primarily a technological and economic process driven by the revolution in telecommunications and computers, massive increases in the movement of capital around the world, greatly expanded capacities for flexible world-wide production sourcing by firms, especially multinational corporations, and growing ecological interdependence and environmental spillovers."[24] There are various indicators of these trends. Since 1945 successive rounds of international negotiations, through first the General Agreement on Tariffs and Trade and now the World Trade Organization, have lowered barriers to the trade of manufactured goods. More importantly, by the mid-1990s one-third of total world trade was actually "intra-firm," or within the branches of multinational corporations with operations around the globe.[25] The various parts of cars, for example, are made in factories around the world and then assembled near or in their target markets. The increase in trade is intensified in regional agreements like the North American Free Trade Agreement (NAFTA) between the United States, Canada, and Mexico (soon to be enlarged), the MERCUSOR (South America), and the European Union. Trade liberalization has been accompanied by the liberalization and integration of financial markets, so that billions of dollars of investment capital moves freely around the globe each day. None of this would be possible without the dramatic improvements in communication and information technologies in the last decades. The Internet is the most visible example of the convergence of telecommunications and computers, but with satellites and fibre-optic cables, the effective cost of a transatlantic telephone call is approaching zero.[26]

What does all this mean in practical terms? The economic consequences are dramatic. With lowered barriers to trade, and with NAFTA requirements like "national treatment" (no discrimination against foreign firms of the partner countries), companies can move to relocate their production more easily if they find more attractive conditions in other countries. Domestic industries cannot be protected from competition. Trading patterns become international rather than national. For example, all the Canadian provinces except Prince Edward Island trade more internationally (primarily with the United States) than they do with one another.[27] The global integration that comes with trade is intensified by flows of capital, so that countries become so closely entwined that economic downturns felt in one will reverberate through others. A distressing example of this integration—and vulnerability—was the decline in the value of the Canadian dollar in mid-1998, ostensibly because of investors' nervousness over economic turbulence in Asia. The communications consequences are no less dramatic. People can connect to one another around the globe, the access to information increases hugely, while the number and types of sources of information increase as well. All this communication implies cultural exchange (dominated by American cultural products, but not exclusively) and to some degree the emergence of global standards and debates (e.g., around human rights).

What does this mean for the nation-state, its institutions, and governance? First, it reduces key policy capacities of nation-states. If they tax too much, companies (and increasing numbers of skilled professionals) can simply shift their operations elsewhere. More and more economic activity is defined by the production of "intangibles" like information/entertainment, and these are notoriously difficult to tax and monitor. And how to tax the massive waves of short-term capital that rollick around the planet? With reduced tax capabilities, spending comes under pressure. It is pressured for other reasons too. Companies facing stiff international competition may pressure for reduced government spending (in order to lower taxes and increase profits) and lower safety and environmental standards. Governments that run deficits have to borrow, and increasingly borrow on highly volatile international markets. If investors do not approve of government policies, or find more attractive options, they will shift their capital elsewhere, sparking currency declines and interest rate fluctuations.

Consider regulation. As markets get more competitive and so-called "natural monopolies" decline, one of the key rationales for government regulation evaporates as well. Substantial deregulation in transportation, communications, and financial services has taken place around the world. Moreover, communication and information technologies make some conventional forms of regulation impossible. What is the sense of Canadian content regulations for TV, or protecting the domestic magazine industry, or restricting pornography, when satellites beam American and international programming directly into our living rooms, when thousands of foreign magazines and newspapers can be freely accessed on the Internet, and when any 15-year-old can send dirty pictures to anyone, anywhere, by e-mail?

A second consequence that flows in part from the first is a diminution of sovereignty or effective power. As policy instruments become constrained, states have less capacity to pursue independent policy choices. Since most states face the same constraints, we can also see a degree of policy convergence as fewer and fewer options become available.[28] Fewer capacities and fewer choices mean weaker states. But power is relative, and if the power of states is now diminished, the power of non-state actors is enhanced. This includes multinational corporations and businesses more generally—with mobility comes leverage. Moreover, it is now widely accepted that modern economies thrive through knowledge, innovation, and flexible responses to rapidly changing circumstances. Governments cannot create these dynamic sectors on their own; they have to attract private capital and private investment. This gives global businesses even greater leverage. But ordinary citizens are also empowered, and this empowerment can cross borders to create effective international social movements. The American militia movement associated with the Oklahoma bombings, to take one frightening example, could not have spread as widely or been as chillingly effective without the Internet.[29] The Zapatista guerrillas of Mexico launched a successful "Netwar" against the government in 1994 with laptop computers, satellite links, and e-mail. The environmental and human rights movements have global reach, visibility, and legitimacy because of modern communications technologies.[30] The international movement to ban land mines, which started in 1992 and culminated in an international treaty signed in Ottawa in December 1997, orchestrated over 1000 non-governmental organizations around the world to put pressure on governments. Technologies of surveillance, like remote satellite sensing, and technologies to resist surveillance, like encryption, which were once almost exclusive to state security apparatuses, are now widely available.[31]

The third consequence takes us back to institutions—states have had to adapt to these new forces, and to do so they have reformed old institutions and created new ones. The state in the new global economy remains important for economic development (e.g., providing the "home base" for multinational corporations, investing in "human capital" in education), and is the "mediator between the domestic society and the global political economy."[32] This means, for example, that states have to redesign themselves in order to be attractive to international investment. Governments everywhere try to be more efficient, so they restructure their departments and agencies, shed many services to the private sector, and slash budgets and tax rates. They redesign their programs and deliver them differently. They shift those services and programs that are not central to dealing with globalization (e.g., welfare, social housing, some aspects of health) to local governments while assuming more responsibility for policy areas deemed important in fostering global competitiveness. They work with other states to address their interdependencies, creating an increasingly dense web of international agreements, standards, and mechanisms that simultaneously constrain and magnify state power. All these strategies have been used in Canada in the last decade.

States remain important, even in a globalized world of flows. Institutional design is, if anything, more important now than ever. Governments around the world are engaged in reforms and experiments to deal with the pressures of a global economy: new forms of public administration, policy delivery, representation, and democracy are appearing everywhere. Canada's recent experiences echo these efforts, for many of the same reasons, even though we add a complex mix of constitutional and jurisdictional issues. One particularly salient effect of globalization in the Canadian context is the centrifugal impact it has on regional economies and, consequently, on regionalism and separatism. Some economists argue that under the stimulus of globalization, Ontario is emerging as the largest region-state in North America.[33] Quebec separatism makes much more economic sense today to those considering it, when the province trades more with the rest of the world than with the rest of Canada. By the same token, some of the efforts to "re-legitimize" the federal state, both in the eyes of Quebec and other provinces and regions, are rooted in the denationalizing impact of globalization.

THE BOOK

The following chapters explore the ambivalence, contestation, and change at the heart of the Canadian state from an institutional perspective, keeping in mind the four guiding questions of institutional analysis set out above. We begin with the most comprehensive institution of all: the constitution. The constitution encompasses not only such prominent formal documents as the Charter of Rights and Freedoms but all the rules, formal and informal, that define or "constitute" the most fundamental aspects of the Canadian state. In this broad sense, the constitution has aptly been called our "master institution"—the institution that includes or decisively shapes all other political institutions. It includes, most obviously, the legislative, executive, and judicial branches of government, and it shapes such extra-constitutional institutions as parties and interest groups. The nature and contested evolution of this "master institution" are explored in Chapters 2 and 3.

Chapters 4 through 8 consider the component institutions of our constitutional structure. Chapter 4 deals with federalism, perhaps the most consistent preoccupation of Canadian institutional politics. Then, in Chapters 5 through 8, we turn

DOSSIER 1.2 THE STATE IN A CHANGING WORLD

The postwar confidence in government bred demands for it to do more. Industrial economies expanded the welfare state, and much of the developing world embraced state-dominated development strategies. The result was a tremendous expansion in the size and reach of government worldwide. State spending now constitutes almost half of total income in the established industrial countries and around a quarter in developing countries. But this very increase in the state's influence has also shifted the emphasis from the quantitative to the qualitative, from the sheer size of the state and the scope of the interventions to its effectiveness in meeting people's needs.

As in the 1940s, today's renewed focus on the state's role has been inspired by dramatic events in the global economy, which have fundamentally changed the environment in which states operate. The global integration of economies and the spread of democracy have narrowed the scope for arbitrary and capricious behavior. Taxes, investment rules, and economic policies must be ever more responsive to the parameters of a globalized economy. Technological change has opened new opportunities for unbundling services and allowing a larger role for markets. These changes have meant new and different roles for government—no longer as sole provider but as facilitator and regulator. States have come under pressure even when governments have previously seemed to perform well. Many industrial countries find themselves grappling with a welfare state that has grown unwieldy, and having to make difficult choices about the services and benefits that people should expect government to provide. Markets—domestic and global—and citizens vexed by state weaknesses have come to insist, often through grassroots and other nongovernmental organizations, on transparency in the conduct of government, and on other changes to strengthen the ability of the state to meet its assigned objectives....

This basic message translates into a two-part strategy to make every state a more credible, effective partner in its country's development:

Matching the state's role to its capability is the first element in this strategy. Where state capability is weak, how the state intervenes—and where—should be carefully assessed....

But capability is not destiny. Therefore, the second element of the strategy is to raise state capability by reinvigorating public institutions. This means designing effective rules and restraints, to check arbitrary state actions and combat entrenched corruption. It means subjecting state institutions to greater competition, to increase their efficiency. It means increasing the performance of state institutions, improving pay and incentives. And it means making the state more responsive to people's needs, bringing government closer to the people through broader participation and decentralization. Thus, the Report not only directs attention to refocusing the state's role, but also shows how countries might begin a process of rebuilding the state's capability.

Source: World Bank, *World Development Report 1997: The State in a Changing World* (Oxford: Oxford University Press, 1998). This summary may be found at http://www.worldbank.org/html/extpb/wdr97/english/wdr97su1.htm.

to the branches of government. Readers should note that our emphasis on the key institutional principles of the parliamentary system have led us to alter the usual order of presentation of these branches. Rather than begin with the cabinet, as most texts do, we address the legislature in Chapter 5, and follow with chapters on the political executive, the administrative state, and the courts. This arrangement reflects the importance of the principle of the "rule of law," which, among other things, requires all governmental action to be rooted in legislation. Chapter 9 marks a transition from institutions formally grounded in the constitution to extra-constitutional institutions that channel societal interests into, and are shaped by, the formal institutions. The first part of Chapter 9 examines Canada's electoral system, a component of the formal institutional structure; the balance of the chapter explores the elections shaped by the formal institutions. Chapters 10 and 11, on parties and interest groups, respectively, continue our examination of extra-constitutional institutions. Together these institutions compose the Canadian state, the parameters of power within and through which the Canadian political community tries to regulate its affairs, articulate its aspirations, and respond to challenges.

The paradox of Canadian political history has been the longevity, stability, and civility of a political system that nonetheless seems to be in perpetual turmoil, if not outright crisis. The constitutional battles of 1990–92 and the Quebec referendum of 1995 may seem distant, but core issues of constitutional renewal were never resolved. Aboriginal self-government, regional alienation, and Quebec's place in the federation remain on the national agenda. Moreover, globalization poses basic questions about both the role and capacity of a national government in the last years of the 20th century. Renewal on all fronts—constitutional, economic, and democratic—will demand careful consideration of institutional constraints and institutional options as we collectively redefine both the potentials and the parameters of Canadian politics.

KEY TERMS

institution
state
logic of an institution
institutional arena
institutional contestation
institutionalized ambivalence
nation-state
globalization

DISCUSSION QUESTIONS

1. In the ongoing debate over the voting rules in the next Quebec referendum, Ottawa insists that the Yes majority must be more than 50 percent plus one, while Quebec argues that a simple majority (50 percent plus one) is sufficient

to take the province out of Confederation. This is a simple but powerful example of the effect that the "rules of the game" can have. Discuss the impact of these voting rules on a referendum outcome, along with another rule that has been proposed: a series of mini-referendums in Quebec among Aboriginal and anglophone communities that would also have to be won in order to secure secession.

2. Courts have generally been more prepared than legislatures or cabinets to extend the rights of gays and lesbians. How would you explain this institutionally?
3. Does globalization affect you personally? If so, how? If not, is it an empty concept? And what do you think the political implications might be?
4. Carolyn Tuohy's notion of "institutionalized ambivalence" seems particularly apt in connection with the February 1998 Supreme Court reference on the constitutionality of Quebec separation. Spend a few minutes reading the sections in this book that describe the case (see "secession" reference in the Index), and discuss what the case reveals about "institutionalized ambivalence."
5. The Australians have decided to hold a national referendum in 1999 to determine whether to replace the monarchy with a president and turn the country into a republic. Despite the fact that the members of the British monarchy perform virtually no role in Australian politics (the same would be true of Canada), this was one of the most heated debates in Australian political history. Why are emotions running so high in this debate? Do you think a decision like this would generate a similar debate in Canada?

SUGGESTED READINGS

Atkinson, Michael M., ed. *Governing Canada: Institutions and Public Policy.* Toronto: Harcourt Brace Jovanovitch, 1993.

Cairns, Alan C. "The Governments and Societies of Canadian Federalism." *Canadian Journal of Political Science* 10 (1977), 695–725.

Dawson, R. MacGregor. *The Government of Canada.* Revised by Norman Ward. Toronto: University of Toronto Press, 1990.

Doern, G. Bruce, Leslie A. Pal, and Brian Tomlin, eds. *Border Crossings: The Internationalization of Canadian Public Policy.* Toronto: Oxford University Press, 1996.

Lusztig, Michael. "Constitutional Paralysis: Why Canadian Constitutional Initiatives Are Doomed to Fail." *Canadian Journal of Political Science* 27 (1994), 747–771.

McRoberts, Kenneth. *Misconceiving Canada: The Struggle for National Unity.* Toronto: Oxford University Press, 1997.

Simpson, Jeffrey. *Faultlines: Struggling for a Canadian Vision.* Toronto: HarperCollins, 1993.

Smith, David E. "Bagehot, the Crown and the Canadian Constitution." *Canadian Journal of Political Science* 28 (1995), 619–635.

Tuohy, Carolyn J. *Policy and Politics in Canada: Institutionalized Ambivalence.* Philadelphia: Temple University Press, 1992.

Weaver, R. Kent, and Bert A. Rockman, eds. *Do Institutions Matter? Government Capabilities in the United States and Abroad.* Washington: Brookings Institution, 1993.

NOTES

1. Alan C. Cairns, *Constitutionalism, Government, and Society in Canada,* ed. Douglas E. Williams (Toronto: McClelland & Stewart, 1988), 15.
2. "Reform MPs Go 'Hollywood,'" *Ottawa Citizen* (September 17, 1997), A3.
3. Joel Brooks, "Abortion Policy in Western Democracies: A Cross-National Analysis," *Governance* 5 (July 1992), 342–357.
4. F.L. Morton, *Morgentaler v. Borowski: Abortion, the Charter, and the Courts* (Toronto: McClelland & Stewart, 1992).
5. Thomas Flanagan, "The Staying Power of the Legislative Status Quo: Collective Choice in Canada's Parliament after Morgentaler," *Canadian Journal of Political Science* 30 (March 1997), 31–53; Leslie A. Pal, "How Ottawa Dithers: The Conservatives and Abortion Policy," in Frances Abele, ed., *How Ottawa Spends 1991–92: The Politics of Fragmentation* (Ottawa: Carleton University Press, 1991) 269–306.
6. Janine M. Brodie, Shelley A. Gavigan, and Jane Jenson, *The Politics of Abortion* (Toronto: Oxford University Press, 1992).
7. The following is based substantially on Edward Greenspon and Anthony Wilson-Smith, *Double Vision: The Inside Story of the Liberals in Power* (Toronto: Doubleday, 1996).
8. Donald J. Savoie, *The Politics of Public Spending in Canada* (Toronto: University of Toronto Press, 1990).
9. See *Highlights from the Report of the Royal Commission on Aboriginal Peoples* [on-line, World Wide Web; cited February 18, 1998; available at http://www.inac.gc.ca/rcap/report/index.html.
10. Notes for an Address by the Honourable Jane Stewart, Minister of Indian Affairs and Northern Development, on the occasion of the unveiling of *Gathering Strength: Canada's Aboriginal Action Plan,* January 7, 1998, Ottawa [on-line, World Wide Web; cited February 18, 1998; available at http://www.inac.gc.ca/info/speeches/jan98/action.html.
11. Sproule-Jones calls these the "basic logic of rule configurations." See Mark Sproule-Jones, *Governments at Work: Canadian Parliamentary Federalism and Its Public Policy Effects* (Toronto: University of Toronto Press, 1993), 23–28.
12. Peter H. Russell, *The Judiciary in Canada: The Third Branch of Government* (Toronto: McGraw-Hill Ryerson, 1987), 3.

13. Kenneth Kernaghan and John W. Langford, *The Responsible Public Servant* (Halifax: Institute for Research on Public Policy, 1990), especially chapters 2 and 3.
14. Peter Aucoin, "The Machinery of Government: From Trudeau's Rational Management to Mulroney's Brokerage Politics," in Leslie A. Pal and David Taras, eds., *Prime Ministers and Premiers* (Scarborough: Prentice-Hall Canada, 1988), 50–68; Colin Campbell, *Governments under Stress: Political Executives and Key Bureaucrats in Washington, London, and Ottawa* (Toronto: University of Toronto Press, 1983).
15. As we shall see in Chapter 8, however, the judicial system is not completely insulated from representational considerations. Judges are often appointed with an eye to regional balance, for example.
16. Anthony Hyde, *Promises, Promises: Breaking Faith in Canadian Politics* (Toronto: Viking, 1997).
17. There may be growing sensitivity to this as well as increasing demand that these "institutional spheres" remain coupled. Parties running for office in Canada have started issuing detailed platforms, of which the Liberals' 1993 Red Book (entitled *Creating Opportunity: A Liberal Plan for Canada*) is perhaps the most famous. It was because of promises made during the 1993 federal election that the Liberals had to adopt a tougher fiscal policy than they had planned and that Sheila Copps had to resign her seat and cabinet post and run in a by-election.
18. United Nations Development Programme, *Human Development Report 1997* [on-line, World Wide Web; cited February 18, 1998], available at http://www.undp.org/hdro/.
19. Carolyn J. Tuohy, *Policy and Politics in Canada: Institutionalized Ambivalence* (Philadelphia: Temple University Press, 1992), 5.
20. Ibid.
21. Expansion of the European Union was launched with the Treaty of Amsterdam of July 16, 1997. This treaty became the new foundation document for the EU, its institutions, and goals. Potential candidates for membership include Bulgaria, Cyprus, the Czech Republic, Estonia, Hungary, Latvia, Lithuania, Poland, Romania, Slovakia, Slovenia and Turkey. The full text of the treaty may be found at http://ue.eu.int/Amsterdam/en/amsteroc/en.htm.
22. The Kyoto Protocol and Canada's Action Plan on Climate Control may be found at http://www.ec.gc.ca/climate/.
23. See David Held, *Political Theory and the Modern State: Essays on State, Power and Democracy* (Cambridge: Policy Press, 1989) and *Democracy and the Global Order: From the Modern State to Cosmopolitan Governance* (Stanford, Calif.: Stanford University Press, 1995).
24. G. Bruce Doern, Leslie A. Pal, and Brian Tomlin, "The Internationalization of Canadian Public Policy," in G. Bruce Doern, Leslie A. Pal, and Brian Tomlin, eds., *Border Crossings: The Internationalization of Canadian Public Policy* (Toronto: Oxford University Press, 1996), 3.
25. Keith Banting, George Hoberg, and Richard Simeon, "Introduction," in Keith Banting, George Hoberg, and Richard Simeon, eds., *Degrees of Freedom: Canada and the United States in a Changing World* (Montreal: McGill-Queen's University Press, 1997), 26.
26. Francis Cairncross, *The Death of Distance: How the Communications Revolution Will Change Our Lives* (Boston, Mass.: Harvard Business School Press, 1997), 6.
27. Statistics Canada.

28. Richard Simeon, George Hoberg, and Keith Banting, "Globalization, Fragmentation, and the Social Contract," in Banting, Hoberg, and Simeon, eds., *Degrees of Freedom,* 391–394.
29. "The Internet was one of the major reasons the militia movement expanded faster than any hate group in history." Kenneth Stern, *A Force upon the Plain: The American Militia Movement and the Politics of Hate* (New York: Simon and Schuster, 1996), 228; cited in Manuel Castells, *The Power of Identity* (Oxford: Blackwell Publishers, 1997), 84.
30. Fred Pearce, "Greenpeace: Mindbombing the Media," *Wired* (May 1996), 51–53, 87–88; David Ronfeldt, "Cyberocracy Is Coming," *The Information Society* 8 (1992): 243–296.
31. Oliver Norton, "Private Spy," *Wired* (August 1, 1997), 114–119; 149–152; David Lyon, *The Electronic Eye: The Rise of Surveillance Society* (Minneapolis: University of Minneapolis Press, 1994).
32. Richard Simeon, George Hoberg, and Keith Banting, "Globalization, Fragmentation, and the Social Contract," in Banting, Hoberg, and Simeon, eds., *Degrees of Freedom,* 396.
33. Thomas Courchene, *Access: A Convention on the Canadian Economic and Social Systems* (Toronto: Ministry of Intergovernmental Affairs, 1996).

THE CONSTITUTION: CANADA'S "MASTER INSTITUTION"

2

The constitution ... may be viewed as the master institution of society.[1]

Canada's constitution reflects three organizing principles: parliamentary democracy, federalism, and the Charter of Rights. Parliamentary democracy governs the relationships between branches of government; federalism describes the relationship between orders of government; and the Charter governs the relationship between governments and citizens. The rules institutionalizing these three principles are found in entrenched constitutional law, ordinary statutes, judicial decisions, and conventional understandings and practices. Constitutional politics often arises out of the tensions between the three governing principles. Federalism and parliamentary democracy, for example, have clashed since 1867, and both have clashed with the Charter since 1982. Constitutional politics also occurs within the institutions established by each of the governing principles. Constitutional politics involves either competing interpretations of existing rules or demands explicitly to change or replace them. When the demands for explicit change become sufficiently comprehensive and radical, when the basic principles of the regime are called into question, ordinary constitutional politics (which is unavoidable) is replaced by megaconstitutional politics. Megaconstitutional politics—the subject of Chapter 3—has been Canada's fate for nearly 40 years.

■ ■ ■

We begin our study of Canadian institutions with the constitution because it is what Alan Cairns has called our "master institution."[2] The degree of importance suggested by this terminology is implicit in the very word "constitution," which shares the same root as the verb "to constitute" and denotes the idea of building and creating, of calling forth into existence. The constitution is the overarching political institution that includes all others, such as federalism and the branches of government. It is the comprehensive set of rules that organizes the distribution and exercise of power within and among all of the state's major political institutions.

The constitution is more than the sum of its parts, however. It is most fundamentally the set of basic principles that breathes life into the particularities of its component institutions. Canada's fundamental constitutional principles are reflected in

FIGURE 2.1 RELATIONSHIPS GOVERNED BY A CONSTITUTION

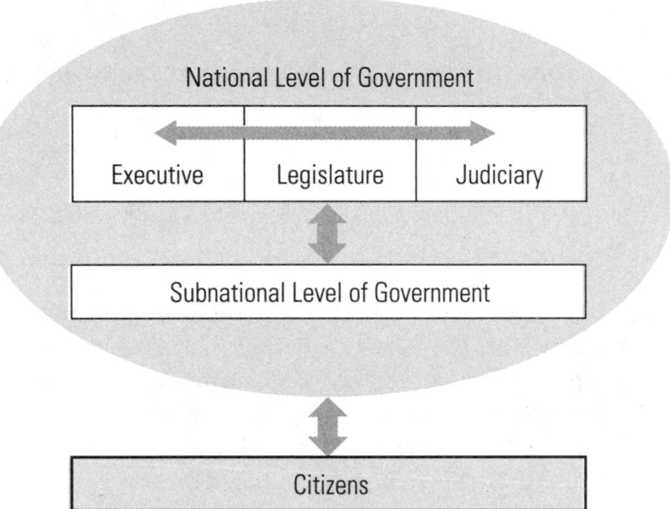

the federal division of the state into two orders of parliamentary democracy constrained by constitutionally entrenched rights. In other words, the constitution embodies three fundamental organizational traits: **parliamentary democracy, federalism,** and the **Charter of Rights and Freedoms.** Important conflicts or tensions exist both within and among the sets of principles underlying each of these three features. Together, the conflicting principles underlying parliamentary democracy, federalism, and the Charter of Rights "constitute" the Canadian regime and its most characteristic political issues.

Each of the three principal features of the Canadian constitution responds to one of the three kinds of constitutional relationships pictured in Figure 2.1. The first relationship concerns the branches of government, namely, the legislature, the executive, and the judiciary. All constitutions specify how each of these is to be organized, the balance of power among them, and, in broad strokes, their relationships to one another. Canada's branches of government reflect mainly the principles of parliamentary democracy it inherited from Britain.

The second key relationship, addressed by some but not all constitutions, concerns the relationship between equally sovereign orders of government. Not all political systems divide sovereignty or the supreme political power[3] between two legally distinct orders. Those that do so are called federal systems. Federalism is characteristic of both Canada and the United States, whose constitutions allocate powers between the central government and provincial or state governments. Indeed, while Canada's parliamentary institutions flow from the British inheritance, its federalism was inspired by the American example.

A third relationship regulated by constitutions is the one between citizens and their governments. Often this relationship is governed by a constitutional bill or charter of rights. Here Canada's primary sources of constitutional inspiration differ markedly. Britain to this day has no constitutionally entrenched bill of rights, while the United States adopted its bill of rights shortly after the ratification of its constitution in 1789. Canada was for much of its history firmly in the British camp on this question. After World War II, however, it wavered between the two models before moving decisively in the American direction with the adoption of the Charter of Rights and Freedoms in 1982.

The constitution that addresses these three relationships is far from a merely technical apportionment of offices, rights, and responsibilities. The allocation, organization, and limitation of political power can never be neutral; it is always grounded in fundamental ideas about the nature of politics itself and sometimes the nature of the polity to which it applies. A constitution, in short, in articulating the "rules of the game" provides a sense of the game itself, its purpose, and its ultimate goal. In any game, moreover, the defining rules obviously influence the kinds of players who are best equipped to compete; thus the typical NBA basketball player would have been unlikely to excel at NHL hockey and vice versa. A game's rules also influence the moves and strategies most likely to succeed—witness the discernible differences between international and NHL hockey, owing partly to differences in the size of ice surfaces and rules concerning fighting. So it is with constitutional rules that constrain the game of politics: players who can dominate under one set of rules might lose influence under another. As we shall see, institutions (and especially the constitution) significantly position different political constituencies in a symbolic order of precedence. Moreover, by giving individuals strong incentives to organize themselves into constitutionally relevant constituencies, the constitution may shape the very identities of citizens.

These characteristics of constitutional rules ensure that they will be controversial and contested, and that constitutional contestation will be an ongoing feature of any country's politics. The degree and scope of constitutional politics will vary, however. At the very least, partisan divisions will emerge over the proper interpretation of particular constitutional rules. The legitimacy of existing rules may also be challenged more directly, raising the prospect of explicit reform or amendment. The latter kind of challenge can range from requests for minor tinkering to demands for wholesale transformation. Among other factors affecting the kind and scope of constitutional politics is the degree of inconsistency within or among a constitution's basic "logic" or principles. In Canada's case, the fires of constitutional politics have been (and continue to be) fuelled by tensions both within and among the central features of parliamentary democracy, federalism, and entrenched constitutional rights.

The constitution that establishes these three central principles is composed of three main kinds of constitutional rules: two forms of constitutional law (entrenched and non-entrenched) and the extralegal category of constitutional

FIGURE 2.2 **KINDS OF CONSTITUTIONAL RULES**

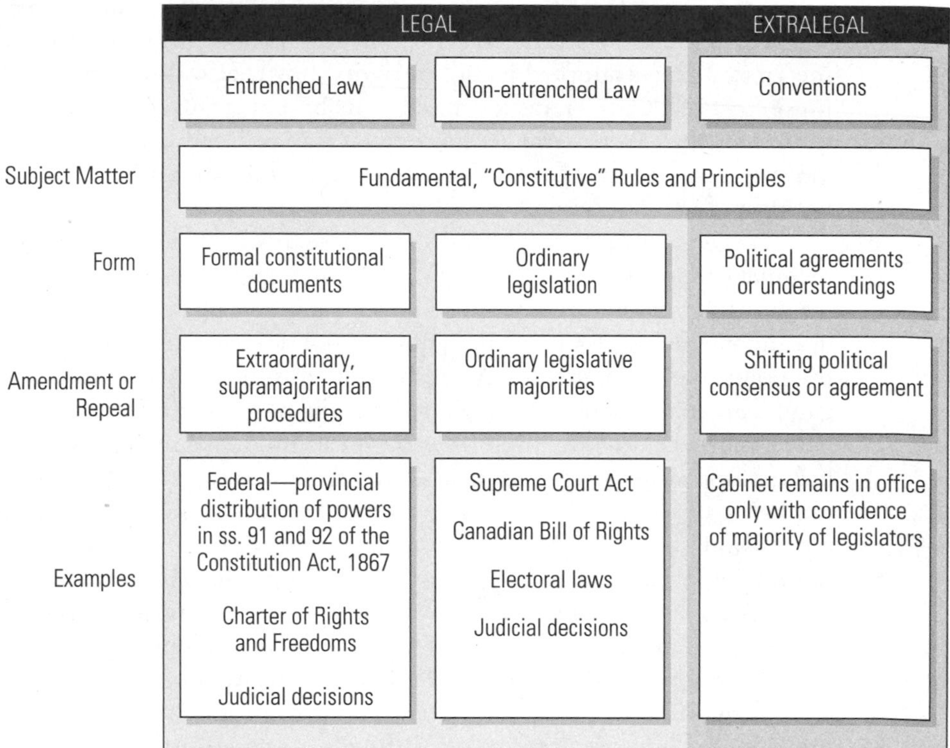

convention. Figure 2.2 provides a schematic overview of our discussion of these different rules.

ENTRENCHED CONSTITUTIONAL LAW

Entrenched constitutional law is considerably more difficult to repeal or amend than ordinary legislation. A normal statute can be changed, just as it was enacted, by a simple legislative majority (50 percent plus one). By contrast, amendments to the United States Constitution, the historical model of modern entrenched constitutions, must first be proposed either by a two-thirds vote in both houses of Congress or by a constitutional convention requested by at least two-thirds of the state legislatures, and then ratified by three-fourths of the states (either through their legislatures or special state conventions). This amending formula is itself part of the entrenched U.S. constitution.

Canada's constitutional law was not entrenched by a similar amending procedure until 1982. Before then, Canada's entrenched constitution consisted mainly of British statutes—the **British North America (BNA) Act, 1867,** and its subsequent amendments—which established most of the familiar institutional structure of the Canadian state, especially parliamentary government and federalism. Although section 92(1) of the BNA Act gave the provinces the power to amend their own constitutions through ordinary legislation ("except as regards the Office of Lieutenant Governor"), this power was not, in fact, a wide-ranging power of amendment,[4] and the federal government originally enjoyed no similar power. In practice, then, most of the BNA Act could be formally changed only by the parliament that passed it. Moreover, since the BNA Act itself was an ordinary statute of the British Parliament, only an ordinary statute of that Parliament was required to amend it. In 1949 Britain added a new section—91(1)—to the BNA Act, giving the federal government a limited authority, comparable to the provincial power in section 92(1), to amend its own constitution. Nevertheless, the essential structure of Canadian parliamentary government and federalism remained under the legal control of the British Parliament at Westminster. Thus, section 91(1) enabled the federal government to make such "housekeeping" amendments as providing for the retirement of senators at age 75[5] and adding representatives for the Yukon and Northwest Territories to both the House of Commons[6] and the Senate,[7] but not to make more substantial changes, such as abolishing or radically transforming the nature of the Senate.[8]

The BNA Act was made legally paramount over conflicting Canadian laws by another British statute, the **Colonial Laws Validity Act,** which invalidated colonial legislation that conflicted with certain British statutes. Enacted in 1865, two years before the BNA Act, the Colonial Laws Validity Act was actually a liberating statute, intended to assure colonial legislatures that the legislation they enacted for local conditions could legitimately differ from, or even conflict with, comparable British legislation. Only "imperial statutes" that applied directly to the colony would override conflicting colonial legislation. The BNA Act, of course, was such an imperial statute, and was thus paramount over domestic Canadian legislation.[9] Whether Canadian legislation conflicted with the BNA Act was a question ultimately resolved by the **Judicial Committee of the Privy Council (JCPC),** an imperial court based in London that served as Canada's final court of appeal until 1949. From the perspective of the British Parliament, neither the Colonial Laws Validity Act nor the BNA Act were formally entrenched; both remained ordinary statutes subject to amendment or repeal through normal legislative procedure at Westminster. For the colonial legislatures, on the other hand, the combination of the two acts provided something akin to entrenched constitutional law.

In the 19th century the lack of a domestic amending formula was consistent with Canada's colonial status. By the 1920s, however, it was clear to all concerned that Britain's major overseas dominions—Canada, Australia, New Zealand, South Africa, the Irish Free State, and Newfoundland—had outgrown their colonial status and were

DOSSIER 2.1 WHY THE BNA ACT CONTAINED NO COMPREHENSIVE AMENDING FORMULA

It is generally known that the British North America Act of 1867 contained no procedure for its own amendment....

It is hindsight to say that this ignored the complexities of federalism, since the men of 1867 thought they had avoided those complexities by discarding the unwanted features of the American model.... John A. Macdonald expressed the view that a province's representatives in the federal Parliament at Ottawa were the only "constitutional exponents of the wishes of the people" with regard to federal–provincial relations, and that the provincial legislatures should not be concerned with such matters. Logically, this could only mean that a request to Westminster for a constitutional amendment would be a unilateral act by the federal government or Parliament. As long as the Macdonald view of federalism prevailed, the question of involving provincial governments or legislatures in the process of amendment could not arise.

F.R. Scott has suggested an additional although related reason why the BNA Act was not provided with an amendment formula of the kind normally found in federal constitutions. The reason was the belief held by the Fathers of Confederation that their distinctive and un-American approach to the problem of dividing legislative powers between the two orders of government had ensured that amendments would be largely unnecessary. In the United States, and subsequently in Australia, the national government was given only a few specified legislative powers, with the residue being left to the states. As time went on and the national government required legislative authority over new subjects, the constitution had to be amended accordingly. In Canada, on the other hand, the national government was supposedly given from the outset almost complete legislative powers, and any authority over unspecified or unanticipated matters was contained in the general power to make laws for the peace, order, and good government of Canada. Thus there was little reason to suppose that many amendments would be necessary.

For both of these reasons the question of adding an American-style amending procedure to the BNA Act only arose in the twentieth century, after Lord Watson and other members of the Judicial Committee of the Privy Council had placed their official stamp of approval on an American-style theory of federalism.

Source: Reprinted with permission from Garth Stevenson, *Unfulfilled Union: Canadian Federalism and National Unity*, rev. ed. (Toronto: Gage, 1982), 199–200.

in practice fully independent sovereign entities. To recognize this evolution, Britain, in consultation with the dominions, agreed to remove the legal trappings of colonialism. This was largely achieved in 1931 through the **Statute of Westminster,** whose section 2 provided that the Colonial Laws Validity Act no longer applied to dominion parliaments.[10]

But if Canadian legislation could no longer be voided on the grounds of conflict with imperial statutes, what would prevent Ottawa or the provinces from disregarding the federal–provincial distribution of powers in sections 91–95 of the BNA Act? The provinces especially found this a worrisome question and successfully pressed to have the following provision (subsection 7[1]) included in the Statute of Westminster: "Nothing in this Act shall be deemed to apply to the repeal, amendment, or alteration of the British North America Acts, 1867 to 1930, or any order, rule or regulation made thereunder."[11] This section in effect exempted the BNA Act from the general rule of the Statute of Westminster and thus maintained its overriding status.

In strictly legal terms, then, Canada's formal constitutional law after 1931 remained ordinary British legislation, subject to repeal or amendment as the British Parliament saw fit. In practice, everyone understood that Britain would amend the BNA Act only at the request of Canada. An understanding gradually developed that such requests would come in the form of a joint resolution of the Canadian Senate and House of Commons, and that Ottawa would submit to Britain resolutions implicating the provinces only with the consent of the affected provinces. Indeed, it was widely assumed in the 1960s and 1970s (though not necessarily earlier)[12] that major amendments required the unanimous consent of the provinces.[13] So long as some understanding of this sort was adhered to, it constituted a de facto domestic amending formula of considerable difficulty, which effectively secured the constitutional entrenchment of the BNA Act. This situation did not change until 1982, when Canada adopted the **Constitution Act, 1982.**

The Constitution Act, 1982, was Britain's last constitutional enactment on behalf of Canada. Future amendments would be covered by the entirely domestic amending formula contained in Part V of that Act. In fact, Part V contains five different formulas. As Kent Weaver notes, "Perhaps the simplest thing that can be said about the history of Canada's constitutional amending formula is that it went from unwritten to unwieldy without ever passing through understandable."[14] First, under the general formula, set out mainly in section 38, some of Canada's entrenched constitutional law can be amended only with the consent of the federal Senate and House of Commons and the legislative assemblies of at least two-thirds (i.e., seven) of the provinces, provided those seven contain at least 50 percent of the population of all the provinces. This has been dubbed the **seven-fifty rule.** A dissenting province may opt out of amendments passed under this formula that "derogate from [its] legislative powers... proprietary rights or any other rights or privileges of [its] legislature or government" (ss. 38[2] and [3]). Second, section 41 subjects the amendment of other parts of our constitutional law to the even stricter requirement of the consent of Parliament and all of the provincial legislatures. With respect to matters covered by this **unanimity rule,** each of Canada's eleven governments enjoys an effective veto. Third, amendments involving one or more, but not all, provinces require the consent of the Parliament of Canada and the affected provinces (s. 43). Together these three formulas govern the kinds of amendments that had previously required British legislation; they brought the entrenched constitution home, or "patriated" it, as constitutional writers usually say. (Thus, the 1982 amendments are often called the **patriation** package.)[15]

Part V of the Constitution Act, 1982, is not exhausted by the amending formula that patriated the constitution. As noted above, both orders of government had previously enjoyed a limited right to amend certain aspects of their own institutional structures through ordinary legislation. These powers have been shifted from their former homes in sections 91(1) and 92(1) of the BNA Act and now appear in sections 44 (federal) and 45 (provincial) of the Constitution Act, 1982; they constitute the fourth and fifth components of the 1982 package of amending formulas.

By virtue especially of the seven-fifty and unanimity rules, Canada acquired the kind of entrenched documentary constitution pioneered by the United States. This entrenched constitution comprises both a series of formal documents and judicial decisions interpreting those documents.

Documents

The new amending procedures apply to the "Constitution of Canada," which, according to section 52(2) of the Constitution Act, 1982, includes not only that act itself but also a series of constitutive British and Canadian laws listed in a schedule to the act entitled "Modernization of the Constitution." These laws include most prominently the British North America Act, 1867, which is renamed the **Constitution Act, 1867,** and its amendments, which also received new titles (usually the Constitution Act of a particular year). Also incorporated into the entrenched constitution by section 52(2) of the Constitution Act, 1982, are the laws and orders that brought other former colonies or territories (Rupert's Land, British Columbia, Prince Edward Island, and Newfoundland) into Confederation or created new provinces (Manitoba, Saskatchewan, and Alberta) out of federal territories. The schedule also lists four pieces of domestic Canadian legislation dealing with such matters as representation of the Yukon and Northwest Territories and the retirement of senators at 75. These amendments were enacted by ordinary legislation under section 91(1) of the BNA Act but can no longer be repealed in the same manner. Although all of these documents are of importance, the central documents are the Constitution Acts of 1867 and 1982.

The Constitution Act, 1867

This act, as amended, remains at the core of Canada's constitutional structure. The Charter of Rights and Freedoms gets much of the public attention nowadays, and is certainly of major importance, but we must remember that the governments it constrains are constituted and fundamentally shaped by the Constitution Act, 1867. Furthermore, the 1867 Act is the ultimate foundation of the courts that enforce Canada's constitutional law, including the Charter. Canada is certainly a different country because of the constitutional entrenchment of the Charter in 1982, but it would be even more different if it were not a federal country based on parliamentary

DOSSIER 2.2 CANADIAN CONSTITUTIONAL DEVELOPMENT FROM 1763 TO 1867

It is common to identify the birth of Canada with 1867, the year of Confederation. Having an official birthday of this sort is certainly useful; without one, Canada would have been unable to hold the official celebrations marking its centennial in 1967 and its 125th birthday in 1992. Constitutionally speaking, however, it is somewhat misleading to date Canada's origins from 1867. The British North America (BNA) Act of that year was certainly a constitutional watershed, but it was far from the beginning of Canada's constitutional development. Three colonies—Canada, Nova Scotia, and New Brunswick—joined together in 1867 to become the new Dominion of Canada's first four provinces (pre-1867 "Canada" was divided into the provinces of Ontario and Quebec). Each of the confederating colonies had a long constitutional history before 1867, and much of that history contributed to our current constitutional structure. The BNA Act, then, was far from a wholly new departure. It built on and incorporated the principles of parliamentary democracy established in the pre-Confederation period.

In the pre-Confederation era, the constitutional history of the colony of Canada is especially significant. The BNA Act was this colony's fifth constitution, not its first. The first British constitution for the former colony of New France was the **Royal Proclamation, 1763,** and the attendant instructions given to the first governor, James Murray. Although the Royal Proclamation was issued shortly after the 1763 Treaty of Paris formally ended the Seven Years' War between France and Britain, New France had in fact been under British military rule since Wolfe's defeat of Montcalm on the Plains of Abraham in 1759 and Montreal's capitulation in 1760. The Royal Proclamation replaced this temporary military administration with the first civilian constitution for the new British colony of "Quebec."

Lasting only eleven years, the constitutional system established by the Royal Proclamation was replaced by the **Quebec Act, 1774.** This second constitution enjoyed somewhat greater longevity, but not much. It was in its turn superseded by the **Constitution Act, 1791,** which divided the colony into two: Upper Canada and Lower Canada. This act had much more staying power than its predecessors, lasting half a century, until the two Canadas were reunified by the **Act of Union, 1840,** the fourth pre-Confederation constitution. The two Canadas were separated again in 1867 when they became the provinces of Ontario and Quebec in the new Confederation of that year.

institutions. The latter characteristics stem in large measure from the Constitution Act, 1867.

The preamble to the Constitution Act, 1867, expresses the desire of the three confederating colonies—Canada, Nova Scotia, and New Brunswick—"to be federally united into One Dominion under the Crown of the United Kingdom of Great Britain and Ireland, with a Constitution similar in Principle to that of the United Kingdom."

Through the last phrase, the Constitution Act continued the British-style parliamentary institutions that had gradually been transplanted to Canada during the pre-Confederation period. At the core of these parliamentary institutions are the institutional principles of representative and "responsible government." Prior to 1867, these principles were highly contested, and lay at the heart of the pre-Confederation constitutional politics summarized in Dossier 2.2. By the time of Confederation, however, the battles fought on behalf of representative and responsible government had been won decisively (see Dossiers 2.3 and 2.6). Indeed, these basic principles of parliamentary democracy were so taken for granted by 1867 that, as we shall see when we discuss constitutional conventions, some of their most important institutional implications were not explicitly spelled out in the Constitution Act; they were simply understood to be part of what it meant to have a constitution similar in principle to that of Britain.

The chief innovation of the Constitution Act, 1867, lay in its somewhat hesitant and ambiguous establishment of federalism. The act reflects federalism most obviously in giving constitutionally entrenched status to two orders of parliamentary government—federal and provincial. Jurisdictional responsibilities are allocated to Ottawa and the provinces mainly by sections 91–95 of the Constitution Act. Section 91 gives to "the Queen, by and with the advice and consent of the Senate and House of Commons," the power "to make laws for the **peace, order and good government** of Canada in relation to all matters not ... assigned exclusively to the legislatures of the provinces." Commonly abbreviated as the **POGG** power, this provision effectively gives to Ottawa what is known as the **residual power** in federal systems. As its name implies, the residual power covers any areas of jurisdiction that are not otherwise accounted for in the formal distribution of powers. The American and Australian constitutions do not give the residual power to the central government; they enumerate the powers of the central government, leaving everything else to the states.[16] The Canadian constitution does the reverse.

Well, not quite the reverse. The American and Australian constitutions simply leave it at reserving all unspecified powers to the residual authority. No further specification of the powers of that authority was deemed necessary. In Canada, by contrast, section 91, having given Ottawa the residual authority, goes on, "for greater certainty, but not so as to restrict the generality of the foregoing," to particularize 29 areas of federal jurisdiction. These encompass most of the powers considered important to economic management in 1867, including jurisdiction over the public debt, trade and commerce, the raising of money by any mode or system of taxation, the borrowing of money on the public credit, navigation and shipping, currency, banking, weights and measures, bills of exchange and promissory notes, interest, legal tender, bankruptcy and insolvency, patents of invention and discovery, and copyrights. Other significant federal areas of jurisdiction include Indians, lands reserved for the Indians, and criminal law. Section 91 ends with the "deeming clause," according to which "any matter coming within any of the classes of subjects enumerated in this section shall not be deemed to come within the class of matters of a local or private

DOSSIER 2.3 CULTURAL DUALITY AND THE STRUGGLE FOR REPRESENTATIVE GOVERNMENT

Representative government involves the election of representatives to an assembly responsible for the enactment of legislation. In the 18th century, British settlers in the New World colonies considered such representative government their birthright, and in many colonies representative institutions were granted with relative dispatch. For example, the first elected legislative assembly met in Nova Scotia (which then included what is now New Brunswick) in 1758. In the colony of Canada, however, representative institutions were not granted until 1791, over three decades after their introduction in Nova Scotia. The delay is explained by the fact that the British authorities did not consider representative government to be compatible with cultural and religious duality. The British authorities thus preferred to delay representative government until a combination of English settlement and public policy had achieved the assimilation of the predominantly French and Catholic population. Thus, while the Royal Proclamation of 1763 promised representative institutions at some point in the future, it conferred immediate governing power on an appointed governor, advised by an executive council (from which Catholics were excluded).

By the 1770s, however, assimilationist expectations no longer seemed reasonable, and the constitutional strategy changed. Large-scale English settlement had not occurred and seemed unlikely to materialize. In addition, the growing restiveness of the American colonies made it prudent to secure the loyalty of Quebec by abandoning assimilationist policies. The 1774 Quebec Act thus strengthened the protection of religious freedom for Catholics and guaranteed the future of French civil law to govern private relationships, though British criminal law would continue to apply. A quasi-feudal system of landholding, known as the seigneurial system, was also retained.

The Quebec Act did not grant representative institutions, however. The imperial authorities concluded that the highly traditional, hierarchical French society they were protecting neither needed nor wanted representative democracy. Certainly the clergy and the seigneurs—the two elements of French society the authorities were most anxious to placate—were not well disposed to this kind of democratic reform, and representative government was thus once again put off. The governor and his executive council remained in charge, though Catholics could now be appointed to the council.

The successful American Revolution changed things again. Quebec had in fact remained loyal (or at least neutral) during this struggle, but for this very reason the northern colony attracted a substantial influx of **loyalists** from the new United States. Having long been accustomed to representative institutions, these new settlers added their voices to those of Quebec's existing English inhabitants in demanding an elected assembly.

By 1791 Britain was prepared to accede to this demand, but once again the problem of linguistic and cultural heterogeneity influenced the institutional calculations. It was still assumed that representative institutions could not effectively serve a community significantly divided along cultural lines. This meant that a single assembly could not be established for the entire colony. The solution lay in the fact that most of the English population (largely loyalist settlers) was concentrated in the western part of the colony. It thus seemed possible to grant representative institutions without abandoning the policy of accommodating the French. Both the French and the English could be given their own assemblies in separate colonies, east and west of the Ottawa River. The Constitution Act, 1791, effected just such a division, establishing the two new colonies of **Upper Canada** (the western portion) and **Lower Canada** (the eastern part), and granting a two-chambered, or bicameral, legislature to each. Representative government was still linked to the idea of cultural homogeneity, but the idea was now to separate the two cultural communities rather than to assimilate one of them. When the two colonies were recombined under the 1840 Act of Union, assimilation was once again the governing policy (see Dossier 2.6).

The 1791 creation of Upper and Lower Canada foreshadowed the similar division of the 1840 Union into the provinces of Ontario and Quebec at Confederation. In both cases, the end was to give the French and English populations control over their own representative institutions. And in both cases, this strategy was beset by the same difficulty: the French and English populations were not (and are not) neatly compartmentalized within jurisdictional boundaries. This has meant that the inevitable division between majority and minority in a representative democracy has not infrequently coincided with the explosive divisions of language, religion, and culture.

The question of whether and to what extent representative institutions can or should represent culturally divided populations remains with us to this day. That this issue continues to animate competing projects of territorial combination and separation, moreover, is evident in modern debates about the separation of Quebec.

nature comprised in the enumeration of the classes of subjects by this act assigned exclusively to the legislatures of the provinces."

The main source of the provincial powers to which the deeming clause refers is section 92, which gives provincial legislatures the "exclusive" power "to make laws in relation to matters coming within" a list of 16 subjects. These include "property and civil rights in the province," hospitals, and the "administration of justice in the province." Section 93 continues the list of provincial powers, giving the provinces authority over education. Two policy areas, agriculture and immigration, were explicitly made areas of **concurrent jurisdiction** (s. 95). In these concurrent areas, both orders of government are allowed to legislate, with federal legislation prevailing in the case of a conflict (known as the rule of federal **paramountcy**).

This original division of powers was clearly intended to embody a much more centralized constitutional logic than the one Canadians became accustomed to in the late 20th century. Indeed, some scholars describe the 1867 Constitution Act as originally establishing a form of **quasi-federalism** at best.[17] A number of constitutional provisions point to such quasi-federal centralization. POGG itself, in giving Ottawa the residual power, was seen by John A. Macdonald as the primary centralizing provision.

> *In framing the constitution, care should be taken to avoid the mistakes and weaknesses of the United States' system, the primary error of which was the reservation to the different States of all powers not delegated to the General Government. We must reverse this process by establishing a strong central Government, to which shall belong all powers not specially conferred on the provinces.*[18]

Macdonald also thought that the powers withheld from the federal government and given expressly to the provinces were quite limited and established no more than "minor legislatures for local purposes."[19] One indication of this is the distribution of financial resources between the two orders of government. Thus, while Ottawa enjoys the right to raise money by any system of taxation, the provinces are limited to "direct taxation within the province." The prime example of direct taxation is the income tax, and in 1867 no income tax existed. Moreover, it was generally assumed that income taxes were undesirable and would never be enacted.[20] Provinces might also raise money through the "management and sale" of provincially owned public lands and timber, or through imposing "shop, saloon, tavern, auctioneer and other licenses," but it is clear that their revenue-generating power was to be much more limited than Ottawa's. "From the start," as Robert Vipond points out, "they depended on federal subsidies."[21]

The centralizing logic of the original constitution is also evident, ironically, in section 92 itself, ostensibly the list of exclusive provincial powers. Section 92(10)(c) grants the provinces power over "local works and undertakings," except for those falling in certain classes. The best-known of these exceptions is the so-called **declaratory power,** which gives Ottawa power over such local works "as, although wholly situate within the province, are before or after their execution declared by the Parliament of Canada to be for the general advantage of Canada or for the advantage of two or more of the provinces." The declaratory power has been used 472 times, mainly to bring local railways under federal jurisdiction.[22] It is also the basis of the Canadian Wheat Board.[23]

Section 93 too contains "local work" under provincial authority that Ottawa may bring into its own sphere of influence. This section gives the provinces "exclusive" authority over education, provided only that they do not "prejudicially affect" any rights and privileges of denominational schools existing at Confederation. If provinces do infringe such denominational rights, the affected groups may appeal to the federal government, which is authorized to step in and enact **remedial legislation.**

The constitutional organization of the judicial system also reflects the quasi-federal logic in the 1867 Constitution Act. Whereas many federal systems divide judicial as well as legislative power, so as to give each order of government its own courts to interpret and apply its own laws, Canada's judicial structure is unitary or integrated. The judges of the most important provincial courts are appointed by the federal government, and these and other provincial courts hear cases under both federal and provincial laws. Interpretive disputes arising under both kinds of law, moreover, are ultimately resolved by the same final court of appeal: the JCPC until 1949 and the Supreme Court since then. As Peter Russell points out, comparatively speaking, "the Canadian judicial system ranks as one of the most integrated, or least federalized."[24]

One important federal power with centralizing implications, the so-called **spending power,** is not mentioned anywhere in the constitution but has been implied from a number of explicit provisions.[25] This power is related to the unequal division of financial resources between the two orders of government. Allowing Ottawa to spend its excess revenues for purposes outside its areas of jurisdiction, the spending power is the basis of the well-established Canadian practice of equalization grants, through which Ottawa redistributes wealth from the richer or "have" provinces (currently British Columbia, Alberta, and Ontario) to the poorer or "have not" provinces (the other seven).[26] The spending power also allows Ottawa to establish shared-cost programs, which provide part of the funding for provincial programs. These shared-cost programs may come with strings attached, requiring provinces to adapt their federally funded programs to standards set by Ottawa. Such "conditional grants" permit Ottawa to influence policymaking in areas of provincial jurisdiction. The spending power that underlies such practices is implied from the federal powers to tax (s. 91[3]), regulate public property (s. 91[1A]), and appropriate federal funds (s. 106).

Perhaps the most dramatic constitutional symptoms of centralization in the Constitution Act, 1867, were the powers of **reservation** and **disallowance,** which established the same kind of quasi-colonial relationship between Ottawa and the provinces as existed between Britain and Canada as a whole. Just as the governor general is given the power to reserve legislation for London's consideration (ss. 55 and 57), so the provincial lieutenant governor, an appointee of the federal government, is given the power to "reserve" legislation for Ottawa's consideration (s. 90). Such reserved legislation is without effect unless it is approved by the supervising government within a specified period. Furthermore, even when legislation is not reserved by the Crown's representative, it is subject to outright "disallowance" by London (vis-à-vis Canada—s. 56) and Ottawa (vis-à-vis the provinces—s. 90).[27]

If the allocation of jurisdictional responsibilities suggests a centralized system, the powers of reservation and disallowance call into question whether Canada was really intended to be a federal system at all, at least if we define federalism in the modern sense of divided sovereignty between two orders of government, each of which owes its power to a constitution rather than to the other order of government, and neither of which is therefore subordinate to the other. In this respect, the early constitution embodied an unresolved tension between conflicting institutional logics. On the one hand, however centralized the division of powers in sections 91 and 92 may have been, both sections clearly refer to "exclusive" provincial powers, suggesting at least some degree of divided sovereignty. The powers of reservation and disal-

DOSSIER 2.4: CONSTITUTIONAL INDICATIONS OF QUASI-FEDERAL CENTRALISM

- POGG/residual power
- unbalanced taxing resources
- federal spending power
- declaratory power
- remedial legislation
- federal appointment of judges in provincially constituted courts
- federal appointment of provincial lieutenant governor
- reservation
- disallowance

lowance pointed in precisely the opposite direction, suggesting that sovereignty was ultimately the preserve of the federal government in Ottawa. The latter reading of the act clearly reflected the views of Macdonald, who explicitly said that the federal government had been given "all the principles and powers of sovereignty" and that the provinces were "subordinate" legislatures, little more than glorified municipalities.[28] In Macdonald's view, as Vipond summarizes it,

> *The extent of provincial autonomy or liberty would depend on the judgment of the federal government just as the extent of colonial freedom depended on the judgment of the imperial authorities. The provinces, like the colonies, might be allowed considerable room to legislate freely on those matters local in nature. But there could be no mistake, according to Macdonald, that in the final analysis the federal government was sovereign over the provinces just as the imperial Parliament was sovereign over Canada.*[29]

This is why we began this discussion of the 1867 Constitution Act by saying that it established the basis for federalism hesitantly and ambiguously.

Like parliamentary democracy, in short, federalism, which we now take for granted, was once a highly contested principle. Unlike parliamentary democracy, however, the battles on its behalf had not been won by 1867, and it was by no means taken for granted at that foundational moment. At best, the BNA Act reflected considerable indecision and ambiguity on the question. In fact, federalism established itself as a central principle of Canada's constitution only by gradually winning a protracted series of post-Confederation political struggles. The story of Canadian contestation over the essential principle of modern federalism is reserved for Chapter 4. For the moment, it is sufficient to indicate one of its chief results: the delegitimation of such powers as reservation, disallowance, and the declaratory power, so that they now exist only on paper and are never used.

As these quasi-imperial powers declined, the emerging federal principle of divided sovereignty clashed with the primary principle of the British constitutionalism Canada had inherited, namely, the principle of **parliamentary sovereignty,** or **parliamentary supremacy.** The British Parliament, in A.V. Dicey's classic formulation, means "the Queen, the House of Lords, and the House of Commons; these three bodies acting together may be aptly described as the Queen in Parliament."[30] Acting together, they had the right to make or unmake any law whatsoever, and no other body had the right to "override or set aside the legislation of Parliament."[31] Among other things, this meant that no parliament could bind its successors; every parliament is supreme and may make laws as it sees fit. As Dicey put it,

> *Parliamentary sovereignty is therefore an undoubted legal fact. It is complete both in its positive and on its negative side. Parliament can legally legislate on any topic whatever which, in the judgment of Parliament, is a fit subject for legislation. There is no power which, under the English constitution, can come into rivalry with the legislative sovereignty of Parliament.*[32]

But this principle of parliamentary sovereignty is surely incompatible with the divided sovereignty characteristic of modern federalism. If power is divided between two constitutionally equal orders of parliamentary government, neither can be truly supreme. As Canada evolved into a modern federation, in short, federalism became one of the reasons why its constitution could only be "similar in principle to," not exactly the same as, Britain's.

As subsequent chapters will show, Canada's institutional structure and political life have been decisively shaped by this marriage of British parliamentary institutions and American federalism. To briefly anticipate, while federalism disperses power among several governments, parliamentary institutions concentrate the power of each government in the hands of its political executive, or cabinet, and especially in the hands of the prime minister or premier. The result is the characteristic pattern of Canadian intergovernmental relations known as "executive federalism," or "federal–provincial diplomacy," and exemplified most dramatically by the centrality of first ministers' conferences in our political life. Debates over the advantages and disadvantages of this feature of Canadian federalism, and battles between its friends and foes, have been central themes of recent Canadian constitutional politics, as both Chapters 3 and 4 will demonstrate. If Canada's early constitutional politics turned on the establishment of parliamentary democracy and federalism, in other words, much of its politics since the establishment of these two central constitutional principles has been generated by the tension-ridden interplay between them.

Although federalism is a limit on the British inheritance of parliamentary supremacy, it did not in itself completely displace the latter principle. Federalism, in fact, places no substantive limits on what government, at some level, may do in Canada. Until 1982 it was largely true that the two orders of government taken together were supreme in the sense that there were few substantive policies that one or the other, or both in combination, could not formally enact. In short, the Constitution Act, 1867, had effected a more or less **exhaustive distribution** of the powers of government between Ottawa and the provinces. The qualification "more or less" is important. The Canadian constitution has always imposed a few substantive limits on both orders of government. Section 133 of the Constitution Act, 1867, for example, states that either English or French may be used in the federal and Quebec legislatures, that both languages must be used in the records and journals of assemblies, that either language may be used in the courts of Canada and Quebec, and that the legislation of both jurisdictions must be printed and published in both languages. The same constraints were imposed on Manitoba by the Manitoba Act, 1870. Similarly, some of the jurisdiction of the "superior" courts established by section 96 of the constitution seems to be fully entrenched and beyond the capacity of either order of government to alter or repeal.[33] These provisions entrench substantive rather than just jurisdictional limits on governments. For the most part, however, it remained true under the 1867 Constitution Act that what could not legally be done by one order of government *could* legally be done by the other. The combined parliaments of Canada remained largely supreme, even if neither order by itself was fully sovereign.

All of this changed in 1982.

The Constitution Act, 1982

This act, as we have seen, "patriated" the constitution, bringing it "home" by giving Canada a formal, fully domestic constitutional amending procedure for the first time. The other major achievement of the act was the addition of the Canadian Charter of Rights and Freedoms to Canada's entrenched constitution. Contained in sections 1–34 of the 1982 Constitution Act, the Charter protects certain individual and group rights and freedoms against violation by all levels of government in Canada. The Charter combines provisions commonly found in such documents throughout the liberal democratic world with provisions reflecting the particularities of Canadian history. Like other bills of rights, the Charter protects a number of "fundamental freedoms" (e.g., freedom of religion and expression), "democratic rights" (e.g., the right to vote), "legal rights" (e.g., the right to a fair trial and protections against double jeopardy), and "equality rights" (e.g., the right not to be discriminated against by the state because of one's religion, sex, or race). The Charter also borrows from the United States the idea that certain rights violations should be enforced through an "exclusionary rule." Under the Canadian version of this principle, a judge must exclude evidence "obtained in a manner that infringed or denied [Charter rights] if it is established that, having regard to all the circumstances, the admission of it in the proceedings would bring the administration of justice into disrepute."

Other Charter rights are more distinctive. Under the section 6 "mobility rights," Canadians can move about the country as they wish, though governments may impede this mobility with programs giving preference to their own provincial residents as long as the program is designed to help those disadvantaged as a result of employment rates lower than the national average. Canada's is thus the only constitution in the world to refer (even obliquely) to unemployment rates. This provision emerges from the peculiar circumstances of Canadian regionalism. Similarly, the Charter protects a series of "official language minority" rights that can be understood only against the background of Canada's linguistic duality. In the same vein, the increasingly prominent issue of Aboriginal rights in Canada is reflected both within the Charter (s. 25) and elsewhere in the 1982 Constitution Act (s. 35).

An interesting feature of the Canadian Charter is section 1, which states that the Charter's rights and freedoms are guaranteed "subject only to such reasonable limits prescribed by law as can be demonstrably justified in a free and democratic society." This has been taken to require a two-stage process of reasoning about Charter violations. First, one must determine whether a law infringes a Charter right; if so, one must then consider whether the contravention can nonetheless be "saved" as a "reasonable limit" under section 1.[34]

Adding entrenched rights to the constitution has deepened the tensions within our master institution and has thus provided a new basis for constitutional contestation. In particular it has furthered the shift away from the British principle of parliamentary supremacy and toward the American principle of entrenched constitutional law. Canadian governments, which had until 1982 been constitutionally

Signing ceremony for the Constitution Act, 1982—Parliament Hill, April 17, 1982.

constrained mainly by the jurisdictional limits of federalism, now face substantive constraints on their freedom even within the areas of jurisdiction assigned to them by the 1867 Constitution Act. At the time the Charter was adopted, many of the provinces saw it as an unwarranted intrusion on their traditional jurisdictional freedoms, and opposed it as a nationalizing and centralizing invention of a hostile federal government. As we shall see in more detail in Chapter 3, Quebec was particularly hostile and never agreed to the Charter. All of the other provinces eventually agreed to accept a Charter, but only if it included an escape hatch of sorts. The result was section 33, the so-called **nonobstante clause,** or **notwithstanding clause,** a feature of the Canadian Charter that is replicated nowhere else in the world. This section allows governments to immunize legislation from challenges under section 2 ("fundamental freedoms") or sections 7–15 (legal and equality rights) for renewable five-year periods. This is done by including in the legislation a clause declaring that it "shall operate notwithstanding a provision included in section 2 or sections 7 to 15 of [the] Charter." The notwithstanding clause in effect preserves a measure of the traditional principle of parliamentary supremacy with respect to at least some of the Charter's substantive rights and freedoms. Although the section grew out of provincial resistance to the Charter, it should be noted that it is available to both orders of government.

In practice, the section 33 legislative override has, with one minor exception, been used only in Quebec, probably because governments find it politically unpalatable to be cast as violators of Charter rights. The language of rights is rhetorically very powerful in our time and constitutes an important constraint on the use of section 33. Quebec has used section 33 fairly extensively, but mainly because it never consented to the adoption of the 1982 Constitution Act (see Dossier 2.5).

Outside Quebec, the Canadian public has enthusiastically adopted the Charter as a cherished constitutional symbol, and overt resistance by other provincial governments has thus ceased. Nevertheless, the tension between the Charter and federalism indicated by the widespread early provincial opposition remains and continues to animate Canada's constitutional politics. Indeed, Alan Cairns's account of Canada's recent constitutional politics is tellingly entitled *Charter versus Federalism.*[35] We explore this opposition in Chapter 3.

The Charter contributes to constitutional contestation not only through its conflicts with federalism but also through its own internal tensions and conflicting principles. As in the case of federalism and the 1867 Constitution Act, the Charter contains language capable of providing solace and inspiration to partisans of opposing views. Just as federalists in earlier constitutional struggles relied on the language of "exclusive" provincial jurisdiction in sections 91 and 92 of the 1867 Act while centralists looked to the reservation and disallowance powers, so those who dislike the censorship of either pornography or hate literature point to the Charter's guarantee of "freedom of expression," while those who support such censorship argue that it gives effect to the Charter's guarantee of "equality rights." Similarly, if some successfully claim that the fundamental "freedom of expression" includes the freedom to solicit for purposes of prostitution, others will respond that restriction of

DOSSIER 2.5: USE OF THE SECTION 33 NOTWITHSTANDING CLAUSE

Section 33 has been used mainly by Quebec. As we will discuss in greater detail in Chapter 3, the Charter of Rights was entrenched in 1982 over the vigorous opposition of Quebec's Parti Québécois (PQ) government under the leadership of René Lévesque. The Quebec government immediately enacted a blanket override, exempting all existing legislation from the application of the Charter. The government also routinely inserted notwithstanding clauses in all new legislation. Because section 33 protects only against challenges based on section 2 and sections 7–15 of the Charter, however, the PQ's policy of universal overrides could not prevent the judicial invalidation of any and all legislation. Thus, in one of its earliest Charter cases, the Supreme Court struck down Quebec's policy of providing English-language education only to the children of parents who had been educated in English *in Quebec*. This policy conflicted with section 23 of the Charter, which guaranteed English-language education rights to children of parents who had been educated in English *in Canada*. Section 23 is not subject to the section 33 override.

The Quebec Liberal Party, under the leadership of Robert Bourassa, defeated the PQ in 1985, and the new government abandoned its predecessor's policy of blanket overrides. Nevertheless, when the Supreme Court invalidated a law that required French-only commercial signs in 1988, the Bourassa government reenacted a slightly amended version of that law with a notwithstanding clause. The original law had been struck down because it violated the Charter's section 2(b) guarantee of freedom of expression, which is one of the sections falling within the scope of section 33. More recently, Quebec has threatened to use section 33 to override a 1997 Supreme Court decision that invalidated the province's spending limits for referendum campaigns.

Outside Quebec, section 33 has been used only once. In 1986 the Saskatchewan government, fearing that a legislative suspension of the right to strike might infringe the section 2(d) guarantee of freedom of association, included a notwithstanding clause in a piece of back-to-work legislation. Saskatchewan's use of section 33 turned out to be unnecessary, however, because the Supreme Court subsequently determined that the right to strike was not protected by section 2(d).

Alberta has occasionally flirted with the idea of an override clause, though it has not yet actually enacted one. In 1983 Alberta threatened to use section 33, with the same aim that Saskatchewan would have later, to defend back-to-work legislation. In 1998 Alberta introduced a bill dealing with compensation for victims of an involuntary sterilization program carried out in the province several decades earlier. Based on the model of workers' compensation legislation, this bill limited the victims' litigation opportunities in favour of an administrative process and capped the amount of compensation they could receive. To forestall a Charter challenge, the government included a notwithstanding clause in the bill. As it turned out, however, commitment to the bill in the caucus (and especially by the premier) was not solid, and faced with a flurry of criticism in the press, the government withdrew the bill the day after it was introduced.

this freedom can be "demonstrably justified" as a "reasonable limit in a free and democratic society" under section 1 of the Charter.

Constitutional law plays an important role in such conflicts, because it provides valuable resources to the partisans. Because it tends to provide such resources to more than one side, however, the bare text of constitutional law does not itself settle the controversy. In many cases, constitutional law provides the occasion for political battles and supplies some of the weapons used in those battles but without clearly determining the outcome. Such battles may be waged in many arenas, including legislative chambers and the arena of public opinion. However, one of the most important arenas is the courtroom. As indicated above, Canada's entrenched constitution consists of both authoritative documents that are difficult to amend and judicial decisions interpreting those documents.

Judicial Decisions

The obvious difficulty of amending entrenched constitutional documents such as the federal–provincial distribution of powers or the Charter of Rights symbolizes the significance attached to them. Constitutional law is a "fundamental" or "higher" law, superior to other laws, and not casually to be tampered with. But this implies that ordinary laws that conflict with entrenched constitutional law must be invalid. Otherwise such conflicting laws would indirectly amend the constitution, turning the apparent difficulties of the official amendment procedure into meaningless formalities. Entrenchment would exist in name only. Thus, section 52 of the Constitution Act, 1982, solemnly proclaims that our entrenched constitution "is the supreme law of Canada, and any law that is inconsistent with the provisions of the Constitution is, to the extent of the inconsistency, of no force or effect."

It is not always clear, however, whether another law infringes the entrenched constitution. For example, section 7 of the Charter of Rights ensures that "everyone has the right to life, liberty and security of the person and the right not to be deprived thereof except in accordance with the principles of fundamental justice." Do all restrictive regulations of abortion infringe section 7 because they deprive women of their liberty, or is restrictive regulation required to protect the fetus's right to life? The language of section 7 does not answer this question in any direct manner, as shown by the fact that the pro-choice and pro-life lobbies have argued opposite sides of the issue.[36] Nor will the closest examination of the federal–provincial distribution of powers in sections 91 and 92 of the Constitution Act, 1867, reveal whether legislation regulating insurance contracts is better characterized as "trade and commerce" legislation, and thus within federal jurisdiction under section 91(2), or "property and civil rights" legislation, which falls within provincial competence by virtue of section 92(13).[37]

There are good reasons why entrenched constitutional law does not settle all constitutional questions. No legal rule can anticipate all of the factual circumstances that might arise within its scope, and interpretive ambiguity is thus inherent in the legal enterprise. This is true even of highly detailed legal codes, such as tax laws, that try to anticipate all contingencies. Tax consultants make a living searching out and exploiting the loopholes created by interpretive ambiguities, and the attempt to put an end to loopholes seems futile; provisions designed to close loopholes often open new ones. Constitutional law, of course, does not aspire to the kind of detailed regulation characteristic of a tax code. Written constitutions set out broad institutional frameworks and establish general principles intended to persist long into the future. Such constitutions tend to be formulated in general terms precisely because their drafters know they cannot anticipate the future. Such broadly phrased legal language is especially prone to the problem of interpretive ambiguity. Seldom are its implications for particular practical questions immediately apparent, so these implications must be established by reasoned argument that draws out more precisely the nature of the principles embodied in the language and shows what those principles require in the circumstances.

In Canada, as in other countries with written entrenched constitutions, it is now generally assumed that the responsibility for authoritatively determining such issues falls to the courts. The reasoning underlying this assumption was stated in its classic form by Chief Justice John Marshall in the 1803 U.S. case *Marbury v. Madison*,[38] the famous case in which the U.S. Supreme Court first claimed the power to invalidate congressional legislation that infringed the constitution. Marshall's reasoning took the form of the following syllogism: (1) "It is emphatically the province and duty of the judicial department to say what the law is"; (2) the Constitution is law—indeed, it is "a superior paramount law"; (3) therefore, it is the province of the courts in disputed cases to say what the constitutional law is. Although it is open to question,[39] this reasoning has gained wide public currency and it sustains the authority of the courts to provide the final and authoritative determination of constitutional meaning. To get a full picture of entrenched constitutional law, therefore, it is not enough simply to read the constitutional text. One must also consult the judicial decisions that put flesh on the constitutional skeleton.

With respect to federalism, for example, early decisions by the JCPC gave the BNA Act a much more decentralized reading than such centralists as John A. Macdonald would have preferred. In general, it gave broad readings to provincial powers and comparatively narrow readings to federal powers, thus promoting and legitimating the transformation of a constitution with strong "quasi-federal" elements into a federalism of coordinate sovereignties. Indeed, JCPC jurisprudence was part (though not a determining cause) of the evolution of Canada into one of the most decentralized federal systems in the world. The JCPC's decentralist orientation is particularly evident in its ruling that federal legislation designed to deal with the Great Depression, such as unemployment insurance legislation, could be justified neither by any of the enumerated heads of power in section 91 nor by Ottawa's general power to enact legislation in relation to "peace, order and good government." It was not justified by POGG because, although that power sometimes allowed Ottawa to legislate on matters otherwise within provincial jurisdiction, it permitted such legislation only temporarily, to deal with emergencies analogous to war or pestilence.[40] According to the JCPC, the Great Depression was not a sufficient emergency.[41]

Dissatisfaction with such rulings ultimately led to the abolition of appeals to the imperial court in 1949. (Appeals begun before 1949 continued to go to the JCPC for a few years thereafter.) Since 1949 the Supreme Court of Canada, while certainly not abandoning JCPC precedents, has shifted Canada's constitutional jurisprudence in a somewhat more centralist direction.[42] On the other hand, the court has steered well clear of the kind of centralism John A. Macdonald would have preferred. On the whole, its jurisprudence reflects the desire to maintain a balanced federalism in which neither government can overwhelm the other.[43]

Such interpretive shifts over time emphasize the importance of going beyond the text to judicial decisions in order to understand the current state of entrenched constitutional law. Indeed, some observers claim that the original constitutional text is largely irrelevant and that the constitution is effectively what the judges say it is. In this view, constitutional provisions are generally too vague to guide or constrain judicial decisions in any meaningful sense. Nor do such observers believe that judges can or should look to the intentions of the constitutional framers for the guidance they cannot find in the text. Different framers often had different reasons for supporting particular constitutional provisions, it is argued, and "founding intention" is thus no less ambiguous than the text itself. And of course the framers of old constitutional provisions could not have had specific intentions about how to resolve modern problems they knew nothing about. Even if a clear founding intention could be discovered, it is often argued that contemporary society should not be governed by the dead hand of the past. But if neither text nor founding intention constrain judicial interpretation—if the constitution is indeed simply what the judges say it is—are we not then governed by judges rather than by the constitution? Have we simply substituted judicial supremacy for parliamentary supremacy? This question points to yet another kind of inter-institutional contestation raised by the Charter. Those who believe the Charter establishes constitutional supremacy applaud the activist judicial enforcement of its provisions and have little patience with such remnants of parliamentary supremacy as the section 33 legislative override. By contrast, those who think the Charter introduces judicial rather than constitutional supremacy counsel judicial restraint or deference toward legislative policy and defend the notwithstanding clause as an appropriate remedy for undemocratic judicial activism.[44] We will touch on this dimension of constitutional contestation in Chapter 8.

NON-ENTRENCHED CONSTITUTIONAL LAW

Judicial interpretation of entrenched constitutional documents is undoubtedly the first thing that springs to mind when most people think of the Canadian constitution. Indeed, it is not uncommon to reserve the term "constitution" for entrenched law that is subject to judicial enforcement. Thus, when the constitution is mentioned, many people think mainly of the federal–provincial distribution of powers in sections 91 and 92 of the Constitution Act, 1867, and the Charter of Rights—the parts of our constitutional law that generate most of the judicial rulings. (Indeed, because it dominates both public and judicial attention, it is not uncommon to find people who identify the entrenched constitution with the Charter, in the mistaken belief that Canada had no constitutional law prior to the Charter's enactment in 1982.) If the constitution is the system of rules constituting the Canadian state, however, it cannot be limited to entrenched law of this sort.

Reserving the term "constitution" for the kind of entrenched law we have been discussing would lead to some rather strange conclusions. It would mean, for example, that Britain has no constitution because it lacks entrenched constitutional law subject to judicial enforcement. As we have seen, the central principle of British constitutionalism is parliamentary sovereignty, which, in its pristine form, makes no distinction between constitutional and any other type of law. In principle, Parliament is simultaneously a legislative body and a constituent assembly. The British constitution, in a strict legal sense, is thus whatever Parliament says it is. This means that nothing is "entrenched" in the sense explained above, and, to repeat, may suggest that Britain has no real constitution.

Yet it seems absurd to exclude Britain, commonly acknowledged as the fountainhead of modern constitutionalism, from the category of constitutional regimes. Britain clearly has a constitution in the sense of a system of fundamental constitutive rules that establish its institutional structure and govern relations between the state and its citizens. The British constitution is often described as "unwritten," but this usage, though widespread and convenient, is misleading. British constitutional rules are often "written" in legislation such as the Act of Settlement (1701), which institutionalized the principles of judicial independence. In designating the British constitution as unwritten, we really mean that its components, though often written down in legal form, are not all collected in a single document styled "the constitution" and entrenched through the kind of amending formula discussed above. As noted above, constitutional statutes in Britain can, in strict legal theory, be repealed or amended at the whim of the sovereign Parliament. Yet these statutes are widely recognized as enjoying fundamental or "constitutional" significance, and are thus entitled to greater reverence and immunity to change than other legislation. Clearly the term "constitution" is legitimately used in a broad sense to encompass non-entrenched constitutive rules, including rules embodied in ordinary legislation.

Canada's constitution is not exhausted by its entrenched legal documents. As in Britain's constitutional structure, important parts of Canada's are found in non-entrenched statutes. For example, the Supreme Court, obviously an important institution of the Canadian state (especially in light of its central role in interpreting the constitution), is not entrenched in the manner of the House of Commons or Senate. Unlike the U.S. Constitution, Canada's Constitution Act, 1867, did not establish a Supreme Court. Instead, section 101 of the Constitution Act enabled Parliament to "provide for the Constitution, Maintenance, and Organization of a General Court of Appeal for Canada." The Supreme Court was created only in 1875,[45] and even then remained subject to the overriding authority of the JCPC for another 74 years. As merely an intermediate appeal court between 1875 and 1949, the Supreme Court, it could be argued, was not truly central to Canada's constitutional structure, and the Supreme Court Act was thus not a piece of constitutional legislation. After 1949, however, the constitutional status of this institution and its founding legislation were no longer in doubt. The **Supreme Court Act,** though an ordinary piece of legislation, subject to amendment or repeal through the normal legislative process, was clearly an important part of Canada's constitution after 1949.

With the advent of the Charter in 1982, the Supreme Court's role as authoritative interpreter of the constitution was dramatically expanded and its constitutional importance underlined. One might think that the court thus deserved to be constitutionally entrenched in the manner of its American counterpart. And, in fact, sections 41(d) and 42(d) of the Constitution Act, 1982, might be understood to confer just such entrenched status. Section 41(d) subjects the "composition of the Supreme Court" to the amending formula requiring the unanimous support of all eleven Canadian governments, while section 42(d) implies that other aspects of the Supreme Court are covered by the general formula requiring the consent of Ottawa and seven provinces having 50 percent of Canada's population. If the Supreme Court cannot be changed without resort to one of the amending formulas, surely it has been entrenched. Yet the Supreme Court Act is not included in the schedule that lists the acts and orders that, together with the Constitution Act, 1982, compose the "Constitution of Canada," which, by virtue of section 52, brooks no conflicting legislation. Is the Supreme Court Act entrenched by sections 41(d) and 42(d) or does it retain its status of ordinary legislation by virtue of its exclusion from the officially listed components of "the Constitution of Canada"? Here we have a prime example of interpretive ambiguity, and arguments have been mounted on both sides.[46] A consensus seems to have emerged that the court was not, in fact, entrenched in 1982,[47] which means that the Supreme Court Act, an ordinary statute, continues to establish a central component of our constitutional structure. Even if the court had been entrenched in 1982, however, that would not affect our conclusion that ordinary statutes are part of the Canadian constitution. The Supreme Court Act certainly fell into that category at least between 1949 and 1982, and there are other pieces of ordinary legislation that have constitutional status.

Another piece of non-entrenched constitutional legislation is the **Canadian Bill of Rights,** which was enacted by the Canadian Parliament as ordinary legislation in 1960 and which, unlike the Charter, applies only to federal legislation. This bill remains in force, although it is not often invoked where its provisions are substantially duplicated by the Charter. The overlap between the Bill of Rights and the Charter is not complete, however. The former contains protections not found in the latter, and courts still occasionally use these in civil liberties cases.[48] Even judges, who tend to reserve the term "constitution" for entrenched law, have sometimes conceded that the Bill of Rights is at least "quasi-constitutional." If we use the term in its broader sense, the bill is clearly of constitutional stature.

The legislation establishing our electoral systems also falls into this category. Whether we continue to employ the single-member, first-past-the-post constituency system so familiar in Canadian politics or move to some version of proportional representation is clearly a question of constitutive importance (for reasons that will become clearer in Chapter 9), even though it is not governed by entrenched constitutional law.

A recent example of non-entrenched constitutional legislation is the **Constitutional Veto Act** of 1996. In effect this law changed the operation of the seven-fifty amending rule. As noted above, constitutional amendments that fall under the scope of the seven-fifty rule require the consent of Ottawa and seven provinces having 50 percent of the Canadian population. Thus, Ottawa can unilaterally veto any amendment that falls under the rule, even if seven or more provinces approve it. By contrast, none of the provinces has a similar veto. Mainly in order to satisfy Quebec's demand for a constitutional veto, and under circumstances to be detailed in Chapter 3, Ottawa decided that it would veto any amendment not approved by Quebec. At the same time, in order to avoid any sense of special treatment for Quebec, Ottawa would similarly veto amendments not approved by any of four other "regions": British Columbia, Ontario, the prairie West (Alberta, Saskatchewan, and Manitoba), and Atlantic Canada. The consent of the latter two regions would be signified by the approval of two provinces with 50 percent of their region's population.

In effect, the Constitutional Veto Act "lends" Ottawa's veto under the seven-fifty rule to each of five Canadian regions. This gives a practical veto to each of four provinces—Quebec, Ontario, and British Columbia (because they coincide with three of the regions), and Alberta (because it has more than 50 percent of the population of the three prairie provinces). By giving four provinces a veto they do not have as a matter of formal constitutional law, the Constitutional Veto Act—an ordinary piece of legislation—radically transforms the constitutionally entrenched amendment formula. Clearly, it falls within the category of non-entrenched constitutional statutes.

Like their entrenched counterparts—indeed, like virtually all law—non-entrenched constitutional statutes are subject to judicial interpretation. Here too, then, one must often consult not only the statute books but also judicial decisions to gain a full understanding of the constitutional law in question. The major difference between entrenched and non-entrenched laws in this respect is that judicial interpretations of the latter can be more easily overridden by the other branches of government. If Parliament doesn't agree with a judicial interpretation of one of its laws (including the kind of constitutional statute we are considering), it can amend the law, by means of the usual majoritarian process, to impose its preference. By contrast, except for the section 33 notwithstanding clause, which is available to override only certain Charter sections, judicial interpretations of entrenched constitutional law can be overcome only by constitutional amendment or by a subsequent change of mind on the part of the judges.

CONSTITUTIONAL CONVENTIONS

Adding constitutional statutes to entrenched constitutional law provides a still-incomplete picture of the constitution. Anyone who looked only in law books to learn about the Canadian state would get a very mistaken impression of how it actually operates. A simple reading of the Constitution Act, 1867, for example, might lead one to conclude that the most powerful figure in Canada's government is the governor general. Indeed, on a literal reading of the Constitution Act, Canada appears to "suffer under a dictatorship, the autocratic rule of one central figure, acting in the place of the Sovereign, who governs the Dominion with little reference to, or control by the people. The only popular element is apparently supplied by a House of Commons, which meets when the governor desires, considers financial legislation which he recommends, and can be forced into an election whenever he deems it desirable."[49]

We would learn nothing from the Constitution Act, 1867, about the fundamental rules of parliamentary **responsible government** that actually govern the exercise of the governor general's powers. Nor would we find mention of the fact that the Crown's extensive powers are exercised only on the advice of the political cabinet, comprising the prime minister and other ministers chosen by the prime minister, and that the governor general virtually always does what these "advisers" propose. Thus, section 54 of the 1867 Constitution Act, which permits "money bills" (legislation involving the appropriation or spending of public funds) to be passed only if they have first been recommended to the House of Commons by the governor general, in practice gives the cabinet the leading role in developing the legislative program to be considered by Parliament.

This conventional rule underlies one of the most prominent features of the British or "Westminster" model of parliamentary government inherited by Canada, that is, the integration of the legislative and executive powers of government. Since the cabinet, which exercises the Crown's executive powers, is drawn from the legislature, the political executive has moved inside the legislature; it is, in a sense, the executive committee of the legislature (see Figure 2.3, page 54). Walter Bagehot called this **integration of powers** "[t]he efficient secret of the English Constitution."[50] Bagehot saw this integration as amounting to "the nearly complete fusion of the executive and legislative powers,"[51] though, as Dossier 2.7 suggests, significant distinctions between the cabinet and the legislature remain, and "fusion" may be too strong a term.

Nor does a reading of the Constitution Act, 1867, reveal the second major principle of responsible government—namely, that the cabinet, which is drawn from sitting members of the two houses of Parliament, is entitled to the de facto exercise of the governor general's powers only so long as it retains the support, or "confidence," of a majority in the House of Commons. A cabinet that loses this confidence must resign, and usually a new election is called. In practice, this means that the leader of the party with the greatest number of seats in the legislature is called on to form a ministry. In this way the executive power of the Crown, which has become

DOSSIER 2.6 THE PRE-CONFEDERATION DEVELOPMENT OF RESPONSIBLE GOVERNMENT

Although representative government in Canada was in place by 1791 (see Dossier 2.3), responsible government would not be achieved until over half a century later. Responsible government had been established in Britain for some time, but its transmission to the colonies was resisted because of the imperial relationship between mother country and colony. A colony by definition is not completely self-governing; it must, to some degree, be subject to imperial control. A colony that has achieved full self-government ceases by that very fact to be a colony. But would a colony not become self-governing if its government became completely responsible to its own locally elected assembly? If the governor was obliged to heed the advice of a cabinet enjoying the confidence of the majority in the assembly, what room would be left for imperial control? Thus, as long as imperial control was considered important, responsible government in the colonies was resisted. The independence of the executive from legislative control was further secured by independent sources of income—such as Crown lands, duties, licences, fines, and forfeitures—whose collection and use were not then under the control of the assembly.

The inevitable result was conflict between the elected assemblies, who were entitled to discuss public policy but had little power to implement their wishes, and the executive branch of government, which exercised real power. The executive branch consisted of the governor, who was appointed by and responsible to Britain, and a council of appointed advisers. In all the colonies, the governor tended to draw his advisers from a social and economic elite, while the assembly was often dominated by representatives of opposing social strata. In Upper Canada the ruling elite was known as the Family Compact; in Lower Canada it was called the Château Clique. Since the legislative councils were also appointed by the governor, they in effect became the legislative arm of these oligarchies, enabling them to veto legislation desired by their opponents in the assemblies. The predictable tension between the branches of government thus came to reflect, and was embittered by, social conflict between different segments of society. In Lower Canada the clash was intensified by the overlap between social and national distinctions: the executive-ensconced ruling elite was largely English, while the French majority controlled the assembly. Here was a classic example of competing interests lining up behind different institutions within the overall constitutional structure, and struggling to make their respective institutions dominant.

By the 1830s, the constitutional conflicts in both Canadas had reached a fever pitch, culminating in the famous rebellions of 1837–38. In response to this crisis, Lord Durham was appointed governor general of all of British North America except Newfoundland, with a mandate to assess the causes of the constitutional ills and to prescribe a solution. Durham's solution was twofold. Regarding the institutional tensions common to all the colonies, he recommended responsible government. "It is difficult to understand," he wrote, "how any English statesmen could have imagined that representative and irresponsible government could be successfully combined." Regarding the particular problems of Lower Canada, he proposed the reunification of the two colonies. He hoped that with neither nationality able to dominate the legislature, cross-national party coalitions would form to secure the prize of executive power offered by responsible government. Such cooperation, he thought, would moderate conflict between the two cultural groups, thus preparing what Durham considered the ultimate solution: assimilation of the French into the more vigorous and enterprising English community. Durham's union proposal was implemented almost immediately through the Act of Union, which was passed in 1840 and came into force early in 1841.

Responsible government, by contrast, was not achieved until 1847–48. In 1847 Lord Grey, the British colonial secretary, informed the Crown's representatives in Nova Scotia and Canada that it was "neither possible or desirable to carry on the government of any of the British provinces in North America in opposition to the opinion of the inhabitants." In short, the governor was to carry out the wishes of his local advisers rather than the wishes of the imperial authority. This implemented the first prong of responsible government: the transfer of effective executive authority from the Crown to the cabinet. Grey also made it clear that the governor was "to abstain from changing [the] Executive Council until it shall be perfectly clear that they are unable ... to carry on the government of the province satisfactorily, and to command the confidence of the Legislature." Thus the second prong of responsible government was established: the cabinet's executive authority now depended on the support of the majority in the assembly. These instructions were put into effect in 1848 when elections changed the partisan composition of the legislatures in both Nova Scotia and Canada. In February of that year, Governor Harvey of Nova Scotia "invited James Uniacke, a leader of the reformers who had won the recent election, to form a one-party cabinet." The following month the newly elected Canadian assembly voted nonconfidence in the existing Tory government, which then resigned. The Canadian governor, Lord Elgin, immediately invited Robert Baldwin and Louis Lafontaine, leaders of the Reform Party, to form the government. Elgin, Durham's son-in-law, thus contributed to the fulfillment of his father-in-law's institutional prescription.

Sources: Janet Ajzenstat, *The Political Thought of Lord Durham* (Montreal and Kingston: McGill-Queen's University Press, 1988; J.M.S. Careless, *The Union of the Canadas: The Growth of Canadian Institutions,* 1841–1857 (Toronto: McClelland and Stewart, 1967; Peter H. Russell, *Constitutional Odyssey: Can Canadians Become a Sovereign People?* 2nd ed. (Toronto: University of Toronto Press, 1993).

"responsible" to the cabinet, is also made "responsible" to the elected legislature. In a purely formal sense, the "government" in a parliamentary system is not elected by the people; it is appointed by the legislature. No one ever votes for a cabinet or a prime minister, though the modern realities of party politics give that impression, because we seem to vote for the party and its leader. In fact, to the extent that we vote for a potential prime minister, we do so indirectly, by voting for the local

FIGURE 2.3 **PARLIAMENTARY INTEGRATION OF LEGISLATURE AND EXECUTIVE**

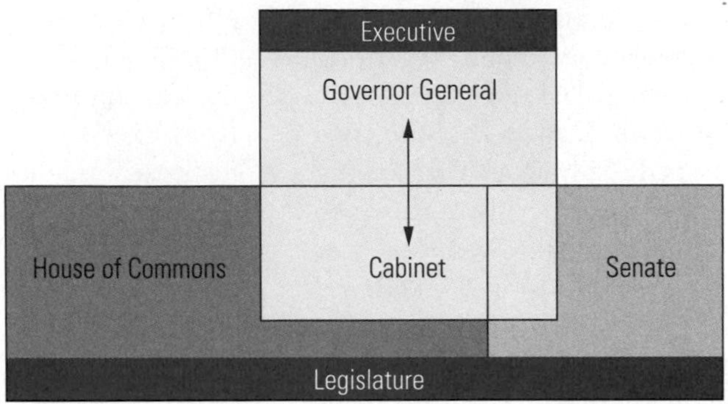

representative of his or her party in the hope that this party elects enough members to form a majority in the House of Commons.

The rules of responsible government are clearly central and distinguishing features of Canada's constitution. Yet it bears repeating that they are not set out in the formal entrenched constitution. The prime minister and cabinet are never even mentioned in the Constitution Act, 1867. Ordinary legislation sometimes refers to them, but it does not establish them. The rules of responsible government are simply not matters of constitutional law, entrenched or otherwise. They lie in the realm of what is called constitutional **convention.**

The pre-1982 rule that major constitutional amendments required the consent of the provinces is another example of constitutional conventions. Our previous discussion of this rule points to what some consider one of the defining characteristics of conventions—that, unlike laws, they cannot be enforced in courts. This was made clear during the political struggles leading to patriation in 1982. As will be explained in Chapter 3, the question of whether Ottawa could proceed unilaterally with the patriation package, without any provincial consent whatsoever, was referred to the Supreme Court. Although the court was prepared to recognize the existence of a convention of "substantial" provincial consent in this "patriation case," it insisted that it was powerless to enforce this rule. It was a court of law, and in strict law Ottawa was entitled to proceed unilaterally. Nevertheless, the court was prepared to say that while such unilateralism might be constitutional in the strict legal sense of the term, it would be unconstitutional in the wider sense, because it would infringe an important constitutional convention.[52]

Conventions are often distinguished from mere custom or habit. We may be in the habit of getting out of bed on the right side, but we would feel no sense of normative unease if we departed from that habit one morning. Similarly, a prime minister who had always consulted his closest advisers promptly at 9:15 each morning might worry about inconveniencing them if he put them off until the afternoon but

DOSSIER 2.7: THE FALLACY OF "FUSION"

It is usual today to say that in the parliamentary system, the political executive and lower house are "fused," emphasizing the fact that members of the cabinet must occupy seats in the lower house. Using "fusion" of the Canadian form of government distinguishes it from the presidential system in which the political executive is not located in the legislature. But the usage obscures the fact that although cabinet ministers sit in the House of Commons, they are in law unlike other members in so far as they wield the powers of the Crown. The two bodies, executive and legislative, are constitutionally distinct....

The requirement that cabinet retain the support of the majority in the lower house on money bills is what necessitates party discipline and gives the government of the day its clout. The dominant cabinet virtually rules over the government-party backbenchers. Some regard cabinet dominance as a deplorable feature of the parliamentary system. The constitutional tradition, however, sees it as crucial because it is the ascendancy of the governing party that leaves members of the other parties in the House free to dissent publicly from government policies. The fact that the cabinet is not supported by the House in toto leaves the minority at liberty to carp, deride and complain—while remaining secure, honoured and constitutionally protected.

Source: Reprinted from Janet Ajzenstat, "Reconciling Parliament and Rights: A.V. Dicey Reads the Canadian Charter of Rights and Freedoms," *Canadian Journal of Political Science* 30, no. 4 (1997), 654–655.

would surely not feel he was breaking a binding rule of great import. By contrast, a cabinet that refused to step aside after losing the confidence of the House of Commons would certainly understand that it was engaged in an act of revolution against fundamental constitutional rules. It is characteristic of constitutional conventions, in short, that they be recognized as binding by those subject to them.[53]

For a convention to be generally recognized as binding, it need not be free of ambiguity and contentious interpretations. Few proponents of parliamentary government would argue that a cabinet that has lost the confidence of the legislature should remain in power, but there might well be disagreement over what establishes such loss of confidence. Obviously a vote explicitly held to test the issue of confidence would meet anyone's criterion. But must all votes on major pieces of government legislation be treated as de facto confidence votes? Here is much room for disagreement. For the most part, Canadian governments have chosen to characterize defeats of their major legislative initiatives as nonconfidence votes requiring resignation. There have been many proposals, however, to reform this practice so that a government would be defeated only on explicitly designated nonconfidence motions. Moreover, there is some variation in parliamentary systems in this respect. In the British Parliament, for example, votes on money bills or the budget are still generally considered matters of confidence, but a somewhat less stringent approach is taken to other legislation. Obviously, treating most defeats on legislative initiatives as de facto nonconfidence motions does not enjoy the same level of agreement or generate the same widespread sense of obligation as the more general principle that loss of confidence unseats a government. The general principle is clearly a much stronger convention than the current Canadian way of institutionalizing it. A change in the Canadian practice would not constitute as substantial a constitutional revolution as abandonment of the general rule.

Many conventions arise from long-established practices that come increasingly to be seen as obligatory. It seems unlikely, however, that the requisite sense of binding obligation arises simply because of the age of the practices. It surely helps to be persuaded that there is a good reason for the rule, that it gives effect to an important and valued principle. This, too, is usually held to be an essential characteristic of constitutional conventions.[54]

The dependence of convention on principle rather than simply on age is particularly evident when conventions emerge fully formed at a well-defined historical moment, much as a law is enacted at a particular moment in time. At two imperial conferences in the inter-war period, for example, Britain and the dominions recognized and agreed to respect the de facto independence of the former colonies. This principle was subsequently given legal effect in the Statute of Westminster, but in the intervening period it was recognized as a binding convention established by the conferences. Although the practice of independence had been growing, no such convention was clearly established before these conferences. This convention rested less on established practice than on explicit agreement that new principles should govern the relationship between Britain and her former colonies.[55]

Similarly, a new convention governing constitutional amendment may have emerged fully formed in 1992, when Canadians rejected a package of amendments known as the Charlottetown Accord. The accord, which will be described in greater detail in Chapter 3, was very complex and contained a wide-ranging series of amendments. It is no exaggeration to say that it would have radically transformed the Canadian system of government. Although the formal amendment procedures require only ratification by legislatures, the Charlottetown Accord was first put to a referendum in all parts of the country, and was defeated by the populations of Canada as a whole and the populations of six provinces. This resounding defeat killed the accord. The Charlottetown Accord has probably made referendums a conventional part of Canada's amending formula. Although single, narrowly focused amendments don't require a referendum, many observers agree that large-scale amendment packages can no longer be passed without first being approved in a referendum.

Conventions often serve to ensure that anachronistic legal rules are operated in a manner consistent with current constitutional principles. Thus, the powers of reservation and disallowance affecting the relations between Britain and Canada and between Ottawa and the provinces have withered by convention as both international and domestic imperialism became unacceptable. Other features of quasi-federal centralism, such as remedial legislation and the declaratory power, have suffered a similar fate. The convention of "nonuse" that has come to govern these powers reflects the defeat of the quasi-federal tendencies in the constitution by the principle of coordinate sovereignty.

Similarly, the conventions of responsible government have from the beginning given a more democratic content to the less democratic legal structure of the Constitution Act, 1867. And the increasing democratization of Canadian sensibilities explains the referendum requirement for wide-ranging constitutional amendment packages.

The ability of conventional rules to overwhelm purely legal rules indicates their potential power. Indeed, in the case of responsible government "it is only because of [the] conventional restraints that the broad legal powers of [the governor general's] office are tolerated within Canada's democratic constitution."[56] Any governor general who attempted to exercise the full range of the Crown's legal powers would succeed only in having those powers abolished and the conventions of responsible government entrenched into formal constitutional law. Such a transformation of constitutional convention into constitutional law is unnecessary only because everyone knows what the Supreme Court proclaimed in the patriation case: that in such cases convention is more important than, and prevails over, constitutional law (see Dossier 2.8). Nowadays we tend to be mesmerized by entrenched constitutional law and to assume that what is not legally entrenched is not effectively guaranteed. The conventions governing responsible government and the nonuse of such powers as reservation and disallowance show that conventional restraints can sometimes be more powerful than legal rules.

Still, one might ask whether it would not be preferable to entrench important conventions into formal constitutional law in order to bring them within the scope of judicial enforcement. Self-restraint being a notoriously unreliable virtue, why depend on the self-restraint of officeholders to secure compliance to constitutional rules when court enforcement of formal law is available? After all, it is often (and rightly) said that the **rule of law** is a leading feature of decent regimes. According to the common formulation, the "rule of law" is preferable to the "rule of men." Should we not conclude that it is also preferable to self-restraint?

This query assumes that law is somehow more securely binding than the self-restraint underlying "mere" convention, but this assumption is open to question. There may be less magic in the judicial enforcement of "law" than first meets the eye. Judges are able to "enforce" the criminal law, for example, only because their orders are backed up by the considerable power of the state's executive branch. They could do very little without the aid of the police, prosecutors, and prisons. But constitutional law governs the state itself. Its judicial enforcement involves the judicial branch of the state, which wields the power of neither sword nor purse, issuing orders to the branches of government that do wield those powers. Where will the enforcement power to back up those commands come from? As Sir Ivor Jennings put it,

> *force cannot be used against those who control the force. A Government cannot coerce itself, though a Government can coerce one of its members. The courts cannot control the*

DOSSIER 2.8: THE SUPREME COURT OF CANADA ON CONVENTIONS

The conventional rules of the Constitution present one striking peculiarity. In contradistinction to the laws of the Constitution, they are not enforced by the courts....

Perhaps the main reason why conventional rules cannot be enforced by the courts is that they are generally in conflict with the legal rules which they postulate and the courts are bound to enforce the legal rules. The conflict is not of a type which would entail the commission of any illegality. It results from the fact that legal rules create wide powers, discretions and rights which conventions prescribe should be exercised only in a certain limited manner, if at all.

Some examples will illustrate this point.... [I]f after a general election where the Opposition obtained the majority at the polls the Government refused to resign and clung to office, it would thereby commit a fundamental breach of conventions, one so serious indeed that it could be regarded as tantamount to a coup d'état. The remedy in this case would lie with the Governor General or the Lieutenant-Governor as the case might be who would be justified in dismissing the Ministry and in calling on the Opposition to form the Government. But should the Crown be slow in taking this course, there is nothing the courts could do about it except at the risk of creating a state of legal discontinuity, that is, a form of revolution. An order or a regulation passed by a Minister under statutory authority and otherwise valid could not be invalidated on the ground that, by convention, the Minister ought no longer to be a Minister. A writ of *quo warranto* aimed at Ministers, assuming that *quo warranto* lies against a Minister of the Crown, which is very doubtful, would be of no avail to remove them from office. Required to say by what warrant they occupy their ministerial office, they would answer that they occupy it by the pleasure of the Crown under a commission issued by the Crown and this answer would be a complete one at law, for at law the Government is in office by the pleasure of the Crown although by convention it is there by the will of the people....

It should be borne in mind however that, while they are not laws, some conventions may be more important than some laws. Their importance depends on that of the value or principle which they are meant to safeguard. Also they form an integral part of the Constitution and of the constitutional system.

Source: Reprinted from *Attorney General of Manitoba v. Attorney General of Canada* (Re Resolution to Amend the Constitution), [1981] 1 S.C.R. 753, at 880–883.

Government. They can give verdicts or judgments against it, but they have no force at their disposal save that controlled by the Government itself.[57]

In the final analysis, judicial commands issued in the name of constitutional law are effective only to the extent that the other branches are willing to abide by them. Constitutional law turns out to be no less dependent on the self-restraint of office-holders than constitutional convention or constitutional statutes.[58]

The contrast between such regimes as Canada and the United States on the one hand and the former Soviet Union on the other illustrates the point. The Soviet Union and its satellites had splendidly written constitutions, which governing authorities routinely ignored. Those authorities considered themselves above the fundamental law of the land. Theirs were regimes of "men, not of laws." Political systems such as Canada's, however, while by no means perfect, clearly govern themselves according to the formal constitution, and in so doing ensure that power is exercised on behalf of the people in the service of the law, not on behalf of the government in the service of its interests. It is this willingness to abide by the formal rules, which we designate by the phrase "rule of law," that forms the ultimate support of constitutionalism. Ironically, this central tenet of liberty is nothing more than a vapour of social commitments. People must believe in the rule of law for it to work, and so in this respect it is terrifyingly fragile—just as fragile, and in much the same way, as the rule of convention. Thus, Jennings maintains that "[t]he constitution of a country, whatever it be, rests upon acquiescence." In this respect at least, he concludes, "Constitutional laws and constitutional conventions are in substance the same."[59] And in fact, in the constitutional realm, we often use the phrase "rule of law" to refer to obedience to all fundamental rules, whether formal or conventional.

THE CONTESTED CONSTITUTION

Institutions, we have argued, are often the very things at stake in politics. This is certainly true of our master institution. The constitution is contested precisely because it is our master institution, because it so decisively constrains and shapes our public life. It does so by creating incentive structures, providing symbolic resources, and shaping the very identities of citizens.

Constitutional rules shape political behaviour most obviously by creating incentive structures that incline political actors to choose certain paths of action over others. Politicians within both orders of government in a federal system, for example, have natural incentives to enhance their own influence and authority, often at the expense of the other order of government. This becomes particularly obvious when politicians who move from one order of government to the other find themselves also shifting their views on federal–provincial conflicts.

Similarly, the conventions of responsible government encourage the relatively strict party discipline characteristic of Canadian politics. Although the governing party's backbenchers (elected members who are not ministers) may dislike legislation proposed by the cabinet, they are unlikely to vote against the government and thereby risk its defeat and the necessity of going to the electorate in a general election with a disunited party. Although the requirement of majority support seems to give the legislature control over the cabinet, in fact it usually has the opposite effect, giving the cabinet great leverage over the legislative party. This accounts for the otherwise inexplicable fact that Canadian cabinets usually prefer to treat votes on most major legislative initiatives as tests of the legislature's confidence. This practice has the consequence of making it next to impossible to defeat a government whose party occupies a majority of legislative seats. (Some of the founders of responsible government understood its executive-strengthening tendency very well, while others did not—see Dossier 2.9.)

The constitution is also important as a source of symbolic resources that may be deployed in the arena of political combat. Although it does not guarantee political victory, it surely helps to have the constitution on one's side. This is why both governments and interest groups go to such lengths to seek favourable judicial interpretations of the constitution.

The constitution is more than a set of incentive structures and political resources, however. According to Cairns, it shapes not only day-to-day political behaviour but also the very nature of society and citizen identities. It does so by placing potential sources of self-definition into a symbolic order of precedence. For example, social classes have no direct constitutional expression, while the geographically based communities that make up Canadian federalism clearly do. This affects the way in which public issues are defined and processed. As E.E. Schattschneider put it, all political organization "is the mobilization of bias. Some issues are organized into politics while others are organized out."[60] Issues that might be presented as class issues, for example, are in Canada more likely to be formulated in the language of federalism. This is partly because the governments of federalism have an interest in emphasizing the federal–provincial aspects of an issue over its other aspects. While an Acadian logger complaining of poverty could explain it as a function of oppression by upper-class anglophones, his government is more likely to explain it as an effect of central Canada's domination of Atlantic Canada's economy.[61] The latter explanation serves the provincial government better in its continuing struggle with the other governments of Canadian federalism, and if the governments, and the parties contending to form governments, privilege some formulations of issues, effectively ignoring all others, then those formulations tend to attain a privileged status in the public psyche. For political purposes, people may bring their membership in the constitutionally recognized communities of federalism into the foreground, leaving other identities and potential sources of political organization in the background.

Non-governmental political interests also fuel this tendency of the constitution to refashion society in its image. Precisely because the constitution is generally acknowledged as fundamental, groups often find it advantageous to argue that their preferred policies are consistent with, or required by, the constitution. But this requires them to argue in terms of the available constitutional categories.[62] This is especially so if political interests wish to make their constitutional claim in court. Thus, in pre-Charter days, when business interests went to court complaining of "unconstitutional" governmental regulation, they had to argue not that the regulation was unconstitutional in itself but that it had been undertaken by the wrong order of government. Or when labour unions participated in a legal challenge to the

DOSSIER 2.9 CONFLICTING VIEWS OF RESPONSIBLE GOVERNMENT AT THE TIME OF ITS FOUNDING

The struggle for responsible government is a fascinating instance of how the same reform can be advocated for quite different reasons by people with radically divergent expectations about its purpose and likely effect, based on competing visions of human nature and community. Two distinct groups lent their support to the Canadian campaign for responsible government, groups that Janet Ajzenstat has helpfully labelled "radical democrats" and "constitutionalists." The radical democrats included such figures as William Lyon Mackenzie and Louis-Joseph Papineau, the leaders of the rebellions in Upper and Lower Canada, respectively. This group enjoyed the support of a number of influential British intellectuals and politicians known as the Philosophical Radicals, among whom John Stuart Mill was the most illustrious figure. Prominent in the constitutionalist camp were Joseph Howe, who led the fight for responsible government in Nova Scotia, and Lord Durham himself. The democrats saw responsible government as transferring power to the legislature and thereby to the people's representatives. They were populists who assumed that "the people" were fundamentally good and that evil flowed from a corrupt system controlled by corrupt elites. Gathering all power into the hands of those who represented the people was thus a way to serve good and thwart evil. Responsible government would ensure this transfer of power to the people.

The constitutionalists took a somewhat dimmer view of human nature and potential. The rule of self-interested and ambitious elites, they thought, was inherent in the nature of things, not something that could be overcome through institutional engineering. Society was naturally divided between the politically ambitious few, who lusted for power, and the unambitious many, who desired primarily comfort and security. Transferring all power to the legislature would secure the rule not of "the people" but of their "representatives," who are always just as much members of the naturally ambitious elite as their less democratic opponents. That such "democrats" compete for power by invoking the name of "the people" does not make them any more trustworthy or less dangerous. The interests of "the people" are, in fact, best preserved not by transferring all power to that part of the natural elite that purports to represent the people but by establishing a moderating system of checks and balances among different parts of the elite. Only effective checks and balances, not unalloyed democracy, could prevent the natural elite from tyrannizing over the people.

The constitutionalists thus supported responsible government for reasons very different from those of the radical democrats. For the constitutionalists, responsible government was the cornerstone of a healthy system of checks and balances within a parliamentary system. Far from weakening the executive, responsible government would, in their view, actually strengthen it, thus creating a "balanced" constitution that would, among other things, check the power of the people's "representatives." The separated executive, constitutionalists thought, was certainly powerful in the limited sense of being able to benefit the Family Compact and Château Clique through personal patronage, but was far too weak in the sense that really counted. It was too weak because, without democratic legitimacy, it lacked both the means and the incentives to promote effective policy for the public good. Bringing the executive within the formal control of the legislature would give it the legitimacy it needed and would forestall the assembly's tendency to gather all governmental power under its direct control. The executive would therefore be able to control the policy process, and the legislature would be restricted to its proper role of oversight and expenditure control.

Sources: Janet Ajzenstat, *The Political Thought of Lord Durham* (Montreal and Kingston: McGill-Queen's University Press, 1988); Janet Ajzenstat, "The Constitutionalism of Étienne Parent and Joseph Howe," in Janet Ajzenstat, ed., *Canadian Constitutionalism: 1791–1991* (Ottawa: Canadian Study of Parliament Group, 1992).

federal government's wage and price controls in the 1970s, their argument had to be that such legislation was beyond Ottawa's jurisdiction.[63] Such tactics, of course, reflect appropriate responses to constitutionally based incentive structures. The federal constitution, in other words, promotes a federalized political discourse, giving it privileged status over other kinds of political discourse, thus further entrenching the salience of federalism in the Canadian political psyche. The Charter of Rights, as we shall see in Chapter 3, was explicitly intended to counteract the federalizing societal effect of the existing constitution and to lay the constitutional foundation for a stronger national identity.[64] This tendency of the constitution subtly to shape, if not to determine, the self-definitions or identities of citizens and communities reveals the sense in which constitutions are more than external frameworks for government. In the words of Alan Cairns, constitutional politics is often about the fashioning and "refashioning of community."[65]

The centrality and significance of the constitution to public life ensures that it will be hotly disputed, that it will give rise to constitutional politics. Interests or constituencies that feel disadvantaged by the existing rules can be counted on to challenge them. For example, those from Canada's less populous regions who believe the central government is biased in favour of central Canada identify the highly disciplined and focused nature of parliamentary government as part of the problem and thus advocate reforming our parliamentary tradition. Similarly, those who dislike the way in which the existing constitution fashions community will engage in constitutional politics in an attempt to refashion it. As Cairns says, we "need to think of constitutional change as the master instrument of community transformation."[66] Canadian history, in fact, reveals little consensus on just what sort of community should be fashioned by the constitution, and thus displays many competing projects of community transformation. Are we to be a single national community based on a British parliamentary heritage, or a partnership of two "founding nations" (English and French)? If the latter, are the two founding nations of equal status throughout the entire country, or perhaps geographically delimited by Quebec and the "rest of Canada"? Or are we really a community of ten equal provincial communities? Or perhaps a partnership of the English, French, and First Nations? Or a multicultural, multiethnic community? Or a citizenry both unified and divided in non-territorial ways by ambiguous rights held in common from coast to coast?

Constitutional politics, whatever its source, involves either competing interpretations of the existing constitution or demands explicitly to change or replace it. Interpretive contestation is generated by ambiguously worded constitutional provisions that can support more than one reading. As we have seen, for example, the protection of "life" in section 7 of the Charter has been claimed as constitutional support for the pro-life side of the abortion debate, just as the same section's protection of "liberty" has been relied on by the pro-choice side. Sometimes entire constitutional acts embody contradictory provisions, pointing to conflicting logics or principles. Thus, the language of "exclusive" provincial jurisdiction in sections 91 and 92 of the 1867 Constitution Act implies the federal principle of divided sovereignty, while the reservation and disallowance powers in the same act imply an imperial–colonial relationship between Ottawa and the provinces. On an even larger scale, conflicting logics are apparent between the major organizing features of the constitution. The British principle of parliamentary supremacy, for example, conflicts with both federalism and the Charter. Similarly, the relationship between federalism and the Charter has been described as "Charter versus Federalism." Interpretive constitutional politics is always about which of the conflicting logics will come to dominate the public realm.

While interpretive constitutional politics is content to work with existing constitutional materials, the politics of explicit constitutional amendment seeks to transform those materials. The politics of constitutional amendment can range from focused, piecemeal tinkering to wholesale constitutional structuring. The 1940 amendment that reversed a JCPC decision by giving Ottawa jurisdiction over unemployment insurance, for example, was much more limited in scope than the project of patriation and the Charter implemented by the Constitution Act, 1982, or than less successful post-Charter constitutional projects such as the Charlottetown Accord. The most radical proposal for formal constitutional change on the agenda of modern Canadian constitutional politics concerns the possible separation of Quebec.

CONCLUSION

The constitution is the most fundamental and comprehensive rule book for the conduct of public life. It is composed of three kinds of rules, which together establish three main organizational features. The three kinds of rules are entrenched and non-entrenched constitutional law (including interpretive judicial decisions in each case) and constitutional conventions. The three main organizational features are parliamentary democracy, federalism, and constitutionally entrenched rights and freedoms. Parliamentary democracy stems from a combination of the entrenched Constitution Act, 1867, and the conventions of responsible government. Federalism is grounded in the division of powers between two orders of government in the 1867 Act, though its precise operation is influenced by the fact that both orders of government are of the parliamentary kind. Rights applicable within both the national and provincial spheres of jurisdiction are found in the Canadian Charter of Rights and Freedoms.

Like other kinds of rule books, the constitution decisively shapes and channels the behaviour it governs, though it does not fully determine that behaviour. The rule book for any sport, for example, does not precisely determine the character or outcome of any particular match, but it does establish the constant parameters of the game. The constitution establishes the most fundamental parameters of power.

The sheer centrality and significance of the constitution ensures that it will be vigorously contested. Such contestation feeds on the kind of ambiguity and conflicting logics that riddle Canada's constitutional structure. These include tensions within and among the three main constitutional features of parliamentary democracy, federalism, and entrenched rights. If the conflicting logics underlying the constitution provide ample opportunity for constitutional politics, the representatives of conflicting interests and visions of community have certainly not permitted the opportunity to pass them by.

Constitutional politics of some kind is normal, indeed inevitable, in almost any regime. There will always be sufficient ambiguity in a polity's constitutive rules to engender at least a politics of interpretation. The intensity and comprehensiveness of constitutional politics can vary considerably, however. When the tensions between conflicting institutional logics and visions of community become sufficiently acute, normal interpretive controversy may give way to "megaconstitutional politics," which poses questions of radical constitutional transformation and may call into question the very survival of the existing polity. Such megaconstitutional politics has preoccupied Canadians for much of the past four decades.

KEY TERMS

- parliamentary democracy
- federalism
- Charter of Rights and Freedoms
- British North America (BNA) Act, 1867
- Colonial Laws Validity Act
- Judicial Committee of the Privy Council (JCPC)
- Statute of Westminster
- Constitution Act, 1982
- seven-fifty rule
- unanimity rule
- patriation
- Constitution Act, 1867
- Royal Proclamation, 1763
- Quebec Act, 1774

Constitution Act, 1791
Act of Union, 1840
peace, order, and good government (POGG)
residual power
loyalists
Upper Canada
Lower Canada
concurrent jurisdiction
paramountcy
quasi-federalism
declaratory power
remedial legislation
spending power
reservation
disallowance
parliamentary sovereignty / parliamentary supremacy
exhaustive distribution
nonobstante clause / notwithstanding clause
Supreme Court Act
Canadian Bill of Rights
Constitutional Veto Act
responsible government
integration of powers
convention
rule of law

DISCUSSION QUESTIONS

1. It has been said that in Britain the constitution is what Parliament says it is, while in Canada and the United States the constitution is what the Supreme Court says it is. What does this imply for the ideal of the rule of (constitutional) law?
2. If one has to choose between parliamentary and judicial supremacy in constitutional interpretation, which would be preferable? In light of your answer, how would you assess section 33 of the Charter?
3. How would one know whether a sharp break with convention violated or amended the constitution?
4. How much, and what parts, of our "master institution" should be constitutionally entrenched? Have we entrenched too little, enough, or too much?
5. Alan Cairns, who has popularized the idea of the "constitutional refashioning of community," says that this idea "may appear vaguely disturbing, with its suggestion of deliberate manipulation of our identities in the service of some higher end." Can the constitutional refashioning of community be avoided or minimized? Should it be? If constitutions should do something other than manipulate identities, what might that be?

SUGGESTED READINGS

Ajzenstat, Janet. "Reconciling Parliament and Rights: A.V. Dicey Reads the Canadian Charter of Rights and Freedoms." *Canadian Journal of Political Science* 30 no. 4 (1997).

Cairns, Alan C. *Charter versus Federalism: The Dilemmas of Constitutional Reform.* Montreal and Kingston: McGill-Queen's University Press, 1992, chapter 2.

Cheffins, Ronald I. *The Revised Canadian Constitution: Politics as Law.* Toronto: McGraw-Hill Ryerson, 1986.

Dicey, A.V. *Introduction to the Study of the Law of the Constitution.* London: Macmillan, 1920.

Heard, Andrew. *Canadian Constitutional Conventions: The Marriage of Law and Politics.* Toronto: Oxford University Press, 1991.

Hogg, Peter. *Constitutional Law of Canada.* 3rd ed. (supp.) Toronto: Carswell, 1992.

Jennings, I. *The Law and the Constitution.* 5th ed. London: University of London Press, 1959.

Knopff, Rainer. "Legal Theory and the Patriation Debate." *Queen's Law Journal* 7, no. 1 (1981).

McConnell, W.H. *Commentary on the British North America Act.* Toronto: Macmillan, 1977.

Reesor, Bayard. *The Canadian Constitution in Historical Perspective.* Scarborough: Prentice-Hall Canada, 1992.

Russell, Peter H., Rainer Knopff, and F.L. Morton. *Federalism and the Charter: Leading Constitutional Decisions.* Ottawa: Carleton University Press, 1989.

NOTES

1. Alan C. Cairns, *Constitution, Government, and Society in Canada,* ed. Douglas E. Williams (Toronto: McClelland & Stewart, 1988), 15.
2. Ibid.
3. For an extended discussion of sovereignty, see Mark O. Dickerson and Thomas Flanagan, *An Introduction to Government and Politics: A Conceptual Approach,* 3rd ed. (Scarborough: ITP Nelson, 1990), 35–44.
4. In *Re The Initiative and Referendum Act,* [1919] A.C. 935 (JCPC).
5. The British North America Act, 1965.
6. The British North America Act, 1975.
7. The British North America Act, 1975 (No. 2).
8. *Reference Re Legislative Authority of Parliament to Alter or Replace the Senate,* [1980] 1 S.C.R. 54.
9. Peter Hogg, *Constitutional Law of Canada,* 3rd ed. (supp.) (Toronto: Carswell, 1992), 3–3 to 3–4.
10. Ibid., 3–4 to 3–7.
11. Ibid., 3–6.

12. Peter H. Russell, *Constitutional Odyssey: Can Canadians Become a Sovereign People?* 2nd ed. (Toronto: University of Toronto Press, 1993), 61–62.
13. Alan Cairns, *Disruptions: Constitutional Struggles: From the Charter to Meech Lake* (Toronto: McClelland & Stewart, 1991), 44.
14. R. Kent Weaver, "Political Institutions and Canada's Constitutional Crisis," in R. Kent Weaver, ed., *The Collapse of Canada?* (Washington: Brookings Institution, 1992), 51.
15. "Patriation" is a Canadian neologism meaning to "bring home"; the dictionary lists only "repatriation," but since the constitution had never legally been in Canada, it could not be repatriated to Canada.
16. The 10th amendment to the U.S. Constitution and section 107 of the Australian Constitution.
17. K.C. Wheare, *Federal Government,* 4th ed. (London: Oxford University Press, 1963), 19.
18. Quoted in R. MacGregor Dawson, *The Government of Canada,* 5th ed., rev'd Norman Ward (Toronto: University of Toronto Press, 1970), 27.
19. Ibid.
20. Hogg, *Constitutional Law,* 6–2.
21. Robert C. Vipond, *Liberty and Community: Canadian Federalism and the Failure of the Constitution* (Albany: State University of New York Press, 1991), 22.
22. Hogg, *Constitutional Law,* 22–15.
23. Ibid., 22–17.
24. Peter H. Russell, *The Judiciary in Canada: The Third Branch of Government* (Toronto: McGraw-Hill Ryerson, 1987), 49.
25. Hogg, *Constitutional Law,* 6–16.
26. The Constitution Act, 1982, provides additional support for equalization payments. Section 36(2) of that act "commits" the federal government to the "principle of making" such payments.
27. On the use of the disallowance power against the Alberta Social Credit government in the 1930s, see J.R. Mallory, *Social Credit and the Federal Power in Canada* (Toronto: University of Toronto Press, 1954).
28. Dawson and Ward, *The Government of Canada,* 27.
29. Robert C. Vipond, "1787 and 1867: The Federal Principle and Canadian Confederation Reconsidered," *Canadian Journal of Political Science* 22 (1989), 11.
30. A.V. Dicey, *Introduction to the Study of the Law of the Constitution* (London: Macmillan, 1920), 39.
31. Ibid., 40.
32. Ibid., 68–70.
33. Russell, *The Judiciary in Canada,* 255–256.
34. For further discussion, see Rainer Knopff and F.L. Morton, *Charter Politics* (Toronto: Nelson Canada, 1992), chapter 3, "The Charter Two-Step."
35. Alan C. Cairns, *Charter versus Federalism: The Dilemmas of Constitutional Reform* (Montreal and Kingston: McGill-Queen's University Press, 1992).
36. F.L. Morton, *Morgentaler v. Borowski: Abortion, the Charter, and the Courts* (Toronto: McClelland & Stewart, 1992).

37. *Citizens Insurance Co. v. Parsons* (1881), 7 App. Cas. 96; 1 Olmsted 94—case 2 in Peter H. Russell, Rainer Knopff, and F.L. Morton, *Federalism and the Charter: Leading Constitutional Decisions* (Ottawa: Carleton University Press, 1989).

38. 1 Cranch 137.

39. *Eakin v. Raub* 12 Sergean & Rawle (Pennsylvania Supreme Court) 330 (1825). For further discussion, see Knopff and Morton, *Charter Politics,* especially chapter 7.

40. In *Re The Board of Commerce Act, 1919,* [1922] 1 A.C. 191; *Fort Frances Pulp and Power Co. v. Manitoba Free Press,* [1923] A.C. 695; *Toronto Electric Commissioners v. Snider,* [1925] A.C. 396—cases 6, 7, and 8 in Russell, Knopff, and Morton, *Federalism and the Charter.*

41. *Attorney General of Canada v. Attorney General of Ontario* (Employment and Social Insurance Act Reference), [1937] A.C. 355; III Olmsted 207; *Attorney General of British Columbia v. Attorney General of Canada* (Natural Products Marketing Act Reference), [1937] A.C. 377; *Attorney General of Canada v. Attorney General of Ontario* (Labour Conventions Case), [1937] A.C. 327—cases 12–14 in Russell, Knopff, and Morton, *Federalism and the Charter.*

42. See Russell, "The Supreme Court's Interpretation of the Constitution," in Paul W. Fox, ed., *Politics Canada,* 5th ed. (Toronto: McGraw-Hill Ryerson, 1982).

43. Peter H. Russell, "The Supreme Court and Federal–Provincial Relations: The Political Use of Legal Resources," *Canadian Public Policy* 11, no. 2 (1985).

44. For a detailed exploration of this debate, see Knopff and Morton, *Charter Politics.*

45. Frank MacKinnon, "The Establishment of the Supreme Court of Canada," in W.R. Lederman, ed., *The Courts and the Constitution* (Toronto: McClelland & Stewart, 1964); Jennifer Smith, "The Origins of Judicial Review in Canada," in F.L. Morton, ed., *Law, Politics and the Judicial Process in Canada,* 2nd ed. (Calgary: University of Calgary Press, 1992).

46. Russell, *The Judiciary in Canada,* 67–68.

47. For example, Canadian governments in both the Meech Lake Accord and the so-called Canada Round of constitutional reform proposed the entrenchment of the Supreme Court, apparently on the assumption that it had not been entrenched by the Constitution Act, 1892. See, for example, *Shaping Canada's Future Together* (Ottawa: Minister of Supply and Services, 1991), 21. Meech Lake and the Canada Round are discussed in Chapter 3.

48. *Satnam Singh et al. v. Minister of Employment and Immigration,* [1985] 1 S.C.R. 177—case 41 in Russell, Knopff, and Morton, *Federalism and the Charter.*

49. Dawson and Ward, *The Government of Canada,* 59.

50. Walter Bagehot, *The English Constitution* (London: Kegan Paul, Trench, Trubner and Co., 1905), 11.

51. Ibid.

52. *Attorney General of Manitoba et al. v. Attorney General of Canada et al.* (patriation case), [1981] 1 S.C.R. 753—case 62 in Russell, Knopff, and Morton, *Federalism and the Charter.*

53. Patriation case—case 62 in Russell, Knopff, and Morton, *Federalism and the Charter,* 746–749; Peter H. Russell, "Bold Statescraft, Questionable Jurisprudence," in Keith Banting and Richard Simeon, eds., *And No One Cheered: Federalism, Democracy, and the Constitution Act* (Toronto: Methuen, 1983), 217.

54. Patriation case—case 62 in Russell, Knopff, and Morton, *Federalism and the Charter,* 749–750; Russell, "Bold Statescraft, Questionable Jurisprudence," 218.

55. Andrew Heard, *Canadian Constitutional Conventions: The Marriage of Law and Politics* (Toronto: Oxford University Press, 1991), 11.
56. Ibid., 18.
57. I. Jennings, *The Law and the Constitution,* 5th ed. (London: University of London Press, 1959), 343.
58. Rainer Knopff, "Legal Theory and the 'Patriation' Debate," *Queen's Law Journal* 7 (1981), 41–65; Knopff and Morton, *Charter Politics,* chapter 11.
59. Jennings, *The Law and the Constitution,* 346.
60. E.E. Schattschneider, *The Semisovereign People* (Hinsdale, Ill.: Dryden Press, 1975), 69.
61. Richard Simeon, "Regionalism and Canadian Political Institutions," in R. Schultz, O.M. Kruhlak, and J.C. Terry, eds., *The Canadian Political Process,* 3rd ed. (Toronto: Holt, Rinehart and Winston, 1979), 294.
62. See Knopff and Morton, *Charter Politics,* 95–97.
63. *Reference Re Anti-Inflation Act,* [1976] 2 S.C.R. 373—case 22 in Russell, Knopff, and Morton, *Federalism and the Charter.*
64. See Russell, "Political Purposes of the Canadian Charter of Rights and Freedoms," *The Canadian Bar Review* 61 (1983); Rainer Knopff and F.L. Morton, "Nation-Building and the Canadian Charter of Rights and Freedoms," in Alan Cairns and Cynthia Williams, eds., *Constitutionalism, Citizenship, and Society in Canada* (Toronto: University of Toronto Press, 1985); Knopff and Morton, *Charter Politics,* chapter 4.
65. Cairns, *Charter versus Federalism,* chapter 2.
66. Ibid., 38.

3 THE MODERN ERA OF MEGACONSTITUTIONAL POLITICS

Constitutional politics at the mega level is distinguished in two ways from normal constitutional politics. First, megaconstitutional politics goes beyond disputing the merits of specific constitutional proposals and addresses the very nature of the political community on which the constitution is based. Megaconstitutional politics, whether directed toward comprehensive constitutional change or not, is concerned with reaching agreement on the identity and fundamental principles of the body politic. The second feature of megaconstitutional politics flows logically from the first. Precisely because of the fundamental nature of the issues in dispute—their tendency to touch citizens' sense of identity and self-worth—megaconstitutional politics is exceptionally emotional and intense. When a country's constitutional politics reaches this level, the constitutional question tends to dwarf all other public concerns.[1]

Canada's constitutional politics since about 1960 has involved the clash of fundamentally incompatible visions of community. Conceptions of Canada as a partnership of two founding nations jostle with claims that other group identities—gender or aboriginality, for example—are of equal or greater foundational importance. Some argue that group diversity or multiculturalism itself is the primary foundational principle. Others see Canada in territorial terms, as a community of equal provinces or regions. All such group-based visions, territorial or otherwise, are in turn challenged by a vision of the country as most fundamentally a community of equal individuals. Moreover, these clashing perspectives are differently distributed across the country; for example, the two-nations view is strongest in central Canada—especially in Quebec, though it also resonates in Ontario—while the equal-provinces vision is particularly prominent in the West.

Clashing views are not unusual in politics, but the stakes are raised and the conflicts become more intense when their advocates attempt to entrench them in the formal constitution. Entrenchment politics of this kind has characterized post-1960 constitutional politics. In this politics, each vision wants itself recognized as constitutionally fundamental, and none will consent to be left uninvited to the constitutional feast, or, if invited, to be seated at the foot of the table. Once at the table, each vision struggles to outrank the others, while watching jealously to ensure that no other vision gets ahead. The result has been ever broader packages of constitutional reform, reflecting the ultimately futile attempt to balance all of the competing claims at the level of entrenched constitutional law. The difficulty of resolving the issues has been compounded by a profound shift from elite accommodation to democratic consultation as the chief mechanism for constitutional change. Accordingly, there has been much sound and fury but with little consequence, except perhaps the deepening fragmentation of the Canadian community. Such is the character of megaconstitutional politics.

■ ■ ■

Constitutional politics from 1867 to about 1960 was what this chapter's epigraph calls "normal constitutional politics." That is, constitutional debate after 1867 tended *not* to involve open challenges to the very legitimacy of the existing constitution. True, there were several formal amendments that changed certain constitutional rules, but they were limited in scope, addressing particular, well-focused issues (e.g., giving power over unemployment insurance to the federal government). Moreover, such amendments occurred sporadically, in piecemeal fashion, not all at once in packages large enough to raise questions about the legitimacy of the entire constitutional structure. On the whole, constitutional politics from Confederation to about 1960 involved competing attempts to interpret, shape, and work the existing rules; it did not openly challenge the legitimacy of the structure in a fundamental and wholesale fashion. During this era, moreover, constitutional politics was of concern primarily to political elites; it did not arouse public passion and involvement.

The 1960s ushered in a qualitative change in Canada's constitutional politics. The prevailing elite-dominated politics of interpretation and piecemeal amendment was replaced by a constitutional politics in which virtually the entire constitution, and thus the integrity of the Canadian political community itself, was periodically challenged in ways that evoked widespread public concern and, increasingly, public participation. Proposals for scrapping the existing constitution and starting almost from scratch were not uncommon, and the disintegration of the country often seemed a real possibility. The challenge came first from nationalism in Quebec, but gradually the discontents of other regions and non-territorial groupings (such as women and Aboriginal peoples) found voice also. Not that the country felt itself to be in a state of perpetual crisis after 1960, for each moment of perceived crisis was followed by a period of relative constitutional calm. Yet the calm never lasted. After each ebb came a new flow, with the sense of crisis building to a new climax. The climaxes were associated with proposals for significant constitutional restructuring—proposals that became more sweeping over time. Most prominent among them were the failed Victoria Charter in 1971; the Quebec referendum on sovereignty-association in 1980; the domestication of constitutional amendments and the entrenchment of the Charter of Rights in the patriation package of 1982; the failed Meech Lake Accord (1987–90); the so-called Canada Round of constitutional reform, which culminated in the October 1992 referendum on the Charlottetown Accord; the 1995 Quebec independence referendum, which like its 1980 predecessor stimulated yet another round of constitutional jockeying. Some commentators speak ruefully of Canada's constitutional "neverendum."

This era of what Peter Russell calls "megaconstitutional politics" has brought to a head the inherent tension in the Canadian constitution between federalism and parliamentary government. While federalism disperses power among governments, parliamentary government concentrates the power of each government in the hands of a cohesive cabinet backed by a highly disciplined party. Parliamentary government thus enhances the ability of majorities within the governing party to ignore or overwhelm minorities. In a large and diverse country such as Canada, the aggrieved minorities are often regional or provincial communities. Thus, disciplined and executive-dominated governing parties in Parliament are often seen as riding roughshod over the interests of some region or province. Quebec, for example, often sees Parliament as serving the interests of the English majority in the rest of Canada, to Quebec's detriment. Similarly, the West complains that Parliament responds most readily to the dominant majority in central Canada (Ontario and Quebec). Such perceptions are, of course, as old as Canada itself, but they have in recent years led to increasingly intense and comprehensive demands for explicit constitutional overhaul.

As one might expect, regional alienation has generated proposals for the reform of both the federal and the parliamentary dimensions of our constitutionalism. One line of reform wishes to decentralize the federal–provincial division of powers, thus taking more regionally relevant powers out of the hands of a regionally insensitive Parliament. The other line of reform wishes to reform our parliamentary institutions. Each of these strategies can itself be broken into two subcategories. Among decentralists are proponents of **asymmetrical federalism**, who believe that Quebec should have more powers than other provinces, and those who insist that all provinces must be treated equally. The parliamentary reform camp has produced two proposals: (1) the as yet unsuccessful proposal to make the houses of Parliament more regionally responsive (thus undermining regional alienation and the need for decentralization); and (2) the successful proposal to entrench a Charter of Rights and Freedoms (thus reducing parliamentary supremacy and increasing the power of the courts).

Whereas decentralization and reform of the two houses of Parliament respond to regionalism by institutionalizing it (though in very different ways), the Charter represents an attempt to counteract or moderate the institutional sources of regionalism. The Charter has not displaced the old parliamentary and federal principles, however. It has merely added to them, thus providing new opportunities for constitutional contestation and new constitutional resources to different kinds of constituencies. In addition to regional communities headed by provincial governments, such players as women, Aboriginals, and multicultural groups have gained new or enhanced constitutional status. Nor has the Charter calmed the turbulent waters of contemporary megaconstitutional politics. It has simply dealt new players, who represent different interests and visions of community, into the game.

The crowded agenda of our megaconstitutional politics involves the clash of several different attempts to refashion the Canadian community in comprehensive but not always compatible ways. Some want to turn the country into a loose confederation of two linguistically and culturally based territorial nations—Quebec and the rest of Canada. Others promote a different version of the two-nations theory, according to which all of Canada is simultaneously the home of both the French and English "founding nations." Still others seek to extend the founding nations idea to include Canada's Aboriginal or "first" nations and to refashion the Canadian community in corresponding ways, especially by institutionalizing forms of Aboriginal self-government. Women's groups extend the founding nations concept even further to encompass the idea of two "founding genders," an idea with its own institutional implications. Adding further spice to this constitutional stew are those who prefer to emphasize the sense in which Canada is an association of 10 equal provincial communities, or a multicultural community, or a community of equal individuals who put their "Canadianness" above all group affiliations. Yet another axis of constitutional politics is the division between the political left and right about social and economic policy, with those on the right seeking constitutional protection for greater domestic "free trade" and competitiveness and those on the left insisting on constitutionally protecting Canada's social programs from being eroded by competitiveness. There is, of course, nothing new for Canadians in the clash of competing visions of community. But in the era of megaconstitutional politics, these visions demand comprehensive revisions of entrenched constitutional law. The conflict of visions thus takes place on the highest level of constitutional symbolism, with the highest constitutional stakes.

The difficulty of resolving or accommodating deep constitutional conflicts, moreover, has been intensified by a broadening of participation in the amending process. An increasing number of the potential players are playing the high-stakes game of major constitutional overhaul, leaving little of the constitution unchallenged and decreasing the prospects of a resolution. In the past, the constitutional politics of conflicting visions of community was conducted almost exclusively by small numbers of political and governmental elites. Non-governmental interests, and certainly the Canadian public at large, were not players in the game of constitutional politics. While the Americans rooted their constitution in the doctrine of popular sovereignty,

Canadians focused instead on the traditional British doctrine of parliamentary sovereignty. The Canadian constitution was legally the act of a sovereign imperial Parliament, and the central domestic issue after 1867 was whether and to what extent the constitution divided domestic sovereignty between two orders of government. The Canadian constitution, as Alan Cairns has written, was primarily a **governments' constitution**, a fact reflected in the predominance of governmental elites in discussing and carrying out its amendment.

The constitutional emphasis on governments changed in 1982, when, as mentioned, the Charter invested non-governmental interests, and indeed individuals as such, with formal constitutional significance. The Charter was the expression of a new **citizens' constitution**,[2] and contributed to irresistible demands for wider public participation in subsequent constitutional amendments. In the contemporary period of megaconstitutional politics, Canadians have demonstrated their rejection of older doctrines of sovereignty in favour of the idea of popular sovereignty. They have made it clear that the constitution belongs to the people and that the people must be involved in its amendment. The Charlottetown Accord represented the most comprehensive game of constitutional politics thus far, with the largest set of players, including the Canadian public at large—which in October 1992 voted on the constitutional package generated by other players.

But the people who claim ownership of the constitution are as fundamentally divided in their visions of community as are their governmental elites, and the people are less likely than their elites to bridge those differences. A small number of governmental leaders in constant face-to-face interaction can come to respect and even like one another, and can agree to fudge or paper over some of their deeper disagreements. At the level of the public at large, deeply conflicting visions of community tend to be less easily reconcilable. The shift from Canada's traditional constitutional politics of elite accommodation to a more popular constitutional politics has thus made our megaconstitutional politics even more "mega." In Peter Russell's words, while the Canadian people have become "constitutional democrats" who believe that a constitution can be legitimate only if it is derived from the people, they have not yet "consented to form a single people." Whether the deeply conflicting visions of community that divide Canadians can be bridged not just by elites but by the broader public is, for Russell, the central question facing Canada at this stage of its "constitutional odyssey." As he phrases it in his book's subtitle, the question is, "Can Canadians become a sovereign people?"

THE ROOTS OF MEGACONSTITUTIONAL POLITICS

Canada was launched on its modern megaconstitutional odyssey by provincial or regional discontent with the existing constitution of parliamentary federalism. Quebec nationalism posed the first major constitutional challenge, but that challenge was soon joined by growing forces of regional alienation and provincialism elsewhere in the country. We shall consider each of these roots of megaconstitutional politics in turn.

Quebec Nationalism

The decisive event in generating demands for major constitutional revision was the **Quiet Revolution** that transformed Quebec politics in the early 1960s. The decade opened with the defeat of the Union Nationale government of Quebec by the provincial Liberals under the leadership of Jean Lesage. The Lesage Liberals ushered Quebec into the modern era of activist states. Prior to 1960 the Union Nationale and its indomitable leader, Maurice Duplessis, had adopted a minimalist, laissez-faire approach to the economy and had allowed the church to dominate the realms of education and social welfare. Whatever the ultimate explanations for this posture, it had often been justified on the basis of a traditionalist ideology according to which the destiny of Quebec francophones was to be a Catholic, agrarian people for whom modern commercial capitalism was a foreign activity better left to English-speaking Protestants.[3] By 1960 this ideology was clearly myth rather than an accurate description of reality, for Quebeckers had for years been leaving their farms in droves and becoming integrated into modern urban, industrial society. The problem was that they had been integrated as workers into enterprises largely controlled and managed by the English community and using English as the language of work, a development that threatened the long-term persistence of French as the primary language in Quebec.

Responding to this reality, the Lesage Liberals abandoned the anti-statism of their predecessors. If French were to survive, the government had to intervene in the economy in order to ensure that it was controlled and operated to a much greater extent by francophones. Commerce was no longer to be disdained as a foreign activity but was to be embraced as a form of secular salvation and, wherever possible, was to be conducted in French. By the same token, education and other social services had to be wrested from the church and directed more explicitly to giving French Quebeckers the skills they needed to take control of economic enterprises rather than just supply their labour. In its newfound interventionism, especially in economic matters, Quebec often wanted to go further than the other provinces and occupy realms of activity that had been filled by the federal government. Ottawa, from this perspective, could not be trusted to exercise its powers in a manner congenial to Quebec. Parliamentary institutions are highly responsive to the majority, and the majority to which Ottawa would naturally respond was the English majority outside of

Quebec. The Quiet Revolution, in short, led to the demand for a transfer of powers from Ottawa to Quebec City, a demand that has dominated Quebec politics and shaped the national constitutional landscape ever since.

Underlying and justifying Quebec's demand for more powers was one of the central visions of community that animates contemporary constitutional politics: the **two-nations vision**. Exponents of the two-nations theory of Canada believe that Canada is primarily the coming together of two founding nations, French and English.[4] There are two versions of this theory, territorial and non-territorial. The non-territorial version argues that all of Canada is home to both of the founding peoples and that the federal government thus represents and expresses the interests of a coast-to-coast bicultural nation;[5] the territorial version insists that Quebec is the primary home of the French nation in North America and that the Quebec government is that nation's chief institutional expression. From the latter perspective, the rest of Canada is the home of an English-Canadian nation, which, as a majority in the federal Parliament, naturally controls the federal government; in short, Ottawa is primarily the government of English Canada, just as Quebec is the true government of the French nation. This territorial version of the two-nations theory implies that Quebec is not a province like the others. Whereas the other provinces are administrative subdivisions of one of the nations composing Canada, Quebec is the institutional expression of the other national partner, and it thus requires more governmental powers than the other provinces do. The territorial version of the two-nations theory, in other words, implies inequality of status and treatment among the provinces, or asymmetrical federalism. It is this vision of community that has driven Quebec's demands for decentralization.

During the early 1960s, however, Quebec's demand for the transfer of powers did not yet express itself as a demand for explicit amendment of the entrenched constitution. The Lesage Liberals preferred to work out administrative arrangements with Ottawa at the subconstitutional level. In response to this strategy, Ottawa agreed that provinces could "opt out" of a variety of federal programs and receive financial compensation for the lost program spending. Significantly, **opting out**, though clearly designed for Quebec, was formally extended to all provinces. Only by making the powers given to Quebec available to all of the other provinces did it seem possible to meet the decentralizing demands of Quebec's two-nations theory without violating the rival **equal-provinces vision**. This strategy for harmonizing the two-nations and equal-provinces perspectives is one we shall encounter again. (See Dossier 3.1 for an account of why this "harmonization strategy" is unlikely to work.)

Quebec immediately availed itself of the new regime and opted out of wholly federal programs, such as grants to universities and youth allowances; federal contributory schemes, such as the Canada Pension Plan; and a variety of federal–provincial shared-cost programs. In return, Ottawa either reduced its taxation in the province by an amount roughly equivalent to its former financial contributions—thereby giving Quebec the "tax room" to raise its own revenue for similar programs—or paid the province cash compensation.

DOSSIER 3.1 WHY ACROSS-THE-BOARD DECENTRALIZATION DOESN'T SATISFY QUEBEC NATIONALISTS

[S]ome people have proposed a radical across-the-board decentralization, so that all provinces would have the same powers currently demanded by Quebec. This is intended to avoid the need to grant "special status" to Quebec. The response by many Quebec nationalists, however, was that this missed the point. The demand for special status was a demand not just for this or that additional power, but also for *national recognition.* As Resnick puts it, "They want to see Quebec recognized as a nation, not a mere province; this very symbolic demand cannot be finessed through some decentralizing formula applied to all provinces." Quebec nationalists want asymmetry for its own sake, as a symbolic recognition that Quebec alone is a nationality-based unit within Canada. This may seem like a petty concern with symbols rather than the substance of political power. But we find the same dilemma in other multination federations, and it is unlikely to disappear.

Source: Reprinted from Will Kymlicka, "Multinational Federalism in Canada: Rethinking the Partnership," in Roger Gibbins and Guy Laforest, eds., *Beyond the Impasse: Toward Reconciliation* (Ottawa: IRRP, 1998), 27.

Although other provinces were free to engage in similar opting out, they tended not to. The result was what Peter Russell calls **soft asymmetry**: the unequal treatment of provinces in fact though not in form. **Hard asymmetry**, by contrast, gives a province **special status** as a matter of formal constitutional law.[6]

Soft asymmetrical federalism can occur at the level of entrenched constitutional law as well as in administrative arrangements. For example, section 94(a) of the 1867 Constitution Act, which was added in 1951, gave Ottawa and the provinces concurrent jurisdiction over pensions, subject to a rule of provincial paramountcy. In effect, the provincial paramountcy rule is a constitutional opting-out provision that allows provinces to stay out of a national pension policy. Again, though all provinces are formally equal in their access to this power, only Quebec has exercised it, thus establishing a constitutionally based soft asymmetry in this policy area.

The fact that the asymmetrical implications of the two-nations theory were institutionalized during the early 1960s in a soft form lessened this theory's clash with the equal-provinces view. The fact that opting out during this period occurred at the administrative level rather than the formal constitutional level further diffused potential opposition. However, the stakes would soon be raised (as would the intensity of conflict among conflicting visions of community) by demands for a radical transformation of the entrenched constitution along two-nations lines, with explicit special status for Quebec.

The impending change in the nature of Quebec's approach to constitutional politics was revealed in the 1966 failure of the so-called **Fulton-Favreau formula** for patriating the formal constitution. Ever since the Statute of Westminster, Canada's political elites had engaged in sporadic and desultory negotiations to find a domestic formula for amending the constitution and thus formally complete Canada's transition from colony to fully independent nation.[7] In late 1964 it seemed that the process of patriating the constitution was finally at an end. Canada's first ministers had unanimously agreed to a new amending formula. Named for the successive federal ministers of Justice who oversaw its negotiation between 1960 and 1964, the Fulton-Favreau amending formula allowed certain parts of the formal constitution, such as the five-year limit on the electoral term of the House of Commons, to be amended with the consent of two-thirds of the provinces having at least 50 percent of the population—an early expression of the seven-fifty rule. But the most important parts of the constitution, and especially the federal–provincial distribution of powers, could be amended only with the unanimous consent of all eleven governments.[8]

The Fulton-Favreau formula, agreed to by Quebec's premier, Jean Lesage, gave Quebec a veto over any attempt to centralize the federal division of powers. Of course, it also allowed any other province to block a Quebec-led attempt to decentralize the division of powers, and we have seen that after the Quiet Revolution Quebec was preoccupied with decentralization. The ability of other provinces to veto formal constitutional decentralization may not have seemed problematic to Lesage because of his emphasis on administrative decentralization. However, this view was not shared by all Quebeckers. The Fulton-Favreau formula was subject to a mounting tide of criticism in Quebec based on the view that the province required formal constitutional decentralization, and that the unanimity requirement of Fulton-Favreau was a straitjacket that would prevent this decentralization. So strong did this line of criticism become that, in January 1966, Lesage withdrew Quebec's support for the Fulton-Favreau formula, thereby killing it. As Russell observes, "Lesage's change of heart meant much more than simply another failure to agree on a constitutional amending formula. The circumstances that prompted the change indicated that Quebec's price for supporting patriation would be nothing less than a [formal] restructuring of the Canadian federation to give sufficient scope for Quebec nationalism."[9] The demand for substantial formal restructuring underlying the failure of Fulton-Favreau is, in Russell's view, what catapulted modern Canada onto the field of megaconstitutional politics.[10]

What was implicit in Lesage's 1966 rejection of Fulton-Favreau became explicit later the same year when the Union Nationale defeated the Liberals and Daniel Johnson became premier. Johnson had been a leader in the fight against Fulton-Favreau and in 1965 had published a book entitled *Égalité ou Indépendance*, which argued for an entirely new formal constitution for Canada, a truly binational constitution that would better reflect the two-nations theory. Johnson's book became the basis of his government's constitutional position,[11] and thus by the mid-1960s Quebec's interest in devolving power from Ottawa to Quebec City had become a matter of formal constitutional confrontation.

The Johnson government's interest in substantial constitutional reform took place against a much broader background of constitutional confrontation, for the 1960s was also a decade of radical and occasionally violent separatist agitation in

Quebec. The Quiet Revolution was not always quiet! Johnson had posed the options as equality or independence—the equality of two national communities within a common constitutional framework or the outright independence of Quebec. The separatists did not think equality within a binational Canada was viable or desirable, and preferred immediate and complete independence. Some chose violent means to promote this end. The violence reached its peak in 1970, when the FLQ (Front de Libération du Québec) kidnapped the British trade commissioner, James Cross, and then kidnapped and murdered Quebec cabinet minister Pierre Laporte. The federal government responded by invoking the War Measures Act and sending in troops. Although the use of emergency measures was controversial,[12] public revulsion at the FLQ actions was widespread both inside and outside Quebec. After 1970, FLQ-style revolutionary separatism virtually disappeared, and separatist energies were channelled into support for the democratic Parti Québécois (PQ).[13] Needless to say, separatism represented the most radical expression of the two-nations theory and involved the most dramatic changes to the formal constitution.

Quebec's shift from administrative bargaining to formal constitutional confrontation was perhaps the primary trigger of the megaconstitutional politics that has periodically preoccupied Canadians ever since. Once the territorial version of the two-nations theory had been elevated to the level of high constitutional principle and symbolism through demands for substantial restructuring of the entrenched constitution, rival constitutional visions rose to the challenge, generating their own projects of formal and large-scale constitutional reform. The two-nations and equal-provinces visions were prominent contenders in the ensuing constitutional struggle, but they were by no means the only ones. Visions of community emphasizing other sources of identity, such as gender, ethnicity, and even unhyphenated Canadianism, were also significant. In eliciting a welter of conflicting constitutional visions, and in forcing the opposition between them into the highly charged atmosphere of formal constitutional change, Quebec's territorially based two-nations proposals pried open a veritable Pandora's box of megaconstitutional politics.

Regionalism and Provincialism

Among the discontents that emerged from the megaconstitutional Pandora's box were those of Canada's West. Just as Quebec considered itself ill served by Parliament, so the West had long nurtured grievances stemming from the perception that its regional interests tended to be overwhelmed by the interests of central Canada in the House of Commons. The problem stemmed not only from the demographic dominance of Ontario and Quebec in the House, which was based largely on representation by population, but also from the conventions of party discipline and cabinet solidarity, which constrained the capacity of western MPs to address regional issues. (These points are discussed in greater detail in Chapter 5.) Such concerns, however, had generally been overshadowed by the constitutional preoccupations of central Canada. From the founding period onward, relations between the English and French communities have often dominated the constitutional horizons of Ontario and Quebec, and this was certainly the case in the 1960s and 1970s. Given the dominant political and economic power of the two central provinces, their constitutional problems became the "national" problems, and the merely "regional" grievances of the West were pushed to the sidelines of the ongoing national unity debate.

This changed dramatically in the 1970s. In 1973 the Organization of Petroleum Exporting Countries (OPEC) launched an international oil embargo, thereby triggering both an economic boom in Western Canada—particularly in Alberta—and economic difficulty for energy-consuming central Canada. Indeed, skyrocketing oil prices almost touched off a fiscal crisis as oil wealth in the West drove up the cost of equalization payments in other provinces—costs borne by a federal treasury that enjoyed only modest financial return from the oil boom. This crisis was exacerbated by what appeared at the time to be a shift in economic power from Toronto to Calgary without a corresponding shift in formal political power.

With the new economic power of the West came an unaccustomed degree of informal political power. No longer could the political and constitutional concerns of the West be ignored by central Canada or the federal government. Thus, by the mid-1970s the "national unity crisis" had come to refer not just to the problem posed by Quebec nationalism and separatism but to the wider phenomenon of regional alienation and the increasingly virulent intergovernmental conflict that attended it. This new constitutional stew was brought to a boil in the West, and particularly in Alberta, by the Trudeau government's introduction of the National Energy Program (NEP) in the fall of 1980. The NEP was designed to control the increase in oil prices, to provide greater oil tax revenues for the federal government, to Canadianize ownership of the oil industry, and to shift exploration from provincial lands to "Canada lands" in the North and offshore. The NEP was viewed as nothing short of confiscatory by the Alberta government, which responded with a series of cuts in the production of oil. While a common bumper sticker reading "Let the Eastern bastards freeze in the dark" did not reflect the formal policy response of the Alberta government, it nicely captured the mood of the times.

The NEP also captured an institutional critique that had been developing over the years in the West and was now being brought to the constitutional table by western provincial governments. The NEP was introduced by a national Liberal government that held only two seats in western Canada—both in Manitoba—but that nonetheless commanded a solid national majority. Thus, even to western Canadians outside Alberta, the NEP demonstrated a serious flaw in parliamentary institutions. The problem was obvious: national parliamentary institutions that were, in fact, not national at all in the exercise of power. Programs such as the NEP were what one could expect when a region was all but excluded from the cabinet and from the government side of the House. Moreover, the NEP's bitter reception in the West also demonstrated what can happen when the national government lacks elected members to sell its programs in the region.

Nor did parliamentary institutions seem to work much better when the West was well represented on the government side of the House. In 1984 western voters helped the Mulroney Conservatives sweep the Liberals from office, and western politicians played a prominent role in Mulroney's cabinet. Nevertheless, in 1986 the federal cabinet awarded a major contract for the maintenance of CF-18 aircraft to a Montreal firm despite the fact that a cheaper and technically superior bid had been submitted by a Winnipeg firm. For many westerners, this event brought into even sharper focus the flaw in Canada's parliamentary regime: even when the West was solidly represented on the government benches, the more populous East would always carry greater weight in a chamber based on representation by population, and western members of the government party would be silenced by party discipline and cabinet solidarity. So powerful was the western discontent with the CF-18 contract that it became the galvanizing event in the formation of a new political party, the Reform Party, which entered national politics under the slogan "The West Wants In."[14]

Quebec and the West were not alone in adopting a combative posture toward Ottawa and in expressing dissatisfaction with existing arrangements. With the development of the modern activist welfare state, provincial areas of jurisdiction over such matters as health, social services, and education assumed a new significance and occupied an increasing proportion of overall governmental resources. In response, the provincial order of government gradually became larger and more sophisticated. Growth and increased power, of course, have a tendency to generate ambitions for even more growth and power. "By the mid 1970s," writes Russell, "the federation was experiencing a high tide of 'province-building,'" a process that often involved struggles with Ottawa for resources and comparative advantages.[15] Among the symptoms of growing intergovernmental conflict was an ever more litigious atmosphere, with the two orders of government increasingly ready to take their quarrels to court. In a number of high-profile cases, moreover, the provinces lost,[16] which further fuelled provincial discontent.

One manifestation of the growing regional alienation and assertive provincialism of Canadian politics was a demand for constitutional decentralization. If parliamentary institutions in Ottawa did not adequately serve certain territorially defined communities in areas of national jurisdiction, the solution was to transfer those areas to the provinces. To this extent, constitutional disaffection in Quebec often dovetailed nicely with that in other parts of Canada. Many Canadians outside Quebec, especially westerners, rejected the two-nations theory and any implication of asymmetrical federalism, but, as in the case of administrative "opting out" in the 1960s, Quebec's decentralizing demands would not lead to asymmetrical federalism if federal powers were formally devolved to all provinces. Nor did decentralists from Quebec care much whether its partner in the two-nations framework wished to decentralize itself. Thus, despite contrasting visions of community, decentralizers in Quebec and the rest of Canada were often able to make common cause in demanding a devolution of powers from Ottawa to the provinces.

Decentralization was not the only constitutional prescription to emerge, however. Regional alienation, though not Quebec nationalism, also produced an alternative and often conflicting line of reform proposals. Instead of further decentralizing the federal–provincial division of powers, some argued for the reform of the national institutions of government to make them more regionally responsive. Proposals for institutional reform, in short, reflected two opposing institutional logics—the logics of what Canadian political scientists have come to call interstate and intrastate federalism.

Interstate Federalism versus Intrastate Federalism

Interstate federalism is based on the existence and interaction of two distinct orders of government. First, it refers to the formal distribution of powers between the two orders of government. Thus, Donald Smiley and Ronald Watts identify the core element of interstate federalism in terms of "the distribution of authority between the general and regional governments whereby jurisdiction, with respect to those matters about which the regional units differ most markedly or which they insist are essential to preserving their distinctiveness, is conferred by the constitution on the states or provinces."[17] Second, interstate federalism refers to the inevitable intergovernmental relations in a federal system. As the prefix "inter" suggests, interstate relations are relations between states or governments.

Because the interstate relations of Canadian federalism often resemble those between states in the international arena, Richard Simeon has gone so far as to label them "**federal–provincial diplomacy**."[18] Like diplomatic relations generally, intergovernmental relations in Canada's federal system are dominated by the executive branch of government. In recent decades this has meant especially relations between political executives (first ministers and cabinets). Thus, what Simeon calls "federal–provincial diplomacy" is also known as "**executive federalism**."

Significantly, much of the politics of constitutional reform during the era of megaconstitutional politics has been played out in the arena of executive federalism, especially in high-profile meetings of first ministers. Of course, the institutional arena in which a political issue is processed shapes the tenor of the discussions and the probable outcomes. Simply put, different institutions, different outcomes. The fact that constitutional reform was discussed most authoritatively in an arena animated by the logic of interstate federalism meant that reform proposals based on the same logic would be strongly promoted. Like any other institutional stage, that of executive federalism favours some voices and actors over others. The natural tendency of the provincial actors in this drama is to demand more power for themselves, to promote a redistribution of powers in favour of the provinces. Indeed, this is generally what happened as constitutional politics unfolded during the 1970s and 1980s. In other words, a constitutional reform process based on the intergovernmental-relations prong of interstate federalism tended to emphasize reform proposals that would enhance the division-of-powers prong of interstate federalism. Nevertheless, reform proposals animated by the logic of interstate federalism were not the only ones to contest the stage of constitutional politics. Increasingly, such proposals had to compete with proposals based on the competing logic of intrastate federalism.

Intrastate federalism is an alternative response to the tensions produced by the marriage of federalism and parliamentary institutions in a large and regionalized country. Instead of responding to regionalism by dividing power *between* orders of government and emphasizing relations *between* those governments, intrastate federalism, as its prefix suggests, responds by bringing regionalism *within* the institutions of the central government. The idea was to reform the parliamentary side of Canada's marriage of parliamentary democracy and federalism in order to make the federal Parliament more regionally responsive, thereby undercutting the need for further decentralization.

Proponents of intrastate federalism argued that the federal division of powers failed to provide sufficient protection for regional interests, even when such protection was augmented by the aggressive defence of regional interests by provincial governments acting within the intergovernmental arena. For westerners especially, the NEP had dramatically underscored this reality. Thus, the argument continued, the division of powers and intergovernmental defence of regional interests had to be complemented by the effective representation of regional interests by national politicians acting within national institutions. In effect, the interstate devices of divided jurisdictions and intergovernmental relations had to be complemented by more effective intrastate mechanisms for the representation of regional interests within the institutions of the federal government. Unfortunately, effective intrastate channels of regional representation in national institutions tend to be choked off by the consequences of parliamentary government, including strict party discipline, cabinet secrecy, regionally unbalanced parliamentary caucuses, and an enfeebled upper house (all of which will be discussed at greater length in subsequent chapters). As a result, provincial governments were able to claim, if only by default, that they were the best representatives of their populations even in matters of federal jurisdiction. This claim fuelled simultaneously the interstate tendency to make national policy through intergovernmental negotiation and the provincial demand for a transfer of powers from Ottawa to the provinces. The national unity crisis, in short, was partly caused by institutions that favoured interstate federalism and would be cured through reforms designed to strengthen intrastate federalism.

The precise intrastate prescriptions varied. In light of the litigiousness of this period and the provincial perception that Ottawa was winning most of the important cases, a common proposal was to reform the Supreme Court to give provincial governments input into Supreme Court appointments. There also emerged advocates for electoral reform and procedural reform in the House of Commons. Senate reform became perhaps the most prominent theme. As we shall see in Chapter 5, the Senate had originally been designed in part to provide regional representation in Ottawa but had never functioned as an effective regional chamber of the legislature.

FIGURE 3.1 **INTERSTATE AND INTRASTATE FEDERALISM**

Interstate Federalism

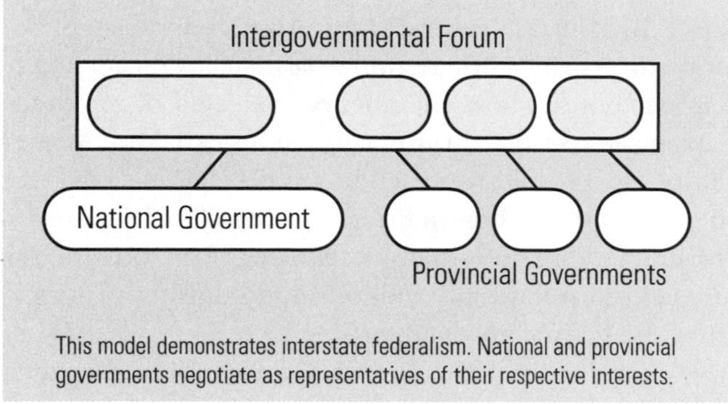

This model demonstrates interstate federalism. National and provincial governments negotiate as representatives of their respective interests.

Intrastate Federalism

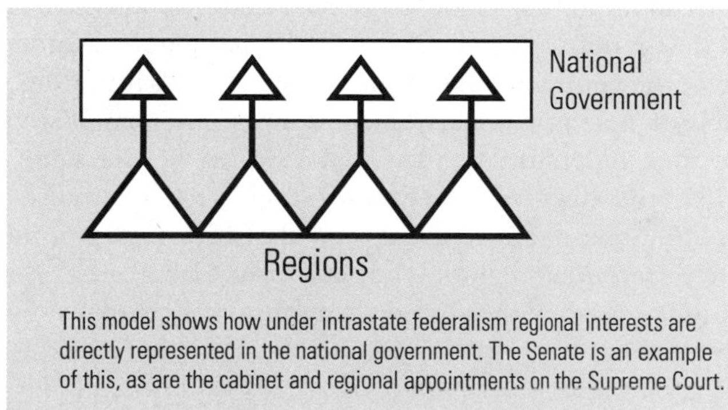

This model shows how under intrastate federalism regional interests are directly represented in the national government. The Senate is an example of this, as are the cabinet and regional appointments on the Supreme Court.

Senate reformers sought ways to enable the upper house more effectively to fulfill the intrastate side of its original logic.

This intrastate approach became especially attractive to certain elements of opinion in the West. Quebec was interested in reform of the Supreme Court but not in other parts of the intrastate movement because it was not particularly in Quebec's interest to enhance the legitimacy of central institutions. Of course, it was not in the immediate interest of provincial governments in the West either, so it was not surprising that prominent western politicians such as former Alberta premier Peter Lougheed were ambivalent about Senate reform. To the extent that western provinces were attracted to intrastate reforms, they often preferred what Alan Cairns has called the "provincialist" version of this approach. **Provincialist intrastate federalism**, which Cairns distinguishes from "centralist" intrastate federalism, refers to mechanisms whereby provincial governments are given a direct voice in central government institutions. The leading proposal in this respect was a new upper house to replace the Senate, one whose members would be delegates of the provincial governments. Inspired by the German *Bundesrat*, this proposed chamber was appropriately called the **House of the Provinces**.[19]

By contrast, **centralist intrastate federalism** gives power within national institutions to provincial or regional *populations* rather than to provincial governments. An upper house whose members are elected by regional or provincial populations is an example. Such a house (the American and Australian senates are examples) attempts to provide representatives of regional concerns who are independent of, and potentially in competition with, provincial governments. Clearly, provincialist intrastate federalism enhances the role of the provinces in the governmental system, while centralist intrastate federalism diminishes provincial authority and strengthens that of the central government.

During the 1970s some provinces added provincialist reforms of central institutions (particularly proposals for a House of the Provinces) to their traditional demand for devolving jurisdictional powers. However, in doing so they were unable to drive centralist intrastate options from the field. Most prominent among these was the demand for a so-called **Triple-E Senate**, an **e**ffective upper house of **e**qual provincial delegations, **e**lected by provincial populations. Indeed, the Triple-E Senate was one of the central planks in the Reform Party's founding platform and accounted for much of that party's early success among alienated westerners. While provincialist intrastate federalism tended to be driven by the same visions of community that fuelled the drive for decentralization, such centralist intrastate proposals as the Triple-E Senate reflected the view that in many important policy areas, even those with differential regional implications, Canada's regional components could be brought together in a single community that expressed itself through its central government.

PATRIATION AND THE CHARTER

Interstate and intrastate federalism were not the only institutional logics through which conflicting visions of community expressed their disagreements. Opponents of the decentralizing logic of interstate federalism relied not only on the intrastate alternative of bringing the regions to the centre but also sought ways to overcome, or at least mute, the salience of provincialism itself in Canadian public life. This project contributed yet another logic to the mix of Canadian constitutional contestation, one that was successfully implemented in the 1982 Charter of Rights and Freedoms.

The chief proponent and architect of the Charter was Pierre Elliott Trudeau, who led the federal government almost from the time the modern period of megaconstitutional politics began (in the 1960s) to 1984, shortly after the entrenchment of the Charter. Trudeau came to federal politics because of a concern with the constitutional aspects of the national unity question, and he remained personally preoccupied during his tenure with constitutional issues. Trudeau was interested in a "balanced" federalism, which he thought was being undermined by proponents of excessive decentralization, especially in Quebec but also in the West. He thus made it his mission to create "counterweights" to the forces of decentralism.[20] Granting provincial demands for a major devolution of power from Ottawa to the provincial capitals did not fit this agenda. Indeed, from Trudeau's perspective such devolution would further fuel the tides of decentralization he was attempting to stem.

Trudeau understood that strengthening the intrastate representativeness of the central government might be one of the counterweights he was seeking. If the federal government was both in fact and perception more regionally responsive, provincial governments could no longer claim to be the best representatives of their populations even in matters of federal jurisdiction, and one of the justifications for further decentralization would disappear. Trudeau thus flirted occasionally with intrastate reform of the constitution. Not surprisingly, however, he preferred centralist versions of intrastate reform, which would emphasize the representation of provincial and regional populations rather than provincial governments in the central institutions.

Intrastate reform was not the central plank in Trudeau's constitutional platform, however, because it continued to concede too much to the very regionalism it was supposed to offset.[21] From the intrastate perspective, regions and provinces remain the fundamental components of the country; intrastate devices merely seek a more centralist or cohesive way of holding the regions together. As Jennifer Smith has written:

> *Intrastate federalism, even the centralist version, risks an identifiable national discourse by promoting a self-consciously regional one. It unavoidably promotes while it accepts and placates regionalism, in which case the remedy exacerbates, not cures, the political ill.*[22]

Trudeau sought to institutionalize a quite different vision of the Canadian community. For him, the federal government had to be seen as more than a locus for regional accommodation. It was the government of all individual Canadians, understood as citizens of a truly national community rather than primarily as citizens of regional or provincial communities composing a broader "community of communities." There existed a national community that was Ottawa's proper constituency; the problem was that the constitutional prominence of an increasingly decentralized federalism obscured this national community. The task was thus to give the national community a form of constitutional expression—a national (and nationalizing) counterweight to the constitutional supports of decentralizing federalism.

The key component of Trudeau's constitutional strategy in this respect was the constitutional entrenchment of rights and freedoms that would apply equally to all Canadians from coast to coast and within both federal and provincial areas of jurisdiction. (Remember that the 1960 statutory Bill of Rights, enacted by the Diefenbaker government, applies only within federal jurisdiction.) The rights in such a constitutionalized charter would belong equally to all Canadians as Canadians, and would emphasize what they had in common as individuals across regions rather than what divided them along regional lines. The charter would thus be the institutional expression of the national community.[23] Many of the other visions of the Canadian community emphasized group identities of one sort or another. For example, the two-nations view emphasizes cultural group identities while the equal-provinces vision stresses the primacy of territorial groups. Trudeau's proposed charter, by contrast, reflected an **individualist vision** of the Canadian community.

The charter could also address Trudeau's concern with the politics of language and culture in Canada. Trudeau had consistently opposed the Quebec-centred version of the two-nations theory, according to which the province of Quebec was coextensive with French Canada. He insisted instead that both French and English speakers should treat the whole of Canada as home, and in 1969 he institutionalized this vision in the federal Official Languages Act. The policy of official, Canada-wide **bilingualism** certainly captured Trudeau's opposition to Quebec nationalism, but that policy failed to find constitutional expression. Entrenching official bilingualism as part of a charter of rights would provide that expression and underscore Trudeau's vision of language rights held in common by all Canadians regardless of their provincial residence.

It should be noted that Trudeau's language policy of countrywide official bilingualism did not imply official biculturalism. His government opposed not only the territorial version of the two-nations theory but also the very idea of Canada as primarily the institutional expression of two national cultures. For Trudeau, language, at least as far as public policy was concerned, was a culturally neutral tool of communication through which many cultures inhabiting the same country could communicate for public purposes.[24] His policy of official pan-Canadian bilingualism, therefore, went hand in hand with a policy of **multiculturalism** rather than biculturalism. Thus, in 1971, two years after enacting the Official Languages Act, Trudeau's government made multiculturalism official government policy. Like pan-Canadian official bilingualism, multiculturalism was a policy designed to emphasize the non-territorial dimensions of Canadian identity. When Canada's non-English and non-French communities pressed in 1980–81 to have multiculturalism recognized by the impending Charter of Rights and Freedoms, Trudeau's government was happy to comply.

In addition to promoting a constitutionally entrenched charter of rights, Trudeau wished to enhance the sense of pride with which Canadians viewed their constitution (including the proposed charter) by formally ending the role of Britain in the process of constitutional amendment. The constitution had to become a truly domestic constitution rather than a statute of the British Parliament, especially in an era when the British connection was of rapidly decreasing relevance. In short, the constitution had to be "brought home" or "patriated." As explained in Chapter 2, this

DOSSIER 3.2 HOW QUEBECKERS VIEW SEA-TO-SEA BILINGUALISM

[T]he main effect of sea-to-sea bilingualism is not to make living outside of Quebec a more realistic option for the Québécois, but rather to ensure that living in Quebec remains a viable option for English-speakers. Sea-to-sea bilingualism may have been intended to strengthen the opportunities for Francophones outside Quebec, but in Quebec it is widely seen instead as protecting the rights of Anglophones in Quebec, whether they are native-born Anglophones or immigrant allophones.

For this reason, unless it is accompanied by recognition of the special status of Quebec, the ideology of sea-to-sea bilingualism is often seen by the Québécois as a threat to their very existence. Most Québécois believe that a vibrant francophone culture cannot survive in Canada unless it survives in Quebec, and that the ongoing viability of the French culture in Quebec depends on ensuring that newcomers to the province, whether from overseas or other provinces, integrate into the francophone society. The Quebec provincial government, therefore, must play a pivotal role in maintaining the viability of the French society in Canada, and to fulfil this role, it must have the ability to regulate certain language rights. Any conception of sea-to-sea bilingualism that denies this fact is likely to be denounced in Quebec.

Source: Reprinted from Will Kymlicka, "Multinational Federalism in Canada: Rethinking the Partnership," in Roger Gibbins and Guy Laforest, eds., *Beyond the Impasse: Toward Reconciliation* (Ottawa: IRRP, 1998), 19–20.

patriation required the adoption of a formally entrenched and wholly domestic amending formula.

From the beginning to the end of his political career, patriation and an entrenched charter remained the twin pillars of Trudeau's constitutional agenda. Obviously, this agenda conflicted with the decentralizing demands that came from many of the provincial capitals. Just as Trudeau opposed the decentralizing agenda of many provincial governments, so the latter resisted the nationalizing implications of his proposed charter of rights. They understood that such a charter would impose national policy standards in areas of provincial jurisdiction, thus diminishing provincial legislative discretion. The tension between these two constitutional agendas bedevilled constitutional politics during the entire period under consideration.

The tension first emerged in earnest during a series of constitutional conferences between 1967 and 1971. Ontario launched the first conference, grandiosely entitled the Confederation for Tomorrow Conference, partly to cement a decentralizing alliance with Quebec against the federal government.[25] The next year, at the first in a series of follow-up conferences, Trudeau, not yet prime minister but attending the conference as Lester Pearson's minister of Justice, clearly placed his stamp on Ottawa's position. Any reallocation of powers between governments, he argued on Ottawa's behalf, should be put off to some undetermined future date. Priority should be given to entrenching a charter of rights—including especially language rights—and reforming such central institutions as the Senate and the Supreme

Court. In later conferences, Trudeau (as prime minister) further developed and promoted these proposals. Needless to say, the gulf between the federal and provincial agendas, together with the widespread assumption that unanimous provincial consent (including, of course, the consent of Quebec) was required, made agreement virtually impossible. Nevertheless, at the last of these conferences, in Victoria in 1971, it seemed that a constitutional miracle had been wrought. The heads of all eleven governments seemed close to agreement on a package of amendments.

The **Victoria Charter**, as this package was known, came closer to fulfilling Trudeau's vision than that of the provinces. To meet the demands of Quebec there was a minor jurisdictional shuffle that would have recognized family, youth, and occupational training allowances as matters of shared jurisdiction with provincial paramountcy, thus allowing Quebec to opt out of national programs and achieve a form of "soft asymmetry." The logic of interstate federalism was also present in a requirement for annual federal–provincial conferences. These nods in the direction of decentralization did not, however, represent the essence of the Victoria Charter. The bulk of the charter dealt with the entrenchment of certain rights (mainly political and language rights) and a new constitutional procedure for appointing Supreme Court justices.

The Victoria Charter also contained an amending formula that would enable the constitution to be patriated. Amendments under this formula would require, in addition to the consent of the federal government, the consent of Ontario, Quebec, any two eastern provinces, and two western provinces having at least 50 percent of the western population.[26] Patriation and constitutionally entrenched rights, the mainstays of Trudeau's constitutional program, were thus at the heart of the Victoria Charter.

The Victoria Charter amending formula reflected a vision of Canada as fundamentally a community of four basic regions, some of which happened to correspond to provinces (Ontario and Quebec) while others comprised several provinces (Atlantic Canada and the West). Such an amending formula suited Trudeau's agenda of constitutionally de-emphasizing the status of provinces and their governments. It did so both in its regionalism (as opposed to provincialism) and in its subordination of provincial equality to the 50 percent population rule as a mechanism of expressing opinion in the western region. Nevertheless, the regionalism of the formula conflicted with his vision of pan-Canadian identity. Moreover, at least Ontario and Quebec enjoyed the double status of regions and provinces. Such a regionalist logic is not new to Canadian constitutionalism. As we shall see in more detail in Chapter 5, the Senate is based on a similar principle of regional rather than strictly provincial representation.

The **regionalist vision** of Canada conflicts in principle with both the territorial two-nations view and the equal-provinces view, just as the latter two views conflict with each other. The conflicts between these perspectives is more or less pronounced, however, depending on the details of particular institutional devices. With respect to amending formulas, for example, a Quebec veto can satisfy both two-nations and equal-provinces theorists if it is part of a "unanimous provincial consent" formula. Outside Quebec, such a formula will be explained as treating all provinces equally; inside Quebec, it can be explained as respecting the right of one of the founding nations to a constitutional veto. Again, from the perspective of two-nations Quebeckers, it is irrelevant if the rest of Canada wishes to subdivide itself into equal provinces. Similarly, as long as Quebec is one of the regions in a regionalist formula, the resulting Quebec veto can satisfy both two-nations and regionalist requirements. By contrast, it is impossible to fudge the differences between a Victoria Charter–style regionalist formula, which treats some provinces as more equal than others, and the equal-provinces view. Similarly, it is impossible to ignore the differences between the equal-provinces and two-nations views in the context of an amendment formula weighting all of the provinces equally but not requiring unanimous consent, thereby depriving Quebec of a veto, such as the seven-fifty rule of the Fulton-Favreau formula and the 1982 Constitution Act.

Although a provisional agreement was reached in Victoria, the conference participants agreed that the governments would have 11 days in which to make a final commitment. This breathing space was created to accommodate the residual reluctance of Quebec premier Robert Bourassa, and in the end Bourassa backed away from the Victoria Charter. Returning from the West Coast to test the waters of Quebec opinion, he found them agitated indeed. The amending formula may have given Quebec a veto, but not nearly enough had been done to accommodate Quebec's interest in a substantive decentralization of powers. Influential Quebec intellectuals mounted an effective campaign of vehement opposition to the Victoria Charter, and the 11 days passed without a commitment coming from Quebec.

With the failure in Victoria, the movement toward constitutional reform slowed considerably until it received a new burst of energy in 1976 with the election in Quebec of the Parti Québécois. The PQ had not campaigned directly on the issue of independence but on a promise to hold a referendum on the question sometime during its first mandate. In response to the PQ's election, the Trudeau government renewed its search for constitutional amendments that might allay a now exacerbated national unity crisis. Over the next three years, a blizzard of task forces, white papers, federal–provincial consultations, and draft legislation was unleashed in an attempt to resolve the problem.[27]

The central initiative during this period was **Bill C-60**, a 1978 piece of draft legislation that would, among other things, have reformed the Supreme Court and Senate. The government believed that, as parts of the federal Parliament's own constitution, both the Court and the Senate could be unilaterally transformed by Parliament under section 91(1). After all, those provinces that had originally had their own upper houses had abolished them under their analogous section 92(1) power of unilateral amendment. If the provinces could abolish their upper houses, Ottawa argued, then surely Ottawa could transform the nature of *its* upper house.

The Supreme Court was to be entrenched in the constitution while being enlarged from nine to eleven members (with four coming from Quebec). The proposed Senate reform was more radical. The new second chamber, to be called the **House of the Federation**, would still be composed of appointed members, although now half the appointments would be made by the provinces. At neither level, however, would the appointments be made by the executive branch of government, as is true of the existing Senate, whose members are appointed by the prime minister. Both federal and provincial members of the proposed House of the Federation would be appointed by the relevant legislatures in partisan proportions reflecting the proportion of seats held by each party in the legislature. Clearly, this was not to be a House of the Provinces composed of delegations of provincial governments. Indeed, as Dossier 3.3 shows, the Trudeau government's proposals were explicitly rooted in the attempt to weaken the voice of provincial governments in national policymaking by giving regional populations alternative voices in the central institutions of government.

Not surprisingly, Bill C-60 also included a constitutionally entrenched charter of rights. Section 91(1), however, obviously did not allow Ottawa to make this reform applicable to the provinces against their consent. Thus, Bill C-60 would have entrenched its charter only with respect to federal jurisdiction but with provision for the provinces to opt in at some future date.

Although the Trudeau government believed it could enact the provisions of Bill C-60 on its own, it proposed to consult with the provinces anyway and gain their consent to the extent possible. In these consultations, the government also hoped to reach agreement on a new domestic amending formula—a reform that, like a universally applicable charter, was clearly not a candidate for unilateral section 91(1) amendment. If agreement on an amending formula was not forthcoming, it would be left to the proposed second stage of the constitutional process, which would address reforms that still required enactment at Westminster. Stage two was also to address the

DOSSIER 3.3 TRUDEAU ON INTRASTATE REFORM OF THE SENATE

Now it may be asked: why not have the provinces appoint the members of the second chamber in a system which would be somewhat attuned to the system of the government in the Federal Republic of Germany? Our view is that the provinces have a function within the Constitution which is to exercise the jurisdiction contained in the Constitution, and particularly in Section 92, or some modification thereof, with authority over the citizens of those respective provinces in areas of provincial jurisdiction. We do not think it would be the right approach to tell the provinces, whose authority is absolute within their spheres of government in the provinces, to determine also how that national government shall be managed and how the national parliament shall be run.

We think it is important for the people of the regions to know that they, as regions, have spokesmen in the second chamber.

Source: Reprinted from Canada, House of Commons, *Debates*, 30th Parliament, 3rd Session (Ottawa: Queen's Printer, June 27, 1978).

federal distribution of powers, though the federal government made no concrete proposals in this regard.[28]

The Trudeau government, however, was in no position to actually implement Bill C-60. In the latter stages of its 1974 election mandate, and at a low ebb in public-opinion polls, it faced vigorous opposition from the provincial governments, many of which had been more recently elected. Sensing blood, the opposition parties in the federal Parliament also joined in a chorus of opposition to the draft bill. Among other things, it was argued that the proposed reform of the upper house could not in fact be accomplished unilaterally under section 91(1)—that this remained an amendment that could be made only at Westminster. When the Joint Committee of the Senate and House of Commons that was studying the bill recommended that the latter issue be referred to the Supreme Court, the government agreed to do so, thereby effectively shelving Bill C-60 until after the court had ruled.[29]

In effect, the delay meant putting Bill C-60 off until after the general election of May 1979. In that election, however, the Joe Clark-led Conservatives defeated the Liberals and formed a minority government. Clark's own constitutional policy, somewhat ambiguously captured by the phrase "community of communities," was assumed to be diametrically opposed to Trudeau's, in that Clark appeared to favour a stronger role for the provinces in Canadian political and institutional life.

With the May election, it seemed that Trudeau's constitutional dreams had been shattered. As if to add insult to injury, some months later the Supreme Court of Canada, apparently flogging an already dead horse, ruled in favour of the provincialist position in the *Senate Reference*.[30] It looked as though Trudeau, and perhaps his constitutional vision, would fade into the pages of Canadian history. Both were rescued from this fate, however, when to everyone's surprise the Clark minority government, having lost a crucial budget vote on December 13, 1979, resigned—a scant six months after taking office! Because Trudeau had stepped down as party leader but had not yet been replaced, and because there was no time to hold a leadership convention before the election, the Liberal Party prevailed upon him to return to his old post. In the event, the disillusioned man who had resigned as leader of the opposition was resurrected as prime minister in February 1980.

The timing was auspicious. The PQ's promised referendum on independence (**sovereignty-association** had now become the rhetorically preferred term) had been scheduled for 1980, and Trudeau, who would almost certainly have fought the independence option even as a private citizen, could obviously fight much more effectively as prime minister. As both the prime minister and a Quebecker, Trudeau was in a position to offer Quebeckers something in return for defeating sovereignty-association in the referendum. What he offered, somewhat vaguely and ambiguously, was a promise to effect constitutional change or renewal.[31] When the referendum question was in fact defeated, Trudeau made good on this promise by immediately inaugurating yet another constitutional reform process, culminating in another first ministers' conference in September 1980.[32]

Many Quebeckers who heard Trudeau's promise of a renewed constitution thought that he was conceding the necessity of a devolution of powers. Indeed, when federal and provincial officials met to set the agenda for constitutional discussions, the reallocation of powers was included as a priority item. Other priority items included reform of the Senate and the Supreme Court, an entrenched charter, and a new amending formula. The situation was not at all like that at the end of Trudeau's previous mandate, however. As Romanow, Whyte, and Leeson remark, "To [the September 1980 conference] came a humbled Quebec, just defeated in the referendum, and a newly elected federal Liberal government, not only armed with a powerful mandate from Quebec but also with a clear majority and drawing strength from central Canada's rejection of the Clark government and its devolutionist policies."[33] Not surprisingly, Trudeau's long-term constitutional commitments came to the fore in these circumstances. Thus "[t]he conference, and the summer-long talks which preceded it, consisted of a vigorous attempt by the federal government to bring confederation back within a more centralist (and from Trudeau's perspective a more cohesive) view of the nation."[34] Many Quebeckers felt that Trudeau had broken his promise of constitutional renewal. In any case, the intensely conflicting interests and visions, in the context of the assumption that unanimous governmental consent was necessary, produced deadlock at the September conference.

In 1980 the Trudeau government decided to break the logjam by challenging the assumption that amendments required unanimous provincial consent. Trudeau had floated the idea of a unilateral amendment request to Westminster as early as 1975, but apparently no one had then taken it seriously.[35] This time, however, it was

DOSSIER 3.4 DID TRUDEAU BREAK HIS REFERENDUM PROMISE OF CONSTITUTIONAL RENEWAL?

Within the framework of constitutional debate in Quebec over the preceding two decades, what could [Trudeau's] pledge of "renewed federalism" reasonably be taken to mean? The pressures of both government and opposition parties in Quebec provincial politics from 1960 onward has been for an enhanced range of autonomy for the authorities of that province and corresponding restrictions on the powers of the federal government over Quebeckers. The Constitution Act, 1982 restricts the powers of the Legislature and government of Quebec and was brought into being by a procedure which was opposed by that Legislature and government. Furthermore, the constitutional reform which was effected in the spring of 1982 was an integral part of a general initiative from Ottawa towards a more highly centralized federal system. The pledges of constitutional reform made to the Quebec electorate by the federal Liberal leaders have not been honoured, and it is not too much to say that this electorate has been betrayed.

Source: Reprinted from Donald Smiley, "A Dangerous Deed: The Constitution Act, 1982," in Keith Banting and Richard Simeon, eds., *And No One Cheered: Federalism, Democracy, and the Constitution Act* (Toronto: Methuen, 1983), 75–76.

[A]nyone not blinded by ideology would certainly be amazed that Trudeau should have made the promise attributed to him. We know that he always opposed the idea of "special status" for Quebec or, indeed, any other form of dualism in Canada. To him Quebec's interests and the French fact are to be furthered through bilingualism and the opening up of Canada rather than through provincial particularisms. And now, against all logic, he was reproached for not having kept his promise to take Quebec's distinct character into account! To believe this we would need to be ignorant of everything he has written or said—or else to be dupes of ideological discourse. In fact, this whole symbolic construct turns on a very brief passage in a speech given in the Paul Sauvé arena at the height of the referendum campaign. Here then is the full text of the "promise":

I address myself solemnly to Canadians of the other provinces: we from Quebec are wagering everything when we urge Quebecers to vote "no." We are telling you that we refuse to interpret a "no" as an indication that everything is fine as it is. We want changes.

This speech, in a public arena at the height of the referendum, was presented during the Meech episode as a kind of policy statement. Yet, not only did it not make any reference to the "distinct" nature of Quebec but it hardly promised anything at all except unspecified "changes." Moreover, Trudeau was addressing his remarks to "Canadians of the other provinces." To whom was the promise made? To Quebec or to the rest of Canada? It would be hard to imagine a more anodyne promise; the most the prime minister could be reproached with was not having promised very much at all.

Source: Reprinted from Max Nemni, "Canada in Crisis and the Destructive Power of Myth," *Queen's Quarterly* 99, no. 1 (1992), 229.

clear that he meant business. There had never been unambiguous agreement on the alleged requirement of unanimity, Ottawa argued, and even if there had been, it was not the kind of constitutional rule that was legally binding. Not being formally spelled out in an entrenched constitutional document, the principle of unanimous provincial consent lacked the status of constitutional *law.* If it existed at all, the unanimity rule fell into the category of constitutional "convention," and conventions had no *legal* status. Legally, according to this view, Ottawa was entitled to transmit requests for amendment to Britain unilaterally, and that is precisely what it proposed to do. The unilateral package would not address all of the matters that had been on the constitutional agenda, only those that the government considered essential. Not surprisingly, the essential elements turned out to be patriation (through a new amending formula) and the entrenchment of a charter of rights. Although two of the provinces, Ontario and New Brunswick, supported Ottawa's initiative, the other eight provinces mounted vigorous opposition.

Among other things, the so-called **gang of eight** provinces promptly challenged Ottawa's unilateralism in the courts, arguing not only that a convention of

DOSSIER 3.5 BOLD STATECRAFT, QUESTIONABLE JURISPRUDENCE

According to Peter Russell, the court's judgment in the patriation case manifested "questionable jurisprudence." If, as the court argued, conventions were really entirely political understandings, not enforceable in court, why did the court decide the dispute about the existence and nature of the convention? In effect, what "was a court of law doing rendering a decision on a non-legal subject?" Russell does not think this circle can be squared as a matter of strict jurisprudential logic. Here is his extralegal explanation:

> *To understand why the Supreme Court judges answered the questions concerning convention we have to look beyond the internal logic of their arguments to their sense of the necessities of judicial statecraft. This is hinted at in the dissenting judges' vague reference to "the unusual nature of these References." The circumstances surrounding these References certainly were unusual. The country was caught in a very difficult constitutional impasse. There was a widely shared assumption by the people and the politicians that a Supreme Court decision was the next essential step in resolving the crisis.*

And in fact, according to Russell, the court's questionable jurisprudence played a considerable role in helping to resolve the crisis:

> *The political consequences of the decision now appear to be essentially positive. The Supreme Court's decision was the decisive event in paving the way for a federal–provincial accommodation that enabled the Canadian constitution to be patriated in a manner acceptable to the federal government and nine provinces. The split nature of the court's verdict gave both Ottawa and the provinces a strong incentive to return to the bargaining table they had abandoned a year earlier. While the decision gave Ottawa a legal green light to proceed unilaterally with its constitutional plans, it cast a heavy mantle of political illegitimacy over the constitutional changes that would result from such a procedure. On the other hand, while the decision confirmed the provinces' claim that their participation in fundamental constitutional change was a constitutional requirement, it warned the provinces that if they failed to work out an agreement with Ottawa, Ottawa could go ahead without them and the courts would do nothing to enforce the provinces' right of participation. When the federal and provincial leaders assembled at the Ottawa Conference Centre on November 2, their opening statements testified to the efficacy of the Supreme Court's decision in restoring their interest in reaching an accommodation on the constitution.*

Although Russell was tempted to "congratulate" the court on the beneficial political results of its "questionable jurisprudence," he could not bring himself to do so enthusiastically:

> *[T]o do so I am afraid may mean that I am subscribing to a "result-oriented" jurisprudence which assesses judicial decisions in terms of whether they support one's personal political preferences. Such a*

jurisprudence is scarcely jurisprudence at all, for in denying the relevance of rationality in the judges' reasons it denies that there is any inherent difference between decision-making by courts and decision-making by the political branches of government. And that is a conclusion which neither I nor, I am sure, the court could accept.

Source: Peter H. Russell, "Bold Statecraft, Questionable Jurisprudence," in Keith Banting and Richard Simeon, eds., *And No One Cheered: Federalism, Democracy, and the Constitution Act* (Toronto: Methuen, 1983).

provincial consent existed but that it was legally binding. Under pressure from opposition parties in the House, Trudeau agreed to postpone any unilateral action pending a court ruling. In September 1981 the Supreme Court handed down a momentous decision in this **patriation case**, agreeing that Ottawa was legally entitled to proceed unilaterally but at the same time declaring that such action would be unconstitutional in a deeper and more important sense. There was indeed a convention of provincial consent, the Supreme Court argued, and although conventions are not legally enforceable, they are often more important than strict constitutional law. The convention at issue, however, required only "substantial," not unanimous, provincial consent.[36]

With this judgment in the background, Ottawa and the provinces made one last attempt to reach a compromise at a constitutional conference in November 1981. This conference resulted in a compromise package that became the basis of the Constitution Act, 1982. Of the several compromises built into the package, two stand out. The first involved a tradeoff between the competing logics of parliamentary supremacy and entrenched rights. Parliamentary supremacy implied the possibility of policy variation among provinces in matters within their jurisdiction. As we noted in Chapter 2, federalism constrained parliamentary supremacy only in a jurisdictional sense; as long as provinces remained within their jurisdictions, they could do as they liked. The very reason for having a provincial order of government, moreover, implied that provinces would often choose to do quite different things with respect to the same or similar policy issues. The logic of entrenched rights applicable to both orders of government, by contrast, implied constraints on policy variation within provincial jurisdiction. The provinces agreed to accept an entrenched charter of rights only if they were permitted to override its provisions under certain conditions, hoping through this residual protection of parliamentary supremacy to preserve a degree of provincial legislative discretion against the charter's nationalizing standards. This was the source of the section 33 "notwithstanding" provision.

The second major tradeoff involved the Charter and the amending formula.[37] In its draft proposals, the Trudeau government had revived the basic structure of the Victoria Charter formula. The consent of Ontario, Quebec, and two each of the eastern and western provinces would be required. As with the Victoria Charter, the two western provinces had to contain at least 50 percent of the western population. This time, however, the same 50 percent rule was applied to the two eastern provinces. A new twist was that the consent of the required provinces and regional blocs could be signified in two ways—either by the provincial legislatures or in referendums initiated by the federal Parliament. Even more than the extension of the 50 percent requirement to the eastern regions, the referendum requirement emphasized Trudeau's desire to weaken the status of provincial governments.

Although the Victoria Charter had gained the support of nine provincial governments in 1971, only two of the premiers involved in that earlier constitutional round were still in office. Significantly, these were the premiers of Ontario (Davis) and New Brunswick (Hatfield), the only two provinces that supported Ottawa's 1980 patriation initiative.[38] The other provinces, at the urging of Alberta, had come to support an alternative formula according to which amendments required the consent of Parliament and two-thirds (in effect, seven) of the provincial legislatures representing 50 percent of the Canadian population. This seven-fifty formula treated provinces more equally than the regionalized Victoria model. Moreover, it required the consent of provincial legislatures rather than provincial populations voting in referendums. The seven-fifty formula, in addition to the section 33 override, became part of the price the dissenting provinces exacted for their acceptance of the Charter.[39]

The November agreement was not unanimous, however. It was reached over the vigorous objection of Quebec. Having lost the independence referendum, the PQ government felt compelled to participate in the attempt to reform the Canadian constitution but never abandoned its long-term sovereigntist inclinations. Certainly Quebec was not about to accept reforms that neglected the province's decentralizing demands and implemented Trudeau's contrary agenda instead. Quebec had thus been an enthusiastic participant in the "gang of eight" opposing provinces. When the other seven members of this group negotiated the compromise agreement, Quebec felt betrayed, a perception fed by the fact that the agreement was hammered out at a late-night meeting (known in Quebec as the **night of the long knives**) to which the Quebec delegation had not been invited.[40] Quebec raised several objections to the package, including the fact that the new seven-fifty amending formula would deprive the province of what it considered its traditional veto over constitutional change. True, this formula had been proposed by the gang of eight (of which Quebec was a member), but Quebec had agreed to the formula somewhat hesitantly, hoping thereby to cement the united front required to derail the constitutional process completely. If its own project were scuttled, Ottawa would certainly not consent to implement the gang of eight's alternative project, which was limited to simple patriation by way of the seven-fifty amending formula, and Quebec would be off the hook.[41] Furthermore, the version of the provincial amending formula to which Quebec had agreed specified that dissenting provinces could opt out of amendments affecting their jurisdiction with financial compensation. This meant that a province would not be penalized for opting out when Ottawa taxed all Canadians for programs that did not apply in that province. In the November compromise agreement, the opting-out principle was retained, but financial compensation was dropped.[42] There is some indication that Lévesque might reluctantly have agreed to the package if financial compensation had been restored, but this would have been completely unacceptable to Ottawa and would thus have killed the deal. Unwilling to see their compromise deal unravel, the premiers refused Lévesque's request. Lévesque then bitterly announced that his government could not accept the accord.[43]

Quebec subsequently argued in court that, as the provincial "homeland" of one of Canada's "founding nations," its agreement was necessary to achieving the "substantial provincial consent" identified by the Supreme Court as a convention of the constitution—that Quebec, in short, continued to possess a veto, even if no other province did, and could use it to derail a patriation package that would deprive it of that veto. The Trudeau government, by contrast, acted on the equal-provinces assumption that any nine provinces out of 10 sufficed to satisfy the "substantial consent" requirement, an assumption confirmed by the Supreme Court.[44] The federal government thus asked Britain to enact the new package, and the resulting Constitution Act—featuring both the new Charter of Rights in Part I (sections 1–34) and the new amending formula in Part V (sections 38–49)—came into force on April 17, 1982.

Trudeau's patriation package was one of the clearest recent attempts to constitutionally refashion community. Trudeau's political purpose in pursuing the Charter was to redefine Canadian identity by counterbalancing the regionalizing effect of the federal constitution. He hoped the Charter would induce Canadians to think of themselves less as members of provincial polities and more as bearers of a set of rights shared in common throughout the country. Trudeau's hope seems to have been fulfilled to a significant extent, at least outside Quebec. Even before the Charter was enacted, it diminished the public influence of the governments of Canadian federalism and gave new prominence to groups of citizens that cared little about the classically Canadian preoccupation with intergovernmental relations. Women, Natives, ethnic groups, the disabled, and the aged all sensed the advantages that potentially flowed from having the constitution on one's side, and thus lobbied hard, and often successfully, to gain constitutional provisions that clearly recognized them and their policy concerns.[45]As a result, all of these groups are explicitly protected against discrimination by section 15(1) of the Charter and assured of the legitimacy of "affirmative action" in their favour by section 15(2). Age and mental or physical ability, for example, were added to the list of prohibited grounds of discrimination in section 15 because of the vigorous lobbying of the groups concerned.[46] In one of the more dramatic events in the Charter-making process, women secured the additional protection of section 28, which states that "notwithstanding anything in this Charter, the rights and freedoms referred to in it are guaranteed equally to male and female persons."[47] Natives are assured by section 25 of the Charter that its other rights and freedoms "shall not be construed so as to abrogate or derogate from any aboriginal, treaty or other rights or freedoms that pertain to the aboriginal peoples of Canada." Section

35 of the Constitution Act, 1982, also "recognizes and affirms [the] existing aboriginal and treaty rights of the aboriginal peoples of Canada." Ethnic groups can look not only to section 15, which extends protection against discrimination based on race, national or ethnic origin, colour, and religion, but also to section 27, which requires the Charter to be "interpreted in a manner consistent with the preservation and enhancement of the multicultural heritage of Canadians."

The constitution-making role played by these **Charter Canadians** (or **Charter groups**, as they have come to be known) in the lead-up to the 1982 Constitution Act was not reflected in the amending formulas implemented by that act. Both the seven-fifty and unanimity rules were forged by provincial governments and, not surprisingly, emphasized the old predominance of governments in constitutional amendment. Indeed, in rejecting Trudeau's referendum proposals these formulas explicitly excluded the public from the formal amending procedure. If the Charter reflected the new logic of a "citizens' constitution," both in its substance and in the informal influence of non-governmental groups in achieving it, the amending formulas represented the continuing logic of the traditional governments' constitution. The Charter reflected the notion that constitutions are the emanations of popular sovereignty, whereas the amending formulas reflected the older assumptions of governmental sovereignty and elite accommodation. As we shall see, the tension between these conflicting logics played an important role in subsequent rounds of Canadian megaconstitutional politics.

Although they were given no formal role in constitutional amendments in 1982, Charter Canadians were dealt permanently and directly into the game of interpretive constitutional politics. Previously, such groups could invoke the constitution as support for their political causes only in the limited and indirect form of supporting the most receptive (or opposing the least receptive) level of government in its jurisdictional battles. But these struggles merely determined which government had jurisdictional authority over their policy concerns. The substantive policy agendas of such groups could be achieved only by working with and through one or both levels of government. The Charter, by contrast, allows these groups to bypass the jurisdictional issues of federalism and claim the direct support of constitutional law for their favoured policies.

Such claims of constitutional support are not just moral claims to be used in lobbying governments and legislatures; more significantly, they can be pursued directly in the courts. The Charter, in short, shifts an important measure of policymaking power from the executive and legislative branches of government to the courts. While courts were previously limited to determining which level of government had the constitutional authority to act in a particular policy area, the Charter enables them to determine more substantively what may or may not be done (sometimes even what *must* be done) in a policy area by whichever level of government has jurisdictional authority. To shift policymaking power from executives and legislatures to courts, however, is to shift it from policymaking arenas that are federally divided to one that is not. As we shall see in more detail in Chapter 8, Canada's judicial system is a unified hierarchy culminating in the Supreme Court, and its decisions on the implications of Charter rights for matters within provincial jurisdiction, inasmuch as they lay down uniform policy standards applicable throughout the country, limit the traditional discretion of provincial governments and legislatures. The Charter was intended to have just such an effect, and was opposed by most of the provincial governments for this reason.

Although the 1982 entrenchment of the Charter represented the institutional implementation of Trudeau's vision of the Canadian community, it did not defeat or decisively displace competing constitutional logics or the other visions of community that animate Canada's modern constitutional politics, and thus did not signal an end to the modern era of megaconstitutional politics. The territorial, Quebec-centred version of the two-nations theory, which had been a major impetus behind the growing sense of constitutional crisis since 1960, found no reflection in the 1982 reforms. Indeed, both the Charter and the new amending formula constituted a forceful denial of the two-nations theory. The two-nations theory did not quietly admit defeat, however. Instead, it led Quebec's government to reject the legitimacy of the 1982 Constitution Act and to demand further constitutional change more congenial to its vision. Similarly, while the Charter was a nationalizing response to the growing provincialism and regional alienation in other parts of the country (especially in the West), it did not address some of the important institutional causes of that alienation. The tension-ridden mixture of parliamentary democracy and federalism underlying the perceived regional insensitivity of Ottawa, and the resulting federal–provincial diplomacy of executive federalism, remained largely intact. Certainly, one could not have expected the Trudeau government to accommodate the decentralizing demands emerging from either Quebec or the West, but neither had anything been accomplished in the way of intrastate reform of Canada's national Parliament to make it more regionally responsive. All of the well-established demands and themes of contemporary Canadian constitutional politics, in other words, remained in place, ready to play a role in the subsequent rounds of constitutional politics that generated the Meech Lake and Charlottetown accords. These new rounds of megaconstitutional politics were not exactly more of the same, or business as usual, however. They were decisively shaped by the new constitutional players rooted in the citizens' constitution.

THE MEECH LAKE ACCORD

The politics of the **Meech Lake Accord** reflected not only the old oppositions between the two-nations and equal-provinces perspectives, or between interstate and intrastate reform proposals, but also the new tension between the logics of the old governments' constitution and the new citizens' constitution.

The accord arose out of the attempt to "bring Quebec back into the Canadian constitutional family." Although Quebec had not consented to the 1982 amendments, it was legally subject to them because the Supreme Court's requirement of "substantial provincial consent" had been fulfilled. Nevertheless, the political legitimacy of the constitution had been seriously wounded in Quebec, and the Meech Lake Accord was driven by the need to heal this wound.[48] Not surprisingly, therefore, the substance of the accord reflected Quebec's demands for some decentralization of powers and explicit constitutional recognition of the province as a "**distinct society**." The accord originated, in other words, from the felt need to respond to Quebec's two-nations sensitivities.

However, as might be expected, the content of the accord was also driven by the desire of other provinces to maintain as much equality of constitutional status among the provinces as possible. This meant that most of Quebec's price for consenting to the constitution—that is, greater influence over certain matters hitherto under federal jurisdiction—could be met only by paying it to the other provinces as well. Thus, Quebec's demand for a constitutionally based role in Supreme Court appointments emerged in the accord as a general right of provinces to submit lists of potential Supreme Court appointees, from which Ottawa would select the winning candidate. Similarly, Quebec's desire for a constitutional role in immigration policy became the right of all provincial governments to negotiate constitutionally entrenched agreements "relating to immigration" with the federal government. Quebec's concern with taming the federal spending power led to a general provincial right to opt out of national shared-cost programs with "reasonable compensation" from Ottawa. This represented yet another provision facilitating soft asymmetry, though the degree of asymmetry was limited by making federal compensation available only if a province that opted out of a national program provided a program of its own that was "compatible with the national objectives" of the shared-cost program. Finally, Quebec's desire to achieve a veto over future constitutional amendments resulted in a proposal to expand the list of subjects that could be amended only with unanimous provincial consent, thus effectively expanding the veto for all provinces.

Most of the accord, in other words, reflected the same strategy of reconciling the two-nations and equal-provinces perspectives that was adopted with respect to the administrative opting-out agreements of the 1960s. Only in recognizing Quebec as a "distinct society," whose legislature and government were entitled to "preserve and promote" this distinctiveness, did the accord suggest a measure of special status for Quebec. Its general thrust was to decentralize powers to all of the provinces. If the Charter had embedded nationalizing forces in the constitution, thus diluting the constitutional status of provincial governments, the Meech Lake Accord would clearly have worked in the opposite direction. Indeed, the accord has been aptly described as "a provincialist revenge against the nationalizing thrust of [the Charter]."[49] It was the attempt by proponents of the old governments' constitution to regain some of the ground they had lost in 1982.

Reproduced with permission from *The Toronto Sun,* a division of Sun Media Corporation.

The Meech Lake Accord reflected the governments' constitution not only in its substantive provisions but also in the way it was formulated and presented to the public.[50] It was simply assumed that the new amending procedures of Part V of the Constitution Act would be implemented in the old way—that governments, and especially first ministers, would retain their old dominance in the politics of constitutional amendment. Thus, the accord was worked out behind closed doors by Canada's eleven first ministers and presented to the public as an unalterable *fait accompli.*

The accord clearly jeopardized the newly won constitutional status of the Charter groups. Its substantive provisions strengthened the constitutional status of provincial governments, and the procedures used to develop it implied that governments remained the dominant constitutional actors, that ultimately the constitution was the peculiar preserve or property of governments, to amend as they saw fit. Stated differently, the accord asserted the symbolic superiority of the governments' constitution over the citizens' constitution. Not surprisingly, the Charter groups fought back.[51] The constitution belonged not to governments but to citizens, they argued, and citizens had to be involved in its amendment. These groups had been major players in the amendments of 1982 and they resented being shut out of the process now. Their concern, however, was not just with the abstract impropriety of excluding citizens from the process of constitutional amendment, though that was clearly involved. In addition, some of the Charter groups believed that Meech jeopardized their particular interests. Thus, feminists worried that Quebec, as a constitutionally recognized distinct society, might be allowed to infringe the Charter rights of women to a greater extent than other Canadian governments—in effect, that a different, more restrictive approach to women's issues might prove to be part of Quebec's distinctiveness. And Aboriginals wondered why only Quebec deserved constitutional recognition as a distinct society within Canada.

In their battle against the Meech Lake Accord, Charter groups were aided by the institutional context established by the new 1982 amending formulas. Recall that under the two most important formulas, certain parts of the constitution could be amended only with the unanimous consent of the federal and provincial governments, while other parts required the consent only of Ottawa and seven provinces having 50 percent of the Canadian population. The Meech Lake Accord was a sizable constitutional reform package, containing amendments subject to both the unanimity and seven-fifty rules. Thus, while entrenching the right to opt out of shared-cost programs with financial compensation fell under the seven-fifty formula, amendment of the amending formulas themselves—to subject more matters to unanimous consent—fell under the unanimity rule. The accord was not presented as a series of discrete amendments to be passed separately under the relevant amending formula, however. As a package of interrelated provisions and delicate compromises, it was too risky to pass it in pieces under different amending formulas. Under such a piecemeal procedure, the parties to the compromise package risked seeing segments they disliked passed while parts they liked were rejected. Thus, the accord was presented as a "seamless web" that had to be passed as a whole or not at all. This meant simultaneously meeting the requirements of both the unanimity and seven-fifty amending formula. In this context, it is important to note that the amendments falling under the seven-fifty procedure have to be passed within a three-year time limit, while those subject to the unanimity rule are not subject to a time limit. Thus, meeting the requirements of both rules simultaneously meant achieving unanimous consent within three years. The three-year clock starts running when the first legislature passes a proposed amendment. Canada's first ministers had signed the Meech Lake Accord on June 3, 1987, and Quebec's legislature approved it in just under three weeks, on June 23. Thus, opponents of Meech could sink the entire package by persuading even a single province not to ratify the accord by midnight, June 23, 1990.

Opponents of Meech were aided by another institutional feature of the 1982 amendment procedures, one that was little noticed and discussed at the time of the patriation package. Although the 1982 rules emphasized governmental institutions rather than people in amending the constitution, they called for legislative consent for future amendments rather than only the executive consent that had been required for the 1982 package itself. (The nine provincial premiers alone, and not their legislatures, had signified provincial consent to the 1982 package.) Often, of course, first ministers at the head of highly disciplined majority parties can pass whatever they like in the legislature in a very short period. But given the importance of this issue, a number of first ministers had committed themselves to legislative hearings before ultimate passage. During the ensuing delays, moreover, elections were held in some provinces and governments changed hands, replacing premiers who had negotiated Meech with others who were not always as favourably disposed to the deal. The most dramatic example was Newfoundland, where the accord had been passed before the election by Brian Peckford's Conservatives, only to have its passage rescinded by the newly elected Liberal government of Clyde Wells.

Governments changed in two other provinces. New Brunswick elected a Liberal government headed by Frank McKenna, a Meech sceptic. In Manitoba, the election produced a minority Conservative government led by Gary Filmon and featuring a Liberal opposition headed by Sharon Carstairs, who was openly hostile to Meech. Passage of the accord through the Manitoba legislature would obviously be especially difficult. These developments gave the Charter group–based opponents of Meech the time needed to mobilize widespread opposition. The longer they could delay final approval, the more likely it was that some province would fail to pass it before the deadline.[52]

In the event, the accord finally passed under Frank McKenna's government in New Brunswick, but it failed to pass in Newfoundland and Manitoba. In Manitoba, yet another institutional feature played a major role in the accord's demise. At the eleventh hour, the difficulties of minority government had been overcome and the leaders of all parties agreed to pass the accord. There was not enough time to do so, however, while respecting all of the procedures of the Manitoba legislature. Those procedures could be suspended and passage expedited, but only with the unanimous consent of all members of the legislature. Elijah Harper, a prominent Aboriginal member of the legislature who reflected the Aboriginal community's opposition to Meech, repeatedly refused to consent to expedited procedures. The fact that the accord did not pass in Newfoundland was at least partly due to the perception in that province's legislature that Harper's action had already killed it in Manitoba. That a single legislator could effectively derail a major constitutional amendment is surely one of the more dramatic illustrations of the power of institutional rules.

The failure of Meech had very different consequences and was given very different interpretations inside and outside Quebec. Outside Quebec, the message was that future constitutional reform would have to address much more than Quebec's agenda and would have to involve the participation of an array of interests much wider than those of the eleven governments. In short, both the package and the process would have to be expanded. In particular, constituencies rooted in the citizens' constitution, and the visions of community they expressed, would have to be more seriously addressed. And the logic of popular sovereignty, with its implications

Elijah Harper blocking the Meech Lake Accord in the Manitoba legislature.

for public participation, would have to be respected. Inside Quebec, the response to the failure of Meech was to insist on a narrowing of participation in any future process of constitutional reform. Thus, Premier Bourassa announced that Quebec would no longer participate in multilateral constitutional negotiations as one player out of many. Instead, and following a strategy consistent with the two-nations theory, Quebec would wait until the rest of Canada came up with its own constitutional proposal. Negotiations would then proceed on a nation-to-nation basis. In the meantime, Quebec would prepare by undertaking its own public consultations on the constitution and developing its own positions. Political sentiment within Quebec also favoured a substantive narrowing of the constitutional agenda, or at least a prioritization of constitutional amendments that would ensure that Quebec's concerns were

Reproduced with permission from *The Toronto Sun,* a division of Sun Media Corporation.

dealt with first. Quebec was not prepared to engage in the linkage politics that outside Quebec was seen as a necessary condition for any constitutional settlement. Needless to say, it would not be an easy task to reconcile these very different reactions to the failure of Meech Lake.

THE CANADA ROUND AND THE CHARLOTTETOWN ACCORD

The collapse of the Meech Lake Accord led to two years of uncertainty and heightened national anxiety as Quebec undertook a comprehensive and energetic reconsideration of its constitutional position and the rest of Canada engaged in more desultory attempts to take its constitutional pulse. In Quebec the constitutional committee of the provincial Liberal Party, chaired by Jean Allaire, undertook extensive public consultation on Quebec's constitutional options. So did the Bélanger-Campeau Commission, a multi-partisan and multi-stakeholder commission established by the Quebec National Assembly with the agreement of both the government and the opposition. The Allaire Committee was more highly nationalistic and decentralist than the Bélanger-Campeau Commission, but both bodies proceeded on classic two-nations assumptions. For its part, the rest of Canada—ROC, as it was beginning to be called—established the Citizens Forum on Canada's Future, chaired by Keith Spicer, and a joint committee of the Senate and House of Commons on constitutional amendment, chaired by Gérald Beaudoin and Jim Edwards. The Spicer forum found considerable discontent with the political process and, to balance Quebec nationalism (to say nothing of provincialism more generally), a desire among Canadians outside Quebec for a strong central government. The Beaudoin-Edwards Committee concerned itself mainly with the process of amendment and made several recommendations, notably that referendums be held to allow the public to have a direct say in matters of constitutional reform.

Matters were brought to a head in May 1991, when Quebec, in response to Bélanger-Campeau recommendations, enacted legislation requiring a provincial referendum on sovereignty in either June or October of 1992. The federal government responded in the fall of 1991 with the release of a new set of constitutional proposals, *Shaping Canada's Future Together.*[53] While Quebec's ultimatum was clearly a motivating factor behind this new constitutional package, its contents were decisively affected by the constitutional dynamics unleashed outside Quebec by the failure of Meech Lake. In particular, every effort was made to avoid the perception of a reform package driven mainly by Quebec's concerns, emanating from private negotiations of first ministers, and presented for legislative approval as a seamless and unalterable web. In other words, this round of constitutional reform had to be the "Canada Round," not another "Quebec Round," and it had somehow to reflect the logic of the citizens' constitution and the emerging demand for public participation; it could no longer proceed on the assumptions of the old governments' constitution.

This attempt to reorient the process of constitutional reform was evident in several aspects of the new initiative. The package addressed several constitutional agendas other than Quebec's, including Aboriginal demands for self-determination and Western interest in a reformed Senate. Procedurally, the handling of the package reflected the logic of the citizens' constitution in several respects. First, *Shaping Canada's Future Together* was released as a document for public and governmental discussion, and was not presented as a seamless web, the product of closed-door intergovernmental negotiations. Second, the package was turned over to a Special Joint Committee of the Senate and House of Commons—the Beaudoin-Dobbie Committee—for extensive public hearings. Third, when the special committee ran into logistical problems and an indifferent public response, the federal government coordinated five major national conferences, in early 1992, on various components of the package—conferences held in Halifax, Montreal, Niagara-on-the-Lake, Calgary, and Vancouver. All of this delayed the onset of traditional intergovernmental negotiation by first ministers and emphasized public participation and consultation. Governments were de-emphasized and citizens were emphasized.

Intergovernmental negotiation could only be delayed, however. For good or ill, the formal amending procedure reflected the logic of the governments' constitution in requiring the consent of federal and provincial legislatures. It is true that governmental executives could no longer act alone, without the participation of their legislatures, but it was still executives (and, in particular, first ministers) who would have to agree on what to present to their legislatures. Thus, when the Beaudoin-Dobbie Committee reported at the end of February 1992, the federal government began a series of intergovernmental negotiations that continued almost unabated into August of that year.

These negotiations were notable in several respects. Although they were carried out behind closed doors, a major effort was made by the federal minister for Constitutional Affairs, Joe Clark, to keep the media and public informed. There was also an expanded set of players, as teams from the territories and four national Aboriginal organizations joined the table. Aboriginals had played a leading role in derailing the Meech Lake Accord. This time, they were to be central participants in the process. Again, these features of the negotiations reflected efforts to graft some of the citizens'-constitution logic onto an amending procedure formally based on a governments'-constitution logic. For many constituencies rooted in the citizens' constitution, however, its logic was not represented in the process as fully as it should have been. Women's groups, for example, felt illegitimately excluded from the negotiations. In a particularly dramatic objection of this kind, Native women's groups, alleging that their interests were not adequately represented by the male-dominated Aboriginal organizations admitted to the negotiations, asked the courts to force the government to fund their participation in the process.

If the process reflected compromises between the competing logics of the governments' and citizens' constitutions, it was also bedevilled by Quebec's two-nations perspective. Living up to its post-Meech commitments, the Quebec government treated the whole process as the effort of one of the national partners in Confederation to work out its own consensus and present a plan for the approval (or rejection) of the other national partner. Thus, Quebec did not participate in the process of intergovernmental negotiations until late July, after an interim agreement had been reached. A curious ambiguity thus infused the whole process. On one hand, much of the process was an attempt to respond to constitutional agendas other than Quebec's, generally in terms of constitutional logics not terribly compatible with Quebec's two-nations perspective. This focus was reflected in the Canada Round label given to these constitutional negotiations. On the other hand, the entire process was also an attempt to arrive at a package that would satisfy Quebec. It should not surprise readers of this book, however, to learn that the package generated by an arena that excluded Quebec would not satisfy Quebec. The July agreement that brought Quebec back into the negotiations included matters of interest to Quebec, such as a "distinct society" provision, but also embodied other constitutional agendas that were not acceptable to Quebec. For example, the July agreement included a Triple-E Senate,

DOSSIER 3.6 THE HOURGLASS PROCESS OF CONSTITUTIONAL REFORM

Think of the process as being shaped like an hourglass. The top part of the glass was fairly wide, representing the public consultation stage of the process when most of the proposals contained in the Charlottetown Accord were discussed and debated. When these proposals were handed over to political leaders and government officials for negotiation and refinement, the glass narrowed. It came to its narrowest point in the summer of 1992 when the final terms of the Charlottetown Accord were hammered out in a process dominated by first ministers. From that narrow neck the process widened out again in the referendum campaign. This bottom part of the glass, though much shorter, was much wider than the upper half.

The short, wide bottom and the tiny neck were not the only unusual features of this hourglass. A much more serious flaw in the process was the structure of the upper part of the glass—the public consultation, negotiation, and refinement stages. The process represented by this part of the glass for most of its length was divided into nearly watertight compartments: Quebec and the rest of Canada....

As the process narrowed in the negotiating and refinement stage, the Quebec section of the glass was nearly empty. Only when it reached the narrowest point of the neck did Quebec, in the person of Premier Robert Bourassa, engage in the process. By then Bourassa confronted what was very nearly "a done deal"—a set of proposals striking a delicate balance among constitutional interests in the rest of Canada.

Source: Reprinted with permission from Peter H. Russell, *Constitutional Odyssey: Can Canadians Become a Sovereign People?* 2nd ed. (Toronto: University of Toronto Press, 1993), 191–192.

which, from Quebec's perspective, gave one-half of Canada's two national components only one-tenth of the representation in an important legislative chamber.

Quebec's return to the bargaining table generated a new round of negotiations and yet another set of compromises. Agreement on a final package was reached in mid-August in Charlottetown. The symbolism associated with Charlottetown was not accidental. The birthplace of Confederation had been selected as the site of a new founding or rebirth.

The **Charlottetown Accord** was a wide-ranging and complex set of proposed constitutional reforms, which, if accepted in full, would have led to sweeping changes in the Canadian federal state. We can do little more here than list the highlights:

- A **"Canada clause"** expressing fundamental Canadian values. This clause was to be the first substantive clause of the constitution and was intended to guide the courts in their interpretation of other parts of the formal constitution, including both the federal division of powers and the Charter of Rights.
- Substantial reform of the nature and interaction of the two houses of Parliament, including an enlarged House of Commons (with at least 25 percent of its

seats guaranteed in perpetuity to Quebec) and a smaller but elected Senate based on equal representation of the provinces.

- A series of reforms relating to Aboriginal peoples, including constitutional recognition of an "inherent" right of self-government, recognition of Aboriginal governments as one of Canada's "three orders of government," and enhanced participation of Aboriginals in the central institutions of government.
- Some decentralization, including controls on the federal government's spending power and the right of provinces to opt out of shared-cost programs with financial compensation; the right to opt out of centralizing constitutional amendments with financial compensation; Ottawa's withdrawal from six areas of exclusive provincial jurisdiction where it had been active through the spending power; and the transfer of jurisdiction over labour market training from the federal to the provincial governments.
- Constitutional entrenchment of the practice of regular first ministers' conferences, which would have responsibility for, among other things, establishing a framework for, and monitoring the exercise of, the federal spending power.
- A constitutional commitment to respecting Canada's "social and economic union."
- A tightening of constitutional amending procedures, by making more of the constitution subject to the unanimity requirement.

Some of these reforms, such as the Canada clause and the proposed Senate, were to be immediately incorporated into entrenched constitutional law; others, such as the framework that would govern the federal spending power, were to be left to future political negotiation. Still others, such as determining the jurisdictional implications of the inherent right to Aboriginal self-government, represented a combination of legal and political approaches: there was a commitment to negotiate, but after five years the inherent right would become justiciable in the courts.

The Charlottetown Accord was the product of conflicting institutional logics and visions of community, and the resulting tradeoffs are everywhere evident in its provisions. Quebec's territorial version of the two-nations theory, for example, was embodied in Meech-like provisions in the Canada clause recognizing the province's status as a "distinct society" within Canada and affirming the role of the province's legislature and government to "preserve and promote" this distinctiveness. However, the Canada clause balanced the distinct-society provisions with one representing the opposing vision of the entire country as equally the home of both official language groups. This provision affirmed the commitment of "Canadians and their governments [to] the vitality and development of official minority language communities throughout Canada."

The Canada clause also reflected the contest between the Quebec-centred two-nations view and the competing equal-provinces perspective. Thus, the recognition of Quebec as a distinct society was offset by a provision confirming "the principle of the equality of the provinces." Both the distinct-society and equality-of-provinces provisions, moreover, were internally ambiguous in ways that reflected tradeoffs between the two principles. The Quebec "distinct society," said the Canada clause, "includes a French-speaking majority, a unique culture and a civil law tradition." This definitional language had its roots in the attempt outside Quebec to limit the scope of "distinctiveness," so that interpreting the constitution in light of this clause would not lead to too much "special status." Yet, in specifying that Quebec's distinctiveness "includes" these three characteristics, the clause suggested that it encompassed other traits as well. And even if the clause were limited to the three listed traits, they included "culture," which can be interpreted narrowly, as reflecting only a part of human activity (the interpretation often assumed outside Quebec), or so broadly as to encompass virtually the whole of human life (the interpretation adopted in Quebec). For its part, the provision confirming the "equality of the provinces" went on to recognize "their diverse characteristics."

The equal-provinces view was also embodied in the proposed new Senate, which was to be based on equal representation of all the provinces. Needless to say, Quebec's government was able to accept this affront to its two-nations sensibilities only with significant concessions to the latter logic in the design of the central legislative institutions. Most prominently, Quebec demanded a guarantee of at least 25 percent of the seats in the House of Commons, even if its share of the national population fell below that level. This was, to be sure, not the 50 percent representation that a strict two-nations logic would require, but it nevertheless implied that the homeland of one of Canada's two nations needed a minimum level of representation, regardless of population. To ensure that the equal-provinces Senate would not be able to overrule the two-nations House, moreover, Quebec (with Ontario's aid) secured agreement to an enlarged House (from what was then 295 seats up to 337 seats) and a smaller Senate (from 104 to 62 seats). Since disagreements between the two houses were to be resolved by majority vote in a joint sitting, the chamber in which Quebec would have at least a 25 percent presence could easily outvote the chamber in which it had only a 10 percent presence.

In addition to representing the equal-provinces view, the Senate reflected the logic of intrastate federalism inasmuch as it attempted to make the central Parliament more regionally responsive. This strengthening of the intrastate side of the constitution was balanced by the proposed entrenchment of the first ministers' conference, one of the key institutions of interstate federalism. The logic of interstate federalism also infused the accord's provisions respecting the division of powers, in the sense both of decentralizing power and providing for endless federal–provincial negotiation of the details.

Both the two-nations and equal-provinces views were evident in the division-of-powers proposals, and they were squared in the now familiar manner of generalizing any explicit decentralization and allowing asymmetry only in its "soft" form through opting-out provisions. For example, provinces could opt out of shared-cost programs with financial compensation. Scepticism about even the soft asymmetrical federalism implied by opting out was evident in provisions guaranteeing provinces that chose to opt out equality of treatment with provinces who had already done so. If Quebec led the way in making a particularly good deal for itself, in other words, other provinces who chose to follow suit were guaranteed an equally good deal.

Quebec's two-nations perspective had to contend not only with Canada-wide bilingualism and the equal-provinces perspective but also with the claim by Aboriginal peoples that they too constituted a distinct society within Canada. To be blunt, equal constitutional status for Quebec and Canada's "first peoples" was something that Quebec could not agree to and that Aboriginal peoples insisted on. These competing claims were fudged by reserving the language of "distinct society" for Quebec but writing the spirit of Aboriginal "distinct society" into another part of the Canada clause. Aboriginal peoples, said this provision, "being the first peoples to govern this land, have the right to promote their languages, cultures and traditions and to ensure the integrity of their societies." Moreover, as in the case of Quebec, Aboriginals were to express their distinctiveness through their own governments, governments to which they had an inherent right and that were said to be "one of the three orders of government in Canada," and thus of equal status with the government of Quebec.

While Aboriginals had joined first ministers in the late stages of drafting the accord, other Charter groups did not. Not surprisingly, many of these other groups did not believe they fared well. In particular, they insisted that they were less effectively represented in the Canada clause than were Quebec and the Aboriginal communities. The role of Quebec's *government* in the preservation and promotion of its distinct society was clearly affirmed. Similarly, "Canadians and their *governments*" were said to be "committed to the vitality and development of official language communities throughout Canada." And again, the right of Aboriginals to promote their cultures and traditions was clearly something they could do through the *governments* to which they had an inherent right and that were on a par with provincial governments. By contrast, it was only "Canadians," not their governments, who were committed by the Canada clause to "racial and ethnic equality" or to "respect for individual and collective human rights and freedoms" or to "the equality of female and male persons." This led to complaints about a hierarchy of rights in the constitution. And, of course, some groups were left out altogether. The disabled, for example, who had secured constitutional status in section 15 of the Charter, were not mentioned in the Canada clause. Nor were other aspirants to constitutional status, such as homosexuals.[54]

The accord also reflected ideological divisions on matters of social and economic policy. Those who decried government intervention and the many barriers to domestic "free trade" erected by provinces sought constitutional recognition of "property rights" and the strengthening of existing (and not very effective) constitutional guarantees of free trade. Proposals to achieve both of these ends were included in Ottawa's original discussion document, *Shaping Canada's Future Together*. Others worried that the constitutionalization of economic "competitiveness" might lead to the dismantling of Canada's network of social welfare policies, and thus lobbied for the addition of a "social charter," which would constitutionally entrench social welfare rights not currently covered by the Charter of Rights. In the end, these opposing camps cancelled each other out. Property rights were not part of the final Charlottetown Accord, and neither domestic free trade nor social welfare rights received strong constitutional protection. Instead, there was a relatively weak "commitment" to respect both the social and economic union of Canada, leaving it to the first ministers subsequently to establish a mechanism to monitor progress in implementing this commitment. The social union entailed such policy objectives as universal public health care, reasonable access to a variety of social services and benefits, high-quality education, and a sustainable environment. The economic union embraced internal free trade and the goal of full employment, among other objectives.

The tension between the emerging logic of popular sovereignty and the older logic of elite accommodation was also clearly evident in the text and politics of the accord. Under the proposed revisions of the 1982 amending procedures, some matters, such as reform of the Senate, were to be shifted from the category of seven-fifty amendment to that of unanimity, but the actual process of amendment was to remain formally the preserve of governments and legislatures. Nevertheless, although the text of the Charlottetown Accord would have continued to embody the logic of the governments' constitution in matters of amendment, the accord itself would not be implemented according to that logic. The actual process of arriving at the Charlottetown Accord and then attempting to pass it suggested the development of a convention that would govern the practical exercise of the formal procedures, much as the conventions of responsible government govern the exercise of the Crown's formal powers. We have seen that, in response to criticisms of how the Meech Lake Accord was handled, public consultation was made a significant feature of the early stages of developing the accord. Now that the accord was complete, the public would be consulted again, in an even broader and much more dramatic fashion. Quebec was committed to holding a referendum in October. It was politically impossible for the province to repeal this legislated requirement altogether, though it was able to change the referendum question from sovereignty to whether or not to accept the Charlottetown Accord. British Columbia and Alberta had also committed themselves to consulting their populations through referendums, and Ottawa had passed legislation enabling a national referendum. In the event, Ottawa and Quebec arranged a synchronized referendum on the accord, held under Quebec's law in that province and the federal law in the rest of Canada. The referendum was held on October 26, 1992. It would seem that minor constitutional amendments can still be passed without such a referendum, but most observers agree that the October 1992 referendum established a conventional precedent for major amendments—certainly for amendment packages of the megaconstitutional scope and significance of the Charlottetown Accord.

As elite agreement on both the Meech Lake and Charlottetown accords demonstrates, the traditional process of elite accommodation can sometimes paper over fundamentally conflicting institutional logics and visions of community. What is difficult but possible for a relatively small group of people engaged over long periods of time in intense face-to-face bargaining may, however, become impossible when the decision-making arena grows to include the participation of the public at large. Different institutional arenas, different outcomes. The accord failed in the referendum because important segments of the public were less willing than their elites to compromise principles and interests. Of all the compromises in the accord, the central one in voters' minds probably concerned the tradeoffs between Quebec's two-nations perspective and its various competitors. As Peter Russell puts it, "The Charlottetown Accord was defeated because, outside Quebec, it was perceived as giving Quebec too much, while inside Quebec it was perceived as not giving Quebec enough."[55] As might be expected, this confrontation of conflicting visions was strongest in Quebec and the West. Figure 3.2 shows that the referendum was soundly defeated in these parts of the country, by majorities ranging from over 55 percent in Quebec and Saskatchewan to 68 percent in British Columbia. The accord was approved in only four provinces—Newfoundland, Prince Edward Island, New Brunswick, and Ontario—and the Northwest Territories. In Ontario the outcome was a virtual tossup; the Nova Scotia outcome was also very close.

Reproduced with permission from *The Toronto Sun,* a division of Sun Media Corporation.

FIGURE 3.2 **THE 1992 NATIONAL REFERENDUM**

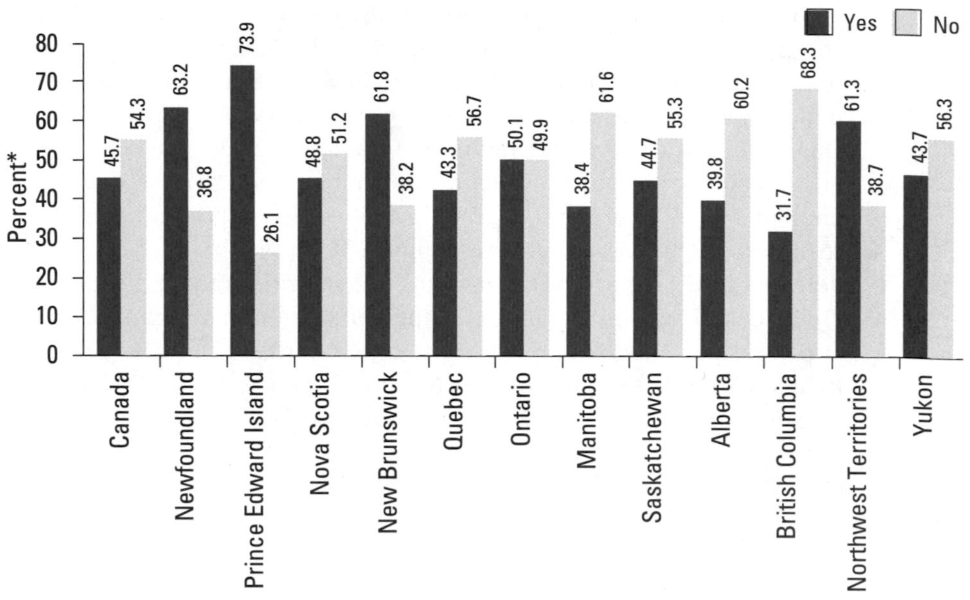

*percentage of the total valid votes cost
Sources: Chief Electoral Officer of Canada and Elections Quebec, 1992.

THE CONSTITUTIONAL NEVERENDUM?

The public rejection of the Charlottetown Accord left Canadians with a profound sense of constitutional weariness and a marked distaste for megaconstitutional politics. Political leaders throughout the land swore oaths not to utter the "C-word" in the foreseeable future and to devote themselves to such matters as the economy instead. But the Pandora's box of megaconstitutional politics has proved difficult to close. Certainly, the conflicting institutional logics and visions of community that have fuelled Canada's modern era of megaconstitutional politics remained in place and at work. Aboriginal peoples continued to search for forms of self-governance, westerners still yearned to make the central institutions of government more regionally responsive, and Quebec nationalists certainly did not give up on sovereignty. Indeed, Quebec sovereigntists (in the form of the Bloc Québécois) and western "reformers" came to dominate the opposition benches in the 1993 and 1997 federal elections, thus keeping their conflicting megaconstitutional visions close to the surface of national politics. Especially important in this regard was the Bloc's overt commitment to the breakup of Canada.

The most important factor in pushing megaconstitutional politics back to the top of the Canadian political agenda was the 1994 election in Quebec of the Parti

Reprinted with permission from The Halifax Herald Limited.

Québécois, under the leadership of the hard-line separatist Jacques Parizeau. The Parizeau government announced that it would hold a referendum on independence in the first year of its mandate. This referendum, which took place on October 30, 1995, plunged Canada into the deepest of its modern megaconstitutional crises.

Parizeau initially wanted to hold a referendum on outright independence. He did not, in other words, want to fudge the issue with a 1980-style vote on sovereignty-association. However, the polls showed that Quebeckers were not prepared to vote for sovereignty unless it was tied to some form of continuing association with Canada. As in 1980, therefore, a compromise position was worked out. Ultimately, Parizeau's Parti Québécois agreed with the federal Bloc Québécois and the provincial Parti Action Démocratique (the third party in the Quebec legislature) that Quebeckers should be asked whether the province "should become sovereign, after having made a formal offer to Canada for a new economic and political partnership." Note that sovereignty was conditional only on an "offer" of partnership, not on Canada's acceptance of that offer. If partnership negotiations broke down, Quebec would end up sovereign anyway.

Even with an ambiguous question, the polls early in the campaign held little hope for a sovereigntist victory. Becoming desperate, Parizeau effectively turned the leadership of the Yes campaign over to the more charismatic Lucien Bouchard, leader of the federal Bloc Québécois. Officially, Bouchard was appointed Quebec's chief negotiator in the anticipated post-referendum partnership negotiations with Canada, but everyone understood that he was now in charge of the referendum campaign itself. An effective campaigner, capable of rousing public emotions, Bouchard soon turned the tide and recaptured momentum for the Yes side. Sensing a looming disaster, Prime Minister Jean Chrétien, who had been content to lie low for much of

DOSSIER 3.7 WHAT DOES "PARTNERSHIP" MEAN?

If Partnership is to be an attractive alternative both inside and outside Quebec, then Canada must have the same autonomy from Quebec that Quebec has from Canada. Partnership that is not symmetrical in this respect is not a true partnership. This implies in turn that Quebec politicians would have no more influence in the internal affairs of the Canadian partner than non-Quebec politicians would have in the internal affairs of Quebec. Simply put, the chances of a Quebec resident becoming prime minister of Canada should be no greater than the chances of a non-Quebec resident becoming prime minister of Quebec.

Partnership, therefore, is not simply asymmetrical federalism dressed up in new rhetorical garments. The principal reason why asymmetrical federalism has not found a significant audience outside Quebec is that it presupposes greater autonomy for Quebec combined with a continuation of Quebec's present role in the federal government. Partnership corrects asymmetry by providing greater autonomy for both Quebec *and Canada,* autonomy which in the latter case stems from Quebec's disengagement from the government of Canada. As Jane Jenson observes, partnership "would allow each society to define equity, justice and equality in its own terms," something that cannot be done when Canada's political leadership comes overwhelmingly from Quebec.

[As Alan Noël] points out, an equal partnership must be built "on solidarity within each national community." For Quebec, a government to give expression to that solidarity is already in place, but for the rest of Canada it remains to be created. (The rest of Canada has governments but no government.) To assume that solidarity within the Canadian partner in a Canada–Quebec partnership can emerge from intergovernmental agreements, or from a "national" government headed by political representatives from the other national community, is to assume the impossible. (It would be similar to the solidarity of Quebec being expressed through Ontario's Mike Harris or British Columbia's Glen Clark.) As Noël goes on to point out, the role of partnership institutions is not only to facilitate harmonization but, more importantly, to protect the partners' autonomy. This in turn requires that the partners have autonomous institutions.

Source: Reprinted from Roger Gibbins, "Getting There from Here," in Roger Gibbins and Guy Laforest, eds., *Beyond the Impasse: Toward Reconciliation* (Ottawa: IRRP, 1998), 402.

the campaign, stepped into the fray in its latter stages. A long-time opponent of the constitutional recognition of Quebec as a distinct society, Chrétien now committed his government to pursuing a distinct-society provision. He similarly agreed to promote a Quebec veto over constitutional amendments.

In the event, the separatists lost the referendum—but only by a whisker. Whereas about 60 percent of Quebeckers had voted No in the 1980 referendum, the result in 1995 was 50.6 percent No and 49.4 percent Yes (with a voter turnout of over 90 percent). Francophones voted 60 percent Yes (up from 50 percent in 1980) while anglophones and allophones voted over 90 percent No, leading an embittered Jacques Parizeau to declare on referendum night that the sovereignty option had been defeated by money and the ethnic vote. Several days later, Parizeau resigned as premier and Lucien Bouchard left federal politics to become the new leader of the PQ and premier of Quebec. Disappointed by the referendum loss but buoyed by how close they came to winning, the Parti Québécois intends to hold yet another independence referendum at an opportune time in the future.

Given the close call of 1995, the separation of Quebec has become a more seriously imagined reality for most Canadians.[56] On one hand, this has led to renewed efforts to make offers to Quebec designed to keep that province within Confederation. On the other hand, it has led to tough-minded thinking about precisely how separation and disengagement can and should occur. The two approaches have become known as **Plan A** (the reconciliation option) and **Plan B** (the "tough love" option).

The Chrétien government's immediate post-referendum strategy was based on Plan A. In particular, the government soon made good on its referendum promise to do something about "distinct society" and the Quebec veto. On the distinct-society front, the House of Commons quickly passed a resolution recognizing Quebec as a "distinct society within Canada." The resolution declared that the House itself would "be guided" by the reality of Quebec's distinct society and "encourag[ed] all components of the legislative and executive branches of government to take note of this recognition and be guided in their conduct accordingly." In other words, distinct society was to become a guiding principle not only for parliamentarians but for all federal government bureaucrats. True, this was only a resolution, not an amendment of the constitution, but it was seen as the first step in a continuing effort to constitutionalize the principle of distinct society.

On the Quebec veto front, the government enacted legislation in early 1996 designed to give Quebec a veto over constitutional amendments. Of course, Ottawa alone could not directly amend the constitution to achieve this end, but it found a way to do so indirectly through ordinary legislation. Remember that the general amending formula requires the consent of Ottawa and seven provinces having fifty percent of the population. Under this formula only Ottawa has an outright veto. In effect, Ottawa passed legislation committing itself to "lending" its veto to the provinces, including Quebec. Under the **Constitutional Veto Act**, Ottawa would pass a constitutional resolution only if it had first been approved by Quebec, Ontario, British Columbia, two of the prairie provinces having 50 percent of the prairie population, and two of the Atlantic provinces having 50 percent of that region's population. As so often in the past, a proposal designed for Quebec was extended to other provinces in order to legitimize it in the rest of the country, though this extension was rooted in the regionalist vision of Canada rather than in the equal-provinces vision.

Ironically, the regionalist veto formula designed to placate Quebec in 1996 is similar to the Victoria Charter formula rejected by Quebec in 1971. Recall that Quebec rejected the Victoria Charter because, although it allowed Quebec to veto changes it disliked, it allowed other parts of the country to block changes that Quebec wanted. Since Quebec had aspirations for positive constitutional change, it saw the Victoria Charter formula as a straightjacket. A similar straightjacket is imposed by the 1996 veto legislation. In effect, that legislation makes constitutional amendments under the general amending formula even more difficult than they had been. This is bound to frustrate such western constitutional projects as formal Senate reform, but as Thomas Flanagan points out, "it may be Quebec, as the province least satisfied with the constitutional status quo, that loses most from the five-region veto."[57]

In addition to the distinct-society resolution and the veto legislation, Ottawa's Plan A strategy for placating Quebec included some administrative decentralization of jurisdictions. In particular, Ottawa agreed to withdraw from the field of labour market training and to transfer funds for that purpose to the provinces.

Ottawa did not, however, rely completely on the Plan A attempt to keep Quebec within Canada. Should Quebec decide to leave despite the blandishments of Plan A, it could not be allowed to unilaterally set the rules for its own departure. To protect its own interests, Canada needed to set clear and demanding rules and conditions under which secession could take place. By making clear the difficulties and costs involved in separation, moreover, such rules might well cause Quebeckers to think twice before voting Yes in the next independence referendum. This was Plan B.

The essential components of Plan B were set out in a remarkable exchange of open letters in the late summer of 1997 between Stéphane Dion, the federal minister for intergovernmental affairs, and the premier (Lucien Bouchard) and deputy premier (Bernard Landry) of Quebec. Dion's version of Plan B had three main elements. First, although Quebec was entitled to separate, a **unilateral declaration of independence (UDI)** would be illegal under both Canadian constitutional law and international law. If Quebec wished to respect the rule of law, separation would have to be achieved through an amendment of the existing Canadian constitution. Since such an amendment would require the consent of other Canadian legislatures, including the Parliament of Canada, the details of disengagement—e.g., the division of the debt—would have to be negotiated first, while Quebec was still part of Canada, not after a UDI. As part of this dimension of its Plan B strategy, the Chrétien government had referred the question of the legality of a UDI to the Supreme Court of Canada (see Dossier 1.1).

Second, Dion questioned the assumption that a 50 percent plus one Yes vote in an independence referendum would be sufficient to trigger even a legal secession process. "Secession, the act of choosing between one's fellow citizens," argued Dion, "is one of the most consequence-laden choices a society can ever make." It is one of those "virtually irreversible changes that deeply affect not only our own lives but also those of future generations," and should thus be subject to more than an ordinary majority decision rule. "It would be too dangerous," he continued, "to attempt such an operation in an atmosphere of division, on the basis of a narrow, 'soft' majority... which could evaporate in the face of difficulties." A more substantial consensus would have to be shown.[58]

Third, Dion raised the contentious issue of the **partition** of Quebec. If Quebec could separate from Canada, he suggested, parts of Quebec might with equal legitimacy secede from Quebec and remain in Canada. Dion highlighted the right of Quebec's Aboriginal peoples to remain in Canada. This example was no doubt strategically chosen, for immediately before the 1995 referendum, three Aboriginal nations held their own votes on whether to stay in an independent Quebec. "The Cree voted 96% No; the Inuit voted 95% No; and the French-speaking Montagnais voted an astonishing 99% No."[59] Clearly, there would be pressure for the partition of Quebec, and Dion asserted that no one could "predict that the borders of an independent Quebec would be those now guaranteed by the Canadian Constitution."[60]

The provinces also played a role in the evolving and shifting balance between Plan A and Plan B responses to the separatist threat. Especially important in this regard was the so-called **Calgary declaration**, which emerged from a September 1997 meeting in Calgary of all provincial premiers and territorial leaders except for the premier of Quebec. The Calgary declaration set out a series of principles to guide public consultation on strengthening the Canadian federation. One of these principles involved the recognition of the "unique character" of Quebec society, an obvious reformulation of the distinct-society principle. This extension of an olive branch to Quebec became a prominent part of the Plan A strategy.

No reader of this chapter should be surprised, however, to learn that the Calgary declaration balanced its support of "unique character" with simultaneous support of the equal-provinces view. Thus, one of the principles insisted that "all provinces, while diverse in their characteristics, have equality of status," and another declared that "if any future constitutional amendment confers powers on one province, these powers must be available to all provinces." Once again, we encounter the now time-honoured strategy of giving to all provinces whatever is given to Quebec.

The Calgary declaration, in other words, embodied the same tensions that destroyed the Meech Lake and Charlottetown Accords. Despite this, the declaration was widely supported in a variety of public consultations undertaken by provincial governments, and by mid-1998 the legislatures of all provinces and territories other than Quebec had passed, or intended to pass, resolutions supporting the declaration. The House of Commons passed a similar resolution. Even the Reform Party, which was the only federalist party to oppose the Charlottetown Accord, endorsed the Calgary declaration. Indeed, it was the Reform Party that introduced the Commons resolution supporting the declaration.

The widespread support for the Calgary declaration is surely explained in part by the fact that it is merely a set of principles for discussion, not a proposed set of constitutional amendments. The stakes are thus much lower, and the tensions between competing principles easier to fudge or ignore. If the history of recent megaconstitutional politics is a guide, any attempt to build another constitutional package on the foundation of the Calgary declaration is likely to meet the fate of the Meech and Charlottetown accords. As Jeffrey Simpson has put it, if the Calgary declaration is indeed, as its proponents suggest, a "candle in the window" to Quebeckers, Canadians should take care not to let the candle "tip over or get blown into a large flame." "Canadians," says Simpson, "know all about constitutional candles that became raging fires. Were the Calgary declaration to launch Canada on another round of constitutional negotiations, grab the asbestos blankets."[61]

By the fall of 1998 the Calgary declaration had receded into the background of Canadian politics. Attention was focused instead on the Supreme Court's pending judgment in the **secession reference**, the aforementioned reference asking the court whether Quebec had the right to secede unilaterally. Nearing the end of its mandate, the Quebec government was considering the timing of an election, and many observers speculated that Premier Bouchard was anxious to use a pro-Ottawa judgment by the court as the pretext for an election call. Quebec had portrayed the reference as an illegitimate tactic by Ottawa to impose its will in a matter that only Quebeckers could decide, and had thus refused to participate in the case. (Ottawa had to appoint an *amicus curiae*, or "friend of the court," to present Quebec's side of the argument.) The PQ government was waiting to pounce on a predictably anti-secessionist judgment by "Ottawa's Court."

The court did not oblige Mr. Bouchard. As in the 1981 patriation case, it gave enough to both sides to make it difficult for either to simply reject the judgment. The court did conclude that Quebec had no legal right to secede unilaterally, that a legal separation would require a negotiated constitutional amendment, as Ottawa had maintained. On the other hand, the court made it clear that if a "clear" referendum question yielded a "clear" result in favour of secession, the rest of Canada had a constitutional obligation to negotiate in good faith with Quebec. The court also implied that such negotiations had to be open-ended enough to include options other than simple separation—"sovereignty association," perhaps, or a "new partnership." This was too good for Quebec nationalists to pass up. No longer could hard-liners say that Canada was indivisible. No longer could they say that they would refuse to negotiate a new "partnership" with Quebec, that separation was a simple in-or-out proposition. Instead of rejecting the decision, therefore, the Quebec government tried to turn it to its advantage, emphasizing the parts it liked and de-emphasizing other parts.

Predictably, both sides were soon engaged in a politics of interpretation, trying to exploit the ambiguities in the decision. What exactly was a "clear" referendum question? Did it have to be clearer than the 1980 and 1995 questions, as Ottawa maintained, or were those questions perfectly clear, as the PQ government argued? And what was a "clear" result in a secession referendum? Would 50 percent plus one suffice, as Quebec had always insisted, or would a more substantial majority be required to break up the country, as Stéphane Dion regularly argued? The court's judgment clearly posed these questions, but the court had just as clearly refused to answer them. A clear result on a clear question was necessary to trigger the constitutional "obligation to negotiate," said the court, but whether the question or the result was sufficiently clear was a matter for political, not legal judgment. In effect, the court has set the questions; politics will supply the answers.

DOSSIER 3.8 THE FUTURE OF THE CALGARY DECLARATION

In spite of [its widespread support in the rest of Canada], the [Calgary] declaration is having zero impact in Quebec, not even on the mythical soft nationalists who allegedly would be glad to remain in Canada if they could just have a little more provincial autonomy. This is not surprising ... because the declaration does not address the consistent demand of Quebec nationalists since passage of the Charter of Rights and Freedoms in 1982—that the Quebec National Assembly be able to override the language rights enshrined in the Charter.

This is exactly what the distinct-society provision of the Meech Lake accord would have done, as Robert Bourassa once admitted in a moment of frankness. [Eventually] the promoters of the Calgary declaration will move on to the next phase of their project, trying to convert it into a constitutional amendment that, whatever its precise wording, will give Quebec its desired power to get around the Charter. Alberta's Ralph Klein, Saskatchewan's Roy Romanow and Ottawa's Stéphane Dion have been remarkably candid about this from the beginning.

At this point the politics will start to get interesting because of Preston Manning and the Reform Party. Mr. Manning is the virtual godfather of the Calgary declaration, having brokered the deal ... when he signalled that he could live with the "unique character of Quebec society" as long as it was balanced by other phrases about provincial equality....

But I doubt that Mr. Manning will want to travel much further along the path to a constitutional amendment.... [He has] recently published a long essay about the way toward national unity. For him, the trail runs through a Triple-E Senate, a smaller federal government and a greater devolution of powers to the provinces. What makes this problematic for Quebec nationalists is his insistence on provincial equality: "Special deals for one province are not acceptable, and any power given Quebec to help protect and develop its uniqueness must also be offered to every province."

Under the heading of devolution, Mr. Manning is quite willing to give Quebec more power over language and culture; but under the heading of provincial equality, all provinces must get the same power. And that's the rub for Quebec nationalists. They want to maintain what Lucien Bouchard once called "asymmetrical bilingualism"—an officially unilingual Quebec in an officially bilingual Canada. They hardly care whether anyone speaks French in Alberta or Saskatchewan, but official bilingualism is the key to preserving Quebec's power in Ottawa.

Ever since passage of the Official Languages Act in 1969, only Quebeckers have been prime minister for longer than a few months at a time. Leaders of three of the five federal parties are from Quebec, as are the Chief Justice of the Supreme Court and the Chief Clerk of the Privy Council.

Mr. Manning caused great consternation when he alluded to these realities in the 1997 federal election campaign. He is not being so tasteless now, but the combination of provincial equality and more provincial control over language and culture remains Reform's greatest challenge to the Canadian status quo, now that fiscal responsibility has become conventional wisdom.

Because of Reform's policy, it will be difficult, if not impossible, for Mr. Manning to support a constitutional amendment of the kind Messrs. Klein, Romanow and Dion have in mind. Since those three are unlikely to embrace Reform's policy, the most likely outcome is further stalemate.

Source: Reprinted from Tom Flanagan, "The Calgary Declaration in 1998," *Globe and Mail,* January 1, 1998, A17.

CONCLUSION

The proliferating constitutional reform proposals of the modern era of megaconstitutional politics reflected competing attempts to fashion and refashion the Canadian community through the mechanisms of entrenched constitutional law. Quebec nationalists promoted the constitutional vision of a binational community territorially divided between Quebec and the rest of Canada. In particular, they envisioned either a loose form of sovereignty-association or an asymmetrical federalism in which Quebec, as a "distinct society," would have substantially greater jurisdictional power than the other provinces. The rest of Canada was not the kind of cohesive national partner posited by Quebec's two-nations theorists, however. The other provinces often shared Quebec's decentralizing aspirations but insisted there be a general decentralization, with little or no special status for Quebec. Underlying such proposals was a vision of Canada as an association of equal provincial communities rather than an association of two equal nations. Because both of these visions shared decentralizing aspirations, they were often able to make common cause against the centralists; nevertheless, their fundamental differences brought them into conflict over such issues as the amending formula, where the two-nations theory implied a special veto for Quebec and the equal-provinces view insisted on a formula that treated all provinces alike. These views could be reconciled with a formula requiring unanimous consent, but not one like the seven-fifty rule, which deprives Quebec of a veto. An intermediate view held that Canada was fundamentally an association of major regions, some of which coincided with provinces (Ontario, Quebec, and, in some versions, British Columbia) while others encompassed several provinces (Atlantic Canada and the West). This vision was reflected in Victoria Charter–style amending procedures requiring the consent of each of the regions. Because the province of Quebec was always one of the regions, this regionalist approach implied the same veto for Quebec as did the two-nations thesis.

In opposition to Canada's decentralizing forces, whether based on two-nations, provincialist, or regionalist theories, were those actors, such as Pierre Trudeau, who sought constitutional expression for a single pan-Canadian identity—based on official bilingualism, multiculturalism, and individual rights—that would

DOSSIER 3.9 HOW TO SECEDE FROM CANADA

The [secession] Reference requires us to consider whether Quebec has a right to unilateral secession. Those who support the existence of such a right found their case primarily on the principle of democracy. Democracy, however, means more than simple majority rule. As reflected in our constitutional jurisprudence, democracy exists in the larger context of other constitutional values.... In the 131 years since Confederation, the people of the provinces and territories have created close ties of interdependence (economically, socially, politically and culturally) based on shared values that include federalism, democracy, constitutionalism and the rule of law, and respect for minorities. A democratic decision of Quebeckers in favour of secession would put those relationships at risk. The Constitution vouchsafes order and stability, and accordingly secession of a province "under the Constitution" could not be achieved unilaterally, that is, without principled negotiation with other participants in Confederation within the existing constitutional framework.

The Constitution is not a straitjacket. Even a brief review of our constitutional history demonstrates periods of momentous and dramatic change. Our democratic institutions necessarily accommodate a continuous process of discussion and evolution, which is reflected in the constitutional right of each participant in the federation to initiate constitutional change. This right implies a reciprocal duty on the other participants to engage in discussions to address any legitimate initiative to change the constitutional order. While it is true that some attempts at constitutional amendment in recent years have faltered, a clear majority vote in Quebec on a clear question in favour of secession would confer democratic legitimacy on the secession initiative which all of the other participants in Confederation would have to recognize.

Quebec could not, despite a clear referendum result, purport to invoke a right of self-determination to dictate the terms of a proposed secession to the other parties to the federation. The democratic vote, by however strong a majority, would have no legal effect on its own and could not push aside the principles of federalism and the rule of law, the rights of individuals and minorities, or the operation of democracy in the other provinces or in Canada as a whole. Democratic rights under the Constitution cannot be divorced from constitutional obligations. Nor, however, can the reverse proposition be accepted. The continued existence and operation of the Canadian constitutional order could not be indifferent to a clear expression of a clear majority of Quebeckers that they no longer wish to remain in Canada. The other provinces and the federal government would have no basis to deny the right of the government of Quebec to pursue secession, should a clear majority of the people of Quebec choose that goal, so long as in doing so, Quebec respects the rights of others. The negotiations that followed such a vote would address the potential act of secession as well as its possible terms should in fact secession proceed. There would be no conclusions predetermined by law on any issue. Negotiations would need to address the interests of the other provinces, the federal government, Quebec and indeed the rights of all Canadians both within and outside Quebec, and specifically the rights of minorities. No one suggests that it would be an easy set of negotiations.

The negotiation process would require the reconciliation of various rights and obligations by negotiation between two legitimate majorities, namely, the majority of the population of Quebec, and that of Canada as a whole. Apolitical majority at either level that does not act in accordance with the underlying constitutional principles we have mentioned puts at risk the legitimacy of its exercise of its rights, and the ultimate acceptance of the result by the international community.

The task of the Court has been to clarify the legal framework within which political decisions are to be taken "under the Constitution," not to usurp the prerogatives of the political forces that operate within that framework. The obligations we have identified are binding obligations under the Constitution of Canada. However, it will be for the political actors to determine what constitutes "a clear majority on a clear question" in the circumstances under which a future referendum vote may be taken. Equally, in the event of demonstrated majority support for Quebec secession, the content and process of the negotiations will be for the political actors to settle. The reconciliation of the various legitimate constitutional interests is necessarily committed to the political rather than the judicial realm precisely because that reconciliation can only be achieved through the give and take of political negotiations. To the extent issues addressed in the course of negotiation are political, the courts, appreciating their proper role in the constitutional scheme, would have no supervisory role.

Source: From the judgment of the Supreme Court of Canada in *Reference Re Secession of Quebec* (1998) (the secession reference). Text of the full decision (and many other Supreme Court decisions) can be found at http://www.droit.umontreal.ca/doc/csc-scc/en.

provide the legitimizing constituency for the federal government. The Charter of Rights, as the centrepiece of a citizens' constitution, was the major triumph of this view, although section 33 of the Charter and the seven-fifty and unanimity amending formulas represented compromises with proponents of a more provincializing governments' constitution. The tension between governments' and citizens' constitutions embedded in the 1982 Constitution Act provided a major subtext for the constitutional imbroglios of the Meech Lake and Charlottetown accords. In particular, a variety of citizens' groups, including women and Aboriginal peoples, demanded the enhancement of their own constitutional status at the expense of the traditional Canadian preoccupations with language, culture, and territory. More generally, the Canadian people, reflecting the modern doctrine of popular rather than governmental sovereignty, have taken ownership of the constitution, and a convention seems to have arisen requiring their direct participation in major constitutional amendments.

The modern era of megaconstitutional politics, in short, saw the steady escalation of constitutional claims. However, the addition of new constitutional claims and players was hardly ever accompanied by the resolution of old issues and the satisfaction of old players. The result was the constant escalation of the constitutional agenda, until, by the time of the Canada Round, it was very crowded indeed—and even then, groups complained bitterly at having been left out or inadequately accommodated. Moreover, the substitution of referendum for elite accommodation as the decisive decision-making device made it more difficult than ever to compromise the proliferating differences.

Since the Charlottetown Accord, Canadians have shied away from any new megaconstitutional amendment packages, though the 1995 Quebec independence referendum, with its harrowingly narrow result, has kept the national unity issue close to the top of the political agenda. In response to this issue, Canadians and their governments have oscillated between Plan A efforts to placate Quebec—e.g., the House of Commons distinct-society resolution, the 1996 veto legislation, the 1997 Calgary declaration—and Plan B speculation about rules and conditions of separation—e.g., the rejection of UDI, the need for a more-than-majority result in an independence referendum, the potential partition of Quebec. None of the Plan A initiatives has resolved the underlying tension between the two-nations view and its competitors, or indeed between and among all of the megaconstitutional visions of Canada. It remains unclear how these issues and expectations will be addressed in the future. The only certainty is that the issues will not soon dissipate, that they will continue to animate Canadian public life.

KEY TERMS

asymmetrical federalism
governments' constitution
citizens' constitution
Quiet Revolution
two-nations vision
opting out
equal-provinces vision
soft asymmetry
hard asymmetry
special status
Fulton-Favreau formula
interstate federalism
federal–provincial diplomacy
executive federalism
intrastate federalism
provincialist intrastate federalism
House of the Provinces
centralist intrastate federalism
Triple-E Senate
individualist vision
bilingualism
multiculturalism
Victoria Charter
regionalist vision
Bill C-60
House of the Federation
sovereignty-association
gang of eight

patriation case
night of the long knives
Charter Canadians / Charter groups
Meech Lake Accord
distinct society
Charlottetown Accord
"Canada clause"
Plan A / Plan B
Constitutional Veto Act
unilateral declaration of independence (UDI)
partition
Calgary declaration
secession reference

DISCUSSION QUESTIONS

1. One of the themes of this chapter is the tension between the logics of the governments' and citizens' constitutions. What do you make of the fact that the core of the citizens' constitution—the Charter of Rights and Freedoms—shifts power away from legislatures elected by citizens to judges appointed by governments?
2. Is the democratization of the process of constitutional amendment good or bad for Canada?
3. Given the analysis in Dossier 3.7, how would you structure a "partnership" between Canada and a newly independent Quebec?
4. Compare the Quebec and Western perspectives on sea-to-sea bilingualism in Dossiers 3.2 and 3.8. Are they compatible or incompatible with each other?
5. In Dossier 3.9 the Supreme Court says that after a secession vote an amendment would have to be negotiated by "two legitimate majorities, namely, the majority of the population of Quebec, and that of Canada as a whole." How would this work in practice? Would the Chrétien government in Ottawa be a legitimate representative of "Canada as a whole"? If not, who else would have to be involved, and how would one structure the "Canadian" delegation at the conference table?

SUGGESTED READINGS

Banting, Keith, and Richard Simeon, eds. *And No One Cheered: Federalism, Democracy, and the Constitution Act.* Toronto: Methuen, 1983.

Cairns, Alan C. *Charter versus Federalism: The Dilemmas of Constitutional Reform.* Montreal and Kingston: McGill-Queen's University Press, 1992.

———. *Constitution, Government, and Society in Canada.* Ed. Douglas E. Williams. Toronto: McClelland & Stewart, 1988.

———. *Disruptions: Constitutional Struggles, From the Charter to Meech Lake.* Toronto: McClelland & Stewart, 1991.

Gibbins, Roger, and Guy Laforest, eds. *Beyond the Impasse: Toward Reconciliation.* Ottawa: IRPP, 1998.

McWhinney, Edward. *Canada and the Constitution 1979–1982: Patriation and the Charter of Rights.* Toronto: University of Toronto Press, 1982.

Milne, David. *The Canadian Constitution.* Toronto: James Lorimer, 1991.

Monahan, Patrick J. *Meech Lake: The Inside Story.* Toronto: University of Toronto Press, 1991.

Romanow, Roy, John Whyte, and Howard Leeson. *Canada ... Notwithstanding: The Making of the Constitution 1976–1982.* Toronto: Carswell/Methuen, 1984.

Russell, Peter H. *Constitutional Odyssey: Can Canadians Become a Sovereign People?* 2nd ed. Toronto: University of Toronto Press, 1993.

Smiley, Donald, and Ronald L. Watts. *Intrastate Federalism in Canada.* Toronto: University of Toronto Press, 1985.

NOTES

1. Peter H. Russell, *Constitutional Odyssey: Can Canadians Become a Sovereign People?* 2nd ed. (Toronto: University of Toronto Press, 1993), 76. Reprinted with permission.
2. The labels "governments' constitution" and "citizens' constitution" are based on Alan Cairns, "Citizens (Outsiders) and Governments (Insiders) in Constitution Making: The Case of Meech Lake," *Canadian Public Policy* 16 (supp.) (1988).
3. Kenneth McRoberts, *Quebec: Social Change and Political Crisis,* 3rd ed. (Toronto: McClelland & Stewart, 1988), chapter 4.
4. Daniel Johnson, *Égalité ou Indépendance* (Montreal: Les Éditions de L'Homme Ltée, 1965).
5. This notion of pan-Canadian biculturalism, which is a version of two-nations thinking, should be distinguished from the policy of bilingualism and multiculturalism later adopted by the Trudeau government, which is based on a rejection of two-nations thinking.
6. Russell, *Constitutional Odyssey,* 178.
7. Ibid., chapter 5.
8. Ibid., 72. See also Donald V. Smiley, *Canada in Question: Federalism in the Eighties,* 3rd ed. (Toronto: McGraw-Hill Ryerson, 1980), 68–69.
9. Russell, *Constitutional Odyssey,* 74.
10. Ibid.
11. Garth Stevenson, *Unfulfilled Union: Canadian Federalism and National Unity,* rev. ed. (Toronto: Gage, 1982), 209.
12. See Ron Haggart and Aubrey E. Golden, *Rumors of War* (Toronto: New Press, 1971); and Denis Smith, *Bleeding Hearts—Bleeding Country: Canada and the Quebec Crisis* (Edmonton: Hurtig, 1971).

13. See Pierre Vallières, *Choose!*, trans. Penelope Williams (Toronto: New Press, 1971).
14. See Tom Flanagan, *Waiting for the Wave: The Reform Party and Preston Manning* (Toronto: Stoddart, 1995), chapter 3.
15. Russell, *Constitutional Odyssey*, 96–97.
16. For example, *Public Service Board v. Dionne*, [1978] 2 S.C.R. 191; *Canadian Industrial Gas and Oil Ltd. v. Saskatchewan*, [1978] 2 S.C.R. 545; *Central Canada Potash Co. Ltd. and Attorney General of Canada v. Saskatchewan*, [1979] 1 S.C.R. 42—cases 23, 24, and 25 in Peter H. Russell, Rainer Knopff, and F.L. Morton, *Federalism and the Charter: Leading Constitutional Decisions* (Ottawa: Carleton University Press, 1989).
17. Donald V. Smiley and Ronald L. Watts, *Intrastate Federalism in Canada* (Toronto: University of Toronto Press, 1985), 4.
18. Richard Simeon, *Federal Provincial Diplomacy: The Making of Recent Policy in Canada* (Toronto: University of Toronto Press, 1972).
19. R.D. Olling and M.W. Westmacott, *The Confederation Debate: The Constitution in Crisis* (Dubuque, Ia.: Kendall / Hunt, 1980), 146.
20. Pierre Elliott Trudeau, *Federalism and the French Canadians* (Toronto: Macmillan of Canada, 1968).
21. Rainer Knopff and F.L. Morton, "Nation-Building and the Canadian Charter of Rights and Freedoms," in Alan Cairns and Cynthia Williams, eds., *Constitutionalism, Citizenship, and Society in Canada* (Toronto: University of Toronto Press, 1985), 142–143.
22. Jennifer Smith, "Intrastate Federalism and Confederation," in Stephen Brooks, ed., *Political Thought in Canada: Contemporary Perspectives* (Toronto: Irwin, 1984), 273.
23. Peter H. Russell, "Political Purposes of the Canadian Charter of Rights and Freedoms," *The Canadian Bar Review* 61 (1983), 33.
24. See Rainer Knopff, "Language and Culture in the Canadian Debate: The Battle of the White Papers," *Canadian Review of Studies in Nationalism* 6 (1979); and chapter 5 in Rainer Knopff, *Human Rights and Social Technology: The New War on Discrimination* (Ottawa: Carleton University Press, 1989).
25. Stevenson, *Unfulfilled Union*, 207.
26. Smiley, *Canada in Question*, 76–77.
27. Pages 129–132 of the previous (1995) edition of this book contain a more detailed discussion of the various constitutional proposals during this period than is undertaken in this edition.
28. Smiley, *Canada in Question*, 81–82; Roy Romanow, John Whyte, and Howard Leeson, *Canada Notwithstanding: The Making of the Constitution 1976–1982* (Toronto: Carswell/Methuen, 1984), 7–8; and Garth Stevenson, *Unfulfilled Union*, 212.
29. Romanow et al., *Canada Notwithstanding*, 157.
30. *Reference Re Legislative Authority of Parliament to Alter or Replace the Senate*, [1980] 1 S.C.R. 54—case 61 in Russell, Knopff, and Morton, *Federalism and the Charter*.
31. Russell, *Constitutional Odyssey*, 109.
32. Romanow et al., *Canada Notwithstanding*, 60–61.
33. Ibid., xx.
34. Ibid.
35. Stevenson, *Unfulfilled Union*, 215.

36. *A.G. Manitoba et al. v. A.G. Canada et al.*, [1981] 1 S.C.R. 753.
37. Cairns, "Citizens (Outsiders) and Governments (Insiders) in Constitution Making," 123.
38. Stevenson, *Unfulfilled Union*, 217.
39. Here it should be remembered that the 1982 amending formula (section 41) also required unanimous provincial consent in matters relating to: "(a) the office of the Queen, the Governor General and the Lieutenant Governor of a province; (b) the right of a province to a number of members in the House of Commons not less than the number of Senators by which the province is entitled to be represented at the time this Part comes into force; (c) subject to section 43, the use of the English or the French language; (d) the composition of the Supreme Court of Canada; and (e) an amendment to this Part."
40. Romanow et al., *Canada Notwithstanding*, 210–211.
41. Ibid., 130–131.
42. Stevenson, *Unfulfilled Union*, 220.
43. Romanow et al., *Canada Notwithstanding*, 210–211.
44. *Re: Objection to a Resolution to Amend the Constitution (Quebec Veto Reference)*, [1982] 2 S.C.R. 793—case 63 in Russell, Knopff, and Morton, *Federalism and the Charter.*
45. Knopff and Morton, "Nation-Building and the Canadian Charter of Rights and Freedoms," 152. For further discussion, see Chapter 11.
46. Romanow et al., *Canada Notwithstanding*, 254–255.
47. Penny Kome, *The Taking of Twenty-Eight* (Toronto: Women's Press, 1983), 23.
48. It was also driven by the fact that Brian Mulroney had led the federal Conservative Party out of the political wilderness in Quebec, where Liberals had dominated for decades, by forging an alliance with Quebec nationalists.
49. Richard Simeon, "Meech Lake and Shifting Conceptions of Federalism," *Canadian Public Policy* 14 (supp.) (1988), 10.
50. Cairns, "Citizens (Outsiders) and Governments (Insiders) in Constitution Making," 122.
51. Ibid., 140–141.
52. Patrick J. Monahan, *Meech Lake: The Inside Story* (Toronto: University of Toronto Press, 1991), 144–145.
53. *Shaping Canada's Future Together* (Ottawa: Minister of Supply and Services Canada, 1991).
54. Russell, *Constitutional Odyssey*, 204.
55. Ibid., 226.
56. See Alan C. Cairns, "The Legacy of the Referendum: Who Are We Now?" *Constitutional Forum* 7, nos. 2 and 3 (Winter and Spring 1996).
57. Thomas Flanagan, "Amending the Canadian Constitution: A Mathematical Analysis," *Constitutional Forum* 7, nos. 2 and 3 (Winter and Spring 1996), 101.
58. Letter from Stéphane Dion to Lucien Bouchard, *Calgary Herald*, August 14, 1997.
59. Cairns, "The Legacy of the Referendum," 36.
60. Letter from Dion to Bouchard.
61. Jeffrey Simpson, "Beware Those Who Would Fan Constitutional 'Candle in the Window,'" *Globe and Mail*, June 23, 1998, A22.

FEDERALISM

4

Canada is in the most elemental way a federal country, and it seems that it is becoming increasingly so.[1]

Federalism is one of the principal foundations for the Canadian state, and is also one of its most pervasive features. It intrudes into most aspects of Canadian political life and shapes a broad array of public policies. Few aspects of public life are immune to the impact of federalism. This is not to say, however, that federalism is well understood either as a set of principles or as a set of institutions and political practices. In part this is because federalism is a dynamic aspect of Canadian politics rather than a fixed set of constitutional rules and institutional manifestations. Canada's federal features have changed dramatically over time, and not entirely in a consistent direction. It is important, therefore, to view federalism in evolutionary terms, to understand its foundational principles, and to realize how deeply embedded it is in contemporary debates about not only constitutional parameters but also the minutia of public policy. There is also an important normative element to federalism. Some Canadians see it reflecting their most fundamental values, while others see it as an irritant at best and at worst an obstacle to the realization of their aspirations. Federalism, therefore, both shapes the institutions through which public policies are contested and provides much of the grist for that contestation.

■ ■ ■

Readers might be excused for wondering why, after completing the first three chapters of this text, they are now confronted with a chapter on **federalism**. After all, discussions of federalism and federal institutions have been woven throughout the previous chapters, and for good reason. It is impossible to understand either the nature of the Canadian constitution or the dynamics of megaconstitutional politics over recent decades without having some rough understanding of federal principles and institutions. Federalism provides much of the grammatical structure and a good deal of the content for Canadian political discourse. Indeed, it is this very centrality of federalism that compels us to step back at this point and focus on federalism itself, to remove it for the moment both from the previous chapter's more detailed discussion of the constitution and from the more detailed discussion of parliamentary institutions to come.

In Chapter 2 we defined federalism as a system of divided sovereignty between two orders of government, each of which owes its powers to a constitution rather than to the other order of government, and neither of which is therefore subordinate to the other. There is, then, a formal, constitutional division of powers or legislative responsibilities. Each order of government has at least one field of jurisdiction in which it is supreme. For the national government, for instance, this could be defence, while for provincial governments it could be primary education. The constitutional division of powers takes the form of a written contract between the two orders of government. This contract cannot be altered unilaterally by either party, and disputes over its interpretation are referred to a neutral arbitrator, the Supreme Court of Canada. All of this, of course, gets somewhat murky when we move from the conceptual terrain to political realities. The spending power, for example, introduces a good deal of fluidity into the constitutional division of powers, and opinions differ as to the Supreme Court's neutrality when that court is asked to adjudicate disputes over the division of powers. (An arbitrator appointed by only one side in a dispute is always open to charges of bias.) Nonetheless, the principles are important, no matter how contested they might be or how imperfect might be their application.

Political scientists commonly treat federalism as the middle term of a tripartite classification, the two poles being **confederalism** and the **unitary state**. According to this usage, Canada, which officially bills itself as a confederation, is misnamed; it is actually a federation. A true confederation in the modern sense is a league of fully sovereign states that join together only for limited purposes, such as foreign policy, defence, and a common currency. These shared matters are administered by a central authority, but this authority does not govern individuals directly; its "citizens" are the component states or polities, who retain full sovereignty over their individual citizens. As a constituent unit of the confederation, each polity, regardless of its size or population, has an equal voice in the councils of the central authority. Having given life to the central authority, moreover, the component polities may also withdraw from or disband it. For this reason, changes in the constitution of the confederation would in strict logic require the consent of all its constituent members. In sum, the central authority depends for its effectiveness—nay its very existence—on the states that created and sustain it.

A unitary state, the other pole of the classification, is the mirror image of a confederation. Although there is usually some degree of decentralization or devolution of governmental authority in a unitary state—to municipal or regional governments, for example—sovereignty is lodged at the centre. Local and regional governments are the creations of, and can be reorganized or disbanded by, the central government in a unitary state. In a confederation, the central government is a creature of the constituent governments; in a unitary state, this relationship is reversed.

While both confederal systems and unitary states have a single locus of sovereignty, either at the centre or in the units, federalism is a system of **divided**

sovereignty. Each order of government governs the same individual citizens, but for different purposes within defined areas of jurisdiction. Yet divided sovereignty and its constitutional expression in the division of powers, though absolutely central to the definition of federal systems of government, are far from the end of the story. Federal systems of government also provide for the representation of sub-national communities within the institutions of the national government. Thus, for example, we find American states, Australian states, and Canadian provinces represented within their respective senates. As the previous chapter illustrates, much of the constitutional contestation in Canada entails disputes over how well such forms of representation work. Modern federalism, moreover, encompasses a vast network of intergovernmental relations and institutions through which the national, provincial, and territorial governments exchange influence and manage complex interdependencies.

In addition, federalism entails a respect for diversity and a spirit of accommodation. Federal institutions, it is assumed, rest on the foundations of a federal society, although, as Alan Cairns has noted, they may shape that society as much as be shaped by it.[2] Federal states are necessarily more diverse than unitary states, if only because governments exist to protect, nourish, and even promote diversity. At the same time, however, respect for diversity is only one face of the federal coin. The other is the promotion of unity in the face of diversity. As the Americans have put it, *e pluribus unum*: from the many, one. Federal systems of government are designed to protect diversity while promoting unity. The resulting tension is an intrinsic feature of federal states, one that is managed but never resolved. As we will see shortly, the Canadian state has swung from one priority to the other, just as different groups within Canada have championed one rather than the other. The point to stress is that stable forms of federal government must both protect, diversity, and promote unity, and must always strive to maintain the delicate balance between the two.

Contemporary federalism is a complex form of governance. It may also strike some as an inevitable form of government for Canada; what else, you might ask, could possibly bridge our regional and linguistic diversities? In 1867, however, it was not at all clear that Canada was, or should be, a federal system in this modern sense. Although we take federalism for granted today, it was a hotly contested issue both at Confederation and for some time thereafter.

THE ESTABLISHMENT OF FEDERALISM

It may be difficult for us to imagine Canada as having anything other than a system of divided sovereignty, but in 1867 federalism was still a new and rather ill-understood American invention. The U.S. Constitution of 1789 had established the world's first federal constitution and, from the perspective of many Canadians in the late 1860s, that constitution had come to grief in the recent American Civil War largely because of its division of sovereignty. This American invention, in short, was viewed with considerable suspicion north of the border. Thus, the 1867 Canadian constitution embodied the logic of federalism only hesitantly and ambiguously. Indeed, as we have seen, on a literal reading of all of its provisions, the constitution of 1867 could at most be characterized as quasi-federal. Opposing principles and logics were embedded in the constitution by the constitutional politics of Confederation itself; subsequently they generated a politics of interpretation, animated by conflicting visions of community, about which logic would prevail. The establishment of Canadian federalism, in other words, involved not only Confederation itself but the subsequent success of a powerful "provincial rights" movement. We shall examine each in turn.[3]

Confederation

Confederation was a response to the sectional deadlock experienced by Canadians under the 1840 Act of Union. Lord Durham, who recommended the union in his famous 1839 report to the British government, hoped that it would encourage the assimilation of the French population (see Dossier 2.6). However, Durham's plan was never implemented in the thoroughly assimilationist manner he proposed. While the formerly separate colonies of Lower Canada and Upper Canada were formally unified, as Durham had recommended, they continued to some extent as legal political entities—**Canada East** and **Canada West**—within the new union. This separation was reflected most prominently in an equal division of legislative seats between the two sections, despite the fact that Canada West's population (450,000) was then considerably smaller than Canada East's (650,000).[4] Also, the different legal, educational, religious, linguistic, and land-tenure systems of the two sections were largely untouched by the Act of Union.[5] As a result, "[t]here was a strong desire that laws affecting but one region be passed only with the concurrence of a majority of representatives from that region, and that laws having common interest be passed only with a majority from each region."[6] This became known as the **double majority principle**. Not surprisingly, this political environment generated the practice of a bifurcated prime ministership, with the position being shared by representatives—English and French—of both sections. Legalized sectionalism and double majorities in the legislative assembly were far from what Durham had envisioned and did little to promote his goal of assimilation.

The double majority rule tended to produce political deadlock when it was respected and political acrimony when a majority from one section was used to enact or prevent legislation of concern primarily to the other section. In 1863, for example, a separate school bill of concern only to Canada West—and not supported by a majority of representatives from that section—was passed with the support of a majority from Canada East.[7] Such actions were particularly galling to Canada West, because, as Durham had predicted, its population had grown more quickly than, and now surpassed that of, Canada East. Having promoted the equal allocation of legislative seats at the outset, when it was smaller, Canada West now shifted ground and began a campaign for representation by population (**rep by pop**), a campaign that would be successfully resisted by Canada East as long as the government to be elected on the basis of that principle would decide all matters of public policy, including those of cultural significance to the French community. The unanticipated consequence of the Act of Union, in short, was political deadlock and deterioration in the quality of public life.

The need to break the political deadlock under the Act of Union became one of the causes of Confederation. By 1864 the sense of crisis had become sufficient to induce John A. Macdonald and George-Étienne Cartier to join their bitter political enemy George Brown in proposing the establishment of two orders of government. Underlying this idea "was a recognition that if English Canadians and French Canadians were to continue to share a single state, the English majority could control the general or common government so long as the French were a majority in a province with exclusive jurisdiction over those matters essential to their distinct culture."[8] In other words, rep by pop could prevail for a common government limited to matters of common concern, with matters uniquely relevant to either linguistic-cultural community being reserved to another, more local, government *within which* rep by pop could also prevail. The resulting division of powers between the central and provincial governments in sections 91–95 of the BNA Act laid the foundation for a

FIGURE 4.1 **MAP OF UNION CANADA**

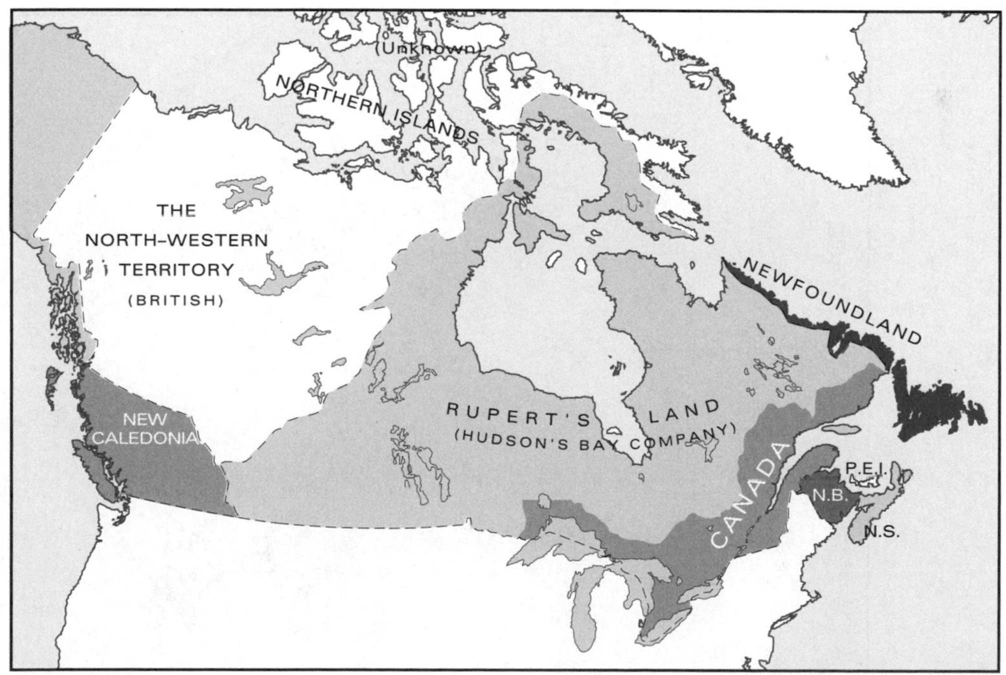

federal interpretation of the constitution. Once again, as in the 1791 Quebec Act, which created separate colonies in Upper and Lower Canada, a policy of disengagement (this time a more partial disengagement) followed on the heels of a project of assimilation.

Although the cultural division that had plagued pre-Confederation politics in the Canadas was a crucial stimulus to the federal division of powers in the new constitution, it was certainly not the only one. Concluding that their project should extend beyond the confines of the existing Canada to embrace a wider British North American confederation, the Canadians arranged to present their proposal to the Maritime colonies at a September 1864 conference the latter were holding in Charlottetown to discuss Maritime union. The Canadians persuaded their Maritime colleagues of the merits of a wider union, and the delegates agreed to meet again the following month in Quebec City to hammer out the details. Two of the Maritime colonies—Nova Scotia and New Brunswick—agreed to join the new Confederation, but, unwilling to submerge their local identities completely, they supported some jurisdictional division between two orders of government. The 72 resolutions drafted by the Quebec conference were then taken to London, where they were refined and enacted into law as the BNA Act, 1867. Ironically, Prince Edward Island, which had hosted the original conference, did not join the new country until 1873.

FIGURE 4.2 **CANADA IN 1871**

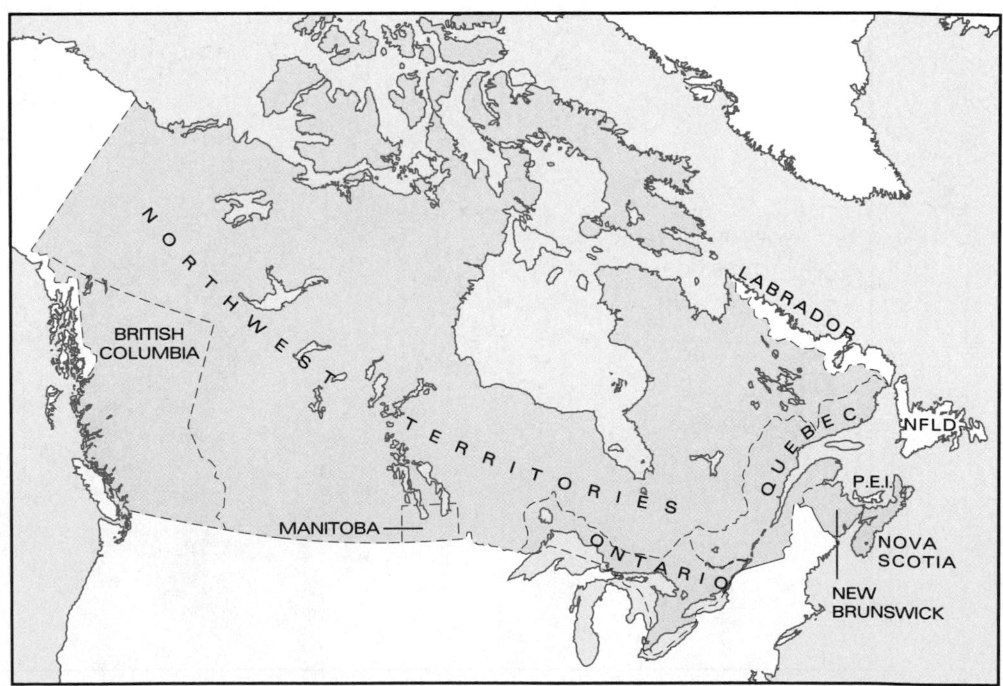

DOSSIER 4.1 THE ADDITION OF PROVINCES AND TERRITORIES, 1870–1949

1. 1870: Admission of Rupert's Land and the North-Western Territory by British order-in-council, effective July 15, pursuant to Constitution Act section 146; and by the 1868 Rupert's Land Act by which the Hudson's Bay Company surrendered those lands to the Crown in anticipation of their transfer to Canada. The Canadian Parliament's 1869 North-West Territories Act provided for the renaming of these lands, upon their admission, as the "North-West Territories."

2. 1870: Formation of the Province of Manitoba from the North-West Territories by the Manitoba Act passed in May. Pursuant to section 1 of the Act, Manitoba was formed on July 15, the date on which Rupert's Land and the North-Western Territory were transferred to Canada. The 1871 Constitution Act amendment confirmed Canada's right to establish provinces from territories admitted to the Dominion and provided also that, once enacted, such statutes could not be amended by Parliament.

3. 1871: Admission of British Columbia by British order-in-council, effective July 20, pursuant to Constitution Act section 146.

4. 1873: Admission of Prince Edward Island by British order-in-council, effective July 1, pursuant to Constitution Act section 146. Except for Newfoundland (including Labrador) and the Arctic islands, Canada had reached its present boundaries.

5. 1880: Admission of "all British Territories and Possessions in North America, and the Islands adjacent to such Territories and Possessions which are not already included in the Dominion of Canada ... (with the exception of the Colony of Newfoundland and its dependencies)," by British order-in-council, effective September 1. The most notable addition was the Arctic islands.

6. 1898: Formation of the Yukon Territory from the North-West Territories by the Yukon Territory Act, June 13.

7. 1905: Formation of the Province of Alberta from the North-West Territories by the Alberta Act, effective September 1, pursuant to the 1871 Constitution Act amendment.

8. 1905: Formation of the Province of Saskatchewan from the North-West Territories by the Saskatchewan Act, effective September 1, pursuant to the 1871 Constitution Act amendment.

9. 1949: Admission of Newfoundland by amendment to the Constitution Act (Nov. 1, 1949), effective March 31. This amendment confirmed the Terms of Union of Newfoundland with Canada Act which was given royal assent on February 18, 1949. Newfoundland was not admitted by British order-in-council, pursuant to Constitution Act section 146, because that section required the approval of a Newfoundland assembly. [In fact] Newfoundland lost its assembly in 1934 and this made section 146 inapplicable.

Source: Reprinted from Bayard Reesor, *The Canadian Constitution in Historical Perspective* (Scarborough: Prentice Hall Canada, 1992), 51–52.

The BNA Act's division of powers between the two orders of government, discussed in detail in Chapter 2, reflected the original Canadian concern to give the most culturally relevant jurisdictions to the provinces and reserve general matters for the central government. Thus, education, a matter of obvious cultural concern, fell within provincial jurisdiction. Similarly, the provincial "property and civil rights" power was intended in part to protect Quebec's civil code from federal interference.[9] A number of social welfare matters, including hospitals, were also assigned to the provinces. The central government, on the other hand, was given most of the important economic powers (which were at the time considered culturally neutral), including "trade and commerce," banking, transportation, and unlimited taxing authority. George Brown expressed the intention behind this division of powers:

> *It sweeps away the boundary line between the provinces so far as regards matters common to the whole people ... and the members of the Federal Legislature will meet at last as citizens of a common country. The questions that used to excite the most hostile feelings among us have been taken away from the General Legislature, and placed under the control of the local bodies. No man need hereafter be debarred from success in public life because his views, however popular in his own section, are unpopular in the other—for he will not have to deal with sectional questions, and the temptation to the government of the day to make capital out of local prejudices will be greatly lessened, if not altogether at an end.*[10]

Brown was exaggerating the extent to which there had been or indeed could be a clean division between culturally relevant matters and culturally neutral matters, with each assigned to its appropriate order of government. Canada's French and English populations do not divide neatly along provincial boundaries. Then as now, important minorities from each community—the English in Quebec, the French in Ontario—lived in provinces dominated by the other. To protect these minorities from the tyranny of cultural majorities, the BNA Act gave Ottawa some authority to interfere in culturally relevant provincial matters. In addition to the blanket powers of reservation and disallowance, the most obvious power of this sort is Ottawa's ability under section 93 to enact "remedial legislation" to protect the educational rights of existing denominational schools. The powers of disallowance and remedial legislation made it almost inevitable that the culturally divisive politics of education would re-emerge on the agenda of pan-Canadian politics. The Manitoba Schools crisis of the 1890s is only one (though the best-known) example.[11]

Although the Confederation settlement exhibited important features of federalism, the emergence of a fully federal constitution remained in doubt for some time. On one hand, the 1867 constitution established the provinces and gave them areas of "exclusive" jurisdiction. Without this, Quebec would never have agreed. Nor would the Maritime colonies have considered dissolving themselves in a fully unitary state. On the other hand, the constitution contained provisions reflecting the views of such influential founders as John A. Macdonald, who did not believe the provinces amounted to much. Macdonald saw the new constitution as an instrument for building a great new nation on the northern half of the continent, extending from coast to coast and expressing itself primarily through its national government. The provinces were a necessary concession to existing local sentiment, but to Macdonald their powers were relatively unimportant in the larger scheme of things. Ottawa had been given all of the powers important to building a vibrant modern state, especially the economic powers and the residual power. As the constitutional project in "community transformation" implicit in these powers took hold, moreover, Macdonald was convinced that the provinces would fade even further into insignificance. From Macdonald's perspective, in short, the principle of divided sovereignty was, at best and appropriately, weakly represented in the 1867 constitution. Indeed, divided sovereignty was arguably not represented at all. Such centralizing devices as reservation and disallowance, as noted in Chapter 2, implied that the provinces were not sovereign even in the spheres of apparently "exclusive" jurisdiction allocated to them by the constitutional division of powers. And yet, despite these indications of centralism, it is difficult to ignore completely the commonsense meaning of the constitutional grant of "exclusive" jurisdiction to the provinces. In other words, the 1867 constitution was at odds with itself in the matter of federalism, providing constitutional resources for the proponents of both unitary centralism and divided sovereignty. How this tension would resolve itself—whether Macdonald or his opponents would carry the day—is a question that would take some time to answer.

Divided sovereignty was ambiguously expressed in the 1867 Constitution Act in part because most Canadians of the later 19th century, whether they were centralist or decentralist in orientation, were highly sceptical about its very possibility. The notion of federalism as an independent principle of government occupying a stable position between confederalism and the unitary state was still relatively new and unproven at the time of Confederation. The term "federalism" itself was certainly a very old one, but it had been put to radically new purposes by the Americans in 1789. Prior to that time, "federalism" was a synonym for "confederalism." The two terms were then used to describe the same thing, much as we now use "inflammable" and "flammable" interchangeably. "Nothing more was involved than the accidental presence or absence of a nonsignifying prefix."[12] And the common regime they labelled was what we now call confederal—that is, a league of fully sovereign states that establish a central authority with no sovereignty of its own. Indeed, this meaning is evident in the etymological origins of the word "federalism," which comes from the Latin *foeder* or *foedus,* meaning "covenant," and is related to *fides,* meaning "faith." Dictionaries in use at the time of the American founding defined federal as "relating to a league or contract."[13] Even the second edition of the *Oxford English Dictionary,* published in 1991, defines "federal" as "pertaining to a convenant, contract, or treaty," and treats "federal" and "confederal" as synonyms. This *OED* definition does not correspond to modern political science usage, but it perfectly captures the pre-1789 understanding. Up to that time, there existed only the two-fold classification of unitary and federal / confederal states.

DOSSIER 4.2 DID THE 1867 PROJECT OF COMMUNITY TRANSFORMATION SUCCEED?

Confederation ... was more than a response to and accommodation of ethnic linguistic duality, or of the colonial diversities in Atlantic Canada. In the same way as the Act of Union of 1840, it had major community-building tasks on its agenda ... There were no Canadians in 1867, partly because, while the colonists were linked to a common British imperial authority, they had been politically shaped in separate colonies, with the partial exception of course of the Act of Union experience of the future citizens of Quebec and Ontario....

Canadians, accordingly, were a project for the future, not an inheritance from the past. They were to emerge as a result of the dominion government's successful performance of its responsibilities, including the essential nation-building tasks of territorial expansion, infrastructure development, and economic growth. From this perspective, the act of 1867 was a mobilizing instrument designed to create a new people whose historically based provincial identifications, derived from separate colonial pasts, were to be supplemented by developing identification with the new central government and the new Canadian community it was fostering. John A. Macdonald, as is well known, was confident that the provinces would become progressively insignificant in the not-too-distant future.

This, however, was not to be, for the BNA Act, 1867, as John Whyte recently reminded us, "contained an equally powerful idea, that of the federal division of legislative powers, which did match the diverse nature of Canada's communities." Macdonald's vision, he notes, "did not ... take. One can only assume that it did not match the economic social and political reality." The failure to "take," of course, was relative. The country survived. Canadians were created, and the result 120 years later is one of the oldest continuing political systems in the world. So this experiment in fashioning a community worked, albeit perhaps not as fully as some had hoped.

Source: Reprinted from Alan C. Cairns, *Charter versus Federalism: The Dilemma of Constitutional Reform* (Montreal and Kingston: McGill–Queen's University Press, 1992), 35–36.

This older view remained the dominant one among Canada's founding generation. True, Canadians were aware of the American experiment in divided sovereignty, but they tended to view this experiment as a dismal failure. Understandably, the recent American Civil War led them to the conclusion that federalism was not a new principle of government with its own inherent stability but an unstable compound of opposing principles that would inevitably foster civil strife. The American experience confirmed many Canadians in their belief that the British legal theorist Sir William Blackstone had been right about sovereignty. According to Blackstone, sovereignty was indivisible, and it was futile or even dangerous to try to divide it.[14] Its location may have migrated over time from the person of the monarch to the collective body of Parliament, but by definition it could not be split between different legislatures. Thus, only unitary states or what we now call confederations were logically possible. "It is a solecism in politics for two coordinate sovereignties to exist together," wrote an American exponent of this view. Any attempt to divide sovereignty would be unstable and over time would tend toward one pole or the other, "subjecting the country in the meantime to 'all the horrors of a divided sovereignty.'"[15]

It was the **Blackstonian theory of sovereignty** that inspired centralists like Macdonald to opt for a more centralized system, with sovereignty securely lodged at the centre. This theory accounts for the presence of such powers as reservation and disallowance in the BNA Act and for the emphasis centralists placed on them in subsequent interpretive battles. Similarly, it accounts for Macdonald's desire to read the division of powers as establishing provinces with little more status than municipalities, subject to the ultimate authority of a superior level of government. In terms of sovereignty, the provinces' relationship to the central government was to parallel Canada's colonial relationship with the British Parliament.

The Blackstonian theory of indivisible sovereignty was not limited to centralists like Macdonald; it was also influential among some Canadian decentralists. Just as **Blackstonian centralists** were logically driven in the direction of a unitary state with sovereignty at the centre, so **Blackstonian decentralists** were driven to support the only other available alternative: a true confederation with sovereignty lodged in the units. Not surprisingly, such confederalists understood the Confederation agreement much as Macdonald did and opposed it for the same reasons that led him to support it. Antoine-Aimé Dorion and Jean-Baptiste-Éric Dorion, for example, two of the most important Quebec critics of Confederation, clearly believed that only the traditional twofold classification between unitary and confederal states was possible, and that the proposed Canadian "Confederation" was thus misnamed. They agreed with Macdonald that the provinces would be little more than municipalities, and that Canada would, for all intents and purposes, become a unitary state. Unlike Macdonald, however, they intensely disliked the idea of a unitary state and would have preferred a true confederation, with the inevitably indivisible locus of sovereignty placed in the component units, not at the centre.[16] This line of confederalist thought has re-emerged occasionally since Confederation, especially in more radical versions of the so-called **compact theory** (see Dossier 4.3) and in Quebec's contemporary demands for some kind of "sovereignty-association" with the rest of Canada.

The founding debate, however, was more than a simple confrontation between such avowed partisans of unitary states as Macdonald and such supporters of the confederal principle as the Dorions. Among Macdonald's allies in supporting the Confederation settlement were the Reformers from Upper Canada, led by George Brown. Although members of this group, like most of the Canadian founding generation, also adhered to the Blackstonian theory of indivisible sovereignty,[17] they were uncomfortable with its practical implications. Like Macdonald, they acknowledged both the instability of confederations and the advantages of a much stronger central government than the confederal principle allowed. Yet, unlike Macdonald, they were not prepared to embrace the unitary state as their preferred principle. Like the Dorions, the Reformers were friends of decentralization, but, unlike the Dorions,

DOSSIER 4.3 THE COMPACT THEORY

The compact theory emerged not long after Confederation as an answer to the question of how to amend the BNA Act. Remember that the act could formally be amended only by the British Parliament, though by convention Britain would not do so except at the request and with the consent of Canada. The crucial question thus became how and by whom the required Canadian input would be manifested. The answer to this question would indicate the true locus of sovereignty in Canada.

Although the compact theorists conceded the legitimacy of Ottawa directly governing the individual citizens of the whole country within its constitutionally specified areas of jurisdiction, they insisted that the provinces were the ultimate sources of sovereignty when it came to formally changing the constitution. According to the theory, the country and its political institutions originated in an agreement or "compact" of the confederating provinces, and thus could be changed only by them. In its strongest form, the theory held that the federal government was entirely irrelevant to the amendment process, that the provincial "creators" of Confederation could initiate and consummate any changes they liked, including changes to the powers of the federal government. Ottawa, having been created by the provinces, was subject entirely to the collective will of its creators. Thus, when Oliver Mowat and Honoré Mercier, the premiers of Ontario and Quebec, respectively, convened an interprovincial meeting in 1887 to amend the BNA Act, they did not think it necessary to invite the federal government, even though their proposed amendments, including repeal of the disallowance power, would have diminished Ottawa's power. In this strong sense, the compact theory was clearly based on a confederalist logic.

In a somewhat weaker sense, one more compatible with the federal logic of divided sovereignty, the compact theory was used not to exclude the federal government from the amending process but to protect provincial involvement in the process—to ensure, in other words, that Ottawa could not secure amendments unilaterally without provincial consent. In strict logic, the theory probably required unanimous provincial consent to major constitutional amendments; occasionally its adherents were prepared to contemplate something less than this, but certainly never less than a substantial majority of the provinces.

The view that Canada is based on a compact of all the provinces may be called the "equal provinces" version of the compact theory. The other version, known as the two-nations theory, holds that Canada was a compact between the two founding nations, English and French. To the extent that the French nation is identified with the province of Quebec, the two-nations version of the compact theory implies special status for Quebec, certainly with respect to the amending process and probably in other respects as well.

From a strictly legal perspective, the compact theory is easily criticized. How, for example, can the federal government be seen as emerging out of a compact among confederating provinces when some of the provinces that allegedly negotiated the Confederation agreement (Ontario and Quebec) did not legally exist to conduct such negotiations but were the product of them? When other provinces (British Columbia and Prince Edward Island), far from joining Canada through negotiations with other sovereign provinces, did so through negotiations with the federal government? And when still other provinces (Alberta and Saskatchewan) were created by federal legislation? Political life is not governed by strict legal logic, however, and the moral claims that Canada is fundamentally either a community of equal provinces or a community of two equal nations remain vibrant.

Sources: Robert C. Vipond, "Whatever Became of the Compact Theory? Meech Lake and the New Politics of Constitutional Amendment in Canada," *Queen's Quarterly* 96, no. 4 (1989); and Patrick Monahan, *Politics and the Constitution: The Charter, Federalism, and the Supreme Court of Canada* (Toronto: Methuen, 1987), 181.

they could not bring themselves to accept the confederal principle.[18] After Confederation, the Reformers formed the core of an increasingly influential **provincial rights movement** that eventually embraced the idea of divided sovereignty and fought to entrench it in the Canadian political psyche.

Thus the principled debate over the nature of the Canadian state was more complex than the dichotomy between Macdonald centralists and Quebec decentralists might suggest. Federalism was not simply a pragmatic compromise between the polar applications of Blackstonian thought. It came to be defended, and defended successfully, as a stable principle of government in its own right.

The Provincial Rights Movement

In order to give unambiguous support to the modern federal theory of divided sovereignty, the provincial rights movement had to resolve the theoretical difficulty posed by the traditional Blackstonian theory of divided sovereignty. The provincial autonomists gradually groped their way to the same kind of resolution discovered by their American predecessors, who had also been followers of Blackstone. The solution lay in the separation of sovereignty from legislative authority, which was accomplished in the American case by lodging sovereignty with the people. This ultimate sovereign power remained undivided, but since it governed indirectly through delegations to governments there was no reason it could not be delegated to more than one order of government. Hence divided sovereignty in the secondary sense of legislative power became a logical possibility. The Canadian solution was similar in form to the American solution but different in substance. Not being as democratic, the Canadian partisans of federalism chose instead to lodge sovereignty in the imperial British Parliament, which, like the American people for American federalists, was an indirect sovereign for Canada because it did not directly exercise domestic legislative power here. This was a convenient, even comfortable, position for the times, given that full and formal Canadian independence from British rule was not on the table and would not be until after the end of the First World War. Thus, again, ultimate sovereignty remained undivided in the British Parliament, but secondary sovereignty was delegated to two orders of government in Canada.[19] The will of the ultimate sovereign in both cases, moreover, was expressed in a written constitution dividing jurisdictional responsibilities between two equal orders of government. Neither order owed its existence to the other; both were creatures of the constitution.

Having arrived at this theory of federalism, the provincial rights movement engaged in a vigorous politics of interpretation, both in and out of the courtroom, to establish it as the dominant reading of the Constitution Act, 1867. The autonomists' project had three main dimensions. First, they had somehow to overcome Macdonald's view that the relationship between Ottawa and the provinces was like that between Canada and Britain, one of imperial–colonial subordination; that is, they had to overcome the constitutional logic inherent in the powers of reservation and disallowance. Second, they had to establish that provincial jurisdiction was truly "exclusive," that the federal government did not have "concurrent" jurisdiction to enact "paramount" legislation in the same areas; that is, they had to establish a jurisdictional division of **watertight compartments**. Third, they had to ensure that the watertight compartments of provincial jurisdiction were ample enough to create a reasonable balance of power between the two orders of government; that is, they had to establish the norm of **balanced federalism**.

Reservation and Disallowance

Overcoming Macdonald's view that the provinces were like colonies of an imperial Ottawa might not seem an easy thing to do, given the powers of reservation and disallowance, which clearly imply such domestic imperialism. Yet the autonomists could point to the language of exclusive provincial jurisdiction in sections 91 and 92 of the BNA Act. Here again we find competing interests that express divergent visions of community and rely on competing principles embodied in an ambiguous set of institutional rules. In this case the autonomists eventually won their interpretive battle.

The provincial autonomists succeeded in part because they were able to exploit a contradiction in the position of the Macdonald centralists. While the centralists were certainly prepared to employ the imperial–colonial thesis to justify the subordination of the provinces, they never fully accepted the implications of the same thesis for Canada's relationship with Britain. It was widely understood virtually from the beginning that Britain would not interfere in Canadian domestic affairs even though the formalities of the imperial relationship would continue, and the powers of reservation and disallowance at that level soon withered. This enabled the proponents of divided sovereignty within Canada to turn the imperial analogy against those Canadian centralists who justified their position by reference to the powers of reservation and disallowance. The provincial autonomists argued that despite the legal veneer, Canada had acquired de facto sovereignty over at least its domestic affairs, and by analogy the provinces should be similarly sovereign within their spheres of jurisdiction. From this perspective, the language of exclusive jurisdictional powers in sections 91 and 92 expressed the true spirit of the constitution, and the powers of reservation and disallowance were constitutional impurities that deserved to fall into the same desuetude as Westminster's analogous powers. The autonomists succeeded in impugning the legitimacy of reservation and disallowance within Canada partly by showing how the centralists were violating the logical implications of their own principles.[20] The powers of reservation and disallowance continued to be exercised for some time, particularly in the western part of the country, where the imperial predisposition on the part of the central government was harder to dislodge, but with their most powerful justification having been destroyed by the provincial autonomists, they ultimately withered away.

Watertight Compartments

In addition to undermining the legitimacy of such imperialistic powers as reservation and disallowance, the autonomists could succeed in establishing the principle of divided sovereignty only if the formal division of powers was read as a set of "watertight compartments." The alternative was to read the powers listed in sections 91 and 92 as substantially overlapping categories, with both orders of government enjoying "concurrent" jurisdiction within the areas of overlap. As an extreme example, the federal power over "marriage and divorce" (s. 91[26]) and the provincial power over the "solemnization of marriage" (s. 92[12]) overlap completely, the latter being a subset of the former. Similarly, if read literally, the federal "trade and commerce" power and the provincial "property and civil rights" power overlap substantially; almost any federal law regulating trade and commerce will affect property and civil rights in the provinces, and the reverse will often be the case too. In fact, this problem of jurisdictional overlap was (and remains) characteristic of much of the federal distribution of powers. On a literal reading, in short, the division of powers would give both governments "concurrent" authority to enact very similar legislation. When two pieces of concurrent legislation conflicted, however, the rule was that federal legislation was "paramount."

The combination of extensive concurrency and the rule of federal paramountcy meant that, for practical purposes, "exclusive" areas of provincial jurisdiction did not exist; provinces would be free to act under the authority of section 92 only to the extent that the federal government did not enact conflicting legislation. Early Supreme Court of Canada decisions gave just such a centralist reading to the division of powers.[21] Not surprisingly, the provincial autonomists strongly opposed this reading. In their view, the BNA Act had explicitly set out only two areas of concurrent jurisdiction—immigration and agriculture (s. 95)—and had thus implicitly rejected concurrency elsewhere. Moreover, if the statement in section 92 that the provincial powers listed there were "exclusive" was to mean anything, practical concurrency between those powers and Ottawa's section 91 powers could not be tolerated. Only if sections 91 and 92 were read as establishing "watertight" jurisdictional compartments, argued the autonomists, would divided sovereignty be a reality.[22]

In these interpretive wars, the provincial autonomists sought—and gained—the support of the judiciary. Although the Canadian Supreme Court in some early decisions read the BNA Act much as Macdonald would have done,[23] the Judicial Committee of the Privy Council (the Supreme Court's superior until 1949) soon overruled the Canadian court and supported the provincial rights reading of the division of powers. Thus, in the 1881 case of *Citizens Insurance Co. v. Parsons*, the JCPC gave its official imprimatur to the autonomists' watertight-compartments reading of the division of powers.[24] Parsons raised the question of whether an Ontario law regulating the terms of insurance contracts could be sustained as provincial legislation under the provincial power over "property and civil rights" or whether it came within the scope of the federal power over "trade and commerce." Here was a clear example of a law that could plausibly be understood as falling under either of two heads of overlapping power. The JCPC concluded that such overlap was intolerable. Using the subject of marriage as an analogy, Their Lordships argued that it was impossible to believe that the federal power over "marriage and divorce" allowed Ottawa to legislate on all aspects of that subject when section 92 gave the provinces the exclusive power to enact laws on the solemnization of marriage. If Ottawa could act in the area of literal overlap, with the assurance that its legislation would be paramount, the provincial power over "solemnization" would not be "exclusive," as advertised, but subject to federal whim. Thus, the literal meaning of these two provisions must be modified in light of each other to negate the overlap and establish the watertight compartments essential to divided sovereignty. In particular, the broader "marriage and divorce" power must be read as excluding matters of "solemnization." Similar **mutual modification** must occur in other cases of apparent overlap, such as that between "trade and commerce" and "property and civil rights." This attempt to carve watertight compartments out of the general and overlapping language of the division of powers, which was characteristic of early JCPC federalism jurisprudence (though it was not maintained consistently in every case), helped to consolidate the federal theory of divided sovereignty.

Balanced Federalism

The early provincial rights movement not only established the federal principle of divided sovereignty in Canada but also ensured that the provinces enjoyed a substantial jurisdictional sphere within which to exercise their sovereignty. The challenge posed to Macdonald-style centralism by modern federalism would not have amounted to much if it had secured the provinces against federal interference only in a restricted jurisdictional sphere. Such an outcome might have qualified as federalism in an abstract legal sense, but it would have been a highly centralized federalism, with most of the important power lodged at the centre. Even without such imperialistic glosses as the power of disallowance, this would have been the kind of "divided sovereignty" even Macdonald might have found congenial. The autonomists could win no more than a hollow victory if they succeeded only in establishing the principle of divided sovereignty. To complete their project, they also had to ensure that the division of sovereignty was relatively balanced. Thus, while the strategy of the autonomists "was on the one hand to render the sphere of provincial jurisdiction resistant to federal encroachments, it was, on the other, to make this exclusive sphere of jurisdiction as capacious as the words of the constitution would allow."[25] The autonomists could achieve this goal only by persuading the courts to adopt their reading of the division of powers.

Once again, *Citizens Insurance Co. v. Parsons* set the tone. Not only did that case follow the lead of the autonomists in reading the division of powers as a set of watertight compartments, but it drew the boundaries between those compartments in a way that favoured provincial power. In effect, it read the federal "trade and commerce" power as if it had said "international and interprovincial trade and commerce," so that all purely intraprovincial trade and commerce became a matter of "property and civil rights." Thus, the provincial regulation of insurance contracts at issue in the case was found to be exclusively within provincial jurisdiction. *Parsons* was only an early example of a pronounced judicial trend. Between 1880 and 1896 the JCPC decided 15 of 18 division-of-powers cases "in favour of the provinces."[26] In doing so, moreover, it "reversed 'every major centralist doctrine of the [Supreme] Court.'"[27] Altogether, the JCPC's early jurisprudence helped to legitimate not only the theory of divided sovereignty but also the view that the substantive powers enjoyed by the two sovereignties were relatively balanced. Macdonald's view that the federal government was a "senior" government and the provinces akin to "junior" municipalities, had been decisively rejected in the authoritative interpretation of the division of powers as well as in the successful attacks on the powers of reservation and disallowance. This interpretation of the division of powers was another way in which Canada was transformed into "a thoroughly federal country" by the turn of the century. That transformation, however, should be seen as a balancing act in itself, for the provincial autonomists did not enjoy an uncontested field.

CENTRALIST CHALLENGES

The kind of federalism established by the early provincial rights movement and blessed by the JCPC—a federalism in which the provinces are at least equal to the federal government in both legal sovereignty and substantive jurisdictional power—did not go unchallenged over the course of Canadian history. In particular, significant centralizing challenges were prompted by each of the world wars and by the economic crisis of the Great Depression during the 1930s.

World War I

At the outbreak of World War I, in 1914, the federal Parliament quickly enacted the War Measures Act. This act gave the federal cabinet wide-ranging "emergency" powers, which the government used aggressively, even in areas normally within provincial jurisdiction. In Donald Smiley's words, the act allowed the establishment of a "'constitutional dictatorship,' with the federal cabinet assuming many of the most important functions of Parliament and overriding the normal legislative jurisdiction of the provinces."[28] Federalism as the division of sovereignty into watertight compartments had come to a quick and complete (though temporary) end, placed in a state of suspended animation by the war.

The suspension of federalism coincided with the nation-building experience of World War I. Although Canada entered the war automatically as a British colony, there is no question that the war helped forge the sense of national identity on which full Canadian independence would be built. The impact of the war on Canada was massive. Canadian casualties were greater in absolute terms, not just relative terms, than American casualties, and even the most casual perusal of war memorials in cities and towns across Canada illustrates the devastating extent of the impact. Even the 1917 conscription crisis, which opened a major fissure between the English and French communities in Canada, was nation building in the sense that it domesticated the wartime experience, giving it added political dimensions unique to Canada. From the perspective of our current discussion, the point to stress is that the emergence of nationalism coincided with the ascent, even if brief, of an assertive federal government.

While the impact of the war on our national identity was to be long-lasting, indeed permanent, the impact on federalism was less so. Not surprisingly, the JCPC was ready to act as midwife for the vigorous rebirth of federalism after the war. It did so most prominently through its interpretation of the general peace, order, and good government (POGG) clause at the beginning of section 91. Macdonald-style centralists, including the early judges on the Supreme Court of Canada, had read the POGG clause as the main grant of federal authority, with the enumerated powers (e.g., trade and commerce or criminal law) being mere examples of that general power. In the centralist interpretation, moreover, federal legislation required for the peace, order, and good government of Canada could be sustained even though it dealt with matters that might otherwise appear to be within provincial jurisdiction. The JCPC agreed that this was possible, but only in response to serious emergencies such as war and pestilence. The JCPC thus gave its retrospective blessing to the wartime suspension of federalism under the War Measures Act, thereby establishing centralized "constitutional dictatorship" through what Smiley calls Canada's "other constitution."[29] It insisted, however, that this "other constitution" must be temporary. Being an "emergency" constitution, it could last only as long as the emergency itself, and emergencies are by definition temporary.[30] The federal cabinet was entitled to considerable discretion in judging when the wartime emergency had ended, permitting it to continue its "constitutional dictatorship" for a reasonable period of postwar reconstruction. But eventually the primary federal constitution of watertight compartments had to be re-established.

Nor did the JCPC lose its prewar interest in pushing out the walls of the provincial jurisdictional compartments. In particular it renewed the prewar attack on the trade and commerce power begun in *Parsons*, extending it to almost ridiculous extremes in the postwar period. Trade and commerce, said the JCPC, was merely an auxiliary power; it could give some additional support to federal legislation that was justified primarily by one of the other heads of power (e.g., criminal law), but it could not justify federal legislation by itself. There was, in effect, no such thing as "trade and commerce" legislation per se. In short, "the trade and commerce power at this stage had been assigned by judicial interpretation to a position in the division of powers inferior to all other heads of power."[31] This extreme depreciation of the trade and commerce power did not last, but it indicates the extent to which the JCPC was prepared to go to protect the provinces against the assertion of federal power. Even when the JCPC eventually commuted this interpretive death sentence for the trade and commerce power, it left the power in seriously weakened condition. Thus, while the First World War may have interrupted constitutional decentralization, it clearly had not defeated it.

The Great Depression

The second major challenge to JCPC-style federalism was triggered by the economic crisis of the 1930s. This challenge arose in response to the constraints imposed by constitutional decentralization on the ability of governments to respond to the Great Depression. In Canada, as in the United States, the Depression provoked new experiments in economic social welfare legislation, including maximum-hour and minimum-wage legislation, unemployment insurance programs, marketing legislation, and the like. Much of this legislative program was undertaken by the federal governments of the two countries. Thus, the American legislative response to the Depression commonly goes under the name of the Roosevelt **New Deal**, in honour of the national president, Franklin Delano Roosevelt, who promoted it. The somewhat weaker program of the R.B. Bennett Conservatives, who were in power in Ottawa at the time, has similarly been dubbed the "Bennett New Deal." In both countries, however, the courts mounted significant opposition to the New Deal policies, striking down many of them as unconstitutional. In the Canadian case, much of the Bennett New Deal was invalidated because, not being justified under the restrictive interpretation of "trade and commerce," it infringed on the provincial power over "property and civil rights." It might still have been sustained as emergency legislation under the POGG clause, of course, but the JCPC refused to consider the Depression an emergency. This was a somewhat ironic conclusion in light of the JCPC's earlier decision that the Canada Temperance Act of 1878 was justified as emergency legislation under POGG because the "evil of intemperance" at the time was "a menace to the national life of Canada so serious and pressing that the National Parliament was called on to intervene to protect the nation from disaster."[32] In any case, if the federal government was legally incompetent to enact the New Deal legislation, the provinces, which had the legal authority, were financially incapable of doing so. Thus, a more effective response to the Depression and the development of a modern welfare state in Canada appeared to be constrained by the kind of federalism engineered by the provincial rights movement and the JCPC.

Not surprisingly, the judicial response to the Depression prompted a significant challenge to the decentralist jurisprudence of the JCPC. The challenge came especially from the Canadian left, which saw in the Depression proof of the inadequacies of laissez-faire capitalism and the need for socialized central planning of the economy. From this perspective, the existing decentralized federal system had to be overcome.[33] Not only did it forestall essential national policies, the critics argued, but decentralized federalism was also based on an illegitimate jurisprudence, one that respected neither the plain language of the BNA Act nor the original intent of the founders who drafted it. The critics, in short, saw the BNA Act largely through the eyes of John A. Macdonald and wished to restore his centralist vision against the decentralist alternative imposed by usurping judges who were based in London and ignorant of both Canadian history and current reality. In this way, an emerging Canadian nationalism, and particularly a nationalism lodged in English Canada, entered the debate over judicial interpretation.

It testifies to the strength and resilience of the constitutional assumptions of the provincial rights movement and the JCPC, however, that the centralist challenge to Depression-era jurisprudence did not succeed—at least not to the extent that a similar centralist challenge succeeded in the United States. The judicial challenge to the American New Deal quickly provoked a vigorous political counterattack by the Roosevelt administration, known as the **court-packing scheme**. Roosevelt proposed to enlarge the Supreme Court and appoint enough new judges favourable to the New Deal to outweigh those against it. As it turned out, the court-packing scheme was not needed, because one anti–New Deal judge backed down and changed sides in 1937, so the existing 5–4 judicial split against the New Deal now became a 5–4 split in its favour. The U.S. court, moreover, not only began to uphold the New Deal but quickly backed away almost altogether from any attempt to place significant jurisdictional constraints on the federal government. As Peter Russell writes, "Since then the US Congress has been virtually free of states rights restrictions on its powers, and the United States has been as centralized as John A. Macdonald hoped Canada would be."[34]

In Canada, the response to anti–New Deal jurisprudence was much more muted and ambiguous. The Bennett government, which had introduced the New Deal legislation, was soundly defeated at the polls by Mackenzie King's Liberals in 1935, before the legislation could be implemented. The King government, far from actively promoting the New Deal against the courts, actually initiated the litigation by referring the legislation to the courts for an assessment of its constitutionality. This was hardly the action of a government committed to the legislation. When the JCPC struck down most of the legislation, moreover, "King, instead of threatening to change the judges, responded in quintessential Canadian fashion and appointed a royal commission (Rowell-Sirois)."[35] In effect, the centralist challenge to decentralist federalism, while intellectually loud and significant, remained at the periphery of Canadian politics. It was influential among intellectual leftists and within the left-leaning Co-operative Commonwealth Federation (CCF), but it was not wholeheartedly embraced by the Liberal government. (The CCF was founded as a new political

DOSSIER 4.4 "SOME PRIVY COUNCIL" BY F.R. SCOTT

"Emergency, emergency," I cried, "give us emergency,
This shall be the doctrine of our salvation.
Are we not surrounded by emergencies?
The rent of a house, the cost of food, pensions and health, the unemployed,
These are lasting emergencies, tragic for me."
Yet ever the answer was property and civil rights,
And my peacetime troubles were counted as nothing.
"At least you have an unoccupied field," I urged,
"Or something ancillary for a man with four children?
Surely my insecurity and want affect the body politic?"
But back came the echo of property and civil rights.
I was told to wrap my sorrows in water-tight compartments.
"Please, please," I entreated, "look at my problem.
I and my brothers, regardless of race, are afflicted.
Our welfare hangs on remote policies, distant decisions,
Planning of trade, guaranteed prices, high employment—
Can provincial fractions deal with this complex whole?
Surely such questions are now supranational!"
But the judges fidgeted over their digests
And blew me away with the canons of construction.
"This is intolerable," I shouted, "this is one country;
Two flourishing cultures, but joined in one nation.
I demand peace, order and good government.
This you must admit is the aim of Confederation!"
But firmly and sternly I was pushed to a corner
And covered with the wet blanket of provincial autonomy.
Stifling under the burden I raised my hands to Heaven
And called out with my last and expiring breath
"At least you cannot deny I have a new aspect?
I cite in my aid the fresh approach of Lord Simon!"
But all I could hear was the old sing-song,
This time in Latin, muttering stare decisis.

Source: Reprinted with permission from *The Canadian Bar Review* 28 (1950), 780.

party in 1933 and was the forerunner of the NDP.) The Depression may have caused some small shift in a centralist direction, but once again the earlier work of the provincial rights movement proved strong enough to withstand a centralist challenge. However, a much larger challenge was to come on the heels of the Depression.

World War II and Reconstruction

"It was the imperatives of war, not the miseries of depression"[36] that placed Canada more seriously on a centralist path. Even if the Depression did not qualify as an emergency that would justify invoking Canada's "other constitution," war clearly did. And so did a significant period of postwar reconstruction. Thus the emergency powers enjoyed by the federal government under the War Measures Act during the war itself were extended in more limited legislative form until 1954.[37] Even after emergency centralism came to an official end, the forces of centralism had established enough momentum to last until the end of that decade. As in the case of World War I, and perhaps even more so, the forces of centralism were bolstered by a powerful Canadian nationalism fuelled not only by the wartime experience but also by a determination that the sense of personal security that had been shattered first by the Depression and then by the war would be restored.

It was during the period of wartime emergency that some of the centralizing lines of thought developed during the Depression began to bear fruit and to find political expression in an electorate battered by depression and war. An early example occurred in 1940, when the BNA Act was amended to give the federal government exclusive jurisdiction over unemployment insurance, thereby reversing one of the JCPC's anti–New Deal judgments. In 1951 another amendment added section 94(a), giving the federal government concurrent jurisdiction with the provinces over old-age pensions, though, in a reversal of the usual rule governing concurrent powers, provincial power would be paramount. Interestingly, although these were largely centralizing changes, they were undertaken only after the unanimous consent of the provinces was sought and obtained. Frank Scott, a leading constitutional scholar associated with the CCF, had argued in 1935 that the federal government was competent to undertake such amendments unilaterally, without any provincial consent whatsoever.[38] Obviously, Canada's governing elites did not agree; centralizing amendments would be undertaken with provincial cooperation. Indeed, even the 1960 amendment imposing compulsory retirement for federally appointed superior-court judges—"an amendment that did not impinge directly on provincial powers"[39]—was achieved with unanimous provincial consent. Peter Russell points out that

> *[f]rom the mid 1930s through to the end of the 1950s the centralist perspective was the dynamic, initiating force in Canadian constitutional politics. Centralism was never stronger than during this quarter-century.*[40]

It is thus all the more striking that, while "[a]ll the constitutional initiatives during this period were centralist ... the most significant of them were accomplished through a process that recognized the provincial governments' share in Canadian sovereignty."[41] "That support for provincial rights could endure, even in times that were least propitious for a federal division of governmental authority," Russell concludes, "demonstrates how rooted federalism had become in the Canadian political culture."[42]

Federalism may have remained well rooted, but the balance of federalism was obviously shifting. Although amendments directly affecting the division of powers were obtained with provincial consent, these amendments were still centralizing. Moreover, a number of amendments not directly affecting the division of powers were achieved by unilateral federal action, without provincial consent. The most significant of these was the 1949 amendment (discussed in Chapter 2) establishing a new section 91(1) of the BNA Act, under which the federal parliament could unilaterally amend its own constitution without going to Britain, just as the provinces had always been able to do under section 92(2).

The same year also saw another significant centralizing initiative, one having its roots in the Depression-induced centralism and controversy of the 1930s. The closest analogue to Roosevelt's court-packing scheme of the late 1930s was a Canadian movement to abolish appeals to the JCPC, thereby making the Supreme Court Canada's final court of appeal. Although this movement found some government support during the 1930s, its implementation was interrupted by the war and was not finally accomplished until 1949. Even then, not everyone supported abolition. The province of Quebec, for example, favoured JCPC-style decentralism, and worried that making the Supreme Court (whose judges were appointed by Ottawa) the final court of appeal would lead to unacceptable centralism. Such centralism, of course, is precisely what many of the proponents of abolition hoped for.[43]

If the centralist supporters of abolition foresaw a full and dramatic reversal of the JCPC's decentralizing jurisprudence, their expectations were not met. The general outlines of JCPC jurisprudence remain at the foundation of our constitutional structure to this day. The Supreme Court after 1949 has never returned to the Macdonald-style centralism it exhibited in its first few years, before it was brought to heel by the JCPC. Nevertheless, as noted in Chapter 2, the court did move somewhat in a centralist direction after the abolition of appeals to London. In particular, the court in the 1950s gave indications that it was abandoning the emergency interpretation of POGG.[44]

The establishment of the Supreme Court as Canada's final court of constitutional appeal appeared to set the stage for an even more important role for the court in defining the evolutionary course of Canadian federalism. And indeed the court continued to play an important role, as the previous chapters have shown and future chapters will further illustrate. However, its role was to a degree overwhelmed by the larger dynamics of megaconstitutional politics in which the court was one but only one player. In the postwar era the primary arena in which the evolution of federalism was to be shaped turned out to be intergovernmental rather than judicial. Canadian federalism became as much what federal and provincial governments defined it to be through intergovernmental agreements, cooperation, and conflict as it was defined by the court.

THE CHALLENGE OF INTERGOVERNMENTAL RELATIONS

Perhaps the most significant and lasting challenge to the kind of federalism promoted by the provincial rights movement and the JCPC took place outside the realm of formal constitutional politics and in the realm of intergovernmental relations. Although the idea of federalism as the division of sovereignty into watertight jurisdictional compartments had been thoroughly established as a central principle of Canada's formal constitution, this idea would be severely tested by the growing informal policy entanglement between the two orders of government. Any politically aware citizen of late-20th-century Canada knows that intergovernmental relations are absolutely central in the conduct of Canadian politics. Indeed, as a matter of political significance, the extensive web of intergovernmental relations that exists today must be considered part of our constitutional "master institution," even though this element of our overall institutional structure has grown up outside the formal constitutional structure of the Canadian federal state. The sheer extent of intergovernmental relations puts paid to the idea of watertight compartments.

The watertight-compartments theory of federalism assumes that there is little involvement of the two orders of government in each other's affairs and thus little need for intergovernmental relations. This was probably never a realistic expectation; some degree of intergovernmental relations exists in all federal states, though the extent of such relations will vary. Certainly the drafters of the 1867 Constitution Act could not have foreseen the degree to which such intergovernmental arenas as first ministers' conferences would come to dominate the Canadian political scene, and in any event they did not spend much time on intergovernmental relations per se. It was assumed that the need for intergovernmental consultation and collaboration would be minimal and could be handled through informal party contacts and representation in the federal cabinet. The only intergovernmental mechanism built into the act was the lieutenant governor, who "... was originally envisaged as being a federal officer entrusted with the responsibility of communicating the views of the national government to provincial authorities and, if necessary, making certain that the provincial governments did not step too far off the path deemed correct for them by the national government."[45] At the same time, the lieutenant governor was not fashioned as a conduit for provincial views into Ottawa. He was primarily an agent of the federal government, armed with the weapons of reservation and disallowance, and not a nascent intergovernmental institution.

What first put these initial assumptions to rest was the discrepancy between the jurisdictional powers of the provinces and their financial resources, a discrepancy that became more pronounced as judicial interpretation affirmed and then expanded the legislative competency of provincial governments. Although the powers of the federal and provincial governments were equalized in many ways by the provincial rights movement and judicial interpretation in the late 19th and early 20th centuries, one important exception stands out: the taxing power was intended to be unbalanced and has remained so. Originally, the provinces were limited to direct taxes, which were not expected to amount to much because income taxes were considered out of the question. Ottawa, however, was given the power to raise money "by any Mode or System of Taxation" (s. 91.3). With the advent of the income tax and the judicial definition of the sales tax as a direct tax, provinces have much greater formal taxing power than was anticipated in 1867. Nevertheless, the extent to which they can employ that power depends on how much tax room is left by Ottawa. Assuming a finite limit to the tax burden that can be imposed on citizens, the higher Ottawa's taxes are, the less room is left for provincial taxation.

One reason for high federal taxes is that Ottawa collects more taxes than required to carry out its direct legislative responsibilities; it does so in order to redistribute income from richer to poorer provinces. On the other side of the jurisdictional fence, competition among provinces for investment places some constraints on their ability to use all of the tax room available to them. Witness, for example, the recent jockeying between Alberta and Ontario to establish the lowest income tax rates in the country. Thus, despite the modern provincial access to more lucrative kinds of taxes than anticipated in 1867, the original discrepancy in the financial positions of the two orders of government remains in place. This means that provinces, including the wealthiest, cannot meet their considerable jurisdictional responsibilities out of their own tax resources. It is this imbalance between the jurisdictional and financial dimensions of the constitution that explains much of the modern phenomenon of policy entanglement and the resulting explosion of intergovernmental relations.

The fiscal imbalance was compounded by the growth of the state in the 20th century, growth that was not evenly spread across the two orders of government. During the early years of Confederation, the discrepancy between the jurisdictional and financial resources of the provinces was less significant than it is today. The late 19th century was still an era of minimal, **laissez-faire government**. Provincial governments in particular were relatively feeble bureaucratic and political organizations. One indication of this fact is that much of the political talent of the day migrated to the new federal government in Ottawa; with the exception of Ontario's Oliver Mowat, who went on to become the province's premier, all of the politicians voting for Confederation opted for elected or appointed federal office.[46] The programmatic activities of the provincial governments were minimal, and bureaucratic resources were limited and underdeveloped. It was a time when people neither expected nor received much from their provincial governments or, for that matter, from the federal government.

Not until the advent of the activist **welfare state** later in the 20th century did the combined jurisdictional strength and financial weaknesses of the provinces begin to impose major strains on the federal system. As the 20th century unfolded, the powers that had been assigned to the provinces, either explicitly in 1867 or implicitly through subsequent judicial interpretation, began to acquire increased importance, as reflected in the skyrocketing expenditures on schools, hospitals, postsecondary education, social services, highways, and public utilities (a point we shall return to in Chapter 7). As their roles and responsibilities expanded, provincial governments became increasingly dependent on federal funds. Thus, the federal government became heavily involved in financing programs within the legislative jurisdiction of provincial governments. Needless to say, intergovernmental relations grew apace and became increasingly complex.

The basis of federal spending within provincial areas of jurisdiction is the "spending power," discussed in the Chapter 2. Recall that although the constitution prohibits the federal government from legislating directly in provincial fields of jurisdiction, there are no similar constitutional constraints on the expenditure of federal funds. As Donald Smiley explains, "according to the constitutional doctrine that came to prevail, the central government might legally spend revenues as it chose, even on matters within the jurisdiction of the provinces, and could at its discretion fix the circumstances under which a potential recipient ... might receive the federal largesse."[47] This lack of constitutional constraint on the federal spending power, combined with expanding federal tax revenues fuelled by sustained postwar economic growth, led to the creation of **shared-cost programs** and **conditional-grant programs**, whereby federal funding was provided for programs administered by provincial governments and falling within the legislative jurisdiction of the provinces. Federal funds were thus used to influence provincial programs, spending priorities, and standards. By attaching conditions to the receipt of federal funding, Ottawa was in effect able to legislate indirectly in provincial fields of jurisdiction.

The name given to the pattern of intergovernmental relations that grew up around conditional-grant programs in the 1950s and 1960s was **cooperative federalism**, a term that belied the fact that cooperation was often a one-way street and that the government paying the piper called the tune. In reality, cooperative federalism was a primary feature of the general centralizing thrust of the postwar period. The nationalism that characterized the era created a receptive electoral audience for the idea of *national* programs and *national* standards across a wide range of social policies. The federal government came to see itself, and to be seen by the electorate, as the most appropriate vehicle for such national programs, standards, and aspirations.

Conditional-grant programs, moreover, constituted only part of an extensive set of fiscal transfers that developed during the 1940s and 1950s, and persist to this day. These transfers from Ottawa to the provinces were designed to accomplish a number of different objectives.[48] The first was to achieve "vertical fiscal balance"—that is, to ensure that the revenues of each order of government approximately matched its expenditures. Thus, transfers from Ottawa to the provinces reflected the heavy programmatic responsibilities and limited tax bases of the provinces, relative in both cases to the federal government. The transfers grouped together under the **Canadian Health and Social Transfer (CHST)** (almost $13 billion in 1998) address this first objective and cover federal transfers with respect to medicare and postsecondary education. The second objective was to achieve a reasonable measure of "horizontal fiscal balance"—that is, to ensure that all provincial governments, both "have" and "have not," had roughly equivalent financial resources to support programs falling within their jurisdiction. **Equalization payments** are the primary although by no means exclusive vehicle for horizontal balance. Equalization payments are not meant to equalize the actual expenditures of provincial governments but rather to equalize the capacity of provincial governments to provide a specified level of services should they choose to do so.[49] The third objective was to ensure that provinces provide specific services at a given level, independent of their ability to pay. Conditional-grant programs such as the **Canada Assistance Program (CAP)**, which was replaced by the CHST, fall into this category; specific services and levels of service are designated, and funding is conditional on such services in fact being provided, something that is generally no longer the case with CHST funding.[50]

Yet another source of intergovernmental entanglement is the discrepancy between the labels used to distribute powers between the two orders of government in 1867 and the kinds of activities engaged in by modern governments. Many of the functions of government today were simply not contemplated by the framers in the late 19th century, and thus both the federal and provincial governments are active in fields that are not explicitly assigned by the constitution to either order of government. For example, the constitution is silent with respect to consumer protection,

DOSSIER 4.5 THE FUNDING OF POSTSECONDARY EDUCATION

The fiscal entanglement of the federal and provincial governments is nicely illustrated by the funding of postsecondary education, in particular for Canadian universities.

The operating grants for most universities come from provincial departments of advanced education. However, a substantial portion of that funding originates with the Established Programs Financing Act, which transfers block funding and tax points from the federal government to the provinces for support of medicare and postsecondary education. (Prior to 1977, EPF funding was tied directly to provincial expenditures in the related fields, but it is now unconditional funding tied to the growth of the GNP.) By the early 1990s federal estimates of annual EPF funding for postsecondary education totalled more than $5 billion.

The funding of university research is particularly complicated and often contentious. The basic salaries of university professors come directly from provincial operating grants and indirectly from the federal government through EPF funding. The research funding other than professional salaries comes primarily from federal sources, including most notably the Natural Sciences and Engineering Research Council (NSERC), the Canada Council, and the Medical Research Council (MRC). Ottawa also funds Centres of Excellence scattered across the university landscape.

Both orders of government provide scholarship support for undergraduate and graduate students, and both are involved in the funding and administration of student loans. Ottawa provides to provincial governments funding that is directed to language training programs and to course offerings in minority official languages. In total, then, the funding picture is complex indeed.

multiculturalism, and environmental protection, fields in which both orders of government are extensively involved. Intergovernmental conflict can therefore occur if the two orders of government impose different standards or program requirements, or if disagreements arise over judicial interpretations of the appropriate distribution of powers. This friction began with the advent of the modern activist state, especially during the 1940s and 1950s, and has become ever more pronounced with time.

Today, for example, environmental protection, a relatively recent addition to the policy agenda, provides particularly fertile soil for both intergovernmental cooperation and conflict. Many environmental concerns are by their very nature impervious to the federal–provincial division of powers or to the "lines on maps" so important to federal states,[51] but the fact that effective environmental protection requires intergovernmental cooperation does not ensure that such cooperation will take place. Legitimate conflict may occur as competing governments articulate inconsistent standards, guidelines, and regulatory procedures. Recent examples of such conflicts are to be found in the environmental assessment procedures brought into play with respect to the James Bay project in Quebec, the Rafferty-Alameda dam project in Saskatchewan, and the Oldman River dam project in southern Alberta. Thus, as Canadians pour new policy wine into the old constitutional bottles established in 1867, policy areas that might seem functionally cohesive have in fact been divided between both orders of government. However, no attempt has been made, or at least no successful attempt, to modernize either the description or division of powers between the two orders of governments. We are still working with labels that are almost 135 years old and in many cases bear only a rough correspondence to the realities of contemporary government.

In combination, these evolutionary lines of development ensured the growth of an elaborate system of intergovernmental relations, a system so pervasive and omnipresent that it flowed into virtually every nook and cranny of Canadian political life. The idea of federal balance bequeathed to us by the provincial rights movement and the JCPC persists, but the notion that this balance is established by watertight jurisdictional compartments does not describe modern reality. The jurisprudence of watertight compartments certainly influences and shapes the phenomenon of intergovernmental relations—for example, it necessitates intergovernmental relations if we are to achieve integrated policies on matters that cut across jurisdictional boundaries—but the fact of extensive intergovernmental policy entanglement shows that the compartments are far from being watertight.

Institutionally, the growth of intergovernmental relations was already evident by the end of the Second World War, when an extensive network of federal–provincial committees had been established in Ottawa. Originally created to orchestrate Ottawa's wartime involvement in provincial fields of jurisdiction, these committees evolved to handle the growing interpenetration of federal and provincial governments in the postwar welfare state. Presently, close to 1000 such committees are in place, committees that play an important role in shaping the multitude of programs and services the governments of Canada provide. A good deal of intergovernmental conference

DOSSIER 4.6 PROBLEMS OF POLITICAL ACCOUNTABILITY

The entanglement of the federal and provincial governments creates significant problems for political accountability. Simply put, it makes it difficult for citizens to know whom to blame when things go wrong and whom to credit when things go right.

Take, for example, the teachers and students in an English as a second language (ESL) program offered by a community college. When faced with significant financial cuts in the program, whom can they hold responsible? Funding may come directly from the provincial government, directly from federal labour market and immigration programs, or indirectly from federal money—conditional or unconditional—channelled through the provinces. Program cuts could reflect federal spending cuts, provincial cuts, or changes in how the provincial government directs federal funding. Each order of government can, if the need arises, blame the other. Meanwhile, students and teachers in the program are at a loss to know where to direct their anger and frustration. Accountable government is thus confounded by the programmatic and fiscal entanglements of the two orders of govern-

activity takes place also, over and above that incorporated in regular committee meetings. For example, throughout the 1980s the government of Alberta participated in two formal federal–provincial conferences a week, on average, every week of the year.[52] Extensive as this federal–provincial web might be, it encompasses only part of the intergovernmental activity that exists. It does not encompass interprovincial meetings, including the annual premiers' meeting, or meetings between provincial and local governments, or between provincial and Aboriginal governments. Moreover, most of the federal–provincial meetings take place at the level of officials, of which 95 percent are not reported.[53] Finally, in addition to the formal meetings and conference activity is the daily flood of phone calls, letters, faxes, and e-mails that ties the two orders of government together in a complex and increasingly seamless web.

During the centralizing era of "cooperative federalism," the routine interaction between federal and provincial officials helped create a "community of interest" that cut across jurisdictional boundaries and facilitated cooperative relationships among governments. There was an understandable tendency of federal and provincial bureaucrats, who were often linked by common professional and educational ties, to cooperate in the pursuit of shared program objectives. Many social and economic problems could best be attacked, and social and economic goals realized, by coordinated intergovernmental action. Effective economic management at one level of the federal system, for instance, could not be pursued in isolation from patterns of fiscal management at other levels. In some fields, intergovernmental cooperation was virtually mandated by the constitutional division of powers. For example, while the Criminal Code falls under the jurisdiction of Parliament, the administration of justice falls under the jurisdiction of provincial legislatures. The result, as Timothy

Woolstencroft notes, was "harmony and cordial relations between the two orders of government."[54] By the late 1960s, however, this professional community of governmental officials came under growing suspicion by provincial politicians who felt that their bureaucrats were not sufficiently sensitive to jurisdictional concerns and might surrender provincial jurisdiction in exchange for federal funds.

As a result of such perceptions, the era of centralizing "cooperative federalism" broke down and was replaced by a more conflictual and decentralizing **executive federalism**, in which more and more of the mass of intergovernmental relations was gathered together under the concentrated and mistrustful authority of cabinets and first ministers. This kind of federalism is, of course, facilitated by the parliamentary system of responsible government, which concentrates power within the cabinet. Generally speaking, federal and provincial ministers can bargain with one another directly because they are assured, through the conventions of party discipline, that they can secure legislative support for whatever bargain might be negotiated. However, the ability to enforce bargains does not necessarily facilitate agreement; executive federalism can be seen not only as a response to conflict but also as a development likely to intensify conflict. Highly competitive politicians, who view much of the world through the lenses of mutual suspicion, are less likely to have harmonious relations than are program specialists immersed in common policy endeavours. Indeed, the development of modern executive federalism contributed in recent decades to the growing sense of "institutional crisis" that Canadians have faced over the past three decades.

The centrepiece of executive federalism and the institution that best captures the federal dispersion and parliamentary concentration of power is the **first ministers' conference (FMC)**. The growing number of FMCs is one indication of the evolution of executive federalism. Only eleven first ministers' conferences (or Dominion–Provincial Conferences, as they were called initially) were held between 1906 and 1946. Six more were held between 1947 and 1956, 11 between 1957 and 1966, 16 between 1967 and 1976, and 17 between 1977 and 1986. The most visible and dramatic manifestation of intergovernmental relations, FMCs tend to focus on the most comprehensive or pressing political problems of the time. In recent years, proposals for constitutional reform have dominated the agendas of first ministers' conferences. When the interest in constitutional reform wanes, FMCs are held less frequently. Instead, the first ministers meet for informal lunches or dinners that are not open to media scrutiny.

In 1972 Richard Simeon introduced the notion of **federal–provincial diplomacy** in an attempt to capture the emerging pattern of intergovernmental relations.[55] This insightful term recognizes that federal–provincial relations, particularly as practised in the first ministers' conference, have taken on many of the trappings of international relations: the importance attached to the symbols of sovereignty, a stress on the formal equality of all actors regardless of province size or order of government, the conduct of "summit meetings" in an atmosphere laden with pomp and ceremony, the treatment of governments as unitary actors rather than as complex packages of

DOSSIER 4.7 CONFLICT OR COOPERATION?

The public's perceptions of intergovernmental relations are often ones of conflict and discord. We hear repeated charges of federal interference, regulatory conflict, and administrative overlap. Such perceptions were instrumental in shaping elements of the Charlottetown Accord and were used by the Yes side to represent the accord to Canadians as a means of reducing overlap, duplication, and inefficiency.

Yet this image fails to capture the fact that Canadian governments cooperate more than they fight—that a complex web of programs, agreements, committees, conferences, and even personal friendships draws the governments together into an elaborate, interdependent, and generally cooperative network. Cooperation extends from major social programs, such as medicare and social security, to detailed issues such as compensation for waterfowl crop damage.

There is no question that overlap and duplication can be problematic. They can create regulatory confusion for businesses and development projects. They can create confusion among the public consumers of social programs. At the same time, overlap creates multiple points of access for citizens and groups trying to influence the political process or to access government services. Some degree of intergovernmental competition may also improve the quality of services and programs available to Canadians and make it less likely that some groups fall between the cracks.

Displays of public rancour should not, therefore, conceal or even overshadow a more productive and harmonious face for intergovernmental relations.

often competing interests, and the use of diplomatic "listening posts" on one another's turf. Diplomatic imagery captures both the formal sovereignty of provincial governments (within their own fields of jurisdiction) and much of the contemporary style of Canadian intergovernmental relations.

In the times to come, first ministers' conferences and the much broader system of intergovernmental relations of which they are a part will face a number of pressing challenges. These include, but are by no means restricted to, the following:

- The proliferation of self-governing First Nations will create an escalating demand for more "seats at the table." While in the short term this demand might be met through the inclusion of Aboriginal peak organizations such as the Assembly of First Nations, over time at least some of the First Nations will demand more direct participation.
- The potential "crowd at the table" will grow further as the three northern territorial governments demand more formal representation. This will strain the diplomatic norm of participant equality. If a decision rule other than unanimous consent emerges, the difference in size between Ontario and the northern territories—a ratio of up to 500 to 1—could be intolerable.

DOSSIER 4.8 THE FIRST MINISTERS' CONFERENCE

While FMCs began as reasonably small affairs, the federal, provincial, territorial, and at times Aboriginal delegations now total more than 200 people. When observers and the media are included, close to 400 people may be in attendance; more than this number of delegates and advisers alone attended the Aboriginal FMCs held in the mid-1980s. In part as a consequence, such formal meetings have been increasingly supplemented, and in some cases almost replaced, by more informal meetings that bring together only the principal players in a more confidential setting. Thus, while a formal FMC will necessarily have a public component—no FMC since 1976 has been held completely in camera—an informal gathering of the first ministers for lunch or dinner need not. At times, the formal and informal components will be woven into a single meeting—short public sessions combined with long private lunches and dinners. As Donald Wallace notes, the "public sessions of the conference are for show, the private lunches and dinners are for work." At other times, the prime minister may simply ask the premiers to join him for an informal working lunch or dinner. However, the practical difference between the two types of events is by no means clear. For example, the Meech Lake Accord first emerged from an informal working session, and then in June 1990 a dinner meeting of the first ministers lasted for close to seven days as the ministers tried to salvage the accord. In the past, informality has been a means by which attendance and public scrutiny could be limited. Whether this strategy will continue to work is at best uncertain.

Source: Donald C. Wallace, "Friends and Foes: Prime Ministers and Premiers in Intergovernmental Relations," in Leslie A. Pal and David Taras, eds., *Political Leadership: Prime Ministers, and Premiers* (Scarborough: Prentice-Hall Canada, 1988).

- The absence of any decision rule other than unanimous consent limits the utility of the FMC. Admittedly, the FMC is not a government and was never intended to be one; it cannot impose decisions on participating governments. However, unanimous consent favours decisions based on the lowest common denominator. If intergovernmental relations are to continue to provide a primary forum for public policy debate and construction, then we may have to implement some form of qualified majority that is binding on dissenting governments.
- The representative character of the FMC, or lack thereof, will come under more critical public scrutiny. For example, feminists will be reluctant to vest social policy control in the FMC or in similar institutions if the women are not at the table in significant numbers. Nor will women be alone in pursuing this line of thought.

Over the past decade, the provincial premiers have made a determined effort to replace federal policy control expressed through the spending power with a form of intergovernmental decision making that reflects and respects the constitutional division of powers. They argue that if national standards are to be set for programs falling under provincial jurisdiction, such standards should be truly national. They should not be unilateral federal government standards but rather standards set by the provinces acting in collaboration with the federal government or by themselves. From a jurisdictional point of view, this argument is compelling. Why should Ottawa set program standards for provincial governments operating within their own jurisdictional domain? Why not replace the Canada Health Act with an intergovernmental agreement?

However, if the provinces were going to act as the effective architects of the national social policy, they may have to come up with a set of decision rules other than unanimous consent. They may have to create a new mechanism to ensure the interprovincial fiscal transfers that come hand in glove with current federal government intervention. More importantly, they will have to come up with some way to ensure that Quebec is at the table. Over the past decade, we have seen an emerging of 9-1-1 federalism. The nine provinces other than Quebec meet and negotiate among themselves, and then negotiate with Ottawa. Quebec remains apart, then negotiates parallel agreements one-on-one with Ottawa. This form of de facto nation-to-nation interaction makes little sense within the conventional context of federalism.

All of this is to say that intergovernmental relations are in a state of flux. It is too early to say if intergovernmental relations will promote greater decentralization, whether Quebec will be singled out, or whether the intergovernmental process will come close to collapsing under its own weight as more players join the fray.

CONCLUSION

Chapter 3 described the period of megaconstitutional politics from 1960 onward. This was not, however, Canada's first period of megaconstitutional politics. Canadian politics from the Royal Proclamation of 1763 to Confederation in 1867 (see Dossier 2.2) represents over a century of megaconstitutional politics. This period was characterized by frequent and wholesale constitutional transformations, including successive experiments in the constitutional fashioning and refashioning of community, such as the alternating experiments in assimilating and accommodating the French population (see Dossier 2.3). For much of that century, the primary institutional battleground was the field of parliamentary democracy, particularly its essential principles of representative and responsible government, and a central question was whether parliamentary institutions should further the ends of assimilation in a unitary state or be the institutional expression of two culturally different peoples in separate states. The different answers to this question resulted in successive unifications and separations of French and English territories, culminating in 1867 with a mixture of both strategies that laid the foundations for Canadian federalism. The resulting division of powers between federal and provincial jurisdictions was also inspired by Nova Scotia and New Brunswick, the other colonies composing the new country, who were not inclined to submerge their local identities in a fully unitary state.

The new constitution was not an unambiguously federal one, however. In addition to the jurisdictional division of powers between two orders of government, it included a number of centralizing features that suggested the superior power and status of the central government. If the language of "exclusive" jurisdictions in sections 91 and 92 of the BNA Act suggested the federal logic of divided sovereignty, the powers of reservation, disallowance, and remedial legislation implied a relationship of imperial–colonial subordination between Ottawa and the provincial capitals. This constitutional ambiguity was resolved in favour of the federal principle of divided sovereignty only gradually through the efforts of a powerful provincial rights movement. Canadian federalism, in short, resulted not only from the politics of formal constitution making that led to Confederation in 1867 but also, and just as importantly, from a post-Confederation politics of constitutional interpretation.

With the aid of the Judicial Committee of the Privy Council, the provincial rights movement established the principle of sovereignty divided into two relatively balanced sets of watertight jurisdictional compartments. However, while this principle underpins the equal status of two orders of government, it has never been an adequate reflection of reality. Especially in the modern era of activist and interventionist government, jurisdictional powers cannot be so easily separated. Even when jurisdictional responsibilities are clear, much of the activity undertaken by one order of government in practice overlaps with, or at least impinges on, the activities of the other order. And, of course, the precise division of jurisdictional responsibilities is often unclear, especially in areas of governmental initiative not contemplated by the original labelling of powers in the 1867 Constitution Act. As a consequence, each order of government is keenly interested in, and often tries to influence, the activities of the other. The result has been a growing web of intergovernmental relations that belies the idea of watertight compartments. At an earlier stage, these intergovernmental relations took place to a considerable extent among professional communities of bureaucrats, a style of interaction known as "cooperative federalism." More recently, cooperative federalism has given way to a highly conflictual "executive federalism," in which interaction is controlled to a greater extent by mutually suspicious political executives.

Contributing to the shift from cooperative to executive federalism, and occupying a central place on the agenda of contemporary federal–provincial diplomacy, has been the increasingly intense and ever more comprehensive politics of formal constitutional reform. Once again, wholesale constitutional restructuring has come into question, including, yet again, the prospect of territorial separation of Canada's French and English territories. The period from Confederation to the 1960s certainly did not lack for constitutional politics, as we have seen. But it was a period of marked stability compared to the megaconstitutional politics of the pre-Confederation era. From the 1960s to the present, contestation over the constitution has been more like pre-Confederation constitutional politics in the sweep and intensity of its challenges to existing federal structures.

And yet, even the expansive politics of megaconstitutional change fail to capture the full extent of the challenge to federalism as we move into the next century.

The effective accommodation of Aboriginal governments into the complex web of Canadian intergovernmental relations poses a huge challenge. The Royal Commission on Aboriginal Peoples suggests that 60 to 70 self-governing First Nations might soon exist in Canada, an estimate that may well be low. How, then, will these First Nations establish effective intergovernmental relations with the existing federal, provincial, and territorial governments? Or, for that matter, among themselves? Will intergovernmental relations with First Nations be similar to or different from existing intergovernmental relations between the federal and provincial governments? Will federalism's respect for diversity be sufficiently elastic to accommodate divergent value systems in Aboriginal communities? None of these questions lends itself to easy resolution.

The federal system is also likely to face growing demands for the formal inclusion of large urban centres. At present, local governments have no formal role in the federal system; they are mere creatures of the federal government. However, these governments dwarf territorial and Aboriginal governments, and the communities they represent are more populous than many provinces. Metro Toronto, for example, is larger than and rivals British Columbia; Calgary and Edmonton are each larger than any Atlantic province and are closing in on the populations of Manitoba and Saskatchewan. Local governments, moreover, are playing an increasingly important role in social program delivery.

The challenge posed by local governments in an increasingly urbanized Canada points to another challenge, and that is the general decline of territoriality in the face of globalization and technological change. Federalism gives primacy to territorial communities and to the lines on maps that separate one from another. Jurisdictional disputes are endemic to formal states, and all relate in one way or another to the defence of territorially defined communities. Globalization, however, acts to sweep away lines on maps. If national boundaries mean less and less as economic containers, or as containers of culture and communication, why should we expect provincial boundaries to continue to be important? If the boundary between Canada and the United States means less and less, what does this say about the boundary between Ontario and Manitoba? Between New Brunswick and Nova Scotia? Alberta and Saskatchewan? Does the preoccupation of federalism with the intricacies of divided sovereignty make sense in a world where sovereignty of any kind is in question? But if the significance of territorial boundaries and communities is in decline, what will be the impact on federalism, a system of government built from territorial communities and emphasizing territorial boundaries?

Much of this has to do with the changing nature of political identities. Federalism assumes the primacy, or at least the importance of, territorial identities. More specifically, it assumes the importance of provincial identities. It may be the case, however, that Canadians are placing more weight on other forms of identity. Some may be local—with Vancouver or Hamilton rather than with British Columbia or Ontario. Some may be ideological—with feminism or environmentalism, for example, both of which are oblivious and even hostile to federal lines on maps. Some identities may be with new Internet communities, which are free of any territorial anchors. In all cases, the nature of the challenge is the same: non-territorial identities are rubbing up against political principles and institutions based on the centrality of territoriality.

None of this is to say that Canadian federalism is on the ropes. However, it is unlikely that the rapid evolution of Canadian society will leave federal principles and institutions untouched. It would be foolish to assume that the institutional parameters put into place in 1867 will necessarily guide us through the troubled waters of the next century.

KEY TERMS

federalism
confederalism
unitary state
divided sovereignty
Canada East / Canada West
double majority principle
rep by pop
Blackstonian theory of sovereignty
Blackstonian centralists
Blackstonian decentralists
compact theory
provincial rights movement
watertight compartments
balanced federalism
mutual modification
New Deal
court-packing scheme
laissez-faire government
welfare state
shared-cost programs
conditional-grant programs
cooperative federalism
Canadian Health and Social Transfer (CHST)
equalization payments
Canada Assistance Program (CAP)
executive federalism
first ministers' conference (FMC)
federal–provincial diplomacy

DISCUSSION QUESTIONS

1. What role did the JCPC play in the development of Canadian federalism? How significant was its role?
2. Is it possible to maintain a stable regime of divided sovereignty in a culturally divided country?
3. Was the development of modern executive federalism good or bad for Canada? If you conclude that it was an undesirable development, what kinds of institutional reform would you recommend to weaken or reverse it?
4. How likely is it that the kind of centralized state preferred by John A. Macdonald would have developed if Quebec had not been part of

Confederation? Is it conceivable that such a centralized regime would develop in the rest of Canada if Quebec were to separate?

5. How do you think Canadian federalism will evolve in the age of globalization?

SUGGESTED READINGS

Ajzenstat, Janet. *The Political Thought of Lord Durham.* Montreal and Kingston: McGill-Queen's University Press, 1988.

Diamond, Martin. *As Far as Republican Principles Will Admit.* Ed. William A. Schambra. Washington: AEI Press, 1992.

Simeon, Richard. *Federal–Provincial Diplomacy: The Making of Recent Policy in Canada.* Toronto: University of Toronto Press, 1972.

Simeon, Richard, ed. *Intergovernmental Relations.* Toronto: University of Toronto Press, 1985.

Simeon, Richard, and Ian Robinson. *State, Society and the Development of Canadian Federalism.* Toronto: University of Toronto Press, 1990.

Smiley, Donald. *Canada in Question: Federalism in the Eighties.* 3rd ed. Toronto: McGraw-Hill Ryerson, 1980.

———. *The Federal Condition in Canada.* Toronto: McGraw-Hill Ryerson, 1987.

Stevenson, Garth. *Unfulfilled Union.* 3rd ed. Toronto: Gage Educational Publishing, 1989.

Vipond, Robert C. *Liberty and Community: Canadian Federalism and the Failure of the Constitution.* Albany: State University of New York Press, 1991.

Watts, Ronald L. "Executive Federalism: The Comparative Context." In David P. Shugarman and Reg Whitaker, eds., *Federalism and Political Community.* Peterborough, Ont.: Broadview Press, 1989.

NOTES

1. Donald V. Smiley, *Canada in Question: Federalism in the Eighties*, 3rd ed. (Toronto: McGraw-Hill Ryerson, 1980), 1.
2. Alan C. Cairns, "The Government and Societies of Canadian Federalism," *Canadian Journal of Political Science*, 10 (1977).
3. Our discussion of the gradual development of federalism relies heavily on Robert C. Vipond, *Liberty and Community: Canadian Federalism and the Failure of the Constitution* (Albany: State University of New York Press, 1991).
4. J.M.S. Careless, *The Union of the Canadas: The Growth of Canadian Institutions, 1841–1857* (Toronto: McClelland & Stewart, 1967), 4.

5. B. Reesor, *The Canadian Constitution in Historical Perspective* (Scarborough: Prentice-Hall Canada, 1992), 40.
6. Ibid.
7. Ibid.
8. Peter H. Russell, *Constitutional Odyssey: Can Canadians Become a Sovereign People?* 2nd ed. (Toronto: University of Toronto Press, 1993), 18.
9. Ibid., 24.
10. Quoted in Donald Smiley, *The Canadian Political Nationality* (Toronto: Methuen, 1967), 7–8.
11. Lovell Clark, ed., *The Manitoba School Question: Majority Rule or Minority Rights?* (Toronto: Copp Clark, 1968).
12. Martin Diamond, *As Far as Republican Principles Will Admit*, ed. William A. Schambra (Washington: AEI Press, 1992), 168–169.
13. Ibid., 112.
14. Robert C. Vipond, *Liberty and Community: Canadian Federalism and the Failure of the Constitution* (Albany: State University of New York Press, 1991), 23.
15. Herbert J. Storing, *What the Anti-Federalists Were For* (Chicago: University of Chicago Press, 1981), 12.
16. Vipond, *Liberty and Community*, 23–24.
17. Thus, George Brown wrote that "the local governments shall be delegated governments and ... the sovereign power shall be vested in the general or federal government." Quoted in Russell, *Constitutional Odyssey*, 21.
18. Vipond, *Liberty and Community*, 25–26.
19. Ibid., 30.
20. Ibid., chapter 5.
21. *Severn v. The Queen*, [1878] 2 S.C.R. 70—case 1 in Peter H. Russell, Rainer Knopff, and F.L. Morton, *Federalism and the Charter: Leading Constitutional Decisions* (Ottawa: Carleton University Press, 1989).
22. Vipond, *Liberty and Community*, chapter 6.
23. *Severn v. The Queen* (1878), 2 S.C.R. 70—case 1 in Russell, Knopff, and Morton, *Federalism and the Charter.*
24. *Citizens Insurance Co. v. Parsons* (1881), 7 App. Cas. 96—case 2 in Russell, Knopff, and Morton, *Federalism and the Charter.*
25. Vipond, *Liberty and Community*, 151.
26. Russell, *Constitutional Odyssey*, 42.
27. Ibid., quoting Murray Greenwood.
28. Donald Smiley, *Canada in Question: Federalism in the Eighties*, 3rd ed. (Toronto: McGraw-Hill Ryerson, 1980), 50.
29. Ibid., 49.
30. *Fort Frances Pulp and Power Co. v. Manitoba Free Press*, [1923] A.C. 695—case 7 in Russell, Knopff, and Morton, *Federalism and the Charter.*
31. *In Re The Board of Commerce Act, 1919, and The Combines and Fair Prices Act, 1919,* [1922] 1 A.C. 191—case 6 in Russell, Knopff, and Morton, *Federalism and the Charter.*

32. *Toronto Electric Commissioners v. Snider,* [1925] A.C. 396—case 8 in Russell, Knopff, and Morton, *Federalism and the Charter.*
33. Russell, *Constitutional Odyssey,* 62.
34. Ibid., 64.
35. Ibid.
36. Garth Stevenson, *Unfulfilled Union: Canadian Federalism and National Unity,* rev. ed. (Toronto: Gage, 1982), 51.
37. Smiley, *Canada in Question,* 50.
38. Russell, *Constitutional Odyssey,* 62–63.
39. Ibid., 65.
40. Ibid., 62.
41. Ibid., 64.
42. Ibid., 63.
43. Russell, *Constitutional Odyssey,* 68–69. See also Peter H. Russell, "The Supreme Court's Interpretation of the Constitution," in Paul W. Fox, ed., *Politics Canada,* 5th ed. (Toronto: McGraw-Hill Ryerson, 1982), 592–593.
44. *Johannesson v. West St. Paul,* [1952] 1 S.C.R. 292 and *Reference Re The Offshore Mineral Rights of British Columbia,* [1967] S.C.R. 792—cases 18 and 20 in Russell, Knopff, and Morton, *Federalism and the Charter.*
45. R.I. Cheffins, *The Constitutional Process in Canada* (Toronto: McGraw-Hill, 1969), 140.
46. W.L. Morton, "Confederation 1870 to 1896," *Journal of Canadian Studies* 1 (1966), 23.
47. Smiley, *The Canadian Political Nationality,* 21.
48. For the more detailed discussion from which this analysis is drawn, see Richard M. Bird, "Federal–Provincial Fiscal Arrangements: Is There an Agenda for the 1990s?" in Ronald L. Watts and Douglas M. Brown, eds., *Canada: The State of the Federation 1990* (Kingston: Institute of Intergovernmental Relations, Queen's University, 1990), 111–116.
49. Ibid., 113.
50. However, the provisions of the 1984 Canada Health Act do inject an element of conditionality into funding under the Established Programs Financing Act. The act imposed financial penalties on provinces that permitted extra billing and user fees and thus effectively ended the practice in those provinces.
51. In a similar fashion, the notion of national sovereignty poses a significant challenge to the control of environmental problems, such as acid rain and global warming, that are indifferent to national and state boundaries.
52. Roger Gibbins, *Conflict and Unity: An Introduction to Canadian Political Life,* 2nd ed. (Toronto: Nelson Canada, 1990), 236.
53. John Reid, "Federal–Provincial Conferences: Their Implications for Legislators and Political Parties," *Canadian Parliamentary Review* 3 (1981), 2.
54. Timothy B. Woolstencroft, *Organizing Intergovernmental Relations* (Kingston: Institute of Intergovernmental Relations, Queen's University, 1982), 9.
55. Richard Simeon, *Federal–Provincial Diplomacy: The Making of Recent Policy in Canada* (Toronto: University of Toronto Press, 1972).

PARLIAMENTARY DEMOCRACY AND THE LEGISLATIVE PROCESS

5

We shape our buildings, and afterwards our buildings shape us.[1]

Canada's system of representative, parliamentary democracy is subject to many overlapping stresses and strains. The claims of provinces and regions for more effective representation in national institutions challenge the core constitutional principle of responsible government, which subordinates territorial interests to tight party discipline in the legislative chamber based on rep by pop (the House of Commons) and minimizes the power of the chamber based on territorial representation (the Senate). The representational claims of territorial interests clash in turn with those of non-territorial interests—e.g., women, ethnic and racial groups, Aboriginals. And representative democracy itself is challenged by a growing demand for more direct democracy. These clashing claims have kept reform of Parliament at the heart of Canada's constitutional and institutional politics.

■ ■ ■

Canadian government is based on the rule of law, and it is within representative legislative institutions that laws are created and legitimized. It is therefore appropriate to place **Parliament** at the centre of the institutional complex that constitutes the Canadian state. Parliamentary institutions provide the primary arenas (although by no means the only ones) within which disputes over the character and direction of public policy are debated and, to a degree and for a while, resolved. However, like other institutions discussed in this text, parliamentary institutions are more than bricks and mortar, more than the particular incumbents who occupy them at any given time. They encompass an elaborate set of rules and norms that shape the personal behaviour of parliamentarians and define the nature of Canadian parliamentary democracy. As Michael Atkinson and David Docherty observe,

> *as a political institution the House of Commons is an arena for the interaction of rules and people. Politicians bring their desires to the institutional setting; the institution establishes the opportunities that help determine whether or not these desires can be accommodated.*[2]

This interplay of rules, norms, and actors is far from static; it has evolved over time and is the subject of ongoing and vigorous debate.

This chapter begins by examining some of the conceptual underpinnings of parliamentary democracy and then moves to a description of the primary institutional components of Parliament, which is not one institution but several. Although many Canadians undoubtedly equate Parliament (and indeed the Parliament Buildings and the Peace Tower) with the House of Commons, Parliament in fact consists of three distinct albeit interlocked institutions: Section 17 of the 1867 Constitution Act states that "[t]here shall be One Parliament for Canada, consisting of the Queen, an Upper House styled the Senate, and the House of Commons." The consent of all three is required before a **bill**—a proposed piece of legislation—becomes an act of Parliament and thus part of the legal structure of the Canadian state. The discussion in the present chapter focuses on the House of Commons and the Senate; the role of the Queen's representative—the governor general—will be discussed in more detail in the next chapter. Once this background discussion is in place, we examine the process by which a bill becomes an act of Parliament. Particular emphasis is placed on the linkages among the institutional actors, linkages relating not only to the flow of legislation but to fundamental characteristics of parliamentary democracy. Thus, the broader intent of the chapter is to locate parliamentary institutions within the web of relationships that constitute the Canadian federal state and to identify contemporary challenges to those institutions.

The challenges come from several directions. The logic of Canadian parliamentary democracy continues to be contested by actors within parliamentary institutions. It is also contested by broader forces of political change pressing in from the outside, forces that include populist discontent and the increasingly litigious character of public life. To date, this contestation has seldom explicitly engaged the basic principles of responsible and representative government. However, the manifestations or outcroppings of those principles—e.g., the importance of party discipline as an organizing rule for parliamentary behaviour, or the manner in which MPs are elected and their social characteristics—have become increasingly contentious, and the ensuing debate is working its way down to the principled foundations of responsible and representative parliamentary democracy.

The challenge to Canada's parliamentary institutions has become more acute since the intensification of constitutional politics that began with the signing of the Meech Lake Accord in 1987. Although this accord would have left parliamentary institutions virtually untouched, the 1992 Charlottetown Accord called into question the legitimacy of the status quo by proposing a reformed Senate and significant changes to the composition of the House of Commons. The challenge gained momentum when the sovereigntist Bloc Québécois became Her Majesty's Loyal Opposition following the 1993 election, and when Reform MPs brought their party's institutional critiques into the heart of Parliament. To date the challenge has not been answered. We still have an unelected but increasingly active Senate in a society that emphatically endorses democratic principles. We still have a pervasive perception in Western Canada, particularly in the Reform heartland of Alberta and British Columbia, that parliamentary institutions fail to provide effective regional representation. We still have rigid **party discipline,** despite growing populist unease about the fundamental tenets of representative democracy.[3] And we still have parliamentary institutions that try to bridge conflicting national visions built around the competing notions of a bicultural community, the equality of the provinces, and the equality of individual citizens. Thus, throughout this chapter we straddle two stools; we describe and assess the parliamentary structures and processes that are currently in place, but we also look forward, albeit with a very clouded crystal ball, to the possible evolution of Canadian parliamentary democracy.

THE CONCEPTUAL FRAMEWORK

The opening line of the 1867 Constitution Act calls for "a Constitution similar in principle to that of the United Kingdom." As noted in Chapter 2, it is through this phrase that the historical traditions of parliamentary democracy, and many of the formal rules and informal conventions governing parliamentary procedure, were constitutionalized in 1867. This historically rooted **Westminster model** of parliamentary democracy not only provides much of Canada's unwritten constitution; it also finds reflection in the procedural and physical architecture of Canadian parliamentary institutions. The fact that both Canada and the United Kingdom have a House of Commons is not of mere historical interest; it illustrates how deeply British constitutional theory and practice have shaped our political landscape. Many of the ceremonies within Parliament—including the Opening of Parliament, the Speech from the Throne, and the introduction of the Speaker to the House—show the continued vitality of British parliamentary traditions.

Canadian practice follows the Westminster model in two fundamental ways. First, it embraces **responsible government;** the government of the day holds office only as long as it is able to command majority support in, or the confidence of, the House of Commons. This is what is meant when the House is referred to as a **confidence chamber.** The parliamentary convention is that when the government is unable to secure majority support in the House, the prime minister is expected to tender his or her resignation to the governor general, who then either dissolves the House and calls for a general election, or, rarely, asks another MP to form a government. Conversely, the Senate is not a confidence chamber; the unlikely defeat of government legislation in the Senate would not force the government to resign. It should be noted that the convention is far from precise, and governments have some latitude in defining which bills should and should not be considered confidence measures. Yet the essential principle is clear; the right to govern rests on the government's ability to command a legislative majority in the House of Commons.

Second, Canadian parliamentary democracy embraces **representative government.** Citizens elect representatives who legislate on their behalf, provide parliamentary support for (or opposition to) the government of the day, and are answerable to the electorate in periodic elections. Parliamentary government is, therefore, based on indirect rather than direct democracy; we elect representatives who vote on our behalf (if not necessarily as we would like) on matters of public policy.

Taken together, representative and responsible government form the heart of our parliamentary institutions and thus also the focus of controversy about those institutions. For example, just what is it that we expect our legislative institutions to represent? Should they be based simply on the principle of representation by population or should this majoritarian principle be modified to accommodate regional diversity? If regional diversity is to count, which of its different versions—two nations, four (or five) regions, or equal provinces—is most important? Or is territorialism perhaps less important than such characteristics as gender, race, and ethnicity? Should our parliamentary institutions represent women or racial groups in proportion to their population? And how is the desire for adequate representation to be squared with the iron party discipline promoted by responsible government? Finally, is representative democracy itself—whether or not it is combined with responsible government—a flawed way of legislating? Should it be replaced (or at least supplemented) by more direct democracy? These are the questions that fuel the ongoing debate about our parliamentary institutions.

THE HOUSE OF COMMONS

The House of Commons is the symbolic and physical centrepiece for Canadian politics. It is the primary stage for elected politicians, whose performance not surprisingly takes on many of the characteristics of political theatre. Yet however bombastic individual performances may be, they should not distract us from the central role played by the House in our system of representative, parliamentary democracy. This centrality, in turn, ensures that debate over the composition of the House, and over the principles that guide its processes, will be ongoing and vigorous. Two principles in particular structure the debate: representativeness and adversarialism.

Representativeness

The composition of the House is important because its task of political representation is so central and intrinsic. As Thomas Hockin has pointed out, the "essential day-to-day business of the Canadian House of Commons is not decision-making but representation."[4] To the extent that MPs are successful in this representational task (and are seen to be successful), the House is able to legitimate and support strong executive government. To the extent that the House is not seen to represent important groups within the society, its capacity in these respects may be constrained and the legitimacy of public-policy decisions may be open to question.

Controversy about what kind of representation is necessary to legitimate the House turns on two of the central issues in Canadian constitutional politics generally. The first concerns the claims of the nation versus the claims of its territorial components. In the context of House of Commons representation, this opposition expresses itself in the competing demands of rep by pop and territorialism. The second issue concerns the competing claims of territorial and non-territorial groupings. The opposition between the logic of the territorially based governments' constitution and the Charter-based citizens' constitution is replicated in representational politics by the competing claims of territorial and non-territorial groups or communities.

Rep by Pop versus Territorialism

We saw in Chapter 4 that in 1867 the establishment of a provincial order of government was supposed to facilitate representation by population in the national House of Commons. The federal division of powers represented the territorial principle, while rep by pop in the House of Commons represented the national principle, although even at that time it was recognized that a complete separation of regional and national matters was impossible. It was thus necessary to implement the principle of intrastate federalism within the national Parliament. It was the Senate, however, not the House of Commons, that was to fulfill this intrastate function. The House was clearly to be based on rep by pop. This founding intention continues to be reflected in the composition of the House, though it has been qualified over time by the principle of territorial representation.

There are currently 301 seats in the House of Commons, with provincial representation ranging from 103 seats in Ontario to four in Prince Edward Island, two in the Northwest Territories, and one in the Yukon. Seats are distributed across the provinces in approximate proportion to their respective shares of the national population. As Table 5.1 illustrates, the principle of representation by population is nonetheless operationalized with some important exceptions. Prince Edward Island and New Brunswick are overrepresented in the House because of the "senatorial floor," a constitutional provision specifying that a province cannot have fewer members in the House than it has senators.[5] The northern territories are overrepresented in a realistic concession to geography; even three northern MPs have a great deal of difficulty covering the remote and demographically complex northern constituencies sprawled across the top of Canada. The overrepresentation of Manitoba, New Brunswick, Newfoundland, Nova Scotia, Saskatchewan, and Quebec is protected by the so-called "grandfather" provision, which ensures that when redistribution occurs, the number of seats held by a province will not be reduced below the number it had in 1985.[6] As a result of these exceptions, three provinces end up with small but significant deficits; the strict application of representation by population would give Ontario 112 seats rather than 103, British Columbia 39 rather than 34, and Alberta 28 rather than 26.

TABLE 5.1 REPRESENTATION BY POPULATION AND PROVINCE IN THE HOUSE OF COMMONS

PROVINCE	% 1996 POPULATION	1999 HOUSE OF COMMONS # SEATS	1999 HOUSE OF COMMONS % SEATS	CURRENT UNDER (–) OR OVER (+) REPRESENTATION (# OF SEATS)
Ontario	37.3	103	34.2	–9
Quebec	24.7	75	24.9	+1
British Columbia	12.9	34	11.3	–5
Alberta	9.3	26	8.6	–2
Manitoba	3.9	14	4.7	+2
Saskatchewan	3.4	14	4.7	+4
Nova Scotia	3.2	11	3.7	+2
New Brunswick	2.6	10	3.3	+2
Newfoundland	1.9	7	2.3	+1
Prince Edward Island	0.5	4	1.3	+2
Northern territories	0.3	3	1.0	+2
Total	100.0	301	100	

The distribution of seats in 1993 was determined by the Representation Act, 1985, which was based on the 1981 census.

The Charlottetown Accord would have added to these exceptions to the principle of rep by pop by guaranteeing Quebec no fewer than 25 percent of the seats in the Commons, even if the province's share of the national population should drop below that proportion. This proposal was clearly based on two-nations territorialism: the representation of the homeland of one of Canada's two nations, if not precisely equal (as the logic of the theory would require), must at least not fall below a minimum level. At the time of the 1991 census Quebec had 25.3 percent of the national population and 25.4 percent of the seats in the House. Any departures from rep by pop caused by this guarantee would thus have occurred in the future, with a relative decline in Quebec's population. Nevertheless, the Charlottetown Accord's 25 percent representation guarantee to Quebec was exceedingly controversial, symbolizing as it did a bicultural vision of community intensely disliked in much of the rest of Canada. Indeed, according to Peter Russell, nothing in the accord alienated voters in the rest of Canada so much as this guarantee, and nothing contributed as much to the accord's defeat in so much of Canada outside Quebec.[7]

A more contentious issue than the distribution of seats across provinces has been the distribution of seats within provinces and, specifically, the extent to which the size of ridings should be allowed to vary.[8] Also controversial has been the electoral system's tendency to distort the translation of regional votes into seats. We shall consider these sources of controversy when we examine Canada's electoral system in Chapter 9.

The Representation of Non-Territorial Groups

Another matter of fundamental dispute in the politics of representation has been the degree to which the composition of the House should mirror the social diversity of Canada beyond its regional and linguistic composition. In a variety of ways, including the Charter of Rights and Freedoms, non-territorial groups have been challenging the preeminence of territorialism in Canadian public life. This challenge has extended to the matter of legislative representation.

MPs have to date been overwhelmingly males, white, and from professional and business backgrounds. Although it is changing to some extent, the composition of the House still does not reflect the diversity of the population. In the 1988 general election, for example, only 39 of the 295 MPs elected (or 13.2 percent) were women, a modest increase from the 10 percent elected in 1984. In 1993, 54 women were elected to the House, but women still constituted only 18.3 percent of the MPs. Most recently, 61 women (20.3 percent) were elected to the House in the 1997 general election. Table 5.2 provides the corresponding data for provincial legislatures. The growing concern about the proportion of women legislators and the growing agitation for reform constitute only the leading edge of a more general challenge to the

TABLE 5.2 WOMEN IN PROVINCIAL LEGISLATURES

PROVINCE	WOMEN AS % OF PROVINCIAL CANDIDATES	WOMEN AS % OF PROVINCIAL LEGISLATORS	DATE OF ELECTION
Prince Edward Island	24.7	11.1	Nov. 1997
Ontario	22.7	12.3	June 1995
New Brunswick	20.4	12.7	Sept. 1995
Nova Scotia	17.8	13.5	Mar. 1996
Newfoundland	15.6	14.6	Feb. 1996
Manitoba	25.5	17.5	Apr. 1995
Quebec	20.4	20.0	Sept. 1994
Saskatchewan	22.5	22.4	June 1995
Alberta	23.9	26.5	Mar. 1997
British Columbia	26.3	26.7	May 1996

representative character of legislative institutions, a challenge that brings into play gender, ethnicity, Aboriginal status, disabilities, and sexual orientation.

Table 5.3 presents some 1990 data, collected for the Royal Commission on Electoral Reform and Party Financing, that maps public perceptions concerning the representation of women in the House of Commons. The table shows a significant although not overwhelming degree of public concern with the underrepresentation of women in the House, and substantial but again not overwhelming agreement with the notion that gender equality in the House would lead to better government. Not surprisingly, more women than men were concerned about the underrepresentation of women and were convinced of the benefits that equality of representation would bring. Perhaps of greater surprise is the degree of public support for gender quotas in the selection of party candidates; more respondents support quotas—a solution to the problem—than believe gender inequality is a problem!

TABLE 5.3 PUBLIC OPINION ON THE REPRESENTATION OF WOMEN IN THE HOUSE OF COMMONS

	TOTAL	MEN	WOMEN
% who say that it is a serious or very serious problem that there are more men than women in the House of Commons	32	26	37
% agreeing that we would have better or much better government if there were as many women as men in the House of Commons	37	32	43
% favouring quotas requiring parties to choose as many female as male candidates	41	35	48

Survey conducted September–October 1990
n = 2947

Source: André Blais and Elisabeth Gidengil, *Making Representative Democracy Work: The Views of Canadians,* Volume 17 of the Research Studies of the Royal Commission on Electoral Reform and Party Financing (Toronto: Dundurn Press, 1991), 65. Reproduced with the permission of the Privy Council Office and the Minister of Supply and Services Canada, 1994.

Questions about the representative character of the House or the Senate are essentially questions about "standing." Who will be present when an issue is debated, a vote called, and or a decision made? The matter of standing is particularly important for women when the issue at hand is legislation dealing with abortion or family violence or with a broad array of social programs that have a significant and differential impact on women. Admittedly, committee hearings may provide standing to groups excluded from direct representation in the House, and "virtual" representation may be provided by sympathetic MPs of either gender. In this last respect, MPs may speak for women in the same way that lawyers represent clients with whom they have little, if anything, in common; just as a male lawyer can represent a female client in court, so too can a male MP represent the interests of his female constituents in the House. Yet the fact remains that many and quite likely most women do not see this as an adequate substitute for direct, elected representation in the House. A second example is provided by Aboriginal peoples, who are no longer prepared to accept indirect or virtual representation. In their case, however, even direct representation in the House is unlikely to provide much legislative leverage, given the small size of the Aboriginal electorate. Hence the preference among Aboriginal peoples for self-government and for intergovernmental rather than legislative representation.[9] It is likely, then, that the representational challenge from women will have a greater impact on parliamentary institutions than will the challenge originating from Aboriginal peoples.

Adversarialism

Public discontent with the House of Commons has much deeper roots than the representation and misrepresentation of various groups and territories; it is also lodged in some of the basic tenets and characteristics of parliamentary democracy. Parliamentary democracy is adversarial in theory and even in architectural design. Government and opposition MPs face one another across a neutral no man's land, separated by the length of two swords, their physical disposition signalling that there are two opposing sides to the issue at hand and little if any common ground. The physical architecture also finds reflection in the equally important normative architecture of rules, customs, and procedures. Government MPs sit on one side of the House and opposition MPs on the other. The Speaker, an MP elected to this position by the House, serves as a referee but not a judge. The electorate is the judge, although with respect only to the global performance of the government and parties, not to specific pieces of legislation. Thus, in many ways the House in its procedures resembles a court of law. The objective of parliamentary debate is not to reach a compromise solution, not to find the best possible outcome, but rather to present two vigorously opposing points of view, with the electorate left to judge. The adversarial character of the House shapes its most basic operating rules and procedures.

The adversarial nature of parliamentary democracy is reflected in the title Her Majesty's Loyal Opposition: the Opposition has a constitutional mandate to

DOSSIER 5.1 A PROPOSAL THAT GOES AGAINST DEMOCRACY—AND HUMAN NATURE

Who are you? Think about it. Are you a man or a woman? Heterosexual or homosexual? Catholic, Protestant, Jew or Hindu, or do you care about religion at all? Are you a senior citizen, a teenager or middle-aged? Is your mother tongue English, French, Greek or something else?

Do you associate with what we might call western values, or those of Islam or Buddhism? Are you working-class, middle-class or upper-class? Are you working or retired? What is your ethnic background: Anglo-Saxon, Ukrainian, Jamaican, Japanese? Do you live in an urban or rural area? Do you have children or not?

For purposes of voting or seeking election in a pluralist democracy, it does not matter how you define yourself or which of the multiple personal characteristics that constitute your humanity you consider paramount. However you define yourself, if you are a citizen you may vote, with very few exceptions. And you may stand with everyone else for election.

Democracies have usually organized themselves this way, by emphasizing that the common humanity of citizens, rather than their personal characteristics, should define their rights. Obviously, democracies must make government practical, so elections usually provide a territorial delineation for representation... But within those territories, all citizens stand equal. People can vote for anyone they want, and no single defining characteristic of their humanity says otherwise.

Sorry about this elementary bit of political philosophy, but it comes in handy in remembering why establishing a system that would allocate certain seats [in the Senate] to women and others to men ... cries out against liberal democracy.

Formal, mandatory sexual equality in electoral politics stands on a false premise—namely that the determining characteristic of citizenship is gender. Gender is indisputably important. For some citizens, it is the most important defining characteristic of individual personality. It is the characteristic that shapes views of public policy.

But for many other citizens—probably the majority—their sex is just one among many characteristics that shape personality and views of public policy. A 75-year-old woman or man may think age is more important than gender. A highly religious person may think religion more important than gender—a Catholic woman who opposes abortion, for example, or an evangelical Christian who wants prayers in the schools....

Opposition to mandatory sexual equality in the allocation of seats does not mean abandoning other means to get greater representation of women in public life. Democracy is best served when it is representative—a mirror for society—but the notion that women or men consider their sex the overriding characteristic on which they base their participation in society is wrong.

Once the pluralistic system yields to one overriding definition of citizenship, there is no logical resistance to the further fracturing of the system by those who would claim another overriding characteristic, be it age, ethnicity, language, class or whatever.... [R]eserving some seats for women, others for men ... is against the most fundamental principles of liberal democracy. It is against what we know of human nature, how people define themselves and what gives them the same rights in a democracy.

Source: Reproduced by permission of *The Globe and Mail.* Reprinted from Jeffrey Simpson, "A proposal that goes against democracy—and human nature," *The Globe and Mail,* September 1, 1992, A18.

oppose, not to cooperate. Indeed, it can be argued that the public is not well served when the opposition parties reject this mandate and cooperate with the government. Certainly, this argument was raised in the debate over the Meech Lake Accord when the opposition parties locked arms with the government and thereby short-circuited, and to a degree delegitimated, public discussion. It should be stressed, however, that the term "Loyal Opposition" also signals that opposition to the government of the day is legitimate—that, to some degree, government and opposition MPs are engaged in a common democratic exercise that can be achieved only through adversarial debate. This interpretation took on a new edge in the aftermath of the 1993 election, when the official Opposition was formed by Bloc Québécois MPs, who were dedicated, as a matter of party policy, to the dismemberment of the Canadian federal state. Not surprisingly, the capacity of Bloc MPs to serve as the Loyal Opposition was contested at the time by the Reform Party, which held 52 seats in the House of Commons, two fewer than the Bloc's 54.

Unfortunately, the adversarial style of parliamentary politics fails to find an appreciative audience in the Canadian public. Voters are exposed to the blunt edge of adversarial politics—to the catcalls and often antagonistic language of parliamentary debate—without seeing any direct evidence that adversarial politics improves the quality of public policy or the sensitivity of government. The style therefore contributes to a growing disenchantment with parliamentary institutions and representative government—disenchantment that has provided an important impetus for, but also a frustrating constraint on, institutional and constitutional reform.

THE SENATE

The Parliament of Canada, like its American, British, and Australian counterparts, is a **bicameral** institution with two distinct legislative chambers. In all four countries there is a "lower chamber" elected on the basis of representation by population: the House of Representatives in Australia and the United States, and the House of Commons in Britain and Canada. In all four countries there is also an "upper chamber": the House of Lords in Britain and the Senate in Australia, Canada, and the United States. Although these upper chambers differ considerably, in all four countries the consent of both chambers is needed before legislative bills become law. These upper legislative

DOSSIER 5.2 THE SPEAKER OF THE HOUSE OF COMMONS

The task of moderating the clashes between partisan adversaries, and keeping adversarialism generally within manageable grounds, falls to the Speaker of the House of Commons. In the early days of British parliamentary democracy, the Speaker was the intermediary between the House and the monarch; he was quite literally "the speaker" and carried out this role at considerable personal risk. Today, the Speaker's primary role as the presiding officer of the House is to oversee parliamentary debate and procedure within the Commons.

Parliamentary debate and procedure are governed by a set of written rules—the "standing orders"—and it is the Speaker who applies and interprets these rules. In a sense, the Speaker is the custodian of a long history of parliamentary norms and conventions, and the rulings of the Speaker play an important role in the evolution of those norms and conventions.

As the umpire or referee in legislative debate, the Speaker is expected to be neutral, to apply the rules of the game in a nonpartisan fashion, and to be an impartial source of appeal for MPs. The Speaker does not cast a vote unless there is a tie. The Speaker is forbidden from taking part in parliamentary debate. In the past, the prime minister nominated an MP from the government side of the House to be Speaker, and thus the Speaker's neutrality was often in doubt. Since September 1986, the Speaker has been elected by all MPs through a secret ballot. However, given the ubiquitous influence of party discipline and the fact that it is impossible to remove all measure of partisanship from procedural wrangles in the House, the Speaker is almost certain to be drawn from the ranks of the majority party in the House.

The Speaker has a number of other roles and responsibilities. He or she is the formal spokesperson for the House in communications with the Senate or the Crown. The Speaker is also responsible for the logistical operations of the House, a task that involves thousands of employees and a substantial budget. Finally, the Speaker is a member of Parliament with constituents to represent.

The Speaker must be able to operate effectively in both official languages, although the position has alternated by convention between English- and French-speaking members. The standing orders of the House state that the deputy speaker "shall be required to possess the full and practical knowledge of the official language which is not that of Mr. Speaker

chambers perform two functions. They are supposed to be institutions of "sober second thought." In all four of the countries we have mentioned —Canada, the United States, and Australia—they are also institutions of intrastate federalism. As regards the latter function, the Canadian Senate is unique in how it tries to marry the traditional conventions of British parliamentary democracy to the American innovation of federalism. The marriage has been uneasy from the start, and it remains a primary source of institutional contestation within the Canadian federal state.

Sober Second Thought

The Senate was created to perform a legislative role similar to that performed by the House of Lords in Britain, though the two institutions had different social and political foundations. At the time of Confederation the House of Lords had deep roots in the aristocratic structure of British society; a powerful landed gentry, the titled aristocracy, and an influential clergy all found symbolic and practical representation within the House of Lords. Therefore, the House of Lords had an important albeit shrinking political constituency. In Canada there were no similar groups requiring or demanding institutional representation: the separation of church and state had proceeded further in Canada than it had in the United Kingdom, and an aristocratic class or landed gentry had not emerged in the colonial conditions of the 19th century. Perhaps the closest the Senate came to the House of Lords in these respects was in the constitutional requirement that senators have "real and personal property" worth $4000 over and above debts and liabilities, a considerable sum in 1867. Yet despite these differences in national circumstances, the legislative role of the Senate was to parallel that of the House of Lords. The appointed Senate was to be a chamber of "sober second thought," an institution within which legislation passed by the House of Commons could be reviewed. In part, that review was meant to provide a check on possible democratic excesses by the elected House, for although the earlier fears of democracy that had played such an important role in shaping American legislative institutions had largely subsided by 1867, they had by no means disappeared. As J.R. Mallory points out, "few of the Fathers of Confederation can have viewed the rising tide of nineteenth-century democracy with much enthusiasm and the Senate must have seemed a natural obstacle to the excessive growth of democratic institutions, or of confiscatory legislation."[10] Nonetheless, the more important function of the Senate was to provide technical review of legislation passed by the democratically elected House, not to question such legislation in principle.

Intrastate Federalism

Sober second thought, even in conjunction with the protection that the Senate was to provide for wealth, was not enough to justify a second legislative chamber in Canada. (Nor was it important enough to sustain provincial second chambers, which have now disappeared from the central and eastern provinces, and were never constituted in the West.) It was the second role of providing regional or federal representation that was decisive in the creation of the Senate, and it was here that the American institutional precedent came into play.[11] The American Senate, unlike the House of Lords, was a federal chamber within which each state, regardless of its population, had two representatives. At first, American senators were indirectly elected by their state legislatures, and the Senate thus represented a state-government– rather than a state-population–oriented form of intrastate federalism, analogous to what Alan Cairns has called provincialist intrastate federalism in Canada. Since a 1911 constitutional amendment,

American senators have been directly elected by state populations, a change that transformed the U.S. Senate into a device of centralist intrastate federalism.

Yet the Canadian Senate, while it was meant to reflect the same federal principles as its American counterpart, did not reflect the specifics of the American model. First, Canadian senators were not selected by provincial legislatures or governments but were appointed by the federal government. In practice, senators have been appointed by the prime minister, who has been under no obligation even to consult with provincial governments.[12] Until 1965, senators were appointed for life; senators appointed after that date must retire at the age of 75. Second, Canadians opted for equal representation by region rather than equal representation by province. Thus, in 1867 Ontario, Quebec, and the Maritimes were each given 24 Senate seats. (The constitutional designation of Ontario and Quebec as both provinces and regions has bedevilled political discourse to this day.) For the one region that was not also a province, Senate seats were divided among the two and then, but not equally, the three Maritime provinces. When a 1915 constitutional amendment recognized Western Canada as a senatorial region, it too was assigned 24 seats divided equally among the four western provinces. Representation for Newfoundland in 1949 and for the two northern territories in 1975 was added to the initial regional allocation of seats. The Senate, in short, was the first institutional representation of the regionalist (as opposed to provincialist) institutional logic that we met in the previous chapter in the form of Victoria Charter–style amending procedures.

Table 5.4 looks at the results of the regionalist formula for allocating Senate seats from the perspective of provinces. There is no equality of provinces here. The table shows that Alberta, Ontario, and particularly British Columbia have the weakest proportional representation in the existing Senate. Such provincial inequities (or, at least, peculiarities) in the distribution of Senate seats are often overlooked in the belief that the Senate provides for equal regional representation, but even regional equality in the Senate takes on some strange twists. The West, for example, is underrepresented in the Senate relative to its share of the national population; the region has 29.5 percent of the 1996 national population but only 23 percent of the Senate seats. Thus, it is not surprising that western Canadians do not see equal regional representation as the appropriate federalist response to a perceived lack of political influence in the House. Atlantic Canada, with just over 8 percent of the national population and 29 percent of the Senate seats, is the primary beneficiary of Senate representation based on regional equality, a principle that was jettisoned in any event when Newfoundland's Senate seats were added to rather than drawn from the preexisting Maritime allotment.

Although the Senate is not an elected chamber, it has formal powers that are virtually identical to those of the House of Commons. If the Senate does not approve legislation passed by the House, its veto cannot be overridden by the House; the one exception is that the Senate has only a suspensive veto on constitutional amendments.[13] Money bills cannot be introduced in the Senate, but the Senate can defeat money bills initiated in the House. It should be stressed, however, that the formal

TABLE 5.4 **CURRENT DISTRIBUTION OF SENATE SEATS**

PROVINCE	# OF SENATE SEATS	POPULATION PER SENATOR*
Newfoundland	6	92,000
Prince Edward Island	4	34,000
Nova Scotia	10	91,000
New Brunswick	10	74,000
Quebec	24	297,000
Ontario	24	448,000
Manitoba	6	186,000
Saskatchewan	6	165,000
Alberta	6	449,000
British Columbia	6	621,000
Yukon	1	31,000
Northwest Territories	1	64,000

* Population figures based on 1996 census.

powers of the Senate have seldom been exercised; only rarely has the Senate attempted to block legislation passed by the House. Thus, the potential problem associated with an appointed chamber having formal powers roughly equivalent to those of the elected chamber was traditionally avoided by the restraint shown by senators in the exercise of their formal powers. Such restraint, which in the past took the form of a widely observed parliamentary convention, ensured a relatively smooth and effective working relationship between the two houses of Parliament. As was observed in Chapter 2, one of the functions of conventions is to ensure that formal constitutional rules are operated in accordance with current constitutional principles. The principle underlying the convention of senatorial restraint is democracy. The greater democracy that Canadians are now insisting on in matters of constitutional amendment, they have insisted on for some time in senatorial behaviour.

As in the case of other norms, however, the exception proves the rule. The parliamentary convention that structured the institutional relationship between the Senate and the House was ruptured in the aftermath of the 1984 election when a Liberal majority in the Senate faced an overwhelming Conservative majority in the House. Given that the Liberal opposition caucus in the House was both decimated and dispirited, the locus of partisan opposition to the Conservative government shifted to the Senate. On a number of key legislative initiatives, including but by no means restricted to the Free Trade Agreement (FTA) and the Goods and Services Tax (GST), the Liberal majority in the Senate set out to block the Conservative majority in the

House. In the case of the FTA, the Senate gave way only after forcing a national election, in which the Conservative government was returned to power. In the GST case, the opposition of the Senate was overcome only when the prime minister used an obscure constitutional provision to appoint eight additional Conservative senators.[14]

Another potential partisan conflict between the Senate and the House was set up by the 1993 election, which left a Progressive Conservative majority in the Senate facing a Liberal majority in the House. In this case, however, the dynamics were somewhat different and more complex. Given that the Conservatives elected only two MPs in 1993, the party's national legislative presence resided almost entirely in the Senate. There was therefore an understandable temptation for Conservative senators to adopt a more aggressive style, if only to provide some national profile for the party. At the same time, the two major opposition parties in the House—the Bloc and Reform—were without representation in the Senate and strenuously resisted any attempt by Conservative senators to preempt their opposition role.

The more general point is that in recent times the partisan behaviour of senators has disrupted, and has the potential to disrupt further, the conventional working relationship between the two chambers. This raises serious questions about responsible and democratic government, which could spur the movement for the reform and even abolition of the Senate.[15] However, once the Liberal party re-establishes its partisan control over the Senate, this pressure will wane.

It is worth noting that when governments change, opposing majorities in the House and Senate are almost guaranteed due to the appointment process and the lags it produces. Because senators are appointed until age 75, those appointed by any given prime minister are likely to remain in place well after the governing party has changed in the House. Thus, the senators appointed by Pierre Trudeau were the ones that confronted Brian Mulroney's governments in the 1980s; those appointed by Mulroney were the ones to confront his successor. There is, then, always a good chance that a new government majority in the House will face an opposition majority in the Senate. It should also be noted, however, that turnover in the Senate is fairly high despite the length of senatorial appointments. Trudeau appointed more than five senators a year throughout his 16 years as prime minister, Joe Clark appointed 11 senators in only nine months, and Brian Mulroney averaged almost nine appointments a year over his time in office. Therefore, a prime minister with two or more terms in office has the opportunity to transform the partisan composition of the Senate. The problem is that by the time this transformation is complete, the opposition may well have come to power. If senators decide to confront the elected House, as they appear increasingly prone to do, then the problems for democratic and responsible government could become acute.

In summary, the Senate reflects a fundamental ambiguity in the institutional structure of the Canadian federal state. It was designed to fulfill a legislative role similar to that fulfilled by the House of Lords in Britain and also a federal role similar to that fulfilled by the American Senate. The roles were not the same and, in trying to fulfill both, it is not surprising that the Senate failed to fulfill either satisfactorily.

Thus, the Senate has come under sustained and growing attack from those who see it as an affront to democratic principles, to federal principles, or to both.

THE LEGISLATIVE PROCESS

To this point we have examined the two primary institutions of Parliament—the House of Commons and the Senate. To understand how these two institutions work together as a coordinated institutional system, we now turn to an examination of the legislative process that spans the two houses of Parliament. As we will see, that process has been dominated by the House and thus by the institutional principles embedded in the House. The federal principles embedded in the Senate, or at least potentially embedded in the Senate, are less visible in the legislative process of Canadian parliamentary government.

Anyone who has tried to run a meeting in which debate occurs and votes are taken knows how complex "parliamentary procedures" can be. It is not our intent to plumb the depths of this complexity or to answer the types of procedural questions that inevitably arise in such meetings ("Madame Chairperson, are we voting on the amendment to the subamendment, or on the whole motion as amended, or as not amended, and do we have a quorum anyway?"). Rather, we provide a road map to the legislative process that illustrates the procedural operation of parliamentary democracy and at the same time shows the terrain of contested principles that legislation must negotiate in its transition from bill to act of Parliament. In doing so, we hope to illustrate the competing needs that the parliamentary process and conventions seek to address. As in the case of a public meeting, there is a need in Parliament for order and control, for some modicum of efficiency in handling the affairs of state. However, there is also a need for flexibility and the capacity to accommodate a diversity of opinion and perspectives. In short, parliamentary procedures try to impose order and control without preventing the full expression of dissent. It is a difficult balancing act and not always successful. It is an act, moreover, whose success is interpreted differently by supporters and opponents of the government of the day.

Most legislation emerges from the complex interplay between the federal cabinet and the public service, between the political and policy imperatives of cabinet ministers, on one hand, and the related expertise—and, sometimes, the policy imperatives—of bureaucrats, on the other. Of course, the initial incentives for parliamentary action may be found in the broader political and social orders, for there are virtually no limits to the domestic and international forces that can shape the legislative agenda; interest groups, special enquiries, court decisions, the actions of other governments, and world events can all come into play. Royal commissions, such as those on Aboriginal peoples and reproductive technologies, can play an important stimulative role. The government **caucus,** which consists of all government MPs and senators, also plays an important role by generating legislative initiatives and providing a sounding board for initiatives originating with the government.[16] The caucus and its committees, including regional caucuses, play such an important role because they provide a representative forum and because frank discussion is protected by norms of secrecy; caucus debate takes place behind closed doors, which enables intraparty disputes to be sorted out before policy initiatives appear on the floor of the House.

Nonetheless, the translation of policy needs and initiatives into concrete legislative proposals takes place primarily in the interplay between cabinet and bureaucracy. Thus, while MPs who are not in the cabinet may be active in the caucus committees and scrums and may introduce legislation in the House as senators may do in the Senate, the great bulk of legislation brought before the House for serious debate is **government legislation.** Other legislative initiatives are inconsequential in volume and policy importance. Here it should be noted that most government bills are **public bills,** which have a general impact on Canadian citizens. The impact of **private bills,** such as those needed to incorporate private companies or charitable organizations (or to change the existing terms of incorporation) is limited to private persons or corporations; these bills are dispatched with little if any parliamentary discussion or debate. Private bills are often introduced in the Senate and receive only perfunctory treatment in the House.

Legislative proposals, or bills, are generally introduced into the House by the responsible minister or initiating MP, and are then given **first reading.**[17] At this stage the bill is simply announced, numbered, and printed in both official languages for distribution; there is no discussion or debate. In effect, the government serves notice to the House, and through the House to the country, that the bill has been placed on the legislative agenda. Substantive debate begins with **second reading,** at which time the bill is discussed in principle. At the end of this stage a vote is taken on the bill as a whole; amendments are not permitted and specific clauses or provisions are not discussed in detail. At this stage too the government defends the need for the legislation and outlines its general policy principles and intended effects. The government also signals the importance it attaches to the bill and thus the extent to which the constraints of party discipline will apply in the subsequent debate.

It should be stressed that parliamentary debate during second reading is not meant primarily to sway opponents on the other side of the House or to shore up supporters. The principal audience is external to the House, as government and opposition MPs write into the public record why the bill is important, why it should be passed or defeated, and how it connects—or fails to connect—to the concerns of voters and to the fabric of the national community. The debate is therefore important even though it may not be dynamic and even though votes in the House may not change as a consequence. It is through parliamentary debate, and through the public record of that debate in Hansard, that the government and opposition meet their responsibility to inform and, at times, even educate the public. While the character of debate in the House may occasionally be trivialized, and while the content of specific debates may be trivial, the role of that debate within the broader context of parliamentary democracy is far from trivial.

If the bill is approved at second reading, it is sent to committee for more detailed, clause-by-clause examination. Bills are usually examined by **legislative committees** (special committees created for specific legislative proposals), although the committee stage may also involve one of the **standing committees** of the House or the entire House (minus the speaker) sitting as a **committee of the whole.** Committee hearings provide an opportunity for some measure of legislative independence from the bureaucratic advice woven into the proposed legislation. Thus, expert witnesses may be called and public hearings held. By this time, however, what is at issue is the fine print, although the line between principle and detail is not always easy to draw. At least under conditions of a majority government, fidelity to the principle of the legislation is ensured by two facts: (1) committees other than the Public Accounts Committee have a majority of members and a chairperson drawn from the government side of the House and (2) the constraints of party discipline that apply to the House as a whole apply with equal force to the votes of its committees. Admittedly, the style and tone of committee debate may be less partisan and more freewheeling, in part because media coverage is much lighter. Amendments are moved, discussed, and voted on, but this all takes place within the constraints of party discipline and with the understanding that the bill has already been approved in principle by the House.[18]

Despite the continuing constraints of party discipline, the **committee stage** has become less formalistic and more important over time. Serious discussion of parliamentary reforms to the committee system began in the early 1960s and culminated in the 1985 McGrath Report,[19] whose recommendations, once implemented, strengthened the role of committees in the legislative process. As a consequence, parliamentary committees are now better equipped, operate with greater independence, and attract greater media attention. They have become a valuable arena within which opposition and backbench MPs can develop policy skills, display leadership abilities, and attract public attention. Although committees have not significantly weakened the overall grip of party discipline on the legislative process, they have provided an enhanced policy role for those MPs outside the inner circle of cabinet. Special committees, including joint House-Senate committees, have played an important policy role both inside and outside the formal legislative process. An example is the Beaudoin-Dobbie Special Joint Committee of the Senate and House of Commons, which handled the federal government's draft constitutional package. The committee came into existence in June 1991, received the federal government's constitutional proposals in September, and disbanded after issuing its report in February 1992. Between September and February, the committee held 78 public meetings across the country, heard presentations from over 700 individuals and groups, received nearly 3000 written submissions, and participated in five national constitutional conferences.

Thus, while today's committees may be a far cry from the freewheeling committees of the American Congress, they are also a far cry from the tame and poorly equipped committees that existed during Canada's first hundred years of parliamentary democracy. Changes to the committee system have enhanced the legislative role of MPs by providing an expanded forum for that role, a forum with greater freedom of expression than that provided by the more stylized and party-bound debate on the floor of the House. The changes have also increased access to, or "standing" within, the legislative process for groups that lack an effective voice within the cabinet or caucus of the governing party. Given the internal pressures for change that have been evident within the House for the last several decades, and given an aggressive search by opposition MPs for some leverage over the policy process, the committee system is likely to continue to evolve along a trajectory of increased independence and policy significance.

After detailed committee examination, the bill is brought back to the floor of the House for the **report stage.** Here all members of the House are able to discuss the details of the bill and any changes emerging from the committee stage. Committee amendments are considered and new amendments are proposed, although all in the context that the bill has already been approved in principle and that amendments that would go to the principled core of the legislation are not permitted. Once all amendments have been put to a vote, the bill as a whole goes to **third reading.** At this last stage, no further changes or amendments are entertained, and members must accept or reject the bill as it stands. The formal vote on third reading brings the legislative process in the House to a close. If the bill is approved on third reading, it is sent to the Senate.

Legislation originating in the House already carries the stamp of democratic legitimacy before reaching the Senate. This stamp in turn curtails Senate debate, which at times is little more than perfunctory. Legislation within the Senate moves through the same stages as it does in the House, but the hurdles are lower at each stage. In most cases the bill is given "sober second thought" rather than a more root-and-branch examination that would touch on the principles of the legislation. Many bills reach the Senate so late in the parliamentary session that the delay entailed in any detailed examination would be tantamount to a veto, and therefore detailed examination is avoided. Thus, the legislative coordination of the House and Senate has been achieved by the joint institutional recognition of the House's greater democratic legitimacy. Despite the formal equality of the two legislative assemblies, the Senate is seen to play (and in fact does play) a decidedly secondary role.

At the same time, there is evidence that the existing legislative relationship between the House and Senate is beginning to unravel. The Senate debates in 1988 on the Free Trade Agreement, in 1990 on the Goods and Services Tax, and in 1991 on the government's abortion bill demonstrate that the Senate is not always willing to forego detailed examination, and that partisanship can overcome the institutional reluctance of appointed senators to challenge the elected House.[20] In the first two cases, the ultimately unsuccessful Senate opposition was mounted despite strong legislative endorsement by the House and on issues that were central to the legislative program of the government. In neither case was the Senate action consistent with conventional motions of responsible government. The abortion case was somewhat different in that the bill, which was not central to the government's legislative program and was not a confidence measure, was handled by a free vote. The final vote in the Senate was a 43–43 tie, which, under Senate rules, meant the defeat of the legislation.

DOSSIER 5.3 THE AMERICAN LEGISLATIVE PROCESS

In Parliament, amendments to legislative proposals are permitted only if they relate in some direct fashion to the core substance of the legislation. The standing orders of the House and the conventional rules of parliamentary procedure would not permit, for example, a bill relating to crop insurance to be amended so as to exempt certain kinds of firearms from import restrictions. By contrast, amendments in the congressional legislative process need not relate in any immediate way to the core of the legislation. As a consequence, bills can be amended in seemingly bizarre ways in order to obtain enough votes for passage. "Logrolling" among members of Congress can result in curious amalgamations that would never be permitted under Canadian rules.

An example of the American case is provided by the Revenue Act of 1992, which began as a response to the Los Angeles riots of that year. Its intent was "to provide tax incentives for the establishment of tax-enterprise zones, and for other purposes." By the time the bill emerged from Congress, it had grown to a $27-billion monster that would have provided benefits for the great majority of the 435 congressional districts. Among other things, the act would have:

- provided tax breaks for 25 city neighbourhoods (presumably including Los Angeles) and 25 similar zones in poor rural districts, plus aid to high-unemployment Indian reservations;
- allowed tuxedos to be written off for tax purposes in two years rather than five;
- permitted court officials to use people's social insurance numbers to weed out convicted felons from jury lists;
- removed the tax on the sale of trucks built in nonprofit schools where students learn by building trucks;
- provided retroactive tax relief for American clergy who worked in Canada before 1984;
- eliminated the tax on the reloading of used rifle and shotgun shells, if customers provide the shells;
- required state authorities to tip off credit-reporting agencies about parents who dodge child-support payments;
- repealed the luxury excise tax on the purchase of yachts, jewellery, furs, and private planes; and
- provided a tax write-off for companies that pay to have their names displayed at college football bowl games.

President George Bush vetoed the bill when it emerged from Congress.

Source: John Saunders, "Tax Bill Offering Pork for All Likely to Wilt under Bush's Veto," *The Globe and Mail,* October 21, 1992, A1–2. Reprinted with permission from *The Globe and Mail.*

A number of points should be stressed with respect to the new level of legislative activity that erupted in the Senate during the Mulroney years. First, it was a marked and important departure from past Canadian experience. Second, its primary roots are to be found in the partisan struggle between the Progressive

Conservative majority in the House, elected in 1984 and reelected in 1988, and the Liberal majority in the Senate, a majority that was the direct legacy of Liberal dominance in the House during the 1970s and early 1980s. The senators who opposed government legislation were Liberals; Progressive Conservative senators did not bend, much less break, party ranks. Indeed, Hugh Winsor argues that Conservative Senator Finlay MacDonald's move in June 1993 to amend (and, in effect, kill) Bill C-93 (the government's reorganization bill that proposed, among other things, the amalgamation of the Canada Council and the Social Sciences and Humanities Research Council) was "... the first time any Conservative senator had attempted to change, improve, modify or defeat any piece of government legislation in the nine years since Mr. Mulroney took office."[21] The third point is that partisan opposition within the Senate has been effectively mobilized only in those cases where the government's legislation was so clearly unpopular that senators could make a plausible case that it was they rather than government MPs who truly spoke for Canadians. As Robert Campbell and Leslie Pal note in the case of the GST debate,

> *Any discomfort [Liberal senators] felt about blocking a piece of financial legislation by the elected House of Commons was assuaged by the incredible public abhorrence of the tax that had built up over the last year. The plummeting popularity of the Mulroney government—a process accelerated by the June 1990 Meech Lake disaster—also bolstered the Liberal senators' sense that they, and not the elected government, were in tune with the people's wishes.*[22]

Within this logic, the unelected Senate became the more democratic chamber!

The Canadian public appears ambivalent about the propriety of the appointed Senate blocking legislation passed by the elected House. When the legislation at issue is unpopular, as was clearly the case with the GST, the public appears to support Senate opposition; by a margin of 2–1 (60 percent compared to 29 percent), respondents to a 1990 Globe and Mail–CBC national survey said they believed that the Senate should not approve the proposed GST legislation.[23] In the case of the Senate's defeat of the government's abortion legislation, public opinion about the legislation itself was more divided and support for the Senate's action less emphatic, although Canadians still sided with the unelected institution. An Angus Reid poll found that 50 percent of 1500 national respondents agreed and 45 percent disagreed that "unelected senators were within their rights to defeat the abortion bill passed by an elected House of Commons."[24] Support for the Senate's defeat of the bill was strongest in Alberta, where Senate reform enjoys its greatest support, and weakest in Quebec, where support for Senate reform is appreciably weaker than it is elsewhere in the country.

To return to the more general legislative process, the Senate can amend legislation passed by the House. In such instances, the House is informed in writing of the amendments, which are put to a vote in the House. If the amendments are defeated and the Senate still insists on amendments before passage, a joint committee meeting of representatives from the two chambers is called by the House to see if the impasse can be broken. In the final analysis, the bill must be passed in exactly the same form by the two chambers. Defeat in the Senate is absolute; it cannot be overridden by the House, which explains in part why in the past the unelected Senate has rarely opposed the will of the elected House. As noted above, in some cases the legislative process will begin in the Senate and then move to the House. This might be the case with legislation incorporating companies, or legislation of limited general effect. It was also the case for the first cut at legislation establishing the Canadian Security and Intelligence Service. The government used Senate debate and hearings as a trial balloon. When it became clear that the legislation needed a major overhaul, it was withdrawn and then later reintroduced, this time in the House.

Passage in the Senate leads to the final step in the legislative process, **royal assent** by the governor general, which has never been refused. (The same is not true for provincial legislation, which was frequently turned back by lieutenant governors in the decades following Confederation.) The title of the bill is read in the Senate by the clerk of the Senate and in the presence of the Speaker and members of the House. The governor general or his or her representative, such as the chief justice or another judge from the Supreme Court, signals royal assent by a nod of the head. It should be noted, however, that although the bill becomes an act of Parliament with royal assent, it does not have the force of law until it is proclaimed. There may often be a delay of months, occasionally even years, between royal assent and **proclamation.** For example, the legislation approving the North American Free Trade Agreement (NAFTA) received royal assent immediately after it had been passed by both houses of Parliament in June 1993, but was not proclaimed until January 1994. In this case, proclamation was prudently delayed pending the outcome of the NAFTA debate in Mexico and the United States.

Not all legislation introduced in the House or Senate is government legislation, although only the government has the right to introduce money bills. MPs and senators have the opportunity to introduce **private members' bills** and thereby initiate legislative debate without the support of the government. At the beginning of the parliamentary session, the names of all MPs who have introduced a private members' bill for first reading in the House are put in a drum and a number of names are chosen at random. Those MPs whose names are chosen are assured that their bill will receive at least one hour of parliamentary debate and will therefore enter the public record. However, such bills are severely constrained because they cannot require the raising or spending of public funds. Little time is allotted for the debate of private members' bills, and it is a rare event when they move through the entire legislative process and are proclaimed. Such bills are used primarily to float trial balloons or to convince the folks back home that the individual MP is actively engaged in the legislative process. (American senators and members of Congress employ this tactic far more often than do Canadian parliamentarians.) Trial balloons that show some potential for liftoff may be co-opted by the government and brought back as government legislation. Yet exceptions to this general assessment do occur. On January 1,

1990, the Non-Smoker's Health Act came into effect, prohibiting smoking in any workplace regulated by the federal government, including the public service, radio stations, shipping companies, and Crown corporations. This act had been introduced into the House not only as a private members' bill but by an opposition MP.

The process described above outlines the events that take place when a bill moves successfully through Parliament's legislative process. It also captures the basic outline of the provincial legislative process—except that no province has a second chamber; provincial legislation thus moves from the elected legislature directly to the lieutenant governor for royal assent. It should be noted as well that the committee stage plays a less important role in most provincial legislatures, and that provincial legislatures face a lighter legislative load than does Parliament. As a consequence, provincial legislatures meet for shorter sessions than does the House of Commons, which sits for an average of 175 days a year.

The speed with which the legislative process moves depends on a number of factors, including the determination and skill of opposition parties in frustrating the government. In doing so, the opposition parties can draw from an impressive arsenal of procedural weapons, including legislative debate itself. As C.E.S. Franks points out,

> *the function of much debate is not to state, convince, prove, persuade, rally, or support, but simply to occupy time. Time is a valuable commodity in the House of Commons, and it is in short supply. The consumption of time through prolonged debate is a weapon the opposition can use in its warfare with the government.*[25]

The speed of the process depends in addition on the priority the government attaches to the bill, the urgency of public concern, the number of other legislative initiatives competing for time and attention, and the degree to which the parties share a common interest in the legislation. Although it normally takes months to complete the process, speed is possible; in 1981 a bill to increase the salaries of MPs moved through all stages in the House in only five hours.[26] On July 9, 1982, with only 13 MPs present in the House (seven short of a quorum), a private members' bill to change the name of the July 1 national holiday from Dominion Day to Canada Day passed with less than two minutes of debate. Here it should also be noted that the government has resources other than public opinion at its disposal in determining the pace of parliamentary debate. At the extreme, closure can be invoked to terminate debate. In some circumstances, the purpose of prolonged debate may simply be to provoke the government into using closure, which in itself becomes another cause célèbre for the opposition. The use of closure is not without risk, for it can give the appearance of a government riding roughshod over legitimate debate and concerns. However, it appears that closure is becoming an increasingly common and less controversial response by the government to even moderately prolonged opposition debate. What used to be extreme has now been routinized to a considerable degree.

But what happens when a bill fails to pass or is defeated? If the parliamentary session ends before final reading and royal assent—if, for example, the House is dissolved for a general election—the bill simply dies. There are no consequences beyond the fact that the proposed legislation is not put into place, and the legislation can be reintroduced in the next session of Parliament. If the bill is a private members' bill, or if the bill is handled as a free vote in which MPs and senators are not constrained by party discipline, the same conclusion applies. However, if the bill is a government bill, particularly a money bill, and if it is deemed by the government or perhaps even by the opposition to be a significant part of the government's legislative program, the defeat of the bill may signal that the government has lost the confidence of the House. (Defeat in the Senate does not signify a loss of confidence, for the Senate is not a "confidence chamber.") In this case, the prime minister may ask or be forced by political opinion to ask the governor general to call an election. The government may also request a formal vote of confidence in the House, or the opposition may call for a formal vote of nonconfidence. In the 1998 debate over the government's compensation package for hepatitis C victims, the opposition Reform Party introduced an amendment that was explicitly not framed as a confidence test, but the government insisted that it was, thereby stemming a revolt within its own ranks. If, in any of these cases, the government's loss of confidence is confirmed, the government has no option but to resign. The governor general has the legal option of dissolving the House and calling an election, or calling on another individual to form a government. This last option would be politically viable only in an unusual circumstance such as might attend an unstable minority government following a general election.

To bring this procedural discussion to a close, it should be noted that the parliamentary environment is very complex. Not surprisingly, MPs and senators take considerable time to learn the rules of the game and even longer to exploit them successfully to their own partisan and personal advantage. Parliamentarians go through a period of socialization and apprenticeship that includes committee assignments and, if they are fortunate, a position as parliamentary secretary to a cabinet minister or, if an opposition MP, a position in the shadow cabinet. MPs need time and experience to sort through the conflicted nature of their role. To what extent and under what circumstances should the MP be bound by the expressed interests of his or her constituents? By the interests of party or by the broader interests of the national community? By the MP's own sense of morality or understanding of the issues at play? The MP's role is a complex and fascinating one to learn and play.

Involvement in the legislative process is only part of the MP's job, indeed a minor part for many MPs. Much time and energy is expended on constituency service—answering letters and phone calls, sorting out bureaucratic problems, attending constituency events, and hosting visitors in Ottawa. The MP serves as an informal ombudsman[27] for constituents who become entangled in disputes about pensions, employment insurance, passports, agricultural subsidies, and a myriad of other program areas in which the federal government plays a role. The MP is also involved in parliamentary committee work that may have little to do with legislation per se, and is responsible for the party organization in his or her constituency. Thus, for many MPs it may be all to the good that what goes on in Question Period and legislative debate is little more than ritualistic combat, for they are freed as a consequence to get on with more important duties.

Finally, we should stress that the above description of the legislative process does not capture many of the nuances of parliamentary procedure that can bedevil the government, empower the opposition, entrance practitioners on both sides of the House, and puzzle if not frustrate the public. Nor does it capture the "theatre" of parliamentary government. In an important sense, the House provides the national stage on which are played the dramas, tragedies, and comedies of Canadian political life. MPs are cast into roles—the Leader of the Opposition, the crusading backbencher, the indignant minister, the embattled prime minister—and these roles are played to the hilt before partisan colleagues and foes, before the audience in the visitors' gallery, and, through the media, before the electorate.

THE QUEST FOR INSTITUTIONAL REFORM

Parliamentary institutions, and particularly the House of Commons, have a commanding presence on the Canadian political landscape. They are more than functional parts of an elaborate system of representative government; they are democratic icons in the political culture. They are also complex clusters of rules, conventions, and norms that shape, even if they do not fully determine, the behaviour of incumbent politicians and the nature of public policy. Not surprisingly, this cluster of rules, conventions, and norms is fluid to a degree and often contested, in whole or in part. At the micro level the rules are often challenged by MPs and senators as they jockey for position and advantage; it is the responsibility of the respective Speakers to uphold the rules, to settle matters of debate, and to permit enough flexibility that the rules can evolve to meet changing conditions. At the macro level, dissension over the rules of the game, over the institutional structures of parliamentary democracy, have become almost endemic to Canadian political life.

Three macro-level challenges to existing parliamentary institutions are particularly noteworthy. The first is the persistent demand for the reform or even abolition of the Senate, which is without doubt the least revered political institution in Canada. The second is the equally persistent attack on party discipline in the House of Commons, an institutional feature that provides a good deal of the structure and form to parliamentary government. The third is an increasingly prominent attempt to supplement or replace representative government with various devices of direct democracy. We examine each of these challenges in turn.

Senate Reform

The movement for Senate reform has been driven by a number of factors, of which the Senate's legislative challenges to the democratically elected House are only the most recent. Indeed, the movement has been laden with a great deal of baggage, as Senate reform has come to be seen as a solution to a variety of problems and as an alternative to reform of the House of Commons. Given that the Senate is the institution that addresses most immediately the reconciliation of parliamentary and federal principles, it is perhaps not surprising that it has been the focal point of much debate over institutional reform.

In the late 1970s and early 1980s, provincialist versions of intrastate Senate reform were proposed as a solution to incessant intergovernmental conflict and, more positively, as a response to the need for more effective intergovernmental coordination. Reform proposals such as those recommended by the Pepin-Robarts Royal Commission envisioned a House of the Provinces to which provincial governments would send delegations that would vote as a bloc on instructions from their government, thereby providing provincial governments with a general check on the legislative activities of the national government and, in some models, with a specific check on the use of the federal spending power in areas of exclusive provincial jurisdiction. This reform model was in keeping with the thrust of Quebec nationalism and with the more general provincialism that was characteristic of constitutional deliberations prior to the passage of the Constitution Act, 1982. The emphasis was on the representation of provincial governments rather than on provincial electorates within the national legislative process.

By the mid-1980s the House of the Provinces model began to lose ground to a model of Senate reform designed to address chronic problems of regional alienation rather than intergovernmental conflict. This new approach to Senate reform, which has been identified most closely with the **Triple-E** vision of an elected, equal, and effective Senate, was built around different representational concerns. Rather than provide an enhanced role for provincial governments, it would provide for the direct popular election of senators. The impact of such reform would be to diminish, not enhance, the role of provincial governments and premiers on the national stage. Regional alienation would be addressed in a number of ways: the election of senators would strengthen ties between citizens and their national government; an equal number of seats for all provinces would give "outer Canada" sufficient legislative clout to counterbalance central Canadian domination of the House of Commons; and an effective Senate would ensure that regional representatives would in fact be heard in Ottawa. While the House of the Provinces model represented provincialist intrastate federalism, the Triple-E model represented centralist intrastate federalism. Its major objective was to strengthen the legitimacy and clout of federal politicians and legislative institutions at the expense of provincial governments.

Support for an elected Senate, although not necessarily for an equal or effective Senate, gained additional momentum from the public discontent with parliamentary institutions documented by the Keith Spicer's Citizens Forum and from the public dissatisfaction with executive federalism that grew out of the Meech Lake debacle. Despite occasional rearguard actions by the proponents of the House of the Provinces model, the Charlottetown Accord proposed a Senate more along the lines of the Triple-E model. The proposed Senate would have been equal, with every province holding six seats. It would also have been elected, though not necessarily directly by the people; in a concession to Quebec, the proposal included the option of indirect election by provincial legislature, or, given the realities of Canadian legislative government, appointment by the provincial cabinet. In other words, the door was left open for a provincialist House of the Provinces, though it seemed that only Quebec was likely to avail itself of that option. Also reflecting the tradition of Canadian dualism was a provision that francophone senators would have had an absolute veto on legislation materially affecting the French language or culture. Aboriginals demanded similar treatment and secured a provision that gave Aboriginal senators an absolute veto on legislation materially affecting Aboriginal peoples. Western memories of the National Energy Policy were addressed by giving the proposed Senate an absolute veto on new taxes on natural resources. Where the vetoes did not apply (which is to say in most cases), the defeat of legislation in the Senate would have triggered a joint sitting of the House and Senate in which a simple majority would have been needed to pass the legislation. In this situation, an enlarged House of Commons would have meant that MPs would outnumber senators by a margin of greater than 5–1 in joint sittings.

The Charlottetown proposal for Senate reform, like the Charlottetown Accord more broadly conceived, tried to balance a number of competing institutional interests and perspectives. It tried to accommodate the West's demand for provincial equality with Quebec's particular interest in institutional protection within the national legislative process. It tried to accommodate the populist quest for more democracy while retaining some role for provincial legislatures in the selection of senators. And it tried to balance the demand for more effective regional representation with emerging demands for Aboriginal representation within national legislations. Like the larger accord of which it was a part, the Senate reform proposal ultimately collapsed under the weight of its accommodative compromises; it offered too little for the champions of Senate reform and too much for its opponents.

The Senate reform debate is interesting not only for its own sake but also because it exposes a number of important institutional tensions in Canadian political life. First, the proponents of Senate reform challenge many of the fundamental tenets of responsible parliamentary government by seeking to weaken executive control over the legislative process. Second, Senate reform of virtually every stripe is designed to shift power to the regional peripheries lying to the east and west of the central Canadian heartland, and thus Senate reformers seek to redefine the power relationship among regional communities in Canada. Third, the quest for Senate reform poses serious complications for the representation of Quebec and the country's sizable francophone minority within national parliamentary institutions. Any move toward provincial equality in the Senate runs up against the awkward demographic fact that Canada's linguistic minority is concentrated in one of the largest provinces; approximately 87 percent of francophones live in Quebec. Therefore, any reduction in Quebec's weight in the Senate would also be a reduction in francophone representation. Here it should be noted that the threat Senate reform poses to cabinet dominance can also be seen as a threat to Quebec and thus to francophone representation. Herman Bakvis shows that since the 1960s Quebec francophones have been slightly overrepresented in the federal cabinet and have occupied major economic portfolios. Quebec ministers, enjoying strong caucus support from Quebec MPs, "have given genuine meaning to the expression 'French power in Ottawa.'"[28] This, Bakvis argues, explains "the reluctance of Quebec to embrace Senate reform in so far as an elected Senate, in which the smaller provinces enjoy over-representation, could derogate power and influence from cabinet."[29]

The striking thing is that Senate reformers have maintained some momentum despite the fact that virtually all of the existing institutional actors would lose by Senate reform. The potential losers go beyond the two central Canadian provinces to include MPs in the House of Commons, who would have to share the stage with a second elected chamber; the cabinet and the prime minister, whose control over the legislative process would be weakened if the reformed Senate was in fact effective; provincial premiers, who would be eclipsed as the primary advocates and defenders of regional interests on the national stage; the existing senators; and perhaps provincial governments in general if, as has been the case in Australia and the United States, more effective regional representation at the centre were to strengthen the role of national institutions. Yet despite this opposition among the very institutional actors whose support is required for constitutional amendment, the Senate reform bus has not yet stalled. In an April 1998 survey of 1500 adult respondents, Angus Reid found that 43 percent of the respondents supported Senate reform, 41 percent supported abolition, and only 11 percent supported the status quo.[30] Support for Reform was highest among Albertans and British Columbians (55 percent and 50 percent, respectively), those with university degrees (54 percent), and those with the highest incomes (48 percent). When Albertans were asked in March 1998 whether the province's "next senator should be appointed by the Prime Minister or elected by all Albertans," 91 percent opted for election and only 7 percent for appointment.[31] A survey of 503 British Columbia respondents in April 1998 found, in a response to the same question, that 84 percent supported election and only 8 percent opted for appointment.[32]

Public opinion with respect to the Senate is divided between those who support the direct election of senators and those who support the Senate's abolition. What is clear, however, is that few Canadians support the status quo. The controversy over Senator Andrew Thompson, who attended fewer than 5 percent of the Senate sittings in the 1990s while maintaining a full-time residency in Mexico, fuelled public anger. Nonetheless, the status quo continues with little sign of governmental enthusiasm for even modest reform. The Senate is still appointed, not elected (though Alberta is spearheading a movement to change that—see Dossier 5.4). The Senate still has formal legislative powers virtually equal to those of the House, powers that the unelected senators seem increasingly inclined to exercise. It is still based on an antiquated formula of regional representation that makes little if any contemporary sense. It is still an institution that attracts unrelenting public criticism and no discernible public support.

This should not lead automatically to the suggestion that the existing Senate is without worth or that senators do not provide reasonable value in return for their salaries and perks. The problem is more that the functions currently performed by the Senate and senators are in large part performed also by other institutional players. Senators may provide sober second thought for legislation, but so do legislative committees within the House, legal advisers within the department of Justice, and courts. The Senate may from time to time provide investigative reports on matters of public policy, but so do royal commissions and special task forces. Senate appointments provide a patronage means by which the government can remove deadwood from the cabinet and reward the party faithful, but, as Chapter 6 points out, such opportunities abound. The question, then, is whether there is anything that the Senate does or might do that could not be done as well by other institutions or actors. Is there a unique and important institutional niche for the Senate? The answer to this question hinges largely on how one reacts to issues of regional representation and alienation. Supporters of Senate reform argue that a reformed Senate could provide a measure of effective and legitimate regional representation that other institutions—notably the House—cannot provide, due to the constraints of party discipline and the principle of representation by population. The supporters of abolition argue either that more effective regional representation is not a serious issue or that such representation could be provided either by a reformed House or through the instrumentalities of executive federalism. In short, they suggest that other actors could pick up the slack if the Senate were to be abolished. Between the proponents of reform and abolition, supporters of the status quo are increasingly difficult to find.

Reform of the House of Commons

The Senate has not been the sole target of parliamentary reform. The House of Commons too has come under criticism both from the public and from parliamentarians themselves. Here the primary concern, one that goes to the core of parliamentary democracy, has been the pervasive impact of party discipline on the procedures of the House and on the capacity of the House to function as a representative institution.

Parliamentary democracy fits hand in glove with party government. Once the legislative process is set in motion by the introduction of a government bill, there is little that opposition parties can do but delay and obstruct. Their leverage is lodged in the complexity of parliamentary procedures, complexity that provides the cover within which opposition MPs lie in wait for the government. Although opposition parties can work to improve legislation through constructive criticism and amendments, the political reality is that better legislation is more likely to work to the electoral advantage of the governing party than of their own. Even in minority government situations, opposition parties do not sit as coalition partners in the government, so the

DOSSIER 5.4 THE ROAD TO SENATE REFORM: ALBERTA'S SENATE ELECTIONS

Contrary to popular opinion, Albertans were not the first champions of a Triple-E Senate for Canada. During the 1864 conferences leading up to Confederation, delegates from Prince Edward Island argued for an elected, effective, and equal Senate. But whatever the history, Alberta leads the crusade today. Not only did the province put Senate reform on the constitutional table in the 1980s, it continues to take the lead by electing Senate nominees.

Alberta's first Senate vote was held on October 16, 1989, and was sparked by a provision in the 1987 Meech Lake Accord that committed the prime minister to appoint senators solely from a list of names provided by the premiers. Confronted with a vacant seat in the upper house and concerned about the accord's potential to block meaningful Senate reform in the future, the province decided to advance the issue by providing the prime minister with a list that contained only one name—the winner of a province-wide Senate election. The prime minister stated his opposition to the vote and vowed not to appoint the winner, but democracy is hard to ignore. Over 640,000 Albertans cast ballots in the election. The winner, Mr. Stan Waters, received 259,292 votes, and after eight months was appointed Canada's first elected Senator by the prime minister.

The 1989 election served notice that Alberta was serious about reform of the upper house and helped ensure that a redesigned Senate would be included in any future effort at constitutional change. Since the 1989 election, Canadians have witnessed the demise of both the Meech and Charlottetown Accords, and four Alberta Senate seats have been filled with appointments made by the prime minister, despite numerous overtures for elected Senators. With future efforts at formal constitutional change unlikely and amidst numerous high-profile Senate scandals, the Alberta government decided to call a second Senate vote on October 19, 1998.

Unlike the 1989 vote, Alberta did not have a vacancy in the Senate when the 1998 election was called. Rather, the intent of the vote was for Albertans to elect two "Senators-in-waiting" who would be available for the prime minister to appoint whenever the next Senate vacancy for Alberta occurred. Because the prime minister refused previous calls from the province to elect Senators, it was decided that an election would have to be held in advance of a vacancy to create a democratic mandate that the prime minister could not ignore.

Alberta's 1998 Senate election led to considerable debate about the Senate, both within the province and across the country. Because only one political party (Reform) decided to enter candidates against two independents, a debate emerged about the legitimacy of the election. Some argued that it was a waste of time because no official position of "elected Senator" existed. Others argued that the prime minister would never appoint the winners. The debate over the merits of the election intensified when an Alberta Senator resigned in the middle of the campaign, and the prime minister quickly appointed a replacement rather than waiting for the results of the vote.

Official results of the 1998 Senate election showed that 892,190 valid ballots were cast. Because each Albertan had up to two votes, the turnout was at least 446,000 Albertans (total valid votes divided by two), but the final results will likely be higher. Bert Brown, a long-time advocate of Senate reform and leader of the Canadian Committee for a Triple-E Senate, topped the polls with 332,985 votes. Ted Morton, a professor of political science at the University of Calgary, came second with 274,272 votes. Guy Desrosiers and Vance Gough, the two independent candidates, received 148,990 and 135,943 votes, respectively.

Whether or not Alberta's 1998 election will eventually result in the appointment of another elected Senator for Alberta remains to be seen. However, other provinces are also lining up to elect Senators. British Columbia has legislation providing for the election of Senators, and efforts at Senate election legislation are currently underway in Manitoba and Ontario. Has Alberta started a trend? Time will tell.

incentives to cooperate are limited. In this critical sense, the function of the House and MPs is to support and criticize the government of the day but not to govern directly.[33] Parliament may be sovereign in the sense that it is not bound by the decisions of past parliaments, but it is not sovereign in the sense of directing the legislative process and determining the nature of legislation. Party discipline, which is perhaps the preeminent operational "rule" for Parliament, ensures that these latter functions remain in the hands of the political executive.

The term "party discipline" may be misleading to some readers in that it draws too much attention to negative constraints on parliamentary behaviour. Admittedly, there are costs associated with breaking party ranks, particularly on matters of importance to the party's leadership. Career prospects, including the golden ring of cabinet appointment, may be hurt and access to key decision makers may be curtailed. In some cases, projects and programs of interest to a dissident MP's constituency may be threatened. Thus the incentive structures of Parliament reinforce party discipline in a variety of ways. It is also true that votes in the House are orchestrated by the party "whips," a term that reinforces the negative connotations of party discipline.[34] However, parliamentarians to a large extent impose party discipline on themselves because of the positive personal benefits that it might bring and because, no matter what the disadvantages might be, MPs know in their bones that the country is better off with their party in power than it would be under any alternative arrangement.

Party discipline plays an indispensable role with respect to responsible and effective government. It provides a means by which regional and social representation can be harnessed to, but not necessarily submerged by, larger policy and national interests. Long gone, and perhaps for the good, is the style of representation epitomized by A.H. Gillmor, member of the 1864 Legislative Assembly of New Brunswick for Charlotte County:

Mr. Speaker, when a bill's before this house I always ask what's it going to do for Charlotte. I ain't got anything to do with the Province. I sits here for Charlotte and if they tells me it'll do good to the Province but do harm to Charlotte then says I, "I go in for Charlotte." If they tells me it'll harm the Province but do good to Charlotte then too says I, "I go in for Charlotte."[35]

If party discipline is a yoke, it is one that is slipped on easily and rests lightly on the shoulders of most MPs.

Be that as it may, there is no question that perceptions of party discipline are the major source of public dissatisfaction with the performance of parliamentary institutions. Certainly, the perceived constraints of party discipline, and the assumed deleterious impact of that discipline on regional sensitivity, have been mainstays of western alienation. Party discipline is the least appreciated, if also the least understood, aspect of parliamentary democracy. The positive functions of party discipline—its role in providing responsible and effective government—are largely overlooked by citizens who perceive their MPs to be little more than trained seals prepared to place the interests of their party above the interests of their constituents, region, and even principles. In this case, of course, appearances are not all that deceiving, for when it comes to formal votes in the House, MPs (and particularly government MPs) have little option but to toe the party line. The loss of confidence that might follow from legislative defeat, and thus the trials and uncertainties of a national election campaign, constitute too great a risk to indulge constituency interests or personal beliefs. However, the appearance of trained seals is also misleading in that MPs may be vigorous spokespersons for constituency and regional interests behind the closed doors of party caucus meetings and in lobbying efforts with cabinet ministers and bureaucrats. Caucus provides a particularly important outlet for dissent and, at the same time, consensus building. Unfortunately, this activity takes place almost entirely in private, is known to only a few, and therefore does little to enhance the public's image of Parliament. Representation takes place, but it is not transparent. In the case of regional representation, more visible if not necessarily more effective forms are left to provincial premiers and the politics of executive federalism.

Party discipline is often seen as an unfortunate constraint on legislative debate, one that reduces what should be a serious, deliberative discussion to little more than a shouting match among partisan camps. While this perception is not without foundation, we must be careful not to misrepresent the character and intention of parliamentary debate. Partisan clashes provide a means of building party solidarity and morale: "A well-fought battle rallies the opposition troops; the opposition does not expect to gain concessions or make changes, but creates its own coherence and enthusiasm through attack on the government."[36] As noted above, the purpose of much debate is simply to consume time and thereby frustrate the legislative timetable of the government. In this context, John Reid has somewhat cynically observed that "the purpose of most debates in the House of Commons is not to enlighten but to beat one's opponents to death by dullness."[37] As Franks points out, "the struggle in the House is not to change the minds and votes of Members of Parliament, but to woo and win the voters in the next election."[38] It is thus irrelevant that debate has no impact on decisions taken in the House, for the primary audience is external to the House.

The public's primary window on effects of partisanship and party discipline is provided by the 40-minute oral **Question Period,** which is held every day that the House is in session. Question Period provides an important and highly visible opportunity for MPs to hold the government responsible to the House. It also attracts the most media coverage—newspaper coverage of Question Period exceeds coverage of debate on government bills by a ratio of 35:1[39]—and generates most of the 10-second clips for television news. MPs are able to question ministers about current events, about charges of corruption and misconduct, and indeed about any matter they may choose. Not surprisingly, Question Period is dominated by opposition MPs and by the leaders of the opposition parties, who have the option to lead off the daily assault. Questions by government backbenchers are much less frequent and, when asked, are often used to set up favourable statements by ministers: "Would the Minister of Finance please explain to the House how he has been so successful in wrestling inflation to the ground, easing unemployment, and setting Canada on the path to economic prosperity?" Question Period is valued because it forces ministers, day in and day out, to respond to their critics. As such, it is a particularly valuable opportunity and stage for opposition parties. However, it is neither an unqualified success nor a blessing. Ministers can evade most questions if they choose to do so, and the prime minister can divert difficult questions to ministers. More importantly, the media coverage of Question Period captures MPs in their most adversarial and abrasive temper. The results of public inquiries such as the Spicer Commission suggest that the abrasive and polemical character of Question Period has contributed to the erosion of public confidence in parliamentary institutions.

Public agitation for a reduction in the role of party discipline is not a new phenomenon. Party discipline has always been a sore point in Western Canada, and radical reform movements such as the Progressives in the 1920s, Social Credit, and the Reform Party have targeted party discipline as a priority for institutional reform. The problems that any significant reduction in party discipline might pose for responsible government, and indeed for electoral empowerment, are largely ignored. However, there may be ways in which the scope of party discipline could be reduced without serious damage to the canons of responsible government. It is interesting to observe, for instance, that party discipline is more relaxed in the much larger British House of Commons. (Size alone may weaken party discipline in that a larger number of MPs reduces the odds of a cabinet appointment and promotes the emergence of "career backbenchers" who maintain electoral visibility by harassing the government.) At the start of the legislative process, bills in the British Parliament are identified by the government as one-, two-, or three-line whips. In the first case, the sponsoring minister may indicate a preference as to how his or her party members should vote, but government MPs are free to vote according to their conscience or constituency preferences. No penalties are applied to MPs who break party ranks, and the defeat of the legislation would not signify that the cabinet has lost the confidence of the House. In the case of a two-line whip, the cabinet and sponsoring minister indicate a considerably stronger preference, and government MPs are expected to follow party lines unless exceptional circumstances prevail. Even in this case, however, the defeat of the bill would not signify a loss of confidence; by designating the bill as a two-line whip, the government has declared in advance that the parliamentary vote will not be interpreted as a confidence measure. Three-line whips are confidence measures; party discipline is strictly enforced, defectors can expect to be sanctioned, and the defeat of the bill would force the resignation of the government and precipitate a general election. It is both ironic and frustrating that Canadian parliamentarians display greater fidelity to the Westminster model at the time of Confederation than they do to the more contemporary British experience. As Joy Esberey notes, the Westminster model has become "petrified" in Canada[40] (see Dossier 6.3).

Popular discontent with parliamentary institutions has not been limited to the representational constraints of party discipline. There is also growing discontent with the financial cost of parliamentary institutions, discontent that has been fed by the more general environment of fiscal constraint and by an incipient taxpayers' revolt in the face of escalating tax loads. As Dossier 5.6 shows, the per capita cost of parliamentary institutions is negligible, but even if this evidence were widely known and appreciated, it would unlikely do much to blunt popular discontent, which has centred not on the total or per capita cost to the public purse but rather on the perks and privileges of MPs and senators. These perks and privileges have come under unrelenting attack from the Reform Party and across the country provide the daily grist for talk shows and letters to the editor. While parliamentarians can argue with justification that many alleged perks are no more than essential prerequisites for a demanding job and are easily matched by those in the private sector, it is unlikely that public discontent will abate so long as the public debt remains significant.

The internal procedures of the House of Commons have evolved considerably over time, and will continue to evolve.[41] However, most of the reforms, important though they may have been, have been apparent only to MPs and aficionados of the Hill. They have not provided much purchase on public dissatisfaction with the House and the behaviour of MPs, or on more general discontent with the responsiveness and representativeness of parliamentary democracy. In the absence of more visible root-and-branch reform to the House, it is not surprising that a good deal of the public's dissatisfaction has come to be focused on the Senate. As Mallory noted prior to the most recent constitutional debate, "because so few people seem to love the Senate, it seems all too easy to use it as a readily salable part of a constitutional reform package."[42] It is also the case that MPs have been resistant to fundamental reform to the House and have been more than happy to have the Senate serve as the lightning rod for public discontent. The irony is that if the Senate had been reformed along the lines proposed by the Charlottetown Accord, it may have acted as a goad

DOSSIER 5.5 QUESTION PERIOD

At 2:15 p.m., four times each week, 11:15 on Fridays, the Speaker of the House of Commons calls for oral questions. The Leader of the Official Opposition rises in his place, is recognized by the Speaker and begins the day's grilling of the government. Nowhere else in the world, even in the "Mother of Parliaments" in the United Kingdom, is the entire government held to daily account in such a fashion, being subjected to questions about virtually any of its programmes and policies.

Amid applause and shouts of encouragement from his caucus colleagues, and catcalls and heckling from those opposite, the Opposition Leader calls on a member of the cabinet to respond to some matter of urgent and pressing need, some great calamity that has befallen Canada since the day before, a question about which the Government has received no official notice.

Usually to similar noise and action, that cabinet minister, or the Prime Minister, will rise and respond, stating that whatever has exercised the Member opposite has been solved already, will be taken under advisement, or, most often, is not really of any consequence or importance to any except those who have been less favoured by the voters. The rhetorical barbs fly in both directions, reminding us why the benches of the House are set two sword-lengths apart. The process of question and answer, supplementary and reply, is repeated 10 to 12 times, in this apparent free-for-all that is the pinnacle of government accountability in Canada—the daily Question Period.

According to the rules and to tradition, the Speaker of the House controls Question Period, which is known as QP to the gaggle of insiders who seemingly make it the central concern of their life. The Speaker will see a Member rising in his or her place and call on the MP to direct a question to the government. Any Member can be called on, in any order, from any party. To those watching the live broadcasts at home this appears to be what is occurring.

But for those on the floor of the House, or in its galleries, there is another reality. While many Members may indeed be rising in their places, the Speaker is calling them not as he sees them, but from lists supplied by the House Leaders of the two opposition parties. These lists are often amended as QP progresses, changes called to the Speaker from House Leaders—who sometimes appear more like baseball managers signaling their on-deck batters and runners to bunt, steal, or run—by waving arms, pointing, nodding and stepping into the fray as the moment dictates....

So, even though it may appear to be mayhem to the uninitiated, the degree of management that goes into the planning of Question Period is considerable. The effort to get the right "spin" onto an issue, to attract the attention of the media and of the government, consumes a great deal of time for a large number of people every day the House is in session, an effort that goes unnoticed, perhaps intentionally so, by those who watch from the outside.

Source: Reprinted with permission from Michael Kalnay, "Managed Mayhem: Question Period in the House of Commons," *Parliamentary Government* 8, no. 4 (Summer 1989), 3–6.

(rather than an alternative) to House reform, forcing MPs to scramble to catch up to a revitalized second chamber and, for the most part, elected senators.

The Challenge of Direct Democracy

Parliamentary institutions are also challenged by proponents of direct democracy, who argue that there is less need today for elected representatives to intercede between voters and the legislative process. In part, the proponents hark back to the mythology of the Greek city-state, to a small-scale political environment in which it was possible for citizens to govern directly. Yet they are not simply nostalgic; many are enamoured with modern technologies that offer the possibility of direct legislative involvement by citizens in a "teledemocracy." At the extreme, the vision is that of an electronic community in which citizens listen to political debates through technology-enhanced town meetings and then vote electronically on matters of public policy. This view dismisses the "art of politics"—the search by elected representatives for creative compromises that might bind a political community together despite the existence of major policy dissension—and reduces politics to a choice among a limited number of alternatives, a choice in which the majority should prevail. A more moderate view wishes to use various devices of direct democracy to supplement, rather than to supplant, representative institutions, thereby creating a better system of "checks and balances."

Short of the electronic city-state, the devices of direct democracy most often under discussion are referendums (or plebiscites), initiatives, and recalls. These devices do not require teledemocracy and have been used (or contemplated) in Canada for some time. In recent years, however, the movement toward such devices has increased.

In **referendums** or **plebiscites** citizens vote directly on the merits of a public measure. The votes could be binding or consultative; they could be used to ratify legislation or constitutional amendments or to test the waters prior to legislative action. A referendum was used in 1949 to decide if Newfoundland would enter Confederation, in Quebec in 1980 to determine if voters were prepared to give their provincial government a mandate to negotiate sovereignty-association with the rest of Canada, and again in Quebec in 1995 to determine if voters supported negotiating a partnership with the rest of Canada. There have been 54 provincial referendums since 1867 and three national referendums: on the prohibition of alcohol (1898), on military conscription (1942), and on the Charlottetown Accord (1992). (The 1992 referendum was triggered in part by the fact that both British Columbia and Alberta have legislation requiring provincial referendums on constitutional amendments. Ontario introduced similar legislation in 1998.) Referendums are used routinely by local municipalities to address such matters as the funding of major public works.

Initiatives provide a means by which a predetermined number of voters can put an issue on a referendum ballot. Initiatives, which are used in many American

DOSSIER 5.6 PER CAPITA LEGISLATIVE COSTS

The total cost of running Parliament and the twelve provincial and territorial legislatures now exceeds half a billion dollars a year. This cost includes salaries, pensions, constituency offices, and a host of operating expenses. However, the following table shows that the per capita costs look less daunting; each and every Canadian, on average, antes up just over $17 a year to support Parliament and his or her provincial legislature. The Senate is the least expensive institution, costing only $1.34 per Canadian per annum.

JURISDICTION	1996–97 LEGISLATIVE BUDGETS (TOTAL)	PER CAPITA COST OF EACH LEGISLATURE
House of Commons	$216,600,000	$7.15
Senate	40,713,000	1.34
Newfoundland	10,667,000	19.33
Prince Edward Island	2,633,000	19.57
Nova Scotia	7,944,000	8.74
New Brunswick	9,903,000	13.42
Quebec	68,599,200	9.66
Ontario	89,002,000	8.32
Manitoba	12,395,000	11.27
Saskatchewan	14,438,000	14.58
Alberta	20,686,700	7.66
British Columbia	24,294,000	6.57
Yukon	3,014,000	97.97
Northwest Territories	9,369,000	145.47

Source: *Flemming's Canadian Legislature. 11 Edition 1997.* From the Alberta Legislature Library.

states, allow voters to legislate directly rather than convey their preferences to legislators who then act on their behalf. In November 1992, 19 states held initiative-triggered votes on such diverse issues as abortion, recycling, nuclear power, euthanasia, homosexual rights, video lotteries, the removal of sales tax on junk foods, and term

DOSSIER 5.7 PARLIAMENTARY SALARIES AND PERKS

In the public's mind, MPs and senators are often seen as overpaid, enjoying a lifestyle well beyond the reach of their constituents. Certainly at first glance, parliamentarians appear to do rather well.

MPs and senators earn a base salary of $64,400; cabinet ministers and the Speaker earn an additional $46,000 each, while House leaders, whips, parliamentary secretaries, and deputy speakers receive somewhat smaller additional incomes. The prime minister earns about $160,000, and the prime minister, the leader of the official Opposition, and the Speaker have official residences supported by public funds. All MPs and senators also receive annual tax-free expense allowances of $21,300 and $10,100, respectively. In total, MPs and senators receive annual compensation equivalent to salaries of $106,000 and $84,000, respectively. Each MP and senator is entitled annually to 64 return-airfare passes to any point in Canada; these formerly provided for first-class seats, but in 1992—coincident with Air Canada's decision to eliminate all first-class seating on domestic flights—the government announced that parliamentarians would now travel executive class.

MPs are entitled to free long-distance telephone service within Canada, a personal computer, two colour television sets, and about $150,000 annually to support offices in Parliament and in their constituencies. Senators receive fewer support services and are entitled to only a single staff member.

It is difficult to determine whether the level of remuneration that MPs and senators receive is appropriate, because it is all but impossible to establish a fair basis of comparison. If the comparison is the average income of constituents, then parliamentarians do well indeed. If it is persons of similar position within the corporate sector, it is less clear that the rates of pay and benefits are inappropriate.

Canadian MPs are not overpaid in comparison with their legislative counterparts in the Group of Seven industrialized democracies. The base annual pay ($US) in the seven countries ranges from $157,000 in Japan to $129,500 in the United States, $108,000 in Italy, $81,926 in France, $73,600 in Germany, $54,680 in Britain, and $54,118 in Canada. Major allowances range up to $537,000 in the United States (enough to support a staff of 20), a figure that dwarfs allowance provisions in the other six countries.

limits for elected representatives. Ontario's 1998 proposed referendum legislation included an initiative component.

The **recall** enables a predetermined number of voters to require that their representative resign before the next election and face the voters in a by-election. Support for the recall emerged in the prairie West between the two world wars and has resurfaced in the populist dissatisfaction associated with the Reform Party. British Columbia has put recall legislation into effect, although it has yet to be used successfully.

The constitutional referendum held on October 26, 1992, at an estimated administrative cost of $165 million, has been Canada's most important experiment with direct democracy. Even though the referendum was not a formal part of the constitutional amendment procedure, and was not legally binding on legislatures other than those in Alberta and British Columbia, it has likely established a firm precedent for future constitutional amendments other than those of a minor character.

Canadians appear to be ambivalent about the use of constitutional referendums. In a massive survey of 3577 respondents conducted by Angus Reid–Southam News two weeks before the 1992 referendum, 50 percent of respondents thought that the referendum was a bad idea. Moreover, 50 percent felt that it would exacerbate regional and linguistic tensions, and 61 percent felt that politicians were using the referendum to push their own ideas; only 34 percent saw the vote as a genuine attempt to consult the people. As Dossier 5.8 shows, there are plausible arguments on both sides of the direct-democracy debate and thus perhaps good reason for this ambivalence.

CONCLUSION

The ongoing debate over parliamentary reform and the more particular debate over party discipline illustrate how some of the basic architectural principles of parliamentary democracy have been and remain contested. Critical attacks have been directed at the Senate, at the means by which MPs are elected, at the inability of the House to represent social and political diversity, at the more specific behaviour of MPs caught up in the ritualistic combat of Question Period and parliamentary debate, at the financial cost of parliamentary institutions, and at the very heart of representative democracy itself. In short, the architectural principles of parliamentary democracy do not rest on a firm foundation of consensual support in the country's political culture. At the same time, it should be noted that discontent with these principles has not been reinforced by nationalist discontent in Quebec, which has focused almost exclusively on the federal rather than the parliamentary aspects of the Canadian state. As a consequence, the major engine of constitutional and institutional change in Canada—the nationalist movement in Quebec—has not driven parliamentary reform. The major engine of parliamentary discontent has been found in the West, and as a consequence it has yet to pose an acute challenge to the parliamentary status quo.

It might be argued that our preoccupation with constitutional politics and the concomitant importance of intergovernmental relations have eroded Parliament's centrality in Canadian political life. To the extent that the major political debates have been fought within the sequestered environment of executive federalism and not on the floor of the House, MPs have joined other Canadians as interested spectators on the sidelines, not as players in the game. Thus, whether the House can provide an adequate institutional bridge across the social, regional, and linguistic cleavages that threaten to fragment the national community is an open question.

DOSSIER 5.8 THE PROS AND CONS OF DIRECT DEMOCRACY

How do citizens ensure that their governments don't act in ways that are misguided, offensive or just plain dumb? For most of Canadian political history, the answer was so obvious that it was rarely articulated: make sure governments are composed of elected representatives rather than imperial officials or appointed elites, and good government will ensue.

That answer is no longer as compelling as it once was. The 1980s brought us the Charter of Rights, which assumes that we can't always count on legislatures to protect individual and minority rights. The 1990s, on the other hand, is the decade of referendums, the political instrument preferred by populist conservatives to remind governments between elections that the people are boss.

Ontario is the latest jurisdiction to catch referendum fever. Actually, Ontario's proposed legislation is three referendum proposals in one. The first provides a legal mechanism for individual citizens to propose province-wide referendums on any matter within provincial jurisdiction. The second, similar to legislation in B.C. and Alberta, requires that a referendum be held before the legislature consents to a constitutional amendment. The third compels the government to hold a referendum before passing any law that increases taxes or creates a new tax....

[T]he centrepiece of the proposed bill is clearly the "no taxation without a referendum" provision. Let us be clear about what it means. The government would continue to have the power to transform the welfare system, close hospitals, change municipal boundaries and overhaul the school curriculum with only the most limited of legislative debates. But if it dared to raise taxes by so much as a penny, it would be required to submit the proposal to the test of a province-wide referendum and abide by its results.

In other words, the referendum legislation puts taxes first. Coming from a government that campaigned on the theme of lower taxes, that is hardly a surprise. The Tories of Mike Harris obviously struck a responsive chord with voters, and the binding referendum has become the means to imbed that preference permanently in provincial legislation.

The problem is that most Ontarians are interested in more than tax cuts. Sure, the promise of a 30-per-cent tax cut sounded very good to many in the province. Yet the polls suggest strongly that many Ontarians including many who voted for Mike Harris, are also deeply concerned when their local emergency room closes, when their kids' education is compromised and when their highways deteriorate.

Naturally enough, most of us want to have it both ways, and it is incumbent on someone to assess the trade-offs, balance priorities and make tough choices. Those aren't the sorts of questions that lend themselves to the "clearly worded, concise and neutral" formulation that the referendum bill requires. Indeed, it is hard to imagine how the process can possibly be neutral when the deck is so obviously stacked on one side. This is a recipe for political escapism, not responsible government.

Imagine what will happen when, faced with rising health-care costs, the government considers that it may have to raise taxes to generate more revenue. One instinct, presumably, will be to avoid going to the people by trying to cook the books to show that there hasn't been a tax increase after all. That strategy, widely used in the United States, breeds hypocrisy and cynicism, not responsibility.

If that fails, a government might attempt to circumvent the referendum requirements by claiming, as the legislation allows, that "the new tax is required as a result of unforeseen and exceptional circumstances." Fine, although exploiting loopholes is hardly a way to build trust either. Of course, someone will challenge the use of the loophole in court—that bastion of democratic accountability. And if the court challenge is successful and the referendum defeated, the government will claim that it really shouldn't be blamed for the long lines in the emergency rooms because the referendum has left it no maneuverability. In short, the referendum initiative is liable to undermine accountability, not foster it.

Is this really how we want our tax dollars spent? Now that's a referendum question I would like to propose.

Source: Robert Vipond, "No Taxation without a Referendum?" Reprinted from *The Globe and Mail,* April 1, 1998, A25.

Former Conservative premier Peter Lougheed and his wife Jeanne are the latest celebrity Calgarians to sign a petition asking city council to hold a referendum on video lottery terminals (VLTs) this fall....

Similar petition drives are under way in Edmonton, Medicine Hat and Fort Saskatchewan, while city councils in Red Deer, Lethbridge and Lacombe have already decided in favour of a referendum. Earlier plebiscites went against VLTs in Rocky Mountain House, Sylvan Lake and Fort McMurray.

The anti-VLT movement began among evangelical Christians in the rural area west of Red Deer, the area of Alberta where that group is strongly represented. Evangelicals and social conservatives are still involved, but they have been joined by a wide variety of other forces, including Roman Catholics, liberal Protestants, Muslims and Sikhs, and the provincial Liberal, New Democratic and Social Credit parties.

The overt opponents of the petition movement come chiefly from the gambling and hospitality industries. The Progressive Conservative government isn't exactly defending the VLTs that it has encouraged to proliferate, but it does stress how hard it would be to replace the revenues (almost $500-million a year) that they generate.

The anti-VLT coalition is interesting because it cuts across normal lines of division and brings together members of all political parties, religions and secular world views. Many oppose the proliferation of VLTs for different and indeed contradictory reasons. Some, emphasizing personal responsibility, think gambling is a moral evil; others, denying personal responsibility, think gambling is a disease or addiction. But all agree that it is not wise for VLTs to be so readily accessible in bars, restaurants and hotels, and for the provincial government to develop such a financial stake in the promotion of gambling.

One of the great merits of direct democracy is that it allows such coalitions to form around single issues. The people trying to limit the availability of VLTs could never form a political party, because they disagree on too many other things, but they can work together for an objective they all support. A side benefit for democracy is that, in working together, all are reminded of how much they have in common with people of different religious convictions and political ideologies.

Political analysts are often critical of single-issue politics, pointing out that you couldn't form a government this way. True enough. But the deeper problem is that modern democracy has systemically confused government and legislation. In a democracy, legislation should have popular assent; but there is no reason why the majority that passes a particular law has to be the same majority that supports the government.

In *Considerations on Representative Government* (1861), John Stuart Mill tried to draw the distinction. The cabinet, he argued, should supervise public administration, subject to debate in Parliament; but neither the cabinet nor Parliament should have full control over the making of law. Legislation would have to be drafted by a legislative commission, appointed by the Crown for long terms and totally distinct from the cabinet and Parliament, before being passed by Parliament.

The point of this scheme was not only to ensure better legislative drafting, but also to prevent law from becoming a party matter. Parties could not campaign on a legislative program because they would not be able to guarantee the passage of legislation.

Mill's view has not prevailed. The Nobel laureate Friedrich Hayek tried to revive it in his magnum opus, *Law, Legislation and Liberty*, but so far without much effect. The notion of an appointed legislative commission is perhaps too far out of joint with our democratic age.

In fact, however, legislatures are losing control of law as, on the one hand, judicial activism gives courts greater control and, on the other hand, direct democracy becomes more widespread. California, with its activist courts, frequent referendums and mammoth petition drives, may give a glimpse of the future.

Cause for concern? Perhaps. But we shouldn't glamorize the parliamentary system, in which the leaders of rigidly controlled political parties calculatingly design legislative programs to win and hold office. The rules by which we live have become the stakes in the game of politics. Turning the law over to judges is even worse than leaving it with career politicians in disciplined parties, but there is a better option: Let the people make, or at least approve, the rules of conduct by which they have to live.

The people will make plenty of mistakes, but so do legislatures and courts. I'll take my chances with the people.

Source: Tom Flanagan, "In Praise of Single-Issue Politics." Reprinted from *The Globe and Mail*, May 21, 1998, A21.

KEY TERMS

Parliament
bill
party discipline
Westminster model
responsible government
confidence chamber
representative government
bicameral
caucus
government legislation
public bills
private bills
first reading
second reading
legislative committees
standing committees
committee of the whole
committee stage
report stage
third reading
royal assent
proclamation
private members' bills
Triple-E Senate
Question Period
referendums / plebiscites
initiatives
recall

DISCUSSION QUESTIONS

1. To what extent might we adopt some of the forms of direct democracy, such as referendums, initiatives, and the recall, without undermining the foundations of responsible government? In what sense and to what degree are the two incompatible?
2. Explain the positive role played by party discipline in parliamentary democracy. To what extent does this role offset the criticisms of party discipline?
3. Discuss the likely impact of Senate reform on your own province. What type of Senate reform, if any, would best suit the interest of your province? Explain your choice.
4. Dossier 5.4 discusses Alberta's elections for "Senators in Waiting." Discuss the pros and cons of holding such elections as a tactic for Senate reform.
5. How would you assess Jeffrey Simpson's argument in Dossier 5.1? Is there a case to be made for gender guarantees? For Aboriginal seats in the House of Commons?

SUGGESTED READINGS

Courtney, John C. "Parliament and Representation: The Unfinished Business of Electoral Redistribution." *Canadian Journal of Political Science* 21, no. 4 (December 1988), 675–690.

Etzioni, Amitai. "Teledemocracy," *The Atlantic* 270, no. 4 (October 1992), 34–39.

Franks, C.E.S. *The Parliament of Canada.* Toronto: University of Toronto Press, 1987.

Jackson, Robert J., and Michael M. Atkinson. *The Canadian Legislative System,* 2nd ed. Toronto: Macmillan, 1980.

Kornberg, Allan, William Mischler, and Harold D. Clarke. *Representative Democracy in the Canadian Provinces.* Scarborough: Prentice-Hall Canada, 1982.

Levy, Gary, and Graham White, eds. *Provincial and Territorial Legislatures in Canada.* Toronto: University of Toronto Press, 1989.

Sancton, Andrew. "Eroding Representation-by-Population in the Canadian House of Commons: The Representation Act, 1985," *Canadian Journal of Political Science* 23, no. 3 (September 1990), 441–458.

Seidle, F. Leslie, ed. *Rethinking Government: Reform or Reinvention?* Institute for Research on Public Policy. Ottawa: Renouf Publishing, 1993.

White, Graham. *The Ontario Legislature: A Political Analysis.* Toronto: University of Toronto Press, 1989.

White, Randall. *Voice of Region: The Long Journey to Senate Reform in Canada.* Toronto: Dundurn Press, 1990.

NOTES

1. Winston Churchill's observation on the architecture of the British House of Commons. Cited in C.E.S. Franks, "The 'Problem' of Debate and Question Period," in John C. Courtney, ed., *The Canadian House of Commons: Essays in Honour of Norman Ward* (Calgary: University of Calgary Press, 1985), 2.
2. Michael M. Atkinson and David C. Docherty, "Moving Right Along: The Roots of Amateurism in the Canadian House of Commons," *Canadian Journal of Political Science* 25, no. 2 (June 1992), 296.
3. For a detailed assessment of public opinion toward representative democracy and its associated institutions, see André Blais and Elisabeth Gidengil, *Making Representative Democracy Work: The Views of Canadians,* vol. 17 of the Research Studies of the Royal Commission on Electoral Reform and Party Financing (Toronto: Dundurn Press, 1991).
4. Thomas A. Hockin, "Adversary Politics and the Functions of Canada's House of Commons," in R. Schultz, O.M. Kruhlak, and J.C. Terry, eds., *The Canadian Political Process,* 3rd ed. (Toronto: Holt, Rinehart and Winston, 1973), 361.
5. Constitution Act, 1867, section 51(A).
6. Constitution Act, 1867, section 51(2). Cf. Elections Canada, "Representation in the Federal Parliament," in J. Paul Johnston and Harvey E. Pasis, eds., *Representation and Electoral Systems: Canadian Perspectives* (Scarborough: Prentice-Hall Canada, 1990), 224–225.
7. Peter H. Russell, *Constitutional Odyssey: Can Canadians Become a Sovereign People?* 2nd ed. (Toronto: University of Toronto Press, 1993), 226.

8. For a detailed discussion, see Andrew Sancton, "Eroding Representation-by-Population in the Canadian House of Commons: The Representation Act, 1985," *Canadian Journal of Political Science* 23, no. 3 (September 1990), 441–458.
9. For discussion on this point, see Roger Gibbins, "Electoral Reform and Canada's Aboriginal Population: An Assessment of Aboriginal Electoral Districts," in Robert A. Milen, ed., *Aboriginal Peoples and Electoral Reform in Canada,* vol. 9 of the Research Studies of the Royal Commission on Electoral Reform and Party Financing (Toronto: Dundurn Press, 1991), 153–184.
10. J.R. Mallory, *The Structure of Canadian Government,* rev. ed. (Toronto: Gage, 1986), 248.
11. See Jennifer Smith, "Canadian Confederation and the Influence of American Federalism," *Canadian Journal of Political Science* 21, no. 3 (September, 1988), 443–464.
12. The brief exception to this rule came during the three years between the initial signing of the Meech Lake Accord in 1987 and its collapse in June 1990. During this interregnum, Prime Minister Mulroney agreed to make Senate appointments from lists submitted by provincial governments.
13. Section 47(1) of the Constitution Act, 1982, states that "an amendment to the Constitution of Canada made by proclamation under section 38, 41, 42 or 43 may be made without a resolution of the Senate authorizing the issue of the proclamation if, within one hundred and eighty days after the adoption by the House of Commons of a resolution authorizing its issue, the Senate has not adopted such a resolution and if, at any time after the expiration of that period, the House of Commons again adopts the resolution." Therefore, the Senate cannot block its own reform.
14. Section 26 of the Constitution Act, 1867, states: "If at any Time on the Recommendation of the Governor General the Queen thinks fit to direct that Three or Six members be added to the Senate, the Governor General may by Summons to Three or Six qualified Persons (as the Case may be), representing equally the Three Divisions of Canada, add to the Senate accordingly." The numbers were changed to four and eight when the West became a senatorial district. For a discussion of this section, see Mallory, *The Structure of Canadian Government,* 249–251.
15. Rebellious upper chambers have not been restricted to Canada. During Prime Minister Margaret Thatcher's term of office in Britain, 102 bills were amended by the House of Lords against the wishes of her government. Canadian Study of Parliament Group, *Responsible Government,* Ottawa, October 27–28, 1989, 5.
16. For a discussion of parliamentary caucuses, see Paul G. Thomas, "The Role of the National Party Caucuses," in Peter Aucoin, Research Coordinator, *Party Government and Regional Representation in Canada* (Toronto: University of Toronto Press, 1985), 69–136.
17. "Resolutions" of the House, including those used to propose constitutional amendments, need not go through the three stages outlined below; they can be introduced and voted on without protracted committee hearings or debate.
18. One of the procedural reforms for the House that is often discussed is to send legislative proposals to committees before the introduction of a formal bill. This reform, it is hoped, would further weaken the constraints of party discipline.
19. *Third Report of the Special Committee on Reform of the House of Commons,* Chairman J.A. McGrath, P.C. (Ottawa, 1985).
20. For a discussion of the FTA, GST, and abortion cases, see Robert M. Campbell and Leslie A. Pal, *The Real Worlds of Canadian Politics,* 2nd ed. (Peterborough, Ont.: Broadview Press, 1991).

21. Hugh Winsor, "Senator Defies Steamroller Politics," *Globe and Mail*, June 3, 1993, A7.
22. Campbell and Pal, *Real Worlds*, 397.
23. *Globe and Mail*, July 9, 1990, A5.
24. *Calgary Herald*, February 27, 1991, A2.
25. Franks, "The 'Problem' of Debate and Question Period," 4–5.
26. Ronald G. Landes, *The Canadian Polity: A Comparative Introduction* (Scarborough: Prentice-Hall Canada, 1983), 165.
27. An ombudsman is a public official empowered to investigate citizen complaints about treatment received from, and within, the bureaucracy. While the ombudsman cannot investigate complaints about the general nature of public policy—one cannot, for example, appeal to the ombudsman about the imposition of the GST—he or she has a wide range of investigative powers relating to the administration of public policy.
28. Herman Bakvis, *Regional Ministers: Power and Influence in the Canadian Cabinet* (Toronto: University of Toronto Press, 1991), 287.
29. Ibid., 287.
30. *Globe and Mail*, May 11, 1998, pp. A1, A7.
31. *Calgary Herald*, March 6, 1998, p. A3.
32. *Calgary Herald*, May 5, 1998, p. A10.
33. John B. Stewart, *The Canadian House of Commons* (Montreal and Kingston: McGill-Queen's University Press, 1977), 14.
34. The whip is an MP charged with orchestrating the legislative behaviour of his or her partisan colleagues. Whips on both sides of the House are appointed by their respective party leaders and ensure that enough members turn up to vote, that committees are staffed, and that legislative procedures run as smoothly as partisan debate allows.
35. Cited in P.B. Waite, "Some Late Reflections on Responsible Government: Irresponsible Government?" *Canadian Study of Parliament Group*, Ottawa, October 27–28, 1989, 2.
36. Franks, "The 'Problem' of Debate and Question Period," 7.
37. Ibid., 9.
38. Ibid.
39. Canada, House of Commons Standing Committee on Organization and Procedure, *Minutes*, November 20, 1975, 9–10.
40. Joy E. Esberey, "The 'Maple Leaf' Mutation," paper presented to the Annual Conference of the British Association for Canadian Studies, Nottingham, April 12–14, 1991, 2.
41. There exists a large literature on parliamentary reform. For example, see Thomas D'Aquino, G. Bruce Doern, and Cassandra Blair, *Parliamentary Democracy in Canada: Issues for Reform* (Toronto: Methuen, 1983); and Magnus Gunther and Conrad Winn, eds., *House of Commons Reform* (Ottawa: Parliamentary Intern Program, 1991).
42. Mallory, *The Structure of Canadian Government*, 269.

THE POLITICAL EXECUTIVE

6

Canada is not an easy country to govern. The huge land mass, two languages, many regional economies, strong provincial governments, the prevailing shadow of the United States, all create centrifugal tensions. The central government, parliament, the executive, and especially prime minister and cabinet, *are the main institutions and forces holding the country together and asserting a national purpose, national standards, and national concerns over and above those of provinces, regions, and particular groups. The federal government has a critical role as the central expression of the nation as opposed to the numerous bodies expressing the concerns of its parts.*[1]

Responsible government and the tight party discipline it generates concentrate political power in the cabinet. At the apex of power within the cabinet is the prime minister or premier, who wields more policymaking power than the American President. Not surprisingly, all of the representational concerns that arise in the legislative arena are played out with even greater urgency in the smaller but more powerful arena of the cabinet. Territorial, cultural, linguistic, religious, ethnic, and racial interests are among those that covet attention at the heart of power in the Canadian political system. The cabinet is expected to be a vehicle of political integration, combining the interests represented by its members into a coherent whole. The need for cabinet solidarity in a system of responsible government certainly helps to unify the cabinet's disparate parts, but the related and equally important need for cabinet secrecy undermines the cabinet's integrative function by hiding it from public view. Under conditions of solidarity and secrecy, cabinet government is easily seen as a convenient way for powerful majorities to dominate minorities. The resulting call for more publicly transparent institutions of integration, such as a Triple-E Senate, directly challenges cabinet government as the most prominent feature of the Canadian political system.

■ ■ ■

When Canadians think about "the government," they usually have in mind particular institutions rather than a complex array of principles and rules. Perhaps because the Government of Canada includes over 400 departments and agencies, not to mention close to 200,000 public servants, we need some way to reduce this complexity and make it comprehensible. This is what a specific institutional focus can do. For example, thinking of government in terms of the **cabinet** enables us to treat the federal government as a single, unitary actor. For citizens and public servants, the cabinet provides a focal point for administrative direction, political authority, and electoral responsibility by playing a central although by no means uncontentious role in the operation of responsible government and executive federalism. It also plays a central role in the broader dynamics of national unity and political integration. In this limited sense, cabinet is the government, and public perceptions that are focused on this particular institution square nicely with political realities.

If the cabinet is at the centre of the governmental web, the spider that rules the web is the **prime minister**. (Visit Prime Minister Chretien's Web site at http://pm.gc.ca.) The prime minister is as important to the operation of cabinet government as the cabinet is to the operation of Canadian government more broadly defined. As the individual to whom voters can attach responsibility when things go wrong and credit when they go right, the prime minister, even more than the cabinet, provides a focal point for voters' perceptions of the government. In all of these respects, the prime minister's role is replicated by provincial premiers, who, within their own bailiwicks, play a pivotal role in the operation of cabinet government and within the broader dynamics of provincial politics. Given that the cabinet and prime minister play such important roles in the federal government, as their counterparts do in provincial and territorial governments, it is striking to note that they are, as was observed in Chapter 2, largely informal institutions. The formal executive powers of the Canadian state are lodged largely in the **Crown,** the **governor general** (and lieutenant governors), and the **Privy Council.** The cabinet itself constitutes the informal political executive whose continuance in office is subject to the whims of the electorate and the maintenance of majority support in the House of Commons. The prime minister holds office by virtue of success in a party leadership convention or selection process,[2] and his or her party's success in a general election, not by virtue of direct popular election.

If we are to come to grips with the various executive institutions that constitute the Government of Canada, we must begin our exploration with a look at formal institutions—specifically, the office of the governor general and the role of the Crown. We can then sketch in the more informal evolution and contemporary operation of cabinet government in Canada. With that backdrop in place, the analysis turns to the role of the prime minister and concludes with a broader assessment of the impact of the political executive on the dynamics of political integration within the Canadian federal state. However, it should be kept in mind throughout this discussion that an understanding of specific institutions tells only part of a complex story. Many of the important connecting links in this story are provided by operating rules and principles that knit executive government into a coherent whole. It is those rules and principles, and the contestation surrounding them, that we attempt to bring into relief with the following institutional analysis.

THE CROWN AND GOVERNOR GENERAL

Canada's formal constitutional documents are replete with mentions of the Crown, the governor general, and, with respect to provincial politics, the **lieutenant governor.** Section 9 of the Constitution Act, 1867, states that "the executive government and authority of and over Canada is hereby declared to continue and be vested in the Queen." Section 12 specifies that executive powers, authorities, and functions are to "be vested in and exercisable by the Governor General, with the advice, or with the advice and consent of or in conjunction with the Queen's Privy Council for Canada, or any member therefore, or by the Governor General individually...." This rather elastic clause appears to give very broad—even sweeping—executive powers to the governor general, who is also, on behalf of the Queen, the "Commander-In-Chief of the Land and Naval Militia, and of all Naval and Military Forces" (s. 15). In the provincial setting, the lieutenant governor holds many of the same formal executive powers, plays the same ceremonial roles, and occupies the same position in the legislative process as does the governor general in Ottawa. Yet while the governor general's and lieutenant governors' formal executive powers are vast, these powers are in practice exercised only on the advice and consent of the cabinet. Canadian constitutional practice therefore makes an important distinction between the **formal executive** and the **political executive.** The former comprises the governor general and the Privy Council at the federal level, and the lieutenant governor and council at the provincial level; the latter comprises the prime minister and cabinet, or premier and cabinet.

There are, however, two powers the governor general (lieutenant governor in provincial politics) exercises without advice and consent. The first is the power of **dissolution;** only the governor general has the power to dissolve Parliament and call a general election. In practice, the governor general acts in response to a request from the prime minister and, since the King–Byng affair in the mid-1920s (discussed below), the governor general has never refused a request. There is nonetheless some real discretionary power in this respect that could come into play in a situation in which the governing party controls less than a majority of seats in the legislative assembly. (This is known as a **minority government,** and is distinguished from a **majority government,** in which the governing party controls the majority of legislative seats.)[3] One could imagine, for example, a minority government situation in which the prime minister's party had received more seats but a smaller share of the popular vote than the principal Opposition party. In this case it is conceivable that the governor general denies a request for dissolution and turns to the leader of the official Opposition to see if he or she could form a government. The second and related power is the power to appoint the prime minister. Here again, the practical exercise of this power is encumbered by parliamentary convention and public expectations. In most situations there is no room for discretion; when Brian Mulroney resigned in 1993, for instance, the governor general did not have the option to call on Jean Charest (the runner-up in the Conservative Party's leadership convention) rather than Kim Campbell (the winner) to form a new government. But there may be room for discretionary action in a situation in which no party is able to secure a parliamentary majority following a general election, or in which the prime minister dies or is incapacitated while in office. In this last case it would still take an extraordinary set of circumstances before the governor general would or could ask someone other than the deputy prime minister to form the government.

The institution of the governor general symbolizes the separation of the government of the day from the Canadian state. Although the prime minister is the political head of the government, the formal executive authority of the state transcends the political personalities of the day and resides in the governor general. (By contrast, the president of the United States is not only the political head of the American government but also its formal and symbolic head.) Thus the Canadian state enjoys an ongoing institutional existence that is formally removed from the vicissitudes of party politics and electoral competition. This important theoretical distinction between government and state finds its roots in the early evolution of parliamentary democracy in Britain, where the House of Commons tried to distance itself from the monarchy. Even if the distinction is not salient to most citizens today, it has important practical consequences for the operation of government. The governor general is able to carry much of the ceremonial load that would otherwise fall on the shoulders of the prime minister—a load that includes the greeting of lesser foreign dignitaries, presiding over ceremonies such as those held on Remembrance Day, handing out awards and honours, meeting with Scouts and Guides, and opening public buildings. The prime minister is thus freed to address other more pressing problems, or at least to choose among ceremonial opportunities, picking those with the greatest promise of partisan gain or the greatest impact on national unity goals. This sharing of the ceremonial load has worked well in Canada and contributes to the efficiency of parliamentary government. (Visit the governor general's Web site at http://www.gg.ca.)

In the United States, the vice president carries out a ceremonial role analogous to that of the governor general but is not so effective in reducing the president's ceremonial load. In a formal sense, after all, the vice president is second best, whereas the governor general is in fact the Canadian head of state. Thus, the governor general "will do" in situations in which the vice president would not. It is worth noting in this context that the vice president is selected according to criteria quite different from those used to select governors general. The vice president's primary role is to balance the ticket in the presidential election by shoring up support among sectors of the electorate or regions in which the presidential candidate might be weak. This electoral emphasis tends to overshadow selection criteria that might be of relevance once the election is over; the vice president's administrative strengths and weaknesses become relevant only if the president should die, resign, or be impeached. The governor gen-

Governor General Roméo LeBlanc inspects the Ceremonial Guard in Ottawa. The inspection marks the start of the Changing of the Guard at Rideau Hall and on Parliament Hill. (CP photo/Jonathan Hayward)

eral, however, has no partisan or electoral role to play and can therefore be selected according to quite different criteria. The governor general must be able to bridge the major linguistic and cultural communities in Canada, which has meant that the office has alternated between Quebec and non-Quebec appointees. It is important that the governor general be fluent in both official languages, although a recent appointment, the Right Honourable Ray Hnatyshyn, may be a partial exception in this respect. To the extent that it is possible, the appointments of governors general and lieutenant governors have also been used to provide symbolic representation for other social groups, including women and ethnic minorities.

The governor general fits into the Westminster model of parliamentary government that Canada inherited from Britain; he or she is the structural (although certainly not political) equivalent of the early British monarchs. The governor general is the Crown's representative in Canada, and for all but the most unusual occasions carries out the formal duties associated with the Crown. (When the constitution was patriated in 1982, Queen Elizabeth II came to Ottawa on a rain-swept day in April to sign the new Constitution Act.) Prior to Confederation, the governor general was the Crown's representative in an active sense; he was appointed by the British government and was responsible for carrying out that government's colonial responsibilities in Canada. The executive power exercised by the governor general was real and immediate, although the achievement of responsible government in the late 1840s marked an important transfer of power from the formal to the political

DOSSIER 6.1 THE CROWN

The turbulent history of executive power, and the problems associated with it in many countries today, indicate that its effectiveness depends greatly on who possesses it. Despite intricate ideological and constitutional arrangements, possessors of power have made many mistakes, and sometimes even destroyed their power and ruined their state through stupidity. Consequently an arrangement gradually evolved through trial and error that separated the possession of power from the wielding of power. That is, one institution would possess the power without wielding it, and another would wield the power without possessing it. This is the arrangement we now have in Canada. Even though we may associate executive power with certain officials, we do not in law or in fact make it the personal possession of any of them. We put it outside the governmental structure, not in someone's hands, but in an abstraction, and we call that abstraction the Crown. Once we did give the power to a person, the sovereign. But that did not always work satisfactorily, because sovereigns, like politicians, are human and fallible. We therefore gradually, and over many decades, separated the sovereign from the Crown by making him just a personification of the Crown and the custodian of its powers. As a custodian, a much-different official from a possessor of powers, the sovereign holds the powers on behalf of the people, and he or she is the personal symbol of authority which man finds necessary to have in every system. But the sovereign may not normally wield these powers personally.

Source: Reprinted with permission from Frank MacKinnon, *The Crown in Canada* (Calgary: Glenbow-Alberta Institute, 1976), 15.

executive. In the decades following Confederation, the governor general's role became increasingly ceremonial in character; few significant powers were exercised without the advice and consent of cabinet, and the governor general's political power extended little beyond moral suasion and the opportunity to offer advice. The power to appoint the governor general passed in practice from the British to the Canadian government, and from 1951 onward only Canadians have been appointed.

The governor general provides the important formal link between the political executive and the monarch, the link that establishes Canada as a **constitutional monarchy.** However, this does not mean that the British crown is at the formal apex of the Canadian state. The governor general represents the Canadian crown, which just happens to reside in the same person, Her Majesty Queen Elizabeth II, as does the British crown. In this Hydra-like position, the Queen plays an important symbolic role in the Commonwealth, serving as the formal head of state for most, although not all, of the member states. Generations have passed since the coincidence of the British and Canadian crowns residing in the same individual has provided the opportunity for British influence in Canadian political affairs. Perhaps the last, and somewhat clouded, example of such influence came in the 1926 general election, when Prime Minister Mackenzie King used the King–Byng affair to his advantage by

DOSSIER 6.2 GOVERNOR GENERAL GEORGES VANIER

On July 1, 1998, *Maclean's* magazine published a survey of the 100 most important Canadians in history. Importance was defined as "a balance of character, ensuring achievement, influence, renown, and an individual's contribution to Canada and the world." At the top of the list was Georges-Philéas Vanier, who served as Canada's governor general from 1959 until his death in 1967.

Vanier served with Canada's Van Doos regiment in the First World War, during which he was severely wounded and received the Military Cross and Distinguished Service Order. In 1925 he left the Van Doos to take up a diplomatic post with the Canadian delegation to the League of Nations. During his diplomatic career Vanier held a number of distinguished posts, including Canadian ambassador to France from 1944 to 1953.

Georges Vanier was the first French Canadian to serve as governor general. With his wife, Pauline, Vanier provided a striking moral example for the country. As Claude Ryan said in the *Maclean's* article, "He set his sights on the goal of giving to Canadian public life a sort of supplement for its soul, an infusion of high patriotism, even of pure and simple spirituality." Today, both Georges Vanier and Pauline Vanier are candidates for sainthood in the Roman Catholic Church.

claiming that the governor general, who at the time was a British official appointed by the government of the United Kingdom, had interfered in Canadian affairs to the advantage of the Conservative Party. Regardless of whether this charge of interference was fair, the incident underscored the established convention that the governor general no longer had an active role to play in Canadian political affairs.

The past several decades of constitutional debate have seen very little discussion of Canada's status as a constitutional monarchy; the governor general and our ongoing connection with the Queen have seldom been placed on the table. It will be interesting to see if this continues to be the case in the years ahead, given the trials and tribulations of the British royal family, a growing British debate on the nature and desirability of the monarchy, and a strong republican movement in Australia.[4] In this context it is unlikely that the monarchy will escape notice should the Canadian constitutional debate resume.

As noted in the previous chapter, the governor general plays a significant formal role in the legislative process. Bills passed by the House and Senate must be presented to the governor general for the Queen's assent before they can become acts of Parliament. The governor general can convey that assent, withhold it, or reserve the bill "for the signification of the Queen's pleasure." In this last case the bill would not be proclaimed unless assent was attained within two years. While this potential hitch in the legislative process has not arisen with the governor general, it arose frequently in the past with the governor general's provincial counterparts.

Lieutenant governors were historically more likely to interfere in provincial politics than was the governor general to interfere nationally. Lieutenant governors were appointed by the prime minister, and not necessarily with the advice, much less the consent, of provincial cabinets. They were thus more prone to reserve provincial legislation for federal scrutiny or to disallow provincial legislation on the advice of the federal government. Lieutenant governors did not suffer the liability of being British actors playing on a Canadian stage; they were drawn from the political class in Canada and were therefore more likely to play an active role. Nonetheless, the lieutenant governors, like the governor general, now play an executive role that is almost exclusively formal and ceremonial. Moreover, the appointment of the lieutenant governor has now passed, in all but the most formal terms, into the hands of provincial governments, thereby paralleling the evolution of the appointment process for the governor general.

The Crown's representatives also play an important symbolic role in the legislative process by delivering the **Speech from the Throne** at the opening of each session of Parliament or the provincial legislature. The Speech from the Throne is designed to outline the government's legislative intentions for the upcoming session; it is therefore written by the government of the day and only delivered by the Crown's representative. Thus, the governor general refers to "my government" even though, in a partisan sense, he or she is assumed to be neutral as Canada's head of state. Beyond outlining the government's legislative objectives, the Speech from the Throne provides a well-publicized opportunity to trumpet the government's past record and, at times, to praise its political leadership. Whether the country or the Crown is well served by these more partisan speeches is another matter.[5]

In summary, the governor general and the symbolic trappings of the Crown are significant elements in the formal institutional configuration of the Canadian state, elements that reinforce a tradition of strong executive government. The governor general also plays an important practical role by taking on much of the ceremonial load that would otherwise fall on the shoulders of the prime minister. However, the governor general and the Crown should not be confused with the reality of political power, the exercise of which resides in the more informal institutions of cabinet government.

CABINET GOVERNMENT

Canadian cabinet government finds its origins in the early history of British parliamentary government. Initial cabinets in the United Kingdom were small groups of ministers who advised and were appointed by the sovereign of the day. As Parliament began to assert its independence from the sovereign, more ministers began to be drawn from the elected House of Commons. With the eventual full flowering of responsible parliamentary democracy, cabinet ministers were drawn almost exclusively from the House. However, they continued to serve as "ministers of the Crown" and thus provided the essential link or "buckle" between the administrative apparatus of the state—the public service—and elected representatives in the House. In this respect, cabinet ministers stood clearly apart from their American counterparts, who were unelected and had no standing in Congress.

The cabinet tenders formal advice to the Crown in the name of the Privy Council, the body formally mentioned in the constitution, and cabinet ministers serve in this capacity as privy councillors. Ministers are appointed to the Privy Council for life; the title continues even though the individual in question may no longer hold office or, indeed, be in public life. However, the Privy Council per se meets only in exceptional and ceremonial circumstances, such as on April 17, 1982, when the constitution was patriated to Canada. The cabinet is, in effect, an informal subcommittee of the Privy Council, that group of privy councillors who hold ministerial positions in the government of the day. Although the cabinet enjoys no formal constitutional recognition, it has an effective monopoly on the right to tender advice to the Crown. The legal instruments through which it and individual ministers act are called **orders-in-council.** These in theory require, and in fact carry, the collective approval of cabinet.

THE CABINET AND RESPONSIBLE GOVERNMENT

When, in 1867, Canadians adopted a system of government "similar in Principle to that of the United Kingdom," cabinet government was part of the British legacy, and Canadian practice departed little from British precedent. The cabinet provided the centrepiece of **responsible government,** with ministers being "responsible" in a number of different ways. First, and perhaps most important, they were collectively responsible to the House of Commons in that they held their positions only as long as they were able to command majority support in, or enjoy the "confidence" of, the House. Responsibility was enforced, at least in theory, by the power of the House both to control future expenditures and to review expenditures that had already occurred. Second, individual ministers were responsible to and in the House for the actions of their subordinates, and might be forced to resign if public servants in their ministry failed to act with discretion or propriety. Third, ministers were responsible to the Crown in the sense that they acted on behalf of the Crown and accepted legal responsibility for their actions. Finally, they were responsible to one another in that the cabinet spoke with a single voice to the Crown, Parliament, and the public, a strategy that S.L. Sutherland maintains "was developed by early cabinets as a shield against the monarch, who might wish to pick off ministers one by one to attain a more collegial group of advisers."[6] This principle, known as **cabinet solidarity,** meant that cabinet deliberations were held in secret, that cabinet documents were secret, and that ministers who could not contain their disagreement with government policy behind the closed doors of cabinet were obligated to resign. The constraints of cabinet solidarity

DOSSIER 6.3 PROBLEMS WITH THE WESTMINSTER MODEL

When Canadians talk about fidelity to the "Westminster model," they generally have in mind a style of British parliamentary government that was in existence at the time of Confederation. Canadian and British practices have evolved considerably since that time, and in some respects the rate of evolution has been faster on the eastern side of the Atlantic. For example, British practice now distinguishes clearly between the inner and outer cabinets, and, as discussed in Chapter 5, has been considerably more flexible and innovative in dealing with the constraints of party discipline and responsible government. Curiously, contemporary Canadian political science is seldom informed by close examination of the more contemporary British experience; our sights tend to be trained on the federal experience of other states rather than the parliamentary experience of Britain.

In the Canadian political community more broadly defined, parliamentary institutions and practices are often defended by reference to their British roots. The irony is that this appeal to tradition may carry less weight in Britain today than it is assumed to carry in Canada; certainly Tony Blair's Labour government is only loosely constrained by tradition. The danger is that even in Canada the appeal may carry little if any weight with the growing proportion of the population that has no ancestral ties with Great Britain. If parliamentary institutions and practices are to be defended in the public arena, it is imperative that greater reference be made to broadly based democratic principles and values, and less emphasis placed on appeals to a British tradition that is increasingly alien to the contemporary electorate.

on ministerial behaviour further reinforce the constraints of party discipline to which all MPs are subject.

This basic framework for responsible government remains largely intact today as a guiding set of parliamentary principles, although our notions of responsible government have evolved with the passage of time. In popular political discourse, the term often means being responsible to the people of Canada, a responsibility enforced through periodic general elections.[7] In this sense, the term responsible government has been diluted to mean little more than "democratic government." Students of Canadian government, however, need to understand its more specific institutional meaning in the British parliamentary tradition. When the term "responsible government" appears in the literature of Canadian government and politics, it is usually used in this institutional sense, not in the broader democratic sense.

Just as the term "responsible government" has acquired a diluted meaning, so too has its component idea of ministerial responsibility for the actions of public servants been diluted over time; ministers are no longer expected to be able to know, control, and thus be held accountable for the actions of their huge number of employees. In fact, ministerial responsibility in its various guises plays a minor role in cabinet resignations. Sutherland examined the 151 ministerial resignations that took place between 1867 and 1990 and found that 62 (41.1 percent) could be traced to ministers taking up other government appointments and 21 (13.9 percent) to ill health.[8] Another 28 (18.5 percent) resigned because they could not agree with their colleagues or, more commonly, with the prime minister. Only two ministers resigned because they accepted responsibility for maladministration in their portfolios! Another 11 resigned for misconduct related to the performance of their ministerial duties, including financial impropriety and undue interference in the legal system. Four resigned for personal misconduct unrelated to their portfolios.

The growing importance of executive federalism has further undermined the notion of responsible government, nationally and provincially, by placing major issues of public policy beyond the realm of effective legislative debate. Both the House and provincial legislatures are often presented with the results of an elaborate process of intergovernmental negotiation, a *fait accompli* not open to legislative debate for fear that the intergovernmental agreement might unravel. For example, the 1987 Meech Lake Accord was submitted to the House as a "seamless web," a product of intergovernmental negotiations that was not open to legislative amendment. If the Charlottetown Accord had survived the 1992 referendum, it too would have arrived at the House as an intergovernmental agreement open for no more than formal, ritualistic debate. Executive authority would have been linked directly to the people through a mechanism of direct democracy rather than indirectly to the people through the traditional mechanism of responsible representative government. While this challenge to responsible government is particularly acute with respect to constitutional politics, the pervasive character of executive federalism and intergovernmental agreements suggests a much wider concern. Here it should also be noted that international agreements can have the same impact on responsible government. The government can negotiate international agreements that, when presented to the House for ratification or for facilitating legislation, are not really open to debate. The hands of MPs have been tied by a process of international negotiation of which they were not a part.

The sheer scope and complexity of contemporary government have also undercut earlier notions of responsible government. As Peter Aucoin notes,

> *the role of Crown corporations and regulatory agencies within the executive system has been significant from the perspective of party government because these organizations have been delegated a degree of autonomy from cabinet direction and control that puts them at "arm's length" from the operation of party government.... the general result has been that a major part of government policy and administration is not under direct cabinet management.*[9]

Perhaps the most significant change to responsible government has come from the growing strength of **party government.** As political parties gained coherence and party discipline began to shape the parliamentary behaviour of MPs to a greater degree, the responsibility of cabinet to the House became increasingly a democratic

DOSSIER 6.4 THE AUDITOR GENERAL

The Auditor General of Canada has the power and authority to examine the accounts of federal departments and agencies and to determine whether decisions were made with "due regard" to economy, efficiency, and effectiveness. The auditor general's annual report to Parliament provides a benchmark against which to measure the economy and efficiency of government expenditures. It also provides a wealth of information for critics of the government, both inside and outside Parliament. The report is an indispensable resource for public-interest groups, such as the National Citizens' Coalition, and for the media.

The Office of the Auditor General is not a part of the government, and its independence is signalled by the fact that its annual report is submitted directly to Parliament, through the Speaker, not to the government of the day. The auditor general is required to assess whether the government's financial statements are complete and fair, and to report instances in which expenditures have not been in line with policy and legislative directives, or appear to have shown a lack of due regard for economy and efficiency. The annual report is an important tool through which Parliament and, specifically, opposition parties can maintain government accountability for the expenditure of public funds, if only by holding the government up to public examination and criticism.

It is important to stress that the auditor general does not second-guess Parliament and assess the merits of various programs; he or she is concerned only with whether the program objectives have been implemented with economy and efficiency, not whether the objectives per se make sense. Nor does the auditor general assess whether the program objectives have been met.

The auditor general's report is given detailed scrutiny by the Public Accounts Committee, which is the only committee of the House chaired by a member of the official Opposition. Although the committee reviews spending only retrospectively, its recommendations and criticisms can have an impact on plans for future expenditures.

In his April 1998 annual report, Auditor General Denis Desautels raised concern with the financial reporting for transfer payments. As he observed, "the emerging practice of recording transfer payments before a recipient signs an agreement [as was the case for GST harmonization payments to the provinces], or even before Parliament has created a recipient, runs against objective accounting standards and even against the government's own rules." In this instance as in others, the auditor general's task is to protect the government's financial integrity and credibility.

fiction. In the case of a majority government, the prospect of the cabinet's losing the confidence of the House has become remote in the extreme. Although opposition parties may routinely move motions of nonconfidence in the government, such motions are just as routinely defeated. The defeat of a majority government on a

DOSSIER 6.5 S.L. SUTHERLAND ON RESPONSIBLE GOVERNMENT

Canadian conventions surrounding ministerial responsibility are in considerable flux. If there is a general direction to recent reforms, it has been to hold officials more directly and publicly responsible for departmental administration, policy implementation, and advice, and thereby to circumscribe more narrowly the responsibility of elected ministers. The reforms have been based on the assumption that it is no longer possible for a minister to know everything that is going on in a department, and that as a consequence more responsibility should be shouldered publicly by senior officials, particularly the deputy minister. The reforms seek to sharpen the demarcation between policy and administration and therefore between the "sphere of action for ministers and civil servants." Sutherland argues that such reforms "may well make government less accessible to the influence of elected ministers and thus the electorate."

Officials are increasingly being called on to appear in public before parliamentary committees without the protection of their minister, and are being held to account for actions taken by their departments and advice tendered to their minister. Sutherland argues that this new "accountability regime" offends natural justice:

> *Public servants whose actions have satisfied administrative standards nonetheless find themselves in a kind of double jeopardy in representative forums where they lack legal standing, where criteria are unclear, where retrospective application of what seems to be a telling argument is normal rhetorical procedure, and where they cannot represent their own case at any length, have no counsel, no right of appeal and no right to compensation. They can find themselves rather brusquely divested of the means to protect their reputations and therefore their livelihoods.*

Sutherland argues that the attempt to demarcate more clearly the line between political and administrative spheres is mistaken and harmful to classical conceptions of responsible government:

> *The genius of the Westminster model of ministerial responsibility is that it is jealous of the sphere of the political, retaining a large scope for politically initiated action. It refuses to become entrapped in trying to separate politics from administration. The system is designed so that it does not matter much to the citizen whether an official or the minister made a decision for which the minister can be responsible in a legal and political sense but not in a personal moral sense, or even whether events as opposed to actors created a "decision." In making everything the minister's, everything can be reopened. In a sense, the classical system prefers political potency and a general political responsibility to address error.... Under a system of ministerial responsibility, questions of public importance and interest are as open as possible to electoral influence because the minister, who is the link to the elec-*

torate, is also the bridge to the department. It is thus through the minister that the democratic loop of accountability to the electorate is closed.

Source: S.L. Sutherland, "Responsible Government and Ministerial Responsibility: Every Reform Is Its Own Problem," *Canadian Journal of Political Science* 24, no. 1 (March 1991). Reprinted with permission.

piece of major legislation could come about only through gross mismanagement on the part of the government whip. Of course, when the governing party does not enjoy a majority of seats, retaining the confidence of the House cannot be taken for granted. (In recent decades, minority governments existed from 1962 to 1965, 1972 to 1974, and for nine months in 1979 and early 1980.) Yet even in a minority situation, the House can only defeat governments; it cannot make new governments, for a loss of confidence is almost automatically followed by the dissolution of Parliament and the calling of a general election. As noted above, an interesting exception occurred in 1925, when Mackenzie King's minority Liberal government was defeated in the House. When King sought a dissolution of the House from the governor general, Lord Viscount Byng, he was refused and the Conservatives were offered the chance to form a new government. When that government was unable to sustain a majority in the House, the Conservative leader sought and received a dissolution of Parliament. In the subsequent 1926 election campaign, which the Liberals won, King charged the British-appointed governor general with interference in Canadian domestic affairs. The **King–Byng affair** has virtually guaranteed the ability of a prime minister to go to the people in the event of a defeat in the House.

Responsible government and party government have thus become almost interchangeable terms. To explain their convergence, we must turn to a closer examination of the relationship between the cabinet and the House of Commons in the contemporary Canadian experience.

Cabinet and the House of Commons

Cabinet government rests on the firm foundation of party discipline in the House of Commons.[10] The ability of the cabinet to govern rests on its capacity to control the legislative agenda and output of the House and, secondarily to this point in time, of the Senate. In Canadian practice, cabinets act with the assurance that their decisions will find faithful reflection in legislation passed by Parliament. The strength of party discipline stems directly from the conventions of responsible government. If the defeat of a government bill in the House signifies that the cabinet has lost the confidence of the House and must therefore resign, the consequence is that government MPs must support government bills willy-nilly or risk losing partisan control of the government. In short, the risks are too high to permit any significant relaxation in party discipline; it would be difficult to convince MPs on the government side of the

House that any bill would be worse for the country than the prospect of a government led by one of the opposition parties.

To be sure, legislative proposals are subjected to extensive parliamentary debate, but this is not to be confused with parliamentary supremacy or control. Government MPs support the cabinet come hell or high water, and thus the cabinet can rest assured of legislative compliance so long as the party in office commands a majority in the House. It should be noted, however, that cabinet's control of the content of legislation is considerably greater than its control of the speed and timing of the legislative process. Cabinet is less likely to face legislative defeat than it is to face delays and obstruction in both the House and Senate, delays that in the end may prevent passage of significant components of the government's legislative agenda.

The cabinet integration of executive and legislative power (and the concomitant strength of party discipline) is the most outstanding feature of Canadian parliamentary democracy, one that concentrates power in the hands of cabinet and therefore, as we will see shortly, in the hands of the prime minister. In the provinces, integration works in an identical fashion to concentrate power in the hands of provincial cabinets and their premiers. This facilitates, in turn, the emergence of executive federalism, whereby federal and provincial governments can negotiate with one another, secure in the knowledge that bargains reached are virtually assured of legislative ratification should it be needed. It is the integration of executive and legislative power that most clearly sets Canadian national institutions apart from those in the United States. Executive and legislative powers in the United States are lodged in distinct branches of government—the presidency and Congress, respectively—with their own institutions and electoral mandates. This **separation of powers** is designed to prevent the very concentration of power that Canadian parliamentary institutions ensure. The separation of powers, along with the sheer number of American states, also prevents the emergence of Canadian-style executive federalism in the United States.[11]

The contemporary strength of party discipline, which plays such an important role in structuring the relationship between the cabinet and the House, should not be seen as immutable. A number of factors could come into play to weaken party discipline. First, as discussed in the previous chapter, party discipline is coming under widespread and growing public attack as a pernicious feature of Canadian parliamentary democracy. This attack has been associated particularly with the populist impulse of the Reform Party, but it has also found vigorous if less frequent expression within the other parties. Although this normative attack on the party-discipline foundation of cabinet government may not be sufficient to produce significant institutional change without a reinforcing reform impetus from other quarters, it is interesting to note that a principled defence of party discipline, one based on notions of responsible government and electoral accountability, is not being mounted with any zeal. Parties differ only in the eagerness with which they embrace parliamentary reform; there is a broad consensus that such reform should be pursued.

Second, the strength of party discipline could be eroded if minority governments are elected in the future. More relaxed party discipline may be promoted as a means by which minority governments could be sustained in office for a reasonable period of time, even in the face of legislative defeat. In short, we could move toward the British practice of designating bills at the outset as confidence or nonconfidence measures. Conversely, a sustained period of minority governments could produce coalition cabinets, although this development would not necessarily weaken party discipline. It is interesting to note in this respect that even though minority governments have been commonplace in Canada, there have never been coalition cabinets at the federal level. In practice, minority government cabinets look exactly like majority government cabinets; they are drawn exclusively from the party with a plurality of seats in the House. This parallels a more general Canadian convention in which minority governments act very much like majority governments—at least until their confidence is successfully challenged in the House.

Third, party discipline might be weakened if there is some significant increase in the ratio of government backbenchers to cabinet ministers. Such an increase could be brought about by the downsizing of cabinet, by an expansion in the size of the House, by landslide parliamentary majorities, or by some combination of the three. As we will see below, the downsizing of cabinets is already occurring, both federally and provincially, and thus the likelihood of an appointment to cabinet has been reduced. This in turn weakens one of the prime minister's most potent weapons—the prospect of cabinet appointment—in controlling potentially rebellious MPs. The combination of a small cabinet and a large parliamentary majority could have a particularly corrosive impact on party discipline. If the size of the House were to be increased in the future, as was proposed in the 1992 Charlottetown Accord, and if the trend toward cabinet downsizing is not reversed, the prospects of a cabinet appointment would become increasingly remote for many MPs. (There is no question that the much larger size of the British House of Commons has contributed to weaker conventions of party discipline in that country.) The same pressure on party discipline could be generated by landslide victories nationally or in particular provinces. In 1997, for example, the Liberals won 101 of 103 seats in Ontario, but Prime Minister Chrétien appointed only eleven Ontario MPs to the cabinet. Some among the remaining Ontario MPs *may* begin to carve out parliamentary careers as constituency representatives, using the breaking of party discipline to demonstrate to their electorate that constituency interests come first.

To this point in Canada's parliamentary evolution, the relationship between the cabinet and the House has been of far greater importance than the relationship between the cabinet and the Senate, which is managed by the Government leader in the Senate, who sits in cabinet. However, as we discussed in Chapter 5, cabinet's dominance of the legislative process in recent years has run up against an unanticipated obstacle—opposition in the Senate. In large part, this senatorial opposition arose from historical accident. Because the Liberals had controlled the federal government for most of the 1960s, 1970s, and early 1980s, Liberal senators outnumbered Progressive Conservative senators by a substantial margin. The Liberal majority in the Senate then became a source of partisan opposition to the legislative agenda of Prime

DOSSIER 6.6 CABINET GOVERNMENT IN THE NORTHWEST TERRITORIES

Although the governmental institutions of the Northwest Territories were originally premised on the Westminster model of cabinet and parliamentary government, Graham White's research shows that those institutions stand apart from the Canadian mainstream. They do so primarily because the majority of the Territories' population is Native, a demographic reality that has shaped the evolution of political institutions in the North.

The Native majority in the N.W.T. Legislative Assembly is linked inextricably to the absence of political parties and thus to the weakness of parliamentary norms that have developed in more partisan environments. The normative model, if not fully the reality, is that of "consensus government." The 24 MLAs are elected in highly personalized campaigns in which party organizations play no role. As White notes, "parties are widely rejected as alien, southern-Canadian political institutions which would impede political development along distinctly Northern lines." The 24 MLAs in turn elect the Government leader and then seven of their own number to serve as ministers. The Government leader's role is restricted to assigning the elected ministers to specific portfolios and, if necessary, disciplining them. As White explains:

Because ministers owe their positions to the Assembly, the Government Leader's control of the cabinet is dependent on skills at conciliating and facilitating rather than on ministers' obligations for their elevation to cabinet and perhaps for their original election as well. Moreover, in the NWT, the calling of an election is the prerogative of the Assembly rather than of the first minister. This is not to say, however, that all conventions of cabinet government are absent. The ministers are still individually and collectively responsible to the assembly, and only the cabinet is able to introduce money bills. A loss of confidence in the assembly triggers the resignation of the government, as it does in the case of Parliament.

White's analysis stresses that many of the principles underpinning government in the Territories are contested. For example, Native MLAs resist the concentration of power within the cabinet and fear that "the majoritarian form of parliamentary decision-making offers no special provision for group interests." As White concludes, "the principles of consensus government conflict fundamentally with the precepts of the British parliamentary model." How this conflict will be resolved within the new Western Arctic and Nunavut territories remains to be seen.

Source: Graham White, "Westminster in the Arctic: The Adaptation of British Parliamentarism in the Northwest Territories," *Canadian Journal of Political Science* 24, no. 3 (September 1991). Reprinted with permission.

Minister Mulroney's government when the Conservatives came to power in 1984. By the early 1990s, eight years of Conservative government had eroded Liberal strength in the Senate to the point that Progressive Conservative senators formed a majority.

This conflict between the Mulroney cabinet and the Liberal majority in the Senate is of interest for two reasons. First, it foreshadowed similar if less severe constraints on cabinet government when, following the 1993 election, the Liberal government confronted a Progressive Conservative majority in the Senate. Second, it illustrates the likely impact that Senate reform would have on cabinet government. The ability and inclination of a non-elected majority in the Senate to frustrate the government of the day pales beside the likely ability and inclination of elected senators to do the same. Indeed, it might be argued that elected senators would have a democratic and institutional mandate to do precisely that. Senate reform would inevitably curtail the cabinet's ability to control the legislative agenda and outputs, for if a reformed Senate could not moderate the existing power of the federal cabinet, it would not be effective. Thus, Senate reform must be seen as a constraint on cabinet government as we have come to know it.

Character and Composition of Cabinet

Although cabinet ministers are formally appointed as ministers of the Crown and are sworn into the Privy Council by the governor general, they are in fact selected by the prime minister of the day and continue to serve in the cabinet only so long as they enjoy the prime minister's confidence. There is no legal or constitutional requirement that cabinet ministers have seats in either the House or Senate. However, political convention dictates that a person appointed to the cabinet from outside Parliament will, if not appointed to the Senate, seek a seat in the House at the first available opportunity, and that he or she will resign from the cabinet if unsuccessful in the bid to be elected. For example, in 1975 Pierre Trudeau appointed the chairman of the Canadian Radio and Telecommunications Commission, Pierre Juneau, to the cabinet as minister of Communications. Juneau then ran in a by-election, lost, resigned from cabinet, and was appointed by Trudeau to the bureaucratic post of deputy minister of Communications.[12] As a rule, cabinet ministers are selected overwhelmingly from those MPs forming a majority or plurality in the House. This, indeed, is the essence of parliamentary systems of government, whether British or non-British in inspiration; the executive is simultaneously part of the legislature and responsible to that legislature.

The principles of responsible government limit the extent to which the prime minister can draw from the Senate for cabinet appointments. Although the Government leader in the Senate is by convention a member of the cabinet, senators cannot appear on the floor of the House, and thus ministers drawn from the Senate weaken the practical responsibility of ministers to the House. In special circumstances, however, additional senators have held cabinet posts. For example, Prime Minister Joe Clark drew on Quebec Progressive Conservative senators to increase that province's cabinet representation after the 1979 general election in which only a single Progressive Conservative MP was elected from Quebec. Similarly, Prime Minister Pierre Trudeau used western Canadian senators to provide regional representation in the cabinet when, following the 1980 election, only two Liberal MPs (both from Manitoba) were elected west of the Manitoba–Ontario border.[13]

By contrast with the Canadian case, the American cabinet is composed of non-elected secretaries appointed by the president; members of the cabinet act as extensions of the president's executive authority and have no autonomous electoral base of their own. (There is a constitutional prohibition, based on the separation of powers, on cabinet members sitting in the House of Representatives or the Senate.) This means that the president has a huge pool from which to draw in making appointments to the cabinet, whereas the Canadian prime minister is restricted to the elected MPs from his or her own party. If, for example, the prime minister sought greater gender balance within the cabinet, any capacity to move in that respect would be constrained by the pool of women MPs in the government caucus, whereas the American president faces no such constraints. (President Clinton's initial administration included 23 cabinet secretaries, of whom six were women, a proportion slightly higher than in the Campbell and first two Chrétien cabinets.) Given this fundamental national difference, and the fact that comparatively high rates of electoral turnover further limit the pool of experienced MPs,[14] it is perhaps surprising to see how well Canadian cabinets compare in quality to their American counterparts.

The size of Canadian cabinets grew considerably over time. Only 13 ministers, including the prime minister, sat in Sir John A. Macdonald's first cabinet. Provincial cabinets and their associated bureaucracies were even leaner. In 1881, for instance, Manitoba had only five civil servants, including four deputy ministers; the provincial attorney general ran his department single-handedly, without a deputy, clerk, or secretary.[15] By the 1980s, however, provincial cabinets averaged more than 20 ministers and Brian Mulroney's largest cabinet had 40, including himself. In part, this growth reflected the increased complexity and scope of contemporary government. At the time of Confederation, no one could have imagined that the federal government would play a role in, much less have cabinet ministers responsible for, such fields as fitness and amateur sport, environmental protection, multiculturalism, and the status of women. Canadian society too became much diverse than it had been at the time of Confederation, and this diversity generated additional pressure for larger cabinets. For example, there were now 10 provinces to be represented, up from four, and there was a need that did not exist in the past to provide representation for women and multicultural communities. (It was not until the late 1950s that Prime Minister John Diefenbaker appointed the first woman, Ellen Fairclough, and the first person of Slavic origin, Michael Starr, to the federal cabinet.) In short, the federal cabinet came to be seen as a mirror, if an imperfect one, of Canadian society. Citizens expected to find their reflection in the composition of the cabinet, and the size of the cabinet grew accordingly as groups within an increasingly complex society jockeyed for both symbolic recognition and the practical political leverage that cabinet representation was thought to provide.

Provincial premiers experienced the same pressure to expand the size of their cabinets. Although provincial cabinets remained smaller in absolute numbers than the federal cabinet, they were proportionately much larger. While just over 9 percent of MPs sat as full ministers in the post-1997 federal cabinet, current provincial cabinets range from 18.5 percent of elected members in Ontario to 38.2 percent in New Brunswick, as Table 6.1 shows. Thus, the odds of securing a cabinet position are much better provincially than they are in Ottawa. The relatively large provincial cabinets have greater weight in the governing party caucuses and in the legislative process than does the federal cabinet. Government MLAs or MPs who are not cabinet ministers are almost the exception in provincial legislatures, whereas backbench MPs on the government side of the House of Commons outnumber their cabinet colleagues by a ratio of roughly 6:1.

Recent years have witnessed a marked decrease in the size of federal and provincial cabinets as prime ministers and premiers respond to a perceived public demand for fiscal restraint and smaller government. While reductions in the number of ministers need not have any significant impact on overall government spending, they can be used to send a symbolic message of restraint to the electorate. For example, Kim Campbell reduced the size of the federal cabinet from 36 to 25 ministers, including herself, when she assumed office in June 1993. Less than five months later, Jean Chrétien's first cabinet had only 23 ministers, including the prime minister, while his 1997 cabinet had 28 ministers. In some cases, however, reductions may be more apparent than real. Incoming premier Ralph Klein reduced the size of the Alberta cabinet from 27 members to 15, but he also appointed a number of backbench MLAs to chair cabinet committees. These individuals sit at the cabinet table, take the cabinet oath of secrecy, and have staffs that look much like ministerial staffs. In all but name they are cabinet ministers of the old breed. Similarly, in his 1997 cab-

TABLE 6.1 ABSOLUTE AND PROPORTIONATE SIZE OF CABINETS

	CABINET SIZE	SIZE OF LEGISLATURE	PERCENT OF LEGISLATURE
Federal	28	301	9.3
Quebec	24	125	19.2
Ontario	24	130	18.5
New Brunswick	21	55	38.2
Saskatchewan	21	58	36.2
Alberta	19	83	22.9
British Columbia	19	75	25.3
Manitoba	18	57	31.6
Newfoundland	16	48	33.3
Nova Scotia	12	52	23.1
Prince Edward Island	9	27	33.3

inet, Prime Minister Chrétien appointed nine secretaries of state to assist ministers in various areas, including multiculturalism, the status of women, youth, parks, Asia-Pacific, and western economic diversifications.

Any prime minister needs to address a number of different and not entirely compatible representational principles in constructing a cabinet. The first, which has been applied more erratically than is often assumed,[16] is to provide territorial representation for the various provincial communities. Given the importance of cabinet as an intrastate institution within the Canadian federal state, and given the role that **regional ministers** (discussed below—see especially Dossier 6.9) play in linking those communities to the national government, it is imperative to represent all provinces around the cabinet table if it is possible to do so. As Donald Smiley and Ronald Watts point out, prime ministers will sometimes go to extraordinary lengths to achieve this objective: after the 1921 election, in which the Liberals were shut out of Alberta, Prime Minister King appointed a former Alberta premier to the cabinet and found him a Commons seat in Quebec.[17]

A second principle is operationally embedded in the principle of territorial representation, and that is the need to represent the two national linguistic communities. This means in practice that Quebec representatives must not only be included in the cabinet but must be included in sufficient numbers to reflect binational visions of the political community. At the Westminster Conference of 1866, which put into place the final details of the Confederation agreement, it was decided that the first Canadian cabinet would have five ministers (including the prime minister) from Ontario, four from Quebec, and two each from New Brunswick and Nova Scotia.[18] In a rough sense, and taking into account the additional provinces, this weighting has prevailed ever since.

The third principle, one captured to a degree by the 1866 formula, is to represent provinces in a manner roughly proportionate to their size. Thus, Ontario has more ministers than any other province, Quebec has more than any province but Ontario, British Columbia and Alberta usually have more than smaller provinces, and so on. If any province is likely to be left out it is Prince Edward Island, where the pool of only four MPs increases the chances that the government will not have an elected member from the Island. To some extent, therefore, the composition of the cabinet is expected to reflect the principle of representation by population rather than the principle of provincial equality, or at least it is expected to reflect rep by pop provided that all provinces, if possible, have at least one representative. Kim Campbell's short-lived cabinet provides a perfect illustration of this principle: it included eight ministers from Ontario, seven from Quebec, three (including Campbell) from British Columbia, two from Alberta, and one each from the remaining provinces except Prince Edward Island, which was left without cabinet representation. Jean Chrétien departed somewhat from this principle in his first cabinet, which included 10 ministers from Ontario, five (including himself) from Quebec, two from Alberta (including the Government leader in the Senate), and only one from each of the remaining provinces, with the exception of Prince Edward Island, which was again excluded. After the 1997 election there were 12 ministers from Ontario, seven (including Mr. Chrétien) from Quebec, two from British Columbia, and one each from the rest of the provinces, including Prince Edward Island.

The fourth principle is to provide representation for a variety of non-territorial communities. In the past it was important that the cabinet provide representation for Protestants and Catholics, including Protestants in Quebec and Catholics outside Quebec. In a similar fashion, representation was provided for anglophones in Quebec and francophones outside the province. More recently, the principle of non-territorial representation has been expanded to include representation for women, multicultural communities, visible minorities, and Aboriginal peoples. For example, gender representation is now automatically addressed, if not necessarily balanced; 7 of the 35 members in Mulroney's last cabinet were women, compared to 5 of 25 in Campbell's cabinet, 4 of 23 in Chrétien's first cabinet, and 6 of 28 in his second cabinet.

Finally, the prime minister must use the construction of the cabinet to promote internal harmony within the party and caucus. It was imperative, for example, that Kim Campbell offer Jean Charest a prominent role in her cabinet in order to heal the internal party wounds caused by the 1993 PC leadership race in which she defeated Charest, just as it was imperative that Jean Chrétien appoint his primary leadership rival, Paul Martin, to the cabinet. The cabinet must represent the party's major ideological camps, and the prime minister must reward supporters without appearing to be too vindictive to enemies and rivals. It is difficult for the prime minister to avoid members of stature within the governing party, even if they fail to share the prime minister's ideological outlook, policy dispositions, or friendship. And of course the prime minister must give attention to competence, particularly with respect to key portfolios. Here the primary concern is not the minister's expertise in the department's sphere of operations but rather his or her general managerial competence and ability to withstand pressure.

Clearly, the ideal cabinet minister is someone who can fill a large number of representational roles. For example, the same individual could represent a particular province, gender, language group, ethnic group, and ideological camp. Even so, the cluster of representational principles outlined above would all but guarantee a large federal cabinet if it were not for other constraints. When the cabinet is unveiled, any group that fails to find its reflection will charge that the government is insensitive to its concerns, hence the constant pressure for an ever more inclusive and larger cabinet. Yet governments are also trying to demonstrate that they are lean, if not necessarily mean, during periods of fiscal constraint, and thus there is a constant pressure to downsize cabinets. These competing priorities are not easily reconciled.

If the cabinet is to serve as a vehicle of political integration for the Canadian federal state, we might expect ministers to be drawn from the ranks of those with extensive experience in provincial politics and government. Certainly this was the case in the post-Confederation period, when prime ministers such as Laurier brought powerful provincial players into the federal cabinet. More generally, however, provincial experience is far from typical among federal ministers. Of all individuals who

Reprinted with permission—The Toronto Star Syndicate.

served in federal cabinets between 1867 and 1984, inclusive, 75 percent had no experience whatsoever in provincial politics.[19] Only 9.1 percent had served in a provincial legislative assembly, while an additional 5.9 percent had also served in a provincial cabinet; 4.8 percent had been provincial premiers, and another 5.2 percent had provincial experience that was limited to running unsuccessfully in a provincial campaign. Provincial experience has therefore been relatively rare among federal cabinet ministers and among the pool of MPs from which they are recruited, and it has been diminishing over time.

The lack of electoral provincial experience among federal cabinet ministers does not close the door to provincial government influence. Extensive federal–provincial intergovernmental networks and regional ministers within the federal cabinet ensure that provincial government interests are brought to the cabinet table. As Herman Bakvis explains, "even under conditions of adversity vis-à-vis specific provinces, federal ministers are still capable of acting as spear-carriers for provincial governments."[20] More important, there is little evidence that the legitimacy or effectiveness of the cabinet as a representative institution has been undermined by the lack of provincial experience among ministers. The fact that regional representation is provided by individuals whose legislative careers have been restricted to the House

Prime Minister Jean Chrétien and Governor General Roméo LeBlanc pose with the federal Cabinet at Rideau Hall, June 11, 1997. (CP photo/Fred Chartrand)

of Commons signals a change in the nature of representation rather than a deterioration. It suggests a progressive shift to intrastate forms of regional representation and away from interstate forms.

Operation of Cabinet Government

In media coverage of the federal government, it is commonplace to encounter such phrases as "the cabinet met to decide" or "cabinet deliberations continued." However, the cabinet in such instances is little more than what columnist Jeffrey Simpson has described as an "amiable fiction." The full cabinet provides an umbrella for a complex array of players who for the most part review decisions that have been made elsewhere. Most meetings of the full cabinet provide little more than an opportunity for the prime minister and other ministers to brief their colleagues and exchange information rather than to make decisions. The full cabinet has become a "mini-caucus" of the governing party,[21] a body too large and cumbersome to be effective at deliberation or decision making. The problem of size is compounded by the fact that the government's most senior bureaucrats, including the Clerk of the Privy Council and the prime minister's principal secretary, attend and participate actively in cabinet

TABLE 6.2 COMPOSITION OF JEAN CHRÉTIEN'S 1998 CABINET

MINISTER	MINISTRY
Jean Chrétien	Prime Minister
Herb Gray	Deputy Prime Minister
Lloyd Axworthy	Foreign Affairs
David Collenette	Transport
David Anderson	Fisheries and Oceans
Ralph Goodale	Natural Resources, Canadian Wheat Board
Sheila Copps	Canadian Heritage
Sergio Marchi	International Trade
John Manley	Industry
Diane Marleau	International Cooperation, La Franco-phone
Paul Martin	Finance
Arthur Eggleton	National Defence
Marcel Massé	Treasury Board, Infrastructure
Anne McLellan	Justice, Attorney General
Allan Rock	Health
Lawrence MacAulay	Labour
Christine Stewart	Environment
Alfonso Gagliano	Public Works and Government Services
Lucienne Robillard	Citizenship and Immigration
Fred Mifflin	Veterans Affairs, Atlantic Canada Opportunities Agency
Jane Stewart	Indian Affairs and Northern Development
Stéphane Dion	Intergovernmental Affairs, President of the Privy Council
Pierre Pettigrew	Human Resources Development
Don Boudria	Leader of the Government in the House of Commons
Bernard Graham	Leader of the Government in the Senate
Lyle Vancliff	Agriculture and Agri-Food
Herb Dhaliwal	National Revenue
Andy Scott	Solicitor General

An updated cabinet list can be found at http://www.parl.gc.ca/36/senmemb/house/cabinet-e.htm

meetings. Officials from departments relevant to the day's agenda may also attend, although their participation is more circumspect. A meeting of the full cabinet may therefore include more than 40 people in addition to the translation staff. (All cabinet documents are prepared in both official languages, and simultaneous translation is provided for all cabinet and cabinet committee meetings.)

Although the cabinet is inevitably complex, different prime ministers have been able to shape that complexity to suit their own personalities. Pierre Trudeau, for example, transformed the cabinet from a "departmentalized" cabinet, which brought together relatively autonomous ministers in a collegial, decision-making forum, into an "institutionalized" cabinet characterized by an elaborate committee structure and supporting **central agencies,** including **Treasury Board,** the **Privy Council Office (PCO),** and the **Prime Minister's Office (PMO),**[22] which bridged and coordinated the activities of such regular **line departments** as the Department of Defence. (These and many other federal government organizations can be accessed on the Internet at http://canada.gc.ca/depts/major/depind_e.html.) This transformation illustrates the prime minister's prerogative and capacity to restructure the machinery of government so that it corresponds to his or her own leadership style. Indeed, Aucoin argues that "the leadership paradigms of prime ministers—their philosophies of governance, their management styles and their political objectives—are the chief determinants in the organizational design of the central machinery of government."[23] In Trudeau's case, transformation meant the strengthening of central agencies to provide a collective cabinet counterweight to the bureaucratic advice on which individual ministers, as heads of line departments, inevitably rely. The enhanced central agencies were also meant to increase interdepartmental coordination and rationality in policy planning.[24] In Mulroney's case, the transformation entailed an increased measure of political control, achieved in part by a shift in power from central agencies to the Priorities and Planning (P&P) Committee of cabinet and to the prime minister himself. Mulroney's style was less bureaucratic and more personal than was Trudeau's.

The Priorities and Planning Committee in the Mulroney cabinet was the Canadian functional equivalent to the British **inner cabinet,** that smaller group of ministers who provide day-to-day executive leadership in Britain. The term "inner cabinet" has been formally avoided in Canada because of the representational pressures noted above. The formal designation of an inner cabinet would generate the same pressures for regional and group representation in the inner cabinet as are currently felt with respect to the full cabinet. Given that such pressures would be all but impossible to accommodate while still maintaining a body small enough to act in a deliberative fashion, more obscure terminology has been preferred. However, the term inner cabinet was used in the short-lived 1979–80 Joe Clark government and became more commonplace in media reports during the Mulroney years.

Jean Chrétien has imposed a more personalized and less bureaucratic decision-making style. Chrétien's first cabinet had only four committees: Economic Development Policy, Social Development Policy, Treasury Board, and a Special

Committee of Council. There is no clear evidence, however, that Chrétien has been able to recapture a collegial style for cabinet decision making, and overcome the time pressure on individual ministers and its corrosive effect on collegiality.

Ad hoc cabinet committees may be created as the situation demands. For example, the Cabinet Committee on Canadian Unity (CCCU) was struck in April 1991 to put together the federal government's proposal for constitutional renewal, *Shaping Canada's Future Together*, which was tabled in the House in September that year. Given the importance of the constitutional task, the composition of the CCCU was almost identical to that of Priorities and Planning, although the committee was chaired not by the prime minister but by the minister of Constitutional Affairs, Joe Clark. The recommendations of the CCCU ultimately flowed upward to P&P, and then to the full cabinet for only perfunctory inspection and discussion. The full cabinet did not see the final text of *Shaping Canada's Future Together* prior to its public release.

Cabinet committees enjoy a good measure of autonomy. Many, perhaps most, act in the name of the cabinet; decisions taken by committees need not be ratified or even discussed by the full cabinet, although all decisions taken are placed before the full cabinet for notification. This committee autonomy was particularly true in the past for the Priorities and Planning Committee, chaired by the prime minister. Nevertheless, the decentralization of decision making within the cabinet has done nothing to decentralize power within the federal government generally. The institutionalized cabinet retains, and may even have strengthened, its commanding presence at the apex of the federal government and the Canadian state. It should also be noted that the committee system has complicated the representation of regional interests within the national government. Given that the most representative body—the full cabinet—is less central to the process, the smaller and less representative committees have become more critical. The role of regional ministers has become more difficult in the institutionalized cabinet: "To be effective, regional ministers now must not only convince the prime minister and their cabinet colleagues of the need to accommodate the regional interests which they represent, but must accomplish this within a decision-making system that has become more formal, structured and complex."[25]

The cabinet and its committee system require extensive logistical support. This support and much more is provided by the Privy Council Office, which is itself a complex organization. In June 1998, approximately 580 people worked within the PCO, of whom 91 were in management positions. (Thirty-four of the management positions were occupied by women, 57 by men.) As the number of management positions might suggest, the PCO's role extends beyond logistical and secretarial support to include detailed policy and strategic advice. The senior officials of the PCO are at the heart of the federal decision-making process and wield considerable policy and political influence. The deputy minister of the PCO, who carries the titles Clerk of the Privy Council Office and Secretary to the Cabinet, is the most senior public servant in the federal government. The clerk of the PCO occupies three principal roles. First, he or she is in effect the prime minister's deputy minister, and in that capacity advises the prime minister with respect to overall policy direction, the functioning and organization of the government, and senior appointments. Second, the clerk is Secretary to the Cabinet, and thus supplies both support and advice to the ministry as a whole. Finally, he or she is the formal head of the public service and is ultimately responsible for its operation and its protection from political interference.

It should also be noted in the context of organizational complexity that cabinet ministers themselves are not solitary actors but rather the heads of elaborate organizational structures. The ministers draw from the public-service resources of their ministries, resources that may range from a few hundred to tens of thousands of public servants, headed by the deputy minister. In addition, ministers have their own **exempt staffs,** averaging about 20 people and including the ubiquitous executive assistants. These are individuals who are "exempt" (hence their name) from the normal Public Service Commission procedures for hiring civil servants. They are political appointees who answer directly to the political minister rather than to the bureaucratic deputy minister. (Douglas Lewis, minister of Public Security in the Campbell cabinet, had an exempt staff of 70!) They provide the minister with administrative support for the political side of the portfolio and also provide strategic policy advice, which in turn gives the minister some independence from the public service. Ministers maintain offices in both the House of Commons and their departments. A minister of the Crown, therefore, should be seen as a political organization with quite formidable resources. One of the primary tasks of prime-ministerial leadership is to harness such resources within a framework of collegial decision making, to preserve ministerial autonomy while maintaining committee effectiveness.[26]

If we turn from the organization of cabinet and its committees to the manner in which decisions are actually made, the first point to stress is that formal votes are not taken in cabinet. Voting makes sense as a decision-making technique only if all participants are considered equal. Indeed, voting *imposes* equality, as each person casts only one vote. In the cabinet context, however, the equality condition is not met. Some ministers will have a greater departmental involvement in the issue at hand than will other ministers. We would expect, for example, that the ministers of Defence and External Affairs would carry more weight in a cabinet discussion of Canadian forces in NATO than would the minister of Justice or the minister of Natural Resources. Some ministers will have a greater regional interest than will other ministers; a minister from Saskatchewan might be expected to contribute less to a discussion of fishing bans and the protection of cod stocks than would ministers from Atlantic Canada. Some ministers will be smarter, more seasoned, and more politically astute, or at least will be seen as such by their colleagues. Simply taking a vote would impose an artificial and unproductive equality. It would also weaken the quality of cabinet discussion by driving the discussion toward polar alternatives rather than a middle ground. Ministers might refrain from useful critical commentary if they had to commit to a yes or no vote. Voting would produce clear winners and losers, logrolling, and possibly long-standing factions, and would thus disrupt the internal harmony of the cabinet. Perhaps most important, making decisions by taking votes would reduce the weight of the prime minister to one vote. This would not only undercut the prime minister's capacity for leadership but would fly in the face of the real differences in status, electoral importance, and power between the prime minister and ministers. Cabinet decisions are therefore taken by consensus; the prime minister articulates the consensus, and ministers are expected to accept the prime minister's articulation, at least publicly, or resign from cabinet. This decision-making style reflects the basic institutional reality of responsible government; the cabinet speaks with a single voice and thus the search for consensus is an institutional necessity.

The second point to stress is that discussions within cabinet and the related cabinet documents are subject to strict secrecy. To some degree, this secrecy is a function of the issues themselves; public disclosure could be damaging to the interests of state, or could be inappropriately advantageous to private interests. More importantly, secrecy allows a frank discussion within cabinet while still retaining cabinet unity before the House and electorate. Only with the conventions of secrecy in place can the cabinet speak with a single voice to the Crown, Parliament, and electorate, and thus maintain collective responsibility. All this is not to say, however, that the cabinet is leakproof. As Bakvis notes, "over the past decade one can find a number of instances in which ministers have flouted the long-standing norms of cabinet secrecy and solidarity, without any apparent harm to their careers."[27]

The downside of cabinet secrecy is that regional and group representation takes place behind closed doors and out of view of the electorate. It may have been the case, for example, that western Canadian ministers in Pierre Trudeau's cabinet vigorously protested the 1980 National Energy Program and that western ministers in Brian Mulroney's cabinet vigorously protested the decision to award a maintenance contract for CF-18 military aircraft to a Montreal firm, despite a lower and technically superior bid by a Winnipeg firm.[28] If so, their protest was not visible; voters saw only their compliance with decisions thought to be harmful to the region. In this respect, Bakvis argues that the failure of regional ministers to provide visible regional representation impairs their ability to promote national unity: "It is in their perceived failure to play a major role in bringing the regions into a larger, shared sense of national identity that the difference between traditional and contemporary regional ministers remains most evident."[29] More generally, the inability of cabinet ministers to provide *visible* representation—and thus evidence to their constituents that they are also providing *effective* representation—means that provincial premiers have been able to claim this role as their own.

In summary, the composition and operating rules of cabinet are linked to the more general principles of Canadian parliamentary democracy. Cabinet is a representative institution par excellence, and cabinets are built with representational issues as the central concern. Cabinet government is responsible government, and the norms of secrecy and collective responsibility are a direct reflection of the conventions of responsible government. However, while many of the principles of representative and responsible government are being contested in the broader political arena, their manifestations in cabinet government have not yet been the subject of public criticism.

CABINET OR PRIME-MINISTERIAL GOVERNMENT?

It is time to bring the prime minister—thus far a somewhat ethereal figure in our discussion of cabinet government—to centre stage. In theory, the prime minister's relationship with ministers is captured by the seemingly contradictory phrase "first among equals." The equality aspect of this description derives from the fact that both the prime minister and cabinet ministers are for the most part elected MPs. Moreover, the prime minister does not occupy a unique formal position within Canada's constitutional framework. In reality, however, equality is far from the case. Individuals become prime minister by being elected as party leader in a national party convention, in which MPs and senators play an important but far from decisive role, and by having led their party to victory in a national election. (In some cases, of course, an individual may take on the office of prime minister before facing a general election; Pierre Trudeau, John Turner, and Kim Campbell all became prime minister by winning the leadership of the incumbent party.) Only the extraparliamentary party can remove the individual as party leader, and this is unlikely to happen prior to electoral defeat. Thus, the prime minister owes his or her position first to the party and second to the electorate, but not to cabinet colleagues. (In the past, prime ministers were selected by and within the parliamentary caucus, and the prime minister was thus more dependent on caucus and ministerial support.)[30] Bluntly put, the prime minister appoints ministers (and their deputy ministers); ministers do not appoint or select the prime minister. Ministers owe their cabinet appointment and their specific ministerial post to the prime minister who appoints them, subject of course to the host of representational constraints noted above. In addition, it is the prime minister alone who decides when an election will be called; cabinet colleagues may not even be consulted.

In assessing the centrality of prime ministers to cabinet government, it is important to note the longevity in office that many Canadian prime ministers have enjoyed, a longevity that has enabled them to put their stamp not only on the government of the day but also on political eras. Canada's first prime minister, Sir John A. Macdonald, was in office for all but four years between Confederation in 1867 and his death in 1891. Wilfrid Laurier was prime minister from 1896 to 1911. William Lyon Mackenzie King occupied the office from 1921 through 1930 (except for a three-month hiatus in 1926), and again from 1935 to 1947. In the case of these three prime ministers, it is all but impossible to separate the first 80 years of Canadian history from their leadership. To take a more recent example, Pierre Trudeau was prime minister from 1968 to 1979, and again from 1980 to 1984. During the same period in the United States Lyndon Johnson, Richard Nixon, Gerald Ford, Jimmy Carter, and Ronald Reagan served as president, and each is identified in the U.S. with a particular political era. Over the first 125 years of Confederation, four prime ministers—Macdonald, Laurier, King, and Trudeau—served for a total of 70 years. Of course, it should be noted that a number of prime ministers had very short tenures: Joe Clark, John Turner, and Kim Campbell together served a total of only 18 months in office.

DOSSIER 6.7 THE PROVINCIAL COMPARISON

Cabinet government in the provinces does not depart radically from the federal experience. As noted in Table 6.1, provincial cabinets are smaller in absolute terms than the federal cabinet but larger in relative terms, with most provincial cabinets having more than 20 ministers. Provincial cabinets have secretariats similar in principle to, but smaller than, the Privy Council Office. Most provincial cabinets have an equivalent of the federal Priorities and Planning Committee, a Treasury Board, standing committees in major policy areas, and a formalized secretariat. The same conventions of secrecy and collective responsibility apply to both the federal and provincial cabinets.

The ability of provincial premiers to dominate their cabinets may exceed that of the prime minister to dominate his or hers. As Rand Dyck explains, "Premiers still select, shuffle, and remove ministers, and they are increasingly the focus of both media and public attention during election campaigns." Premiers have access to advisers, public-opinion polling, and party resources that ministers do not share, or do not share to the same extent. Thus, Dyck concludes that "while ministers are said to be individually responsible for their departments and collectively responsible for government policy, determined premiers can still make their presence felt throughout the government's operations." The degree to which premiers do so may be largely a matter of personal style. For example, former Alberta premier Peter Lougheed had a reputation as a hands-on premier who did not hesitate to monitor and interfere in the departmental affairs of his cabinet colleagues. Lougheed's successor, Don Getty, had a different reputation; he practised a hands-off style of leadership that gave greater autonomy to his ministers.

Source: Rand Dyck, *Provincial Politics in Canada* (Scarborough: Prentice Hall Canada, 1991), 10–11.

Only the prime minister can energize and orchestrate the complex cabinet machinery described above; no minister has either the authority or resources to do so. For political authority the prime minister can draw on success at the polls—many MPs and ministers will be elected on their leader's coattails—and election as party leader by the extraparliamentary party. More than any other individual, the prime minister is able to define the election mandate and link that mandate to his or her own leadership. For resources, the prime minister can draw on the considerable bureaucratic and strategic support of the Privy Council Office and Prime Minister's Office. The PCO serves principally as the prime minister's department, and provides the prime minister with information and policy advice on all issues of national importance. In this respect, its role overlaps and complements that of the PMO, which serves prime ministers in their capacity as both party leader and head of government.[31] Thus, as regards political and organizational resources, the prime minister is much more than a single actor; the prime minister commands the immediate resources and personal loyalty of close to 1000 public servants and political aides. The formalized identification of a deputy prime minister in the Mulroney, Campbell, and Chrétien governments, and the increased muscle of the Deputy Prime Minister's Office within the cabinet committee system, have augmented rather than diffused the prime minister's influence and reach. The prime minister also has unparalleled access to the media and to the public. Finally, it should be remembered that it is the prime minister who articulates the cabinet consensus and thus ultimately decides government policy. Although the prime minister cannot consistently or wildly depart from the views of cabinet colleagues, there remains a large element of discretion through which prime-ministerial leadership can be exercised. For example, the federal government's millennium scholarship fund is largely a prime-ministerial initiative that emerged with little cabinet input or discussion.

In many ways, then, the prime minister occupies a position in the Canadian government that is similar to the position of the American president. Admittedly, the prime minister does not have the same opportunity that the president has to refashion the federal bureaucracy in his or her own image; an incoming prime minister will make only a fraction of the roughly 2600 appointments made by an incoming president. Over time, however, the prime minister has considerable capacity to shape the institutional environment by moving and promoting people within the public service; by recruiting new blood; by determining the staffing of key central agencies, including the PMO and PCO (the PMO itself plays a key role in staffing and personnel decisions); and by making a large number of appointments to government boards and agencies. These latter appointments are overwhelmingly **patronage** appointments (i.e., rewards for loyal party supporters), which allow the prime minister to place a significant personal and partisan stamp on the institutional apparatus of the Canadian state.[32] For example, Brian Mulroney made close to 700 appointments in the six months between his announcement of retirement and his replacement by Kim Campbell. These included appointments to the Senate, to federal courts, and to a wide range of regulatory agencies.

The prime minister, like the American president, is able to convert high-profile action on the international stage into political authority and resources at home. Meetings such as the Rio Summit on the Environment or the annual gathering of the leaders of the Group of Seven industrialized countries provide domestic political exposure and leverage. (A similar argument might be made with respect to prime-ministerial action in the arena of intergovernmental relations, although recent constitutional experience shows that the prime minister can just as easily be burned in this arena.) However, the most important point of comparison with the American president is that the prime minister exercises greater control over the legislative process. The integration of executive and legislative power in Canada means that, in most cases, the prime minister is able to secure legislative approval for policy initiatives; the cabinet dominates the House and the prime minister dominates the cabinet. The prime minister has no need to bargain with the House in the way in which the president must continually bargain with both houses of Congress; the American Congress is an emphatically autonomous institution, and even a strong president with

DOSSIER 6.8 PATRONAGE APPOINTMENTS WITHIN THE FEDERAL GOVERNMENT

The prime minister has the opportunity to make a wide range, and substantial number, of patronage appointments. Some of the most important and lucrative opportunities are listed below.

- The Senate: senators are appointed to age 75 and receive an annual salary of $64,400 plus a tax-free expense allowance of $10,000, in addition to travel and other expenses.
- National Parole Board: 45 full-time members earn between $80,100 and $94,500, and an unlimited number of part-timers earn $400–$475 a day.
- Citizenship Court: judges swear in landed immigrants as new Canadian citizens and earn $61,800–$72,900 a year.
- National Transportation Agency: nine full-time and six part-time members earn $88,000–$103,000 a year.
- International Joint Commission: three commissioners earn $88,000–$103,600 a year.
- Immigration and Refugee Board: 95 full-time members earn $73,400–$86,400 a year; an unlimited number of part-time members earn $355–$420 a day.
- Atomic Energy of Canada Limited: 11 directors receive an annual retainer of $4,600–$5,500 and a daily rate of $385–$475.
- National Energy Board: nine permanent members and six temporary members all earn $98,100–$115,000.

Other important players in the patronage game include the Canadian Radio-television and Telecommunications Commission, the Security Intelligence Review Committee, the Canadian Ports Corporation, the Canadian National Railway, VIA Rail, the CBC, the Export Development Corporation, the Bank of Canada, Canada Post, the National Capital Commission, the Advisory Council on the Status of Women, and the National Arts Centre.

Source: Stevie Cameron, "So long, and thank you very much," *The Globe and Mail*, June 5, 1993, D1, D3.

a partisan majority in both the House of Representatives and Senate cannot be assured of legislative support. It is impossible to imagine a Canadian prime minister having anything close to the degree of difficulty that Democratic president Bill Clinton has experienced with even a Democratic-controlled Congress.

In a rough sense, therefore, Canadian government can be seen as prime-ministerial government rather than cabinet government. The prime minister is the focal point of the party's electoral strategy and the lightning rod for public discontent. At the same time, the federal government is too large and too complex to be directed by a single individual, even when backed by the resources of PCO and PMO. In the trench warfare of public policy formulation and administration, cabinet ministers retain real influence and discretionary power. The prime minister's time, energy, and attention are carefully rationed out to a relatively few areas of special interest, political sensitivity, or expertise. Beyond that, cabinet government flourishes and shapes the public policies of the federal government.

CABINET GOVERNMENT AND POLITICAL INTEGRATION

At the time of the Confederation debates, when Canadians wrestled with the problems of regional representation in the new federal government, the cabinet was seen as the first line of defence for regional interests. Though the Senate consumed a good portion of the Confederation debates, it was assumed that this chamber would play a subordinate role to cabinet representation; partly as a consequence, the Senate slid to the margins of Canadian parliamentary and political life. At that time, it was not envisioned that provincial premiers would play the role that they have come to play as ardent defenders of provincial interests on the national stage and within the institutional matrix of executive federalism. With respect to political institutions, the emphasis of the time was on intrastate rather than interstate representation. It was the cabinet that was given the primary (albeit implicit and constitutionally undefined) role of national integration.

President Bill Clinton and Prime Minister Jean Chrétien say goodbye after meeting in Seattle.

To a fair degree, cabinet government has lived up to these early expectations. The federal cabinet has provided a common political forum within which the major communities and interests of Canada have found expression, one in which the principal players have been at the table and have had cards to play. If the cabinet has not provided a "fair shake" for the West, if Aboriginal representation has been sparse, if women have not played a role commensurate with their share of the national population, if language tensions remain unresolved, then it must also be recognized that these shortcomings are shared by the larger political community. They are not shortcomings of cabinet government alone. The failures have largely stemmed from the fact that the federal cabinet does indeed reflect the realities of a diverse and often divided country.

However, the cabinet's record with respect to national integration has not been unblemished and may in fact be deteriorating with the passage of time. The major constraint on the cabinet comes from the secrecy of cabinet deliberations. Cabinet government operates behind closed doors, and thus while regional and other forms of justice may be done, they are not seen to be done. The delicate task of knitting together a complex and divided national community is carried out in a forum that is largely invisible to Canadians. Therefore, we are not exposed to the trade-offs that make the country work, the sometimes crude deals that hold us together, and the delicate abeyances that lie beneath the surface of public debate.[33] In short, we are not educated in the realities of Canadian political life. It can be argued, of course, that secrecy is essential if deal making is to be effective, and that cabinets, like sausage factories, are best kept from public view. Yet if a degree of secrecy is necessary for the politics of political integration, then cabinet government may face a formidable challenge in an age when voters are demanding political processes that are more transparent. This challenge will be particularly acute if future cabinets are not adequately representative and exclude regional or social communities.

It is important to recognize that many of the principles and principal characteristics of cabinet government remain contested and are likely to become more contested in the future. Cabinet's dominance of the legislative process will continue to provoke calls for more effective representative government and for more freedom of manoeuvre for backbench and opposition MPs. Although it can be argued that party discipline quite appropriately keeps policymaking in the control of government and less in the hands of special-interest groups than would be the case if Parliament were more involved in policymaking,[34] those same groups will argue vehemently for a more open process. The secrecy of cabinet decision making will be contested by court challenges. Perhaps most important, the conventions of cabinet government and parliamentary democracy will be severely tested if the national party system fragments to the degree that majority governments can no longer be formed, or if only one party has a reasonable prospect of forming the government because the other parties occupy overly narrow regional or socio-demographic niches.

The outcome of the 1992 referendum on the Charlottetown Accord may also challenge the foundations of cabinet government. If the No vote in the referendum

DOSSIER 6.9 HERMAN BAKVIS ON REGIONAL MINISTERS

Regional ministers are those designated by the prime minister as the "head" or "political" minister for a province, for a region within a larger province, or even at times in the past for a broader geographical area such as the Prairies or Atlantic Canada. Regional ministers are responsible for the health of the party organization in their region, for dispensing patronage, and for monitoring expenditures affecting their province or region. They are also responsible for "communicating the decisions and views of the centre to the regions, explaining the less palatable outcomes of Ottawa's deliberations to provincial or local constituents, and helping ensure that local supporters remain within the fold."

The position of the "Quebec lieutenant" within the federal cabinet can be seen as a special but by no means atypical case of the regional minister. Ministers who have taken on regional responsibilities beyond those embedded in their particular portfolio, and who have consciously and forcefully played a regional role, include such notables as Lloyd Axworthy, John Crosbie, Pierre De Bané, James Gardiner, Herb Gray, Romeo Le Blanc, Allen MacEachern, Don Mazankowski, Lowell Murray, Gerald Regan, and Eugene Whelan.

Herman Bakvis disputes a common assumption that strong regional ministers are a thing of the past, and argues instead that they have survived remarkably well throughout the transformations of the federal cabinet that occurred under Pierre Trudeau and Brian Mulroney. Nor, he argues, has the role of regional ministers been seriously eroded by the growth of institutionalized federal–provincial relations. Indeed, the failures of executive federalism in the constitutional sphere may make the cabinet and regional ministers within the cabinet even more important as "instruments of national conciliation":

> *the prospect remains strong ... that the cabinet as we know it will continue to stand at the apex of federal government institutions. Equally likely, this body will continue to be thoroughly alive to the myriad pressures and nuances involved in the representation of regional interests.*

In such representational politics, regional ministers play a central role. Their influence comes first and foremost through the resources of their own portfolios, which are then "logrolled" to provide the minister with broader influence throughout cabinet. Bakvis is careful not to exaggerate the influence of regional ministers, noting that it may be found primarily at the margin of federal expenditures, mainly affecting the timing and specific location of federal projects. At the same time, "it is still ... a good-sized margin, one that could conceivably expand in the future."

Regional ministers are also likely to play a continuing role in providing provincial governments with access to the federal cabinet:

[T]he regional minister system still represents a significant means by which provincial governments can make their influence felt within the federal cabinet. By establishing links with the senior minister in their province, these governments have been able to sway discussion of, and decisions on, a wide range of federal issues of importance to them.

Source: Herman Bakvis, *Regional Ministers: Power and Influence in the Canadian Cabinet* (Toronto: University of Toronto Press, 1991). Reprinted with permission.

was in significant measure a rejection not only of the Charlottetown Accord but also of executive federalism more broadly defined, it is unlikely that the political challenge will stop short of the operating norms and conventions of cabinet government. Conversely, if the defeat of the accord effectively shuts down constitutional politics, we may miss some important reform opportunities. For example, Bakvis suggests that elected senators could provide a new and more effective breed of regional minister, one empowered by a broader electoral mandate and operating from a more secure electoral base.[35] In the absence of Senate reform, the imperatives of institutional evolution could seek other outlets in a more fundamental challenge to parliamentary democracy.

CONCLUSION

We began this chapter by stressing the centrality of the cabinet to parliamentary government and the centrality of the prime minister within the cabinet process. We concluded by again emphasizing the importance of the prime minister within the political executive broadly defined. It may seem, therefore, that Canadian parliamentary government is highly personalized, and that prime ministers have an inordinate ability to place their personal stamp on cabinet as well as on the times in which they live.

At the same time, however, we stressed that there is a principled foundation to parliamentary government. Neither the prime minister nor the cabinet operates in a vacuum; together they operate within a complex web of principles and conventions that define a system of responsible and representative government. In an important sense they are the creatures of that system; they reflect its principles rather than operate outside its boundaries. Their ability to govern, and the way in which power is exercised within and by the political executive, stem directly from the principled foundations of Canadian parliamentary government. While those foundations are not uncontested, they have operated with a reasonable degree of continuity since Confederation. Thus, to understand the nature of the political executive in Canada, one must understand not only the players of the day but also the institutional rules by which they play and through which they exercise their influence on Canadian political life.

KEY TERMS

cabinet
prime minister
Crown
governor general
Privy Council
lieutenant governor
formal executive
political executive
dissolution
minority government
majority government
constitutional monarchy
Speech from the Throne
orders-in-council
responsible government
cabinet solidarity
party government
King-Byng affair
separation of powers
regional ministers
central agencies
Treasury Board
Privy Council Office (PCO)
Prime Minister's Office (PMO)
line departments
inner cabinet
exempt staffs
patronage

DISCUSSION QUESTIONS

1. Many parliamentary reforms have been proposed to weaken cabinet's grip on the legislative process. What might be the impact of such reforms on responsible government? On government efficiency?
2. Consider the possible implications of reducing the size of the federal cabinet even further, to less than 20 ministers. What might be some of the advantages? Disadvantages? What representational costs might be incurred?
3. Discuss the advantages and disadvantages of cabinet secrecy. On balance, can a case be made for less secrecy?
4. It has been suggested from time to time that the governor general be elected. What consequences for parliamentary government might flow from such a reform? On balance, is this suggestion worthy of pursuit?
5. Public discontent with parliamentary government often entails a strong distaste for party discipline and for the partisanship that such discipline reflects and engenders. How might you try to convince a public audience that party discipline may, in fact, be a positive feature of Canadian parliamentary democracy (i.e., an essential component of effective and responsible government)?

SUGGESTED READINGS

Aucoin, Peter. "Regionalism, Party, and National Government." In Peter Aucoin, ed., Research Coordinator, *Party Government and Regional Representation in Canada.* Toronto: University of Toronto Press, 1985, 137–160.

Bakvis, Herman. *Regional Ministers: Power and Influence in the Canadian Cabinet.* Toronto: University of Toronto Press, 1991.

Campbell, Colin. *Governments under Stress: Political Executives and Key Bureaucrats in Washington, London, and Ottawa.* Toronto: University of Toronto Press, 1983.

Franks, C.E.S. *The Parliament of Canada.* Toronto: University of Toronto Press, 1987.

Marshall, Geoffrey, ed. *Ministerial Responsibility.* Oxford: Oxford University Press, 1989.

Pal, Leslie A., and David Taras, eds. *Prime Ministers and Premiers: Political Leadership and Public Policy in Canada.* Scarborough: Prentice-Hall Canada, 1988.

Punnett, R.M. *The Prime Minister in Canadian Government and Politics.* Toronto: Macmillan, 1977.

Sharp, Mitchell. "Depoliticizing the Speech from the Throne." *Parliamentary Government* 8, no. 4 (Summer 1989), 16–18.

Sutherland, S.L. "Responsible Government and Ministerial Responsibility: Every Reform Is Its Own Problem." *Canadian Journal of Political Science* 24 no. 1 (March 1991), 91–120.

Thomas, Paul. "Theories of Parliament and Parliamentary Reform." *Journal of Canadian Studies* 14 (1979), 57–66.

NOTES

1. C.E.S. Franks, *The Parliament of Canada* (Toronto: University of Toronto Press, 1987), 268. (Emphasis added.)
2. Some provincial party leaders have been selected through a direct vote by party members rather than through a party leadership convention. As we will discuss in Chapter 10, the continued use of leadership conventions at the federal level is a matter of growing debate within the party organizations.
3. In virtually all cases, minority governments in Canada look like majority governments in that all members of the cabinet come from a single party.
4. It should be noted, however, that constitutional monarchies are not generally under attack around the world. The unrest in Australia and Britain is largely idiosyncratic.
5. Mitchell Sharp, "Depoliticizing the Speech from the Throne," *Parliamentary Government* 8 (Summer 1989), 16–18.
6. S.L. Sutherland, "Responsible Government and Ministerial Responsibility: Every Reform Is Its Own Problem," *Canadian Journal of Political Science* 24, no. 1 (March 1991), 95.
7. Until the late 1920s, ministers appointed during Parliament's term were obligated to resign their seats and run in a by-election before assuming office.
8. Sutherland, "Responsible Government and Ministerial Responsibility," 102. Several reasons for ministerial resignations are not provided: these include "other" (7); private reasons not elaborated (5); task finished (8); and private sector opportunity (3).

9. Peter Aucoin, "Regionalism, Party, and National Government," in Peter Aucoin, Research Coordinator, *Party Government and Regional Representation in Canada* (Toronto: University of Toronto Press, 1985), 144.
10. Ibid., 137.
11. For an extended discussion of this point, see Roger Gibbins, *Regionalism: Territorial Politics in Canada and the United States* (Toronto: Butterworths, 1982), chapter 4.
12. Franks, *The Parliament of Canada*, 12.
13. The Senate reforms proposed in the 1992 Charlottetown Accord would have removed this option by prohibiting senators from sitting in the federal cabinet.
14. Franks, *The Parliament of Canada*, 75–79.
15. Nelson Wiseman, "The Questionable Relevance of the Constitution in Advancing Minority Cultural Rights in Manitoba," *Canadian Journal of Political Science* 25, no. 4 (December 1992), 701.
16. Herman Bakvis, *Regional Ministers: Power and Influence in the Canadian Cabinet* (Toronto: University of Toronto Press, 1991).
17. Donald V. Smiley and Ronald L. Watts, *Intrastate Federalism in Canada* (Toronto: University of Toronto Press, 1985), 65.
18. Ibid., 4.
19. See Doreen Barrie and Roger Gibbins, "Parliamentary Careers in the Canadian Federal State," *Canadian Journal of Political Science* 22, no. 1 (March 1989), 137–145.
20. Bakvis, *Regional Ministers*, 297.
21. Jeffrey Simpson, "Operations Unlimited," *The Globe and Mail*, May 19, 1988, A6.
22. Stéphan Dupré, "The Workability of Executive Federalism in Canada," in Herman Bakvis and William Chandler, eds., *Federalism and the Role of the State* (Toronto: University of Toronto Press, 1987). See also Colin Campbell, *Governments under Stress: Political Executives and Key Bureaucrats in Washington, London, and Ottawa* (Toronto: University of Toronto Press, 1983), 351.
23. Peter Aucoin, "The Machinery of Government: From Trudeau's Rational Management to Mulroney's Brokerage Politics," in Leslie A. Pal and David Taras, eds., *Prime Ministers and Premiers: Political Leadership and Public Policy in Canada* (Scarborough: Prentice-Hall Canada, 1988), 66.
24. Ibid., 54.
25. Aucoin, "Regionalism, Party, and National Government," 146.
26. Aucoin, "The Machinery of Government," 54.
27. Bakvis, *Regional Ministers*, 286.
28. For a full discussion of the CF-18 issue, see Robert M. Campbell and Leslie A. Pal, *The Real Worlds of Canadian Politics: Cases in Process and Policy* (Peterborough, Ont.: Broadview Press, 1989), chapter 1.
29. Bakvis, *Regional Ministers*, 300.
30. The practice of caucus selection is still used in Australia and Britain. Alternative methods of leadership selection are discussed in Chapter 10.
31. Aucoin, "The Machinery of Government," 63.

32. Patronage appointments are made directly by the prime minister or responsible minister and are not routed through the Public Service Commission. They can provide not only lucrative reward for party supporters but also a means of ensuring that "friends of the government" staff important advisory and regulatory positions.
33. Roger Gibbins and David Thomas, "Ten Lessons from the Referendum," *Canadian Parliamentary Review* (Winter 1992–93), 2–5.
34. C.E.S. Franks, "The 'Problem' of Debate and Question Period," in John C. Courtney, ed., *The Canadian House of Commons: Essays in Honour of Norman Ward* (Calgary: University of Calgary Press, 1985), 10.
35. Bakvis, *Regional Ministers.*

THE ADMINISTRATIVE STATE

7

The challenge of governing within limits is not only to establish and meet limits, but also to design and apply them creatively, as a tool for achieving wider public policy and public management goals. While budgetary positions are now improving in many OECD countries, the careful application of limits and working through of their consequences for public services remains a constant preoccupation. The fundamental goal remains better government, whether or not that is also thought to require smaller government.[1]

The postwar period in Canada, as in other Western countries, saw the rise of the welfare state and, as a consequence, the growth and complexity of the public bureaucracy. Characterized by expensive social programs and detailed regulation, and financed by massive borrowing, the administrative welfare state has come under attack by market-oriented conservatives and by exponents of the so-called New Public Management (NPM). The result has been cutbacks, deregulation, and privatization. Public bureaucracies have been downsized and redesigned. Nevertheless, the state remains a large and imposing presence in our lives. We have hardly reverted to the limited "night watchman" state that preceded the welfare state. And although some state programs and regulations have been downsized or eliminated, others have emerged to take their place.

■ ■ ■

Government has come to play a large and ubiquitous role in our lives. Sometimes its role is visible and easily identified, as when it provides money for such services as public universities, hospitals, or police protection. The government's reach into our lives, and into our pocketbooks, is also felt at the checkout counter, where provincial sales taxes and the Goods and Services Tax add substantially to the cost of our purchases, and on payday, when income tax is deducted from our paycheque. At other times, government influence is less visible. Indeed, there are many areas of government activity of which we may be scarcely aware. Leaving aside the explicitly covert activities of such government agencies as the Canadian Security Intelligence Service (CSIS), Canadians may take little notice of the impact of government regulations on such things as the packaging of consumer goods, the quality of air and water, or the kind of protective gear that must be worn on construction sites. Whether they are visible and obvious or more subtle and hidden, governmental activities add up. We live in an era in which vast areas of social, economic, and personal life are publicly administered. We live in the era of the administrative state. This is true even at a time when the size and role of the state is being reduced.

The administrative state grew hand in hand with the **welfare state**. The welfare state has its roots in the industrial revolution of the 19th century and developed in a variety of forms in different countries at different times.[2] At the end of World War II, however, most Western states committed themselves in one form or another to the development of a welfare state.[3] What did this mean? First, it meant that governments were prepared to stimulate employment in economic downturns and put the brakes on during periods of inflationary growth. Government would be the flywheel for the economy, principally through its budget and other economic measures. The use of the state to manage economic growth this way was the hallmark of Keynesianism.[4] Second, it meant that governments would develop social programs to deal with the critical needs of their citizens: health, education, child care, disability, unemployment, and old age. Third, it meant that governments would try to ensure a greater degree of equality among citizens, in terms of wealth and income and in terms of life opportunities. This involved governments in income redistribution through taxation and spending, and in a variety of regulatory schemes designed to moderate the inequalities generated by economic and social markets.

While some of the commitment to welfare-state principles was rhetorical, and varied in practice and according to the political ideology of incumbent governments, all Western governments grew steadily between 1945 and the early 1980s. They grew in terms of expenditures, taxes, programs, employment, regulations, and a host of small and large interventions in society and the economy. Naturally, the public bureaucracy required to implement and manage this new activity also grew. Government departments proliferated and expanded; new kinds of departments—central agencies—arose to coordinate the state's increasingly complex activities; regulatory agencies of all kinds were established; task forces, commissions, and advisory boards came to litter the public landscape. The whole enterprise was expensive, and governments financed it through substantial borrowing, building up massive public debts over a 30-year period.

Then it stopped. The story of the welfare state in recent years involves painful adjustments, spending cuts, increased taxation, public-sector layoffs, and program restructuring. Conservative attacks on the traditional welfare state, which had been muted and marginal in the postwar period, began to gather momentum in the 1980s—the decade of the elections of President Ronald Reagan in the United States, Prime Minster Margaret Thatcher in Britain, and Prime Minister Mulroney in

Canada.[5] With budget deficits widespread among the Organization for Economic Cooperation and Development (OECD) countries (proportionally, Canada had one of the largest), it became routine to argue that public sectors were too large, that bureaucracies were inefficient, and that government programs were often inefficient and ineffective. The key ideas behind the welfare state came under attack. There was less confidence that governments could actually control their economies, greater willingness to target social programs for the needy and encourage others to provide for themselves, and more acceptance of the idea that individuals, not governments, should make their own opportunities.

The late 1980s and early 1990s saw this conservative rhetoric replaced by action in several countries. Broadly similar strategies have been adopted to "reinvent" or "re-engineer" public sector institutions around the world,[6] and in early 1998 even Communist China was embarking on plans to fire millions of bureaucrats, close key central planning ministries, privatize many agencies, and generally redesign government to meet the needs of a market economy.[7] Since 1993 the federal Liberal government has adopted much the same approach under the rubric of "Program Review" and "Getting Government Right." While the results have sometimes been less radical than similar initiatives in other countries,[8] there is no doubt that the Canadian public sector (including the provinces) is being dramatically reformed.

It is important to put these developments in perspective. While they are getting smaller in some ways, and less intrusive, states remain the largest and most powerful institutions in society. Government spending has declined as a proportion of the **gross domestic product (GDP)**—the total value of all goods and services produced in a country in one year—but remains substantial. Thus, while total government program spending in Canada dropped from 43 percent of GDP in 1992 to about 34 percent in 1998, the presence of the state remains visible—one in every three dollars is still spent by the federal, provincial, or municipal governments. More importantly (see below), this money is spent primarily on social services such as health, education, and social assistance. Indeed, in some instances the presence of government in our lives is bound to grow in policy areas such as environmental standards, the enforcement of trade agreements, education, health, and retirement. Finally, now that deficits have been eliminated in most jurisdictions in Canada, governments may get interested in activism once more, and activism is usually associated with growth in programs, departments, and interventions. Nonetheless, the changes we have witnessed in the administrative state in the last decade are important and not entirely reversible. The institutional nature of the Canadian administrative state is changing.

This chapter chronicles both the rise of the administrative welfare state and the more recent challenges it has faced. The story is told from several perspectives. The growth and then partial retrenchment of the welfare state is evident in patterns of public spending and employment, the evolution of social programs, changes in public regulation, and transformations of the public bureaucracy. We shall examine each in turn. The story, moreover, involves both levels of government, and we thus end with a discussion of state retrenchment in Alberta and Ontario, two of the leaders in reforming the provincial state.

THE FISCAL PICTURE

One of the key responsibilities of any government is the management of the fiscal affairs of the state. As governments became larger, this task grew in complexity. Revenues and expenditures provide an important indicator of the size and scope of the state because they are a fiscal measure of societal resources channelled through state institutions for public-policy purposes. A "large" state presumably is one that absorbs substantial financial resources, thereby leaving less for private citizens to determine how they will spend. This is true even of programs that essentially involve little more than transferring funds from one pocket to another. Many social programs are redistributive in this sense, in that the government collects taxes from all citizens and then returns those taxes through programs such as child benefits or pensions. It is sometimes argued that redistributive activities of this sort should not count in determining the "size" or economic cost of government, since in the end it is money that is returned to citizens and spent by them. In the wider sense of the state's centrality and importance in society, however, these types of expenditures certainly count. It is because of them that governments engage in a host of minutely calibrated interventions associated with tax collection and program administration.

It should be remembered that government spending does not always follow the lines of federal–provincial legislative jurisdiction. The spending power (introduced in Chapter 2) has allowed Ottawa to launch social and welfare programs that, strictly speaking, fall under provincial jurisdiction. The spending power can be used in this way only if the monies are transferred to a person or organization, and only if the recipient may refuse the transfer. No one is forced to apply for a Canadian Millennium Scholarship, for example, so Ottawa can use its spending power in education, clearly a provincial jurisdiction. However, when Ottawa and the provinces decided in 1940 that the federal government should provide unemployment insurance, a constitutional amendment was required because the UI scheme was compulsory and therefore affected the civil rights of citizens (something within provincial jurisdiction). The spending power has been behind a host of key Canadian welfare programs, from family allowances in 1945 (now replaced) to medicare. Ottawa is permitted to attach conditions to the monies it offers, and this allows some degree of policy control.[9]

In 1997–98, federal and provincial program spending accounted for 28.4 percent of GDP, down from 37.5 percent in 1992–93.[10] (The higher figures reported above—34 percent in 1998, down from 43 percent in 1992—include municipal government spending.) Figure 7.1 shows that the trend in the 1990s has been downward and that Canada has led the G-7 countries in reducing overall spending. This is a remarkable turnaround. Total government expenditures in Canada have risen steadily from the 1960s and by the late 1980s, as a percentage of GDP, were higher in

Canada than in the United States and in most other developed countries. The 1960–73 Canadian average, for example, was 31.8 percent—close to that of Canada's major trading partners. By 1984 the Canadian proportion was almost 47 percent, a full 10 percentage points higher than the U.S. average and roughly six percentage points higher than the G-7 or OECD averages.

What happened? Part of the story of growth in the size of expenditures was growth in the size of annual deficits and public debt (the **deficit** is the annual shortfall that is covered by borrowing, and the total of all deficits is the **debt**). In other words, the provinces and Ottawa funded these growing expenditures in large part by borrowing. By the mid-1980s, for example, for every dollar Ottawa collected in tax revenues, it spent $1.33 on programs.[11] By 1993–94, 33 cents of every dollar of revenue collected by Ottawa went in interest payments on the national debt.[12] In 1992 the total Canadian government deficit (national accounts basis) was 7.4 percent of GDP, almost double the G-7 average. From that period to 1997, however, through a combination of economic growth and program cuts and revenue increases at both levels of government, Canada reached the point where its total deficit as a proportion of GDP was half that of the G-7 countries. Indeed, by 1998, as a result of a balanced federal budget and a majority of balanced provincial budgets, the total government sector in Canada was actually running a small surplus (about 1 percent of GDP, national accounts basis), the best performance in the G-7.[13]

How is total government spending divided among levels of government? In 1994–95, federal, provincial, and local governments spent a total of $357 billion, of which 48 percent was spent by the federal government alone.[14] The key expenditure areas for government as a whole are in the social policy field broadly defined, which includes health, education, income security, and social assistance. As the next few pages will show, the federal government still controls the largest single expenditure programs in these areas, but the provinces control expenditures in the hugely expensive areas of health and education. Keith Banting has called this federal–provincial balance a "bifurcated welfare state."[15]

The February 1998 federal budget provided a glimpse into where the money goes at the federal level. Table 7.1 breaks down the major program spending categories of total federal government expenditures. Elderly benefits and employment insurance comprise the bulk of transfers to persons, a total of $34.2 billion in 1997–98, and were projected to rise somewhat in each of the next two years. Major transfers to other levels of government are principally for two purposes: the Canada Health and Social Transfer and equalization payments (whereby Ottawa equalizes provincial tax revenues). Total cash transfers to other governments amounted to $19.9 billion in 1997–98 and were projected to decline marginally in the next two years. Transfers to persons and cash transfers to provinces together account for almost exactly one-half of all federal government program spending.

Until the 1998 budget, a major component of federal spending was servicing the public debt. In 1993 annual debt charges of $42 billion amounted to one-quarter of all federal expenditures. In 1998, for the first time since 1971, the federal

FIGURE 7.1 **INTERNATIONAL FISCAL COMPARISON**

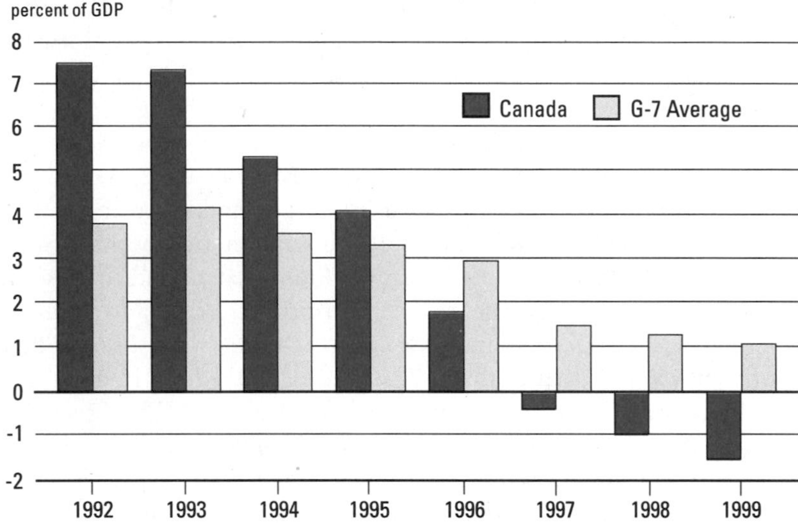

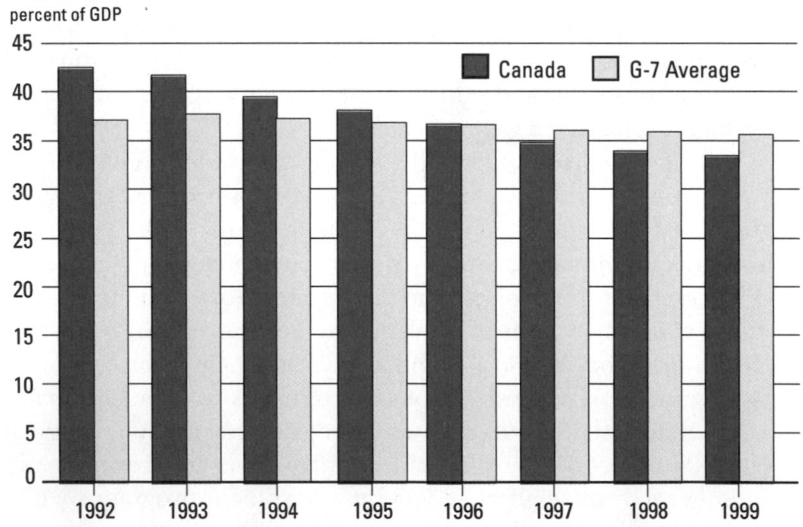

Source: *The Budget Chart Book, 1998,* 79, 81.

Note: The OECD has not yet adjusted its national accounts data to incorporate recent revisions in the Canadian System of National Accounts.

TABLE 7.1 FEDERAL BUDGETARY EXPENDITURES

	1996–97	1997–98	1998–99	1999–00
		(billions of dollars)		
Major transfers to persons				
Elderly Benefits	21.6	22.2	22.9	23.6
Employment insurance benefits	12.4	12.0	12.6	13.2
Total	34.0	34.2	35.5	36.8
Major transfers to other levels of government				
CHST				
Total entitlements	26.9	25.3	26.0	26.6
Tax point transfer	−12.1	−12.8	−13.5	−14.1
Cash payment	14.8	12.5	12.5	12.5
Equalization	8.7	8.8	8.5	8.7
Transfers to territories	1.1	1.1	1.1	1.1
Other fiscal transfers	−0.4	−0.4	−0.4	−0.5
Alternative payments for standing programs	−2.0	−2.1	−2.2	−2.3
Total cash transfers	22.2	19.9	19.5	19.5
Reference: Total entitlements	36.0	34.2	34.7	35.4
Direct program spending				
Departmental transfers				
Agriculture	1.1	1.0	1.0	0.9
Industry and Regional Development	1.6	1.9	2.0	1.8
Foreign Affairs	2.1	2.2	1.9	1.9
Health	0.9	0.9	1.1	1.1
Human Resources Development	2.1	2.1	2.2	2.0
Indian and Northern Development	3.9	4.0	4.1	4.1
Other	6.1	7.6	4.7	5.1
Total	17.9	19.6	17.0	16.8
Crown corporations	3.6	3.9	3.8	3.8
Defence	8.5	8.4	7.9	8.2
Other	18.7	20.0	20.9	21.9
Total direct program spending	48.7	52.0	49.5	50.7
Total program spending	104.8	106.0	104.5	107.0
(percent of GDP)	(12.8)	(12.4)	(11.7)	(11.5)

Numbers may not add due to rounding.

Source: *The Budget Chart Book 1998,* 67.

government announced a balanced budget—no deficit. It projects that it will have balanced budgets (possibly surpluses) over the next several years and that the proportion of debt-to-GDP will decline from 70 percent to just over 60 percent in five years. All Canadian governments are expected to be in surplus by the end of the decade.

The other side of government budgets is revenues, or taxation. All three orders of government may raise revenues for their own purposes, though revenue collection by municipalities is constrained by provincial legislation. Ottawa's taxing authority is technically greater than the provincial taxing authority because it has access to both "direct" and "indirect" forms of taxation, whereas the provinces are limited to direct taxation. Constitutionally, this distinction was understood as the difference between levying a tax that could not be passed on to others (e.g., income taxes) and levying a tax that could (e.g., a tax on manufacturers or the customs tariff). It has not been possible to clearly maintain this distinction, however. Sales taxes, for example, which seem to be the classic example of an indirect tax that is passed on to the consumer, are levied by all provinces except Alberta. The provinces gained access to this lucrative source of income through some judicial sleight of hand, according to which the tax was imposed not on the retailer, who passed it on to the customer, but directly on the customer, with the retailer acting as the government's tax collector.[16]

The two most lucrative sources of government revenue are income and corporate taxes, which both provincial and federal governments have undoubted power to levy. The personal income tax is the single most lucrative tax field, contributing $102.5 billion to government coffers, compared with only $18 billion from corporate taxes.[17] Looking at only the federal government once more, the 1998 budget projected $71 billion in personal income taxes and $20.5 billion in corporate income tax in 1998–99.[18] Employment insurance contributions alone for the same year will be almost as much as corporate taxes, though about half of those contributions come from employers. The projected trends are for increased revenues from both personal and corporate taxes in the next three years, though this is the result of economic growth rather than increased levels of taxation. In fact, for the first time in decades there is serious discussion of cutting taxes. This is due to Canada's comparatively high levels of taxation (compared to those of the United States) and the arrival of the "fiscal dividend" at the federal level. It is also ideologically motivated to some degree—Conservative governments in Alberta and Ontario have cut taxes, and in Ontario's case the cut came before the deficit was eliminated.

Both federal and provincial governments levy sales and excise—or consumption—taxes as well, and these are not insignificant. According to Statistics Canada, in 1994–95 they accounted for 20 percent of total government revenues. The trend, therefore, has been to reduce reliance on corporate taxes and increase revenues from taxes on persons. One result of this trend has been a more finely grained integration of the public treasury with the body politic. Citizens confront government with virtually every purchase. Purchasers of cigarettes and liquor bear the heaviest load—in the form of so-called sin taxes—but all provinces except Alberta have sales taxes on virtually all commercial transactions. The latest and least-loved entry in the tax field is the Goods and Services Tax (GST), a federal levy introduced in January 1991. It replaced the Manufacturers' Sales Tax, an inefficient and hidden tax on manufactured goods only. The GST is almost universal in application, visible because it is paid at the retail level, and applicable to services as well as to goods.[19]

Behind these fiscal details lie some important fiscal policy decisions taken by all governments, but particularly by Ottawa. Whereas revenues fell short of expenditures at the federal and provincial levels for most of the 1980s, the reverse has been true in recent years. The provinces, particularly New Brunswick and Alberta, led the way well before Ottawa devised a plan to cut its deficits. But from 1995 to 1998 Ottawa applied itself single-mindedly to cutting program expenditures and raising revenues. It was fortunate to have done so during a period of low interest rates (so debt charges were controlled) and economic growth (which stimulated more tax revenues). Ironically, in a period of five years Ottawa's biggest problem went from controlling the deficit to wondering how to apportion surpluses, though by late 1998, after the global economic downturn and the dramatic fall in the value of the Canadian dollar, the Finance minister was attempting to dampen expectations of steadily growing surpluses.

Apart from good luck and dogged determination, this federal fiscal performance depended on a mix of institutional and fiscal policy decisions. The institutional ingredients were strategic support from the prime minister and the implementation of a new budgeting system, the **Expenditure Management System (EMS).** When Paul Martin became Finance minister in 1993 he was convinced that the deficit was a problem, but he was not convinced that it would have to be dealt with through dramatic cuts in expenditure. He thought that economic growth would meet the Liberals' deficit target of 3 percent of GDP. His officials spent a year convincing him that the target could not be met that way, and were vindicated when the initial 1994 deficit projections proved to be significantly higher than first thought. In the spring of that year, Martin had to convince his cabinet colleagues to implement a spending freeze. In the context of the cabinet, only the minister of Finance and the secretary of the Treasury Board are "fiscal guardians"; the rest are spenders. At this point Martin received strong support from Prime Minister Chrétien, and the freeze was imposed. A year later, Martin proposed deep cuts, driven by the aforementioned program review exercise that would scrutinize every program in terms of efficiency and effectiveness. Once again, the prime minister intervened and beat back cabinet opposition. From that point forward, Martin and the department of Finance began to drive the entire government agenda.[20]

The second institutional ingredient was the EMS. Ottawa had tried a variety of different schemes to manage the expenditure process in the last 25 years and none had been successful.[21] Four principles guide the EMS system: (1) "fiscal and expenditure planning provides a stable environment where changes to spending and programs can be planned well ahead of implementation"; (2) "strategic planning for the medium to long term emphasizes examining existing programs and delivery systems and reallocating expenditures to new priorities"; (3) "parliamentarians and Canadians are consulted in the expenditure planning process;" and (4) "incentives encourage effective planning, resource allocation, and performance information and management."[22] In practice Martin and his officials introduced several key innovations that made it possible to keep control of federal expenditures. First, there were no "policy reserves." Departments wishing to develop new programs would have to find the funds internally, usually by cutting something else. Second, the process of program review was instituted, whereby Finance officials delivered spending cut targets to departments, who then reviewed their own programs to see how they might meet them. Third, a contingency reserve was established by the minister of Finance to cover unexpected expenditures, but it lay entirely within his discretion. Fourth, Treasury Board did have a small operating reserve, but departments that asked for money would have to pay it back. Fifth, forecasts for economic growth, interest rates, and revenues were deliberately conservative.

The other main ingredient in the federal government's strategy was a series of fiscal policy decisions, primarily to cut selectively but deeply and to raise revenues. As for cuts, there was no magic or mystery as to what the key targets were: transfers to governments and transfers to persons. As described in Chapter 4, a complex system of transfers from Ottawa to the provinces developed after Confederation. By the 1970s the federal government was transferring billions of dollars to the provinces in equalization payments and to pay roughly half of the costs of postsecondary education, health, and social services. In 1978 transfers for health and postsecondary education were consolidated under the Established Programs Financing (EPF) Act, and support was divided equally between cash transfers and "tax points" (Ottawa lowered its personal taxes by several tax points and the provinces increased theirs by the same number). Ottawa was seeking more predictable funding formulas, while the provinces received greater discretion over how to spend the monies. Ottawa also transferred funds for social assistance through the Canada Assistance Plan (CAP), paying half of all welfare costs in the provinces. In 1985 Ottawa capped the growth in EPF transfers to the provinces, and in 1990 it froze per capita entitlements for two years. In the 1991 budget these expenditures were frozen once more to 1994–95, after which time they were to be constrained to the rate of growth of gross national product (GNP) minus three percentage points. (GNP is GDP plus total net income from abroad.) Equalization payments to the provinces were exempted from the expenditure control plan, but growth in CAP payments to the three richer provinces—Ontario, Alberta, and British Columbia—was capped at 5 percent per year. The 1995 federal budget announced that CAP and EPF would be combined within a year in a new program entitled the Canadian Health and Social Transfer (CHST). We discuss the program features of CHST in more detail below, but from a fiscal point of view the most important feature of the CHST was that it promised to reduce federal cash transfers to the provinces by $4.5 billion annually by 1997–98.

Transfers to persons were also cut and various steps taken to increase revenues from contributions and charges. In 1995 the government announced that the former Unemployment Insurance program would be changed to the Employment Insurance (EI) program. This was on top of cuts to the program in the previous year, and together the changes succeeded in cutting benefits by $2.5 billion annually in 1995. Insurance premiums, however, continued to funnel money into federal coffers, and by 1998 the EI fund had a surplus of close to $10 billion. Starting in 1996 Old Age Security (OAS) pensions were clawed back at a steeper rate from high-income retirees, saving $300 million annually. Because of the aging of the population, federal projections showed massive increases in public pension expenditures, so the 1996 federal budget announced plans to consolidate the OAS and income-related pension supplements into the Seniors Benefit.

These institutional changes and fiscal strategies paid off handsomely. By late 1997 it seemed clear that the federal government was headed toward a budget surplus, and the February 1998 budget confirmed that Ottawa's fiscal fortunes had been completely reversed. Because of decisions to spend on several new programs, what might have been a surplus was converted into a balanced budget, the first since 1970. The key spending initiative was a set of measures entitled the Canadian Opportunities Strategy. It included a $2.5-billion endowment for the establishment of the Canadian Millennium Scholarship Fund, designed to provide annually 100,000 scholarships of about $3000 each to low- and middle-income students. Students were also to be given a tax credit toward the interest payments on their student loans. Other measures provided grants to students with children, education credits to part-time students, and allowed Canadians to withdraw money from their RRSPs for full-time education and training. Several other educational initiatives, combined with some measures aimed at increasing youth employment, raised the cumulative total for the strategy over four years to $4.6 billion, of which the scholarship fund accounts for over one-half.

On the social policy side, Martin reaffirmed the government's earlier commitment to raising the CHST floor of transfers to the provinces from $11 billion to $12.5 billion annually. Spending on the Canada Child Tax Benefit was increased by $850 million over the next two years, and the limit on the child-care expense deduction was raised. If the previously announced increase in the CHST floor is excluded, the cumulative total of these and some other measures amounted to $1.4 billion, of which about half was allocated to new Aboriginal programs (including the previously announced $350 million healing program for victims of abuse in residential schools).[23] Unlike the 1997 budget, this one offered some measure of general and targeted tax relief, primarily to lower-income Canadians, but in measure to the middle class as well. The cumulative amount of tax relief over three years was to be $7 billion.

Finally, Martin pledged to pay down the national debt. Since he did not think the $3 billion contingency reserve would be needed, he pledged to dedicate it in its entirety to debt reduction—$9 billion over three years. As well, the relative size of the debt as a proportion of GDP was expected to decline significantly even without any special measures, simply as a consequence of a growing economy. The debt-to-GDP ratio was projected to drop to 63 percent in 1999–2000, and Finance officials claimed that even with special measures it would decline to about 30 percent of GDP by 2015.[24] Again, as the global financial crisis deepened during 1998, Martin's rhetoric grew considerably more cautious.

A key point to be emphasized in this discussion is that fiscal measures of the state's size and scope should be understood as more than mere monetary figures. Social programs are not merely transfers of dollars; they represent a set of relationships between the state and citizens, a structure of rules that subtly and sometimes directly establishes interests and encourages certain political processes. The most obvious of these is the status of "beneficiary." Millions of Canadians receive transfers from the federal government under one or a combination of transfer programs, and thus to a greater or lesser degree, depending on their employment income, are dependent on the state for their well-being. One of the arguments in favour of universal income security programs that paid benefits to everyone regardless of income (e.g., Old Age Security) was that they encouraged the political solidarity of citizens as well as their willingness to support state programs. If everyone is a beneficiary, everyone in theory gains from government programs in some way. Programs that target specific groups, especially lower-income groups, are openly redistributive, and those who give without receiving in return will be less than willing to give. Whatever the merits of this argument (and it is moot, since universality is effectively dead in Canada), it is important to realize that programs are not merely "cash transfers." Like constitutional categories, social programs establish identities and interests. The very concept of a "senior citizen" is supported by a host of government programs, from pensions to housing allowances, social services, special tax treatment, and even reduced bus fares. Ironically, the private sector then mimics the public sector and designates "senior citizens" as a separate category of persons. If there is any doubt about age, of course, some form of government identification is produced (senior citizens have special federal government cards).

From this perspective the welfare state is more than a matter of money. It is an institutional patterning of relationships between citizens and the state and between different categories of citizens. We interact, in part, in terms of the identities that have been established for us through welfare state programs. While unemployment carries no dishonour, for many Canadians the idea of receiving EI benefits, outside of narrowly defined circumstances, is tinged with shame. For others, reliance on EI poses no difficulty at all, but they avoid welfare like the plague. There are good practical reasons for doing so, of course (social assistance is often deliberately unpleasant), but other norms apply as well. Programs, in short, define recipients in particular ways. If programs have to change, as the fiscal pressures described above suggest they will, then the definitions will necessarily change. The rights and obligations that currently apply in some programs will be altered, as will the relationships between the state and its citizens. Cutbacks are not merely cutbacks in expenditures—they are redefinitions of the institutional matrix of the welfare state itself. That is why the 1998 federal budget is so intriguing. It did include some cautious spending initiatives, but at the same time maintained that it would "stay the course" of previous fiscal policy. But will it? There is increasing concern in some circles about the Canadian "social union," that is, the bonds among Canadians that encourage national identity and solidarity.[25] The welfare state, especially federal transfers to persons, was from this perspective a key ingredient in forging certain relationships between Canadians and their government. The cuts of recent years may have frayed the fabric of the social union by undermining these relationships.

PUBLIC-SECTOR EMPLOYMENT

Government can be measured in fiscal terms, and, as the preceding section argues, its fiscal dimensions imply something about the way it connects to society. Another way of understanding the relationships between state and society is in terms of personnel and employment, or how many people work in the state or quasi-state sector. This is an even more direct institutional relationship, of course, since it defines people as employees and a good part of every day is lived in that role. Inevitably, this relationship carries over into other arenas of social life.

The ubiquity of government employees is only slightly less than the ubiquity of state taxes. Police officers, bus drivers, doctors, teachers, professors, social workers, street crews—it would seem scarcely possible to avoid interacting with a living representative of the state apparatus at some point in any given day. In addition, there is the host of government employees we rarely see but who help structure the private institutions that make up the social landscape: liquor-control inspectors, food inspectors, customs officials, municipal building-code inspectors, city planners, and so forth.

The preceding paragraph suggests that the state employment sector is large, but it also used the term "government employees." In fact, the size of the public sector is really a function of the definitions one uses. Richard Bird, Meyer Bucovestsky, and David Foot, for example, distinguish between civil-service employment, government employment, and public employment.[26] **Civil-service employment** includes those with full-time appointments to a government position made through a central personnel agency attached to the federal or provincial governments. It is the narrowest definition and applies to what the public usually thinks of as "government bureaucrats." The concept of **government employment,** on the other hand, includes the civil service along with certain non-civil service occupations as well as municipal employment. The final category, **public-sector employment,** is the broadest of the three and includes the first two along with those sectors that are clearly government-funded and -controlled but whose employees work for semiautonomous institutions. Teachers and school-board employees, as well as most hospital employees, are examples.

Even within this set of categories, however, it is sometimes not easy to pigeonhole people. The armed forces and employees of government enterprises are treated differently by different statistical sources. As well, the term "teacher" sometimes refers to a full-time equivalent that might actually consist of 10 supply teachers. Finally, it is possible that a significant chunk of the "self-employed" sector (consisting of lawyers, accountants, notaries, engineers, architects, and those who refer to themselves as consultants) actually depends on government contracts for its livelihood. This group would not normally be embraced by any of the definitions of state employment, and while this makes little difference at the statistical level, since the numbers are small, in the institutional sense it might be quite important, since it implies that a significant proportion of the professional class is intimately bound to the state.

In 1929 Ottawa had 42,790 civil servants on the payroll. The single largest departments at the time were the Post Office (10,871), National Revenue (5771), and Marine and Fisheries (4283). There were more convicts in Canadian penitentiaries than there were civil service employees in most federal government departments.[27] By contrast, Bird et al.'s analysis of state-sector employment, based on data from 1975 (in the midst of the period of greatest government employment growth), gives a snapshot of government employment at perhaps its peak. The federal government that year employed 273,000 civil servants, more than six times the 1929 number. And provincial civil servants—who had been significantly less numerous than their federal counterparts until after World War II—now almost equalled this number.

Moreover, federal and provincial civil servants together accounted for only 24 percent of total public-sector employment in 1975. Even the category of "government employment" (which includes civil-service employment as well as other federal and provincial full-time employees, the armed forces, and municipal employees) surprisingly accounted for only 46 percent of total public-sector employment in 1975. Over half of those who worked in the public sector in 1975 worked in education, hospitals, or government enterprises. Moreover, if hospital and postsecondary workers are classified as provincial employees and other education institutions are classified as municipal, then the federal government employed only about a quarter of the total public sector. Provincial governments accounted for 44 percent and municipalities an astonishing 31 percent. Bird et al. drew several surprising conclusions from their analysis.

> *In the first place, less than one-quarter of all public employees are, strictly speaking, "civil servants," with all that is commonly taken to imply for security of tenure, methods of selection and promotion, and so on. Secondly, while more than half of all civil servants in Canada work for the federal government, that government is in total by far the least important employer of the three levels of government. The provincial level is the most important by a considerable margin, and the provincial and local levels together account for three-quarters of all public employees in this country. Finally, the "typical" public employee—if such a concept has any meaning—is more likely to work for a hospital or educational institution than to be a direct employee of any of the three levels of government (excluding government enterprises).*[28]

These conclusions confirm what we learned from the evolution of expenditure patterns, namely, that the provincial sector has grown dramatically in relation to the federal sector.

The story of recent years, however, has not been growth in public-sector employment but cutbacks. At the federal level, close to 50,000 employees left the public service between 1995 and 1998. Between 1996 and 1997 alone, there was a net drop of 13,581 or 6.5 percent, to a total of 194,396.[29] The largest proportion of this drop came from reductions in staff at Transport Canada, as many were shifted from the department's Air Navigation System to the newly created agency Nav Canada. These aggregate figures mask some important details, however. First, some departments, like Correction Services and Statistics Canada, actually grew marginally while the overall number of public-service employees declined. Second, federal cuts since 1995 have not been of the traditional pattern of small nicks to all departments. In keeping with the vision of Program Review and its idea that each program should be reviewed on its merits and that consequently not all reductions and cuts would necessarily be proportionate, some departments (e.g., Transport Canada) faced deeper cuts in personnel and programs. These "MAD" (most affected departments) departments received some compensation. The other point that is obscured by the aggregate figures is that the federal public service is poised for a period of substantial renewal. According to the clerk of the Privy Council, "Over 30 percent of the current executive group will be in a position to retire by the year 2000, and this will rise to about 70 percent by 2005. A similar pattern exists in some of the professional and scientific categories."[30]

It seems unlikely that there will be net growth in public-sector employment. By Statistics Canada measures, total public-sector employment has been in steady decline since 1994 (though local administration has grown slightly).[31] This decline is due in part to the fiscal strategies undertaken by Canadian governments in the last 10 years—in order to balance budgets, they have had ultimately not simply to cut programs but to cut people as well. However, it is also due to new public-management philosophies (to be discussed below). Government is increasingly seen not as a direct service provider (which requires many staff) but a strategic partner that establishes frameworks and provides leverage.

SERVICES AND PROGRAMS

Money and personnel are important measures of the scope and size of the state, but they only indirectly capture what the state actually does. To grasp the full impact of the state on society, we must also assess the services and programs it offers. The most visible programs in expenditure and personnel terms are health, education, and income security, along with the protection of persons and property. The growth in each of these areas over the last 50 years has been remarkable and is virtually synonymous with the growth of the state itself. The first three areas in particular reveal a pattern of growing state dominance in what were formerly considered to be activities in the private or voluntary and charitable realm. In highlighting this point we are not trying to suggest any peculiarity to the Canadian pattern. A complete reliance on volunteers and charity, such as existed at the turn of the century, was long ago abandoned in all Western states, even the United States. What this pattern does reveal is the degree to which the modern state is integrated with social institutions. It is the centrepiece in an institutional matrix of relationships, and this very centrality mediates other apparently private actions. Going to university, for example, is a decision often made in terms of available student loans and government funding for universities. People who are planning their finances in anticipation of retirement begin their calculations by trying to guess the value of their public pensions. Indeed, the very notion of retiring at a particular age is a function of legislation and government policy.

In the health field, government expenditures amounted to only $41.73 per person in 1890.[32] The earliest Canadian hospitals were run by religious orders, and later were supplemented by public institutions for—as they were called then—the deaf and dumb, the blind, orphans, and the insane. In the mid-19th century, volunteer secular groups began to build and administer hospitals on a nonprofit basis. Community leaders and wealthy philanthropists sat on local boards of trustees, sometimes with appointees from local and (rarely) provincial governments, if the institution received grants from the public purse. But before 1930 there was only one provincially owned hospital in the entire country (Victoria General in Halifax).[33] The number of hospitals grew after the turn of the century, and public acceptance of them as places to receive care increased as well. Provincial and local governments provided grants so that the hospitals would care for the indigent. The western provinces experimented with arrangements to hire physicians for remote communities and in some cases to establish municipal hospitals. Calls for hospital insurance and even medical insurance were heard throughout the period, but not until 1944—as part of an initiative from the first socialist government in North America, the Co-operative Commonwealth Federation (CCF) in Saskatchewan—was there legislation for a provincial hospital insurance scheme. Ottawa had actually proposed in 1945, at the end of the war, to support a national health insurance plan in exchange for almost exclusive access to tax sources, but the provinces declined. In 1948 Ottawa announced the National Health Grant Program to support designated provincial health expenditures. The program included grants to conduct health surveys of services and facilities, improve general public health, deal with special needs such as mental health and venereal disease, and help the provinces build more hospitals. This was the foundation of the modern Canadian health-care system; over the next 10 years provincial governments expanded their public facilities and services and gradually introduced hospital insurance. In 1958 Ottawa offered to pay half the costs of hospital insurance and diagnostic services, and by 1960 every province had a plan. In 1968, after considerable opposition from Canadian doctors, Ottawa introduced a similar shared-cost program to support provincial medicare plans. Within three years all 10 provinces had plans that met federal guidelines and were eligible for federal support.

The modern Canadian health-care system has evolved dramatically from its voluntary and largely private nature at the turn of the century. Combined federal and provincial government financing is now virtually the sole source of support for health institutions. Physicians constitute a self-regulating profession but one that receives its powers from government legislation. Public health programs and health research are funded and in many cases conducted by government. Voluntary groups and agencies still play an important role in the system, but they are linked to and organized around services provided by the public sector. Many of these organizations receive government funding and support. Virtually anything that has to do with health is touched in one way or another by government, either through dollars or through regulations. Private actions are channelled through this fine institutional web of rules.

A roughly similar pattern of expansion and growth took place in the educational field. Before Confederation, education was dominated by the church and local authorities and school boards. It varied tremendously across the country and, like health, was made a provincial jurisdiction in 1867. In the mid-19th century, Ontario led the way by establishing a provincially controlled and regulated educational system: standardized textbooks, teacher certification, curricula, and subject requirements. Local boards of education still raised part of the revenues from local ratepayers and had some discretion in the management of educational facilities, but the story of the educational system, especially in the 1960s, is one of consolidation and centralization. Private schools still exist, of course, and in some provinces receive provincial subsidies, but whereas 100 years ago they were typical of the education system, now they are clearly peripheral—though the current interest in **privatization** has led to calls for the increased privatization of education as well. The educational system has also become more complex and costly, involving community colleges, technical and vocational training, publicly supported universities, kindergartens, and daycare. To say that everyone is touched by the state educational system is to state the obvious.

Income-security programs are perhaps less visible, but they are just as important in defining the relationship between the state and its citizens. We consider these programs so normal a part of the policy landscape that it is sometimes difficult to imagine a time when they did not exist. In fact, most of the major income-security programs in Canada are a product of the postwar period. Prior to that period, with a few exceptions, the role of government was small compared to that of private charities and voluntary agencies. The assumption was that income security was something people provided for themselves through employment and savings and family support. Those who could not care for themselves in this way received assistance from local government welfare (with provincial funding) or charitable agencies. Government's role was residual, and the dominant institutional assumption was that of welfare and charity, not income security. There were some exceptions. Workers' compensation, for example, was instituted by the provinces around the turn of the century. Mothers' allowances and veterans' benefits were products of World War I. Old-age pensions were cost-shared by the federal government after 1927 but were provided only to indigent Canadians over the age of 70. In 1941, however, as a result of a constitutional amendment, Ottawa established a national unemployment insurance plan. In 1945, in its White Paper on Employment and Income, the federal government acknowledged for the first time a state responsibility to encourage full employment and to assist those who could not find employment. The pension system was elaborated in the 1950s, with the establishment of Old Age Security, which was paid to all elderly Canadians regardless of income. In the mid-1960s this pension was supplemented with the Canada and Quebec pension plans, funded through employee and employer contributions. Various federal shared-cost assistance programs were consolidated in the 1960s in the form of the Canada Assistance Plan (CAP), whereby Ottawa paid half the costs of provincial social-assistance programs. Thus, in little over 30 years, the core of the income-security system was established: Old Age Security and the Canada and Quebec pension plans for retirees, family allowances, unemployment insurance, and the CAP.

As noted above, CAP has been consolidated with transfers for health and postsecondary education under the CHST, and this entailed a significant reduction in federal government funding for social programs. The reduction in government spending and state employment is linked to cutbacks in welfare state programs.

REGULATION

Health, education, income security, and protection of persons and property (through police services) are the key functions of the modern Canadian state and, from a citizen's point of view, among its most visible. But there are other equally important if more subtle ways in which the state affects our lives. It can use its regulatory powers to structure our social and political environment in ways that we may not realize. The state does so through government departments as well as through a panoply of **regulatory agencies**—statutory bodies "charged with responsibility to administer, to fix, to establish, to control, or to regulate an economic, cultural, environmental, or social activity by regularized and established means in the public interest and in accordance with general policy guidelines specified by the government."[34] What we watch on television and listen to on radio, for example, is a direct result of broadcast regulations established by the Canadian Radio-television and Telecommunications Commission (CRTC). The availability of certain telecommunications services is also subject to CRTC regulation. Marketing boards set the prices and quantities of chickens, eggs, turkeys, milk, and a host of other farm and agricultural products. Even something as mundane as your morning coffee and lunch-time peanut butter and jam sandwich are structured by the state through its regulatory powers. While product standards are not set directly by the federal government, national standards are voluntarily established by the Standards Council of Canada through powers granted to it by the Standards Council of Canada Act (1970).

The major federal and provincial regulatory agencies were established in bursts, usually around some major economic or technological stimulus. Agricultural marketing boards, for example, were established for the most part around the Depression to deal with plummeting prices. Oil and gas regulation grew apace with the industries, as the resources were first discovered and then distributed to markets. Television and telecommunications regulation of course developed with the new technologies.

Like other aspects of government activity, regulation has come under more scrutiny, control, and constraint in the last 10 years. The regulatory agencies (or in some cases, departments that retained regulatory control) pursued laudable public-policy objectives (e.g., orderly marketing, the prevention of monopoly dominance, the preservation of the family farm) but operated under three key assumptions. First, rules governing private behaviour, and emanating from the regulatory agency, were thought to be the best way of achieving the policy objectives. Second, there was relatively little examination of the social cost of regulations—that is, the broader impact beyond the specific target. Finally, it was assumed that regulations could be tailored as necessary to domestic circumstances, without much concern about conflicting international obligations. All three assumptions have been attacked, particularly in the last decade.

From the perspective of the more conservative political ideologies that began to dominate public affairs in the 1980s, it is not clear why rules made on high, through public intervention, are necessarily better than rules that emerge from private transactions. Not that regulation should be discarded altogether, but it is argued that the means should be different. For example, instead of stipulating that an entire industry meet a certain fixed standard of airborne emissions by a certain date, a regulatory agency might allow tradable pollution permits, so that companies with better performance might "sell" their quotas to those with worse. The end result would be the same, but the process would allow more flexibility.

DOSSIER 7.1 THE FUNCTIONS OF REGULATORY AGENCIES

Robert Adie and Paul Thomas list the following as being among the phenomena regulated by governments:

- entry into or exit from a particular economic activity (e.g., broadcasting licences and trucking licences);
- prices (e.g., rent controls, telephone rates, and airfares);
- the volume of output (e.g., the management of supply of agricultural products under marketing boards);
- the rate of return allowed to the providers of a service (e.g., telephone and hydro rates);
- the health and safety of activities and products (e.g., occupational health and safety and consumer-product safety);
- the environment (e.g., regulations restricting pollution and requirements for environmental impact assessments);
- information and fairness (e.g., regulations against misleading advertising and protection against fraud); and
- culture (e.g., Canadian content rules and language legislation).

Source: Robert F. Adie and Paul G. Thomas, *Canadian Public Administration: Problematical Perspectives*, 2nd ed. (Scarborough: Prentice-Hall Canada, 1987), 331.

Coupled with this scepticism about bureaucracy was a concern with the aggregate social cost of regulation. Why should regulations protect the Canadian publishing industry, say, or dairy producers? Such regulation allows these sectors to profit—or, to put it in policy terms, it encourages indigenous Canadian writing and protects the family farm and security of Canadian food supplies, but at what cost to others?

Increasingly, regulation is also constrained by international agreements. The North American Free Trade Agreement, for example, forces Canadian authorities to treat American and Mexican companies exactly as they would Canadian companies—thereby eliminating a host of discriminatory regulations that used to be the mainstay of Canadian industrial policy. Agricultural marketing boards feel pressure to open access to (cheaper) foreign supplies, and even the protections for cultural institutions are hedged and constrained. The World Trade Organization, a host of United Nations bodies, and eventually the Multilateral Agreement on Investment are examples of international bodies and agreements that (with Canadian participation and support) gradually limit the old practices of regulation.

A good illustration of the more careful approach to regulation is the **Regulatory Impact Analysis Statement (RIAS)** and the **Federal Regulatory Policy,** both of which date from the mid-1980s and the Mulroney regime's effort to bridle government. The current regulatory policy was revised and implemented in 1995. It describes its policy objective as follows:

> *Canadians view health, safety, the quality of the environment, and economic and social well-being as important concerns. The government's regulatory activity in these areas is part of its responsibility to serve the public interest.*
>
> *Ensuring that the public's money is spent wisely is also in the public interest. The government will weigh the benefits of alternatives to regulation, and of alternative regulations, against their cost, and focus resources where they can do the most good.*
>
> *To these ends, the federal government is committed to working in partnership with industry, labour, interest groups, professional organizations, other governments and interested individuals.*[35]

The Federal Regulatory Policy lays out broad principles and guidelines that must be followed by all departments. It demands that the problem or risk be clearly defined, that federal intervention be justified, that Canadians be consulted in the design and implementation of regulations, that benefits outweigh costs and that costs be minimized. Perhaps most importantly, it insists on broad consultations with stakeholders, transparency, and accountability:

> *Regulatory authorities must clearly set out the processes they use to allow interested parties to express their opinions and provide input. In particular, authorities must be able to identify and contact interested stakeholders, including, where appropriate, representatives from*

public interest, labour and consumer groups. If stakeholder groups indicate a preference for a particular consultation mechanism, they should be accommodated, time and resources permitting. Consultation efforts should be coordinated between authorities to reduce duplication and burden on stakeholders.[36]

The RIAS is a procedural guide that puts the principles of the regulatory policy into practice. The RIAS process demands that departments explain what the proposed regulation will be, what alternatives there are, what the benefits and costs of the regulation will be, who has been consulted, what compliance and enforcement mechanisms will be used, and who the contact person in the government is to explain the initiative. All RIAS proposals must go through the Special Committee of Cabinet. There is an extensive consultation process, and RIASs are published in *The Canada Gazette* (Parts I and II). The system is by no means flawless, and the key decision on what counts as a regulatory or policy decision lies with ministers. Subsequent scrutiny of proposed regulations is not always perfect. But the federal system for reviewing proposed departmental regulations in 1998 was completely different from the one used in 1978. One small indication of this is the annual publication of a federal regulatory plan. It lists all planned regulatory initiatives by all federal departments and regulatory agencies for the coming year. Each initiative is identified by a unique tracking number, and agencies must indicate costs and benefits as well as planned consultative activities. Regulatory initiatives also have to be categorized by anticipated costs: low-cost initiatives are under $100,000; intermediate cost initiatives are between $100,000 and $50 million; major initiatives are over $50 million.[37]

Technological changes, globalization, and the prominence of more ideologically conservative governments in the 1980s all contributed to the sense that the last decade has been one of massive **deregulation.** In specific sectors this is true. Aviation is perhaps one of the prime examples. Over the last decade, much more competition has been allowed domestically, as well as internationally (through so-called "open sky" agreements). Recently the federal government even shed itself of air navigation services. There have also been important moves to deregulate telecommunications, broadcasting, trade, drug testing, food inspection, and the environment. However, as the preceding paragraphs show, the story is much more complex. Some aspects of domestic regulation have been shifted upward to international agreements such as NAFTA and international agencies such as the World Trade Organization—the Federal Regulatory Policy makes explicit reference to them. In other cases, regulatory activities that once were undertaken by government departments have been shifted to private, non-commercial agencies—as the Nav Canada example illustrates. In other cases, the regulatory approach is changing. Environment Canada, for example, states that since 1992 it has been shifting to "pollution prevention" rather than "react and cure," and encouraging the adoption of new regulatory techniques such as economic instruments, non-regulatory tools, and voluntary agreements. As the department's 12 pages of planned regulatory initiatives for 1997 indicate, government is not out of the regulatory game—it is simply changing the rules and its strategies.

Not surprisingly, state retrenchment has affected the size, shape, and structure of the public bureaucracy. We have already noted the decline in the number of civil servants. But the reshaping of the bureaucracy extends far beyond simple "downsizing." Precisely what is to be cut or downsized, and how the remaining body is to function and be organized, is affected by new ideas about public institutions and the services they provide, ideas that are loosely gathered under the banner of the **New Public Management (NPM).**[38] NPM challenges two traditional ideas about government. The first concerns the purpose of government as a provider of **public goods**—services and support that would not or could not otherwise be provided through markets or civil society. A public good is a service or commodity that is provided to all citizens in equal measure (e.g., clean air). Once it has been provided, no one can be excluded from the enjoyment of a public good. This can be contrasted with a private good, which is purchased for the exclusive use of the purchaser (e.g., a house or a car). Because private goods can be sold for a price, private producers have an incentive to provide them. By contrast, private enterprise has no incentive to produce a public good such as a clean atmosphere, which consumers, who cannot be prevented from breathing, would have no reason to pay for. If public goods are to be produced, the theory goes, governments must play a central role in securing their production. A highway, for example, has traditionally been thought of as a public good. A well-developed highway system is an essential component of an advanced economy. However, on the assumption that they are not commercially viable—because there are so many alternative routes to any destination that it is impractical to charge for the use of a highway—governments typically provide highways. While the idea that public goods should be publicly provided or secured has not been abandoned, the contemporary evaluation of public goods suggests that their core is small and that governments have provided services in the past that could be delivered through private means. For example, schools, postal services, and even highways, which used to be generally accepted as public goods to be provided in large measure by governments, are now subject to significant pressure for privatization.

The second traditional idea challenged by NPM is that government has to be organized hierarchically, with a chain of command that stretches from top to bottom. Corresponding to Max Weber's ideal type of bureaucratic organization, a government department was to be organized in the shape of a pyramid, with few persons on top and increasing numbers of people in the lower levels. This hierarchical structure was supposed to facilitate a unity of command in which each bureaucrat has one person to whom he or she is directly answerable. Tasks within the organization are fragmented to facilitate an efficient division of labour. Recruitment or selection to the organization, and promotion within, are based on merit. Therefore, appointment and promotion are based on what you know and what you can do instead of whom you know and who you are.

Weber's hierarchical model describes the traditional organization of government departments under the British-model parliamentary system. This system is often described as a line system. Quite simply, each function of government is administered by a department, and each department limits its activities to those matters that fall within its specialized jurisdiction. Responsibility in each department (or "ministry") is ensured by the appointment of a political head or "minister," and coordination of policy and administration is provided by the coming together of ministers in the cabinet. In this model, civil servants are nonpartisan professionals who implement the policy goals set for them by their political masters. Moreover, to secure their independence and impartiality, civil servants, like judges, are granted secure tenure. (The system of **line departments** was never practised in its pure form—that is, with no administrative overlap between departments; it has been compromised especially by the emergence and dramatic increase in power of **central agencies.** See Dossier 7.2.)

The Weberian ideal has its attractions, but it comes at a cost. The Kafkaesque vision of this idea of the administrative state is well known: thousands of faceless bureaucrats shuffling paper up and down the chain of command, devoid of inspiration or sympathy, empty of emotion, bereft of intelligence or autonomy. For proponents of the NPM, the Weberian model overemphasizes rules at the expense of responsiveness and limits innovative practices. David Osborne and Ted Gaebler argue that preoccupation with rules and regulations and hierarchical chains of command generate a sluggish, centralized bureaucracy that cannot keep up with the rapid pace of change driven by new technology and an information-based society and economy.[39]

Proponents of NPM advocate quite different models of governance, including market-based reforms and the "dialectic" or participatory organizational form in which public organizations seek the input of lower-level employees and clients in the decision-making process as well as negotiate contracts for the provision of services rather than implement them directly using standard administrative tools. Similarly, NPM calls into question the permanence of government organizations and of employment tenure and roles. Alternative organizational models reflect a more flexible pattern of governance, which might include task forces and interdepartmental committees and clarification of the terms of tenure in the public service to include protection from dismissal for partisan reasons but no guarantee of lifetime employment. Finally, the tradition of an "acquiescent" public service is countered by the notion that politicians should take greater advantage of the creative and problem-solving skills of public employees and encourage entrepreneurship in the performance of duties rather than insist on control and accountability as their preeminent concerns.[40]

Taken as a whole, this set of ideas about the organization and procedures in public administration points to a significantly different state, "a leaner, more flexible and swiftly responding creature than it had become during the decades of easy growth that followed 1945."[41] Donald J. Savoie argues that the ideas and dynamics of the new public administration represent nothing less than a cultural shift in the way

DOSSIER 7.2 CENTRAL AGENCIES

Line departments tend to be large, service-delivery organizations with a limited jurisdiction. They are responsible for a functional area of government policy such as agriculture, health, or transportation. Central agencies, by contrast, tend to be small in number of personnel but powerful in jurisdiction. Their responsibilities cut across the functional areas of government and emphasize the coordination of policy rather than the delivery of services. Because of the different responsibilities of central agencies, their personnel are different from those in line departments. The staff of central agencies, sometimes called **superbureaucrats,** are less likely to be career public servants and more likely to move from one agency to another. They tend to be more highly educated than their counterparts in the line departments and often have considerable career experience outside the bureaucracy in either business or academia. The Privy Council and the Treasury Board are central agencies. Although the department of Finance looks like a line department in many respects, it is often considered a central agency because of its function in coordinating the activities of other departments. Similarly, the Justice department has assumed the function of "Charterproofing" legislation emanating from many other departments and has thus taken on some of the features of a central agency.

we think about government, a shift away from "bureaucratic government" and toward "entrepreneurial government" that is "competitive and customer driven."[42] In this model of governance, the central role of the state is not necessarily to provide goods and services but to set frameworks wherein public goals can be achieved by separating policymaking from policy-delivery functions. Osborne and Gaebler describe the new ideal of **entrepreneurial government** as follows:

> *Most entrepreneurial governments [promote]* competition *between service providers. They* empower *citizens by pushing control out of the bureaucracy, into the community. They measure the performance of their agencies, focusing not on inputs but on* outcomes. *They are driven by their goals — their* missions *— not by their rules and regulations. They redefine their clients as* customers *and offer them choices — between schools, between training programs, between housing options. They* prevent *problems before they emerge, rather than simply offering services afterward. They put their energies into* earning *money, not simply spending it. They* decentralize *authority, embracing participatory management. They prefer* market *mechanisms to bureaucratic mechanisms. And they focus not simply on providing services, but on* catalyzing *all sectors — public, private, and voluntary — into action to solve their community's problems.*[43]

Given the profound nature of the changes, it is not surprising to hear cautionary notes and voices of outright opposition. Christopher Pollitt warns against the religious fervour that accompanies "claims from the political pulpit about the 'reinvention of government.' Says Pollitt:

> *It would be sensible to ask, for example, how widely the new techniques are being put in place. It would also seem wise to enquire whether, once in operation, the techniques are producing the desired results — or whether they seem to carry 'side effects' as well. Do rank and file public officials support the reforms? Do citizens notice any difference? In short, are there any implementation gaps between the promise and the performance, and, if so, what is their nature?*"[44]

Other critics focus on the appropriateness of importing private management techniques to the realm of the public service. Here we find contested views of the language, the procedures, and the larger vision that new ideas about public management bring to public administration. Is it right to discuss citizens as clients, as customers, as consumers of public services? Should the administration of government reflect a vision of society as shared public interest or as a collection of private interests? Can we reconcile the ideas and techniques of the new public administration with the importance of public debate and accountability that are the bedrock of democratic government?

The critics notwithstanding, it would be difficult to find a government today that has not been affected by the NPM movement. There is evidence everywhere of the structures and practices that serve as its hallmarks: decentralized budgeting practices, the implementation of performance indicators and performance-related pay, the establishment of standards for quality control, the contractualization of relationships that were traditionally hierarchical with the involvement of private nonprofit and for-profit actors, and, finally, systematic evaluation to determine the most successful policies and procedures with an emphasis on "value for money."[45]

Regardless of partisan stripe, governments in the Anglo-American democracies have introduced reforms (and acronyms to go with them), including the National Performance Review Exercise (NPR) in the United States and the Citizen's Charter in Britain. The most oft-cited example is New Zealand, the country that has "gone farthest along the entrepreneurial path."[46] Changes since the mid-1980s, under the Labor government and then the National government elected in 1990, included the restructuring of commercial projects of government—in sectors ranging from natural resources to banking to communications as state-owned for-profit enterprises and the privatization of other government agencies; the new functional organization of the government service according to roles of policy management, regulation, and social welfare; significant changes to social policy, including the implementation of user fees, increased contracting with private and public service providers, and reduced regulation in the public and private sectors to increase competition. Public-sector managers were also given the power to negotiate contracts with employees.[47]

Of course we need not look so far afield for examples of administrative reform in action. While Canada remains steeped in the practices of traditional public

DOSSIER 7.3 THE DEBATE OVER NPM

"I argue that the new public management is basically flawed. By its very nature the public administration field does not lend itself to Big Answers because private sector management practices very rarely apply to government operations. As James Q. Wilson explains, public administration 'is a world of settled institutions designed to allow imperfect people to use flawed procedures to cope with insoluble problems... Because constraints are usually easier to quantify than efficiency we can often get a fat government even when we say we want a lean one.' To be sure, the manner in which programs are conceived and delivered can be improved. This however, usually happens incrementally and on a program-by-program basis....

The new public management has yet to deal head-on with accountability in government. The principle of ministerial responsibility makes the minister 'blamable' for both policy and administration but he in turn can reach into the bureaucracy, organized as it is along clear hierarchical lines, and secure an explanation as to why things have gone wrong as well as how things can be made right.... [I]t is the centrally prescribed rules and regulations that so inhibit effective management, force governments not only to steer but also to row, and to concentrate on inputs that underpin the principle of ministerial responsibility.

Lest we need to be reminded, there is also a world of difference between citizens and clients. Clients are sovereign. They can hold business accountable through their behaviour in a competitive market.... Citizens, on the other hand, have common purposes. They hold politicians accountable through the requirements of political institutions and through exposure via the media. The solution lies in fixing our political institutions and the laws of Parliament rather than in 'periodic preaching from the pulpit' that resorts merely to emotive words about the failings of bureaucrats and public servants....If nothing else, we need a fundamental review of the merits of advising on policy from a sectoral or departmental perspective. The current machinery of government tends to compartmentalize such advice.... If key issues are more and more lateral or horizontal in their implications, then the bureaucratic policy formulation and advisory structures must become horizontal as well. Public servants will have to bring a far broader and more informed perspective to bear on their work since issues are now much more complex and interrelated....

The point to bear in mind is that the solutions that work are practical, rooted in the political and legal realities of government. They should not be expected to represent anything more than gradual and incremental improvements in public administration."

Source: Donald J. Savoie, "What Is Wrong with the New Public Management," *Canadian Public Administration* 38 (Spring 1995), 112–121.

"The new public management is not a simplistic Big Answer. Rather it is a normative reconceptualization of public administration consisting of several inter-related components: providing high quality services that citizens value; increasing the autonomy of public managers particularly from central agency controls; measuring and rewarding organizations and individuals on the basis of whether they meet demanding performance targets; making available the human and technological resources that managers need [in order] to perform well; and, appreciative of the values of competition, maintaining an open-minded attitude about which public purposes should be performed by the private sector, rather than the public sector. The new public management *has* thought about the question of accountability and argues that the two enemies of accountability are unclear objectives and anonymity. By emphasizing clear objectives and written performance contracts, the new public management should increase rather than diminish the accountability of public servants to ministers and of ministers to Parliament. [P]eople—whether one calls them citizens or consumers—are demanding quality and service from both public and private sector producers, and comparing the performance of all organizations."

Source: Sandford Borins, "The New Public Management Is Here to Stay," in *Canadian Public Administration* 38 (Spring 1995), 122–132.

The Canadian Centre for Management Development also weighs in on the debate, affording some guidance that we might use to come to grips with its proponents:

"One of the most important issues in public management today is the dynamic tension between empowerment and accountability, between devolution and horizontal coordination, between delegation and strategic leadership. The application of contemporary management ideas in government points in the direction of a government structure that is more variegated and fragmented than in the past, one in which decision-making authority is pushed away from the centre and out toward the front lines of service delivery. However, this impulse finds itself in tension (though not necessarily in contradiction) with traditional notions of political accountability and of administrative uniformity and equity, as well as with such contemporary needs as fiscal control and horizontal policy coordination.... What the literature suggests is that the management of tensions or dualities is the essence of organizational life, and that wisdom lies not in attempting to resolve such tensions once and for all, forcing the organization to choose between them, but in balancing the dualities in creative and appropriate ways. It is perhaps in seeking to balance the twin impulses ... in ways that meet genuine contemporary needs yet are faithful to the enduring requirements of parliamentary democracy that we will achieve genuine progress in public administration in our time."

Source: "A Word from CCMD," in B. Guy Peters and Donald J. Savoie, *Managing Incoherence: The Coordination and Empowerment Conundrum* (Ottawa: Minister of Supply and Services, 1995).

DOSSIER 7.4 A POLICY EXAMPLE: EDUCATION POLICY IN NEW ZEALAND, 1994

"The aim [of increasing the responsiveness of the education system and the satisfaction of all significant stakeholders] was to be achieved by altering the incentive structure within the administration of education through two major structural changes. The first was to abolish all layers of administration between the central state agencies and the local school in order to locate decision making as close as possible to the point of implementation and thereby achieve greater administrative efficiency and responsiveness.

The second was to alter the balance of power between the providers and clients of education by providing communities with the means for a greater say in the running of their schools and for expressing expectations about their children's education."

Source: Education Review Office, *Effective Governance: School Boards of Trustees,* quoted in Jonathan Boston, John Martin, June Pallot, Pat Walsh, *Public Management: The New Zealand Model* (Auckland: Oxford University Press, 1996), 172.

administration, the integration of new public management principles and the redesign of governments have become important features in the contemporary Canadian political landscape. Indeed, the story of federal governance in Canada in recent years has been colourfully described as "orgies of reform hardly punctuated by even the briefest period of routine" in the Canadian civil service.[48] One of the earliest reforms was the emergence of the central agencies described in Dossier 7.2. This was designed to bring greater rationality and coordination to government policymaking. Central agencies, however, exist in some tension with the principles of NPM (see Dossier 7.5).

More recently, and more directly as a consequence of NPM, the idea that governments have done too much, at too high a cost, has been institutionally reflected in the phenomena of privatization and deregulation.

Privatization has affected a host of **public enterprises.** Welfare-state governments have worked not only through line departments, in other words, but also through state-owned (or partially owned) businesses. In Canada, public enterprises include Crown corporations and mixed enterprises. **Crown corporations** are "companies in the ordinary sense of the term, whose mandate relates to industrial, commercial or financial activities but which also belong to the state, are owned by the government or the Crown, or whose sole shareholder is the government or the Crown."[49] **Mixed enterprises** are those companies "in which the federal government has taken a direct equity position in common with other participants for the purposes of implementing a public policy or satisfying a public need."[50] They are no different from other companies, except that government is one of the major shareholders. Mixed enterprises include such things as bridge or tunnel authorities, domestic and international development activities, and commercial ventures such as Petro-Canada and Telesat Canada. (Governments can also participate in commercial enterprise through **chosen instruments**—see Dossier 7.6.) Dossier 7.7 lists the public enterprises

DOSSIER 7.5 CENTRAL AGENCIES VS. NPM

Central agencies are at the heart of the tension between the old and new principles of public administration. B. Guy Peters and Donald J. Savoie describe the "coordination and empowerment conundrum" as the tension between, on one hand, the push to decentralize and empower front-line employees and to restructure the delivery of services, often in partnership with agencies outside government, and, on the other hand, fiscal pressures and the demands of the global economy, which impose a need for better coordination of policies and programs by governments.

Peters and Savoie argue that one of the questions yet to be resolved is the future role of central agencies and the reconciliation of decentralization of decision making and accountability. They write: "Finally, central agencies should be losing power in a world that emphasizes empowerment and decentralization. Central control is privileged in traditional administrative structures that depend on hierarchical and legal and political control. In a world of government that is more concerned with the empowerment of lower echelons of the public service and of their clients, central agencies appear to be anachronisms."

However, in their study of the impact of the National Performance Review on the behaviour of central agencies in the American federal government, Peters and Savoie conclude that "despite the changes over the past year, the fundamental nature of central agencies has not been transformed: they are still very much in the business of imposing central policy and management controls." The lessons they learned in their study have implications for Canada:

> *The important lesson ... is that the tension and contradictions between the need for greater coordination and central direction and managerialism left unresolved in the United States are also unresolved in Canada. This has important implications for how policies will be made, for how the expenditure budget will be struck, and for the ability of the political leadership to point to a government-wide strategy and stick to it.... It is also clear that the push to decentralize decision making and to free managers from too much central control holds implications for accountability. The danger is perhaps stronger for Canada than it is for the United States. In a parliamentary system, as compared to a presidential system, there are precious few accountability mechanisms.... The push towards empowerment and removing constraints to management may well force us to revisit the application of the principle of ministerial responsibility.*

Source: B. Guy Peters and Donald J. Savoie, *Managing Incoherence: The Coordination and Empowerment Conundrum* (Ottawa: Canadian Centre for Management Development), 1995.

privatized between 1985 and 1997. This impressive list gives some sense both of the traditional importance of public enterprise in Canada and the strength of the recent challenge to it.

Dossier 7.7 also contains a lengthy list of advisory boards or committees that have been eliminated. Such **advisory councils** are created by the government to provide an independent and ongoing source of policymaking advice. They are staffed by private citizens, but there is a strong tendency to appoint members of interest groups concerned with the relevant policy area. Thus, to a considerable extent advisory councils provide a means for governments to fund the lobbying efforts of interest groups, efforts that are often directed at obtaining greater funding. This scenario is made more controversial by the fact that not all interest groups are equally likely to gain representation on advisory councils. Under the influence of conservative ideology and NPM, many of these advisory bodies have become dispensable.

So have some of the less prominent regulatory agencies, such as the Anti-Inflation Board and Appeal Tribunal, which do play some role as regulatory and adjudicative agencies. It is important to repeat, however, that while the contemporary deregulatory thrust is certainly evident in Dossier 7.7, there continues to be a lot of regulatory activity. Prominent institutions such as the Canadian Wheat Board, the CRTC, and the Canadian Human Rights Commission come readily to mind, though these too are under varying degrees of attack. And, as noted above, as old forms of regulation are abandoned, new ones often come into being.

In addition to privatization, cutbacks, and deregulation, reform initiatives have included various attempts to make government decision making more efficient, empower managers and public servants in the delivery of services, and cut through red tape.[51] These initiatives go by such names as Increased Ministerial Authority and

DOSSIER 7.6 CHOSEN INSTRUMENTS

As an alternative to taking a direct equity position in a private or quasi-private organization, the government may also pursue its objectives by providing either one-time or ongoing financial support to a wholly private company. Spar Aerospace Ltd., of Ste-Anne-de-Bellevue, Quebec, provides an example of how the Canadian government can pursue a number of its objectives—both political and economic—through such a chosen instrument. During one of Kim Campbell's first visits to the province of Quebec as prime minister, her newly appointed Science minister, Rob Nicholson, announced the awarding of a $92-million contract to Spar Aerospace for the completion of a new Canadian satellite system called RADARSAT. This system contributed to the research and development sector of the Canadian economy in the area of high-technology development and would, in the words of the minister, "keep Canada on the leading edge of earth-observation satellite capacity." Ottawa's support of Spar Aerospace was also a financial boon to the electorally important province of Quebec in the months leading up to a federal election. Such government investment in private industry has come under increasing attack from the ideological right and from the perspective of the New Public Management.

DOSSIER 7.7 CHANGES TO FEDERAL DEPARTMENTS AND AGENCIES, 1985–1998

FEDERAL GOVERNMENT PRIVATIZATIONS, 1985–1997

Air Canada
Air Navigation Systems
Canada Communication Group
Canada Development Corporation
Canadair Limited
Canadian Arsenals Limited
Canadian Commercial Corporation
Canadian Sports Pool Corporation
Canadian Mining and Energy Company
Canarctic Shipping Company Ltd.
Canadian National Railways
CNCP Telecommunications and Telecommunications Terminal Systems
CN Hotels
CN Route
Canagrex
CN Exploration
CN (West Indies) Steamship Ltd.
Co-enerco Resources Ltd.
Eldorado Nuclear Ltd.
Enterprise Cape Breton Corporation
Fishery Products International Ltd.
de Havilland Aircraft of Canada
Loto Canada Inc.
Nanisivik Mines Ltd.
National Sea Products Ltd.
Nordion International Inc.
Northern Canada Power Commission
Northern Transportation Company Ltd.
Nortwestel Inc.
Oromocto Development Corp.
Pêcheries Canada Inc.
Petro-Canada
Saskatchewan Mining Development Corp.
Teleglobe Canada
Telesat Canada
Terra Nova Telecommunications Inc.
Uranium Canada Ltd.
Varity Corporation

THINK TANKS ABOLISHED

Economic Council of Canada
Law Reform Commission
Science Council of Canada
Medical Council of Canada

ELIMINATED BOARDS / COMMITTEES / TRIBUNALS

Advisory Committee on La Francophonie
Advisory Committee on Lay Members of the Competition Tribunal
Advisory Committee on Le Musée de la Nouvelle France
Advisory Committee for Le Musée des Arts du Spectacle Vivant (de la Science)
Agriculture Products Board
Alachlor Review Board
Anti-Dumping Tribunal
Anti-Inflation Board and Appeal Tribunal
Atlantic Development Council
Atlantic Enterprise Board
Atlantic Regional Council
Atlantic Regional Freight Assistance Program
Canada–Norway Sealing Commission
Canadian Aviation Safety Board
Canada Employment and Immigration Advisory Council
Canadian Environmental Advisory Council
Canadian Environmental Assessment Research Council
Canadian Industrial Renewal Board
Canadian Institute for International Peace and Security

Canada Oil and Gas Lands Administration
Canadian Saltfish Corporation Advisory Board
Canadian Transport Commission
Canadian Transport Commission Committee
Canadian Veterinary Drug Advisory Committee
Communications Research Centre Advisory Committees
Copyright Board and Appeal Board
Defence Industrial Preparedness Advisory Committee
Defence Minister's Advisory Board on Canadian Military Colleges
Demographic Review Secretariat
Eastern Rockies Forest Conservation Board
Enterprise Development Board and Regional Enterprise Development Boards
Emergency Planning Canada
Fisheries and Oceans Research Advisory Board
Health Minister's Business Advisory Council on Canada's Drug Strategy
Immigration Act Special Advisory Board
Interim Postal Services Review Committee
International Aviation Advisory Task Force and Committee
International Centre for Ocean Development
International Commission for the Northwest Atlantic Fisheries
International Cultural Programs
International North Pacific Fisheries Commission
International Pacific Salmon Fisheries Commission
Machinery and Equipment Advisory Board
Marine Advisory Board on R&D
Montreal Science and Technology Museum Advisory Committee
National Advisory Committee on Development Education
Natal Advisory Council on Physical Fitness and Amateur Sport
National Defence Consultative Committee on Social Change
National Design Council
National Marine Council
National Museums of Canada
Natal Transportation Agency
Office of the Administrator Anti-Inflation Act
Office of the Administrator of the Maritime Pollution Claims Fund
Office of the Inspector General of Banks
Oil and Gas Commission
Patent Appeal Board
Pay Research Bureau
Pension Review Board
Petro-Canada International Assistance Corporation
Petroleum Monitoring Agency
Prairie Farm Assistance Act Board of Review
Preparatory Commission for Conversion to the Metric System
Procurement Review Board
Queen Elizabeth II Canadian Research Fund Board
Refugee Status Advisory Committee
Restrictive Trade Practices
Statute Revision Commission
Tariff Board
Textile and Clothing Board
Trade Marks Opposition Board
Veterans Land Administration
War Veterans Allowance Board

Source: "Federal Government's Shrinking Image," *The Ottawa Citizen,* February 21, 1998, A4.

Accountability, Shared Management Agenda, Total Quality Management, and **Public Service 2000 (PS 2000).**

Introduced in 1989 to make the public bureaucracy more responsive to the complex political and economic environment of the 1990s, the PS 2000 initiative proposed three key objectives: to improve service to Canadians by decentralizing decision-making authority to deputy ministers, line managers, and people on the front lines in the federal civil service in every region of Canada; to create a better system for the management of personnel so that authority attached clearly to individuals and, in turn, personal accountability was increased; and, finally, to make the public service more flexible and responsive, in particular by tapping the resources and experience of employees.[52] By 1992, however, the PS 2000 initiative faltered under the weight of budget reductions, wage restraint, and restructuring, which "corroded the perceived legitimacy of PS 2000 within the public service."[53]

Administrative reform was not abandoned, however. On June 25, 1993, the same criteria of efficiency and effectiveness that had led to PS 2000 generated a somewhat different reorganization under the short-lived leadership of Prime Minister Kim Campbell. This time the emphasis was placed on reducing the number of government departments. Ten seats around the cabinet table were eliminated and departments were restructured with the goal of improving the federal government's responsiveness to new policy demands and shifting resources from the top to the front lines of service provision. Stringent budgetary requirements included forced savings of $600 million from administrative costs.

Not surprisingly, in 1993 the newly elected Liberal government, under Prime Minister Jean Chrétien, stamped its own mark on the reform process. Chrétien accepted Campbell's reduction and reorganization of government departments and gave further impetus to administrative reform by creating a new cabinet position responsible for public-service renewal. The new minister, Marcel Masse, "lost no time in declaring his intention to "get government right," and launched a major **Program Review** to do so. His agenda for action borrows heavily from the new public management movement and its literature.[54] The government claimed to be responding not only to dissatisfaction with "big government" but also to citizens' loss of faith in government and their doubts that their interests, "as citizens, clients and taxpayers, were sufficiently and effectively reflected in the actions of their governments." The Program Review was to examine federal programs and activities, clarify roles and responsibilities, and ensure that resources were directed to the highest priorities. The review examined all federal programs and activities, with the exception of money transfers to persons and other levels of government, to "identify the federal government's core roles and to re-focus resources on priority areas while reducing overall spending."[55]

Other major initiatives by the Liberal government reflect a concern for quality control in public-sector management and in program delivery.[56] Following the development of a Declaration of Quality Service, the Treasury Board issued a Framework for Alternative Program Delivery in 1995 that set out strategies, including many of the

DOSSIER 7.8 ROYAL COMMISSIONS AND TASK FORCES

Royal commissions and task forces are similar and can be contrasted with advisory councils. Commissions and task forces are temporary organizations created by the cabinet to investigate either specific events or general matters of policy. They are usually dissolved after submitting a report to government. Royal commissions differ from task forces in that they represent a more formal organization—their members are appointed and their mandate is assigned by an order-in-council. They tend to be used for major or highly salient issues, operate in public, and produce a public report. Task forces, by contrast, are less formal, often examine narrower issues, and submit a private report.

Royal commissions and task forces have been popular instruments of Canadian governments; from Confederation to 1979, royal commissions were used more than 400 times. Recently, there have been a number of high-profile and important royal commissions. Perhaps the most significant was the Royal Commission on the Economic Union and Development Prospects for Canada, headed by former Liberal Finance minister Donald Macdonald. Appointed by Prime Minister Trudeau in 1981, the Macdonald Commission filed its report in 1985, together with 72 volumes of research studies. Among the major recommendations was that Canada negotiate a free-trade agreement with the United States. This recommendation led Prime Minister Mulroney to abandon his opposition to free trade, an opposition he had stated clearly during his successful bid for the Conservative Party leadership in 1983. The Free Trade Agreement was negotiated and implemented on January 1, 1989. Mulroney also appointed a number of important royal commissions, including ones on new reproductive technologies, electoral reform and party financing, and Aboriginal peoples.

From the government's perspective, there are a number of advantages to using commissions or task forces. Perhaps most important, they allow the government to isolate a specific concern or policy area and to focus considerable energy and wide-ranging expertise on exploring policy alternatives. Commissions and task forces are often used to bring together experts from the public bureaucracy, the private sector, and academia to provide in-depth, but also varied, analyses in developing policy options. Furthermore, commissions and task forces enable the government to focus expertise for a finite period of time without creating a permanent bureaucratic infrastructure. From a practical, political perspective, they also provide the government with a convenient place to consider, and possibly defuse, an embarrassing political issue. The major criticism of this organizational form is that it has no power of implementation. Since recommendations may be ignored at the discretion of the government, considerable money and time may be spent with little or nothing to show in the way of new policy initiatives. On the other hand, the research and recommendations of royal commissions may lead to the establishment of a more permanent organization for interest representation. For example, in 1970 the Royal Commission on the Status of Women led to the creation of the National Advisory Council on the Status of Women.

familiar tenets of managerialism, for service delivery. **Alternative Service Delivery (ASD)** is a strategy for innovation and change in management. It is not an objective but the means to an end—good management. It is rethinking and redesigning program and service delivery from a citizen-centred perspective to better respond to the needs of Canadians, and to meet other key government objectives: more responsive and results-oriented governance; improved cost-effectiveness; collaboration and citizen engagement; a federation that works."[57] Institutional support comes from the Treasury Board Secretariat, the administrative arm of the Treasury Board. In particular, the ASD sector of the Treasury Board Secretariat supports the Getting Government Right initiatives with policy development and coordination, assistance to departments, and research and communications. The Treasury Board Secretariat outlines how Alternative Service Delivery principles are integrated into departmental practices:

> *Ministers lead organizational restructuring within their portfolios. Departments are encouraged to redesign program and service delivery where there are better means for serving Canadians and meeting the government's obligations and fiscal objectives. The current approach encourages the design of tailor-made solutions depending on the needs, circumstances and opportunities on a case-by-case basis, using the Framework for Alternative Program Delivery ... as a guide for the choice of options.*[58]

DOSSIER 7.9 THE CHANGING SHAPE OF THE PUBLIC SERVICE

The Program Review asked departments to review and assess their activities and programs against the following guidelines:

Public Interest Test: Does the program area or activity continue to serve a public interest?

Role of Government Test: Is there a legitimate and necessary role for government in this program area or activity?

Federalism Test: Is the current role of the federal government appropriate, or is the program a candidate for realignment with the provinces?

Partnership Test: What activities or programs should or could be transferred in whole or in part to the private/voluntary sector?

Efficiency Test: If the program or activity continues, how could its efficiency be improved?

Affordability Test: Is the resultant package of programs and activities affordable within the fiscal constraint? If not, what programs or activities would be abandoned?

Source: *Getting Government Right: A Progress Report.* Appendix I. March 7, 1996. Canada. Minister of Supply and Services, 30.

[Program Review] affirms that the Government of Canada can best serve Canadians by concentrating its activities around five core roles:

1. Ensuring that Canada speaks with one voice in the community of nations on issues of concern to all Canadians. This role addresses the need to defend Canada's sovereignty in a global environment, and includes areas such as foreign policy, international trade, peacekeeping, immigration and defence.
2. Protecting and strengthening the efficiency of the Canadian economic union. The Canadian economic union is the base from which Canadian firms and industries learn to compete in the global economy. It is also the economic space where Canadians exchange goods and services, and where wealth and jobs are created. The role of the government includes setting framework laws that ensure the effective operation of the marketplace, such as bankruptcy, competition, and intellectual property laws, as well as sectors of regulatory activity, such as environmental or consumer protection.
3. Protecting and strengthening the Canadian social union and the solidarity of Canada. The social union contributes to the quality of life, security and safety of all citizens. It is the sharing community. It also contributes to attracting and retaining domestic and international investment, and it plays a key role in the creation of jobs. To those in need, it provides a system of mutual help, such as assistance to youth, to the elderly and to the unemployed, through transfer and equalization programs. It is therefore a contributor to a strengthened federation.
4. Managing the pooling of resources for the pursuit of collective goals where a single program or centre of expertise would be more efficient and where there is a limited need for diversity. This role recognizes the contribution of the Geological Survey of Canada, the Canadian Hydrographic Service, the Atmospheric Environment Service, and Statistics Canada, among others. It recognizes that there are occasions when citizens are best served by pooling resources.
5. Acting as the guardian of citizens' rights in a democratic society of parliamentary tradition, governed by the rules of law that protect and promote Canadian values and identity while celebrating our diversity. This role addresses a wide range of issues, from the government's fiduciary responsibility to Native people to official languages to law enforcement. Security of life and property is one of the hallmarks of Canada, and it contributes to the quality of life and the standard of living of Canadians.

Implementation is always the most difficult part of any reform. It requires courage, persistence and resolve. It is also the test that reveals the true quality of reform.

As decisions are implemented to their full conclusion, Canadians will discover the real extent of the reform that is under way. The most visible sign to date has been "less government." This results from the many difficult decisions that governments have made to reduce services in some areas and eliminate them in others, in order to realign the role of government to address contemporary needs within society's collective means.

A more careful look, however, reveals that while governments are making decisions to reduce the level of indebtedness and bring Canada closer to the goal of balanced budgets, they are at the same time contributing to a profound change in Canadian society. This change includes

Forging a new relationship among governments

Laying the basis for new partnerships with other sectors of society

Strengthening the relationship between government and citizen

Source: Clerk of the Privy Council, *Fourth Report to the Prime Minister on the Public Service of Canada* (Ottawa, 1997) [on-line, World Wide Web; cited March 13, 1998]; available at http:canada.gc.ca/depts/agencies/pco/4report96/chap2 e.htm.

A second major initiative, the Quality Services Initiative, outlines the service standards that Canadians can expect from the federal government. Criteria range from prompt, dependable, and accurate services to guarantees of compliance with the Official Languages Act, to willingness to listen to client suggestions, concerns, and expectations and to improve services accordingly.[59] The Liberal government's drive to change the managerial environment was also directed toward increasing accountability of the public service in Parliament. The Improved Reporting to Parliament Project (IRPP) was implemented to improve the expenditure-management documents supplied to Parliament and to produce and distribute departmental planning and performance information to Parliament and the Canadian public more efficiently and economically, using new developments in information technology.[60]

REFORM IN THE PROVINCES: TALES FROM ALBERTA AND ONTARIO

Like governments everywhere, the provincial governments in Canada have embarked on the exercise of administrative reform. Here we touch on two of the "heavyweights," Alberta and Ontario, and their politics and processes of "reinventing government." Both governments have embraced similar goals of public-sector reform: reduce the role of state and expand the scope for private sector activity while creating a more "business-like" government, although there are both similarities and differences in their choice of policy instruments. Both governments implemented spending cuts, reorganized the machinery of government, and combined centralization of policy-making power with decentralization of service delivery. Ontario premier Mike Harris cut spending and income taxes; his Alberta counterpart, Ralph Klein, promised to balance the budget in four years, using spending cuts, and did so in three years.

DOSSIER 7.10 GETTING GOVERNMENT RIGHT

It is hard to argue with the concept of "getting government right," but what evidence does the Liberal government use to convince citizens that it is, indeed, succeeding? Its *Getting Government Right Progress Report* (1996) highlights a number of initiatives and outcomes:

Program Spending: The yardsticks used to measure progress are decreases in program spending in absolute terms and as a proportion of GDP. As well, the government discusses new and shifting priorities: setting framework policies rather than directly supporting business, maintaining elements of the social union, reflecting the important role the federal government plays in securing public safety and promoting Canadian values and identity in the fields of culture and heritage.

Clarifying Federal Roles and Responsibilities: "Costly overlap and duplication are being reduced in many areas and the federal government is focussing its resources on areas best addressed at the national level." Stimulated by Program Review, "the federal role in building a stronger Canadian economy is being transformed" through deficit reduction, the use of framework policies to create more favourable conditions for job creation and sustained economic growth, and specific changes in the major sectors of the economy, including transportation, agrifood, and other resource sectors. On the social union front, the federal government's key objective is "to maintain universal access to a comprehensive package of publicly funded health services and to basic social services of comparable quality for all Canadians, regardless of where they live in Canada." In other policy fields, "the federal government launched a comprehensive and progressive reform agenda to redefine its relationship with First Nations....Given the importance of trade to all sectors of the Canadian economy, international trade promotion is increasingly being done in partnership with the provinces and private sector....Following on an extensive review of defense policy, infrastructure and expenditures are being significantly reduced and adjusted to reflect Canada's priorities in the post-cold war environment....In affirming and strengthening its core roles, the federal government has chosen to focus its resources on those functions and activities that it is best placed to deliver. In some cases, the federal government is working in partnership with others in the federation to make its involvement more effective. The Efficiency of the Federation initiative offers important examples of this partnership process."

Making the Federal Government Work Better: The federal government's embrace of the principles and practices that inform the new public management are evident in its commitment to "make efforts to improve the quality of all its programs and services to make them more effective, efficient, affordable, accessible and fair. Central to this commitment are:

- better use of information technology to get government closer to Canadians;

- more responsive and flexible approaches to program delivery;
- changes in the way government makes decisions; and
- putting government operations, where appropriate, on a results-based footing, with a client-centred focus on quality service."

Source: *Getting Government Right: A Progress Report* (Ottawa: Minister of Supply and Services, 1996), 7–25.

Klein was elected premier of Alberta in May 1993, and his government took an aggressive approach to eliminating the government deficit without raising taxes as well as to restructuring the public sector. Overall spending by the provincial government was cut by 20 percent, and the $3.4-billion annual deficit was replaced by a $958-million surplus by June 1995. Provincial government spending per capita was reduced by 33 percent, "marking a massive withdrawal of government from the economy in a remarkably short time."[61] In addition, the Klein government laid out its plans for redesigning the public service: its goals were improved managerial, accounting and reporting systems, a reduction in the size of the public service, less regulation, greater focus on efficiency and accountability in the public service, and privatization of the delivery of some government services.

The political and economic backdrop in Alberta was one of deficit spending in the wake of a dramatic drop in revenues in the mid-1980s. Despite the collapse of oil and grain prices—oil prices per barrel fell from $40 to $13—the provincial governments of the late 1980s and early 1990s continued to spend. By the time Klein took over the leadership of the provincial Progressive Conservative Party in late 1992, there was a great deal of public concern over the government's deficit. At the same time, the federal Reform Party was demanding major spending cuts in order to attack the federal deficit, which contributed generally to the increased public awareness of the problems of deficit spending and, especially in Alberta, to heightened support for tighter strings on the public purse. Based on a platform of aggressive cuts to the deficit, the Klein government carried 44 percent of the popular vote and a large majority of seats in the 1993 election. However, even these figures fail to capture the extent of popular appeal of the deficit-busting agenda in Alberta. Indeed, during the 1993 campaign there was little to choose between the Progressive Conservatives and Liberals on the major issue of the day. Both parties campaigned for "brutal" and "massive" cuts and together they amassed 84 percent of the popular vote.[62]

Given the climate of support for a smaller and leaner provincial government in Alberta, the Klein government also embarked on a major reorganization and downsizing of the public service. The stage was set in the months before winning the election of 1993, when the Progressive Conservative government eliminated six deputy minister positions and 1000 jobs in a public service that numbered about 30,000 employees. However, it was the budget of 1993 that illustrated the government's determination to cut the size and cost of government: salaries of MLAs and senior officials were cut, the number of departments was reduced from 26 to 16, the public-service payroll budget was cut by 5 percent and more than 2000 full-time jobs were eliminated. In controversial moves to restructure the relationship of the provincial government to local administrative boards, the province eliminated 80 of 140 school boards and took over the job of administering the education portion of local taxes. Local health boards were eliminated and administration was consolidated into 17 regional health authorities in order to streamline costs and planning. In the legislature, opportunities were opened up for backbench MLAs to contribute to policymaking by appointing all Conservative MLAs to one of four standing policy committees. The effect has been to limit the power of cabinet ministers and senior officials and to encourage a more holistic approach to policymaking. Performance measures were established, following the introduction of three-year business plans for all departments and agencies. The business plans were used to review the mandate and effectiveness of every department and to improve accountability both for performance and efficiency. The review of government programs also allowed the government to identify areas of public service that could be privatized. Famously, even before the implementation of business plans in early 1994, liquor stores and registry office services were contracted out in September 1993.

The Klein government also developed an important procedural innovation in 1993 when it embarked on a consultation process to determine the extent of public- and private-sector support for its fiscal plan. While questions about the significance and influence of the consultation process have been raised, it did serve to gauge the high level of support for attacking the deficit and to communicate with community leaders the extent of the problems facing the government. The "roundtable approach" proved so successful that it was also used to examine and make recommendations on health care and education.[63] The development of this consultation process, like many other features of the Alberta experience, reflects the interaction of the institutions of the government with the political world in which they operate.

When we shift our focus to the Ontario experience with "reinventing" government, we find a similar policy agenda but a different political landscape. In order to tailor a plan to the Ontario government, the Progressive Conservative Party outlined its policy agenda in advance of the 1995 election and labelled it "the Common Sense Revolution" (CSR). There were five key elements of the plan: "cuts to government spending, removing barriers to growth, doing better for less, balancing the budget, and lowering taxes."[64] The CSR document was launched on May 3, 1994, and on June 8, 1995, the Progressive Conservative party won 44.8 percent of the popular vote in Ontario and 83 of 130 seats. While it might be overstating the case to herald the new government as revolutionary, major policy and organizational changes began immediately and were hard-hitting. As well, and in contrast to Alberta, the CSR was met with public protests and resistance.

Despite the popular perception of "revolution" in Ontario, the NDP government under Premier Bob Rae in fact implemented instruments of budgetary policy—the Expenditure Control Plan and the Social Contract, initiated in 1993—that reflected growing concern for deficit-spending and a new approach to ministerial organization. Indeed, 1993 marked the end of an era that began with the appointment of the Committee on Government Productivity in 1969 under Premier John Robarts. Richard A. Loreto describes the period from 1969 to 1992 as the era of "institutionalization" of cabinet government in Ontario:

> *In short, the institutionalized system reflected the expansion of the state's role and the notion that every set of interests, both inside and outside government, needed voice in the policy-development process. Political sensitivity competed with political neutrality as the key criterion for senior administrative appointments. It was a system that was complex and, at times, cumbersome. It was also a system that often placed structural and procedural sophistication ahead of clarity of purpose and the execution of political will.*[65]

While Ontario's NDP government entered the 1990 election with a policy platform entitled "An Agenda for the People," a rapidly accumulating deficit that approached $17 billion forced it to demonstrate to the public and to financial markets that it was addressing the fiscal problems. The Expenditure Control Plan slashed ministry spending by $4 billion in 1993–94 and the Social Contract overrode collective bargaining agreements with public-sector wage cuts. These shifts in the policy agenda returned to haunt the NDP. The response of unions and social justice groups was a sense of having been "deeply betrayed" by the first NDP government in Ontario's history. "They felt it had perverted the NDP's social democratic mandate in many ways and especially by imposing on workers a Social Contract."[66] The NDP lost the election to Mike Harris's Conservatives.

If the policy and administrative shifts under Bob Rae signalled a shift in the winds of governance, the Conservative CSR agenda hit like a "tornado." Major policy changes included a decrease in overall government spending of 11 percent and cuts of up to 20 percent in non-priority government spending (priorities were identified as health, classroom education, and law enforcement); a 30-percent cut in provincial income tax rates; reductions in regulations of the labour market and economic investment, to stimulate growth; cuts to welfare benefits and the implementation of workfare for all able-bodied recipients up to the age of 65 and single mothers whose children were over the age of three years; promises that 725,000 jobs would be created over a five-year period; and, finally, a pledge to balance the budget in five years.

As well as major policy changes, administrative reform continued apace under Premier Harris. He streamlined the cabinet system, eliminating several cabinet positions, including ministers without portfolio, implemented cuts to departmental and central agency staff, and eliminated policy committees. Nineteen ministerial portfolios remained, and the system was supported by three coordinating committees—the Policy and Priorities Board, Management Board, and Legislation and Regulations—and was given administrative support by the Cabinet Office and the Premier's Office. The Policy and Priorities Board, chaired by Harris, was the most powerful committee and included the minister of Finance and chair of the Management Board, and it was here and in Management Board meetings that significant policy decisions were made. The new cabinet system was one "built for speed."[67]

DOSSIER 7.11 EVALUATING THE "REVOLUTIONS" IN THE PROVINCES

"Mike Harris won the 1995 Ontario election on a 'get tough platform' involving a massive 30 percent cut in taxes and social services. Able-bodied recipients will be forced into workfare. Those who cannot make it in the tough job market of the 1990s will be on their own. This sounded more like the dog-eat-dog ethos of Alabama but not Ontario....But it isn't Ontario that is leading Canada down this path towards a new market-based morality. It's Ralph Klein's Alberta. Instead of blaming the rich and the corporations for fleeing their responsibilities to invest and pay taxes in Canada, they have lashed out at the poor, at various minorities, at public sector workers as the causes of their tax woes and their financial insecurities."

Source: Trevor Harrison and Gordon Laxer, *The Trojan Horse: Alberta and the Future of Canada* (Montreal: Black Rose Books, 1997), 1.

"The significance of the Klein Government's achievement is that they actually put into practice the heretofore merely verbal criticisms of the welfare state. Beginning with the 1993 budget, the Government of Alberta has undertaken to reduce the intrusion of the welfare state in the lives of citizens....

To summarize the achievements of the Klein government: It is the first in the country to have shown a genuine and realistic commitment to fiscal prudence and less government. Moreover, it has done so not as an end in itself but as a means to ensure economic development: balance the books and investment will come."

Source: Barry Cooper, *The Klein Achievement* (Toronto: University of Toronto Press, 1996), Introduction.

Debates over the merits of the significant administrative and policy changes in Alberta and Ontario have taken place not only in the legislatures and not only by political analysts and the media but also in classrooms, union halls, and community centres and by students, workers, activist groups, and individual citizens. The different public responses in the provinces is striking. In Ontario, the Labour Council of Metropolitan Toronto and York Region and other activists organized a large rally of protestors to oppose the Tories on the day of their first budget speech in 1995 and this protest was followed by "Days of action"—one-day strikes and demonstrations rotating through Ontario cities. Students, teachers, public-service unions, daycare workers, and advocates for the poor have expressed outrage at the massive spending cuts and changes to public service in Ontario.

On the other hand, the story in Alberta has generally been one of quiescence and public support. Certainly there have been public demonstrations of opposition by students, doctors, nurses, community groups, and concerned citizens opposed to cuts in public spending and social services. But they have not been on the same scale or of the same intensity as those in Ontario. Keith Archer and Roger Gibbins describe the public-opinion landscape in Alberta as "characterized by enthusiastic and moderate supporters of balanced budgets, program cuts, government restructuring, and more broadly defined neoconservative policies. The absence of polarization makes the landscape a very difficult one for opposition parties and leaders, as large groups of discontented voters are difficult to find, categorize, and mobilize."

In the search for answers to the question of why there have been such different public responses in the provinces we turn to the arena outside institutions, to political culture and voter behaviour. Linda Trimble writes:

> *Ontario doesn't share Alberta's one-party state characteristics, especially the discomfort with opposition parties evidenced here. Ontario has a history and tradition of strong opposition parties and a three-party legislature; Alberta doesn't. In many ways, Alberta is idiosyncratic. In Alberta, opposing the government is viewed as unseemly, anti-Albertan, and, to some extent, traitorous.... It's as if criticism of the government is seen as criticism of Alberta itself. The Alberta legislature is arguably the most opposition-unfriendly legislature in Canada.*

Source: Keith Archer and Roger Gibbins, "What Do Albertens Think? The Klein Agenda on the Public Opinion Landscape," in Christopher Bruce, Ronald Kneebone, and Kenneth McKenzie, eds., *A Government Reinvented: A Study of Alberta's Deficit Elimination Program* (Toronto; Oxford University Press, 1997), 462–485.

The central administrative innovation was to adopt a businesslike approach to planning as the focal point of the expenditure-budget process, including the creation of ministry business plans to ensure that managers synchronized fiscal management and spending. Business plans are reviewed by the Policy and Priorities Board and Management Board and signed by the minister and deputy minister, and coordination of the process is provided by the cabinet office. The purpose of the planning process was to link the government's policy and fiscal agendas, to empasize fiscal planning and sustainability, and to improve accountability.[68]

Under the rubric of "modernizing government" and "doing better for less," the introduction of business plans and the demand for departments to focus on core services clearly reflect elements of both the Ontario government's ideological preference for reducing the role of the state and the pursuit of the NPM philosophy: "Concentrating on core services will mean a more accountable, innovative and efficient government that focuses on priorities and does better with less. New performance measures, based on results, will mean that taxpayers will be enabled to determine the effectiveness of these core services." By April 1996 the Ontario government reported that "downsizing" of the public service would eliminate 10,600 jobs by 1997–98 and that further cuts would occur.[69]

CONCLUSION

Recent years have seen substantial challenges to the administrative welfare state that emerged and flourished in the postwar period. Under the influence of conservative ideology and the New Public Management movement, the state has been downsized in some respects and significantly redesigned in others. We must not, however, lose sight of the fact that government continues to loom large in the lives of Canadians and that any full-scale return to the limited state of the prewar period seems highly unlikely. One reason is that while there is interest in redesigning welfare-state social programs, there is little interest in abandoning them altogether. Another reason is that the evolution of the state involves the emergence of new forms of intervention and regulation as old ones are reduced or abandoned. For example, replacing domestic regulatory regimes with international ones may reduce the significance of the Canadian state, but it does not necessarily reduce the overall scope of regulatory activity—though it certainly tends to change its nature and consequences (whether for good or for ill remains a matter of controversy).

Controversy also exists about how best to organize government and how far governments should go in modelling their operations on business practices. In particular, the principle of accountability, which is central to responsible government, seems most fundamental to the way questions of government organization are answered. The issue concerns not only analysts and citizens looking in on government but the very people involved in public administration, including politicians and officials at the highest echelons of the federal government. Their concern is reflected in a recent report by deputy ministers on the Task Force on Public Service Values and Ethics, who found that almost every issue they examined led back to the principles of democratic life in a parliamentary system and especially to the principle of accountability.[70] How can accountability be maintained under a system of public management that emphasizes decentralization and entrepreneurial innovation? In wrestling with this question, the report insists that accountability must be retained and that while ministers can delegate specific authority to an executive officer of service-delivery agencies, the officer would remain accountable to the minister and the minister to Parliament.[71] How exactly this is to be achieved is, to say the least, unclear. The tension between the "new" public management approach and the "old" public administration approach is likely to animate bureaucratic politics for some time.

KEY TERMS

welfare state
gross domestic product (GDP)
deficit
debt
Expenditure Management System (EMS)
civil-service employment
government employment
public-sector employment
privatization
regulatory agencies
Regulatory Impact Analysis Statement (RIAS)
Federal Regulatory Policy
deregulation
New Public Management (NPM)
public goods
line departments
central agencies
superbureaucrats
entrepreneurial government
public enterprises
Crown corporations
mixed enterprises
chosen instruments
advisory councils
Public Service 2000 (PS 2000)
Program Review
Alternative Service Delivery (ASD)

DISCUSSION QUESTIONS

1. Trace the contours of the Canadian welfare state as it evolved between its emergence, after World War II, and the mid-1970s. What were its key dimensions in terms of spending, employment, and programs, and how have these changed in recent years?
2. How did the federal government manage to achieve a balanced budget in 1998, after more than 20 years of running up deficits?
3. What key challenges does New Public Management (NPM) theory present to traditional concepts of public-sector service provision? Does NPM go too far?
4. This chapter lists several initiatives undertaken by the federal government in order to "get government right." Can you discern a "Canadian style" of administrative reform in these initiatives?
5. The government administrative reform projects described in this chapter share many important features, despite important differences among them. What factors drove these similar agendas, regardless of different party stripe and political circumstance?

SUGGESTED READINGS

Aucoin, Peter. *The New Public Management: Canada in a Comparative Perspective.* Montreal: Institute for Research on Public Policy, 1995.

Banting, Keith G. *The Welfare State and Canadian Federalism,* 2nd ed. Kingston and Montreal: McGill-Queen's University Press, 1987.

Bourgault, Jacques, Maurice Demers, and Cynthia Williams, eds. *Public Administration and Public Management—Experiences in Canada.* Sainte-Foy, Que.: Les Publications du Québec, 1997.

Charih, Mohamed, and Arthur Daniels, eds. *New Public Management and Public Administration in Canada.* Toronto: Institute of Public Administration of Canada, 1997.

Ford, Robin, and David Zussman, eds. *Alternative Service Delivery: Shaping Governance in Canada.* Toronto: Institute of Public Administration of Canada, 1997.

OECD. *In Search of Results: Performance Management Practices.* Paris: OECD, 1997.

Osborne, David, and Ted Gaebler. *Reinventing Government: How the Entrepreneurial Spirit Is Transforming the Public Sector.* Reading, Mass.: Addison-Wesley, 1995.

Pal, Leslie A., ed. *How Ottawa Spends 1998–1999: Balancing Act: The Post-Deficit Mandate.* Toronto: Oxford University Press, 1998.

Peters, B. Guy, and Donald Savoie, eds. *Taking Stock: Assessing Public Sector Reforms.* Ottawa and Kingston: Canadian Centre for Management Development and McGill-Queen's University Press, 1998.

Savoie, Donald J. *The Politics of Public Spending in Canada.* Toronto: University of Toronto Press, 1990.

NOTES

1. Organization for Economic Co-operation and Development, *Issues and Developments in Public Management: Survey 1996–1997* (1977) [on-line, World Wide Web; cited October 19, 1998]; available at http://www.oecd.org/puma/gvrnance/surveys/summary.htm.
2. On the welfare state, see Hugh Heclo, *Policy and Politics in Sweden: Principled Pragmatism* (Philadelphia: Temple University Press, 1987); Peter Flora and Arnold J. Heidenheimer, eds., *The Development of Welfare States in Europe and America* (New Brunswick, N.J.: Transaction Books, 1981).
3. The seminal British blueprint for the postwar welfare state was the Beveridge Report; see Great Britain, Parliament, House of Commons, *Social Insurance and Allied Services* (London: HMSO, 1942). The Canadian version was drafted by Leonard Marsh; see Canada, Parliament, House of Commons, Special Committee on Social Security, *Report on Social Security for Canada* (Ottawa: King's Printer, 1943).
4. Keynesianism is named after the British economist John Maynard Keynes (1883–1946), whose key work was *The General Theory of Employment Interest and Money* (London: Macmillan, 1936). Keynes argued that capitalist economies could experience almost permanent recession, and only state spending—incurring a deficit—could stimulate the economy. Government deficits could then be paid down during periods of economic growth, when governments would generate surpluses. See Robert Skidelsky, *Keynes* (Oxford: Oxford University Press, 1996).

5. Barry Cooper, ed., *The Resurgence of Conservatism in Anglo-American Democracies* (Durham, N.C.: Duke University Press, 1988); and Paul Pierson, *Dismantling the Welfare State: Reagan, Thatcher, and the Politics of Retrenchment* (Cambridge: Cambridge University Press, 1994).
6. For an overview of international trends, see B. Guy Peters and Donald J. Savoie, eds., *Governance in a Changing Environment* (Montreal: Institute for Research on Public Policy, 1995); Organization for Economic Co-operation and Development, *Issues and Developments in Public Management: Survey 1996–1997* (1977) [on-line, World Wide Web; cited October 19, 1998]; available at http://www.oecd.org/puma/gvrnance/surveys/summary.htm.
7. "Zhu Takes on the Red-Tape Army," *The Economist* (March 14–20, 1998), 45.
8. Peter Aucoin, *The New Public Management: Canada in a Comparative Perspective* (Montreal: Institute for Research on Public Policy, 1995), 16.
9. The federal spending power has been controversial for decades, precisely because it permits federal intrusion in provincial policy fields, often forcing provinces to spend on programs they might not have supported independently. Then, if Ottawa decides to back out, the provinces are left to run the programs themselves. The ill-fated 1988 Meech Lake Accord had a clause that, for the first time in Canadian constitutional history, would have entrenched the spending power but given provinces the right to opt out with compensation. In December 1997 the provinces succeeded in extracting a concession from the federal government on the use of the spending power to construct the social union. Afterward, however, Ottawa claimed that it would respect no restrictions on its current powers or legislation such as the Canada Health Act. See Jim Brown, "Power Politics over Budget Surplus," *Ottawa Citizen,* December 10, 1997 [on-line, World Wide Web; cited March 13, 1998]; available at http://www.ottawacitizen.com/cpfs/national/971210/n121029.html.
10. *The Budget Chart Book 1998* (Ottawa: Public Works and Government Services Canada, 1998), 74.
11. Canada, Department of Finance, Budget Papers (Ottawa: February 25, 1992), 9.
12. Canada, Department of Finance, Budget Papers (Ottawa: February 27, 1995), 87.
13. *The Budget Chart Book 1998,* 80.
14. Statistics Canada [on-line, World Wide Web; cited October 19, 1998]; available at http://www.statcan.ca/english/Pgdb/State/Government/govt02b.htm.
15. Keith G. Banting, *The Welfare State and Canadian Federalism,* 2nd ed. (Kingston and Montreal: McGill-Queen's University Press, 1987), 54.
16. *Atlantic Smoke Shops Ltd. v. Conlon,* [1943] A.C. 550.
17. Statistics Canada, *Consolidated Federal, Provincial, Territorial and Local Government Revenue and Expenditure* [on-line, World Wide Web; cited October 19, 1998]; available at http://www.statcan.ca/english/Pgdb/State/Government/govt01a.htm.
18. *The Budget Chart Book 1998* (Ottawa: Public Works and Government Services Canada, 1998), 66.
19. On April 1, 1997, Ottawa announced the creation of the Harmonized Sales Tax (HST) in cooperation with New Brunswick, Nova Scotia, and Newfoundland. The HST combined the GST and the PST charged in those provinces with a single flat 15-percent tax.

20. Edward Greenspon and Anthony Wilson-Smith, *Double Vision: The Inside Story of the Liberals in Power* (Toronto: Doubleday, 1996), 163–170.

21. Donald J. Savoie, *The Politics of Public Spending in Canada* (Toronto: University of Toronto Press, 1990).

22. Treasury Board Secretariat, *The Expenditure Management System* (Ottawa, 1994).

23. *The Budget Chart Book 1998,* 61.

24. Joan Bryden, "Battle for Bucks Begins," *Ottawa Citizen,* February 25, 1998, A6.

25. Margaret Biggs, *Building Blocks for Canada's New Social Union* (Kingston, Ont.: Canadian Policy Research Networks, Working Paper No. F02, 1996).

26. Richard M. Bird, in collaboration with Meyer W. Bucovestsky and David K. Foot, *The Growth of Public Employment in Canada* (Ottawa: Institute for Research on Public Policy, 1979), Chapter 3.

27. *Canada Year Book, 1930,* 1008–1012.

28. Bird, *The Growth of Public Employment in Canada,* 32–33.

29. Treasury Board of Canada, *Employment Statistics for the Federal Public Service: April 1, 1996 to March 31, 1997.*

30. Clerk of the Privy Council, Fourth Report to the Prime Minister on the Public Service of Canada (Ottawa, 1997).

31. Statistics Canada, *Employment and Average Weekly Earnings (Including Overtime), Public Administration and All Industries, 1994–1996* [on-line, World Wide Web; cited October 19, 1998]; available at http://www.statcan.ca/english/Pgdb/State/Government/govt18.htm.

32. *The Statistical Year-Book of Canada for 1890,* 464.

33. G. Harvey Agnew, *Canadian Hospitals, 1920 to 1970: A Dramatic Half-Century* (Toronto: University of Toronto Press, 1974), 23.

34. Kernaghan and Siegel, *Public Administration in Canada,* 3rd edition. (Scarborough, ON: ITP Nelson), 226.

35. Treasury Board of Canada, *Government of Canada Regulatory Policy* (Ottawa: 1995). [on-line, World Wide Web; cited October 19, 1998]; available at http://www.info.tbs-sct.gc.ca/SIGS/html/TB_B3/text/files/RP1-1E.html.

36. Treasury Board of Canada, *Government of Canada Regulatory Policy* (Ottawa: 1995). [on-line, World Wide Web; cited October 19, 1998]; available at http://www.info.tbs-sct.gc.ca/SIGS/html/TB_B3/text/files/RP1-1E.html#appb.

37. Treasury Board of Canada, *Federal Regulatory Plan, 1997: A Guide to Planned Regulatory Initiatives* (Ottawa, 1997) [on-line, World Wide Web; cited October 19, 1998]; available at http://www.tbs-sct.gc.ca/tb/rad/plan97/title.pdf. The categorization scheme is a bit more complicated than this, since it also is supposed to include some assessment of the acceptance to the public.

38. "New Public Management" is the label given to the bundle of principles that informs contemporary thinking about administrative reform and reflects the assumption that "there is something called management which is a generic, purely instrumental activity embodying a set of principles that can be applied to public business as well as private business." See Jonathan Boston, John Martin, June Pallott, and Pat Walsh, *Public Management: The New Zealand Model* (Auckland: Oxford University Press, 1996), Chapter 2; Peter Aucoin, "Administrative Reform in Public Management: Paradigms, Principles, Paradoxes and Pendulums," *Governance* 3 (1990), 115–131. See also Kenneth Kernaghan,

"Keeping the New Public Management Pot Boiling," *Canadian Public Administration* 38 (1995), 481–484, for a discussion of the "several terms and concepts that are central to the NPM debates but which are used in a bewildering variety of ways."

39. David Osborne and Ted Gaebler, *Reinventing Government: How the Entrepreneurial Spirit Is Transforming the Public Sector* (Reading, Mass.: Addison-Wesley, 1995).
40. B. Guy Peters, *The Public Service: The Changing State and Governance* (Ottawa: Minister of Supply and Services, 1993), 3.
41. Christopher Pollitt, *Management Techniques for the Public Sector: Pulpit and Practice,* Research Paper No. 17, Canadian Centre for Management Development (Ottawa: Minister of Supply and Services), 1.
42. Donald J. Savoie, "What Is Wrong with the New Public Management," *Canadian Public Administration* 38 (Spring 1995), 113.
43. Osborne and Gaebler, *Reinventing Government,* 19–20.
44. Pollitt, *Management Techniques for the Public Sector,* 3.
45. Pollitt, *Management Techniques for the Public Sector,* 2.
46. In their discussion of the New Zealand case, Boston et al. note that there are "well-recognised risks associated with the emulation of one country's practices by another. Differences in political culture, administrative ethos, technological advancement, legal conditions and constitutional conventions all make the transfer of ideas and policies between countries a complex and hazardous business." Nevertheless they argue that many of the approaches to and policy instruments associated with administrative reform in New Zealand are "transportable." *Public Management: The New Zealand Model,* 363–364.
47. Osborne and Gaebler, *Reinventing Government,* 330.
48. Donald J. Savoie, "Reforming Civil Service Reforms," *Policy Options* 15 (April 1994), 3.
49. Patrice Garrant, "Crown Corporations: Instruments of Economic Intervention—Legal Aspects," in Ivan Bernier and Andrée Lajoie, eds., *Regulations, Crown Corporations and Administrative Tribunals,* Research Study for the Royal Commission on the Economic Union and Development Prospects for Canada (Toronto: University of Toronto Press, 1985), 5.
50. Canada, Royal Commission on Financial Management and Accountability, *Final Report,* 358–359, cited in Kernaghan and Siegel, *Public Administration in Canada,* 187.
51. Savoie, "Reforming Civil Service Reforms," 3.
52. Paul M. Tellier, "Public Service 2000: The Renewal of the Public Service," *Canadian Public Administration* 33 (Summer 1990), 126–127.
53. Ian D. Clark, "Restraint, Renewal and the Treasury Board Secretariat," *Canadian Public Administration* (Summer 1994), 227. For a different perspective see Robert J. McIntosh, "Public Service 2000: The Employee Perspective," *Canadian Public Administration* 34 (Autumn 1991), 503–511.
54. Savoie, "What Is Wrong with the New Public Management," 112.
55. *Getting Government Right: A Progress Report* (Ottawa: Minister of Supply and Services, 1996), 5–6.
56. Treasury Board Secretariat, *Response to the Fifth Report of the Standing Committee on Public Accounts on Quality Service* (available at Web site http://www.tbs-sct.gc.ca/Pubs_pol/partners/RFR1-1E.html).

    There is a plethora of information exchange mechanisms to spread the word about successful departmental innovations and to share research on organizational and service delivery practices. The Treasury Board Secretariat is the coordinator of knowledge and expertise for the federal government and facilitates information exchange through a number of other agencies: the Canadian Public Sector Quality Association, the National Quality Institute of Canada, the Interdepartmental Quality Network, and the Citizen-Centred Service Delivery Network.

57. Treasury Board of Canada, *ASD Defined* (available at Web site http://www.tbs-sct.gc.ca/tb/irpp/irppe.html).

58. Treasury Board of Canada, *Alternative Service Delivery: Role of the Treasury Board* Secretariat (available at Web site http://www.tbs.-sct.gc.ca/tb/irpp/irppe.html).

59. Treasury Board, *Quality Services: A Progress Report,* "Introduction," 1996. The report lists extensive departmental examples, and highlights the following service standards: "with the use of electronic filing of individual income taxes, many returns are processed in 10 days or less; by September of 1997, turnaround times for processing first applications for veterans' disability pensions will be cut in half; a passport can be processed and read for pick-up in 5 days when a request is submitted in person."

60. Treasury Board Secretariat, *Improved Reporting to Parliament Project* (available at Web site http://www.tbs-sct.gc.ca/tb/irpp/irppe.html).

61. Christopher J. Bruce, Ronald D. Kneebone, and Kenneth J. McKenzie, "Introduction," in Bruce, Kneebone, and McKenzie, eds., *A Government Reinvented: A Study of Alberta's Deficit Elimination Program* (Toronto: Oxford University Press Canada, 1997), 1.

62. Robert L. Mansell, "Fiscal Restructuring in Alberta: An Overview," in Bruce et al., *A Government Reinvented,* 31.

63. Mansell, "Fiscal Restructuring in Alberta," 51.

64. Ontario Progressive Conservative Party, "The Common Sense Revolution—Doing What We Said We Would Do," May 3, 1996 (Web site http://www.ontariopc.on.ca/news-general.cfm?docid=174). The document promised that Harris would do the following: "Cut overall government spending by 11 per cent without taking money from health, classroom education and law enforcement. As part of the spending cuts, welfare rates would be rolled back ... and all able-bodied welfare recipients under the age of sixty-five, including single mothers with children over the age of three, would be required to work for their cheques. Cut the provincial income-tax rate by 30 per cent across the board while replacing the existing employers' health tax with a new, revenue-neutral but progressive income-tax supplement. Balance the provincial budget within five years. Create 725,000 net new jobs over five years." Thomas Walkom, "The Harris Government: Restoration or Revolution," *The Government and Politics of Ontario,* 4–3.

65. Richard A. Loreto, "Making and Implementing the Decisions: Issues of Public Administration in the Ontario Government," in Graham White, ed., *The Government and Politics of Ontario,* 5th ed. (Toronto: University of Toronto Press, 1997), 97.

66. Diana Ralph, "Introduction" in Ralph Andre Regimbald and Neree St.-Amand, eds., *Open for Business, Closed to People: Mike Harris's Ontario* (Halifax: Fernwood Publishing, 1997), 1.

67. Loreto, "Making and Implementing the Decisions," 103.

68. Ibid., 107. There were four required elements to the business plans: ministry vision and core businesses, strategy for change, performance measures and reporting, and a marketing and communications strategy.

69. Ontario Progressive Conservative Party, "Restructuring Government/Eliminating MPPs' Pensions" / "Sunshine Laws," April 11, 1996 (Web site http://www.ontariopc.on.ca/news-general.cfm?docid=160).
70. John Tait, "A Strong Foundation: Report of the Task Force on Public Service Values and Ethics (The Summary)," *Canadian Public Administration* 40 (Spring 1997), 1–22.
71. Ibid., 5.

THE COURTS

8

Judges are reluctant virgins, reluctant to admit that they make law and that they are perceived as making law. The lawmaking role of judges is increasing steadily. This would be so even without the Charter, but it is even more so the case because of it.[1]

The courts have become increasingly prominent political and policymaking institutions. It is impossible, for example, to understand recent megaconstitutional politics without reference to the patriation case, the Quebec signs case, and the 1998 secession reference, to name only three of the relevant judgments. Courts have been central players in the politics of abortion, censorship, gay rights, minority language education, and criminal justice policy. Judges have gone from invalidating laws on constitutional grounds to rewriting their provisions and requiring the expenditure of public funds. Should institutions designed for the impartial adjudication of narrowly defined disputes undertake such wide-ranging policymaking? Can they avoid doing so? Can they be redesigned for better policymaking without compromising their adjudicative role? These are among the questions that have placed the courts and judicial power squarely on the agenda of Canada's institutional politics.

■ ■ ■

Courts have become increasingly important players in Canadian politics. In the 1998 secession reference, for example, the Supreme Court addressed the question of whether Quebec can legally issue a unilateral declaration of independence (see Dossier 3.9). This case thrust the court into the heart of Canada's biggest and thorniest political thicket. A few months earlier, the Supreme Court handed down the blockbuster decision in *Delgamuukw*,[2] which made it easier for natives to assert claims of "Aboriginal title" to lands not covered by treaty. In British Columbia, where the entire province is subject to such claims, the ruling cast a pall of uncertainty over many natural resource projects, jeopardizing new investment and job creation. Like the Quebec separation case, *Delgamuukw* aroused a storm of controversy, including pointed criticisms of what some British Columbians considered the "foreign court" in Ottawa that decided the case.[3]

Nor was British Columbia happy with *Eldridge,*[4] in which the Supreme Court ruled that the province had to divert money from other purposes, including perhaps other health-care purposes, to pay for interpreters for deaf patients in its hospitals.

In neighbouring Alberta, public debate during the spring of 1998 was dominated—indeed, convulsed—by *Vriend,*[5] in which the court rewrote Alberta's Human Rights Act to include homosexuals in the law's list of groups protected against discrimination. There was much discussion about whether the province should use section 33 of the Charter to override *Vriend* (see Dossier 2. 5), and this debate quickly made the case a national *cause célèbre.*

The four cases just discussed, all heard or decided within months of one another, represent only a handful of the significant and controversial Supreme Court cases in 1997–98. Moreover, the Supreme Court itself is only the tip of the judicial iceberg; many more policy-relevant judgments are issued by lower courts, and, as we shall see, they are often just as important as Supreme Court decisions. Scarcely a week goes by that a court somewhere in the land does not attract substantial media attention for a controversial policy decision. Can women go topless on city streets?[6] Can adult children be required to maintain and support formerly neglectful but currently needy parents?[7] Should those who kill out of compassion for the victim be given more lenient sentences?[8] Should "spousal benefits" be extended to homosexual couples?[9] Nowadays, these and many similar questions are as likely to be authoritatively answered by courts as by legislatures. To understand the public-policy answers to such questions, one must look as much to the case law as to the statute books.

Judges may be increasingly important policymakers, but as this chapter's epigraph indicates, they are loath to admit this political role. And judges are not alone in resisting the view that they are political actors. When we think of a court, most of us do not think first of a political and policymaking institution. Political battles, waged between forces mobilized by conflicting visions of public policy, take place most obviously and prominently in legislatures, the executive branch, and the arena of public opinion, not in the courtroom. Courts, we rightly think, engage in **adjudication,** the authoritative resolution of particular disputes arising in the course of everyday life. In doing so, courts appear to undertake the non-political function of applying law, not the political role of making it. Judges even more than bureaucrats have traditionally been understood as policy implementers rather than policymakers. Dossier 8.1 presents a classic statement of this view by the late Supreme Court Justice John Sopinka (but compare page 360–361).

It is true, of course, that there is an entire area of law, known as the **common law,** that is not governed by statutes enacted by legislatures but consists entirely of judicial decisions.[10] This is certainly a kind of "judge-made" law, but at least since the advent of parliamentary supremacy in Britain, it has been considered a decisively subordinate kind of law.[11] Under the doctrine of parliamentary supremacy, non-statutory areas of judge-made common law persist only to the extent that the legislature

DOSSIER 8.1 THE SEPARATION OF LAW AND POLITICS

One of the basic principles underlying the liberal democratic approach to government [is this]: There is a difference between politics and law.

There is a difference between making decisions according to how popular they are, how many people will support them, how organized the opposition might be or whether people are willing to pay for them—these are political calculations—and making decisions according to whether a particular result is rational, logical, consistent with past practice, appropriate in light of liberal democratic principles and morally defensible. These are legal determinations.

To insist that the courts must be independent of the political arms of government is to insist that law is and must be separate from politics. It is to believe that a decision can be *legally* correct even through it is *politically* insupportable.

Shielding the judiciary from inappropriate influences means, first and foremost, shielding it from other branches of government—because it is in these branches of government where political interests are most powerfully felt. Political power and interests are the lifeblood of a legislature, a cabinet, a constituent assembly or a presidency. Their halls are filled with people who would love to be able to determine the outcome of legal disputes. Indeed, such people, especially if they represent a majority, would prefer that all disputes be political, rather than legal, because politics lets the powerful win. Only the law allows the weak to win against the strong....

Recent changes in our Constitution and in the dynamics of society have made it more difficult for judges to maintain the appearance of impartiality. Until 1982 the role of judges in relation to legislation was to interpret the law. In addition, because we are a federation in which the power to pass legislation is divided between the federal government on the one hand and the provinces on the other, the courts were empowered to decide whether legislation was properly within the sphere of the branch of government that passed it.

In 1982 all that changed. With the adoption of a Charter of Rights and Freedoms, there are areas in which neither the federal Parliament nor the provinces can legislate. As well, all government action can be subjected to judicial scrutiny. These new powers have brought the court into the political arena. By way of example, our court struck down legislation in our Criminal Code, a federal statute, which prohibited abortion except under certain stringent terms; struck down federal legislation prohibiting all federal civil servants from engaging in partisan political activity; and passed upon the validity of a federal government order-in-council which authorized the testing of cruise missiles by the United States on Canadian soil.

This politicization of the courts has resulted in attacks on the courts from two fronts. Public-interest groups have become more vocal, waging long and loud campaigns seeking to influence the decision of a court or to influence the government to change a decision made by the court. Political figures both in power and opposition, spurred on by public clamour, indulge themselves in public criticism of judges and even demands for discipline....

The paradox created by the Charter is that it was adopted by means of a democratic process to protect the individual against an abuse of power by the majority, but many feel that it is undemocratic for unelected judges to overrule the majority. The majority does not like to be told it is wrong.

The unfortunate fact is that the Charter has turned the court into the messenger who is likely to get shot for bringing bad news. By enacting the Charter, the legislative branch of government enacted a permanent invitation to the judiciary to tell the majority that it is wrong—that it cannot do what it wants to do, or at least that it cannot do it in a way it wants to do it. If the majority is in a particularly surly mood, bringing this kind of bad news can be a singularly unpleasant business.

How does this relate to the topic of judicial independence? In a very direct way. The Charter is a law. It is the supreme law of the land. It is the duty of courts to apply the law. In order to apply the Charter, courts must be willing to declare laws enacted by elected representatives unconstitutional—to say, in effect, that the majority is breaking the law.

Now if the courts are subject to effective political pressure, whether that be through public criticism aimed at shaming judges into changing their rulings, or through the threat of disciplinary proceedings at the instigation of the executive branch, then the judicial system will be less capable of telling the majority that it is wrong. They will be less able to apply the Charter in an effective manner. And this means the end of the rule of law.

Source: From a speech given by the late Mr. Justice John Sopinka of the Supreme Court of Canada. Reprinted from *The Globe and Mail*, November 28, 1997.

chooses not to displace them with statutes—that is, only when judge-made law does not differ appreciably from the law the legislature would have made. Even in the common-law realm, in short, judges can be seen as applying implicit legislative policy. In any case, the legislative displacement of common law has steadily increased, and certainly judges were understood to be applying legislation.

In fact, the traditional view of the judicial role as non-political has never been an adequate reflection of reality even with respect to statutory law. Lawmaking has always been an integral, if generally unacknowledged, corollary of adjudication, whether that adjudication arose in the context of legislation or common law. Nowadays, the lawmaking function of the courts is more significant and prominent than it was in the past. Still, the adjudicative and lawmaking dimensions of judicial decision making remain conceptually distinct and have different institutional implications. The judiciary is an institution caught between the competing institutional purposes of adjudication and policymaking. The resulting institutional controversy is the subject of this chapter.

DOSSIER 8.2 ADJUDICATION IN COMPARATIVE CONTEXT

Adjudication is distinct from other dispute-resolution systems such as **negotiation, mediation,** and **arbitration.** Once a party takes a dispute to court, the opposing party must also appear or face sanctions determined by the state. Unlike negotiation or mediation, it is the judge who decides the controversy, not the disputing parties. Like mediation and arbitration, in adjudication there is a neutral third party (the judge), but unlike a mediator, the judge has the power to decide the dispute rather than simply encourage a settlement. And unlike most forms of arbitration, the judge must decide in conformity with the whole body of relevant law.

Adjudication is appropriate for disputes whose settlement is necessary for the preservation of order in a society. Adjudication is inappropriate in cases where public order is not so important and where the disputing parties could reach a satisfactory settlement themselves (here, negotiation is more appropriate) or with some help from a neutral third party (here, mediation is more appropriate). Adjudication is also inappropriate in cases where an imposed settlement is necessary, but where that settlement need not be decided according to the whole body of relevant law (here, arbitration is more appropriate).

One of the disturbing trends in modern society is the use of adjudication to settle disputes for which another form of dispute resolution would be more appropriate. The reasons for the overuse of adjudication ... relate to a lack of public knowledge of alternative forms of dispute resolution, the private interests of some members of the legal profession, and the breakdown of community and the resulting personal isolation connected with industrial and postindustrial society. This latter trend makes it difficult for many to understand opposing points of view, so that when they are involved in a dispute there is a tendency to believe that they are "in the right" and the other person is clearly "in the wrong." Given these assumptions about right and wrong, it is easily concluded that a court of law will decide in favour of the "right" party, and therefore the most logical means to settle the dispute is to take it to a court of law.

Source: Reprinted from Ian Greene, "The Courts and Public Policy," in Michael M. Atkinson, ed., *Governing Canada: Institutions and Public Policy* (Toronto: Harcourt Brace Jovanovich, 1993), 182–183.

The chapter begins with an examination of the courts from the perspective of their adjudicative purpose, and shows how this purpose is institutionalized through the central constitutional norm of judicial independence. We then show why even the most adjudicative of courts cannot avoid some degree of policymaking, and how courts, cases, and judges can be positioned at different points on the continuum between adjudication and policymaking. The institutional change and contestation caused by the ongoing tug of war between the competing logics of adjudication and policymaking is our penultimate topic. Finally, we consider how interest groups and governments make political use of this apparently apolitical arena for policymaking.

JUDICIAL INDEPENDENCE AND THE SEPARATION OF LAW AND POLITICS

One of the two purposes underlying the judiciary—the adjudicative purpose—emphasizes the non-political character of courts and judges. This view is institutionally reflected in the great care we take to make judges as independent of political pressure as possible. For example, judges are appointed, not elected, and enjoy security of tenure. In the case of most of our "higher" courts—the **superior courts** mentioned in section 96 of the Constitution Act, 1867—tenure is entrenched by section 99 of the 1867 act. Originally, section 99 simply granted judges tenure "during good behaviour," making them "removable by the Governor General [only] on Address of the Senate and House of Commons," a rare occurrence. In effect, this section originally granted Canada's superior court judges tenure for life, a privilege still enjoyed by American federal judges. In 1960, however, section 99 was amended to impose a mandatory retirement age of 75. Below this age limit, tenure "during good behaviour" still applies.

Although the judges of the **section 96 courts** are appointed by the federal government, the courts over which they preside are "constituted" by the provinces. The "cooperative federalism" thus required to establish and staff these courts may also help to protect judicial independence. It can also make for some interesting intergovernmental relations (see Dossier 8.3). The independence of section 96 court judges is further enhanced by the fact that their salaries are protected from easy political manipulation by section 100 of the Constitution Act, 1867.

Because of their high status and constitutionally entrenched independence, the section 96 superior courts have become the centrepiece of our judicial system. Included in this category is the superior trial court in each province—variously known as the Court of Queen's Bench, the High Court, the Supreme Court, or the Trial Division of the Supreme Court—which tries the most important criminal and civil cases. This is the only court in which jury trials are available. The superior courts also include the provincial "courts of appeal" (sometimes called the Appeal Division of the Supreme Court), which exercise a supervisory appellate jurisdiction over a variety of "lower" courts, subject only to the ultimate supervision of the Supreme Court of Canada. Of Canada's roughly 2000 judges, over 40 percent staff these superior courts. These figures include **supernumerary judges**—that is, judges who "have reached retirement age, but have been reappointed for a specified period on the recommendation of the chief judge or judicial council or have opted for semi-retirement prior to retirement age."[12]

Despite the constitutional centrality of the section 96 trial courts, much of the trial work in Canada is actually done by "lower" or "inferior" courts, which do not enjoy constitutionally entrenched guarantees of independence to quite the same degree as their "superiors." These courts are both constituted and staffed by the provinces and are thus known as **provincial courts.**[13] The jurisdiction of the provincial courts overlaps substantially with that of the higher trial courts, and in fact they

DOSSIER 8.3 THE SASKATCHEWAN JUDGES AFFAIR

In 1982, shortly after coming to power, a Conservative government led by Grant Devine passed an order-in-council decreasing the Saskatchewan Court of Appeal from seven to five judges. The Court of Appeal had been expanded from five to seven a few months earlier but the two new positions had not been filled when the Devine government took office. The new Conservative administration was determined to check what it regarded as unrestrained Liberal patronage in filling section 96 judgeships and chose the tactic of closing off vacancies until the federal minister of justice agreed to consult with the government of Saskatchewan on appointments....

This was by no means the end of the affair. During 1983 and 1984 there was open warfare between the provincial and federal governments over judicial appointments in Saskatchewan. The provincial cabinet passed an order-in-council which would close each vacancy on the Court of Queen's Bench until its strength fell from thirty to twenty-four judges. The intention was to block any further appointments by the Trudeau government to the Saskatchewan courts. A group of Saskatchewan trial lawyers, frustrated by the effect this cutback on judicial manpower was having on the processing of cases, challenged the legality of this manoeuvre. Justice Wimmer of the Court of Queen's Bench ruled that while there is no doubt about the constitutional power of the provincial legislature to alter the size of the courts, the statute governing the Court of Queen's Bench with its provisions requiring judges in specific locations did not permit the cabinet by order-in-council to eliminate positions on that court.

Source: Reprinted with permission from Peter H. Russell, *The Judiciary in Canada: The Third Branch of Government* (Toronto: McGraw-Hill Ryerson, 1987), 122–123.

try the vast bulk of criminal cases,[14] with only a few serious crimes, such as murder and treason, reserved for the exclusive jurisdiction of the superior courts. Indeed, the "vast criminal jurisdiction" exercised by these courts "appears to be unmatched by the lower criminal courts of any other liberal democracy."[15] Despite their obvious importance, these entirely provincial courts do not come under the constitutionally entrenched guarantees of independence in either section 99 or 100. Over 50 percent of Canada's judges work in the lower provincial courts.[16]

Like the provinces, the federal government is also able to establish and staff its own non-section 96 courts. Section 101 of the 1867 Constitution Act states that Ottawa may "from time to time provide for the constitution, maintenance, and organization of a general court of appeal for Canada, and for the establishment of any additional courts for the better administration of the laws of Canada." The most prominent **section 101 courts** are the nine-judge Supreme Court of Canada and the Federal Court, the latter of which hears cases arising under federal administrative law. In 1990 the Federal Court was composed of a 16-judge trial division and an 11-judge

FIGURE 8.1 **THE CANADIAN JUDICIAL SYSTEM**

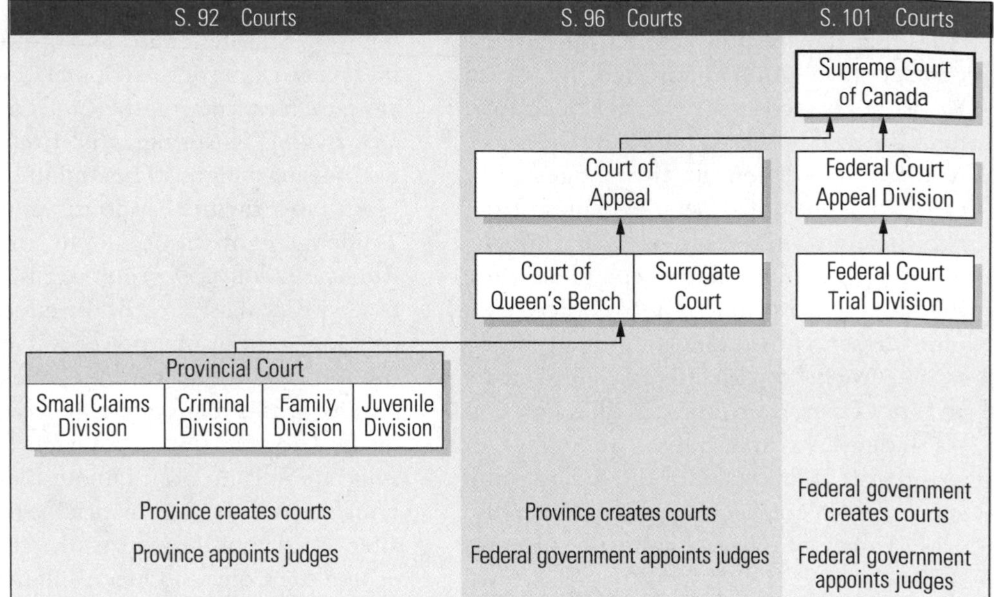

Source: F.L. Morton, ed., *Law, Politics and the Judicial Process in Canada*, 2nd ed. (Calgary: University of Calgary Press, 1992), 64, figure 1.

appeal division.[17] Another section 101 court is the Tax Court of Canada, which in 1990 had 15 judges.[18] The 50-odd judges of section 101 courts constitute just 3 percent of Canada's judiciary. Like the judges of the provincial lower courts, they do not enjoy the guarantees of independence in sections 99 and 100 of the constitution, which apply only to section 96 courts.

The fact that sections 99 and 100 of the Constitution Act, 1867, apply only to section 96 courts does not mean that the provincial courts and the federal section 101 courts lack independence. Judicial independence has long been a central constitutional convention and has been protected for non-section 96 courts by ordinary legislation. Further, insofar as they make determinations of guilt and innocence, non-section courts have since 1982 been subject to section 11(d) of the Charter of Rights, which guarantees the right "to be presumed innocent until proven guilty according to law in a fair and public hearing by an independent and impartial tribunal." This section secures a measure of independence, though it does not guarantee the full extent of section 99 protection. As the Supreme Court put it in *Valente v. The Queen*, "The essence of security of tenure for purposes of s. 11(d) is a tenure, whether until an age of retirement, *for a fixed term, or for a specific adjudicative task*, that is secure against interference by the Executive or other appointing authority in a discretionary or arbitrary manner."[19] Most Canadian judges enjoy protections that meet this standard.[20]

Section 11(d) of the Charter also implies salary protections for provincial court judges. This became clear in litigation arising out of government salary rollbacks in the early 1990s. As part of their effort to put an end to deficit spending, several governments during this period imposed wage rollbacks for all public-sector employees, including judges. Angry judges claimed that such salary cuts threatened their independence and thus undermined their status as "independent and impartial" tribunals under section 11(d) of the Charter. In 1997 the Supreme Court ruled that provinces could indeed freeze or reduce judicial salaries but that they had to establish **judicial compensation commissions (JCCs)** to review any proposed changes.

DOSSIER 8.4 JUDICIAL SALARY DISPUTES

Alberta judges should resist the temptation to take their pay dispute with the province into their courtrooms.

Lawyers in Calgary are warning of a possible widespread revolt by the province's 107 judges as a result of the government's decision to award them an 8.8 percent salary increase. [P]rovincial court Judge John James [has] adjourned his court cases citing concerns that the province's position undermined judicial independence....

When the province attempted to roll back judges' salaries in 1994, as part of a wider restructuring of public-service wages, the judges appealed to the Supreme Court, which ruled that provincial governments could not arbitrarily reduce judges' salaries without violating judicial independence. It ordered the province to establish an independent body to oversee salary adjustments.

The commission, made up of three lawyers, recommended ... a two-part pay increase of 33 percent, which would make Alberta judges the highest paid in Canada.

While the tribunal convincingly argued the need for a raise, it did not, in our view, make a case for paying Alberta judges more than their colleagues in every other province.

The recommendation for a 33 percent hike clearly backed the province into a corner. It had been ordered to leave salary matters to an independent body, but how could it justify such rich remuneration to a public that had given it a mandate for fiscal restraint?

It had little choice, we believe, but to opt for a lower figure.

Unfortunately, Justice Minister Jon Havelock then muddied the waters by including in the order-in-council the implication that one of the reasons judges weren't getting more was because they "did not shoulder a share of the (1994) cuts."

Judge James, among others, read this as evidence the province was "punishing" judges for their Supreme Court appeal and indicating the absence of the proper arm's-length relationship between the two bodies....

Source: Reprinted with permission from "Out of order," an editorial in the *Calgary Herald*, August 28, 1998, A18.

Furthermore, a government that ignored the recommendations of a JCC would have to justify its actions in court.[21]

Why do we consider judicial independence important enough to elevate it to constitutional status? The reason has to do with the traditional perception of courts as non-political adjudicative institutions. Judicial independence is essential to the adjudicative function of courts, for it is the foundation of impartiality, the necessary condition of any publicly legitimate system of dispute resolution. If, in cases that arouse public interest and passion, judicial decisions could be influenced by political pressure through the manipulation of tenure or salary, both the perception and the reality of impartiality would be eroded. So important is this principle that, in addition to the entrenched guarantees of tenure and salary, we have evolved a constitutional convention that politicians refrain from discussing with judges the merits of cases before them. Cabinet ministers who violate this convention do so at the risk of their ministerial careers. The impartiality flowing from judicial independence is especially significant when the government itself is one of the parties in a courtroom battle, as when the state prosecutes someone for allegedly committing a crime, or when someone challenges the constitutionality of state action.

Judicial independence from the realm of political controversy has two sides. Not only must public figures refrain from meddling in judicial affairs but judges must resist speaking out on public issues. This tradition of "judicial silence" reflects the need for judges to appear impartial to litigants who come before them. A judge who takes a public stand on a controversial law, for example, may subsequently seem biased in a case involving the interpretation or the constitutionality of that law. Thus, when Justice Thomas Berger of the B.C. Supreme Court in 1981 criticized parts of the proposed Charter of Rights and Freedoms, he was roundly criticized by the Canadian Judicial Council and ultimately felt compelled to resign.[22] Although the tradition of judicial silence on public matters is long-standing and powerful, Chief Justice Antonio Lamer of the Supreme Court of Canada recently wondered whether it should be loosened enough to permit judges to reply to criticisms of the courts and their role (see Dossier 8.5).

It is worth reflecting on the fact that the lack of political accountability we strive so hard to achieve for judges is seen as a much less desirable trait in senators. In a democratic age, election seems to be the necessary condition of political legitimacy, which is why Canada's appointed Senate—on paper, virtually the equal of the House of Commons—is (with the exceptions discussed in Chapter 5) largely a toothless tiger. That our judges have not suffered the decline in public legitimacy that has befallen senators indicates the persistence of the traditional view that the central judicial activity—the adjudication of disputes—is decisively non-political.

In the United States, by contrast, where the political nature of judging has been more widely acknowledged, some judges are elected. Even in the U.S., however, the pull of the adjudicative perspective remains strong. Only state court judges in some states are elected; judges of the higher federal courts, including the Supreme Court, are appointed. Even when judges are elected, moreover, the process in most

DOSSIER 8.5 SHOULD JUDGES DEFEND THEMSELVES?

Since 1982, judges as a whole have been subject to increasing criticism, especially of course in respect of controversial decisions made under the Charter. By no means would I ever suggest that this kind of criticism should be stifled. Of course not. It is valuable and healthy to our democracy.... [Nevertheless] I wonder whether judges, or maybe through their Chief Justices, should be rolling up the sleeves of their judicial robes and involving themselves in these public discussions more directly.

... I am sure it seems peculiar to the public that the judges simply make their decisions and then remain mute while the rest of society reacts to them. The public hardly ever hears any reaction from the judges. From the judges' point of view, it is certainly frustrating sometimes to stand by when there are errors made, whether innocent or deliberate, by those who write about or comment on judicial decisions....

... But our tradition, and it is a strong one, is one of silence on such matters. I have always thought that this was proper—that the judiciary should keep silent lest it sacrifices its independence or, at least, the perception of impartiality.

But lately I have begun to wonder whether that tradition of silence continues to be appropriate....

It used to be the case that, while judges themselves were silent, the judicial perspective was supplied by the law officers of the Crown and by the bar. Accordingly, the tradition of judicial silence was paired with an equally strong tradition of support from other quarters.... It appears to me, however, that the latter tradition of support for the judiciary has faded somewhat, which leads me to wonder whether the tradition of judicial silence itself should be revisited. I do not blame anyone for this state of affairs. It strikes me that it be another inevitable by-product of the Charter. Perhaps as judicial decisions have become more entwined with political issues, the more difficult it has become for public figures and lawyers themselves to speak up. There is political risk in their doing so. But the consequence is that the judiciary has no voice and no champion. In turn, public understanding of such fundamental concepts as judicial review under the Constitution and judicial independence is, I fear, fast eroding.

I admit that I do not have a clear solution to offer. I would be certainly reluctant to see judges enter the political fray. There would be enormous risks in this. On the other hand, I worry that there is also a risk in having judges hold their tongues. Perhaps there is some other solution.

Source: Reprinted from "Remarks of the Right Honourable Antonio Lamer, P.C., to the Canadian Bar Association," August 23, 1998, St. John's.

cases is best described as a "confirmation" election. That is, the state governor appoints a judge from a short list generated by a nonpartisan nominating commission, and, after the judge has served a probationary year, the electorate is given the opportunity to confirm or reject the appointment.[23]

JUDICIAL POLICYMAKING

If adjudication is one side of the judicial coin, policymaking is the other. Although policymaking is an inevitable byproduct of much adjudication, its significance can be enhanced or intensified by several contextual factors, including the level of court making the decision, the kind of case being decided, the kind of law at issue, and the attitudes of judges. We shall look first at judicial policymaking in general and then at each of these contextual intensifiers.

The Inevitability of Judicial Policymaking

Despite its commonsense attractiveness, the traditional separation of adjudication from the political realm of policymaking has never been an entirely adequate account of reality. In the early decades of this century, a school of thought known as **legal realism** showed that the courts cannot avoid some share in policymaking. Judges cannot avoid policymaking because the law they apply to settle a dispute is often unclear, so they have to choose between competing interpretations. Such choices in effect "make" new law. There are cases, it is true, in which the law seems quite clear, and the only judicial task is to decide between competing versions of the facts. Did Harry really rob the store? Does his alibi stand up? In many cases, however, the dispute (or at least a significant component of it) is generated not by conflicting accounts of the facts but by conflicting interpretations of an ambiguous law. The facts clearly show that the heroin found in Dick's suitcase was planted there by someone else without Dick's knowledge. Is the law prohibiting possession of this narcotic an "absolute liability" law, making Dick guilty regardless of how the heroin came to be among his possessions? Or does Dick get off because the law requires a showing of *mens rea* (guilty mind)? The law is unclear, and, such a case never having arisen before, the judge must choose, thereby setting policy not only for the case at hand but also, because of ***stare decisis*** (the rule of **precedent**), for similar cases in the future.[24] The particular case yields a general rule of law.

To some extent, interpretive judicial lawmaking is inevitable. Unlike rule by decree, which applies only to particular situations, the "rule of law" uses abstract and general language to govern entire classes of situations. But language is notoriously slippery and indeterminate. Dossier 8.6 provides a humorous account of just how much interpretive room can be found in what might appear to be a perfectly clear law.

The hypothetical case of *Regina v. Ojibway* described in Dossier 8.6 is, of course, a caricature, which is to say it exaggerates for comic effect. But like all caricatures it brings into the foreground important aspects of reality. For a more realistic example of interpretive ambiguity, consider a bylaw prohibiting vehicles in the park. This law obviously applies to a pickup truck, but what about tricycles, or bicycles, or motor scooters? Whom does one arrest for breaking a bylaw prohibiting sleeping in the railway station? The traveller who nodded off while waiting for a late train or the

DOSSIER 8.6 REGINA V. OJIBWAY

Blue, J.: This is an appeal by the Crown by way of a stated case from a decision of the magistrate acquitting the accused of a charge under the Small Birds Act, R.S.O., 1960, c. 724, s. 2. The facts are not in dispute. Fred Ojibway, an Indian, was riding his pony through Queen's Park on January 2, 1965. Being impoverished, and having been forced to pledge his saddle, he substituted a downy pillow in lieu of the said saddle. On this particular day, the accused's misfortune was further heightened by the circumstance of his pony breaking its right foreleg. In accord with current Indian custom, the accused then shot the pony to relieve it of its awkwardness.

The accused was then charged with having breached the Small Birds Act, section 2 of which states: "Anyone maiming, injuring or killing small birds is guilty of an offence and subject to a fine not in excess of two hundred dollars."

The learned magistrate acquitted the accused, holding, in fact, that he had killed his horse and not a small bird. With respect, I cannot agree. In light of the definition section, my course is quite clear. Section 1 defines "bird" as "a two-legged animal covered with feathers." There can be no doubt that this case is covered by this section.

Counsel for the accused made several ingenious arguments to which, in fairness, I must address myself. He submitted that the evidence of the expert clearly concluded that the animal in question was a pony and not a bird, but this is not the issue. We are not interested in whether the animal in question is a bird or not in fact, but whether it is one in law. Statutory interpretation has forced many a horse to eat birdseed for the rest of its life.

Counsel also contended that the neighing noise emitted by the animal could not possibly be produced by a bird. With respect, the sounds emitted by an animal are irrelevant to its nature, for a bird is no less a bird because it is silent.

Counsel for the accused also argued that since there was evidence to show the accused had ridden the animal, this pointed to the fact that it could not be a bird but was actually a pony. Obviously, this avoids the issue. This issue is not whether the animal was ridden or not, but whether it was shot or not, for to ride a pony or a bird is of no offence at all. I believe that counsel now sees his mistake.

Counsel contends that the iron shoes found on the animal decisively disqualified it from being a bird. I must inform counsel, however, that how an animal dresses is of no concern to this court.

Counsel relied on the decision in *Re Chicadee,* where he contends that in similar circumstances the accused was acquitted. However, this is a horse of a different colour. A close reading of the case indicates that the animal in question there was not a small bird, but, in fact, a midget of a much larger species. Therefore, that case is inapplicable to our facts.

Counsel finally submits that the word "small" in the title Small Birds Act refers not to "Birds" but to "Act," making it The Small Act relating to Birds. With respect, counsel did not do his homework very well, for the Large Birds Act, R.S.O., 1960, c. 725, is just as small. If pressed, I need only refer to the Small Loans Act, R.S.O., 1960, c. 727, which is twice as large as the Large Birds Act.

It remains, then, to state my reason for judgment, which simply is as follows. Different things may take on the same meaning for different purposes. For the purpose of the Small Birds Act, all two-legged, feather-covered animals are birds. This, of course, does not imply that only two-legged animals qualify, for the legislative intent is to make two legs merely the minimum requirement. The statute therefore contemplated multi-legged animals with feathers as well. Counsel submits that, having regard to the purpose of the statute, only small animals "naturally covered" with feathers could have been contemplated. However, had this been the intention of the legislature, I am certain that the phrase "naturally covered" would have been expressly inserted just as "Long" was inserted in the Longshoreman's Act.

Therefore, a horse with feathers on its back must be deemed for the purposes of this Act to be a bird, and a *fortiori,* a pony with feathers on its back is a small bird.

Counsel posed the following rhetorical question: If the pillow had been removed prior to the shooting, would the animal still be a bird? To this, let me answer rhetorically: Is a bird any less of a bird without its feathers?

Appeal allowed.

Source: Reprinted from *Criminal Law Quarterly* 8 (1965), 137. Reproduced with the permission of Hart Pomerantz, Steve Breslin, and Canada Law Book Inc., publisher, 240 Edward Street, Aurora, Ontario L4G 3S9.

still-conscious drunk who is settling in on the bench? Obviously these laws do not apply to everything that might fall within the dictionary meanings of "vehicle" or "sleep." But where to draw the line? Because legislators cannot anticipate all the circumstances to which their laws might apply, our system leaves it to judges to fill in the blanks (or "interstices") when unanticipated situations generate a courtroom dispute. In short, **interstitial lawmaking** is an inevitable component of much adjudication. The political task of lawmaking cannot be completely separated from the judicial task of settling disputes arising under the law.

Such judicial lawmaking does not end with the establishment of a judicial precedent. The interstitial law judges make usually generates new interpretive ambiguities even as it settles old ones. Because judicial decisions are precedents, they too involve rules designed to govern like cases in the future. Indeed, another way of stating the rule of *stare decisis* is to say that "like cases must be treated alike." But of course no two real-life situations are ever entirely alike. Thus, the rule really means that cases alike in the relevant respects should be treated alike. Interpretive ambiguity, and hence the opportunity for new judicial policymaking, arises in determining what the relevant criteria are for judging two cases alike or different. A whimsical but revealing example is the interpretive debate about the precedent *Re Chicadee* in *Regina v. Ojibway* (Dossier 8.6).

Blue J.'s treatment of *Re Chicadee* is an example of **distinguishing cases** that seem alike. As one Alberta judge put it, "you can always distinguish [a case from an apparent precedent] if you want to."[25] Another judge spoke of working hard to "distinguish [a precedent] out of existence." [26] As part of distinguishing cases, judges can limit the scope of precedents by allocating part of the earlier case's reasoning to the category of ***obiter dicta.*** Traditionally, only that part of a court's reasoning that is strictly necessary to deciding the immediate factual dispute between the parties, known as the ***ratio decedendi,*** is binding precedent for subsequent cases. All other reasoning, though it may be related and interesting, is considered a judicial aside (an *obiter dictum*) and does not establish binding law. As one might expect, however, the line between *ratio* and *obiter* tends to be fuzzy, and judges can move it around to bring a current case within or exclude it from the ambit of an apparent precedent. Sometimes judges dispense with any pretense at distinguishing cases, and escape the constraints of a precedent simply by ignoring it. Finally, the Supreme Court of Canada has explicitly said that it is not bound by its own precedents, and is free to overrule them in subsequent cases; it does so rarely, however, preferring to rely on the device of distinguishing cases. [27] In sum, precedent, though important, is not an ironclad constraint on judicial discretion, and thus on judicial policymaking.

Judicial Power and Judicial Hierarchy

Although both adjudication and policymaking occur in all courts, the balance between them differs with the level of court. As one moves up the judicial hierarchy, from trial to appellate courts, policymaking becomes more prominent and adjudication less so.[28]

At trial, the case is before the court primarily because the dispute between the litigants must be resolved. Does the accused go free or go to jail, and, if the latter, for how long? Which of two divorcing parents gets custody of the children, or is custody to be shared? Has there been a breach of contract, and, if so, what is the remedy? These are the kinds of day-to-day conflicts that trial judges must decide. The focus is often on the facts of the immediate situation: Was the gun fired in anger or with cool deliberation, or was it fired in self-defence? Of course, once the facts are determined, the law must be applied to them, and this often involves interpretive choice. At trial, however, interpretive judicial lawmaking is no more than the inescapable and subordinate corollary of the court's primary task: to resolve the dispute before it.

Once the case moves on to appeal, the lawmaking dimension of judicial decision making becomes more prominent. From an adjudicative perspective, appeal courts secure fairness for litigants. As we understand the adjudicative process today, we are entitled not only to our "day in court" but also to our day in a higher court that can "correct injustices or errors that may have occurred in the lower court."[29] In correcting errors, however, an appeal court does not retry the entire case before it. It generally accepts the factual determinations of the trial court and focuses its attention on whether the lower court correctly interpreted the relevant law. In appellate courts, in short, interpretive lawmaking moves from the background to the foreground of the judicial process.

The law made by an appellate court is further enhanced by the wider scope of its application. Strictly speaking, the decision of a lower trial court is binding precedent only for that court in its future decisions. It may have persuasive influence on other judges of the same rank, but they are not obliged to follow it. The judgment of an appellate court, by contrast, is binding on all lower courts within its jurisdiction.[30] Thus, the legal interpretations of the appeal court of any province become the law for the entire province.[31] The appeal courts of the provinces stand in relation to one another just as trial courts do. Being of equal rank, they are free to disagree with one another about the interpretation of the same or similar laws unless a higher court chooses to decide the issue.[32] For provincial appeal courts, the higher court is the Supreme Court of Canada. Sitting atop the judicial hierarchy, the Supreme Court, through its legal interpretations, makes law for the entire country.[33] It is the supreme judicial policymaker.

The judicial hierarchy, in other words, exists not simply to provide an avenue of appeal for disgruntled litigants in the immediate case. It also exists to bring uniformity to the application of the law, ensuring that the same law is not applied in dramatically different ways by courts throughout the relevant jurisdiction—in other words, that the law is the same for all to whom it applies. This is another reason why the immediate case loses its prominence, in a sense becoming the vehicle through which an important question of legal policy is placed before the court. At trial, interpretive lawmaking is no more than the side effect of adjudication; at appeal, adjudication is little more than the background for interpretive lawmaking.

The predominance of legal policymaking over adjudication is especially marked at the level of the Supreme Court, which generally chooses the cases it wishes to decide, selecting only those that raise substantial issues of legal policy. The court's freedom to control its own docket in this way clearly indicates that policymaking, not adjudication, is its primary function. From the adjudicative perspective, which emphasizes error-correcting fairness to the litigants, the freedom to appeal is a fundamental right. And, indeed, our system grants the right to at least one appeal in the vast majority of cases. Prior to 1975 this adjudicative perspective was also applied to the Supreme Court. Of course, not everyone could be given the right to yet another appeal; such an unrestricted right would swamp any national court of reasonable size. But the principle that governed the rationing of the court's scarce resources, especially in civil-law cases (see Dossier 8.7), still focused on the interests of the litigants. The standard in civil suits was the amount of money at stake. If not everyone could be allowed to appeal, certainly those who had a bigger monetary stake in the outcome should be given that right. In particular, there was a right to appeal to the Supreme Court in any case involving more than $10,000. Thus, "[t]he criterion which determined most of the cases [the Supreme Court] heard was the amount of money in dispute, not the importance of the legal questions at issue."[34] This order of priorities was reversed in 1975, when an amendment to the Supreme Court Act abolished the

DOSSIER 8.7 DIVISIONS OF LAW

The term "common law" arose early in this chapter, and the term **civil law** has come up in our discussion of the abolition of the right to appeal to the Supreme Court in civil-law cases involving more than $10,000. These terms are ambiguous and are used in ways that differ with the context, as part of a more comprehensive classification of laws and legal systems. It is worth pausing to unravel some of the complexities.

At the most general level, common law is used in contradistinction to civil law to differentiate entire legal systems. Civil-law systems include the countries of continental Europe, Scotland, Louisiana, and Quebec. Common-law jurisdictions include the remaining Canadian provinces and American states, England, Australia, and New Zealand. Civil-law systems are based on Roman law and usually feature a comprehensive civil code. The common-law jurisdictions derive from the English tradition of emphasizing judicial decisions. Although statutory law has displaced judicial decisions as the primary source of law in most common-law jurisdictions, these jurisdictions do not have a comprehensive code.

In addition to designating a kind of legal system, the term "common law" has a second and more particular meaning: as we saw at the outset of this chapter, it is also used within common-law jurisdictions to distinguish judge-made law from statutory law.

Civil law also has a more particular meaning. Within common-law systems, it is often used as a synonym for **private law,** and it is in this sense that we used it in speaking of the right to appeal to the Supreme Court in civil-law suits involving more than $10,000. Private law applies to disputes between individuals, and is distinguished from **public law,** which concerns disputes between individuals and the organized community, and between different governments in a federal system. Public law comprises constitutional law, criminal law, and administrative law. Private law deals with quarrels between individuals about contracts, property, and torts (breaches of duties of care owed to others, such as repairing a dangerously damaged stairway in one's home).

In common-law legal systems, judge-made common law has been largely displaced by statutes in the public-law realm. In such systems, judge-made common law remains more significant in the private realm—or, as one might say more confusingly, common law remains prominent in the civil-law realm.

$10,000 rule and directed the Supreme Court to choose most of its own cases according to the criterion of "public importance."[35] At the heart of this amendment lay the conviction that the adjudicative function of error correction was sufficiently served by intermediate courts of appeal and that the Supreme Court should concentrate on the lawmaking side of its function, taking cases not because of their importance to private litigants but because of the public importance of the legal issue involved. While the litigant is often concerned with the legal issue only as a means to winning a dispute, the Supreme Court is concerned with the litigants (whose dispute, after all, has been addressed by at least two courts) only as a means to the legal issue.

Some constraints on the Supreme Court's discretion to control its own docket remain. For example, criminal-law cases can still be appealed as a matter of right when there is a dissenting legal interpretation in a provincial court of appeal.[36] Nevertheless, the abolition of the monetary criterion in civil suits removed the most important constraint. Peter Russell points out that in the early 1970s, before the $10,000 rule was abolished, "only 15 percent of the Court's cases reached the Court through the Court's granting of leave." By contrast, a decade later, after the rule had been repealed, "roughly three-quarters of the Court's cases came by this route."[37] The Supreme Court's role as a law-developing body, rather than an error-correcting court in the adjudicative sense, is thus well established.

The Canadian Supreme Court can exercise its lawmaking function over a more extensive range than can the comparable courts of other federal states. In such federations as the United States, Switzerland, and Germany, the national court of appeal ensures the uniform application of federal and constitutional law but is not the final court of appeal for validly enacted laws of the federal subunits. The authoritative interpretation of sub-national laws is left to the highest court of the subunits; only if the constitutionality of the law or its interpretation is called into question will the matter end up in the national high court. In Canada, by contrast, the Supreme Court is the final court of appeal for provincial as well as federal and constitutional law. If federalism is the jurisdictional division of lawmaking authority, and if judicial interpretation is a kind of lawmaking, this interpretive authority of the national high court in matters of provincial law is clearly a departure from the federal principle. In other federal regimes, judicial as well as legislative lawmakers at the local level are free to "legislate" differently within their jurisdiction. In other words, not only can local laws differ in their surface wording, but similarly worded laws might come to differ because of different interpretations. In Canada, similarly worded provincial laws receive a uniform interpretation whenever they are considered by the Supreme Court. Ottawa's ability to make the Supreme Court the final court of appeal for provincial as well as for federal and constitutional law was confirmed by the JCPC in 1947.[38] Given the JCPC's evident concern with protecting provincial lawmaking power from centralized intrusion, this decision almost certainly reflects the traditional view that courts are not political, lawmaking bodies.[39]

The Supreme Court's tendency to unify the interpretation of provincial law in modern-day Canada should not be exaggerated, however. It is true that at an earlier period the Court exercised considerable influence over provincial law. Indeed, "[f]rom its foundation in 1875 until well into the modern period, cases involving provincial laws were the predominant element in [the Court's] caseload."[40] So important were these cases, moreover, that they produced greater legal uniformity within the provincial area of "property and civil rights" than was achieved under section 94 of the constitution "through legislative co-operation between the common law provinces and the federal government."[41] In recent decades, however, and especially since it gained control of its own docket in 1975, the court has increasingly become a public-law court, steering clear of the provincially dominated private-law sphere.[42] Moreover, the court has tended to focus on federal public law (criminal and administrative) and constitutional law. The court still interprets provincial laws, but more rarely, and usually only in cases that concern more than one province. Thus, in Russell's words, "without any formal constitutional change, provincial courts of appeal in Canada increasingly assume the role of their counterparts in the United States as final courts of appeal on questions of provincial law."[43] The Supreme Court continues to exercise a unifying influence on provincial law, but it does so now less through simple interpretation of such law and more through its "application of the norms contained in the ... Charter of Rights to the activities of provincial governments."[44] Within the limits of the constitution, however, provincial courts of appeal now exercise substantial power to shape the law of their own jurisdictions.

Indeed, provincial courts of appeal exercise considerable influence even on the interpretation of federal and constitutional law. Outside the area of federal administrative law, which is the preserve of the Federal Court, most cases arising under federal and constitutional law work their way through the section 96 courts to

DOSSIER 8.8 INTEGRATED VERSUS DUAL COURT SYSTEMS

The Supreme Court of Canada's appellate authority over provincial as well as federal and constitutional law is a leading feature of Canada's **integrated court system,** just as the limitation of high-court jurisdiction to national and constitutional law in other federal systems is a feature of their **dual court systems.** The integration of the Canadian court system is also evident in the fact that superior-trial courts are **courts of general jurisdiction,** which can try and hear appeals on cases arising under both federal and provincial law. In light of this, the cooperative federalism involved in establishing and staffing these courts seems particularly appropriate.

In addition, we have noted that most criminal cases in Canada, which clearly involve federal law, are tried by the entirely provincial courts. In the dual court systems of other federations, the federal and local courts are to a greater extent separately responsible for their own legal systems. In allowing Ottawa to establish not only a general court of appeal for Canada but also "any additional courts for the better administration of the laws of Canada," section 101 of the 1867 Constitution Act permits some movement toward a dual court system. That is, it allows Ottawa to remove areas of federal law from the jurisdiction of the section 96 courts of general jurisdiction and give them to wholly federal courts. The Federal Court of Canada's responsibility for federal administrative law is an example. However, there appear to be limits to how far the federal government can move in this direction (see Peter H. Russell, *The Judiciary in Canada,* 68–69).

the provincial courts of appeal. And most end there. Some go no further because the losing party does not appeal. Others do not proceed because the Supreme Court refuses to grant leave to appeal. After all, the top court has limited resources and can afford to hear only a small fraction of those who seek its services.

If intermediate courts of appeal disagree about an issue of federal law, of course, the Supreme Court is more likely to take a case that allows it to impose uniformity. But even this is not certain. For a variety of reasons,[45] the number of cases heard by the second-highest courts of appeal has risen severalfold in recent decades—quintupling between 1960 and 1980, for example[46]—while the number of cases heard by the Supreme Court has actually declined.[47] This means that the proportion of intermediate appeal cases that proceed to the Supreme Court has also declined. In 1987 Russell reported that only 1–2 percent of the cases decided by the provincial and federal courts of appeal are heard by the Supreme Court.[48] He speculated that the "demands on the Supreme Court's resources may become so heavy" that the court will no longer be able to impose uniform interpretations even in matters of federal law, with the result "that the Criminal Code and other federal statutes [may] come to mean very different things in different parts of the country."[49] Thus, while the Supreme Court is the ultimate legal policymaker in theory, the policymaking significance of the second-highest appeal courts will often play that role in practice. And even in cases that do go to the Supreme Court, intermediate appellate courts play an important role in shaping the issues and arguments to be addressed there.

Sometimes circumstances enable even a trial court to set long-term and controversial policy for the country as a whole. For example, in 1984 a Court of Queen's Bench judge in Calgary struck down a federal law limiting the amount that could be spent on election advertising by anyone other than political parties.[50] This law, the court determined, violated the Charter's guarantee of freedom of expression. The timing of this decision did not permit an appeal before the 1984 federal election, and, in order to ensure that the same rules applied throughout the country, the expenditure limitations were not enforced elsewhere. Thus, the decision of a single trial judge set election-spending policy for the entire country. Non-party individuals or groups were free to spend as much as they liked on election advertising not only during the 1984 election but also during the 1988 "free trade" election, when pro–free trade business groups, provincial governments, and labour unions spent millions of dollars to influence opinion.[51]

Not until 1993 did the government enact a new law re-imposing spending limits, only to have that law invalidated by another Calgary Queen's Bench judge in June of that year.[52] This decision too came with an election in the offing, and once again it was decided not to enforce the law elsewhere. This time, however, Ottawa chose to appeal the decision, although it lost in the Alberta Court of Appeal and decided against a further appeal to the Supreme Court of Canada.[53] The 1997 election was thus also fought without any spending limits.

Reference Cases

The policymaking prominence of a judicial decision can be intensified not only by the level of court but also by the kind of case. **Reference cases** have special policy significance. Since reference cases are heard only by appellate courts, moreover, the intensifying effects of level of court and kind of case overlap.

Reference cases take the form of questions posed by governments to their highest courts of appeal in the absence of the kind of concrete dispute that generates adjudication. In 1875 the federal government gave itself the power to submit questions "on any matter whatsoever," and all of the provinces soon followed suit. References to provincial courts of appeal are one of the kinds of cases that may still be appealed as a matter of right to the Supreme Court. The Quebec secession reference discussed in Chapter 3 (and excerpted in Dossier 3.9) is the most dramatic recent reference case.

Although governments are free to pose any reference question they like, they often pose the kinds of legal questions that appeal courts face in ordinary litigation. The difference is that the resulting decisions are more obviously and directly policy decisions. One indication of this is that reference cases, unlike normal adjudication, need not turn on existing laws. Governments, unlike ordinary litigants, are free to pose reference questions about proposed laws that may not even be fully drafted.[54] In addition, while lawmaking in ordinary litigation becomes more prominent than adjudication as one moves up the appellate ladder, the adjudicative context is always present. The case begins as a concrete dispute, and even as the original litigants fade into the background during the appeal process, the case is still in some sense theirs. What started at trial as the case of *The Queen v. Smith* remains *The Queen v. Smith* when it reaches the Supreme Court, though that court is more concerned with setting general legal policy than with resolving the immediate dispute. After all, though policymaking may now assume centre stage, the result will also resolve the original dispute. In form at least, judicial policymaking in such cases can still be said to be a corollary of adjudication. In reference cases, by contrast, the normal adjudicative context falls away altogether and policymaking becomes the sole focus.

Reference cases bring the tension between the lawmaking and adjudicative dimensions of judicial decision making into sharper relief than do other cases. Because they depart so radically from adjudication, it is often argued that reference questions may not legitimately be addressed to the judiciary. Indeed, in the United States and Australia the posing of non-adjudicative reference questions to the judiciary is unconstitutional, because it compromises the essential nature of the judiciary as an adjudicative institution. In the United States, article 3 of the constitution extends the judicial power only to "cases and controversies," a phrase understood to encompass only traditional adjudicative disputes. Similar arguments were made in Canada in the early 1900s, and a challenge to the constitutionality of reference cases reached the JCPC in 1912. The imperial court accepted the claim that reference cases were not really judicial in nature, but, in the absence of an American-style "case and controversy" limitation, saw nothing in the Canadian constitution that prevented governments from adding such non-judicial tasks to the judicial workload.[55] The Supreme Court of Canada took the same position in the 1998 Quebec secession reference.

Both the JCPC and the Supreme Court tried to maintain some distance between reference cases and normal adjudicative litigation by treating the former as generating only legal advice, not binding law. This is why the decisions in reference cases are sometimes called **advisory opinions.** Posing a reference question to a court, our judges have said, is akin to posing the same legal question to the government's own legal advisers.

In the JCPC's view, advisory opinions rendered by judges should be seen as having "no more effect" than similar opinions given by non-judicial legal advisers.[56] As substitute legal advisers, moreover, judges were not bound by their own advice when the same issue comes before them in the course of normal litigation. Just as they are free to ignore the opinions of the government's non-judicial legal advisers in deciding the cases that come before them, so they were free to ignore their own advisory opinions. In short, reference cases were not to be binding precedents. This rather legalistic distinction, however, has never withstood the test of human nature. Why would governments ask judges rather than their own legal advisers if they did not think they were getting a more authoritative and certain opinion—i.e., an opinion that would settle the issue? And why would one expect judges to be more resistant than anyone else to the embarrassments of retreating from their public pronouncements? As common sense leads us to expect, judicial decisions in reference cases have always been given as much precedential weight as decisions arising out of ordinary litigation.

Judicial Power and Constitutional Law

The kind of law at issue in a case can also intensify the policy significance of the decision. Constitutional cases, whether they come by way of references or ordinary litigation, are particularly important in this respect. To be sure, one must reject what Russell calls the "worst kind of legal formalism," namely, the view that courts are "powerful only when they are interpreting a constitution."[57] As we have seen, judicial interpretation shapes policy in important ways at all levels of law. Nevertheless, judicial policymaking at the constitutional level is set apart by special characteristics that magnify its policy impact. This is all the more true of judicial policymaking under one of the newest components of Canada's constitutional law, the Charter of Rights and Freedoms.

Judicial policymaking in the name of constitutional law is, in principle, more powerful than policymaking under other vague laws. A legislature that does not like what judges have done with one of its laws can, in theory, simply rewrite the law.

Nothing more than an ordinary legislative majority is required. Of course, what is possible in theory is not always easy in practice. The new law judges make tends quickly to become an established legal status quo, and like any status quo it attracts vested interests to defend it, making it more difficult to dislodge than it was to implement in the first place. Judicial implementation of new law, after all, requires only the decision of a judge (or panel of appeal judges) in a single, narrowly focused case. Reversal by the legislature often requires more widespread political mobilization.[58] Still, legislative reversal of judicial interpretations of ordinary laws is likely to be easier than reversal of constitutional interpretation through the extraordinarily difficult process of constitutional amendment.

In the case of section 2 and sections 7–15 of the Charter, of course, legislative reversal of judicial decisions is, in theory, no more difficult than the reversal of decisions turning on ordinary legislation. Legislation invalidated under these sections of the Charter can, as we have seen, be reenacted with a section 33 "notwithstanding clause," and this can be done by a normal legislative majority. Nevertheless, section 33 lacks public legitimacy, and there have been calls for its repeal. Moreover, outside Quebec it has been used only once (see Dossier 2.5). As Christopher Manfredi puts it, "Whether by explicit amendment or through the emergence of a new constitutional convention, there is a real possibility that section 33 will become a non-operative part of the Charter."[59] In practice, then, judicial decisions under even those sections of the Charter subject to section 33 are as difficult to reverse as decisions under any other part of the entrenched constitution.

Constitutional law is a particularly fertile source of discretionary judicial power because, as we noted in Chapter 2, it is (for good reason) virtually always phrased in broad, general, and ambiguous language. Newer constitutional documents, like the Canadian Charter of Rights and Freedoms, are especially significant in this regard because they tend to provide the most open-ended scope to judicial policymaking. The "newness" of the Charter needs to be put in perspective, however. Many of the rights and freedoms protected by the Charter are in fact not new to our legal system. What the Charter mostly does is elevate to formal constitutional status principles—such as freedom of religion or speech, the right against self-incrimination, or the right to be presumed innocent until proven guilty—that were already established in our tradition. Legally, they were embedded in a variety of statutes, common-law precedents, and conventional understandings. There was a good deal of ambiguity and indeterminacy in this older legal structure as well, and thus considerable room for ongoing, incremental interpretive discretion. So how has constitutional entrenchment of the same principles increased interpretive discretion?

One answer is that, for all the remaining indeterminacy, the older body of law relating to rights and freedoms had already answered many important questions that the Charter then reopened. Rights can be defined more or less broadly, extending to more or fewer interests and activities. Does the right to freedom of expression extend to libel or pornography, for example? Does religious freedom, which obviously prohibits criminalizing membership in a mainstream religion, also prohibit the criminalization of activities that may be promoted by a religion, such as polygamy or the use in religious ceremonies of illegal drugs? In addition to these definitional questions, there are circumstances when interests or activities clearly covered by a right must be limited because of countervailing considerations. In section 1, the Charter itself recognizes that the rights and freedoms it protects are subject to "such reasonable limits, prescribed by law, as are demonstrably justifiable in a free and democratic society." The existing legal system had already settled many questions about the definition of rights and their proper boundaries. Whereas courts were previously constrained to some extent by established legal determinations of these matters—whether in the form of legislative provisions or their own precedents—the Charter allows them to address many legal questions afresh. By reopening previously settled questions, it increases indeterminacy and hence judicial power.

Consider the right against self-incrimination. This right, now protected by sections 11(c) and 13 of the Charter, is not new to our legal tradition. Among other things, this well-established right has always meant that a person accused of a crime did not have to take the stand in his or her own defence. It was up to the prosecution to prove guilt beyond a reasonable doubt without help from the accused. On the other hand, the accused always had the option to testify if that seemed a prudent strategy. In doing so, however, the accused accepted the risk of being caught in self-incriminating statements under cross-examination. What happens if an accused who has incriminated himself or herself in this way gets a new trial because the judge made technical mistakes while directing the jury about the meaning of the law? If the accused, having learned from previous mistakes, chooses not to testify at the second trial, should the prosecution be entitled to read the first-trial testimony into evidence? Prior to the Charter, it had been established that the prosecution could introduce such prior testimony without infringing the right against self-incrimination. Section 13 of the Charter does not obviously alter this policy. It protects a witness against the use of self-incriminating testimony in "other proceedings," but it is hardly clear that a second trial of the same accused on the same charge comes within the meaning of "other proceedings." If Sally testifies against Jim at his trial, incriminating herself in the process, that testimony cannot subsequently be used against her at her own trial, which clearly falls within the category of "other proceedings." But if Jim incriminates himself at his own first trial, is his second trial on the same charge another proceeding or is it a further stage in the same proceeding? Section 13 raises this question, though it does not answer it in any obvious way. Simply by reopening a question that once was settled, however, it provides new scope for discretionary judicial policymaking. In fact, when this question came before the Supreme Court in *Dubois*,[60] the court used its discretion to change the established rule. Defining the second trial of the same accused on the same charge as another proceeding, the court ruled that henceforth the right against self-incrimination will prevent first-trial testimony from being introduced in the second trial. Using the indeterminate language of the Charter, the court made significant new policy not clearly established by the language of the Charter.

Judicial Activism versus Judicial Restraint

Changing the rules of the game, we have argued, shapes but does not determine behaviour. Although expanding the realm of ambiguous constitutional law—as Canada did in 1982—provides increased opportunity for dramatic exercises of judicial power, it does not require them. Whether judges make use of the opportunities such law affords them depends on their own attitudes—i.e., on their inclinations to be "activist" or "restrained." At the constitutional level, **judicial activism** refers to the judicial "readiness to veto the policies of other branches of government on constitutional grounds." **Judicial restraint,** by contrast, "connotes a judicial predisposition to find room within the constitution" for established legal traditions, and especially for "the policies of democratically accountable decision makers."[61] Activist judges can also square off against other branches in their interpretation of statutory and common law, just as restrained judges can defer to the interpretation of such law by the other branches. In this section, however, we focus on constitutional activism and restraint.

There are many examples of judicial restraint with respect to important constitutional provisions. In the United States, the Bill of Rights was in place for about 130 years before the Supreme Court began to use it in an activist fashion.[62] In Canada, the quasi-constitutional 1960 Bill of Rights was used only once during its first 22 years to invalidate a piece of federal legislation.[63]

On the other hand, there are well-known episodes of judicial activism in both countries. During the 1930s the United States Supreme Court and the Judicial Committee of the Privy Council used broadly phrased constitutional language to block the new forms of social welfare policy—such as maximum-hour and minimum-wage legislation—that emerged in response to the Great Depression in both Canada and the United States. (Such activism on behalf of economic conservatism is no longer in evidence in either country.) In the 1960s and early 1970s, while Canada's Supreme Court was exercising great restraint in its application of the Bill of Rights, the U.S. Supreme Court embarked on a dramatic period of **liberal activism.** Under the leadership of Chief Justice Earl Warren, it invalidated such policies as racial segregation,[64] school prayers,[65] and flag salutes;[66] required equally sized electoral constituencies;[67] and established a strict rule for the exclusion of constitutionally tainted (though reliable) evidence in criminal trials.[68] The momentum generated by the Warren court persisted into the early years of Warren Burger's tenure as chief justice. Although the Burger court generally displayed greater restraint, it nevertheless issued one of the most explosively activist decisions of our time, *Roe v. Wade* (1973),[69] which struck down the restrictions on abortion that prevailed in most states.

This liberal activism differed from the earlier **conservative activism** not only in political orientation but also in the kinds of orders courts were prepared to issue to the more obviously political branches of government. Hitherto it had been assumed that courts could use their interpretation of constitutional provisions only

DOSSIER 8.9 HOW TO READ A CASE CITATION

A	B	C	D	E	F	G
1. **The Queen v. Oakes**	[1986]	1	S.C.R.	103	at 110.	
2. **R. v. Oakes**	(1986)	26	D.L.R. (4th)	20,	27–29	(S.C.C.).
3. **Roe v. Wade**		410	U.S.	335,	340	(1973).

Column A. The name of the case (technically known as "Style of Cause"), set in italics. When the state is one of the parties in a Canadian case, it is often represented synonymously by the "The Queen" (example 1), "Regina" (the Latin for "Queen"), or simply "R" (short for Regina—example 2).

Column B. The year in which the case was decided or reported. In Canadian citations, it is placed after the style of cause. (For the American practice see point G, below.) Dates appearing in square brackets (as in example 1) refer to the year the decision was reported rather than to the actual date of decision. This format is used when the date is essential to finding the decision because the law report in which it appears (column C) is organized primarily by year. Dates appearing in round brackets (as in example 2) refer to the actual date of decision rather than the date of reporting; they are used when the reporting year is not essential to finding the case because the law report is organized primarily by volume.

Column C. The volume of the law report. In reports subdivided primarily by year, volumes are numbered consecutively through each year, with the next year's reports beginning again at volume 1. Other reports number volumes consecutively for many years.

Column D. The name of the law report in short form (usually just the initials). S.C.R. refers to Canada's Supreme Court Reports, D.L.R. to the Dominion Law Reports ("4th" refers to the fourth series of D.L.R. volumes, which began with a new volume 1 in 1984). Provincial reports are easily identified: O.R. (Ontario Reports), A.R. (Alberta Reports), etc. The initials "U.S." designate the United States Reports, the official reports of the American Supreme Court.

Column E. The page number at which the cited case begins.

Column F. The page number(s) of specifically cited material within the case report, separated from the decision's first page by either "at" (as in example 1) or a comma (as in the other two examples).

Column G. In American cases the date of decision is placed in round brackets at the end of the citation (example 3). In both Canada and the United States, concluding round brackets also serve to indicate the deciding court (example 2). This is not necessary when the law report itself is court specific (S.C.R. or U.S.) but is useful in reports that cover courts at several levels or across several jurisdictions (D.L.R.). In Canadian citations, identification of the court is the only function of the concluding round brackets; in American citations, both court identification (when necessary) and the year of decision are placed in these brackets.

negatively, to tell the other branches what they could not do, as opposed to what they must do. But during the modern period of liberal activism, the U.S. Supreme Court pioneered and established the practice of positive orders. For example, it not only told school boards that they must stop forcing students into segregated schools against their will but insisted they take steps to ensure integration or proportional racial balance in the schools. In practice this meant bussing students from predominantly black neighbourhoods to schools in white neighbourhoods, and vice versa.[70] Similarly, the courts

> *have laid down elaborate standards for food handling, hospital operations, recreation facilities, inmate employment and education, sanitation, and laundry, painting, lighting, plumbing and renovation in some prisons; they have ordered other prisons closed. Courts have established equally comprehensive programs of care and treatment for the mentally ill confined in hospitals. They have ordered the equalization of school expenditures on teachers' salaries, established hearing procedures for public school discipline cases, decided that bilingual education must be provided for Mexican-American children ... [etc.].*[71]

The addition of **positive activism** to the older tradition of **negative activism** has obviously enhanced the policymaking significance of judicial review.

When the Canadian Charter of Rights came into effect, in 1982, some observers speculated that the courts would continue with the posture of restraint they had adopted toward the 1960 Bill of Rights. This did not happen. On the whole the Supreme Court in its early jurisprudence welcomed the advent of the Charter as an opportunity for a new—and activist—departure. Even where the wording of the Charter and the Bill of Rights did not differ appreciably, the court attributed to Charter provisions meanings that were different from those it had attributed to the corresponding Bill of Rights provisions. Thus, while the federal Lord's Day Act did not infringe the guarantee of religious freedom in the Bill of Rights,[72] it was found to violate religious freedom under the Charter.[73] Similarly, though both the Bill of Rights and the Charter guarantee the right to counsel upon "detention" or "arrest," those asked by the police to provide a Breathalyzer sample did not enjoy this right under the Bill of Rights because the Supreme Court decided that demands did not amount to "detention";[74] in *Therens*, an early Charter case, the court changed its mind, bringing Breathalyzer demands within the definition of "detention," thereby giving everyone subject to such a demand the right to consult a lawyer before blowing.[75] In these and similar cases, the Supreme Court significantly altered established policy, though no relevant changes in legal language required such changes. Even where the Charter embodied new legal language, it often did not require the changes actually wrought by the court. Thus, the section 13 guarantee of the right against self-incrimination, though more expansive than the Bill of Rights protection, did not clearly settle the question of whether a second trial of the same accused on the same charge comes within the category of "other proceedings" or whether it is another stage of the same proceeding. It was possible to construe the section as preserving existing policy, but the court chose the interpretation that changed that policy.[76] The mere existence of the Charter obviously does not account for such judicial policy reform; it can be explained only by a greater judicial receptivity to the claims and attractions of judicial activism.

In addition to the foregoing examples, activist decisions by the Supreme Court invalidated a refugee determination process that had been lauded by the United Nations as one of the best among Western nations.[77] The additional "fair hearing" requirements imposed by the court cost taxpayers hundreds of millions of dollars and contributed to wild swings between unmanageable backlogs in refugee claims and general amnesties designed to clear these backlogs.[78] In the criminal justice area, the court has made it increasingly difficult for police to acquire admissible statement, lineup, and blood-sample evidence,[79] and has placed stringent limits on the power of police to enter homes without a judicial warrant.[80] In perhaps its most controversial criminal-law decision—*Morgentaler*[81]—the court in 1988 invalidated Canada's abortion law. In the volatile realm of language politics, the court has struck down Quebec laws limiting the right to be educated in English to those whose parents had had such an education in Quebec[82] and requiring French-only commercial signs[83] (although Quebec reinstated the latter law by resorting to the section 33 notwithstanding clause). Nor does the Supreme Court have a monopoly on judicial activism. In the lower courts we find decisions "striking down restrictions on pornography, voluntary school prayer, boys-only hockey leagues, discrimination against single-mothers and illegitimate children, homosexuals, and the poor."[84]

Not all activist judicial decisions have been of the liberal variety. There are also examples of conservative activism. The successful challenges to election spending limits by the National Citizens' Coalition are prominent examples. Similarly, the Reform Party persuaded a court to relax (if not completely to invalidate) restrictions on paid broadcast time for parties during federal elections.[85] As McCormick and Greene note, moreover, there have also been "many decisions that have benefited middle-class drinking drivers because police failed to inform them of their right to counsel before the breathalyzer test."[86] And feminists have been concerned by cases, brought by men, that strike down laws benefiting women.[87] Feminists have been particularly concerned with a series of cases in which the courts struck down "rape shield" laws that protect women from certain invasions of their privacy during rape trials.[88]

The courts have not limited themselves to the negative activism of striking down laws. The Supreme Court has required provinces to provide additional French-education services and facilities, indicating that positive activism is part of its arsenal. Other examples of positive activism include the already discussed rulings ordering B.C. to spend money on interpreters for the deaf and requiring governments to establish judicial compensation commissions. In *Schachter*,[89] the court went even further, indicating that in certain circumstances courts could do more than tell the government what it must do; they could actually undertake the positive action for the government. In particular, if the violation of the constitution lay in excluding some group from a legislative benefit provided to others, a court could read the neglected group into the statute's list of beneficiaries, in effect rewriting the act. Such **reading in** is how the Supreme Court, in *Vriend*, added "sexual orientation" to the list of prohibited grounds of discrimination in Alberta's Human Rights Act.[90]

The story is not one of unremitting activism, however; the Supreme Court has also handed down its share of restrained decisions. While the court struck down

Quebeckers march in downtown Montreal to demonstrate their support for the province's "sign law" after the Supreme Court ruled the law unconstitutional.

the federal Lord's Day Act, it upheld secular "day of rest" legislation at the provincial level.[91] Back-to-work legislation was declared compatible with the Charter because the "right to strike" was not deemed to be part of the "freedom of association" protected by section 2(d) of the Charter.[92] Although the Charter's language-rights provisions entitled one to speak either English or French in a New Brunswick court, the court found that these provisions did not protect the corresponding right to be directly understood by the judge (though the right to be understood in any language, most likely through an interpreter, was protected by fair-trial provisions found elsewhere in the Charter).[93] In *Rodriguez*, the court refused to establish a right to doctor-assisted suicide, leaving this controversial issue in the hands of the legislature.[94] In *Schachter*, the very decision that legitimated the practice of "reading in," the court did not engage in this practice. The last example points to an important difference between the bottom-line result of a case and the reasoning involved in reaching that result: the result in *Schachter* was clearly restrained, though the reasoning opened up new avenues of activism.[95]

There is obviously an evolving balance between judicial activism and restraint in any court. In the 1930s the highest courts of Canada and the United States engaged in a conservative activism on economic matters; since then they have been remarkably restrained on these issues. In the 1960s and early 1970s the U.S. Supreme Court engaged in the most dramatic period of liberal judicial activism the world has seen. Since then, especially under the current chief justiceship of William Rehnquist, it has leaned more in the direction of judicial restraint. From the enactment of the Canadian Bill of Rights to the advent of the Charter in 1982—during much of which time activism was rife in the U.S.—the Supreme Court of Canada's rights-and-freedoms jurisprudence was clearly situated at the restrained end of the continuum. More recently, as the U.S. court has demonstrated greater restraint, the Canadian court, armed with the new Charter, has increased its activism. Even in the short history of the Charter, however, ebbs and flows of activism are evident. Up to 1986, for example, 60 percent of Charter claims were upheld by the Supreme Court. Since then, the success rate has dropped to about 20 percent. This lower rate still represents greater activism than was exhibited by the pre-Charter court, but obviously some of the initial glow of Charter enthusiasm has worn off.[96] Institutionally, where a country's judiciary falls on the continuum between activism and restraint at any time clearly shapes the balance of power between the branches of government. The more activist the courts, the greater their influence on public policy.

INSTITUTIONAL CHANGE AND CONTESTATION

The adjudicative and policymaking roles of the courts have different, and often incompatible, institutional implications. The institutional structures and procedures appropriate to adjudication, in other words, may not always facilitate good policymaking. In recent decades, many of the courts' traditionally adjudicative institutional features have been reformed to accommodate their more openly acknowledged and increasingly prominent policymaking role. We have already discussed how reforms that allowed the Supreme Court to control its own docket reflected the policymaking perspective. The aforementioned decision by the Supreme Court to consider itself free to overrule its own precedents can be seen in the same light. After all, good policymaking implies the flexibility to adjust to changing circumstances and new insights. Related changes have occurred, or have been proposed, in rules and practices governing access to the courts, the kind of evidence judges may consider, the decision-making procedures of the higher courts, and the modes of selecting and training judges. We examine each of these below.

Institutional reforms to accommodate policymaking have not consistently won out over competing adjudicative institutional rules, however. After all, to the extent that the judiciary as a whole continues to perform both functions, as it clearly does, one would expect the adjudicative perspective to continue to exert its institutional claims. Thus, as we shall see, while the decision-making procedures of the Supreme Court increasingly reflect and accommodate its policymaking role, effective policymaking by the highest appeal courts in the provinces is hampered by continuing institutional pressure stemming from their role in the adjudicative process. Similarly, the process of judicial selection and training continues to be caught in the tension between adjudicative and policymaking principles.

The Rules of Access

The involvement of the courts in the political and policymaking process has been enhanced by changes—made by the courts themselves—in the rules governing access to their services. For example, there has been a significant loosening of the rules of **standing.** Virtually all institutions or rule systems have rules of standing that determine who can trigger the institution's activity and participate in that activity. In Parliament, for example, only elected members of the House of Commons have standing to ask questions during Question Period; those in the public gallery can only observe. In the case of the courts, rules of standing determine who is entitled to place a legal argument before a court. In the past, only someone embroiled in the kind of concrete dispute courts were designed to resolve had standing. And, of course, courts were not designed to resolve all disputes. They were not designed to resolve partisan disputes about what the law should be. Such "political" disputes were to be left to the political arena. As one judge put it, "If you want to give a speech, rent a hall. The court is there to apply the law, not to provide a soap box."[97] Thus, one could not ask a court to rule a censorship law unconstitutional simply as a concerned citizen who did not like such laws. Such an action would constitute an illegitimate transfer of ordinary political partisanship from the legislative realm into the courtroom. By contrast, the owner of a bookstore hauled into court for illegally selling obscene materials had standing to challenge the constitutionality of the law under which he was charged.[98]

Under this rule, Joe Borowski, Canada's famous antiabortion crusader, could never have launched his well-known courtroom battle on behalf of his cause. What stake, other than that of a concerned citizen, did Borowski have in a case in which constitutional arguments were raised against the permissive aspects of Canada's abortion law? The fetus obviously had a stake, and so might a father trying to save his unborn child from the mother's determination to abort. Joe Borowski was neither. In fact, he was no more than "Joe Public," who was politically opposed to the law and who under the old rules of standing would have been stopped at the courtroom door and told to take his arguments where they belonged: to the political realm of legislative politics. It is a measure of the liberalization of Canada's rules of standing that the Supreme Court's majority granted Borowski standing to launch his constitutional assault on Canada's abortion law.[99] In effect, the court permitted Borowski to trigger a legal

DOSSIER 8.10 A TRADITIONAL VIEW OF STANDING

I start with the proposition that, as a general rule, it is not open to a person, simply because he is a citizen and a taxpayer or is either the one or the other, to invoke the jurisdiction of a competent Court to obtain a ruling on the interpretation or application of legislation or on its validity, when that person is not either directly affected by the legislation or is not threatened by sanctions for an alleged violation of the legislation. Mere distaste has never been a ground upon which to seek the assistance of a Court. Unless the legislation itself provides for a challenge to its meaning or application or validity by any citizen or taxpayer, the prevailing policy is that a challenger must show some special interest in the operation of the legislation beyond the general interest that is common to all members of the relevant society. This is especially true of the criminal law. For example, however passionately a person may believe that it is wrong to provide for compulsory breathalyzer tests or wrong to make mere possession of marijuana an offence against the criminal law, the Courts are not open to such a believer, not himself or herself charged or even threatened with a charge, to seek a declaration against the enforcement of such criminal laws.

The rationale of this policy is based on the purpose served by Courts. They are dispute-resolving tribunals, established to determine contested rights or claims between or against persons or to determine their penal or criminal liability when charged with offences prosecuted by agents of the Crown. Courts do not normally deal with purely hypothetical matters where no concrete legal issues are involved, where there is no *lis* [lawsuit] that engages their processes or where they are asked to answer questions in the abstract merely to satisfy a person's curiosity or perhaps his or her obsessiveness with a perceived injustice in the existing law. Special legislative provisions for references to the Courts to answer particular questions (which may be of a hypothetical nature) give that authority to Governments alone and not to citizens or taxpayers.

Source: Chief Justice Bora Laskin dissenting in *Minister of Canada v. Borowski,* [1981] 2 S.C.R. 575.

"case" even though he was not involved in the kind of concrete controversy courts were designed to resolve. Chief Justice Bora Laskin's dissenting opinion in that case, which is excerpted in Dossier 8.10, reflects the more traditional approach to standing.

A related rule held that courts should not decide legal issues in cases that become **moot.** A case was moot, or no longer "live," when the concrete dispute underlying it no longer existed. For example, when Borowski, having cleared the standing hurdle, was finally able to place his arguments before the Supreme Court, his case had become moot because the law he was challenging had already been struck down by the court in the case of *R. v. Morgentaler.* Of course *Morgentaler* effectively established abortion on demand, an even more permissive situation than the one Borowski had challenged. Borowski thus had an even sharper quarrel with the absence of a law than he had with the former law. But the Supreme Court drew the line at the claim that opposition to the absence of a law could constitute a valid case. Without a law to challenge, Borowski was no longer embroiled in a valid legal dispute; his case had become moot.[100] In what seemed like an application of the traditional rule against deciding moot cases, the court refused to decide Borowski's. However, even as the court turned Borowski away, it claimed authority to decide moot cases whenever it seemed important to do so. And in fact the court had already done so on important occasions. In *Mercure,* for example, it rendered judgment in a challenge to English-only speeding tickets in Saskatchewan, even though the litigant, Father Mercure, had died—the classic example of mootness.[101] Similarly, in its first major Charter case the court addressed the question of whether a provincial law requiring Canadian citizenship as a condition of membership in the legal profession violated the Charter's section 6 mobility rights, even though the original litigant had in the meantime become a citizen and a member of the bar.[102]

These changes in the rules of standing and mootness indicate a transformation of the judiciary's self-understanding. The older, stricter rules institutionally reflected the traditional view of the courts as adjudicative, dispute-resolving bodies. Without a concrete dispute, they were not entitled to act. If such a dispute existed, it could perhaps be resolved only by choosing between rival interpretations of legal language, thereby making new law interstitially. But this lawmaking function of the courts was seen as the sometimes unavoidable corollary of their primary dispute-resolving function, not as a primary judicial function in its own right. Hence, without a concrete, live dispute before it, a court had no authority to issue interpretive pronouncements. The traditional rules of standing and mootness guaranteed the primacy of the judiciary's dispute-resolving function.

The more flexible rules prevalent today have evolved to accommodate a different order of priorities in judicial functions. No longer is interstitial constitutional lawmaking seen as corollary to dispute resolution; nowadays the judiciary (especially the Supreme Court) sees itself, and tends to be seen by others, as the oracle of the constitution, as the body charged with authoritatively settling major questions of constitutional interpretation. Setting constitutional policy is increasingly seen as the primary judicial function, especially of the higher appellate courts. To the extent that this is so, concrete disputes can no longer be the necessary condition of judicial action, as they were under the old rules of standing and mootness. This is because the old rules, strictly applied, meant that some important constitutional issues might never come before the courts. For example, who, under those rules, would have had standing to bring a Borowski-like challenge to the permissive aspects of abortion law? Neither the mother who is taking advantage of the law's permissiveness nor the doctor who is performing the abortion is likely to raise such a challenge. The fetus, which most clearly satisfies traditional standing requirements, is obviously in no position to bring the case. The father probably comes closest to the kind of litigant who might have been granted standing under the old rules, but even a case brought by the father would almost certainly have become moot before it got far up the appellate ladder, either because the abortion had occurred or because the child had been born.

In short, the constitutional issues raised by Borowski would probably never reach the Supreme Court in a concrete case of the kind contemplated by the traditional rules of standing and mootness. This was perfectly acceptable in the past, when dispute resolution was seen as the courts' primary function, but it is unacceptable to the modern **oracular courtroom.**[103] Why, after all, should the constitution's chief oracle be denied the opportunity to exercise its central function of issuing authoritative pronouncements on important matters of constitutional debate merely because the traditional adjudicative context is lacking? In order for the oracle to be free to hear and decide all constitutional issues, the traditional rules of standing and mootness had to be relaxed.

As pointed out by Chief Justice Laskin's dissent in Borowski's 1981 standing case (Dossier 8.10), reference cases used to be the only major exception to the traditional rules of access to the courtroom. Under the reference-case procedure, governments could bypass the normal adjudicative context, placing questions before the courts simply because they were considered important, not because they had to be answered in order to settle a concrete dispute. Private citizens, by contrast, could ask for a legal opinion only as the byproduct of dispute-resolving adjudication. The logic of the oracular courtroom, however, required that the privileged access of governments be extended to concerned private citizens. Because not all important constitutional issues were likely to come before the courts through normal adjudication or through government-initiated reference cases, the path had to be cleared for what amounts to "private references."[104] This is the ultimate significance of the newly relaxed rules governing access to the decision-making services of the courts.

In addition to relaxed rules of standing and mootness, the oracular view implies similarly easy access for **intervenors.** Intervenors are individuals or (more likely) groups that are not parties to a dispute before the courts but have an interest in the constitutional issues raised by the dispute and are permitted by the court to make legal arguments about those issues. If setting constitutional policy, rather than resolving concrete disputes, is central to the judicial function—if the actual parties are simply convenient vehicles for raising the constitutional issues—it follows that legal representation and debate about those issues need not be limited to the parties.

After all, as in any policymaking context, there are likely to be many interests that have a stake in the outcome, and there is no reason to believe that all of those interests will be adequately represented by the two formal opponents before the court. As the important policymaking role of the courts becomes apparent—not least to the courts themselves—the pressures mount to allow diverse interests to make representation. This is achieved by granting intervenor status to such non-party interests. The federal and provincial governments have the right to intervene; non-governmental interests can intervene only with the court's leave. Completing its own logic in relaxing the standards of standing and mootness, the Supreme Court has recently been fairly generous in granting intervenor status to non-governmental interests.[105] The result is often to turn the courtroom into something more closely akin to a legislative committee hearing than to a traditional judicial proceeding.

DOSSIER 8.11 THE ADJUDICATIVE AND ORACULAR VIEWS

The traditional adjudicative perspective was well stated by Alexis de Tocqueville in his famous analysis of the United States in the mid-19th century. "Under this system," he wrote, judicial review "cannot cover all laws without exception, for there are some laws which can never give rise to that sort of clearly formulated argument called a lawsuit."

Compare Tocqueville's remark with Justice Ronald Martland's approach to the standing issue in *Borowski* (1981):

> *[T]o establish status as a plaintiff in a suit seeking a declaration that legislation is invalid, if there is a serious issue as to its invalidity, a person need only to show that he is affected by it directly or that he has a genuine interest as a citizen in the validity of the legislation* and that there is no other reasonable and effective manner in which the issue may be brought before the Court *(emphasis added)*.

And consider the following statement from *The British Columbia Government Employees' Union v. British Columbia:*

> *Of what value are the rights and freedoms guaranteed by the Charter if a person is denied or delayed access to a court of competent jurisdiction in order to vindicate them? How can the courts independently maintain the rule of law and effectively discharge the duties imposed by the Charter if court access is hindered, impeded or denied? The Charter protections would become merely illusory, the entire Charter undermined.*

Sources: Alexis de Tocqueville, *Democracy in America,* ed. J.P. Mayer, trans. George Lawrence (Garden City, N.Y.: Anchor, 1969); *Minister of Justice of Canada et al. v. Borowski,* [1981] 2 S.C.R. 575; *The British Columbia Government Employees' Union v. The Attorney General of British Columbia,* [1988] 2 S.C.R. 214.

The Rules of Evidence

The courts have also transformed the rules of evidence in ways that facilitate their heightened policymaking role. The traditional courtroom is well designed to elicit what are known as **adjudicative** or **historical facts,** the facts relating to the history of the immediate dispute: who did what to whom under what circumstances. Policymaking, on the other hand, looks not to any particular case but to the general run of cases. Policy is made for entire classes of people or situations, not for any single circumstance. To make effective policy, policymakers thus need **social** or **legislative facts,** facts about what happens on average, not what happened in this or that case.[106] The legislative and executive branches have the tools to acquire and analyze such facts. They can do studies, appoint royal commissions, hold committee hearings, and the like. The adjudicative form permits none of these things. Strictly speaking, the classically adjudicative court, though it may make general policy as a byproduct of its decision, depends entirely on evidence placed before it, in a highly adversarial context, by the immediate parties to the dispute,[107] who are naturally more concerned with the outcome of the dispute than with its policy byproduct. The result is that general policy, applicable to the run of cases, may be founded on the facts of an entirely unrepresentative case.[108]

As courts, especially higher appellate courts, have become more prominent in the policy process (and more conscious of their policy role), they have become more hospitable to new kinds of evidence. When their adjudicative function was emphasized, courts tended to focus on adjudicative facts and to steer clear of the kinds of social-science evidence legislative policymakers might solicit. However, as they faced up to their policymaking role, especially in constitutional cases, they saw the need for less traditional kinds of evidence.[109] This has become especially apparent with respect to section 1 of the Charter of Rights and Freedoms, which says that rights are subject to "such reasonable limits as can be demonstrably justified in a free and democratic society." Early in its Charter jurisprudence, the Supreme Court signalled that deciding the question of "reasonable limits" would require the courts to deal with social-science evidence to an unprecedented degree.[110] Lawyers have responded by commissioning expert studies and putting social scientists on the stand as expert witnesses. Psychiatrists and ballistics experts in criminal trials now have their counterparts in constitutional cases.

The enhanced access for intervenors can be understood as another way of getting the required information before the court. If the sole purpose of the courts were to resolve the dispute between the immediate litigants, it would be hard to justify permitting anyone other than the litigants and their lawyers to play a significant role. When the courts' policymaking role is emphasized, on the other hand, it is equally difficult to justify limiting participation to the litigants. To the extent that the judicial decision will set general policy, it will affect more people and interests than the immediate litigants, and it seems sensible for those interests to be heard. When a legislature makes policy, we generally want to consult as widely as possible to discover all of the relevant facts. To the extent that a court is "legislating," why should it not consult just as widely? In fact, the ability of intervenors to provide policy-relevant facts and arguments not likely to be presented by the litigants is the main justification for granting them access to the courtroom. The consequence of such changes, as mentioned above, is to make the court look less like an adjudicative body and more like a legislative committee hearing, in which academic experts and interest group representatives also play a prominent role.

A related change concerns *obiter dicta.* To make effective policy, a court inevitably has to deal with matters ranging beyond the factual specifics of the dispute before it. Comments on such matters would traditionally have been considered non-

DOSSIER 8.12 JUDICIAL PASSIVITY: A CONTINUING CONSTRAINT ON EFFECTIVE POLICYMAKING

While courts have come to look more and more like legislative bodies, they are certainly not indistinguishable from them. Courts retain many adjudicative features, with important consequences for their policymaking role. An important feature of adjudicative institutions, for example, is that they are passive rather than proactive; they do not seek out disputes to resolve but wait until the disputants call on their services. In taking cases as they come, however, they also take the attendant policy issues as they come. The more overtly political and policymaking branches of government can be more proactive in identifying policy problems they wish to address and in establishing an order of priorities among them.

Even in this respect, however, the Supreme Court, as the highest judicial policymaker, has moved closer to the legislative model. Part of the significance of its post-1975 freedom to select its own cases is surely that it can now more easily shape its own policy agenda, though this freedom remains more limited than that of the executive or legislative branches. The court can choose its issues only from those that come before it, and while virtually every plausible issue will get there eventually, they may not come at the times and in the order the court would prefer. (This institutional comparison, while generally valid, should not be overstated. Circumstances often revise the preferred order of priorities for the political branches as well.)

Judicial passivity has another important policy-relevant consequence. It makes it more difficult for courts to monitor and adjust the policies they set. The political branches can keep a watching brief in a policy area and launch a reform process when it seems necessary. Judges, by contrast, generally have no official (as opposed to private) knowledge of policy difficulties and can do nothing about them unless and until a new case comes before them. In general, the continuing influence of adjudicative principles makes the judicial policymaking process more piecemeal and haphazard.

binding *obiter dicta.* In 1980 the Supreme Court indicated that all of its comments, including those that would formerly have been considered *obiter dicta,* would be binding on lower courts.[111] This is appropriate from a policymaking perspective, though it is anomalous from an adjudicative perspective.

Appellate Court Decision-Making

The increasing policy role of appellate courts is also reflected in changes to their decision-making procedures, especially those of the Supreme Court. Unlike trial courts, in which cases are heard before a single judge, appeal courts sit in panels of several judges. In provincial appeal courts (which range in size from three in P.E.I. to 24 in Quebec),[112] cases are heard by panels of three or (less commonly) five or (very rarely) seven judges. The Supreme Court sits in panels of five, seven, or all nine judges. From an adjudicative perspective, the important thing is to settle the dispute of the litigants, to decide either to sustain or overrule the outcome in the trial court. Although the immediate litigants may have some interest in the reasoning that justifies the result, they will naturally be more interested in the result itself. The dispute-settling logic of adjudication, in short, places little emphasis on a single coherent reason for the final outcome. It is enough for each judge on an appellate panel to retire to his or her study after hearing the case and produce an opinion. Whether the opinions mesh in any coherent way is less important than counting the bottom-line scores to produce wins or losses for the parties. Such individualistic, separate opinion writing, known as **seriatim opinion writing,** was indeed the practice in Canadian appellate courts in the past, when adjudication was emphasized as their primary function.

As the Supreme Court's policymaking function came to be emphasized, however, seriatim opinion writing came under sharp criticism. After all, the policy dimension of a case inheres not in the immediate outcome for the parties but in the reasoning that justifies that outcome. It is the justifying reasons that apply beyond the confines of the immediate cases. Seriatim opinion writing, with its welter of independently arrived-at reasons, is unlikely to produce a coherent set of policy guidelines. Recognizing this, the Supreme Court has transformed itself into a much more collegial institution, one that attempts to be coherent in the reasons it gives for its decisions. Like its U.S. counterpart, the very prototype of a policymaking high court, the Canadian Supreme Court now precedes opinion writing with conferences designed to produce an overall consensus, or at least to focus the issues and reduce the number of opinions. Whether unanimity is achieved or not, an effort is made to produce collective opinions, with one judge writing on behalf of all those sharing a particular point of view or with several judges coauthoring a collective opinion. Furthermore, evolving opinions are circulated among the judges, allowing for a narrowing and sharpening of any disagreements that occur. **Dissenting** and **concurring opinions** are not uncommon (see Dossier 8.13), but in most cases there are far fewer opinions now than there were in the days of seriatim opinion writing. It is also more likely, even with multiple opinions, to discern fairly clear majorities and minorities on the major important legal issues before the court.

The more publicly controversial a case is, the harder the Supreme Court tries to achieve unanimity. The reason is obvious. The decision of an appointed body is more likely to have the weight and authority necessary to settle a very divisive issue if it represents the opinion of all of its members than if it is supported by a bare majority of five to four, or seven to three (or even three to two). For the same reason, it is better for the court to sit in larger panels in publicly divisive cases, preferably as a complete court of all nine judges. Again, this increases the authority of its decisions. If unanimity cannot be achieved, it is better to divide five to four than four to three. In the latter case the public cannot be sure that the two judges not hearing the case would not have turned the three-judge minority into a five-judge majority had they been on the bench. This problem is even more acute in the case of a five-judge panel.[113] As F.L. Morton puts it, "If a final appellate court hands down a single unanimous opinion in a potentially controversial case, it sends a subtle but important message to the 'losing' side that continued litigation or resistance to the decision would be futile."[114] Again, the U.S. Supreme Court most completely fulfills the logic of a policymaking high court: it sits as a full court of all nine judges in virtually all cases. Although the Supreme Court of Canada continues to sit in smaller panels,[115] it strives to sit as a full court in the most controversial and divisive cases. A good example is the "patriation case" (discussed in Chapters 2 and 3), which addressed the constitutionality of Ottawa's proposal to bring the constitution home and add the Charter of Rights with no (or minimal) provincial consent.

When the court manages to achieve unanimity, it sometimes enhances the authority of its judgment by presenting it as an unsigned **opinion of the court** (also known as a ***per curiam*** **opinion**)[116] rather than as the opinion of any one judge with whom others happen to concur. This has happened in cases turning on such "politically volatile issues [as language rights], Quebec's claim to a unilateral veto over constitutional amendments, the federal government's claim to unilateral authority to reform the Senate, and Newfoundland's jurisdictional claim to the offshore Hibernia oil fields."[117] Not surprisingly, the court issued a *per curiam* opinion in the 1998 Quebec secession reference.

Although provincial courts of appeal are important policy-makers, they have been unable to institutionalize their policymaking role to nearly the same extent as the Supreme Court. As intermediate courts of appeal, they remain more squarely caught in the tension between their adjudicative and policymaking dimensions. In the case of the Supreme Court, the adjudicative, error-correcting function of appeal courts can be entirely discounted because litigants have already had an appeal. Thus, the Supreme Court can be given the discretion to choose its own cases on grounds of policy importance rather than litigant-centred error correction. Provincial courts of appeal, by contrast, are the major error-correcting appeal courts in most cases. Thus, if litigants are to enjoy a right to appeal, they must have the right to proceed to the

DOSSIER 8.13 SUPREME COURT PROCEDURE

After argument is concluded the judges retire to a conference room to express their tentative views on the case. It is our practice for each judge to state his or her views in reverse order of seniority, beginning with the most junior judge and concluding with the most senior. The thinking behind this tradition was to avoid the more junior members of the Court simply adopting the views of their elders and betters. I may say that whatever may have been the case in the past, there is very little risk of this happening today; the members of the Court are, as the Chief Justice euphemistically puts it, "fiercely independent." It is interesting to note that the United States Supreme Court does it the other way round, proceeding on the basis of seniority, with the Chief Justice expressing his views first.

The first tentative expression of views at our conference will usually disclose whether there is any prospect of unanimity or whether there is clearly going to be more than one judgment. We decide at this conference who is going to prepare the first draft. This will be a member of the group which appears likely to form the majority. One of that group will normally volunteer or, if there is no volunteer, the Chief Justice will ask one of the group to take it on. The other judges then set aside their record in the case until a draft is circulated. Depending on the complexity of the case and the number of other judgments which a particular judge is working on, it may take several weeks or, regrettably, even months before a judgment is circulated. When this happens the judges on the panel get their papers out again, review their bench notes and any memoranda they may have dictated immediately following the hearing, study the draft, and decide whether or not they are going to be able to concur. They may at this point ask their law clerks to do some additional research.

Sometimes members of the panel will make suggestions for amendment which the author of the draft may accept or reject. Sometimes these suggested amendments are proffered in terms that the judge's concurrence is premised on their adoption. More often than not they are put forward on the basis that the judge views them as an improvement or clarification or as additional support for the result but would be willing to concur in any event. If amendments are made, the draft is recirculated and approval sought for the changes from those proposing to concur. The changes may be dropped at this point or, if not, they may spark concurring reasons.

A member of the Court may find the draft reasons totally unacceptable and will memo his or her colleagues that he or she proposes to dissent. This grinds the process of concurring to a halt since it is viewed as "bad form" to concur with the original reasons until you have seen the dissent. The same process of suggested amendment may take place with respect to the dissenting reasons. Two and maybe three sets of draft reasons are now in circulation. It is agreed at the next court conference that this is an appeal on which judgment should be released soon, on the next judgment day, if possible. The pressure is on. At this point, if not before, the individual judge's approach to decision-making becomes very important. This is particularly so in a court with a very heavy caseload. The ideal would, of course, be if all the judges could spend as much time on the cases assigned to their colleagues as they spend on the ones they are writing themselves. This is simply not possible. As the late Chief Justice Laskin put it: "If the case load is heavy, the tendency will be for judges to concentrate their limited time and their energy on opinions that have been assigned to them; and to show generous institutional faith in opinions in other cases prepared by others." Laskin concluded, therefore, that in a busy court "there is an institutional preference to support a majority result by reasons acceptable to a majority." I have no doubt that this is correct, and it should, of course, be the focal point of our concern about overworked courts. Under the pressure of a heavy caseload, the delicate balance which should exist between judicial independence and collegiality may be displaced and collegiality may give way to expediency. This is an extremely serious matter for an appellate tribunal because the integrity of the process itself is threatened. The only answer is to grant fewer leaves and make sure that the balance between the Court's sitting time and its non-sitting time is appropriate and correct, one that allows adequate time for research and reflection, for conferring with one's colleagues, and for the drafting and redrafting of reasons for judgment.

Source: Bertha Wilson, "Decision-Making in the Supreme Court of Canada," *University of Toronto Law Journal* 36, no. 3 (1986): 236–237, published by University of Toronto Press. Reprinted by permission of University of Toronto Press Incorporated.

provincial courts of appeal. This means that these courts are swamped by appeals they have no discretion to turn away. To handle the large caseloads, courts of appeal in the larger provinces have grown beyond the size of the Supreme Court itself (Ontario, Quebec, and British Columbia all have 20 or more, including supernumerary judges; Alberta has 15). Moreover, they can rarely afford to sit in panels of more than three.[118] This not only makes it virtually impossible to maintain the collegiality necessary for jurisprudential policy coherence, but it also undermines the institutional authority of any particular decision. After all, a two-thirds majority on a panel of three represents only 10 percent of a 20-judge court.[119] Furthermore, caseload pressures are so great that, in a majority of cases, judges do not **reserve judgment** in order to produce carefully considered written opinions. Instead, decisions are handed down from the bench at the conclusion of the hearing. In some provinces, over 90 percent of cases are dispatched in this manner.[120] Since appeal cases by definition raise contested issues of legal interpretation, this means that most provincial appeal court judgments will contribute little of deep or lasting significance to the resolution of these issues. If it is important for appeal courts to develop the law of their jurisdictions, provincial courts of appeal, because of the pressures of their adjudicative function, are poorly placed to do the job. Since they are the de facto final authority for so many cases, moreover, no other existing court can fill the gap.[121]

Judicial Selection

The modes of selecting judges also reflect the conflicting logics of adjudication and policymaking. The adjudicative perspective places a premium on selection procedures that focus on technical legal competence, good character, and diligence—traits required for the impartial adjudication of concrete disputes. This emphasis on technical, "professional" qualifications, together with the concern for independence discussed earlier, militates against any significant political influence over the selection process. The most obvious manifestation of the adjudicative perspective, as pointed out above, is that Canadian judges are appointed, not elected.

However, while appointment is less overtly political than election, it is not immune to political influence. Those who wish to keep politics out of judicial selection have always had to contend with a temptation to base judicial appointments on considerations of political **patronage,** by which we mean the tendency of the government of the day to reward loyal party workers with plum positions, such as ambassadorships, seats in the Senate, and judgeships. Such rewards of loyal service should be distinguished from **ideological appointment,** which seeks to fill important policy-relevant positions with those who share the government's ideological perspectives and thus can be trusted to implement its policy preferences. Both kinds of political motives may be present in any particular appointment, of course, but in the past, when the courts were not perceived as important policymaking institutions, judicial appointments were more often a reward for loyal service than for ideological commitment.

Political considerations in judicial appointments are possible because elected politicians ultimately make the appointments. Federally controlled appointments to the section 96 and section 101 courts, for example, "are made by the Cabinet on the advice of the Minister of Justice, except for chief justices, who are recommended by the Prime Minister."[122] Provincial court judges are appointed by provincial attorneys general. Until recently in Canadian history, these politicians were relatively unfettered in their control of appointments and, not surprisingly, patronage was a leading basis of the appointments they made. The most obvious kind of patronage is the appointment of former political candidates. Studies have shown that anywhere between one-third and 80 percent of judges appointed to various courts up to about World War Two had been politicians, and that between 80 and 90 percent of those appointments were made by governments of the same political stripe.[123] In addition, many appointees who had not actually been political candidates had been active behind the scenes in party affairs.[124]

In recent decades, patronage in judicial appointments has been much criticized, and procedural reforms have been implemented to constrain the discretion of the political appointers in all jurisdictions except the three Maritime provinces.[125] Two major strategies—**screening committees** and **nominating committees**—are in use. Both are designed to inject some politically independent assessment of professional adjudicative qualifications into the selection process. Screening committees assess a list of potential candidates proposed by the appointing cabinet minister and declare them qualified or unqualified. Nominating committees draw up a list of qualified people from which the government then chooses. British Columbia and Alberta use nominating committees; the other provinces use screening committees, obviously the weaker alternative from the perspective of adjudicative professionalism.

At the federal level, in a combination of both approaches, a **Commissioner for Federal Judicial Affairs** develops a list of potential candidates and then refers them to provincial screening committees for further assessment in relation to particular appointments. The "nominating" function of the commissioner is limited, however, because he or she only ensures that candidates have the minimal technical qualifications required by law: membership in the provincial or territorial bar association and at least 10 years' experience in legal practice or on the bench.[126] The screening committees are not allowed to rank candidates but simply label candidates as qualified or unqualified. Reasons must be given for declaring a candidate to be unqualified, and such a determination can be overruled on appeal to the minister of Justice.

While these reforms reflect the influence of the adjudicative perspective, they do not represent the victory of that perspective. Plenty of room for patronage remains, especially where full-scale nominating commissions are not in place. Not surprisingly, actual practice replicates this process of partial reform. That is, while patronage has certainly declined, it continues to play a significant role. Certainly, concern about patronage remains, including (as indicated in Dossier 8.3) concern by provincial governments about the local superior court appointments made by the federal government. While the most dramatic form of patronage—the appointment of former politicians—has declined significantly,[127] it still occurs. A particularly prominent modern example was former Prime Minister Trudeau's appointment of three of his cabinet ministers—Mark MacGuigan, Bud Cullen, and Yvon Pinard—to the Federal Court in 1984, just before he turned the prime ministership over to his successor, John Turner.[128] Appointments of "behind-the-scenes supporters of the government party" seem not to have declined as much.[129] Overall, patronage continues to be substantial. For example, almost half of the Mulroney government's judicial appointments "had a known political association with the Conservative party."[130]

We indicated above that, of the two kinds of politically motivated appointment, patronage, as a reward for loyal service to the governing party, is most likely to predominate when the courts are seen as non-political adjudicative bodies. As the courts come to be understood as significant policymaking bodies, one would expect that policy-relevant ideological considerations would come to replace party loyalty as the prime political consideration in judicial selection. Ideological appointment has certainly replaced patronage in the United States, where the policy significance of the courts has long been recognized. At least since the 1960s, presidents have worked hard to fill federal judicial vacancies with judges most likely to generate preferred policy outcomes. The ideological aspects of judicial appointment have become spectacularly public because presidential nominations must be confirmed by the Senate, which, in the American separation-of-powers system, is often controlled by the president's partisan opponents. Thus, President Reagan's nomination of Robert Bork to fill a Supreme Court vacancy in 1987 generated an all-out, eventually successful war by political liberals to defeat the nomination in the Senate.[131] The appointment of Bork, the liberals feared, would transform the existing 5–4 balance in favour of maintaining the most prominent liberal policies mandated by the court—such as the invalidation of most restrictions on abortion—into a 5–4 tilt in the opposite direction.

There have been occasional examples of such ideologically motivated appointments in Canada, though they are much rarer than in the United States. Prime Minister Trudeau's 1973 elevation of Bora Laskin to the chief justiceship of the Supreme Court is a case in point. Laskin's elevation violated a tradition of replacing the previous chief justice with the most senior judge from the other language group. In 1973, this meant that retiring Chief Justice Fauteux would normally have been succeeded by Ronald Martland, the senior anglophone judge, who had served on the court since 1958. Laskin, a junior judge who had been on the court only four years, would not have been in the running. F.L. Morton gives the following explanation for Trudeau's sidestepping of tradition.

> *There were two major categories of political issues facing the Supreme Court in the early seventies: federalism and the 1960 Bill of Rights. Trudeau's position on both issues was no secret. He was simultaneously a centralist and a civil libertarian. Martland, an Albertan, had a judicial track record that was sympathetic to provincial rights and hostile toward the Bill of Rights. By contrast, Laskin had built an illustrious legal career as a strong defender of the section 91 powers of the national government. In the area of civil liberties, Laskin had distinguished himself as an activist by writing several stinging dissents criticizing his colleagues for refusing to interpret the Bill of Rights more broadly.*[132]

In short, Trudeau's elevation of Laskin to the chief justiceship was an instance of ideological appointment.

With the new policymaking prominence of the Canadian courts under the Charter of Rights and Freedoms, some commentators suggested that ideological considerations would begin to play an increasing and more public role in Canada's judicial-appointment process. For example, Peter Russell wrote that "[f]illing Supreme Court vacancies ... has always been a little bit political in a subterranean way, and now it will be right at the surface [with] the political interest groups lobbying and pressing the appointing authorities to put people on the court of their persuasion."[133] Interest groups have certainly undertaken such lobbying, but not with the same public visibility or the same dramatic effect as occurs in the United States. Moreover, governments themselves have not taken public stands of their own on the appropriate ideological direction of judicial appointments. The central reason for this is that there is no equivalent in the Canadian appointment process of the highly public and explicitly partisan confirmation hearings in the U.S. Senate, in which ideological considerations tend to be thrust onto centre stage.

As the policy and ideological implications of judicial power become more apparent, criticism of the secretive nature of Canadian judicial appointments has grown, and it is increasingly common to hear support for an American-style politicized appointment process. *The Globe and Mail*, for example, has been calling for "much broader participation in fashioning the Court,"[134] and the Reform Party wants to establish a committee of the House of Commons that would, among other things, "hold hearings into the qualifications and judicial philosophy of any person proposed for appointment by the Prime Minister to the Supreme Court." Similarly, the Reform Party recommends that "No person shall be appointed a judge of a provincial Court of Appeal unless that person has been nominated after hearings by the legislature of the province in question into the person's qualifications and judicial philosophy."[135]

Group representation is another influence on judicial appointments that goes beyond the traditional logic of adjudicative professionalism. As with other public institutions, there has always been pressure to ensure the representation of important politically relevant groups in the judiciary. Not surprisingly, all of the characteristic and conflicting representation claims of Canadian politics came into play. For example, the classic divide between Quebec and the rest of Canada has always been an important representational consideration. One indication of this importance is the practice of alternating the chief justiceship of the Supreme Court between anglophone and francophone judges. The ever-iconoclastic Prime Minister Trudeau violated this tradition, as he had earlier violated the seniority rule, when he appointed Brian Dickson to replace Laskin in 1984. Prime Minister Mulroney, however, may have re-established the tradition in 1990 by naming Antonio Lamer as Dickson's replacement. Canadian dualism is also institutionalized in a legal requirement that several of the Federal Court's judges and three of the Supreme Court's judges come from Quebec. (Had the Charlottetown Accord been passed, the requirement of three Quebec judges on the Supreme Court would have become entrenched constitutional law.) The remaining six judges are, by convention, distributed in a way that reflects the competing claims of provincialism, regionalism, and rep by pop. Thus, Ontario generally receives two to three judges, Atlantic Canada one to two judges, and the western provinces one to three judges.

Non-territorial claims are also at work. At an earlier period, the religious division between Protestants and Catholics was a conventional basis for representation on the court, though it has declined as this religious division has become publicly less relevant. More recently, the representation of non-traditional minority religions and ethnic groups on the court appears to have played a role in appointments. Thus, the court's first Jew (Bora Laskin) was appointed in 1970, the first Ukrainian-Canadian (John Sopinka) in 1988, and the first Italian-Canadian (Frank Iacobucci) in 1991. Together these appointments seem to reflect the conventional institutionalization on the Supreme Court of the growing theme of "multiculturalism" in Canadian public life.

Aboriginal peoples have also begun demanding some influence on the Supreme Court. Thus, the Charlottetown Accord provided for Aboriginal peoples to be consulted on Supreme Court appointments. In addition, the accord exhorted the

DOSSIER 8.14 PUBLIC SCRUTINY OF JUDICIAL APPOINTMENTS

[F]or those Canadians who think that the question of who is to occupy the seat of [judicial] power is really none of our business, because public scrutiny of judges would somehow undermine the justice system, consider the cases of Mr. Justice Josep Kompalla.

Mr. Kompalla, you may recall, officiated at the final game of the 1972 Canada–Russia series, and his hockey-is-a-non-contact-sport interpretation of the rules nearly cost us the game. Mr. Kompalla was, of course, in his day a respected international official, learned in the written constitution of hockey. When he retired after a long and distinguished career on and off the bench, he was given an award.

Mr. Kompalla's particular interpretation of the rules on September 28, 1972, disagreed with that of the Canadian team—but he could always say that he was simply enforcing his best reading of hockey's broadly worded constitution. Which he probably was. And anyway, who could argue with him? Jean-Paul Parise tried and got thrown out for the on-ice equivalent of contempt of court. From his decision, like those of the Supreme Court, there was no appeal.

In the constitution of hockey, as with the Constitution of Canada, who you set up as the arbiter of the rules is as important as the rules themselves. As the interventionist interpretations of Mr. Kompalla demonstrated, different readers can arrive at competing yet equally plausible readings of the same text. Mr. Justice Don Cherry of the Court of Hockey Night in Canada starts from the same rule book as Mr. Kompalla, yet reaches entirely different verdicts.

All of which is to say that Canadians might want to think about who is reading our constitutional rule book. Problem: Whenever someone suggests that, seeing as Supreme Court justices are easily the most powerful political figures in the land, we ought to have some kind of a public discussion about the kinds of views and philosophies we want on the bench, the idea is immediately batted down. Too American.

The collective wisdom among the cozy elite that has long controlled judicial appointments in this country... seems to be that public scrutiny of appointees would somehow politicize the judiciary. Whatever exactly that means, it would be a bad thing because, well, it would be just like the United States.

Here's the rub: Our judiciary is already politicized, just like the United States. That's because, since 1982, we have had a Charter of Rights, just like the United States, and judicial review of democratic decision-making, just like the United States.

If you don't think the judiciary is politicized, it's because you're one of the vast majority of Canadians who aren't in on the lobbying process. In the United States, that lobbying is at least public and above board; conservatives, liberals, activists, deferentialists, strict constructionists and all the rest work hard to elevate their candidate to the bench. In Canada, this all takes place behind doors, involving a few favoured, powerful interest groups, with the rest of us entirely shut out.

So someone about whom Canadians know nothing, and whose appointment has received the clandestine sponsorship of people who would have trouble winning an election for dog-catcher, may end up with virtual life tenure in the most powerful office in the land. There was, for example, a serious back-room lobbying campaign a few years ago to put activist lawyer Mary Eberts on the Supreme Court. But of course, the process is not politicized. Shouldn't the Canadian public, and not just a few well-connected law professors and litigators with agendas, get to vet the selection?

Americans have judicial hearings, public debates and long-running journalistic fights over who should be the next Supreme Court justice, and bitter dust-ups over the Court's decisions, because they understand that such things matter. Like the rest of us, judges make mistakes, sometimes show bias, sometimes are misled; after 200 years of swings of the judicial pendulum, Americans are more than happy to acknowledge this.

Even if judges are paragons of honesty, and most strive to be, the nature of their work means that their values and views must inform their decisions. It's an unspoken part of the job description. Because of the broad wording of the Constitution, judges are asked to provide answers to questions of law where the law often offers no indisputably right answers. How they weigh the possible solutions will have as much to do with their personal opinions and principles as with the law.

Consider [the case of] Delwin Vriend, a gay man living in Alberta ... whose human-rights code [did] not prohibit discrimination on the basis of sexual orientation. The court [had] to decide whether it [believed] it [had] the power, under the Charter, to order Alberta to add protection for homosexuals to the code. That [meant] deciding how far it [thought] the Charter should reach, and how much power the court should wield in relation to democratically elected legislatures.

You may think the answer to this question is hidden in the text of the Constitution, and you would be half right. When it comes to easy cases, the text is clear: If the law says no dogs in the park and you take your Labrador retriever for a walk in the park, the decision is automatic. Unfortunately, cases that make it to the Supreme Court are almost never that simple: In the *Vriend* case, the decision of each judge [had] more to do with his or her pre-existing views about what makes a good society and what is the proper balance between judiciary and legislature than it [did] with anything to be discovered in legal texts and precedents. Those precedents [justified] the decision, but they [did] not create it.

The Alberta Court of Appeal, for example, rejected Mr. Vriend's argument.... That was not because the appeal-court judges had a better understanding of the legal precedents than the trial judge [or the Supreme Court], who upheld Mr. Vriend's Charter challenge. Both [positions] are well supported by legal principle and precedent—depending on the assumptions one makes about the proper role and reach of the Charter. The key is those assumptions.

Canadians need to know what kinds of people, with what sorts of ideological assumptions, are being put on the bench. Because, unlike elected officials, their word is final. And unlike elected officials, once we put them in their seats, they're there for a long, long time.

Source: Anthony Keller, "Wanted: A Public Word with the Would-Be Judges," *The Globe and Mail*, December 1, 1997.

federal government to examine, "in consultation with Aboriginal groups, the proposal that an Aboriginal Council of Elders be entitled to make submissions to the Supreme Court when the court considers Aboriginal issues."[136]

The representation of women has also become a major theme, as reflected in the appointments of Justices Bertha Wilson (1982), Claire L'Heureux-Dubé (1987), and Beverly McLachlin (1989). When Justice Wilson retired in 1991 she was not replaced by another woman. Nevertheless, F.L. Morton speculates that a "convention of having at least two women justices is here to stay."[137] There has also been a push to appoint more women to other courts at all levels. Between 1980 and 1990, for example, the proportion of women among federally appointed judges rose from 3 percent to 10 percent. Once a distinct minority in the legal profession, women now constitute about half of current law students, and one would thus expect their representation in the judiciary to increase over time. In the meantime, feminists have advocated, and the Canadian Judicial Centre has implemented,[138] seminars on gender bias for the still predominantly male judiciary.[139]

Group representation in such highly coveted positions as judgeships can be promoted for several (often overlapping) reasons. First, representation in particular offices or positions may be desired and granted as a symbolic acknowledgement of the worth of a particular group. In this sense, representation is a matter of public recognition. It suggests that a group is worthy of sharing in desirable public offices. All of the claims discussed above fulfill this symbolic function. Second, representation may be required for certain practical reasons. For example, Quebec representation on the Federal Court is designed to ensure some degree of bilingualism on that national court. Quebec representation on the Supreme Court may also fulfill that function, but its main purpose historically was to ensure that the court, when it interprets Quebec law, has members familiar with that province's Civil Code. As the court increasingly steers clear of provincial law, this purpose has declined somewhat in significance, while the symbolic dimension—recognition of the "special status" or "distinctiveness" of Quebec—has become more important. Finally, representation may be sought to ensure that a group's perspectives and interests are taken into account in significant policy decisions. The convention of regional representation on the court is seen as desirable by the provinces partly for this reason. To put it bluntly, the provinces want to have their views represented in an institution that determines the limits of federal and provincial jurisdiction and gives practical meaning to the national standards sketched out in the Charter of Rights and Freedoms. Of course the provinces worry that, even if judges come from different parts of the country, those selected by the federal government alone will represent the regions symbolically, not practically, in a significant policy-relevant sense. This is why provinces have consistently pushed to gain influence over Supreme Court appointments. Thus, both the Meech Lake and Charlottetown accords contained provisions requiring Ottawa to appoint Supreme Court judges from lists supplied by the provinces.

The concern with policy influence also underlies the evolving conventions for ethnic and gender representation in the judiciary. Indeed, the concern with rep-

The Supreme Court of Canada sits in Ottawa, February 16, 1998, for the landmark case on whether Quebec can secede. Supreme Court judges are (from left) Michel Bastarache, Frank Iacobucci, Peter Corey, Claire L'Heureux-Dubé, Chief Justice Antonio Lamer, Charles Gonthier, Beverley McLachlin, John Major, and Ian Binnie. (CP photo/Tom Hanson)

resentativeness as a vehicle for policy influence is becoming increasingly prominent and is displacing symbolic recognition as the primary representational concern. This, of course, reflects the increasingly obvious policy relevance of the courts. Women and ethnic and racial groups seek representation in the vice-regal (and policy-impotent) offices of governor general or lieutenant governor largely for purposes of symbolic recognition. The symbolic motive may also be present when they seek representation in the House of Commons, but in this case the desire to influence policy is likely to be dominant. Nowadays the courts are much closer to the House of Commons than to vice-regal offices on this continuum of representational claims.

POLITICS IN THE COURTROOM

The increasing relevance and accessibility of the courts as a policymaking forum has escaped the notice of neither interest groups nor governments, both of which strive to turn judicial decision making to political advantage.

The Courts and Interest Groups

Political interest groups direct their lobbying efforts to important policymaking arenas, and their increasing tendency to pursue their agendas through the courts shows that the latter are becoming more prominent as such an arena.[140] The broad rules of access have certainly facilitated such interest group use of litigation as a policy reform strategy.

Sometimes interest groups are permitted to become direct parties to the litigation, as when Operation Dismantle, a coalition of antinuclear peace groups, claimed that Ottawa's decision to allow testing of the American cruise missile in Canadian airspace violated the Charter's section 7 right to "life, liberty and security of the person."[141] Operation Dismantle lost this case, but the fact that the Supreme Court heard and decided it was a major public-relations victory for the group. In the same vein, the conservative National Citizens' Coalition (NCC) was a direct party in the successful legal challenges to federal rules attempting to impose limits on third-party advertising on behalf of election candidates. In other cases, interest groups fund more traditional litigants with whose causes they sympathize, enabling such litigants to take what would be for many of them a prohibitively expensive journey to the Supreme Court. Thus pro-choice groups spent more than half a million dollars to fund Dr. Henry Morgentaler's successful challenge to Canada's abortion law.[142] Similarly, Joe Borowski, who had already benefited from relaxed rules of standing, became in effect the front man for the pro-life forces that funded his litigation.[143] The Legal Education and Action Fund (LEAF), a feminist organization dedicated to pursuing feminist policies through litigation, has similarly aided sympathetic litigants by funding their cases and supplying legal counsel. On the other side of the ideological divide, the NCC provided the same kind of assistance to Merve Lavigne in his unsuccessful challenge to the use of compulsory union dues for partisan political purposes.[144] In other cases, especially when the views of interest groups clash with those of the formal litigants, the groups take advantage of intervenor status to place their arguments before the judges. This tactic has often been used by LEAF. Through a variety of strategies, in sum, interest groups have become the de facto (if not the de jure) forces behind much important constitutional litigation. This development surely signifies the maturation of courts as full-fledged policymaking institutions.

Governments and the Courts

Litigation of public-policy relevance always implicates governments. After all, it is the policy preferences of governments that stand to be diverted, obstructed, or invalidated by activist jurisprudence. However, governments and their policies are not always the passive targets of courtroom attacks by individuals, interest groups, or (in the case of federalism quarrels) other governments. Governments sometimes make active use of litigation for their own strategic and tactical reasons. This is particularly evident with respect to reference cases, which are launched by governments. Sometimes reference cases are simply a way for governments to get the inevitable over with; when the constitutionality of a policy is uncertain and is being (or may be) challenged in ordinary litigation, a government anxious to resolve the resulting policy uncertainty can speed up the process by referring the question immediately to its highest court of appeal.[145] Reference cases can be used as a more independent and proactive component of government strategy, however. For example, with respect to federalism, one level of government can use the reference procedure to challenge policies of the other. [146]

With respect to its own policies, a government may find the reference procedure particularly useful when it is faced with a highly divisive policy issue it would prefer to shelve for a while. Since reference-case litigation can be about proposed laws rather than existing laws, a government can refer a policy proposal to the courts before making a final decision. In doing so, the government triggers an often lengthy judicial process that effectively puts the issue on the back burner. If the issue remains divisive when the Supreme Court has spoken, moreover, the decision may still be useful to the government. If the court declares a proposed policy unconstitutional, for example, the government can back away from it gracefully, telling the policy's supporters that it tried to satisfy them but was prevented from doing so. If the court finds the policy constitutional, the situation is trickier because a policy that is constitutionally permissible is not necessarily constitutionally required; a constitution that permits capital punishment, for example, does not require legislatures to enact it or prevent them from abolishing it. Still, this is a subtle distinction that may be lost on the general public. Certainly, a government that decides to go ahead with the policy will be tempted to trumpet an alleged judicial seal of approval.

Such strategic considerations almost certainly informed the reaction of Ontario's minority Liberal government in the mid-1980s to the question of extending public funding for the Catholic school system from Grade 10—the level to which they had traditionally been funded—through to the end of high school. This was an exceedingly controversial issue (one over which the previous Conservative government had come to grief), and rather than face it head-on the Liberal government referred the issue to the Ontario Court of Appeal and awaited the inevitable appeal to the Supreme Court. Not only would this tactic delay the need to decide but, if the funding extension was found unconstitutional, the government could tell its supporters that it had tried. If the policy was upheld, it "could tell equal-funding opponents that their constitutional objections had been found invalid."[147]

Governments can also find normal adjudicative litigation to be of strategic benefit. For example, when Borowski's pro-life case arrived at the Supreme Court, the federal government could easily have asked the court to quash it as being moot, since the law Borowski was challenging had already been struck down in *Morgentaler.* Ottawa chose not to do so because it "wanted to keep the issue before the Court so as to avoid taking a stand on abortion during the [upcoming 1988] election campaign [, it being] considered a violation of judicial independence for a politician to comment about a case before the courts."[148]

Similarly, the *Vriend* litigation in Alberta helped to keep a serious division within the governing Alberta Conservatives in the background, at least for a while. Although the provincial Conservatives were united by "fiscal conservatism," they were badly split on such social issues as abortion, censorship, and gay rights. As long as fiscal conservatism dominated the public agenda, the party functioned as a cohesive whole; whenever the controversial social issues came to the forefront, so did intra-party squabbling. The *Vriend* case shifted the divisive issue of gay rights off the legislative stage and into the courtroom, and the Alberta government was quite content to leave it there. Ultimately, of course, the litigation came to an end and the Conservative caucus had to confront the question of how to respond—in particular whether to use section 33 of the Charter to override the decision. The party nearly came apart over this issue, though it finally settled on an uncomfortable compromise.[149] No doubt, many members of caucus would have preferred that the litigation had dragged on even longer!

Another intriguing example of governments benefiting from normal litigation occurred in a lower-court precursor of *Vriend*. In 1992 the Ontario Court of Appeal did to the Canadian Human Rights Act what the Supreme Court did to the Albert act in *Vriend*: it added "sexual orientation" to the list of prohibited grounds of discrimination.[150] The question of whether to extend the protection of the act to homosexuals was as controversial for the government of Brian Mulroney as it subsequently was for Alberta's Conservatives. Kim Campbell, then Mulroney's Justice minister, wanted to amend the legislation to include sexual orientation. Significant opposition within the Conservative caucus stymied all attempts to pass such legislation, however. When two gay men took the issue to court, it was Campbell's Justice department, the same department that helped develop her legislative proposals, that was responsible for defending the challenged law. Not surprisingly, when this defence failed and the court of appeal rewrote the act to include sexual orientation, the Justice department decided not to appeal. After all, the minister's policy preference, which could not be achieved through the legislature, had been achieved in court.[151] Chapters 2 and 6 showed how the political executive, though nominally under legislative control, in fact controls the legislature. This case indicates how litigation can sometimes serve executive policy preferences on the rare occasions when legislative support is not forthcoming.

CONCLUSION

While courts, especially appellate courts, have always played an important policymaking role, that role has expanded dramatically in recent times, particularly because of the expansion of vaguely worded constitutional law. The Supreme Court's policymaking role has become especially evident, leading to reforms giving it more discretion to choose cases on the basis of their policy importance. Canadian judges have themselves raised the profile of their own policymaking power by adopting a more activist posture, by relaxing rules of access to their policymaking services, by accepting new kinds of policy-relevant evidence, and (in the case of the Supreme Court) by transforming their own internal decision-making procedures. As these developments have shifted power from the legislative and executive branches to the courts, political interest groups, responding to the new rules and opportunities, have shifted some of their lobbying efforts into the courtroom. Moreover, governments, as might be expected, have sometimes found ways to turn litigation to strategic advantage. In sum, the courts have emerged as major players on the political stage. Judges may continue to pose as policymaking "virgins," but informed Canadians can no longer afford to treat them as such.

KEY TERMS

adjudication
common law
negotiation
mediation
arbitration
superior courts
section 96 courts
supernumerary judges
provincial courts
section 101 courts
judicial compensation commissions
legal realism
stare decisis / precedent
interstitial lawmaking
distinguishing cases
obiter dicta
ratio decedendi
civil law
private law / public law
integrated court system
dual court system
courts of general jurisdiction
reference cases
advisory opinions
judicial activism / judicial restraint
liberal activism / conservative activism
positive activism / negative activism
reading in
standing
moot
oracular courtroom
intervenors
adjudicative facts / historical facts
social facts / legislative facts
seriatim opinion writing
dissenting opinion / concurring opinion
opinion of the court / *per curiam* opinion
reserve judgment
patronage / ideological appointment
screening committees / nominating committees
Commissioner for Federal Judicial Affairs

DISCUSSION QUESTIONS

1. Which is preferable—judicial activism or judicial restraint?
2. Should Canadian Supreme Court appointments be made more open and politically accountable through a process analogous to the confirmation hearings held in the U.S. Senate?
3. Should Canada move further in the direction of a dual court system?
4. Should section 33 of the Charter be repealed?

5. Discuss the controversy about the judicial role implicit in Dossiers 8.1, 8.5, and 8.14.

SUGGESTED READINGS

Beatty, David. *Constitutional Law in Theory and Practice.* Toronto: University of Toronto Press, 1995.

Glendon, Mary Ann. *Rights Talk: The Impoverishment of Political Discourse.* New York: The Free Press, 1991.

Hutchinson, Allan C. *Waiting for Coraf: A Critique of Law and Rights.* Toronto: University of Toronto Press, 1995.

Knopff, Rainer, and F.L. Morton. *Charter Politics.* Scarborough: Nelson Canada, 1992.

Mandel, Michael. *The Charter of Rights and the Legalization of Politics in Canada,* rev. ed. Toronto: Wall and Thompson, 1994.

Manfredi, Christopher P. *Judicial Power and the Charter: Canada and the Paradox of Liberal Constitutionalism.* Toronto: McClelland & Stewart, 1993.

McCormick, Peter, and Ian Greene. *Judges and Judging.* Toronto: James Lorimer, 1990.

Monahan, Patrick. *Politics and the Constitution: The Charter, Federalism, and the Supreme Court of Canada.* Toronto: Methuen, 1987.

Morton, F.L., ed. *Law, Politics and the Judicial Process in Canada,* 2nd ed. Calgary: University of Calgary Press, 1992.

Morton, F.L. *Morgentaler v. Borowski: Abortion, the Charter and the Courts.* Toronto: McClelland & Stewart, 1992.

Rosenberg, Gerald N. *The Hollow Hope: Can Courts Bring About Social Change?* Chicago: University of Chicago Press, 1991.

Russell, Peter H. *The Judiciary in Canada: The Third Branch of Government.* Toronto: McGraw-Hill Ryerson, 1987.

Schneiderman, David, and Kate Sutherland, eds. *Charting the Consequences: The Impact of Charter Rights on Canadian Law and Politics.* Toronto: University of Toronto Press, 1997.

Seidle, F. Leslie, ed. *Equity and Community: The Charter, Interest Advocacy and Representation.* Ottawa: Institute for Research on Public Policy, 1993.

Silverstein, Mark. *Judicious Choices: The New Politics of Supreme Court Confirmations.* New York: W.W. Norton & Company, 1994.

Snell, James G., and Frederick Vaughan. *The Supreme Court of Canada: History of the Institution.* Toronto: University of Toronto Press, 1985.

Sniderman, Paul M., Joseph F. Fletcher, Peter H. Russell, and Philip E. Tetlock. *The Clash of Rights: Liberty, Equality, and Legitimacy in Pluralist Democracy.* New Haven: Yale University Press, 1996.

NOTES

1. Remarks of a Court of Appeal judge. Quoted in Peter McCormick and Ian Greene, *Judges and Judging* (Toronto: James Lorimer, 1990), 233.
2. *Delgamuukw v. British Columbia,* [1997] 3 S.C.R. 1010.
3. Gordon Gibson, "Good Fences Would Make Good Judges," *Globe and Mail,* April 14, 1998, A23.
4. *Eldridge v. British Columbia,* [1997] 3 S.C.R. 624.
5. *Vriend v. Alberta,* [1998] 1 S.C.R. 493.
6. *R. v. Jacob* (1996), 31 O.R. (3d) 350.
7. *Dobson v. Dobson,* (1997), 143 D.L.R. (4th) 189.
8. *R. v. Latimer* (23 November 1998, Sask. C.A.), unreported.
9. *Rosenberg v. Canada* (1995), 25 D.R. (3d) 612.
10. For further explanation of the term "common law," see Dossier 8.4. See also McCormick and Greene, *Judges and Judging,* 8–9.
11. See Donald Horowitz, *The Courts and Social Policy* (Washington: Brookings Institution, 1977), 1–2.
12. McCormick and Greene, *Judges and Judging,* 21.
13. The terminology is somewhat confusing, because section 96 courts are also "provincial" in the sense that they are constituted by the provinces under section 92(14) of the 1867 Constitution Act. Section 96 courts are not fully "provincial," however, because their judges are appointed by Ottawa. Thus, some commentators refer to the "inferior" provincial courts as "pure provincial courts" or capital-P "Provincial courts." See McCormick and Greene, *Judges and Judging,* 17.
14. In fact, they try over 90 percent of all cases heard in Canadian trial courts. See ibid., 18.
15. Peter H. Russell, *The Judiciary in Canada: The Third Branch of Government* (Toronto: McGraw-Hill Ryerson, 1987), 204.
16. McCormick and Greene, *Judges and Judging,* 21. As in the case of the figures reported above for section 96 courts, these figures include supernumerary judges.
17. Ibid. Three supernumerary judges (two on the trial division and one on the appeal division) are included.
18. Ibid. Two of these were supernumerary judges.
19. *Valente v. The Queen,* [1985] 2 S.C.R. 673, at 698. (Emphasis added.)
20. McCormick and Greene, *Judges and Judging,* 5–6.
21. *Manitoba Provincial Judges Association v. Manitoba,* [1997] 3 S.C.R. 3. Cf. Jacob S. Ziegel, "The Supreme Court Radicalizes Judicial Compensation," *Constitutional Forum* 9, no. 2 (1998).

22. F.L. Morton, ed., *Law, Politics and the Judicial Process in Canada*, 2nd ed. (Calgary: University of Calgary Press, 1992), 147–153.
23. McCormick and Greene, *Judges and Judging*, 36.
24. See Paul Weiler, *In the Last Resort* (Toronto: Carswell / Methuen, 1974), Chapter 4.
25. McCormick and Greene, *Judges and Judging*, 219.
26. Ibid., 220.
27. For further discussion of these matters, see McCormick and Greene, *Judges and Judging*, Chapter 8; and Morton, *Law, Politics and the Judicial Process*, Chapter 9.
28. This is reflected in the opinions of judges themselves. Trial court judges are less likely, and appeal court judges more likely, to think of themselves as lawmakers. See McCormick and Greene, *Judges and Judging*, 230–235.
29. Russell, *The Judiciary in Canada*, 289.
30. McCormick and Greene, *Judges and Judging*, 9.
31. Indeed, the very existence of separate courts of appeal in all of the provinces probably reflects a recognition of this substantial policy role. At an earlier stage in Canadian history, appeal court judges were simply trial judges assigned on an ad hoc basis to hear appeals. As long as error correction is considered to be the main function of an appeal, this is a perfectly satisfactory way of proceeding.

    "Once the policy-making elite in the justice field come to recognize that the court of appeal is not simply correcting error but is also developing the law of the province, there is a greater emphasis on the need for continuity and collegiality in its structure and operation. An ad hoc rotating membership of trial judges is unacceptable for a body of jurists writing the jurisprudence of a province" (Russell, *The Judiciary in Canada*, 293).
32. McCormick and Greene, *Judges and Judging*, 180.
33. But the authority of its decisions, and the willingness (even the ability) of lower courts to follow them, will vary with the number and coherence of opinions expressed by its judges. And of course even coherent opinions can be distinguished. See the section on appellate court decision making below; and McCormick and Greene, *Judges and Judging*, 212–214.
34. Russell, *The Judiciary in Canada*, 334.
35. The amendment was actually passed in late 1974 and came into effect in 1975.
36. The other examples are described in the Canadian Bar Association Committee Report, *The Supreme Court of Canada* (Ottawa: Canadian Bar Association, 1987), 23–24.
37. Russell, *The Judiciary in Canada*, 345.
38. *Attorney General of Ontario v. Attorney General of Canada*, [1947] A.C. 128—case 17 in Peter H. Russell, Rainer Knopff, and Ted Morton, eds., *Federalism and the Charter: Leading Constitutional Decisions* (Ottawa: Carleton University Press, 1989).
39. Case 17 in Russell, Knopff, and Morton, *Federalism and the Charter*, 123.
40. Russell, *The Judiciary in Canada*, 65.
41. Ibid., 66.
42. Patrick Monahan, *Politics and the Constitution: The Charter, Federalism, and the Supreme Court of Canada* (Toronto: Carswell / Methuen, 1987), 18.
43. Russell, *The Judiciary in Canada*, 66. Cf. McCormick and Greene, *Judges and Judging*, 172.
44. Russell, *The Judiciary in Canada*, 67.

45. See ibid., 294–296.
46. Ibid., 294.
47. Ibid., 295.
48. Ibid., 333; McCormick and Greene, *Judges and Judging*, 172, 208.
49. Russell, *The Judiciary in Canada*, 305.
50. *National Citizens' Coalition Inc. and Brown v. Canada* (A.G.) (1984), 5 W.W.R. 436.
51. Rainer Knopff and F.L. Morton, *Charter Politics* (Scarborough: Nelson Canada, 1992), 25.
52. *Somerville v. Canada*, unreported.
53. Janet L. Hiebert, "Money and Elections: Can Citizens Participate on Fair Terms amidst Unrestricted Spending?" *Canadian Journal of Political Science* 31, no. 1 (1998), 96.
54. For example, *Reference re Legislative Authority of Parliament to Alter or Replace the Senate*, [1980] 1 S.C.R. 54—case 61 in Russell, Knopff, and Morton, *Federalism and the Charter.*
55. Knopff and Morton, *Charter Politics*, 188.
56. Russell, *The Judiciary in Canada*, 91.
57. Ibid., 349.
58. For an American expression of the same point, see Robert Bork, *The Tempting of America: The Political Seduction of the Law* (New York: Free Press, 1990), 102.
59. Christopher P. Manfredi, *Judicial Power and the Charter: Canada and the Paradox of Liberal Constitutionalism* (Toronto: McClelland & Stewart, 1993), 38. See also McCormick and Greene, *Judges and Judging*, 197. Manfredi's book constitutes a defence of section 33 (see especially Chapter 7). For a review of the debate about section 33, see Knopff and Morton, *Charter Politics*, 228–232.
60. *Dubois v. The Queen*, [1985] 2 S.C.R. 350.
61. Russell, Knopff, and Morton, *Federalism and the Charter*, 19.
62. *Moore v. Dempsey*, 261 U.S. 86 (1923); *Gitlow v. New York*, 268 U.S. 652 (1925); *Powell v. Alabama*, 287 U.S. 45 (1932). See also F.L. Morton, "The Politics of Rights: What Canadians Should Know about the American Bill of Rights," in Marian C. McKenna, ed., *The Canadian and American Constitutions in Comparative Perspective* (Calgary: University of Calgary Press, 1993), 109.
63. *The Queen v. Drybones*, [1970] S.C.R. 282—case 37 in Russell, Knopff, and Morton, *Federalism and the Charter.*
64. *Brown v. Board of Education*, 347 U.S. 483 (1954).
65. *Engel v. Vitale*, 370 U.S. 421 (1962); *School District of Abington v. Schemp*, 374 U.S. 203 (1963).
66. *West Virginia State Board of Education v. Barnette*, 319 U.S. 624 (1943).
67. *Baker v. Carr*, 369 U.S. 186 (1962); *Reynold v. Sims*, 377 U.S. 533 (1964).
68. *Mapp v. Ohio*, 367 U.S. 643 (1961).
69. *Roe v. Wade*, 410 U.S. 113 (1973).
70. *Swann v. Charlotte—Mecklenberg Board of Education*, 402 U.S. 1 (1971).
71. Horowitz, *The Courts and Social Policy*, 4.
72. *Robertson and Rosetanni v. The Queen*, [1963] 1 S.C.R. 651.
73. *Her Majesty the Queen v. Big M Drug Mart Ltd.*, [1985] 1 S.C.R. 295—case 42 in Russell, Knopff, and Morton, *Federalism and the Charter.*
74. *Chromiak v. The Queen*, [1980] 1 S.C.R. 471.

75. *The Queen v. Paul Mathew Therens,* [1985] 1 S.C.R. 613—case 44 in Russell, Knopff, and Morton, *Federalism and the Charter.*

76. *Dubois v. The Queen,* [1985] 2 S.C.R. 350.

77. *Satnam Singh et al. v. Minister of Employment and Immigration,* [1985] 1 S.C.R. 177—case 41 in Russell, Knopff, and Morton, *Federalism and the Charter.*

78. Knopff and Morton, *Charter Politics,* 22–24, 159; Michael Mandel, *The Charter of Rights and the Legalization of Politics in Canada* (Toronto: Wall and Thompson, 1989), 175.

79. Knopff and Morton, *Charter Politics,* 54—identification lineup: *R. v. Ross,* [1989] 1 S.C.R. 3 (SCC) 16; blood sample: *R. v. Dyment,* [1988] 2 S.C.R. 417.

80. *R.v. Feeney,* [1997] 3 S.C.R. 1008.

81. *Morgentaler v. The Queen,* [1988] 1 S.C.R. 30.

82. *Attorney General Quebec v. Quebec Association of Protestant School Boards,* [1984] 2 S.C.R. 66—case 55 in Russell, Knopff, and Morton, *Federalism and the Charter.*

83. *Quebec v. Ford et al.,* [1988] 2 S.C.R. 712—case 52 in Russell, Knopff, and Morton, *Federalism and the Charter.*

84. F.L. Morton and Rainer Knopff, "The Supreme Court as the Vanguard of the Intelligentsia: The Charter Movement as Postmaterialist Politics," in Janet Ajzenstat, ed., *Canadian Constitutionalism: 1791–1991* (Ottawa: Canadian Study of Parliament Group, 1991), 61–62.

85. Lisa Young, "Party, State and Political Competition in Canada: The Cartel Model Reconsidered," *Canadian Journal of Political Science* 31, no. 2 (1998), 351.

86. McCormick and Greene, *Judges and Judging,* 243.

87. Ibid.

88. *R.v. Seaboyer,* [1991] 2 S.C.R. 577.

89. *Schachter v. Canada,* [1992] 2 S.C.R. 679.

90. *Vriend v. Alberta,* [1998] 1 S.C.R. 493.

91. *Edwards Books and Art Ltd. v. The Queen,* [1986] 2 S.C.R. 713—case 48 in Russell, Knopff, and Morton, *Federalism and the Charter.*

92. *Reference re Public Service Employees Relations Act (Alberta Labour Reference),* [1987] 1 S.C.R. 313.

93. *Société des Acadiens v. Association of Parents,* [1986] 1 S.C.R. 549.

94. *Schachter* [1992].

95. For further discussion of the difference between a decision's bottom line and its justifying reasoning, see Knopff and Morton, *Charter Politics,* Chapters 5 and 13.

96. Such numbers can be no more than suggestive. For a meaningful assessment of a court's activism one must take into account not only the success rate of claimants but also the prominence and significance of the issues on which the court is willing to be activist.

97. McCormick and Greene, *Judges and Judging,* 235.

98. *R.v. Butler,* [1992], 1 S.C.R. 452.

99. *Minister of Justice of Canada et al. v. Borowski,* [1981] 2 S.C.R. 575.

100. *Borowski v. Canada,* [1989] 1 S.C.R. 342—case 51 in Russell, Knopff, and Morton, *Federalism and the Charter.*

101. *R. v. Mercure,* [1988] 1 S.C.R. 234.

102. *Law Society of Upper Canada v. Skapinker*, [1984] 1 S.C.R. 357—case 40 in Russell, Knopff, and Morton, *Federalism and the Charter.*

103. Knopff and Morton, *Charter Politics*, Chapter 7.

104. This term was used in *Borowski*, [1989] 365.

105. Knopff and Morton, *Charter Politics*, 193–195.

106. Horowitz, *The Courts and Social Policy*, Chapter 7.

107. See McCormick and Greene, *Judges and Judging*, 245.

108. For further discussion, see Knopff and Morton, *Charter Politics*, Chapter 8.

109. Knopff and Morton, "Nation-Building and the Canadian Charter of Rights and Freedoms," in Alan Cairns and Cynthia Williams, eds., *Constitutionalism, Citizenship, and Society in Canada* (Toronto: University of Toronto Press, 1985), 165.

110. *Law Society of Upper Canada v. Skapinker*, [1984] 1 S.C.R. 357—case 40 in Russell, Knopff, and Morton, *Federalism and the Charter.*

111. See McCormick and Greene, *Judges and Judging*, 224.

112. Eighteen regular judges and six supernumerary judges in 1990 (ibid., 21).

113. This has actually happened, in the case of a rehearing with more judges; see ibid., 205.

114. Morton, *Law, Politics and the Judicial Process in Canada*, 433–434.

115. Panels of seven account for 80 percent of Supreme Court hearings. See McCormick and Greene, *Judges and Judging*, 28.

116. The U.S. term is "per coram opinion."

117. Morton, *Law, Politics and the Judicial Process in Canada*, 435.

118. "For cases that raise extraordinary legal or constitutional issues, they will sometimes sit in panels of five or, even more rarely, of seven. For the smaller appeal courts, this means that the entire court may hear some cases; for the larger appeal courts, it means that even the most significant and unusual cases are considered by only a portion of the full membership" (McCormick and Greene, *Judges and Judging*, 168).

119. One response is the practice of circulating draft opinions for comment by all judges on the court, not just those on the panel. Given caseloads, this practice is likely to be increasingly perfunctory. It also raises intriguing dilemmas if the panel deciding a case is opposed by the majority of the court. See ibid., 183–184.

120. Russell, *The Judiciary in Canada*, 296. For further detail, see McCormick and Greene, *Judges and Judging*, 168–170. It is worth noting that prior to 1975 the same was true for the Supreme Court; ibid., 194.

121. For reform proposals, see Russell, *The Judiciary in Canada*, 298–300.

122. Morton, *Law, Politics and the Judicial Process in Canada*, 69.

123. Russell, *The Judiciary in Canada*, 114–115; Morton, *Law, Politics and the Judicial Process in Canada*, 73.

124. Russell, *The Judiciary in Canada*, 114.

125. Morton, *Law, Politics and the Judicial Process in Canada*, 70.

126. Ibid., 69.

127. Russell, *The Judiciary in Canada*, 114–115.

128. Morton, *Law, Politics and the Judicial Process in Canada*, 74.

129. Russell, *The Judiciary in Canada*, 115.

130. Peter H. Russell and Jacob S. Ziegel, "Mulroney's Judicial Appointments and the New Judicial Advisory Committees," in Morton, ed., *Law, Politics and the Judicial Process in Canada*, 89.

131. Bork, *The Tempting of America;* Morton, *Law, Politics and the Judicial Process in Canada*, 107; Knopff and Morton, *Charter Politics*, 135.

132. F.L. Morton, *Morgentaler v. Borowski: Abortion, the Charter, and the Courts* (Toronto: McClelland & Stewart, 1992), 72–73.

133. Peter Russell cited in Morton, *Law, Politics and the Judicial Process in Canada*, 79.

134. William Thorsell, "What to Look for, and Guard Against, in a Supreme Court Judge," *Globe and Mail*, December 20, 1997, D6.

135. "New Canada Act: An Act to Modernize Our Government for the 21st Century," sections 11 and 12.

136. These proposals are in section 20 of the accord.

137. Morton, *Law, Politics and the Judicial Process in Canada*, 76.

138. The Canadian Judicial Centre was established in 1988 to provide continuing-education courses to judges.

139. These seminars have provoked some controversy. See Morton, *Law, Politics and the Judicial Process in Canada*, 82–83.

140. This is a matter of degree. There has always been some interest group use of the courts. See Kent Roach, "The Role of Litigation and the Charter in Interest Advocacy," in F. Leslie Seidle, ed., *Equity and Community: The Charter, Interest Advocacy and Representation* (Ottawa: Institute for Research on Public Policy, 1993).

141. *Operation Dismantle Inc. v. The Queen*, [1985] 1 S.C.R. 441—case 43 in Russell, Knopff, and Morton, *Federalism and the Charter.*

142. Morton, *Morgentaler v. Borowski*, 129.

143. Ibid., 92, 131–132.

144. *Lavigne v. Ontario Public Service Employees Union*, [1991] 2 S.C.R. 211. For discussion of this case, see Christopher P. Manfredi, "Re Lavigne and Ontario Public Service Employees Union: Public Administration and Remedial Decree Litigation under the Charter of Rights and Freedoms," *Canadian Public Administration* 34 (1991), 395–416.

145. *Reference re Anti-Inflation Act*, [1976] 2 S.C.R. 373—case 22 in Russell, Knopff, and Morton, *Federalism and the Charter.*

146. For example, the original provincial references in the patriation case.

147. Knopff and Morton, *Charter Politics*, 33.

148. McCormick and Greene, *Judges and Judging*, 31.

149. The compromise was to accept the judgment where it concerned the protection of homosexuals against discrimination in employment, housing, and services, but to resist its extension to such matters as same-sex marriage and spousal benefits.

150. *Haig and Birch v. Canada et al.* (1992), 57 O.A.C. 272.

151. Thomas Claridge, "Ontario Court Uses Power to Read in Words Not in Law," *Globe and Mail* (August 8, 1992), A1, A5.

ELECTIONS AND VOTING

9

By whatever measure is used, Canada has one of the most disproportional electoral systems among established democracies. [1]

How is it that Canadian political parties can form majority governments with less—sometimes substantially less—than 50 percent of the popular vote? How can federal parties be shut out of a region where they get 20 percent of the votes and at the same time win crushing landslides—as much as 100 percent of the seats—in regions where they receive little over 50 percent of the votes? How can a party with only 14 percent of the national vote form Her Majesty's Loyal Opposition, while another party, with more votes, wins only two seats? Why, despite shifting partisan allegiances among a majority of voters, has a single party formed the government in Ottawa for 70 percent of the 20th century? Short-term factors of political leadership and issues play a role, but a large part of the answer lies in the electoral system, which provides one of the clearest and most dramatic examples of how institutional rules shape political outcomes.

■ ■ ■

Our system of government is essentially an "indirect" democracy. Citizens do not govern themselves directly; instead, they elect representatives to govern them. In this way, the consent of citizens is secured, however indirectly and imperfectly.[2] The right of adult citizens to elect the government in periodic competitive elections is perhaps the most fundamental of all democratic rights. Whether democracy requires more than periodic competitive elections is, of course, a matter of controversy. While some theorists are content to define democracy in terms of electoral politics, others insist that the term should be reserved for an ideal political system characterized by a high level of citizen involvement and participation in all aspects of collective welfare, not just elections.[3] There is widespread agreement, however, that periodic competitive elections based on universal adult suffrage constitute at least a necessary, if not the sufficient, condition for democratic government.

This chapter examines the way in which the principle of periodic competitive elections is given institutional form in Canada. Like other political institutions, the electoral system is subject to variations and has alternatives. We begin with a discussion of these alternatives. If periodic competitive elections are a necessary condition of democracy, there are many pathways to democratic government. The chapter then considers how the Canadian electoral system shapes political behaviour and outcomes. As with other institutions, the electoral system is anything but neutral in its effects, and its inherent biases generate controversy and the search for alternatives. As might be expected, Canada's electoral system is controversial in some of the same ways as are other political institutions. For example, the electoral system is accused of exacerbating regional alienation, and alternative systems are canvassed for their potential to achieve a better intrastate integration of regional interests. Similarly, the growing democratic and egalitarian propensity of Canadians has challenged the traditional practice of giving urban constituencies much larger populations than rural constituencies, in violation of the principle of rep by pop. Likewise, conflicting definitions of citizenship have led to demands that non-territorial groups, such as women or Aboriginal Canadians, receive proportionate electoral representation. Ultimately, the electoral system is important because of its impact in defining voter choices and influencing the development of the party system. This chapter concludes by examining the determinants of voting behaviour. Chapter 10 explores party system development.

ELECTORAL SYSTEMS

In all representative democracies, there is a set of rules known as the **electoral system**, which prescribes how citizen preferences, expressed through votes, are translated into seats in a legislative assembly. In interpreting the outcome of elections, it is conventional to focus on the distribution of seats in the legislature. However, the way in which preferences are expressed, and the rules used to aggregate those preferences, can have an important bearing on how seats are distributed among legislative parties. Electoral systems are not neutral. Electoral outcomes often owe as much to the effects of the electoral system itself as they do to the preferences of citizens in a democracy.

Douglas Rae, in *The Political Consequences of Electoral Laws*,[4] identified the three major dimensions of electoral systems: (1) the preference articulation of voters, (2) the nature of electoral districting, and (3) the electoral formula. Each of these dimensions involves choices among several alternatives, choices that will affect electoral outcomes, sometimes profoundly.

Preference Articulation

How are citizens able to express their opinions about candidates in an election? Voting is only one way. One can also campaign actively for a favourite candidate, contribute money to the campaign, place a campaign sign on the lawn, and do other things to demonstrate political support. However, in deciding who has won the election, these things are not directly taken into account. The winner is not the candidate with the most money, or the most volunteers, or the most lawn signs. The preferences expressed when votes are cast are the only ones that count, the only ones that are counted. Suppose, then, that there are three candidates and that a voter likes candidate A, dislikes candidate B, and is indifferent to candidate C. To what extent is the voter able to express this range of feeling on the ballot?

The simplest and crudest way of expressing preferences on an electoral ballot is through a categorical choice. Sometimes referred to as **simple preference**, the categorical-preference option enables the voter to identify one, and only one, of the candidates as the preferred candidate. Given a choice between candidates A, B, and C, one could put an "X" beside one of them or beside none of them (thereby spoiling the ballot). Note that with this method the voter is able to express a preference for A over both B and C but is unable to express any feelings about B and C. There are times when the voter may dislike candidate B more intensely than he or she likes candidate A. Under a simple preference system, this may lead to **strategic voting**—that is, voting for the candidate most likely to defeat a strongly disliked candidate. Thus, a voter who thinks that her second preference is more likely than her first preference to defeat the despised third candidate may end up voting for her second preference. Under this condition, the voter has made a complex calculation, but little of it was communicated through the ballot. This simple-preference vote articulation is the method used in federal and provincial elections in Canada.

Alternatively, one could express preferences through an **ordinal choice**, which involves ranking candidates from most preferred to least preferred. The voter is able to express a fuller range of preferences, identifying the positioning of each of the candidates relative to the others. On the part of the voter, the choice is more complex. Australia uses a version of ordinal voting in electing its Senate and House of Representatives.

Electoral Districting

What are the contours of an **electoral district** (also known as a **constituency**, or sometimes **riding**) and how many seats are allocated to each district? An electoral district is typically a geographic unit within which votes are translated into legislative seats. For example, in 1998 the city of Calgary spanned seven federal and 21 provincial districts. Electoral districts vary according to the number of representatives they elect. One alternative is for a single member to represent each constituency. Such **single-member districts** generate unambiguous winners and reduce a complex array of preferences into the choice of a single individual. Elected bodies based on single-member districts include the House of Commons in both Canada and Britain, the House of Representatives in both the U.S. and Australia, and Canadian provincial legislatures. The other alternative is to have **multi-member districts**, in which as few as two and as many as 100 or more members are selected from a constituency. The Canadian Senate, although not elected, uses multi-member provincial and territorial districts in all provinces except Quebec, which is divided into 24 Senate districts. At the provincial level, British Columbia retained a number of multi-member districts until 1990. Other institutions based on multi-member constituencies include the United States and Australian senates, the legislatures of Israel and many European countries, and some city councils in Canada.

Electoral districts can be either simple or complex. Simple electoral districting exists where the area is divided into a set of mutually exclusive constituencies with a given number of representatives from each constituency. There may be a large number of constituencies, such as the 301 single-member districts in the Canadian House of Commons, or a small number, such as the single multi-member electoral district in the Israeli Knesset.

Complex electoral districts are those that provide for multiple layers, or tiers, of representation over a particular geographic area. Germany uses complex electoral districting in that its lower house, the Bundestag, is composed half of members elected from single-member constituencies and half of members chosen by proportional representation within each of the *länder* (the sub-national units of German federalism). A single vote is used in determining the one winner from the constituency as well as the proportion of *länder* seats to be allocated to each party in the lower house.[5] This system, often referred to as **mixed-member proportional (MMP)**, has recently been adopted by New Zealand and has been suggested in Canada.

The Electoral Formula

An electoral formula is the rule or set of rules used to determine when a candidate can be declared a winner. Each electoral formula answers two interrelated questions: (1) How many votes are required to win a legislative seat? (2) Is a party's share of seats in proportion to its share of the vote? As to the question of how many votes are required to win a seat, the answer depends on whether single-member or multi-member districts are used. In the case of single-member districts, there are two main alternatives. In a **plurality system**, sometimes called **first-past-the-post**, the winner is the one who receives more votes than the other contestants. He or she need not (and often does not) obtain the support of a majority of the voters in the electoral district. The plurality system is used at the federal, provincial, and municipal levels in Canada.

Under a **majority system**, by contrast, the winner must receive at least 50 percent plus one of all votes cast. Since it is often the case that a majority does not support any candidate on a single ballot, majority systems often entail **multiple ballots.** In legislative elections in France, for example, if the first ballot results in no clear winner, all candidates except the top two are dropped from the ballot and a **runoff election** is held between them. [6] The winner of such a two-person runoff election will necessarily receive a majority of votes cast. Similarly, federal parties in Canada have traditionally chosen their leader by majority vote at a convention of delegates (though they are increasingly shifting to systems of direct election by party members).[7] After each ballot at the convention, the candidate who receives the smallest number of votes is eliminated and another vote is held; this procedure continues until one candidate receives the support of 50 percent plus one of the voters.[8]

Something similar to the traditional Canadian party-convention system can be achieved with only one ballot, if that ballot incorporates the principle of ordinal preference ranking. In other words, voters rank all candidates in order of preference, and if no one gets a majority of first-preference votes, then second, third, or subsequent preferences can be used until someone emerges with a clear majority. This electoral formula, known as the **single transferable vote (STV),** or **alternative vote (AV),** is used to achieve clear majorities in single-member district elections for the Australian House of Representatives.

Neither the plurality nor majority rules make sense in multi-member districts, which elect several members. One way of electing members for such districts is the so-called **party-list system.** Citizens vote not directly for individual candidates but for parties, which are then allocated seats in proportion to the votes they receive. Parties fill these seats from a previously established prioritized list of candidates. In a 100-seat district, for example, a party would draw up a ranking of 100 candidates. If the party received 30 percent of the vote, it would receive 30 percent of the seats, which it would fill with the top 30 candidates on its list.

When citizens vote directly for individual candidates in a multi-member district, a winning candidate must get a predetermined proportion of the total votes cast. The proportion is typically just over the proportion of the electoral district's seats represented by the one seat the candidate hopes to fill. Thus, one seat would represent 12.5 percent of an eight-member district, and the quota of votes required to fill that seat would be set at just over 12.5 percent. To deal with situations in which no one achieves the quota, or in which not enough candidates achieve the quota to fill the available seats, the single transferable vote may be used. Again, voters rank the candidates, and if the distribution of first preferences does not fill all of the seats, unused lower preferences are successively counted until all the seats are filled. Australia uses this version of STV to fill seats in its multi-member Senate districts. (Some authors reserve the STV label for such multi-member situations and use AV—alternative vote—to describe ordinal preference ranking in single-member districts.)[9]

As to the second question answered by an electoral formula—whether a party's share of legislative seats will be proportional to its share of the vote—it is clear that the party-list system produces such **proportional representation (PR).** The single transferable vote in multi-member districts also achieves a degree of proportionality. Single-member plurality systems, by contrast, do not result in proportional representation. Indeed, such systems distort the translation of votes into seats, sometimes dramatically so. Suppose, for example, that the same three parties contest every district in an election based on the single-member plurality system. In order to win a seat, a party's candidate need only garner more votes than his or her competitors. If those opponents split the opposition vote evenly, a candidate can win with just over one-third of the vote. If the same party wins in this manner in every district, it could win 100 percent of the seats with, say, 35–40 percent of the vote. This hypothetical example, though extreme and improbable, illustrates the tendency of the single-member plurality electoral system.

Both proportional representation and the single-member plurality system have their defenders and opponents. Proportional representation has the obvious merit of ensuring that a party's strength in the legislature is roughly equivalent to its popularity among the electorate. On the other hand, some kinds of PR, especially the party-list system, can encourage the fractionalization of political parties and decrease the likelihood of any one party controlling a majority of legislative seats. Consequently, it increases the likelihood of **coalition governments,** in which governments are often required to invite fringe parties or extremist parties into the cabinet in exchange for their legislative support. Proportional representation has been most popular in continental Europe and in the summer of 1998 was even being considered seriously for the British Parliament, traditionally the flag bearer for the first-past-the-post electoral system.

THE CANADIAN ELECTORAL SYSTEM

In Canada the electoral system for national and provincial elections is a simple-preference, single-member-constituency plurality system. This system is also used in the United States to elect members of the House of Representatives. It is rapidly falling out of favour in parliamentary regimes, however. Australia abandoned it in favour of STV several decades ago, and New Zealand recently abandoned it in favour of MMP. Indeed, among advanced industrial nations with parliamentary systems, only Britain and Canada retain the single-member plurality system, and, as just mentioned, even Britain is considering a system of proportional representation. In Canada, too, the first-past-the-post electoral system is a frequent object of attack, though governments (who, by definition, have succeeded under the system) are understandably reluctant to change it.

Controversy over the single-member plurality system has tended to focus on three matters: (1) the tendency to translate imperfectly the votes cast for a party into the share of seats it wins, and especially the tendency to produce strong regional bias in the distribution of legislative seats; (2) the tension between the principle of representation by population and territorial factors in the apportionment of electoral districts; and (3) the difficulty of adequately representing non-territorial groups, such as women and Aboriginals.

The Translation of Votes into Seats

For reasons just explained, the national and provincial electoral systems taken as a whole distort the way in which parties are awarded seats following elections. Table 9.1 presents the results of each federal election between 1945 and 1997 as a ratio of a

TABLE 9.1 RATIO OF POLITICAL PARTIES' SHARE OF POPULAR VOTE TO THEIR SHARE OF SEATS, 1945–1997

YEAR	RANK ORDER OF PARTIES (PERCENTAGE OF VOTE)				
	1	2	3	4	
1945	Lib 1.24	PC 1.00	CCF 0.73	SC 1.29	
1949	Lib 1.49	PC 0.53	CCF 0.37	SC 1.03	
1953	Lib 1.32	PC 0.62	CCF 0.77	SC 1.06	
1957	Lib 0.97	PC 1.09	CCF 0.88	SC 1.09	
1958	PC 1.45	Lib 0.55	CCF 0.32	SC 0	
1962	PC 1.17	Lib 1.01	NDP 0.53	SC 0.97	
1963	Lib 1.17	PC 1.09	NDP 0.49	SC 0.76	
1965	Lib 1.23	PC 1.13	NDP 0.44	Cdt 0.72	
1968	Lib 1.29	PC 0.87	NDP 0.49	SC 1.21	
1972	Lib 0.93	PC 1.16	NDP 0.66	SC 0.75	
1974	Lib 1.24	PC 1.02	NDP 0.39	SC 0.82	
1979	Lib 1.01	PC 1.34	NDP 0.52	SC 0.46	
1980	Lib 1.18	PC 1.13	NDP 0.57		
1984	PC 1.51	Lib 0.51	NDP 0.57		
1988	PC 1.33	Lib 0.88	NDP 0.72		
1993	Lib 1.46	Ref 0.94	PC 0.04	BQ 1.37	NDP 0.39
1997	Lib 1.34	Ref 1.03	BQ 1.36	NDP 0.64	PC 0.35

Legend
Lib: Liberal Party
PC: Progressive Conservative Party
CCF: Co-operative Commonwealth Federation
NDP: New Democratic Party
SC: Social Credit Party
Cdt: Creditiste
BQ: Bloc Québécois
Ref: Reform

Note: Very small parties and independents are excluded.

Sources: F. Leslie Seidle, "The Canadian Electoral System and Proposals for Its Reform," in Alain G. Gagnon and A. Brian Tanguay, eds., *Canadian Parties in Transition: Discourse, Organization, Representation* (Scarborough: ITP Nelson, 1989), 251. Reprinted with permission; calculated from data from Chief Electoral Officer of Canada, *Thirty-Fourth General Election, Report of the Chief Electoral Officer, 1988;* Appendices (Revised), (Ottawa: 1988), 20–21. Reprinted with permission of the Minister of Supply and Services Canada, 1994. Data from 1993 and 1997 elections taken from the Web site of Elections Canada: http://www.elections.ca.

party's share of the popular vote to its share of seats. Each entry in this table is the percentage of a party's seats divided by the percentage of the vote it received. Thus, a ratio of 1.0 indicates that a party's seat percentage equalled its vote percentage. It received, for example, 30 percent of all seats and 30 percent of all votes. A ratio of greater than 1.0 indicates that the party received a higher percentage of seats than votes, whereas a ratio of less than 1.0 indicates the party received a lower percentage of seats than votes. One could interpret these lower ratios as instances in which a party is penalized by the electoral system.

Prior to the 1993 election, both the Liberals and Conservatives had been well served by the electoral system. In 12 of the 17 elections since 1945, the Liberal Party's share of seats has exceeded its share of the popular vote. Likewise, the Conservative Party's share of seats has exceeded its popular vote in 12 of the 17 elections. The party most consistently penalized by the electoral system was the NDP, which between 1961 and 1997 always received less than two-thirds of the seats it would have won had the same votes been cast under a system of proportional representation. In 1997 this trend continued for the NDP: the party won 7.0 percent of the seats in the House of Commons and 10.7 percent of the popular vote. One of the more striking features of these data is the degree to which parties are over-rewarded once their percentage of the vote approaches 50. In the three elections during this series when a party received around 50 percent of the vote (Liberals in 1949, Conservatives in 1958 and 1984), the electoral system worked to produce a legislative landslide. For example, in 1949 the Liberals received 73.7 percent of the seats on the basis of 49.5 percent of the votes, for a ratio of 1.49. In 1958, the Conservatives received 78.5 percent of the seats based on 54 percent of the votes, for a ratio of 1.45, while in 1984 they received 74.8 percent of the seats based on 49.7 percent of the votes, for a ratio of 1.51.

In addition to magnifying the size of election victories, the electoral system can also affect which parties are designated as winners and losers. For example, in both the 1957 and 1979 elections, the Liberal Party received more votes than any other party but the Conservatives received more seats. The data in Table 9.1 show that, in both elections, the Conservatives translated votes into seats more effectively than did the Liberals; in both cases, the governor general invited the Conservatives to form the government.

Perhaps the upper limit in the distorting effects of the Canadian electoral system was reached in the 1993 federal election. The Liberal Party received 60 percent of the Commons seats based on 41.1 percent of the vote, for a ratio of 1.46, one of the highest representation ratios on record. At the other extreme is the Conservative Party, which won two Commons seats (0.67 percent) on the basis of 16 percent of the votes, for a representation ratio of 0.04. In other words, the Conservative Party received 4 percent of the seats to which it would have been entitled in a system of proportional representation. Parties that aspire to a national base of support but finish well behind the winner are severely penalized under Canada's electoral system. The NDP, which had national aspirations in 1993, had a low representation ratio of 0.39.

The imperfect translation of votes into seats has been attacked on two grounds. The first concerns one of the classic themes of Canadian constitutional politics: the tension between institutional features that promote regionalism or provincialism and the intrastate logic of national integration. The single-member plurality electoral system exacerbates regional alienation, which has led proponents of improved national integration to recommend a shift to proportional representation. The second ground of criticism concerns the way in which the system complicates and distorts the interpretation of electoral mandates.

REGIONALISM

In an influential article on the effect of the electoral system, Alan Cairns has argued that the tendency of the system to over-reward the party with the largest number of seats has a regional dimension and a regionalizing bias.[10] According to Cairns, parties tend to benefit from the distorting effect of the electoral system in some provinces or regions and to suffer its disadvantages in other regions. A party that wins 50 percent of the votes in the West and 25 percent in central Canada, for example, will win much more than 50 percent of western seats and probably much less than 25 percent of central Canadian seats. Another party may experience the same phenomenon in reverse. The results are pernicious because the representation of parties in the Commons has a stronger regional hue than their support among the national electorate. Instead of being institutions of national integration, parties can become more concerned with representing the regional interests of their members in the Commons, thereby reinforcing regional differences and regional tensions.

The regionalizing effect of the electoral system was especially dramatic in the 1993 election, providing strong support for Cairns's argument (see Table 9.2). The losing parties with regionally concentrated support tended to do much better than the losing parties whose support was more thinly spread. For example, the most regional of the parties, the Bloc Québécois, had a representation ratio of 1.36, indicating that it was highly over-rewarded for its support. The representation ratio of the Reform Party, whose support was less regional than the Bloc's but much more regional than the NDP's or Conservatives', was 0.94, indicating a modest degree of underrepresentation on the basis of its electoral support. Compare this to the representational ratios of 0.45 and 0.04 for the NDP and Conservatives, respectively—two parties whose support was more thinly spread across the country in 1993—and the regionalizing effects of the electoral system become even more apparent.

Table 9.3 shows a similar pattern for the 1997 election. Again the two losing parties with regionally concentrated support did very well; the BQ's representation ratio of 1.36 was identical to its 1993 ratio, while Reform climbed from just below the neutral point to just above it. Similarly, although the representation ratios of the PCs and the NDP climbed somewhat, both remained very low, meaning that their more thinly spread votes were substantially under-rewarded in terms of seats.

TABLE 9.2 **POLITICAL PARTIES' SHARE OF POPULAR VOTE AND SEATS, BY PROVINCE, 1993 GENERAL ELECTION**

PROVINCE	LIBERAL		BLOC QUÉBÉCOIS		REFORM		NEW DEMOCRATIC		PROGRESSIVE CONSERVATIVE		OTHER	
	% vote	% seats	% vote	% seats	% vote	% seats	% vote	% seats	% vote	% seats	% vote	% seats
Ontario	52.9	99.0	0.0	0.0	20.1	1.0	6.0	0.0	17.6	0.0	3.4	0.0
Quebec	33.0	25.3	49.3	72.0	0.0	0.0	1.5	0.0	13.5	1.3	2.7	1.3
Nova Scotia	52.0	100.0	0.0	0.0	13.3	0.0	6.8	0.0	23.5	0.0	4.4	0.0
New Brunswick	56.0	90.0	0.0	0.0	8.5	0.0	4.9	0.0	27.9	10.0	2.7	0.0
Manitoba	45.0	92.9	0.0	0.0	22.4	7.1	16.7	0.0	11.9	0.0	4.0	0.0
British Columbia	28.1	15.6	0.0	0.0	36.4	75.0	15.5	9.4	13.5	0.0	6.5	0.0
Prince Edward Island	60.1	100.0	0.0	0.0	1.0	0.0	5.2	0.0	32.0	0.0	1.7	0.0
Saskatchewan	32.1	35.7	0.0	0.0	27.2	28.6	26.6	35.7	11.3	0.0	2.8	0.0
Alberta	25.1	15.4	0.0	0.0	52.3	84.6	4.1	0.0	14.6	0.0	3.9	0.0
Newfoundland	67.3	100.0	0.0	0.0	1.0	0.0	3.5	0.0	26.7	0.0	1.5	0.0
Yukon	23.3	0.0	0.0	0.0	13.1	0.0	43.3	100.0	17.8	0.0	2.5	0.0
Northwest Territories	65.4	100.0	0.0	0.0	8.4	0.0	7.7	0.0	16.2	0.0	2.3	0.0
Total	41.3	60.0	13.5	18.3	18.7	17.6	6.9	3.1	16.0	0.7	3.6	0.3
Ratio	1.46		1.36		0.94		0.45		0.04		0.08	

Source: *Report of the Chief Electoral Officer, Thirty-Fifth General Election, 1993* (Ottawa: Minister of Supply and Services, 1994), 27–30. Reprinted with permission of the Minister of Supply and Services Canada, 1994.

Such regional distortion of votes into seats has reinforced regional alienation in Canada. In the 1970s and early 1980s the Liberals were all but shut out of the West and the Progressive Conservatives were all but shut out of Quebec, despite significant electoral support in each case. As a consequence, western Canadians lacked significant elected representation on the government side of the House and within the cabinet when the National Energy Program was introduced in 1980. Not only was the legislation less sensitive to regional concerns than it might have been, but the Liberal government lacked elected members to sell the package in the West. Distortions in the electoral system thus reinforced long-standing sentiments of regional alienation and further eroded the legitimacy of parliamentary institutions within the region. Similarly, in Quebec the electoral system contributed significantly to the "Tory syndrome";[11] it bedevilled Conservative efforts to build the party within Quebec and to convince Canadian voters at large that the Progressive Conservatives were indeed a national party that could span linguistic divisions within the country. For those who decried the decentralizing trends of Canadian regionalism, and who sought mechanisms of intrastate federalism to enable the national institutions to play a stronger integrative function, the single-member plurality electoral system became an obvious

TABLE 9.3 **POLITICAL PARTIES' SHARE OF POPULAR VOTE AND SEATS, BY PROVINCE, 1997 GENERAL ELECTION**

PROVINCE	LIBERAL		BLOC QUÉBÉCOIS		REFORM		NEW DEMOCRATIC		PROGRESSIVE CONSERVATIVE		OTHER	
	% vote	% seats	% vote	% seats	% vote	% seats	% vote	% seats	% vote	% seats	% vote	% seats
Ontario	49.5	98.1	0.0	0.0	19.1	0.0	10.7	0.0	18.8	1.0	1.8	1.0
Quebec	36.7	34.7	37.9	58.7	0.3	0.0	2.0	0.0	22.2	6.7	1.0	0.0
Nova Scotia	28.4	0.0	0.0	0.0	9.7	0.0	30.4	54.5	30.8	45.5	0.8	0.0
New Brunswick	32.9	30.0	0.0	0.0	13.1	0.0	18.4	20.0	35.0	50.0	0.6	0.0
Manitoba	34.3	42.9	0.0	0.0	23.7	21.4	23.2	28.6	17.8	7.1	1.1	0.0
British Columbia	28.8	17.6	0.0	0.0	43.1	73.5	18.2	8.8	6.2	0.0	3.7	0.0
Prince Edward Island	44.8	100.0	0.0	0.0	1.5	0.0	15.1	0.0	38.3	0.0	0.3	0.0
Saskatchewan	24.7	7.1	0.0	0.0	36.0	57.1	30.9	35.7	7.8	0.0	0.6	0.0
Alberta	24.0	7.7	0.0	0.0	54.6	92.3	5.7	0.0	14.4	0.0	1.2	0.0
Newfoundland	37.9	57.1	0.0	0.0	2.5	0.0	24.8	0.0	36.8	42.9	0.9	0.0
Yukon	22.0	0.0	0.0	0.0	25.3	0.0	28.9	100.0	13.9	0.0	9.9	0.0
Northwest Territories	43.1	100.0	0.0	0.0	11.7	0.0	20.9	0.0	16.7	0.0	7.6	0.0
Total	38.5	51.5	10.7	14.6	19.4	19.9	11.0	7.0	18.8	6.6	1.6	0.3
Ratio	1.34		1.36		1.03		0.64		0.35		0.19	

Source: *Report of the Chief Electoral Officer, Thirty-Sixth General Election, 1997* (Ottawa: Minister of Supply and Services).

object of challenge. In addition to (or as an alternative to) promoting intrastate reforms to the Canadian Senate, it was often suggested that a system of proportional representation would lead to truly national and thus integrative parties in the federal parliament, parties whose seats in various parts of the country would reflect the votes cast for them there, rather than the unnecessarily regionalized parties produced by the current electoral system.

Electoral reform to dampen the fires of regionalism seemed less necessary by 1984, when Brian Mulroney finally overcame the "Tory syndrome" to lead a Conservative government with strong representation from all parts of the country. Mulroney managed this feat largely by knitting together a national alliance that encompassed Quebec nationalists and alienated westerners. In 1993, however, this alliance came apart. Quebec nationalists left the Conservative Party for the Bloc Québécois, while westerners migrated to the Reform Party. The major beneficiary of this electoral fractionalization in 1993 was the Liberal Party. The Liberals won 100 percent of the seats in Nova Scotia, Prince Edward Island, Newfoundland, and the Northwest Territories on the basis of 52 percent, 60.1 percent, 67.3 percent, and 65.4 percent of the votes, respectively. More important, the Liberals won 98

(99 percent) of the 99 seats in Ontario on the basis of only 52.9 percent of the vote. However, the Liberal Party's seats were underrepresented in both Alberta and British Columbia. The Bloc Québécois was rewarded with 72 percent of the seats from Quebec based on 49.3 percent of the votes in that province. The Reform Party received 84.6 percent of Alberta seats based on 52.3 percent of the Alberta vote and 75 percent of British Columbia seats based on 36.4 percent of the B.C. vote. Regionalized party representation had returned with a vengeance, and again it was exacerbated by the electoral system.

The 1997 election reinforced the regional character of the Canadian party system, solidifying Reform's hold on the West, maintaining the Bloc's strength in Quebec, and continuing the Liberals' stranglehold in Ontario. Both the Conservatives and the NDP continued to be heavily penalized by the electoral system. The regionalization of Canadian party politics has led many observers to argue the need to abandon the first-past-the-post electoral system in favour of some alternative that could lead to greater proportionality.[12] However, to date there has been no groundswell of opinion behind this view and no sign that the Liberal government is anxious to embark on fundamental reform of the electoral system.

ELECTORAL MANDATES

Nowhere was the way in which the electoral system complicates the interpretation of electoral mandates more evident than during the 1988 federal election. During its first term of office following the 1984 election, the Conservative government negotiated a free-trade agreement with the American government, subject to legislative ratification in both countries by January 1, 1989. The enabling legislation was passed expeditiously by the House of Commons and required passage in the Senate to complete the process of legislative approval. However, as noted in Chapter 5, the Liberal Party controlled a majority of Senate seats, and the Liberal leader in the Senate, Allan MacEachen, refused to give Senate approval unless and until the government received a mandate from the Canadian people through a general election. After some heated debate, the government decided to request that the governor general dissolve the Commons and call an election.

That election, held on November 21, 1988, represented a rare instance of an election dominated by a single issue. The Conservatives were the only major party in favour of the Free Trade Agreement, while both the Liberals and New Democrats were opposed. Together the Liberals and New Democrats received 52 percent of the popular vote, while the Conservatives were supported by 43 percent of voters (the remaining 5 percent of the voters supported independents or candidates of other parties). The Canadian people had spoken. To the extent that votes in the election were based on attitudes toward the Free Trade Agreement, the conclusion seemed obvious: Canadians were in opposition to the agreement.

However, those preferences, as always, needed to be given meaning by the electoral system. The electoral system translated 43 percent of the votes for the Conservatives into 169 seats (57 percent) and a majority government. Armed with its "mandate" from the people, the victorious Conservatives returned to Parliament with new vigour and again passed the free-trade legislation in the Commons. This time the legislation went on to pass easily in the still Liberal-dominated Senate, and the process was completed before the January 1, 1989, deadline. The constitutionality and legitimacy of the Conservative government's actions were never in doubt. Whether those actions were consistent with the preferences Canadians expressed in a national election, and thus deserving of being labelled democratic, is less certain.

An equally striking outcome of the electoral system can be seen in electoral politics in the province of Quebec, particularly in support for the Parti Québécois (PQ). The provincial election of 1970 was the first contested by the PQ. The PQ received 23.1 percent of the popular vote and was rewarded with seven of the 108 seats in the National Assembly. Three years later, in the election of 1973, the party increased its popular support to 30.2 percent. Despite this significant increase, and despite the fact that the total number of seats in the National Assembly had increased to 110, the PQ's number of seats actually decreased from seven to six. The PQ's marginal position in the legislature concealed the fact that the party was gaining supporters and adherents at a steady pace. With this momentum in mind, it is not surprising that the PQ was able to receive 41.4 percent of all votes in 1976. However, unlike the situation in 1970 and 1973, the PQ had attained a level of support at which the electoral system began to work in its favour. Its 41.4 percent of the popular vote was translated into 71 of the 110 legislative seats and a majority government. The party's appeal to a minority (albeit a substantial minority) of Quebeckers was translated into majority control of the legislature.

Nine years later, after having served two terms in office, the PQ suffered a humiliating electoral defeat. In a legislative assembly of 122 seats, the PQ held only 23 seats. Much of the popular commentary of the day suggested that the PQ was a spent force in Quebec politics, that its message was no longer relevant to Quebeckers. Those conclusions, based as they were on the distribution of seats in the National Assembly, seemed reasonable and consistent with the outcome of the election. The interpretation is different if one focuses on the preferences expressed by Quebeckers through the popular vote. In 1985 the PQ received 39 percent of all votes cast, barely 2 percent less than it had received in 1976. Changes in the nature of the opposition (it had been divided among several parties in 1976, and was united behind the Liberals in 1985) had a tremendous effect on the way that support was translated into legislative seats. If 1976 was in fact less than a ringing endorsement of the PQ's independentist policy, then 1985 can hardly be interpreted as a resounding repudiation of that same policy.

In fact, assessing support for the PQ's constitutional policy is even more complex. The party was supported by a significant minority of the voters in both elections, some but not all of whom supported sovereignty-association. The simple-preference ballot provides Canadians with a crude instrument for expressing their electoral preferences. Once expressed, the preferences are filtered through a highly distorting electoral system, in which modest differences in votes received can lead to substantial differences in seats won. The leaders of political parties then take it upon themselves to define the type of mandate they have received. As the cases discussed above have illustrated, the electoral system provides one of the most striking examples of the dramatic effect institutions may have in structuring political outcomes.

Controversies over Electoral Districting

The manner in which constituency boundaries are drawn, and the principles used to guide that process, are aspects of the electoral system that have generated considerable debate in recent years. The controversy is a prime example of the impact that institutions may have in channelling political debate on questions of importance to Canada's representative democracy. As the institutional environment concerning electoral districting began to change, so too did the definition of the principles that guided redistricting. Electoral districts drawn under the new institutional environment differ in important ways from those drawn under the old environment.

At the centre of the controversy is the principle of **representation by population,** often called simply **rep by pop.** As noted in previous chapters, in 1867 rep by pop in the House of Commons reflected the nationalizing principle in Canada's central Parliament, while the division of powers and the Senate reflected the regionalizing or federal principle. In Chapter 5 we observed that although the principle of representation by population in the allocation of seats to the provinces still exists, it has been significantly diluted since Confederation by the "senatorial floor" and "grandfather clause," and that it would have been diluted further by the Charlottetown Accord's proposed 25 percent guarantee of Commons seats for Quebec. The present formula for electoral districting for House of Commons elections, adopted in the Representation Act, 1985, reflects the balance between rep by pop and territorially based modifications to this principle. The formula has four steps, which are set out in Figure 9.1.[13] The point of departure is 282 seats, which was the number of seats in the Commons following the redistribution of 1976[14] and in effect when the 1985 rules were adopted. Two seats are then assigned to the Northwest Territories and one to the Yukon, leaving 279 for allocation to the provinces. Canada's provincial population is divided by 279 to calculate the **electoral quotient.** The provincial population is then divided by the electoral quotient to determine the initial allocation of seats to each province.

The first three steps of the formula are dominated by the principle of representation by population, according to which each province should be represented in the House of Commons in proportion to its share of the Canadian population. In step 4 the principle of rep by pop is adjusted by the senatorial floor and the grandfather clause. Today the senatorial floor has the effect of increasing the number of seats in the Commons beyond what rep by pop would provide not only for Prince Edward

FIGURE 9.1 **ALLOCATING SEATS IN THE HOUSE OF COMMONS**

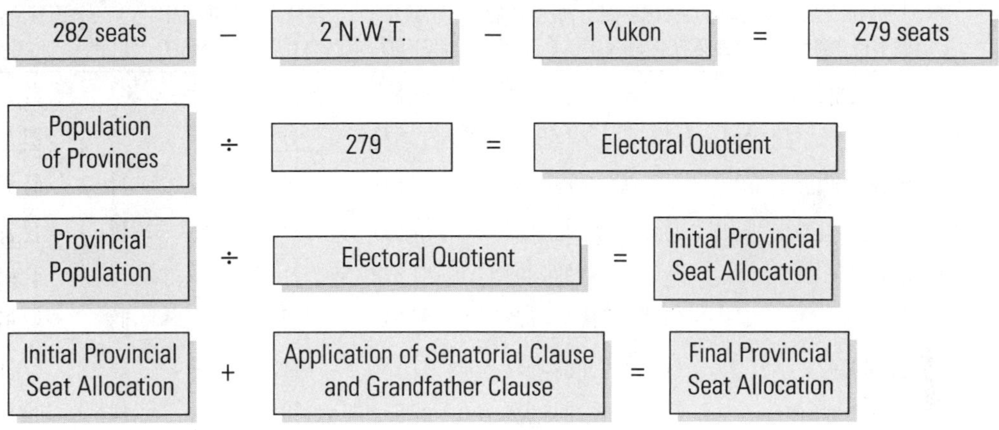

Source: Adapted from Chief Electoral Officer of Canada, *Representation in the Federal Parliament,* (Ottawa: 1993), p. 8.

Island, for which the provision was originally designed and which receives four seats,[15] but also for New Brunswick, which is entitled to 10 seats.[16]

The second adjustment in step 4 of the formula, based on the grandfather clause, prevents provinces from losing seats. Without this clause, Canada's shifting demographic profile in recent decades—particularly its reflection of population growth in Ontario, British Columbia, and Alberta—would (given a constant number of seats) have decreased the representation in such provinces as Nova Scotia, Manitoba, and Saskatchewan. To provide adequate provincial representation, Parliament passed the grandfather clause to guarantee that no province could lose seats. If the districting formula ended at step 3, seats would be transferred from provinces with declining populations to those with increasing populations within a House of constant size. Step 4 requires that these losses be compensated to some extent through the addition of new seats. Step 4, in short, ensures a gradual increase in the size of the House of Commons. In the redistribution of 1996, for example, higher-than-average population growth in Ontario and British Columbia entitled Ontario to four and British Columbia to two additional seats. Since no province could lose seats, the net effect was a growth in the size of the House of Commons from 295 to 301 seats.

Step 4 of the 1985 formula means that not all provinces will be represented in proportion to their population. Table 9.4 shows the calculations for seat allocation following the redistribution of 1996. In the left column is the number of seats allocated to each province in 1976. Each province's population is divided by the national

TABLE 9.4 REPRESENTATION IN THE HOUSE OF COMMONS, BY PROVINCE AND TERRITORY

PROVINCE OR TERRITORY	NUMBER OF SEATS ESTABLISHED IN 1976 AND CONSTITUTING 33RD PARLIAMENT[1]	POPULATION 1991	CALCULATIONS NATIONAL QUOTIENT[2]	ROUNDED RESULT	SPECIAL CLAUSES[3]	TOTAL	ELECTORAL QUOTIENT
Newfoundland	7	568,474	97,532	6	1	7	81,211
Prince Edward Island	4	129,765	97,532	1	3	4	32,441
Nova Scotia	11	899,942	97,532	9	2	11	81,813
New Brunswick	10	723,900	97,532	7	3	10	72,390
Quebec	75	6,395,963	97,532	71	4	75	91,946
Ontario	95	10,084,885	97,532	103	—	103	97,912
Manitoba	14	1,091,942	97,532	11	3	14	77,996
Saskatchewan	14	988,928	97,532	10	4	14	70,638
Alberta	21	2,545,553	97,532	26	—	26	97,906
British Columbia	28	3,282,061	97,532	34	—	34	96,531
Northwest Territories[4]	2	57,649	—	—	—	2	
Yukon Territory	1	27,797	—	—	—	1	
Total	282	27,296,859				301	

1. Assign two seats to the Northwest Territories and one to the Yukon Territory (three seats).
2. Use 279 seats and population of provinces to establish national quotient (27,211,413 ÷ 279 = 97,532).
3. Add seats to provinces pursuant to "Senatorial Clause" guarantee in the Constitution and new "Grandfather Clause" (based on 33rd Parliament).
4. There is no quotient for the Northwest Territories and Yukon; criteria other than population apply.

Source: Elections Canada, *Representation in the Federal Parliament* (Ottawa: Minister of Supply and Services, 1993), 17.

electoral quotient to identify the initial seat allocation. The number of seats is then adjusted by the application of the senatorial and grandfather clauses for a final seat allocation. In the far right column, the provincial population is divided by the final seat allocation, producing the effective electoral quotient in each province. The data indicate that Ontario is the most underrepresented province in the House of Commons, with 97,912 citizens for each seat in the Commons. It is followed closely by Alberta (97,906), British Columbia, (96,531), and Quebec (91,946). By contrast, Prince Edward Island is substantially overrepresented in the Commons, with one member for every 32,441 citizens.

During the first century after Confederation, the concern for rep by pop in the distribution of Commons seats *between* the provinces was not matched by a similar concern for applying this principle *within* provinces. The fact that a province is represented in proportion to its population does not necessarily mean that constituencies within the province are equal in size and that all parts of the province are represented in proportion to their populations. Once constituencies have been allocated, in other words, how are their boundaries drawn? The Constitution Act, 1867, is silent on the application of rep by pop to Commons constituencies within the provinces. Section 51 of that document states only that the size of the House of Commons and the allocation of seats to the provinces must be adjusted after each decennial census "by such authority, in such manner, and from such time, as the Parliament of Canada from time to time provides."[17] The size and shape of electoral districts was of such little interest to the Fathers of Confederation that "not a single word of significance appears on the matter in the recorded negotiations leading to Confederation."[18]

Lacking a clear statement of principle in the Constitution Act, 1867, the rules for the determination of electoral boundaries came about through convention. Since redistribution was required every 10 years, since it had to pass in the Commons and was therefore controlled by the government, and since a party could exact substantial rewards in its seat distribution if it practised political **gerrymandering** (see Dossier 9.1), there was a strong incentive to develop districting theories that were to the government's advantage. Norman Ward speaks of four such theories as "frequently masquerading as principles." "[S]ince the beginning," he writes, "these theories have been used indiscriminately as genuine guiding principles and as excuses to justify perversions of representation."[19]

Ward's four theories of districting are: (1) that constituencies should have approximately equal populations; (2) that existing county lines should be preserved; (3) that one should interfere with the boundaries of a constituency only when increased population requires allocating more seats; and (4) that rural areas require greater representation than urban areas.[20] The application of one or another of the above "principles" could enable one to justify any manner of electoral redistribution. Rather than define the end or purpose of distribution, these "principles" were more often employed as a means to serve the ends of self-interest and personal political advantage. Thus, political expediency overshadowed representational principles in the design of electoral boundaries throughout much of Canada's history.

Two significant changes since the early 1960s have had an impact on the way in which the principle of rep by pop has been interpreted and implemented in the drawing of electoral boundaries. The first was the passage of the Electoral Boundaries Readjustment Act of 1964, which shifted responsibility for drawing electoral boundaries from Parliament to 11 federal electoral boundaries commissions—one for each province and one for the Northwest Territories. (The Yukon does not require a commission because it constitutes a single constituency.) The second was the adoption of the Charter of Rights and Freedoms in 1982, which drew the courts into the process of electoral districting.

DOSSIER 9.1 ORIGINS OF THE TERM "GERRYMANDER"

The term "gerrymander" was coined to describe an 1812 Massachusetts constituency designed to pack many supporters of the opposition Federalist Party into a single district, thus reducing the number of representatives they could elect. Since the Federalists did not all inhabit a conveniently focused locality, the district was twisted and elongated, rather resembling a salamander. The Federalists dubbed it a gerrymander in honour of Governor Elbridge Gerry, who signed the electoral map into law. A gerrymander is thus the drawing of electoral boundaries intentionally to advance the partisan interest of one party by reducing the effective voting strength of other parties.

Source: Reprinted from Rainer Knopff and F.L. Morton, *Charter Politics* (Scarborough: ITP Nelson, 1992), 333.

The creation of electoral boundaries commissions at the federal level in 1964 and in most provinces subsequently was intended to achieve two goals: to remove partisanship from among the factors used to readjust electoral boundaries, and to set the rules that were to guide the process. Ward describes the readjustment process during the first 99 years of Confederation as "a freelance operation in which any rational boundary drawing was likely to be the result of coincidence or accident."[21] The "irrationality" of the process should not be confused with "randomness." Quite the opposite. Partisan advantage was the "principle" that guided redistribution when it was conducted by Parliament.[22] This problem with the readjustment process was resolved by creating electoral boundaries commissions that were entirely free of partisan pressure. The commissions are chaired by a judge designated by the chief justice of the province and have two other members appointed by the Speaker of the Commons.[23] The use of nonpartisan commissions has almost completely silenced critics' concerns over the use of redistricting to partisan advantage. Indeed, there has been more controversy over the application of the rules to be applied by the boundaries commissions during the redistricting process.

The commissions are charged with striving for equality of constituency size, but they are also required to temper this ideal to accommodate such non-population-based considerations as different population densities and "communities of interest." Thus, sparsely populated rural areas may be given constituencies with smaller populations than densely populated urban areas. With some exceptions, however, constituencies are not permitted to deviate from the provincial average by more than 25 percent. Note, however, that the 25 percent deviation limit concerns the amount of variation that can occur in the size of constituencies *within* provinces. Because of the use of the senatorial and grandfather clauses, the population of constituencies *between* provinces can vary by more than 25 percent. As Table 9.4 illustrated, the average constituency in Prince Edward Island had little more than 32,000 residents, about 67 percent below the Canadian average.

The 25 percent deviation limit is subject to two competing interpretations. First, it can be seen as legitimizing (and even encouraging) variation up to the limit in order to accommodate non-population-based factors. According to this interpretation, the primary purpose of the deviation limit is to permit an entirely legitimate degree of constituency inequality, one that should be fully exploited in drawing the electoral map. Thus, one would expect many rural constituencies to be well below (approaching 25 percent below) the average population and many urban constituencies to be well above the average.

The second way of understanding the 25 percent deviation limit is as an extreme outer limit, which may sometimes have to be used but which should generally be avoided. In this view, equality should be the primary concern of electoral boundaries commissions and deviations from that ideal as large as plus or minus 25 percent should be undertaken reluctantly and rarely. Under this interpretation, one would expect to find most constituencies clustering around the average, with only the occasional outlier straying toward the limit.

It is clear from the debate in the Commons over redistricting plans, as well as from a subsequent amendment to the Electoral Boundaries Readjustment Act, that legislators tended to favour the former interpretation.[24] Equally clear is the fact that the boundaries commissions have tended to take the latter view, not in eliminating the systematic differences in constituency size between largely urban and rural constituencies but in reducing the differences and moving toward greater equality.[25] Here we find another example of how different institutional arenas, with their different incentive structures, produce different outcomes.

The inevitable tension between legislatures and commissions can generate some interesting institutional politics. For example, Parliament temporarily suspended the 1994 redistribution process, in part because of the predictable displeasure of MPs with the commissions' often radical restructuring—even deletion—of their constituencies. Rural MPs who would have lost their seats altogether because of a redistribution of seats from declining rural to growing urban areas had special reason to feel aggrieved, but their concerns tended to be shared even by MPs who had not been entirely displaced. By definition, MPs have experienced success in existing constituencies and dislike both the risk involved in running in reconfigured ridings and the extra work of building new constituency organizations. Similar discontent with a provincial electoral map proposed by a badly divided commission in Alberta led that province's government in 1992 to reject the commission's map and give the job of drawing a new one to a legislative committee. Obviously the practice of having electoral boundaries readjusted by independent commissions has not entirely depoliticized the process.

The issue of electoral districting entered yet another institutional arena, the courts, with the 1982 adoption of the Charter of Rights and Freedoms as part of the

DOSSIER 9.2 THE ELECTORAL BOUNDARIES READJUSTMENT ACT

15. (1) In preparing its report, each commission for a province, except the commission for the Northwest Territories, shall, subject to subsection (2), be governed by the following rules:

(a) the division of the province into electoral districts and the description of the boundaries thereof shall proceed on the basis that the population of each electoral district in the province as a result thereof shall, as close as reasonably possible, correspond to the electoral quota for the province, that is to say, the quotient obtained by dividing the population of the province as ascertained by the census by the number of members of the House of Commons to be assigned to the province as calculated by the Chief Electoral Officer under subsection 14(1); and

(b the commission shall consider the following in determining reasonable electoral district boundaries:

(i) the community of interest or community of identity in or the historical pattern of an electoral district in the province, and

(ii) a manageable geographic size for districts in sparsely populated, rural or northern regions of the province.

(2) The commission may depart from the application of the rule set out in paragraph (1)(a) in any case where the commission considers it necessary or desirable to depart therefrom

(a) in order to respect the community of interest or community of identity in or the historical pattern of an electoral district in the province, or

(b) in order to maintain a manageable geographic size for districts in sparsely populated, rural or northern regions of the province,

but, in departing from the application of the rule set out in paragraph (1)(a), the commission shall make every effort to ensure that, except in circumstances viewed by the commission as being extraordinary, the population of each electoral district in the province remains within twenty-five percent more or twenty-five percent less of the electoral quota for the province.

Source: Reprinted from Canada, the Chief Electoral Officer of Canada, *Electoral Boundaries Readjustment Act* (Ottawa: Minister of Supply and Services, 1993), 5–6.

entrenched Constitution. The Charter guarantees to all citizens "the right to vote" in elections to the House of Commons and provincial legislatures (s. 3), and the right to equal treatment under the law (s. 15). With respect to the Charter-guaranteed right to vote, the courts have been asked whether the Charter guarantees only the "equal right to vote" or also the "right to an equal vote."[26] If the Charter guarantees the right to an equal vote, perhaps that right is violated when voters in high-population constituencies cast less weighty votes than their counterparts in low-population districts.

DOSSIER 9.3 TWO VIEWS ON ELECTORAL DISTRICTING

The various commissions, in keeping with the exhortation of the Act, have shifted grounds for redistribution in Canada from the more traditional territorial and geographic ones to a more egalitarian one. The one man–one vote notion, which was at the centre of the representational disputes adjudicated by American courts when the Electoral Boundaries Readjustment Act was adopted and which had no history of sustained or wholehearted parliamentary support in Canada, may well with time emerge in some form suitable to the Canadian political condition as the distinguishing representational principle to evolve from the work of the commissions.

Source: Reprinted with permission from John C. Courtney, "'Theories Masquerading as Principles': Canadian Electoral Boundary Commissions and the Australian Model," in John C. Courtney, ed., *The Canadian House of Commons: Essays in Honour of Norman Ward* (Calgary: University of Calgary Press, 1985), 157.

Representation-by-population has two distinct implications for Canadian federal politics. The first is that provinces should be represented in the House of Commons in proportion to their share of the total populations of the country. This version of "rep by pop" was the rallying cry of the Clear Grits prior to 1867 and was implemented as part of the Confederation settlement by section 51 of the Constitution Act, 1867. The second implication is that federal electoral districts—particularly those within the same province—should be roughly equal in population. This principle was not expressed in Canadian law until the passage of the *Electoral Boundaries Readjustment Act* in 1964.... *The Representation Act, 1985* amended both the Constitution Act, 1867 and the *Electoral Boundaries Readjustment Act*. In each case the amendments increase the likelihood that federal electoral districts across the country will have widely varying populations and that they therefore undermine representation-by-population with respect to both its Canadian implications.

Source: Reprinted with permission from Andrew Sancton, "Eroding Representation-by-Population in the Canadian House of Commons: The Representation Act, 1985," *Canadian Journal of Political Science* 23, no. 3 (September 1990), 441–442.

The courts have elaborated on the right to vote in several decisions, all arising from challenges to provincial electoral boundaries.[27] The judicial foray into the redistricting controversy was launched in *Dixon,* a 1989 British Columbia case.[28] Robert Dixon, a philosophy professor and president of the Canadian Civil Liberties Association, challenged British Columbia's constituency boundaries. At the time of the challenge, almost one in three provincial constituencies in British Columbia varied from the average constituency population by more than 25 percent, which had been the intraprovincial standard for federal constituencies since 1966. Furthermore, the population distribution was systematically uneven, in that rural areas had populations below average while urban areas were above average. The fact that the Social

Credit government received disproportionate support from rural areas, while the New Democratic opposition received stronger support from urban areas added a partisan dimension to the controversy.

The case was argued before Justice Beverley McLachlin of the British Columbia Supreme Court (now of the Supreme Court of Canada). Justice McLachlin argued that "the concept of representation by population is one of the most fundamental democratic guarantees. And the notion of equality of voting power is fundamental to representation by population.[29] However, although the principle of voter equality is "the single most important factor to be considered in determining electoral boundaries,"[30] it should not be interpreted as requiring absolute or near absolute equality in constituency populations. Instead, McLachlin interpreted section 3 as requiring **relative equality of voting power,** a concept that allowed some deviation to accommodate factors such as geography and population density in the interest of "better government."[31]

But just how much deviation from absolute equality did the concept of "relative equality" condone? Justice McLachlin did not set a clear standard, though she suggested that the deviation limit of plus or minus 25 percent recommended by the province's Fisher Commission,[32] and used by the federal government within provinces, was a "tolerable limit."[33] British Columbia's electoral system was not within tolerable limits, however, and was thus declared invalid.

McLachlin's suggestion of a 25 percent deviation limit did not settle the issue of how much inequality could be tolerated under the Charter. Court challenges thus proceeded in Saskatchewan and Alberta despite the fact that each province had recently passed, or soon would pass, legislation limiting the amount of deviation from the average constituency size to 25 percent.[34] Concern over the Saskatchewan legislation centred on the division of the province's constituencies into urban, rural, and northern categories, with each category allocated a fixed number of seats out of proportion to its share of the population. Thus, the urban areas contained 47.6 percent of the population and received 43.9 percent of seats, while the rural and northern categories combined contained 52.4 percent of the population and received 56 percent of the seats.[35] The greater support received by the Progressive Conservative government from rural areas and by the New Democratic opposition from urban areas (note the parallel with British Columbia) led to considerable speculation that the legislation was an attempt by the government to redistribute to partisan advantage.

The redistribution plan for Saskatchewan was challenged by a group of university professors and lawyers who formed a nonprofit corporation called the Society for the Advancement of Voter Equality (SAVE), as well as by a group called Equal Justice for All. SAVE challenged the redistricting plan in a lawsuit before the lower courts, and, to save time, the government referred the matter directly to the Saskatchewan Court of Appeal.[36]

The Saskatchewan Court of Appeal went considerably further than had Justice McLachlin in *Dixon,* arguing that although some deviation from equality is a "practical necessity,"[37] nonetheless the basic aim of redistribution must be "fair and effective representation" of all citizens, a principle requiring constituencies of "substantially equal voter population."[38] The court viewed the division of the province into urban and rural constituencies as "arbitrary" and therefore unjustified.[39] The fact that all but two northern ridings fell within the 25 percent deviation from the average was insufficient to guarantee "relative or substantial equality of voting power."[40] The addition of the adjective "substantial" to Justice McLachlin's "relative equality" implied a more rigorous standard.

Philosophically, the Saskatchewan Court of Appeal decision suggested a much greater emphasis on equality as the measure of the constitutionality of electoral boundaries legislation. Practically, the decision caused great concern for the Saskatchewan government, which was within five months of the end of its five-year term of office and thus faced an imminent election without valid electoral boundaries. Not surprisingly, Saskatchewan appealed within two weeks, and the Supreme Court, aware of the time pressures, agreed to expedite the hearing, scheduling arguments for a mere six weeks later, at the end of April 1991. On June 6, 1991,[41] by a 6–3 majority, the court overturned the decision of the Saskatchewan Court of Appeal, thereby reinstating the Saskatchewan Act and the boundaries map. The majority decision was written by Justice McLachlin, the same judge who had decided the *Dixon* case in British Columbia in 1989.

Justice McLachlin argued that the debate over the meaning of the right to vote enshrined in the Charter centred on two competing interpretations of the section 3 right to vote. She noted that

> *those who start from the premise that the purpose of the section is to guarantee equality of voting power support the view that only minimal deviation from that ideal is possible. Those who start from the premise that the purpose of section 3 is to guarantee effective representation see the right to vote as comprising many factors, of which equality is but one.*[42]

Justice McLachlin took the latter view, arguing that the purpose of the section 3 right to vote "is not equality of voting power per se, but the right to 'effective representation.'"[43] Absolute equality of voting power is not guaranteed under section 3. Although the first condition of effective representation is "relative parity of voting power,"[44] "factors like geography, community history, community interests and minority representation may need to be taken into account to ensure that our legislative assemblies represent the diversity of our social mosaic."[45] Based on this interpretation of the right to vote, the court upheld Saskatchewan's electoral boundary legislation and the maps drawn by the boundaries commission. In doing so, it supported the general deviation limit of plus or minus 25 percent, as well as the limit of 50 percent for areas with an extremely sparse population.

In upholding Saskatchewan's use of the traditional urban–rural distinction in its districting plan, Justice McLachlin was careful to note that this was not the only non-population-based factor that could justify departures from strict equality. She especially emphasized "minority representation" and "cultural and group identity" as matters that might legitimately be taken into account in drawing constituency boundaries. At the time of this decision there was speculation that her remarks might be used to justify the creation of electoral districts for Aboriginal peoples and possibly for other minority groups.[46] However, to date no Canadian government has done so.

The increased involvement of both electoral boundaries commissions and the courts in the drawing of electoral boundary maps has had several implications. First, partisan considerations have been reduced significantly in the redistribution process. The temptation to gain political advantage from redistricting proved irresistible for legislators during the century that followed Confederation. The use of boundaries commissions has transformed this process from a political exercise into an administrative one. Second, there has been a notable increase in the equality of electoral districts within provinces. The use of the grandfather and senatorial clauses at the federal level has meant that many provinces have seats added to their initial allotment, thereby producing different House of Commons electoral quotients from one province to another. However, within provinces, for both federal and provincial elections the amount of voter inequality has decreased significantly over time. Third, recent court decisions have made it clear that systematic inequalities that significantly transgress the 25 percent deviation standard are not constitutionally permissible, though a less dramatic balancing of equality and non-population-based factors is entirely legitimate. Certainly the courts in Canada have not adopted a rigid formula for voter equality, as has the Supreme Court in the United States, where near mathematical equality has become the standard for congressional districts.

Although these changes have been important, they also serve to illustrate that institutional changes can at times distract attention from more important and fundamental issues. For example, recall that the goal of the Charter's guarantee of voting rights is to produce "fair and effective representation." One interpretation of this goal is for each vote to have *relatively equal weight in electing a member of Parliament.* But that represents a narrow interpretation of the goal. "Fair and effective representation" could be broadened to mean that the right to vote guarantees each voter *an equal (or relatively equal) voice in electing a government.* Stated another way, it would imply that a vote for the Liberals or the New Democrats would have the same weight as a vote for the Conservatives.

If that is what is meant by voter equality, then changing the size of electoral districts could appear to be little more than institutional tinkering. The fact is that the single-member plurality electoral system affects voter equality more dramatically than the kinds of constituency inequalities characteristic of contemporary Canada. For example, Table 9.5 shows the deviation between the percentage of votes and percentage of seats received by each of the parties since 1878. A positive number indicates the margin by which the percentage of seats exceeds the percentage of votes, and a negative number shows the margin of votes over seats. In the far-right column, the absolute deviations (i.e., excluding the sign) are summed.

The data indicate significant deviation in Canadian elections between parties' share of the vote and their share of seats. For example, in 1878 the Conservatives

TABLE 9.5 **DEVIATIONS BETWEEN PERCENTAGE OF LEGISLATIVE SEATS AND PERCENTAGE OF POPULAR VOTES, 1878–1997**

(% SEATS–% VOTES)

YEAR	PC	LIB	NDP	SC	REF	BQ	OTHER	TOTAL DEVIATION
1878	+15	−13					1	29
1882	+12	−12						24
1887	+9	−8						17
1891	−5	−4					−1	10
1896	−5	+10					−6	21
1900	−9	+10					−1	20
1904	−12	+13					−1	26
1908	−8	+10					−1	19
1911	+10	−9					−1	20
1917	+8	−5					−3	16
1921	−9	+8	+5				−4	26
1925	+1	0	+1				−3	5
1926	−8	+6	+3				−2	19
1930	+7	−8	+2				−1	18
1935	−14	+26	−6	+3			0	49
1940	−15	+23	−5	+1			−5	49
1945	0	+10	−5	+1			−7	23
1949	−14	+25	−8	0			−2	49
1953	−12	+16	−2	+1			−2	33
1957	+3	+1	−2	0			0	6
1958	+25	−15	−6	−2			−1	49
1962	+7	+1	−7	−1			0	16
1963	+3	+7	−7	−3			0	20
1965	+5	+9	−10	−4			0	28
1968	−4	+14	−9	−1			−1	29
1972	+6	+3	−6	−2			−1	18
1974	+1	+10	−9	−1			−1	22
1979	+12	0	−9	−3			−2	26
1980	+4	+8	−9	−1			−2	24
1984	+25	−14	−8	0			0	47
1988	+14	−4	−5	0			−4	27
1993	−15	+19	−4	0	−2	+5	−4	49
1997	−12	+13	−4	0	+1	+4	−1	35

Source: Calculated from data in Hugh G. Thorburn, ed., *Party Politics in Canada*, 6th ed. (Scarborough: Prentice Hall, 1991), 553; Chief Electoral Officer of Canada, *Thirty-Fifth General Election, 1993, Official Voting Results* (Ottawa: 1994); and Chief Electoral Officer of Canada, *Thirty-Sixth General Election, 1997, Official Voting Results* (Ottawa: 1997).

received 68 percent of the seats and 53 percent of the popular vote, for a deviation of +15. The Liberals received 45 percent of the vote but only 32 percent of the seats, for a deviation of –13. "Other" parties received 1 percent of the seats and 2 percent of the votes, for a –1 deviation. Thus, the total deviation in 1878 was 29 percentage points. The total absolute deviation since Confederation has ranged from a low of 5 in 1925 to a high of 49 on several occasions, including 1993. It has been highest during the landslide elections of 1935, 1940, 1949, 1958, 1984, and 1993. Significantly, there was no systematic reduction in the magnitude of deviations following the redistribution of 1966 (the first conducted by the boundaries commissions). Because the absolute deviations represent a measure of voter inequality in electing governments, one must conclude that changing the rules for drawing electoral boundaries, and the resulting shift toward more equal constituencies, has not affected the level of voter inequality in this area.

A closer examination of the data for the 1993 and 1997 elections may help sharpen the focus of this issue. The Liberal party received 5,593,524 votes in 1993 and 177 seats in the House of Commons. This translates into a vote-per-seat ratio of 31,601 votes for each seat. The Conservative party, by contrast, won 2,177,412 votes but only two seats, for a ratio of 1,088,706 votes per seat. The votes per seat for the other parties were as follows: NDP (103,869), Reform (49,578), and Bloc Québécois (33,838). Had each of these four parties received the same number of votes per seat as the Liberals, the House would have had 82 Reformers, 69 Conservatives, 58 BQ members, and 30 New Democrats.

Compare this to the 1997 election. The Liberal party received 4,992,932 votes and 155 seats, meaning that for every 32,212 votes the Liberal party won a seat. The Bloc required 31,492 for every seat as they garnered 44 seats with1,385,630 votes. The Reform party received 2,512,570 votes and 60 seats, or 41, 876 votes per seat. The NDP received 1,434,705 votes and 21 seats, or 68,319 votes per seat. The Conservatives received 2,446,340 votes and 20 seats, or one seat for every 122,317 votes. Certainly the way in which votes are counted through the electoral system has a profound impact on the outcome of the elections. The problem (if it could be called such) of voter inequality in electing MPs lies less with the size of electoral districts and more with the single-member plurality electoral system.

A solution to this problem could be found in adopting proportional representation as a system for electing MPs. Making the number of legislative seats won by each party reflect more accurately its proportion of the vote would ensure that the value of each vote is more equal. However, adopting such a radical institutional change would have implications that extend far beyond merely changing the parties' vote-per-seat ratio. It would have profound effects on the likelihood of coalition governments, on the degree of governmental stability, on the effectiveness of executive federalism, on the relative strength of the various parties in the legislature and the electorate, and likely on the policies that emanate from government. The possibility of such dramatic changes, while perhaps cautioning against a headlong rush toward proportional representation, serves as a powerful reminder of the importance of institutions in shaping and channelling interests in the Canadian state.

Territorialism versus Non-Territorial Representation

Territorialism has been a central dimension of controversies about electoral districting and the translation of votes into seats. For example, apportioning districts to protect the representational levels of less populous provinces and sparsely populated rural areas is a clear and increasingly contested attempt to accommodate territorially based social differentiation at the expense of the principle of rep by pop. Similarly, one of the chief complaints about the single-member plurality system is that its tendency to distort the translation of votes into seats exaggerates regional cleavages at the expense of effective national integration.[47] But while territorialism remains a central theme in almost all contestation about Canada's political institutions, and about the electoral system in particular, it is by no means the only one. Chapter 3 explored the growing significance of non-territorial groups in Canada's megaconstitutional politics, for instance, and Chapter 5 noted the growing demand by such groups as women and Aboriginals for increased representation in the legislative institutions.

This latter demand implicates the electoral system. How precisely is the demand for increased representation of certain groups to be achieved? Should "affirmative gerrymandering" be employed to increase the electoral influence of specific groups?[48] Should guaranteed levels of Aboriginal representation be achieved through separate Aboriginal districts?[49] If a certain level of female representation is desirable, should it be achieved through separate (though geographically overlapping) districts for men and women, with each sex electing its own member, or should there be two members, one a woman and one a man, elected by both sexes in each district? If guaranteed quotas of seats for certain groups are undesirable (see Dossier 5.1), could their increased representation nevertheless be promoted through some form of proportional representation? These are perplexing and controversial questions. The only certainty is that it would be difficult to adapt the existing system of plurality elections in single-member districts to ensure increased legislative representation for groups other than territorial communities.

Here, incidentally, we encounter a somewhat ironic situation vis-à-vis the Senate. If the Senate were to remain an appointed institution, it would take no more than an act of political will to make it more representative of the Canadian population. To take an extreme case, a prime minister could appoint only women and Aboriginals to the Senate. (Whether either group would be satisfied with representation in an appointed Senate is another matter.) However, should we move to an elected Senate, we would confront many of the same electoral dilemmas that arise with respect to the House of Commons. The advantage would be that any elected format would be a radical departure for the Senate, and thus there may be more room for experimentation in the design of an elected Senate than in electoral reform for the more tradition-bound House of Commons.

There is no consensus at present on the need for electoral reform to enhance group representation in legislative assemblies. Nor is there clear evidence of significant public support, much less majority support, for quotas or for electoral districting along lines of gender or ethnicity. However, some of those who are sceptical about the need for guaranteed representation in legislative assemblies still support efforts by political parties to ensure that more "balanced" slates of candidates are run in federal and provincial elections. There is, then, an implied belief that if only the parties could be more responsive to group demands, we might be able to avoid formal renovations to the electoral system. We consider the ways in which parties are responding to this belief in the next chapter.

THE ELECTORAL FRANCHISE

The right to vote in open, competitive elections is among the most basic of all democratic rights. The fundamental character of voting rights is illustrated by the fact that they are among the select few rights provided in the Charter of Rights and Freedoms that are not subject to the section 33 legislative override. The right to vote can be denied only where it can be demonstrably justified as a reasonable limit under section 1 of the Charter. The application of the Charter right to vote and its subsequent interpretation by the courts represent the most recent steps in the long march toward **universal adult suffrage.** Today, the major impediments to voting stem from factors other than institutional impediments or prohibitions: a lack of interest, the perception that politics is not relevant, a recent move, illness, or bad weather. This is not to imply that nonvoting is an issue about which one need not be concerned. But it does suggest that institutional factors may have a limited role in addressing the issue in contemporary Canada.

At the time of Confederation, the **franchise** was neither universal nor consistent across the country. Although the intention of the founders was to produce a consistent federal franchise, no agreement was reached on who would have the right to vote. Consequently, section 41 of the 1867 Constitution Act provided for the use of provincial franchises for federal elections until a federal franchise was adopted. Because the provinces had different franchises, the effect was to produce several different federal franchises for the first five elections in the new Dominion. Certain features were common to all the provincial franchises. In particular, each was limited to males 21 years of age or older, and each had a property requirement. The differences came in the particularities of the property qualifications. In Ontario and Quebec, an adult male living in an urban area could vote if he owned, occupied, or rented real property assessed at $300 or with an annual value of $30. In rural areas the property requirement was a $200 assessment or annual value of $20. In New Brunswick the franchise was held by adult males who had real property worth $100 or who had personal property or an annual income of $400. In Nova Scotia the requirement was real property of $150 or personal property of $300. The effect of these property, age, and gender requirements was that only about 15 percent of the total population could vote in federal elections.[50] The proportion of the adult male population entitled to vote was much higher. As Ward notes, these restrictions in effect constituted a "householders franchise" in which most male heads of households were entitled to vote.[51]

The first major reform of the franchise occurred with the Franchise Act of 1885, which finally introduced a common federal franchise. Like the provincial franchises it replaced, the federal franchise was limited to adult males. Like the Ontario and Quebec franchises, its property qualification distinguished between urban and rural dwellers. Eligible to vote were those who owned property worth $300 in cities, $200 in towns, or $150 in rural areas. Furthermore, otherwise eligible sons of property owners could qualify with their fathers' surplus property.[52] This reform increased the size of the electorate by an additional 5 percent, to approximately 20 percent of the population.

The second major reform to the franchise occurred in 1898 under the Liberal government of Wilfrid Laurier. By the end of the century, there were increasing calls for universal manhood suffrage through a removal of all property requirements for voting. Indeed, most provinces had by this time removed all property requirements from their franchises. However, the principle of universal manhood suffrage was strongly opposed in Quebec. In what is perhaps a quintessential Canadian solution, the federal government returned to using provincial franchises for federal elections. Thus, universal adult male suffrage was effected in most of Canada, while Quebec retained its distinctive franchise restrictions at the federal level. The importance of adopting universal adult male suffrage in most of Canada was well captured by Ward:

> *It is a fair statement that some time between 1885 and 1898 the notion that the franchise was a trust accompanying property, rather than a right normally accompanying citizenship, all but disappeared in federal politics. The shift to popular democracy was effected quietly and painlessly.*[53]

The change from regarding the franchise as a "trust" to thinking about it as a right of citizenship was indeed important. Yet this "right" was, at first, extended only to men. Women still could not vote. The gender barrier in voting at the federal level was finally abandoned through a series of measures beginning in 1917, some 50 years after Confederation. The first step was the Military Voters Act, 1917, which extended the franchise to women who had husbands, sons, brothers, or fathers in the Canadian or British armed forces. The following year, the federal government extended the franchise to all women, provided they met the same qualifications as male electors in their province. Finally, in 1920 the federal government abandoned the use of provincial franchises for a uniform and federal franchise that included women among qualified voters.

The 1920 legislation did not enfranchise all adult Canadians, however. There remained some limits on foreign-born Canadians. These were removed in 1922.[54] A relatively small number of groups or individuals continued to be excluded from voting even after 1922. For example, in Quebec provincial elections women were not enfranchised until 1940. In addition, at the federal level, Inuit were explicitly restricted from voting until 1950; they gained the de facto right to vote only with the creation of the Northwest Territories constituency after 1961. Similarly, status Indians were excluded from voting until 1960.

In 1969 the voting age was reduced from 21 to 18 years, providing a significant extension of voting rights to youth. Today the only exclusions that remain in the Canada Elections Act are for minors (those under 18 years), a small number of election officials (the chief electoral officer and the returning officers in each constituency), most federally appointed judges,[55] and some inmates of prisons and mental institutions. The exclusion of prisoners has frequently and sometimes successfully been challenged as an unreasonable limitation of the Charter's section 3 voting rights and has led to prisoner voting in some cases, but at the time of writing, the issue has not been fully decided by the Supreme Court.

In all but the most formal sense, Canada's franchise is now based on universal adult suffrage. The institutional barriers to voting have been removed. Yet the active electorate in Canadian elections can change substantially from one election to the next. There is a continual flow of voters into and out of the electorate. For example, in any four-year election cycle, the electorate can change by as much as 25 percent as new voters enter and **transient voters** move into or out of the active electorate.[56] In addition, 10–15 percent of eligible voters never vote in elections. Whether for reasons

A Suffragette rally, 1913.

of old age, poor health, lack of mobility, lack of interest, or political alienation, this group constitutes what can be termed the voluntarily disenfranchised.

Efforts to examine the reasons for nonvoting in Canadian elections thus far have borne little fruit. One explanation for this is methodological—many people will not admit that they do not vote. For example, the reports of the chief electoral officer indicate that usually about 75 percent of registered voters vote in an election. Public-opinion surveys, however, typically show that only about 15 percent of respondents admit to not voting.[57] In addition, many of the characteristics that distinguish people in their level of political participation generally, such as their gender or ethnic background, have little if any effect on their likelihood of voting. Indeed, one recent study that contrasted three different models of participation—focusing on social background characteristics, political attitudes, and a cost-benefit self-interested calculation—found that none of these models had a powerful effect on voting. However, it also found that the strongest predictor of voting was the amount of information people had about politics and the election.[58] Although it may be tempting to conclude that rates of voting could increase by making more information available to voters, it is difficult to ignore the fact that a vast amount of information already is available during elections. A more cautious interpretation may be that the factors that lead some people to "tune out" political information are the same factors that lead to nonvoting. Research to date suggests that these factors may be more idiosyncratic than systematic.

THE CANADIAN VOTER

Elections in Canada exhibit elements of stability and change. Stability is evident in the fact that only the Liberal and Conservative parties have ever formed the government at the national level and in four of the 10 provinces. In addition, there have been prolonged periods of one-party government both federally and provincially. The Conservatives governed continuously from 1867 to 1896, except for a brief stint in opposition from 1873 to 1878, and most of the 20th century has been a period of Liberal governance. During the 50-year period stretching from the Depression-era election of 1935 to the election of Brian Mulroney's Conservatives in 1984, the Liberal Party governed for 42 years. Following nine years of Conservative party governance under Brian Mulroney and then Kim Campbell, the Liberals returned to government in 1993. Furthermore, this trend has been repeated, with variations, at the provincial level. The Union Nationale governed Quebec from 1936 to 1960, with the exception of the four years the party spent in opposition during World War II. The Social Credit Party governed continuously in Alberta from 1935 to 1971 and in British Columbia from 1953 to 1991 (with the exception of three years of NDP government, from 1972 to 1975). The record for longevity in office belongs to Ontario's Conservative Party, which governed without interruption from 1943 to 1985.

One must be careful not to read too much into this aggregate level of stability in Canadian elections. First, it can obscure the fact, discussed earlier in the chapter, that the electoral system tends to over-reward parties with the greatest support and penalize others. Thus, majority governments and **legislative dominance** can be based on population minorities, and shifting minorities at that. Second, the existence of aggregate stability in governing parties may also hide considerable changes in the government's position relative to the legislature. For example, in 10 of the 14 federal elections from 1957 to 1997, the governing party changed hands or the same party held government but shifted between minority and majority status.

Third, and perhaps most important, one should not infer that the aggregate stability in Canadian election outcomes is produced by similar levels of stability in the voting behaviour of Canadians. Paradoxically, the considerable amount of aggregate stability in elections has coexisted with a high level of instability among Canadian voters. Flexibility in voting patterns is the hallmark of the Canadian electorate. This flexibility is illustrated by the recent experience of the Conservative Party. In 1984, although the Mulroney Conservatives won a landslide victory, their success did not represent a historic realignment of the electorate. Such realignments are not common features of the Canadian political landscape. Instead, the Conservatives in 1984 benefited from high levels of support on a large number of short-term policy and leadership issues. The government's precarious hold on its newfound supporters was illustrated by its dive in the public-opinion polls in 1987,[59] and by its fluctuating levels of support throughout the 1988 election campaign.[60] Although the party was re-elected in 1988, its victory once again owed a greater debt to the vagaries of the electoral system, and to the party's positioning on the Free Trade Agreement, than to an electorate of realigned Conservative partisans. The final proof of the malleability of the partisan leanings of Canadians was evident in the 1993 election, when the Conservatives plummeted to only 16 percent of the vote and two seats in the House of Commons. The 1993 election dispelled any doubts about a Conservative realignment in 1984.

The decision to vote for one party or candidate instead of another, or to vote at all, represents the distillation of a wide variety of factors based on the voter's past, on his or her present circumstances, and on perceptions of who is best suited for governing in the immediate or long-term future. For some voters, the processes of early childhood socialization mark them as Conservatives, Liberals, or New Democrats, and they carry their partisan self-images into adulthood. Those partisan self-images can serve as powerful filters through which they perceive other political objects such as political leaders, local candidates, and political issues. Other voters may be influenced much more directly by the election campaign itself, attuning themselves to the thrust and parry of the leaders' debates, evaluating the merits of the parties' position on issues, or remaining attentive to the parties' revenue and expenditure plans, particularly those directed at the region or groups with which they identify. Of course, this collage of factors influencing voting decisions, and the way in which it is presented to voters, is itself part of the contest for electoral success. Political leaders, together with the parties' campaign organizations, actively engage in efforts to "prime" the electorate to respond to the campaign on their terms and with their party's agenda.[61] The experience of the Conservatives in 1993 illustrates the limits of a party's ability to successfully prime the electoral pump.

The number of factors that can be brought to bear in the voting decision makes it difficult to draw simple conclusions or present simple models of this complex process. Nonetheless, a quarter-century of detailed survey research on the Canadian voter has shown that three types of factors interact to shape and direct the voting decision, namely, partisanship, attitudes toward party leaders, and attitudes toward issues.

Partisanship

The idea of **partisanship** is rooted in the concept of **party identification,** which was developed from research on the voting behaviour of Americans in the 1950s. A group of researchers at the University of Michigan, headed by Angus Campbell, conducted the first large-scale national voter surveys following the 1952 and 1956 presidential elections. The portrait of the electorate that emerged from their surveys was surprising. They found that voters were less interested and involved in the campaign, and had a poorer understanding of the parties' positions on issues, than they had anticipated. However, they also found that most voters had a psychological identification with one of the parties—they thought of themselves as Democrats or Republicans—and that these identifications had a strong effect on their vote.

Equally important was their analysis of the acquisition and durability of party identifications. For most voters, party identification was passed from generation to generation through the socialization process in the family. It was more likely to be an *affective* tie to a party—a generalized feeling of like or dislike—than a *cognitive* one arrived at through a critical appraisal of party policies. The importance of party identification on voting was twofold. First, research showed that this stable, enduring, affective identification with parties was the single most important determinant of a person's voting behaviour—that is, party identification had a powerful, direct effect on voting. Second, party identification had a significant effect on the way voters thought about political issues and the candidates for office. In other words, most American voters in the 1950s did not become Democrats or Republicans because of their views on Dwight Eisenhower or Adlai Stevenson (respectively, the Republican and Democratic presidential candidates in 1952 and 1956); instead, they supported Eisenhower or Stevenson because they were already Republicans or Democrats and were so usually as a result of the political "cues" they had received from parents and others in their youth.

Research on the voting behaviour of Canadians has shown that partisanship operates differently in the Canadian context than it did in the early American studies.[62] Identification with a political party in Canada was found by Harold Clarke and his colleagues to be less consistent across the two levels of the federal system, in that many voters in Canada had a split identification—they identified with different parties at the federal and provincial levels of government. In addition, party identifications are less stable, and Canadians are more likely to change their partisan self-image when they change their vote intention.[63] There is no Canadian equivalent to, for example, "Democrats for George Bush [the Republican president from 1988 to 1992]," in which one retains a long-standing partisan identification while voting for another party.

The reason for this difference between the two countries is mainly institutional. Many U.S. states require voters to register as supporters of one of the political parties, so that they can participate in the state's primary elections to choose a presidential nominee for their party. There is no counterpart to this public declaration of partisanship in Canada. In addition, general elections in the United States, both in presidential election years and in off-year congressional elections, usually feature a large and complex ballot. In addition to voting for candidates for the presidency, one may also participate in elections for the U.S. Senate, House of Representatives, governor, state legislatures, and a host of county and municipal offices. Party identification provides an efficient and effective way of managing a complex election process. It also provides a way to choose among the candidates running for less salient offices (such as county sheriff) without having to depend on detailed information about these individuals (gathering and assessing such information can be relatively costly).

Elections in Canada are markedly different from their American counterparts. The typical Canadian ballot in a federal election has a short list of three to seven contestants for a single seat in the House of Commons. Provincial election ballots are usually equally simple. In voting for a single office, there is a less pressing need for a party label to simplify electoral choice. There is also less of an institutional requirement to retain one's party identification if, in the current election, it proves inconsistent with candidate preferences.

As a result, analysts of voting in Canada developed a measure of partisanship that is sensitive to the way in which party attachments operate within our institutional framework. The measure of partisanship developed by Harold Clarke, Jane Jenson, Lawrence LeDuc, and Jon Pammett is based on the three components of stability, consistency, and intensity of attachment to a party. Stability of partisanship refers to its persistence over time—has one always identified with one party, or was there a period in which one felt closer to another party or to no party? Consistency is a measure of partisanship at the federal and provincial levels. Partisanship is consistent if the same party attachment is held at the two levels of government. Intensity refers to the strength of attachment, and ranges from very strong to moderate to weak. Voters who have stable, consistent, and strong attachments to parties are called **durable partisans,** and typically constitute between 34 and 37 percent of the electorate.[64] Those who deviate on one or more measures of stability, consistency, and strength of attachment are called flexible partisans; they constitute 63 to 66 percent of the electorate.

Party identification among durable partisans acts as a long-term stabilizing force on the electorate, similar to the effect of party identification in the United States in the 1950s. However, the impact of party identification for the electorate as a whole is reduced because of the predominance of flexible partisanship. The phenomenon of flexible partisanship, together with the strength of short-term forces (e.g., attitudes toward leaders and issues), led to the depiction of the Canadian electorate as an example of **stable dealignment,** in which the possibility of substantial electoral change is ever present.[65]

The magnitude of the change is illustrated in Figure 9.2, which shows the behaviour of a significant portion of the electorate during the three federal elections from 1984 to 1993. In the first two of these elections, a little under two-thirds of voters reported voting for the same party they supported in the previous election. This represents a small decline from the 67 and 68 percent of party loyalty reported for the 1974 and 1979 elections, respectively, and a significant decline from the 72 percent reported in 1980. In 1993, only 43 percent reported voting for the same party as in 1988, a finding consistent with the dramatically transformed Parliament that emerged from that election; over half the electorate changed its vote in 1993.

Among the factors responsible for such shifts in partisan support are attitudes toward party leaders and issues.

Party Leaders

Modern election campaigns are conducted largely on television. Campaign strategists are acutely aware of this fact, and campaigns are organized to conform to the

FIGURE 9.2 **VOTE SWITCHING AND ABSTENTION, 1984, 1988, 1993**

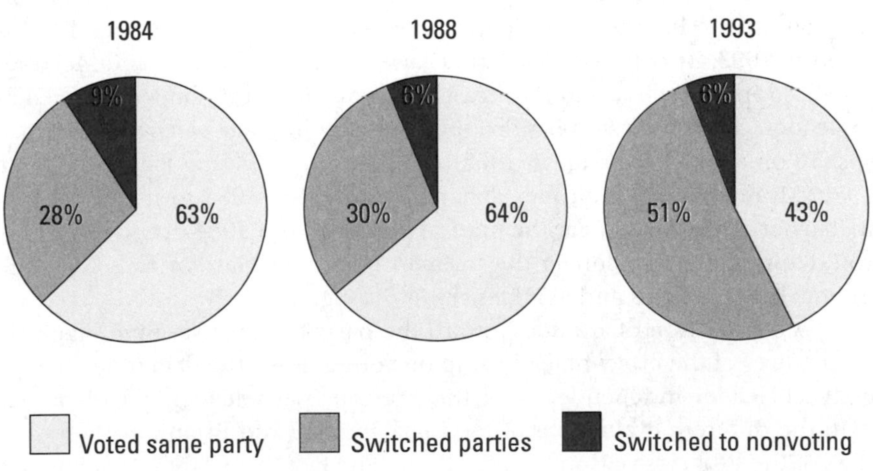

Source: Harold D. Clarke, Jane Jenson, Lawrence LeDuc, and Jon Pammett, *Absent Mandate: Interpreting Change in Canadian Elections,* 3rd ed. (Toronto: Gage, 1991), 106.

requirements of television. Since television is a visual medium, its most basic requirement is for an image to project. In the presentation of policies, television requires a spokesperson—someone who is able to articulate and defend a party's policy platform. As their parties' chief spokespersons, party leaders have come to play an increased role in the voting behaviour of Canadians. The greater level of attention that is focused on party leaders, in Canada as well as in other modern democracies, has not always been flattering to them. As captured and presented through the jaundiced eye of the media, party leaders almost invariably become less popular the longer they remain in the public arena. Elections are sometimes cast as contests between groups of leaders who differ mainly in their level of unpopularity, where voters are left with little choice but to "throw the rascals in."[66]

Data on attitudes toward party leaders in recent decades confirm the overall decline in popular evaluations of party leaders and also the complex ways in which leadership affects voting. Figure 9.3 shows evaluations of federal party leaders in the six elections from 1974 to 1993, as well as during the Charlottetown Accord referendum in 1992. Nine of the leaders portrayed in this figure fought more than one of this series of campaigns. Although Preston Manning and Lucien Bouchard are included in this multiple-campaign group, the figure shows only their 1993 data because in 1992 only Quebeckers were asked about Bouchard while only Canadians outside Quebec were asked about Manning; their 1992 results were thus not comparable to those of Chrétien, McLaughlin, and Mulroney, whose ratings were based on a national survey. Consequently, Figure 9.3 displays trend lines for only seven of the nine multiple-campaign leaders.

All but two of the seven trend lines dropped consistently over time. The two exceptions to this trend were Ed Broadbent in 1984, when his public image improved over the previous election, only to fall off dramatically by 1988, and Jean Chrétien, whose rating rose between the Charlottetown Accord referendum of 1992 and the election in 1993. By contrast, Trudeau, Clark, Mulroney, Turner, and McLaughlin all saw their support decline—in most cases dramatically—the longer they remained as party leader. Trudeau's support dropped steadily in each election, from a high of almost 70 on a 100-point scale in 1968 (the election predating Figure 9.3) to only 55 in 1980. More recently, Mulroney dropped from 62 in 1984 to the mid-50s in 1988. John Turner, who started near the neutral point at 51 in 1984 dropped to 41 in 1988. It would appear that the longer they remain under the glare of TV's klieg lights, the more our leaders' warts and wrinkles shine through.

A comparison of attitudes toward the party leaders over time suggests several other features of the effect of leadership on voting. First, the data indicate that voters assess each leader independently of the previous party leader. This is most clearly seen in the different evaluations of Joe Clark in 1980 and Brian Mulroney in 1984 as leaders of the Progressive Conservative Party. The fact that Clark was held in relatively low esteem when he led the Conservatives, with a rating of 42, did not affect the rating of Mulroney four years later—a score of 63. Likewise, Ed Broadbent in 1979 was not harmed by the negative ratings of David Lewis, the NDP leader in 1974. Nor did John Turner's low evaluation in 1988 negatively affect Jean Chrétien in 1993. Furthermore, there is as much variation in evaluations of most of the leaders over time as there is between each leader and his or her successor. Put another way, leadership is a short-term factor in Canadian elections. The variability in party-leader evaluations from one election to the next, with or without a change in leadership, can make a significant impact on the magnitude of change in the election.

Second, the data in Figure 9.3 caution against an oversimplified interpretation of the importance of leadership in Canadian elections. There is no direct relationship between attitudes toward leaders and voting. For example, in each election in the series except 1993, the leader of the New Democratic Party was the second most popular leader. In 1974, David Lewis was only marginally more popular than Robert Stanfield, the Progressive Conservative leader. However, from 1979 through 1988 NDP leader Ed Broadbent was consistently rated substantially higher than the least popular leader and came close to the ratings of the most popular leader. Despite the generally strong ratings of New Democratic Party leaders during this period, the party invariably finished in third position (in what were then three-party races), usually trailing the second-place finisher by 10 percentage points and sometimes as many as 20 points. Thus, popular leadership is no panacea to a party's troubles, particularly if the party's program and policies are unpopular among the electorate. On the other hand, lack of popularity at the national level does not spell disaster for a party, as long as national unpopularity is offset by strong regional popularity. Thus

FIGURE 9.3 THERMOMETER RATINGS OF PARTY LEADERS, 1974–1993

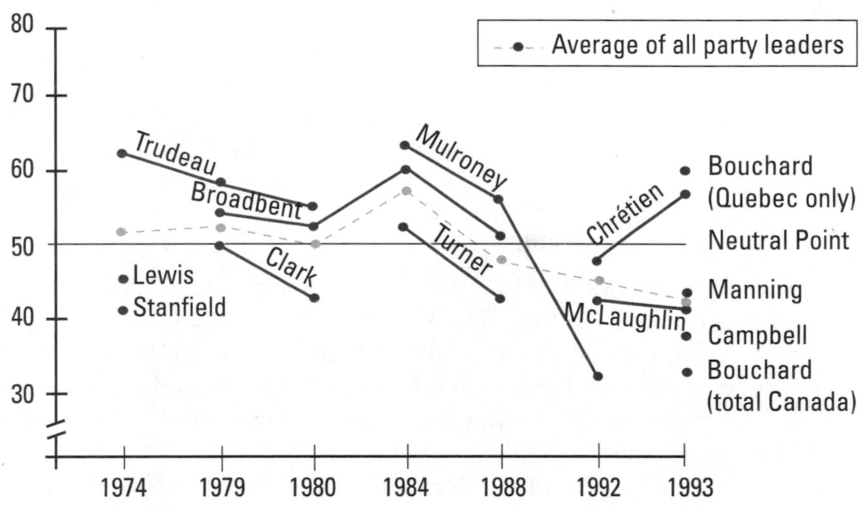

Source: Harold D. Clarke et al., *Absent Mandate: The Politics of Discontent,* 3rd ed. (Toronto: Gage), 77.

Lucien Bouchard, the least popular leader nationally in 1993, led his party to a second-place finish in the House of Commons on the strength of high popularity in Quebec. As already noted, such regional distortions are a function of the electoral system.

Third, although positive leadership evaluations do not constitute a guarantee of electoral success, the data indicate that leadership can be an important factor in the voting decision. Except in 1979, the party leader with the highest rating nationally was elected as prime minister. Furthermore, recall that although the Progressive Conservatives led by Joe Clark won a minority election victory in 1979, they received only 36 percent of votes, 4 percent less than the Liberals led by Pierre Trudeau. In addition, the two most dramatic reversals of electoral fortune during this series coincided with equally dramatic shifts in the popularity of party leaders. The first of these reversals occurred between 1980 and 1984, when the government shifted from a Liberal majority under Trudeau to a massive Progressive Conservative majority under Mulroney. The period between these elections saw a leadership change for the Progressive Conservatives in 1983 and the Liberals in 1984. In 1980 Trudeau held a 12-point edge over Clark in leader evaluations, while in 1984 Mulroney held a 12-point edge over Turner. Thus this period witnessed a shift of 24 points in the evaluations of Liberal and Progressive Conservative leaders. A similarly large shift took place between 1988, when Mulroney enjoyed a sizable lead over John Turner, and 1993, when Turner's successor, Jean Chrétien, turned the tables on Mulroney's successor, Kim Campbell. This shift coincided with the precipitous decline of the Conservatives from a majority government in 1988 to a precarious two-seat rump in 1993 and their replacement by a Liberal majority government. (Given Mulroney's remarkably low rating in 1992, one shudders to think what might have happened to the Conservatives had he led them in the 1993 election.)

In addition to the summary assessment of party leaders provided by the "feeling thermometer," one can also compare the substantive content of leader evaluations. In *Letting the People Decide,* Richard Johnston and his colleagues distinguished between assessments of the competence and the character of party leaders.[67] The trait of competence was assessed on the basis of whether the leader was viewed as intelligent, knowledgeable, and able to provide strong leadership and a vision of Canada. The character of leaders was assessed on the basis of whether they were perceived as moral, trustworthy, and compassionate. Johnston et al. showed that Mulroney significantly outscored Turner in assessments of competence, though both leaders rated low in assessments of character. Furthermore, their research indicates that Ed Broadbent scored relatively high on assessments of both competence and character, and that these ratings remained high throughout the campaign. However, the NDP was not able to translate this relatively positive leader evaluation into strong electoral support.

Changes based on short-term factors such as leadership are always precarious, as the Conservative and New Democratic parties were to learn in 1993, when evaluations of Kim Campbell and Audrey McLaughlin declined relative to those of their predecessors in the previous election. On the other hand, a decline in leader evaluations, or a relatively low assessment for a party leader, does not spell immediate defeat for a party, as the Liberals found throughout Trudeau's tenure and as the Conservatives found under the leadership of both Clark and Mulroney. The instability in voting behaviour produced by short-term leadership effects can be neutralized, reversed, or reinforced by additional short-term issue effects. It is the interaction of the public's assessment of leaders and its view of issues that determines the extent to which individual-level instability is reflected in instability in election outcomes.

Issues

The short-term character of voting behaviour in Canada is both produced by and reflected in the changing features of political issues. One of the more important features of issues in elections is their remarkable variability. Despite the oft-voiced perception that political debate revolves around a repetition of a limited set of questions—Quebec's place in Confederation and the constitutional issue, Canada's relationship to the United States, the balance of power between Ottawa and the provinces (including their fiscal relationship), and the state of the economy—the past two decades have witnessed a high level of change in election issues. Furthermore, it is rare for one political party to "win" the issue debate decisively. Rarer still is the election in which one party wins decisively the contests over leader popularity and political issues. Double victories of this sort are recipes for election landslides, as occurred in the 1984 election. Typically the government receives a mixed and limited mandate based on more ambiguous leadership and issue effects.

Three conditions must be met for issues to have an important effect in an election outcome: the issue must be salient, it must be linked to the parties, and opinion must be skewed. **Issue salience** refers to the visibility and perceived electoral importance of an issue. An issue is salient if large numbers of voters think about that issue when deciding how to vote.

The linking of an issue to the political parties is also a critical step in the issue becoming an important factor in the election outcome. No matter how salient an issue may be to some voters, if the parties collectively refuse to tie themselves to a distinctive position on it, the issue will be of diminished importance. For example, proponents of capital punishment have difficulty basing their votes on this issue because none of the major parties in Canada supports capital punishment. Furthermore, whenever a vote on capital punishment reaches the floor of the Commons, party discipline is relaxed to enable all members to vote according to their conscience. Likewise, advocates of both the pro-life and pro-choice positions on the abortion issue are frustrated in their attempts to politicize this issue because of the ambiguity of party positions on abortion.[68] Even when parties do take relatively clear and distinctive positions on issues, the **party linkage** may not be drawn completely for all voters. For example, although research on the 1988 federal election has shown that one of the major effects of the campaign was to establish and solidify the connection between an individual's position on the Free Trade Agreement and his or her partisan support, a significant number of Canadians nonetheless voted for the party that opposed their own position on this key issue.[69]

The third condition that must be met for an issue to be important in an election is that opinion must be skewed. **Skewness** refers to the distribution of support on an issue. Opinion is skewed when significantly more people are on one side of an issue than on the other side. In addition, as was the case with the free-trade issue in 1988, opinion also is skewed if there are similar proportions of the electorate on either side of an issue but with one side linked to one party and the other side linked to two or more parties.

It is unusual for all of these conditions—salience, party linkage, and skewness—to be met in an election. Although many elections provide evidence of issues being salient to voters, they tend not to be clearly linked to parties with a skewed opinion. To illustrate this more clearly, we examine the fluctuations in issue importance during the last two decades. The data in Table 9.6 indicate the variability in issue salience over time. In each election between 1974 and 1988, respondents to a national survey were asked which issues were most and second most important to them during the election.

Several features of this table merit discussion. In the first four elections portrayed in the table, a significant proportion of the electorate—usually about one-quarter—did not think about the election on the basis of issues, and could not mention a single issue as important to them. This changed in 1988, when all but 5 percent could mention an important issue (for most it was free trade), and this trend continued through the 1993 election, when 7 percent of respondents could not think of an election issue. Stated differently, a majority of Canadians, anywhere from 70 to 95 percent, approach elections at least in part on the basis of issues.

Note, however, that although issues are important to most Canadians, there is a high degree of variability in issue mentions over time. In 1974 the election appeared to be dominated by the inflation issue, but by 1984 and 1988 the concern with inflation had evaporated. The 1979 election saw a decrease in the salience of inflation, an increase in the importance of constitutional issues (the separatist PQ had come to power in Quebec in 1976), and an increase in the salience of leadership as an issue. During the 1980 election the government's deficit and the budget increased in salience (the Clark government fell in debate on its first budget), as did resource issues (through the rising cost of oil and gas and the government's controversial proposal to introduce an 18-cent-per-litre tax on non-renewable energy resources). By the 1984 election the fight against inflation in the United States and Canada had led to a significant increase in unemployment rates and an increased salience of the unemployment issue. Constitutional and resource issues had all but disappeared from the public mind, although social issues had increased, along with the sentiment that it was time for a change. During the 1988 election all issues were dwarfed by the overwhelming salience of free trade. By 1993 the free-trade issue had all but disappeared, although economic issues continued to prevail.

TABLE 9.6 MOST IMPORTANT ELECTION ISSUES, 1974–1993

	1974	1979	1980	1984	1988	1993
ECONOMIC ISSUES						
Economy in general	5%	11%	9%	17%	2%	23%
Inflation, cost of living, wage and price controls	46	154	14	2	–	–
Taxes	3	8	3	3	4	2
Government spending, deficit, budget	3	4	17	12	7	21
Unemployment, jobs	3	10	4	36	2	34
Free trade	–	–	–	–	88	2
Other economic issues	3	1	1	3	–	–
CONSTITUTIONAL ISSUES						
National unity, inter-governmental relations	2	10	7	2	6	3
Bilingualism, language	3	3	–	1	–	–
Quebec, separatism, referendum	1	15	6	2	–	–
RESOURCE ISSUES						
Oil prices, energy policy, development	2	4	31	1	–	–
Environment, pollution	–	5	1	1	9	1
SOCIAL ISSUES						
Housing, health, medicare, pensions, women's issues	12	5	2	11	14	5
OTHER ISSUES						
Foreign policy, defence	2	2	3	3	1	1
Leadership, leaders	6	14	15	8	5	3
Change, parties, retrospective evaluations	1	8	8	14	1	3
Trust, patronage, majority government, the polls	7	1	4	4	1	4
All other issues	3	2	2	4	3	2
None, No important issues, Don't know	30	28	22	25	5	7

Source: Harold D. Clarke, Jane Jenson, Lawrence LeDuc, and Jon Pammett, *Absent Mandate: Canadian Electoral Politics in an Era of Restructuring*, 3rd ed. (Toronto: Gage, 1996), 29.

Although each election witnessed at least 15 percent of voters (and, in most elections, considerably more than 15 percent) mentioning one issue as most important to them, not all of those voters should be thought of as "issue voters." That is, one should not infer from Table 9.6 that 46 percent of voters in 1974 switched to one party because of the inflation issue or that the inflation issue accounted for a 46 percent difference in the outcome of the election. Instead, 46 percent represents the absolute upper limit in the importance of inflation in 1974. Its true independent effect can be determined only after taking into account linkage to parties, skewness of opinion, partisanship, and leader effects. A fuller understanding of the effect of issues in elections can be obtained through a more detailed examination of the economic issues of inflation and unemployment from 1974 to 1984 and the free trade election of 1988.

Inflation and Unemployment, 1974–1984

The rate of inflation rose to unprecedented heights in the 1970s and early 1980s. From an average rate of less than 3 percent in the 1960s, the rate of inflation skyrocketed to 11 percent in 1974. From then until 1982 inflation dropped below 9 percent only twice, peaking at 12.5 percent in 1981. During the same period, the rate of unemployment rose from an average of less than 4 percent in the 1960s to an average of over 6 percent in the 1970s. It peaked at 12 percent in 1983. Thus, the decade from 1974 through 1984 saw chronic high levels of inflation (although with a dramatic decline leading to 1984) and chronic high unemployment, with an equally dramatic surge leading to 1984.

Recall from Table 9.6 that inflation was the most salient issue in 1974 and unemployment the most salient issue in 1984. Neither inflation nor unemployment were the most important electoral issues in 1979 or 1980. Table 9.7 isolates the independent effect of inflation in 1974, while Table 9.8 repeats the analysis for unemployment in 1984. The tables begin with a series of logical steps to identify the presence of a linkage of the issue with a party. For example, in 1974 the total who considered inflation a leading issue was 44.3 percent. A smaller total—34.3 percent of the electorate—mentioned inflation as important and saw a party as closest to them on this issue; the remaining 10 percent of those who considered inflation important saw no party as closest to them on this issue, and thus this issue could not affect their vote (although it could affect their decision on whether to vote). Taking the analysis one step further, 27.6 percent voted for the party closest to them on the issue of inflation. For unemployment in 1984, 19.7 percent voted for the party closest to them on the issue of unemployment.

Sections B and C in Tables 9.7 and 9.8 control for party attachments and for attitudes toward the party leaders. The assumption behind section B is that some voters are durable partisans who not only identify strongly with a party at both levels of government but also never change their partisanship and always vote for the same party. Although such voters may say that a particular issue was important to them and decided their vote, it is more likely that their partisanship was responsible for their vote and their issue position on inflation or unemployment. After controlling for partisanship, the tables show that 15.2 percent of voters in 1974 and 12.3 percent in 1984 could have voted on the basis of the inflation and unemployment issues, respectively.

Section C adopts a similar control for party leaders. The assumption is that when one party leader is preferred over all others by a wide margin, leader evaluations likely comprise the largest effect. In 1974 the control for leadership attitudes leaves 10.5 percent of voters classified as inflation voters, while 9.4 percent are classified as unemployment voters in 1984.

The test of issue skewness is applied in section D of Tables 9.7 and 9.8. The 10.5 percent of the electorate who were inflation voters were about one-and-a-half times as likely to support the opposition as they were to support the government (6.6 percent versus 4.0 percent). However, the opposition vote also split among the Progressive Conservatives and the New Democrats, favouring the Conservatives by a ratio of nearly three to one. The net result was that the Liberals retained the support of almost as many inflation voters (4.0 percent of the electorate) as did the Progressive Conservatives (4.9). Thus, despite rates of inflation at levels unprecedented in the post–World War II period, and despite its high level of salience as an issue, inflation had at best a marginal effect on the outcome of the 1974 election.

When one applies the skewness test to 1984, however, the opposite conclusion is reached about unemployment. The Liberal government was widely blamed for high unemployment levels and the opposition was able to capture support among unemployment voters by a ratio of greater than 10 to 1. Furthermore, among the opposition, Progressive Conservatives enjoyed a substantial advantage over New Democrats in the skewing of opinion. The net result was a very large advantage (5 total percentage points) for the Progressive Conservatives on the unemployment issue. When their issue advantage on unemployment was combined with their leadership advantage (recall Figure 9.3), the result was a significant increase in votes for the Conservatives in 1984. When that vote outcome was processed through the electoral system, the result was a landslide in legislative seats.

THE FREE TRADE ISSUE OF 1988

Rarely in Canadian electoral history does one issue dominate an election to the extent that the free-trade issue dominated the 1988 election. Table 9.6 indicated that almost nine out of 10 respondents to a national election survey thought that free trade was an important election issue. This proportion is far above the average issue salience. For example, in the six elections from 1974 to 1993, no other issue was mentioned by as many as half of the sample, and in three of the six elections no more than one in three voters could agree on the most important issue of the campaign.

TABLE 9.7 EFFECT OF INFLATION ON VOTING BEHAVIOUR, 1974

	PERCENTAGE	(N)
Total weighted sample	100.0	(2445)
A. General		
1. Mentioned inflation as first or second most important issue	44.3	(1083)
2. Saw a party as being closest to them on inflation	34.3	(838)
3. Voted for the party closest to them on inflation	27.6	(676)
B. Controlling for party attachment		
4. Vote in 1972 and 1974 federal elections		
a. same party (standpatters)	18.5	(453)
b. different parties (switchers)	5.3	(129)
c. eligible but did not vote in 1972 (transients)	1.8	(43)
d. not eligible in 1972 (new voters)	1.8	(43)
5. If voted same party in 1972 and 1974, always voted same party?		
a. yes	11.9	(292)
b. no	6.4	(156)
Total inflation vote due to party	11.9	(292)
Total inflation vote not due to party	15.2	(371)
C. Controlling for party and attitudes toward party leaders		
6. Evaluation of leader of party voted for exceeds second most liked leader by 20 points or more (100-point scale)	4.7	(115)
Evaluation of leader of party voted for does not exceed most liked leader by 20 points (inflation voters)	10.5	(256)
D. Direction of vote of inflation voters		
Liberal	4.0	(96)
Progressive Conservative	4.9	(119)
New Democrat	1.7	(41)

Source: Keith Archer and Marquis Johnson, "Inflation, Unemployment and Canadian Federal Voting Behaviour," *Canadian Journal of Political Science* 21 (September 1988), 578. Reprinted with permission.

TABLE 9.8 EFFECT OF UNEMPLOYMENT ON VOTING BEHAVIOUR, 1984

	PERCENTAGE	(N)
Total weighted sample	100.0	(3380)
A. General		
1. Mentioned unemployment as first or second most important issue	36.3	(1227)
2. Saw a party as being closest to them on unemployment	25.1	(847)
3. Voted for the party closest to them on unemployment	19.7	(667)
B. Controlling for party attachment		
4. Vote in 1980 and 1984 federal elections		
a. same party (standpatters)	10.2	(344)
b. different parties (switchers)	5.3	(178)
c. eligible but did not vote in 1980 (transients)	2.0	(68)
d. not eligible in 1980 (new voters)	2.0	(69)
5. If voted same party in 1980 and 1984, always voted same party?		
a. yes	7.1	(240)
b. no	3.0	(101)
Total unemployment vote due to party	7.1	(240)
Total unemployment vote not due to party	12.3	(416)
C. Controlling for party and attitudes toward party leaders		
6. Evaluation of leader of party voted for exceeds second most liked leader by 20 points or more (100-point scale)	2.9	(98)
Evaluation of leader of party voted for does not exceed most liked leader by 20 points (unemployment voters)	9.4	(318)
D. Direction of vote of unemployment voters		
Liberal	0.8	(29)
Progressive Conservative	7.2	(242)
New Democrat	1.4	(47)

Source: Keith Archer and Marquis Johnson, "Inflation, Unemployment and Canadian Federal Voting Behaviour," *Canadian Journal of Political Science* 21 (September 1988), 581. Reprinted with permission.

Because of the way in which the free-trade issue unfolded prior to the 1988 election, its high salience was both expected and predictable. The Royal Commission on the Economic Union and Development Prospects for Canada, headed by Donald Macdonald (formerly Trudeau's Finance minister), had been established by Trudeau in 1982. One of the key recommendations of the Macdonald Commission was for the government to negotiate a free-trade agreement with the United States. Its report was tabled in 1985, by which time the Liberals had been defeated by the Progressive Conservatives under Brian Mulroney. Although Mulroney had not appointed the commission, and although he had spoken against free trade when he ran for the Conservative leadership in 1983, nonetheless he had become a supporter of the principle of a Canada–United States free-trade agreement. In late 1985 he initiated discussions on free trade with the Reagan administration. An agreement in principle was reached by late 1987, subject to the agreement's enabling legislation receiving passage into law in both countries by January 1, 1989.

The Conservative government's large majority in the House of Commons ensured that the legislation received quick passage in the lower house of Parliament. However, recall from Chapter 5 that for a bill to become law, it must be passed by both the House of Commons and the Senate and must then receive royal assent. The appointed Senate was controlled by a majority of Liberal members—not surprisingly, since the Liberal Party had controlled the government (and, therefore, appointments to the Senate) almost without interruption since 1963. The Liberal leader in the Senate, Allan MacEachen, also a former Trudeau Finance minister, declared that the Senate would not pass the legislation unless the Mulroney government received a mandate to that effect through a national election. As the January 1, 1989, deadline for ratification drew nearer, Mulroney recognized the intransigence of the Liberal senators' position and requested the governor general to dissolve Parliament and call a general election. The election was held November 21, 1988.

Against this backdrop, the salience of the free-trade issue in the election is understandable. But did it meet the other conditions of affecting the outcome of the election, namely, being linked to the parties and manifesting skewness of opinion? The data indicate that the answer is a qualified yes. It is qualified because on first blush the distribution of opinion appears relatively even rather than skewed. During the final week of the campaign, for example, 38.4 percent of respondents to the national election study survey supported the free-trade agreement while 45.1 percent were opposed. The remaining 16.5 percent were neither supporters nor opponents of the agreement.[70]

Although that distribution indicates a lack of skewness, when one factors in the way in which the issue was linked to the parties, the opinions become less evenly divided. Table 9.9 illustrates the linkage of the issue of free trade to the parties in 1988. During the final week of the campaign, 88.3 percent of free-trade supporters intended to vote Progressive Conservative, compared to only 6.4 percent and 2.8 percent of free-trade supporters intending to vote Liberal and New Democrat, respectively. Among the opponents of free trade, the division of support was less decisive.

TABLE 9.9 **FREE-TRADE OPINION AND VOTE INTENTIONS, NOVEMBER 14–20, 1988**

VOTE INTENTION	ATTITUDE TOWARD FREE TRADE			
	SUPPORT	NEITHER	OPPOSE	TOTAL
Progressive Conservative	88.3	56.0	7.3	47.5
Liberal	6.4	28.1	61.0	33.8
New Democrat	2.8	10.5	29.0	15.7
Other	2.6	5.5	2.7	3.0
Total	42.3	12.3	45.4	(417)

Source: Richard Johnston, André Blais, Henry E. Brady, and Jean Crête, "Free Trade and the Dynamics of the 1988 Canadian Election," in Joseph Wearing, ed., *The Ballot and Its Message: Voting in Canada* (Mississauga: Copp Clark Pitman, 1991), 321. Originally published by the American Political Science Association.

For example, 61 percent of free-trade opponents intended to vote Liberal, whereas 29 percent of this same group were New Democrat voters. Only 7.3 percent of opponents of the free-trade agreement intended to vote Conservative. Thus, there was a clear linkage to the Conservatives as supporters of the agreement, but more ambiguity in linking the issue to the two major opposition parties, both of which opposed the agreement. The greater ability of the Conservatives to rely on supporters of the agreement altered the effect of the distribution of opinion. The existence of two parties on one side of the issue and one on the other side transformed a relatively equal distribution of opinion to one that clearly favoured the Conservatives. Thus, free trade played a key role in the election outcome. And, of course, so too did the electoral system, which turned the PC's 43 percent of the votes into 57 percent of the seats and a legislative majority.

CONCLUSION

Competitive elections are one of the givens in a representative democracy, one of its defining characteristics. They perform the critically important function of enabling a political community to choose who will (and who will not) govern. They provide an important opportunity to evaluate the past performance of a government and render judgment on that performance. Knowing that a country's political leaders are chosen through competitive elections tells a great deal about the relationship between citizens and their government.

However, the existence of competitive elections can raise as many questions as it answers about that relationship. Elections are both part of the institutional structure of the Canadian state and a separate, quasi-independent check on the political regime that controls the state apparatus. As with other state structures, the form of elections affects the outcomes they produce. In particular, the nature of the electoral system has had a profound effect on the development of the party system and on the partisan configuration of the government. The observation that institutions matter in politics is as well illustrated by the electoral system as it is by any institution of the Canadian state.

On the other hand, considerable effort has been made to remove "politics" from the administration of the electoral mechanism. The use of boundary commissions in electoral districting has partially depoliticized what had been a highly partisan exercise. In addition, the gradual extension of the franchise greatly expanded the opportunities for all citizens to participate in the selection of the government.

Elections are determined not only by the characteristics of the electoral system or of the electorate. They are determined also by the complex array of beliefs, attitudes, and behaviours that form an essential component of the electoral process. Whether we choose to vote or abstain is a decision rooted in both our social context and our individual experiences. General patterns of nonvoting are weak and not readily susceptible to explanation or prediction. Likewise, partisan choices in Canada are not deeply rooted in class, religious or educational backgrounds. Voting is remarkable as much for its diversity and instability as it is for its constancy. Short-term factors tend to predominate but often pull voters in opposite directions. The known biases in the electoral system, combined with the high degree of flexibility in voting patterns, suggest that elections will continue to be marked by volatility and change. These factors also suggest that Canadian governments will continue to have considerable latitude when it comes to interpreting the meaning and defining the mandate of their election victories.

KEY TERMS

- electoral system
- simple preference
- strategic voting
- ordinal choice
- electoral district / constituency / riding
- single-member district
- multi-member district
- mixed-member proportional (MMP)
- plurality system / first-past-the-post
- majority system
- multiple ballots
- runoff election
- single transferable vote (STV)
- alternative vote (AV)
- party-list system
- proportional representation (PR)
- coalition governments
- representation by population / rep by pop
- electoral quotient
- gerrymandering

relative equality of voting power
universal adult suffrage
franchise
transient voters
legislative dominance
partisanship
party identification
durable partisans
stable dealignment
issue salience
party linkage
skewness

DISCUSSION QUESTIONS

1. It has been said that Canada is an exception to the tendency of the first-past-the-post electoral system to produce two-party systems. Why would one expect this electoral system to favour two-party systems? Why is Canada an exception? Use Tables 9.2 and 9.3 to determine the extent to which the electoral system produces two-party systems *within* provinces or regions, if not in the country as a whole.
2. Should we change Canada's electoral system? If so, which alternative do you favour and why? What are the obstacles to such change and how could they be overcome?
3. How equal in population should Canadian federal constituencies be within provinces? Within the country as a whole? How equal should provincial constituencies be?
4. Should we keep or abolish the senatorial floor and/or the grandfather clause?
5. What is the significance of the fact that the anti-free-trade vote in the 1988 election was divided between the Liberals and the NDP? Does this fact have any bearing on the legitimacy of the Conservative government proceeding with the agreement even though a majority of voters cast ballots for parties opposed to it?

SUGGESTED READINGS

Bakvis, Herman, ed. *Voter Turnout in Canada.* Vol. 15 of the Research Studies of the Royal Commission on Electoral Reform and Party Financing. Toronto: Dundurn Press, 1991.

Canada. Royal Commission on Electoral Reform and Party Financing. *Reforming Electoral Democracy.* Vol. 1. Toronto: Dundurn Press, 1991.

Carty, R. Kenneth, Lynda Erickson, and Donald E. Blake, eds. *Leaders and Parties in Canadian Politics: Experiences of the Provinces.* Toronto: Harcourt Brace Jovanovich, 1992.

Clarke, Harold D., Jane Jenson, Lawrence LeDuc, and Jon H. Pammett. *Absent Mandate: The Politics of Discontent.* 3rd ed. Toronto: Gage, 1996.

Courtney, John C., Peter MacKinnon, and David E. Smith, eds. *Drawing Boundaries: Legislatures, Courts and Electoral Values.* Saskatoon: Fifth House, 1992.

Dalton, Russell J. *Citizen Politics in Western Democracies: Public Opinion and Political Parties in the United States, Great Britain, West Germany and France.* Chatham, N.J.: Chatham House, 1988.

Frizzel, Alan, Jon H. Pammett, and Anthony Westell, eds. *The Canadian General Election of 1997.* Toronto: Dundurn Press, 1998.

Johnston, J. Paul, and Harvey E. Pasis, eds. *Representation and Electoral Systems: Canadian Perspectives.* Scarborough: Prentice-Hall Canada, 1990.

Johnston, Richard, André Blais, Henry E. Brady, and Jean Crête. *Letting the People Decide: Dynamics of a Canadian Election.* Montreal and Kingston: McGill-Queen's University Press, 1992.

Wearing, Joseph. *The Ballot and Its Message: Voting in Canada.* Mississauga: Copp Clark Pitman, 1991.

NOTES

1. Donley Studlar, "Will Canada Seriously Consider Electoral System Reform?" *Inroads* 7 (1998), 56.
2. Canada, Royal Commission on Electoral Reform and Party Financing, *Reforming Electoral Democracy,* vol. 1 (Toronto: Dundurn, 1991), 26.
3. Robert Dahl, *Democracy and Its Critics* (New Haven, Conn.: Yale University Press, 1989).
4. Rev. ed. (New Haven, Conn.: Yale University Press, 1971), 16.
5. Guido Goldman, "The German Political System," in Samuel H. Beer, Adam B. Ulam, Suzanne Berger, and Guido Goldman, eds., *Patterns of Government: The Major Political Systems of Europe,* 3rd ed. (New York: Random House, 1973), 554–557.
6. Suzanne Berger, "The French Political System," in Beer et al., *Patterns of Government,* 385.
7. In 1998, for example, the Progressive Conservative Party used a version of direct election by party members to select its leader. Although Preston Manning was selected leader of the Reform Party by a traditional party convention, the party constitution calls for the leader to be directly elected by members in the future.
8. Joseph Wearing, *Strained Relations: Canadian Parties and Voters* (Toronto: McClelland & Stewart, 1988), 212–216.
9. For example, Tom Flanagan, "The Alternative Vote: An Electoral System for Canada," *Inroads* 7 (1998).
10. Alan Cairns, "The Electoral System and the Party System in Canada," *Canadian Journal of Political Science* 1 (1968).
11. George C. Perlin, *The Tory Syndrome: Leadership Politics in the Progressive Conservative Party* (Montreal and Kingston: McGill-Queen's University Press, 1980).

12. See *Inroads* 7 (1998), a special issue devoted to electoral reform.
13. This system is described in Canada, Elections Canada, *Representation in the Federal Parliament* (Ottawa: Minister of Supply and Services, 1986), 2–18.
14. Although the legislation was passed in 1974, it was first applied in the redistribution of 1976.
15. On the basis of population, it would be entitled to one seat.
16. On the basis of population, it would be entitled to eight seats.
17. Constitution Act, 1867, section 51.
18. Norman Ward, "The Basis of Representation in the House of Commons," *Canadian Journal of Economics and Political Science* 15, no. 4 (November 1949), 487.
19. Norman Ward, *The Canadian House of Commons: Representation,* 2nd ed. (Toronto: University of Toronto Press, 1963), 35.
20. Ward, "The Basis of Representation," 490–491; Ward, *The Canadian House of Commons,* 19–35; Terence Qualter, "Representation by Population: A Comparative Study," *Canadian Journal of Political Science* 33 (1967), 248–252.
21. Norman Ward, "A Century of Constituencies," *Canadian Public Administration* 10 (1967), 107.
22. In the words of C.G. "Chubby" Power, a long-time member of Parliament in the 1930s and 1940s, the process of redistribution was an "unseemly, undignified and utterly confusing scramble for personal or political advantage." The House of Commons, *Debates,* 1939, 1808.
23. In 1979 an eleventh commission was created from the two seats in the Northwest Territories. The Yukon, with one seat, has no boundaries commission.
24. For a report of the debates, see Ward, "A Century of Constituencies." The act was amended in 1985 to enable commissions to exceed the 25-percent limit wherever, in their opinion, circumstances warranted such a deviation. For a discussion of the changes in 1985, see Andrew Sancton, "Eroding Representation-by-Population in the Canadian House of Commons: The Representation Act, 1985," *Canadian Journal of Political Science* 23, no. 3 (September 1990), 441–457.
25. Keith Archer, "Conflict and Confusion in Drawing Constituency Boundaries: The Case of Alberta," *Canadian Public Policy* 19, no. 2 (June 1993), 177–193.
26. The issue is cast in this way in Rainer Knopff and F.L. Morton, *Charter Politics* (Scarborough: Nelson Canada, 1992), Chapter 12.
27. A good description of recent cases can be found in John C. Courtney, Peter MacKinnon, and David E. Smith, eds., *Drawing Boundaries: Legislatures, Courts and Electoral Values* (Saskatoon: Fifth House, 1992).
28. *Dixon v. B.C. (A.-G.)* (1989) 4 W.W.R. 393.
29. Ibid., 286.
30. Ibid., 293.
31. Ibid., 294.
32. British Columbia, the Honourable Judge Thomas Fisher, Commissioner, *Report of the Royal Commission on Electoral Boundaries in British Columbia, 1988* (Fisher Report). See also Norman Ruff, "The Right to Vote and Inequality of Voting Power in British Columbia: The Jurisprudence and Politics of the Dixon Case," in Courtney, MacKinnon, and Smith, eds., *Drawing Boundaries.*

33. *Dixon,* 311.

34. The legislation in each province contained a minor exception to the 25-percent deviation rule. The Saskatchewan legislation provided for two northern constituencies that could deviate from the average by up to 50 percent. Similarly, the Alberta legislation provided for a maximum of 5 percent of seats (i.e., four seats) that could fall below the average by up to 50 percent.

35. Knopff and Morton, *Charter Politics,* 337.

36. Ibid.

37. *Reference re Provincial Electoral Boundaries* (Sask.) (1991), 90 Sask. R. 185.

38. Ibid., 186.

39. Ibid., 189.

40. Ibid., 197.

41. *Reference re Provincial Electoral Boundaries* (Sask.), [1991] 2 S.C.R. 158.

42. Ibid., 182.

43. Ibid., 160.

44. Ibid.

45. Ibid.

46. Although such special-group-based constituencies have been much discussed, they have not often been implemented in electing national or sub-national legislatures. The idea has gained ground in other parts of the political system, however. Thus, each of the major national parties now guarantees that a substantial proportion of delegates to its leadership conventions are women and youth, although the New Democratic Party—perhaps surprisingly, given its rhetoric of representing political "outsiders"—has lagged behind both the Liberals and Progressive Conservatives on this matter. See John C. Courtney and George Perlin, "The Role of Conventions in the Representation and Accommodation of Regional Cleavages," in George Perlin, ed., *Party Democracy in Canada: The Politics of National Party Conventions* (Scarborough: Prentice-Hall Canada, 1988), 124–130.

47. For a classic article on this issue, see Alan Cairns, "The Electoral System and the Party System in Canada, 1921–1965," *Canadian Journal of Political Science* 1, no. 1 (1968), 55–80.

48. Knopff and Morton, *Charter Politics,* 361.

49. For a thorough discussion of this issue, see Robert A. Milen, ed., *Aboriginal Peoples and Electoral Reform in Canada,* vol. 9 of the Research Studies of the Royal Commission on Electoral Reform and Party Financing (Toronto: Dundurn Press, 1991).

50. Norman Ward, *The Canadian House of Commons: Representation,* 2nd ed. (Toronto: University of Toronto Press, 1963), 212.

51. Ibid.

52. Ibid., 212–213.

53. Ibid., 225. Reprinted with permission.

54. Dominion Elections Act, 1920. See also ibid.

55. The Royal Commission on Electoral Reform and Party Financing (Lortie Commission) recommended in 1991 that the prohibition on judges' voting be removed.

56. Harold D. Clarke, Jane Jenson, Lawrence LeDuc, and Jon Pammett, *Absent Mandate: Interpreting Change in Canadian Elections* (Toronto: Gage, 1991), 131.

57. Keith Archer, "The Meaning and Demeaning of the National Election Studies," *Journal of Canadian Studies* 24 (Winter 1989–90) 122–140.

58. Janet Harvie, "Political Participation in Canada," unpublished M.A. thesis, University of Calgary, 1989, Chapter 4.

59. Clarke et al., *Absent Mandate.*

60. Alan Frizzel, "The Perils of Polling," in Alan Frizzel, Jon H. Pammett, and Anthony Westell, eds., *The Canadian General Election of 1988* (Ottawa: Carleton University Press, 1989).

61. Richard Johnston, André Blais, Henry E. Brady, and Jean Crête, *Letting the People Decide: Dynamics of a Canadian Election* (Montreal and Kingston: McGill-Queen's University Press, 1992), 4.

62. Subsequent analyses in the United States from the 1960s through the 1990s indicate that the importance of party identification was at its zenith during the relative calm of the 1950s.

63. Harold Clarke, Jane Jenson, Lawrence LeDuc, and Jon Pammett, *Political Choice in Canada* (Toronto: McGraw-Hill Ryerson, 1979).

64. Clarke et al., *Absent Mandate,* 48–49; Harold D. Clarke, Jane Jenson, Lawrence LeDuc, and Jon Pammett, "Voting Behaviour and the Outcome of the 1979 Federal Election: The Impact of Leaders and Issues," *Canadian Journal of Political Science* 15, no. 3 (1982), 517–552.

65. Clarke et al., *Absent Mandate,* 48–49; Harold D. Clarke, Jane Jenson, Lawrence LeDuc, and Jon Pammett, "Voting Behaviour and the Outcome of the 1979 Federal Election: The Impact of Leaders and Issues," *Canadian Journal of Political Science* 15, no. 3 (1982), 517–552; Lawrence LeDuc, "Canada: The Politics of Stable Dealignment," in Russell Dalton, Scott Flanagan, and Paul Beck, eds., *Electoral Change in Advanced Industrial Democracies* (Princeton: Princeton University Press, 1984).

66. Clarke et al., *Absent Mandate.*

67. Johnston et al., *Letting the People Decide,* 169–196.

68. Barry Kay, "Single Issue Politics," paper presented at the 1990 Annual Meeting of the Canadian Political Science Association.

69. Richard Johnston, André Blais, Henry E. Brady and Jean Crête, "Free Trade and the Dynamics of the 1988 Canadian Election," in Joseph Wearing, ed., *The Ballot and Its Message: Voting in Canada* (Toronto: Copp Clark Pitman, 1991), 321.

70. Johnston et al., "Free Trade and the Dynamics of the 1988 Canadian Election," 317.

POLITICAL PARTIES

10

[R]egionalization of the political / party system ... has now reached an extreme in Canada. Only the Liberal Party still has any claim to be a national party, and its claim is rather weak.[1]

The Canadian federal party system evolved early in this century from a two-party system into a multiparty system dominated by two major parties but with the significant presence of "third" parties. This was often described as a "two-party-plus" system. In recent decades, the Liberals and the Conservatives were the two major parties, while the NDP constituted the "plus" side of the two-party-plus equation. In the 1993 election two new parties—the Reform Party and the Bloc Québécois—broke through to create a five-party system. One might describe this change as the addition of two parties to the "plus" side of the "two-party-plus" system, except for the fact that the two additions have been more than also-ran minor parties. Each has formed the official opposition in the House of Commons, while the Conservatives—traditionally the main alternative to the Liberals—have found themselves in fifth place in the Commons. On the other hand, neither of the new parties has yet demonstrated that it can be an electorally viable alternative to the Liberals (the BQ, understandably, makes no attempt to be one). It thus seems more accurate now to describe the system as a one-party-plus system, in which all five parties, including both the "one" (the Liberals) and the "pluses" (Reform, BQ, NDP, and PC) are to a considerable extent regionally based. With the benefit of hindsight one can see the five elements of the current party system playing a central role in Canadian party politics since the 1920s.

■ ■ ■

Political parties perform a crucial role in the functioning of democratic government in Canada. They are an important link between some of the formal institutions of government—especially Parliament and the prime minister and cabinet—and between government and the enfranchised citizenry it purports to serve.

Parties are intimately involved in the relations between the executive and the legislature in the parliamentary tradition. Canadian parties arose in response to the institutional requirement in Westminster-style governments for the political executive to have the confidence of the House of Commons. The political executive is most likely to maintain the confidence of the Commons when its supporters hold a majority of the seats. Thus, the norms of cabinet government in Westminster-style parliamentary government encourage legislators to band together in ongoing political alliances, groupings that have become known as political parties.

Parties serve not only to provide intraparliamentary linkages between legislators, however; they also function as extraparliamentary organizations by bridging the gap between legislators and citizens. In performing this latter function, parties are engaged in selecting and recruiting candidates for elective office, selecting political leaders, and providing the organizational framework for electoral competition.[2]

The relationship between parties and the state is ambiguous and contested. On the one hand, unfettered competition between political groupings is a core value for democratic government. From this perspective, parties are voluntary citizen associations. They are institutions of the citizenry, not the state, and the key role of the party system is to represent the diversity of citizens' views. Parties should thus be subject to little if any state regulation. On the other hand, because parties perform functions that are essential to the health of the political system, they could properly be viewed as institutions of the state. This latter perspective might lead one to suggest that parties should be both funded and regulated by the state. In fact, while recognizing that parties are quasi-public institutions, the Canadian state has subjected them to relatively little explicit regulation. This does not mean, however, that the shape of the Canadian party system has not been influenced by the institutions of government. Quite the opposite. Parties are profoundly affected by the institutional environment within which they operate.

This chapter begins with a discussion of the determinants of party development. We canvass competing theories among scholars of party politics about why parties develop as they do. While parties themselves reflect debate over governing perspectives, research on party development is characterized by controversy over theoretical and methodological perspectives. These academic disputes are politically relevant because of their implications for party strategies. In other words, the kind of electoral appeal one believes a party should pursue depends in large measure on what one believes is crucial to party development. After reviewing the analytical perspectives on party development, we apply them to an understanding of the historical development of the Canadian party system. This discussion highlights the interplay between citizen demands, party strategies, and institutional characteristics. The chapter concludes with an examination of the parties as organizations, and examines the interplay between their internal institutional structures, approaches toward policy development, and methods of leadership selection.

PARTY DEVELOPMENT: A THEORETICAL OVERVIEW

Political parties do not simply appear, as if from nowhere, on the political scene. They arise at particular points in time in response to a variety of opportunities and constraints, with the purpose of achieving particular representational or governing objectives. An examination of party systems across the range of countries typically called liberal democracies reveals two striking features—a remarkable diversity in the number and political orientation of parties across countries, and an equally remarkable stability over time in party systems within countries. For example, in France and Italy more than 10 political parties are represented in the legislature, whereas only two parties have seats in the United States Congress. In Canada, three parties won seats in the federal elections between 1980 and 1988, and five parties did so in the 1993 and 1997 elections. On the other hand, of the more than 40 postwar Italian governments, the Christian Democrats have been the major actor in all but one,[3] and in federal politics in Canada only the Liberals and Conservatives have ever formed the government.[4]

Analysts of politics need to develop a model of party development that accounts for cross-national diversity and at the same time offers an explanation for national stability. To make matters more complicated, the model must also help account for the opposite outcomes—namely, instances of cross-national consistency in party systems and of change in party systems within countries. Why, for example, do both Britain and the United States have two-party systems? And how is it that the Conservative Party in Canada could win 211 of 282 seats in the House of Commons in 1984 but only two seats of 295 in 1993. The three major theories of party development emphasize societal, mobilizational, and institutional explanations, respectively.[5]

The Societal Approach

Societal approaches to the development of the party system emphasize the role played by changes in the economy, social relations, or political culture of a society. From this perspective, a party system is largely determined by and reflective of social relations and/or attitudes of individuals. To understand why a party system has developed as it has, one must examine the development of the underlying social relations. By implication, a party system would change only if the underlying social forces also changed. Although there are many variants of the societal approach to party development, two have been particularly popular in Canada, the **political culture** model and the **class politics** model.

Political culture can be defined as "attitudes toward the political system and its various parts, and attitudes toward the role of the self in the system."[6] It is what Gabriel Almond and Sidney Verba refer to as a society's **civic culture**,[7] or what others call "national character."[8] Political culture is often likened to a camera filter—the filter selectively blocks out certain colours, or, in the case of political culture, certain political ideas, so that political decisions involve choosing among a limited range of options. How restrictive or permeable the filter is—how many attitudinal and ideological options it filters out—will differ from one society to another.

For students of political parties, this approach suggests that the number and ideological diversity of parties in a society will reflect the range of options permitted by the filter of political culture. A prominent example of the approach was developed by Louis Hartz and his followers to explain American and Canadian party systems. Hartz propounded the so-called **fragment theory** of political cultural development to explain the comparative lack of ideological diversity in the American party system. Unlike Europe, where parties ranged from the tradition-oriented right to the socialist and even communist left, the United States was characterized by two parties whose disputes fell within the liberal middle ground. Left-leaning political opinions were not only unrepresented by major parties but were considered positively un-American and during the 1950s were indiscriminately persecuted by the Congressional Committee on Un-American Activities chaired by Senator Joe McCarthy. For Hartz, the narrow ideological range of legitimate American opinion stemmed from the fact that the United States was founded and settled by people who represented an ideologically narrow "fragment" of the European society from which they came.[9]

In Europe itself, Hartz argued, modern socialism was the natural product of a rich interaction between liberalism and the feudal past. Feudalism was a collectivist ideology that emphasized the organic connectedness of different parts of society. This connectedness was understood to be hierarchically arranged. Just as the head naturally ruled the limbs in the bodily organism, so nobles naturally ruled peasants and serfs in the social and political organism. Feudalism, in short, was both collectivist and hierarchical. Liberalism rejected both dimensions of feudalism by conceiving society as a collection of equal and naturally unconnected individuals who were not by nature subject to anyone's rule and who established government by consent. Liberalism, in short, was individualistic and egalitarian. Socialism, for its part, is egalitarian (like liberalism) but collectivist (like feudalism). This combination of parts of both liberalism and feudalism, Hartz argued, was possible in Europe because the raw materials were available there. Both liberalism and feudalism, as sources of socialism, were well reflected in European political culture.

The United States, by contrast, lacked a significant tradition of feudal collectivism that could have provided the collectivist orientation required for the development of socialism. American political culture was established by the liberal fragment of European society that came to the New World at the time of the liberal enlightenment. The American Revolution then institutionalized liberal values and culture in the country's political institutions.[10] The minority that held somewhat more traditional and conservative views migrated north to become Loyalist settlers in Canada, and the remaining feudal element in American society—slavery—was ultimately defeated in the Civil War. By the time American political culture congealed, then, it was trapped inside liberalism. Illiberal ideas are un-American, and the culture allows only small "l" liberal parties to develop and flourish.

Gad Horowitz applied Hartz's fragment theory to Canada to explain Canadian political culture and the Canadian party system.[11] Although Hartz believed that English Canada had a liberal political culture similar to that of the United States, Horowitz was struck by the relative strength of social-democratic ideas and parties in Canada—particularly the Co-operative Commonwealth Federation (CCF) and its successor, the New Democratic Party (NDP)—as well as by the greater willingness of all parties to use government to effect desirable social purposes. Horowitz suggested that English-speaking Canada developed a more social-democratic culture because there were more feudal elements in Canada at the point at which its culture congealed. Specifically, the immigration of United Empire Loyalists at the time of the American Revolution provided English Canada with a cultural element loyal to the Crown and to social and political hierarchy. This element was present and powerful during Canada's counterrevolutionary beginnings, and during the period of industrialization it provided Canada with the makings of social democracy.[12] The influence was not as great as in Britain, to be sure, and thus social democracy in Canada lacked the legitimacy that it enjoyed in Britain. But its legitimacy in Canada was substantially greater than in the United States.[13]

The Hartz–Horowitz cultural development theory sees parties as epiphenomena, that is, as organizations that are not responsible for their own development. The culture of society is either open to the articulation of a particular ideology in the form of a political party or it is not. In other words, the primary source of a party's success rests with societal attitudes toward the ideas that the party seeks to represent.

There are several questions about the Hartz–Horowitz thesis that merit reflection.[14] Is the model historically accurate? Can it explain change in party performance over time? Must parties have an ideological base and, if so, must that base be liberal, conservative, or socialist? What about religious, agrarian, environmental, or populist parties? Do parties not have some strategic role to play in carving their own social base of support? Do parties have to accept society as a given? Can they not take an active role in reshaping societal attitudes and culture? As one might imagine, these questions have led many researchers to look for other explanations of the party system in Canada and elsewhere. Among the alternative explanations that have been developed, the neo-Marxian class-based model also focuses on the determining role of society.

Whereas the cultural approach focuses on the attitudes of individuals or groups in society, neo-Marxian class-based approaches highlight the relations between groups or individuals. Most political scientists who use this approach draw a fundamental dichotomy between the interests of capital and labour in a market or mixed economy, and suggest that this tension is reflected in the party system. Perhaps the best illustration of the neo-Marxian class-based approach in Canada is John Porter's classic study of social class and power.[15] In an exhaustive study of elites in the areas of business, politics, public administration, and the media, Porter found a complex web of linkages through common schooling, strong social and familial ties, and overlapping memberships within the country's corporate structure, especially on the

DOSSIER 10.1 CULTURAL APPROACHES TO POLITICAL PARTIES

I would not put any great stress on the party system as an explanation of the weakness of American socialism. The Hartzian cultural analysis shows why socialism as an ideology must die in the United States. If cultural forces kill socialism as an ideology, it will die—regardless of the party system.... The Hartzian analysis applied to Canadian conditions shows why socialism as an ideology could become a significant force in Canada. Institutional analysis can show why permanent, significant third parties arise, but it cannot explain why one of the parties should be socialist. The cultural analysis is necessary to explain the relative strength of a socialist ideology in Canada; the institutional analysis is necessary to explain why this ideology can easily find expression in a permanent separate party.

Source: Reprinted from Gad Horowitz, *Canadian Labour in Politics* (Toronto: University of Toronto Press, 1968), 49.

The strong cultural similarities between English-speaking Canada and the United States has often led citizens of the latter to wonder why the two remain in separate politics. Yet, although these two peoples probably resemble each other more than any other two nations on earth, there are consistent patterns of difference between them.... The great mass of literature on these two North American democracies suggests the United States is more achievement-oriented, universalistic, egalitarian, and self-oriented than Canada.... Although many factors in the history of these nations have determined the current variations between them, three particular factors may be singled out: the varying origins of their political systems and national identities, religious traditions, and different frontier experiences. In general terms, the value orientations in English-speaking Canada stem from a counterrevolutionary past, a continuing need to differentiate itself from the United States, the influence of monarchical institutions, a dominant Anglican religious tradition, and a less individualistic and more governmentally controlled frontier expansion than was presented on the American frontier.

Source: Reprinted from S.M. Lipset, "Revolution and Counterrevolution: The United States and Canada," in Orest Kruhlak, Richard Schultz, and Sidney Pobihushchy, eds., *The Canadian Political Process* (Toronto: Holt, Rinehart and Winston, 1970), 13–14.

boards of directors of major companies. He argued that the inequality of wealth and political resources, coupled with social interconnectedness, enabled the privileged class to manipulate politics and wield power at the expense of everyone else. Furthermore, Porter viewed the major parties as willing agents in the politics of manipulation. This perspective was captured graphically by Frank Underhill when he argued that the Liberals and Conservatives "provide a screen behind which the controlling business interests pull the strings to manipulate the Punch and Judy who engage in mock combat before the public."[16]

DOSSIER 10.2 CLASS-BASED APPROACHES TO POLITICAL PARTIES

The political elite in Canada is not representative of the population which it leads.... The predominance of some occupational groups and people of one class background means that limited perspectives are brought to bear on public issues. In Canada, it is the homogeneity of political leaders in terms of education, occupation and social class which gives the political system its conservative tone.

Source: Reprinted with permission from John Porter, *The Vertical Mosaic* (Toronto: University of Toronto Press, 1965), 388–391.

The political transition of the Canadian west is a non-party tradition.... In [the Prairie provinces], two characteristics, not found together in any of the other provinces, combined to discourage the introduction and development of a party system. One was their relatively homogeneous class composition, the other their quasi-colonial status. The former seemed to make a party system unnecessary, the latter led to a positive aversion to party. The absence of any serious opposition of class interests within the province meant that alternate parties were not needed either to express or to moderate a perennial conflict of interests. There was apparently, therefore, no positive basis for an alternate-party system. The quasi-colonial position of the western provinces made it a primary requirement of their provincial political systems that they should be able to stand up to the national government.... In view of all this, what needs to be explained is not why there was a non-party tradition in the west, but why the party system ever made any headway there at all. The answer is to be found in the exigencies of the federal parties.

Source: Reprinted with permission from C.B. Macpherson, *Democracy in Alberta: Social Credit and the Party System*, 2nd ed. (Toronto: University of Toronto Press, 1962), 20–21.

As with political cultural approaches, class-based approaches may not provide a fully satisfactory explanation of the party system. Although a market economy may produce a fundamental conflict between the interests of those who own or control businesses and those who do not, the range of conflicting interests in a complex industrial or postindustrial society extends far beyond simple class conflict. Differences between various ethnic, linguistic, or religious groups, between those on the ideological left and right, between one region and another, between young and old, men and women, farmers and industrial workers, and many others may be found in modern societies—and all these differences may be reflected in the party system. To focus on only one social cleavage produces an incomplete, static, and unsatisfactory view of party development. It also fails to consider the institutional constraints and party strategies that can play a profound role in transforming a societal cleavage into the organizational form of a political party.

Mobilizational Approaches

Ascribing an independent role to political actors in shaping their own environment has been an important development in the study of political science and is a central theme of this book. Politics is about more than responding to inputs and channelling them into governmental or policy outputs. It is also about establishing priorities, setting goals, and implementing strategies that enable one to pursue objectives. Political actors are strategic actors. The view of parties generated by this analytical framework is vastly different from the view generated by society-centred models. Parties are no longer viewed as epiphenomena; instead they are strategic actors engaged in defining the issues of importance in political conflict and in mobilizing voters behind their issue positions. Societal attitudes are viewed not as given or immutable. Instead, they are precisely the domain of political conflict. In the words of Janine Brodie and Jane Jenson, the most widely cited proponents of this view of party development, parties actively engage in a contest to "define the political."[17] Parties lead political debate, they do not follow it. They define what is acceptable for political debate and discussion instead of responding to the constraints imposed by society.

Brodie and Jenson develop their theory of party development in an analysis of class voting in Canada. Like society-centred analysts who emphasize the importance of class relations, Brodie and Jenson also argue that social and political relations are influenced by economic relations. In a mixed economy such as Canada's, they believe that economic relations are characterized by class conflict. However, Brodie and Jenson take the view that class conflict will become part of the political cleavage structure only if parties choose to highlight the importance of class. The Liberal and Conservative parties, as the parties of the business class, attempt to "define the political" in ways that minimize and downplay the political significance of class. Instead, they have championed the issues of race, ethnicity, language, and region. As parties of the business class, the Liberals and Conservatives appeal to the working classes through the latter's identities as Quebeckers, westerners, Catholics, or francophones.[18]

The NDP shares responsibility for defining class out of Canadian politics, according to Brodie and Jenson. Canada's erstwhile social democratic party has accepted the Liberal and Conservative liberal view of political debate by moderating and watering down its commitment to socialism, by accepting as a given the business unionism[19] that Canadian unions inherited from their American counterparts, and by acquiescing to the principles of individual inequality inherent in a mixed economy. The failure of both the CCF and NDP to offer a radical alternative to a liberal definition of the political has resulted in alternative (i.e., socialist) ideologies being considered illegitimate.[20]

Although the theory that parties are strategic decision makers provides an important corrective to cultural theories that seem to rob parties of their active role in pursuing partisan objectives, it also can attribute more autonomy to parties than they in fact possess. At its most extreme, the theory that parties are strategic actors

DOSSIER 10.3 MOBILIZATIONAL APPROACHES TO POLITICAL PARTIES

[A] particular conception of political parties is used in this book, one which sees parties less as aggregators of individual voters' preferences and more as the actual creators of the pattern of those preferences.... This conception assigns political parties in liberal democracies a crucial role in the definition of what the substance and form of electoral politics will be. They identify which among a broad range of social differences and tensions will be raised and debated in elections, and they nurture and sustain the criteria by which an electorate will divide against itself in a more or less stable system of partisan alignments. Parties are not alone in this process of issue creation and consideration. Other institutions play important roles, but it is parties, as the organizers of elections, which ultimately have the greatest influence on the "definition of politics."

Source: Reprinted from M. Janine Brodie and Jane Jenson, *Crisis, Challenge and Change: Party and Class in Canada* (Toronto: Methuen, 1980), 1.

able to play a role in defining societal values may devolve into the view that anything goes—that parties are free to champion any issue or cause, the pursuit of which is equally likely to end in political success. Thus, Brodie and Jenson suggest that by becoming more radical the NDP would become more successful at the polls. They provide no convincing support for this view. Likewise, Claude Galipeau chastises all the parties for not putting forward a radical feminist definition of the political, with the implication that doing so would increase the legitimacy of both this ideology and the party that championed it.[21] More likely, parties that champion issues or positions few voters support will find themselves relegated to the electoral wilderness. This is especially true if they do so in a political system that uses a single-member constituency, plurality electoral system. Communist or fascist parties have had remarkably little success in Canada because their "definition of the political" is at odds with the view of the vast majority of Canadians. Likewise, there is no antiabortion party, no gay and lesbian party, and no strong libertarian party because such parties' "definition of the political" would constitute a distinct minority view.

Working from a different theoretical perspective, Anthony Downs also argued that parties adopt a strategic approach to building political support.[22] Downs did not suggest, as do Brodie and Jenson, that parties attempt to shape societal attitudes and values. Instead he began by assuming that political parties' first task is electoral victory, and that they act as self-interested utility maximizers in pursuing that goal. In other words, they try to get as much support as they can for the least cost. Based on these assumptions, Downs adapted Harold Hotelling's **spatial model** of party behaviour. Hotelling based this model on his analysis of the location of department stores within a city.[23] Arguing that department stores try to maximize their clientele by decreasing the distance that customers must travel to shop, Hotelling showed that the distance is shortest in the middle of the city, and that a department store should therefore locate itself at that point. A second department store, however, would reach exactly the same decision—its optimal location is in the centre of the city too, directly across from the first store. To the extent that minimizing distance travelled was an important factor in choosing between stores, Hotelling argued (and observation confirmed) that the two stores would be located in close proximity. Applying his model to party competition, Hotelling argued that the choice of ideological location by parties was similar to the choice of geographical location by department stores. To maximize voter appeal, parties try to move toward the position of the "median" voter—that is, the voter who occupies the middle position between the ideological right and left. As they do so, parties become indistinguishable from one another on the ideological scale just as department stores gravitate toward each other in physical space.

Downs adjusted Hotelling's model by suggesting that the decision of the parties on their optimal location depends on the underlying distribution of opinion among the electorate.[24] Societies that are ideologically polarized will have a polarized two-party system. Societies that are characterized by a "normal" distribution of opinion, with relatively small numbers holding extreme views and large numbers of citizens taking moderate positions, will have two similar parties. Finally, societies with relatively equal numbers across the entire ideological spectrum will be characterized by a multiparty system. In taking societal values and attitudes as a given, in discovering the distribution of those positions, and in locating themselves at their electorally optimal position, the parties of Downs's analysis are "rational" but uncommitted policy brokers. They hold policy positions for instrumental reasons only—because the policy increases their electoral appeal. In light of this model, parties engage in a continual strategic calculus in responding to the shifting positions of other parties and adjusting to the distribution of opinion in society.

Downs's model has not been without its critics. Allan Kornberg and his colleagues tried to apply the Downs model to Canadian parties by examining the political attitudes of the Canadian electorate and of the leadership of Canadian parties.[25] Their results demonstrated that the model did not fit well. One reason for this was a lack of consistency in the political attitudes of the electorate. Thus, individuals who hold a leftist position on social policy may hold a rightist position on defence and a centrist position on economic policy. This is usually referred to as a lack of ideological constraint. A model that suggests individuals and parties can be arrayed along a simple left–right continuum is therefore problematic. Furthermore, Kornberg et al. showed that views on many important issues in Canadian politics, such as language or constitutional reform, do not align on a left–right ideological continuum. They may be entirely independent of one's left–right political views. The ideological views of Canadians are therefore multidimensional. This characteristic must be taken into account when one tries to apply a spatial model to party development in Canada.[26]

Institutional Approaches

Political institutions set the framework within which party competition takes place. The importance of the institutional framework of party competition has long been recognized, but it is the rare study that systematically takes that importance into account in combination with either the societal or mobilizational explanations. This may be partly because the importance of institutions seems so obvious. Who would dispute the fact that the institutional requirement of responsible government in Westminster-style parliamentary systems produces parties that are different from those produced under the American separation-of-powers system? Or that a federal system of government might impose on parties challenges for unity and diversity that differ from those in unitary systems? Or that the electoral system would profoundly influence the distribution of legislative seats among parties? Or that state regulation of party finances or campaign advertising would affect party development? Let us briefly summarize the impact of these four institutional factors.

The Westminster-model parliamentary system is best characterized by the term "responsible government." As described in previous chapters, responsible government exists when the executive depends for its continued existence on support from the legislature. The executive stays in power only as long as it maintains the support—in parliamentary terms, the confidence—of the legislature. This close relationship between the executive and the legislature encourages the formation of relatively strong parties with disciplined voting patterns. The party or parties supporting the government are likely to vote as a unified bloc in favour of the government's initiatives, and the opposition parties are equally likely to vote as a bloc against their initiatives. Failure to do so, especially on the part of the government party, jeopardizes the life of the government—it can be defeated on a vote of confidence. In contrast to the Westminster model, the American separation of powers provides the executive with a base of support independent of the legislature. There is a less pressing need for disciplined parties, and, as a result, the parties tend to be weaker and more fragmented.

A second important institutional feature that affects a party system is whether the country has a federal or unitary system, and, if so, the relative strength of the subnational units. The Canadian pattern of strong provincial governments and substantial differences between provinces in the timing and pattern of their development has led to relatively distinct party systems at the federal and provincial levels.[27] For example, Social Credit sprang to power in Alberta long before it appeared at the national level, and it retained considerable vigour in British Columbia long after it disappeared from the national stage. In Quebec, both the Union Nationale and the Parti Québécois, among others, chose not to develop federal counterparts, although there have been strong informal linkages between the PQ and the Bloc Québécois. Throughout the late 1980s and early 1990s, the Reform Party resisted pressure to form provincial wings, choosing instead to organize only at the federal level. The asymmetry in federal and provincial parties goes beyond the separate provincial or national arenas adopted by certain parties. Even where their names are the same, the parties are organizationally distinct. For example, in Alberta both the Liberal and Progressive Conservative parties have voted to formally sever their connection with their federal namesakes, and so has the Liberal Party in Quebec. The feelings of discomfort and disaffection with their counterparts at the other level of government is not the exclusive prerogative of provincial parties. In 1989 the federal NDP found itself at loggerheads with its provincial section from Quebec, and the provincial wing broke with the federal party. The practice of executive federalism, the absence of synchronicity between federal and provincial elections, and the difficulties inherent in mediating the differences across the diverse Canadian regions all point to the importance of federalism in fragmenting the Canadian party system.

The electoral system is probably the most widely studied institutional determinant of the party system. As we noted in Chapter 9, the electoral system overrepresents parties with a regional base of support (Bloc Québécois and, to a lesser extent, Reform in 1997); over-rewards the party with the most votes (Liberals in 1997); underrepresents parties whose appeal extends across several regions but to a minority in each region (Conservatives and New Democrats in 1997); and awards seats to each party in such a way as to highlight its regional distinctiveness. Thus the CCF and NDP have generally received more seats from the West than from Ontario while receiving more votes (albeit a smaller percentage) from Ontario. Historically, the CCF–NDP has looked more like a western party from the perspective of the legislature than from that of the electorate. In 1997 the NDP combined its traditional western support with newly developed support in Atlantic Canada, owing at least in part to the party's new leader, Alexa McDonough, from Nova Scotia. As well, prior to the 1984 election Conservative seats were significantly underrepresented in Quebec. In 1984 and 1988, however, the Conservatives were overrepresented in Quebec. The Liberals, by contrast, generally have fewer seats in the West than their share of votes would warrant. Thus, among other things, the electoral system has regionalized the party system and systematically strengthened some parties while weakening others. Simultaneously, the use of single-member constituencies rather than proportional representation has minimized the number of parties represented in the legislature. Groups with newly emerging political interests, such as environmentalists, may find it more effective to work at reshaping one or more of the existing parties to accommodate their position than to create and support a new issue-oriented political party.

Government regulation of party financing and campaign advertising also has an important impact on party development. Through the first 100 years after Confederation, the government turned a blind eye to party financing. Although data on party financing prior to 1974 are notoriously scarce, it is known that the Liberal and Conservative parties obtained the great bulk of their funding from the Toronto and Montreal business communities. The New Democrats, and the CCF before them, were chronically underfunded, drawing the bulk of their support from individuals and unions.[28] The Election Expenses Act, passed in 1974 and amended in 1977 and 1983, has significantly transformed the system of party financing. Chief among the changes introduced by the act is the use of a tax-credit system to finance the parties. Parties must register with Elections Canada to be eligible for the tax credits, and all registered parties must file audited financial statements annually, providing the names of all donors who contributed $100 or more. The act also provides for a system of reimbursement for 50 percent of local campaign expenditures for candidates receiving 15 percent of the vote, a policy that has favoured established parties and hindered the others. Features that have a similarly detrimental effect on new-party development include the procedures to register a party (it must have 12 seats in the Commons or have contested 50 seats in the previous election), provisions to allow parties to keep local campaign surpluses but that require independents to turn over any surpluses to the Consolidated Revenue Fund of the treasury, provisions to allot broadcast time in an election campaign in proportion to a party's performance in the previous election, and ceilings on campaign financing.[29]

Paradoxically, though some of these provisions have been regarded as hindrances to the emergence of new parties, the 1993 election showed that at times they can have a negative impact on more established parties. For example, both the Progressive Conservatives and New Democrats lost their official party status in the House of Commons after falling below 12 seats in 1993 (the Conservatives won two seats; the NDP won nine). In addition, many of the Conservative Party's election expenses were not reimbursed because its candidates failed to get 15 percent of the vote in most constituencies. By contrast, the regional strength of the Reform Party in the West and the Bloc Québécois in Quebec resulted in these parties' winning a much larger number of seats (hence gaining official party status) and getting reimbursed for more of their election expenses than were the Conservatives, despite the closeness in the number of overall votes won by the three parties.

Institutional features of the state have a complex effect on the development of the party system. Several of these features have effects that oppose and counterbalance one another. For example, we noted that the Westminster-model parliamentary system encourages parties to be cohesive and disciplined, though the federal system and certain aspects of the electoral system tend toward the fragmentation of parties. Similarly, a fragmented party system and systems characterized by one-party dominance may encourage the emergence and rapid growth of new parties,[30] though government regulation of campaign expenditure and access to broadcasting outlets may provide advantages to established parties. The many conflicting institutional factors combine to create an environment for party development that is highly contingent. When one adds to this the factors of stability and change in society as well as the parties' changing mobilizational strategies, the model of party development becomes even more complex and dynamic. Let us briefly apply this model to sketch an outline of party development in Canada.

DOSSIER 10.4 THE ELECTION EXPENSES ACT AND ITS IMPACT ON POLITICAL PARTIES IN CANADA

Contrary to the impact of the Federal Election Campaign Act in the United States, which stimulated the campaign financing activities of ideological, corporate and interest-group political action committees, the Canadian Election Expenses Act has consolidated the position of the three major parliamentary parties. Despite the successful constitutional challenge against the ban on third-party spending by the right-wing National Citizens' Coalition, there is as yet no sign of the PAC [Political Action Committee] phenomenon in Canada. Furthermore, there is little evidence that minor parties or independent candidates have benefited from the controls.... In the light of the foregoing, it may be concluded that the reform of Canadian party finance reinforced the party orientation of the Canadian electoral system through the creation, with the help of public funding and tax incentives, of a regular, reliable and predictable source of funds for institutionalized parties.

Source: Reprinted with permission from Khayyam Zev Paltiel, "Political Marketing, Party Finance, and the Decline of Canadian Parties," in Alain G. Gagnon and A. Brian Tanguay, eds., *Canadian Parties in Transition: Discourse, Organization, Representation* (Toronto: ITP Nelson, 1989), 348.

PARTY DEVELOPMENT: AN INTERPRETATION

A useful way of understanding party development is to identify specific periods of continuity and change in party function and/or party alignments. If one looks to the number of parties represented in Parliament, the federal party system falls into four periods, each of which corresponds to unique patterns of political organization and behaviour. The differences in the parties from one period to another have been manifested in their internal structure and behaviour and in the nature of their support in the electorate.[31]

Table 10.1 presents the results of national elections from 1878 to 1997 and demarcates the four periods of the federal party system. The first period, from Confederation to 1917, was characterized by a two-party system in which the Liberals and Conservatives captured all but a handful of seats. The second period, from 1921 to 1962, witnessed the partial breakdown of the two-party system and its replacement by a "two-plus" party system. During this period a number of third parties, generally with regionally concentrated seats, arose to challenge the established parties, with limited success. The third period, from 1963 to 1988, saw the number of third parties dwindle to one. This was still a two-plus party system, but by the end of this period only one third party, the NDP, was left on the "plus" side of the ledger. The fourth period was inaugurated by the 1993 election, which produced a dramatic regional fragmentation of the party system. With that election Canada moved away from a two-plus-one party system to the regionally arrayed five-party system now represented in Parliament.

TABLE 10.1 PARTY SEATS AND VOTES IN FEDERAL ELECTIONS, 1878–1993

Combined Election Results

Election Year	Partly Forming Federal Government	Total Seats	Conservative Seats	Conservative Votes (%)	Liberal Seats	Liberal Votes (%)	Progressive Seats	Progressive Votes (%)	CCF—YOP Seats	CCF—YOP Votes (%)	Social Credit Seats	Social Credit Votes (%)	Reconstruction Seats	Reconstruction Votes ($)	Bloc Québécois Seats	Bloc Québécois Votes (%)	Reform Seats	Reform Votes (%)	Other Seats	Other Votes (%)
1878	Con.	206	140	53	65	45													1	2
1882	Con.	211	138	53	73	47														
1887	Con.	215	128	51	87	49														
1891	Con.	215	122	52	91	46													2	2
1896	Lib.	213	88	46	118	45													7	9
1900	Lib.	213	81	47	132	52														1
1904	Lib.	214	75	47	139	52														1
1908	Lib.	221	85	47	135	51													1	2
1911	Con.	221	134	51	87	48														1
1917	Con.	235	153	57	82	40														3
1921	Lib.	235	50	30	116	41	65	23											4	6
1925	Lib.	245	116	46	99	40	24	9											6	5
1926	Lib.	245	91	45	128	46	20	5											6	4
1930	Con.	245	137	49	91	45	12	3											5	3
1935	Lib.	245	40	30	173	45			7	9	17	4	1	9					7	3
1940	Lib.	245	40	31	181	51			8	8	10	3							6	7
1945	Lib.	245	67	27	125	41			28	16	13	4							12	12
1949	Lib.	262	41	30	193	49			13	13	10	4							5	4
1953	Lib.	265	51	31	171	49			23	11	15	5							5	4
1957	Con.	265	112	39	105	41			25	11	19	7							4	2
1958	Con.	265	208	54	49	34			8	9	0	2								1
1962	Con.	265	116	37	100	37			19	14	30	12								
1963	Lib.	265	95	33	129	42			17	13	24	12								
													Créditiste Seats	Créditiste Voters (%)						
1965	Lib.	265	97	32	131	40			21	18	5	4	9	5					2	1
1968	Lib.	264	72	31	155	45			21	17	0	1	14	5					0	1
1972	Lib.	264	107	35	109	38			31	18	15	8							1	1
1974	Lib.	264	95	35	141	43			16	15	11	5							1	1
1979	Con.	282	136	36	114	40			26	18	6	5							0	2
1980	Lib.	282	103	33	146	44			32	20	0	1							0	2
1984	Con.	282	211	50	40	28			30	19									1	
1988	Con.	295	169	43	83	32			43	20									0	4
1993	Lib.	295	2	16	177	41			9	7					54	13	52	19	1	4
1997	Lib.	301	20	19	155	38			21	11					44	11	60	19	1	2

Note: 1997 results from Elections Canada.
Source: Hugh Thorburn, *Party Politics in Canada*, 6th ed. (Scarborough: Prentice Hall Canada, 1991), 533.

Although we will use these four periods to organize our discussion of party development, they do not tell the whole story. For example, if one looks not to the number of parties in the legislature but to their character and mode of operation, a different pattern emerges. From this perspective, one can superimpose three lines of demarcation on our four historical periods. The first period was characterized by patronage politics and caucus parties, the second by brokerage politics and ministerialist parties, and the third and fourth by electronic politics and personal parties.

Similarly, when one examines underlying social and ideological formations, yet another picture comes into view. As Stephen Harper and Thomas Flanagan have argued, the dramatic changes in the number and kinds of parties during the last three of our historical periods obscures a remarkable stability in Canada's essential political factions. In Dossier 10.5, Harper and Flanagan argue that since the 1920s the changes in Canada's federal party system represent mainly the periodic reshuffling of five basic social and ideological groupings: the Liberals, the Progressive Conservatives, the CCF–NDP, right-wing western populists, and Quebec nationalists. From this perspective, the five-party system that emerged in 1993 simply brings to the foreground what had been in the background of all variations in the party system since the end of the first two-party period.

Keeping these overlapping perspectives in mind, let us look in more detail at each of the four historical periods.

First Period: 1867–1917

The party system extant at the time of Confederation had developed largely as a result of institutional factors under the Act of Union. Although legislatures had existed in Upper and Lower Canada from 1791 onward, the absence of responsible government until the late 1840s meant that there was no need for stable coalitions of like-minded legislators to support the government. Members of the executive council held their position at the pleasure of the governor and could remain in office indefinitely, with or without the support of the legislature.

When responsible government was introduced in the United Province of Canada in 1848 (see Dossier 2.6), there emerged a pressing need for more stable coalitions of legislators. The legislature of Canada at that time comprised equal numbers of representatives from Canada West and Canada East, and building a legislative majority thus meant bridging the linguistic, cultural, and religious divide that separated French-speaking Catholics in Canada East from English-speaking Protestants in Canada West. The tendency of the pre-Confederation period was for relatively weak coalitions of conservative English-speaking representatives to form an alliance with their conservative French-speaking counterparts under the Liberal–Conservative label; this group was opposed by an equally weak alliance between more liberal anglophones and francophones under the Liberal banner. These alliances were made less stable by their linguistic, cultural, and religious differences (governments often fell on debates relating to such issues).

DOSSIER 10.5 FIVE LONG-TERM COMPONENTS OF THE PARTY SYSTEM

Ever since 1921, Canada has had a multi-party system. Parties have come and gone, but not these five components to the system:

- A Liberal party with a national coalition capable of governing. At times in the 1970s and 1980s the Liberals were virtually shut out of the West, as they are today in francophone Quebec, but they have usually maintained appreciable strength in all parts of the country....
- A Conservative or Progressive Conservative party claiming a national base, but in fact coming to power only in exceptional circumstances and then governing only for short periods of time....
- A social democratic party claiming to be national but with real strength only in Western Canada and Ontario. This element became visible as early as the mid-1920s, when a group of left-wing MPs emerged amid the wreckage of the disintegrating Progressive party. These MPs went on to help found the Co-operative Commonwealth Federation in 1932. The CCF regrouped in 1961 as the New Democratic Party....
- A right-wing populist party based in Western Canada. Social Credit, the first modern example, entered the House of Commons in 1935. Despite a long history of ups and downs, it continued to elect western members through 1965. Provincial Social Credit parties governed Alberta until 1971 and British Columbia until 1992. The Reform party inherits the conservative populist tradition. Its first and so far only leader is Preston Manning, himself a federal Socred candidate in 1965 and the son of Ernest Manning, the long-serving Social Credit premier of Alberta.
- A francophone nationalist party in Quebec, such as the Bloc Populaire in 1945, the Union des Électeurs in 1949, the Raliement Créditiste in 1962 through 1979, and the Bloc Québécois in 1993. Plus nationalist parties that ran for office at the provincial level—Maurice Duplessis's Union Nationale, which replaced the Conservatives and dominated provincial politics from the 1930s until 1960; the Parti Québécois, which has governed on and off since 1976; and, most recently, Mario Dumont's Action Démocratique. Interestingly, these nationalist parties have spanned almost the entire ideological spectrum, from socialist left to monetary-reform right.

Source: Reprinted from Stephen Harper and Tom Flanagan, "Our Benign Dictatorship," *The Next City*, Winter 1996–97, 38.

As noted in Chapter 4, the genius of Confederation was to adopt a federal form of government and to relegate to provincial jurisdiction those issues that most clearly divided English from French. George Brown's hope (reported in Chapter 4) that Confederation had entirely removed such cultural divisions from federal politics was never completely realized, of course, and the French–English divide continued to play a role on the national stage, sometimes dramatically so (the hanging of Louis Riel and the conscription crises of both world wars are cases in point). Nevertheless the institutional arrangements of federalism, coupled with the incentive for majority control of the legislature in a Westminster-style parliament based on the first-past-the-post electoral system, encouraged legislatures to form relatively broad and diverse electoral coalitions that cut across the cultural divide. There could not be too many broad coalitions, of course, and those that emerged were inevitably quite similar precisely because of their attempt to appeal broadly to all of the same political interests. Thus little differentiated the Liberal and Conservative parties at the centre of the political spectrum during this period.[32]

The early Liberal and Conservative parties also minimized the impact of cultural factors by remaining largely parliamentary parties. As classic examples of what Maurice Duverger characterized as **cadre parties,**[33] the Liberals and Conservatives were slow to develop **extraparliamentary wings** and instead remained centred in the legislature. In the first 50 years after Confederation, the Liberal Party only once held a convention of its supporters outside Parliament; the Conservatives held none. The strategy of both parties was to limit political debate to the parliamentary forum and to encourage support through the widespread use of patronage. This was a strategy of elite accommodation rather than one of mass participation.

Unlike many other democracies, Canada did not develop a strong party of the working class during this period. The reasons can be found in the complex web of institutional, societal, and strategic factors. The Westminster-model parliament encouraged the formation of majority governments and thus a small number of parties. Both the Liberal and Conservative parties emerged from among the alliances that existed within the legislature at the time responsible government was implemented. Once these parties formed within Parliament, it became more difficult to replace them. In the words of Seymour Martin Lipset and Stein Rokkan, a party system already in existence provides a threshold for the development of new parties.[34] Therefore, since a working-class party did not develop at the outset of the party system, the cost of doing so later became greater.

One key to the development of working-class parties lies in the nature and political strategy of other working-class organizations, particularly trade unions.[35] Where trade unions have played an active role in the development of a political party, they tend to have met with considerable success. In Canada the union movement developed in a strongly nonpartisan way. The National Policy of the Macdonald government instituted a development strategy that encouraged capital inflow through direct foreign investment. The Canadian manufacturing and industrial sector developed as "branch plants" of multinational, particularly American, firms.[36] The importation of American companies usually was accompanied by the importation of American unions to organize Canadian workers. The strategy of political nonalignment—made famous by American union leader Sam Gompers ("Reward your friends, punish your enemies") and referred to earlier as business unionism—was similarly imported into Canadian labour.[37] Canadian unions thus chose a political strategy that was more suitable for the American separation-of-powers system than for Canada's Westminster-style parliament. There was no concerted effort on the part of Canadian labour to establish a strong working-class party. As a result, such a party failed to emerge and instead labour worked within the two-party system.

Second Period: 1921–1962

During the first two decades of the 20th century, Canadian society underwent important changes that placed considerable strain on the party system. The continual movement toward urbanization and industrialization (especially in Ontario and Quebec), the rapid agrarian settlement of the prairie provinces, and the continued support by both political parties of the National Policy—which was perceived (correctly) as favouring the industrializing centre at the expense of the agrarian periphery—led many in the outlying regions to question the degree to which their interests were, or could be, adequately represented in either existing party.[38]

The tensions within the party system were heightened during the conscription crisis of the First World War. The Conservative government of Robert Borden favoured conscription, whereas the Liberal opposition, led by Wilfrid Laurier, was opposed. Many Liberal candidates outside of Quebec supported conscription, however, and together with the Conservatives ran under the banner of Unionists. Two consequences flowed from the emergence of the conscription issue. First, it undercut the distinction between the two political parties and confused political allegiances because of the election of a Unionist coalition government. The Liberal Party was not a unified alternative to the Conservatives. Second, in repoliticizing the French–English cleavage, the conscription crisis contributed to an important sectional realignment of the party system. The selection of Wilfrid Laurier, a French Canadian, as Liberal Party leader in the 1890s had strengthened the Liberal allegiance of Quebeckers, but with the conscription crisis of World War I the support of Quebeckers for the Liberal Party became overwhelming.[39] In 1917 the Liberals won 62 of the 65 seats in Quebec; in 1921, they won all 65.

A significant institutional change also affected party development during this era. Recall that during the first period of party development, political patronage was the lifeblood of parties, the route through which most positions in the civil service were obtained. However, the Civil Service Commission Act, 1918, placed the authority for recruitment into the civil service squarely in the hands of the commission (i.e., the bureaucracy). This institutional change removed one of the central rationales of parties and could have led to a decline in their importance and role. However, their structural necessity in a Westminster-model parliamentary system provided an incentive for parties to transform themselves to meet the changing requirements of the political system—or disappear. The representational requirements of parties in post–World War I Canada were to mediate the important differences that were either emerging or becoming more politicized in a geographically diverse, economically fragmented, and ethnically and religiously divided country.[40]

The Liberal and Conservative parties responded to this new representational requirement by attempting to act as brokers between the country's diverse interests.[41] Instead of attempting to represent one class, one region, or one ethnic, linguistic, or religious group, they attempted to represent them all. This **brokerage party** strategy was based on the premise that the conflict between these groups could best be mediated within the parties outside of Parliament rather than between parties inside Parliament. The brokerage strategy was represented especially in the development of **ministerialist parties** in which individual cabinet ministers would function as the representatives of particular regional, cultural, or economic groups within the party decision-making process and simultaneously act as party spokespersons in explaining and communicating decisions to the affected interest.

If one measures the success of the brokerage strategy by the level of electoral support obtained by the parties, the Liberal Party was without question the better broker of competing interests. It won eight of the nine elections held from 1921 to 1957 and governed for 31 of those 36 years. Its only defeat during this period occurred shortly after the onset of the Great Depression, when the Conservative Party under R.B. Bennett captured 137 of 245 Commons seats, only to plummet to 40 seats five years later. The Liberals were led throughout this period by William Lyon Mackenzie King and Louis St. Laurent, both of whom were noted conciliators.

However, the electoral record also illustrates the limitations inherent in the brokerage model. Those groups that believed that the Liberal and Conservative parties were either unwilling or unable to effectively represent their interests had an incentive to go outside these parties and develop other parties that might prove more effective. Bear in mind that the costs of doing so in representational terms could be high. The winner-take-all character of the electoral system means there is no reward for finishing second or third. If a new party cannot defeat both established parties in a constituency, it cannot win the seat. In addition, the Canadian tradition of majority or minority (but not coalition) governments reinforces the winner-take-all feature of elections. In devising their strategy, groups must ask themselves whether their interests are better served if they have a small voice in a governing party or a loud voice in an opposition party. This is not to say that new parties cannot emerge within Canada's electoral institutions. The strong tradition of third parties in Canada suggests otherwise. Nevertheless, emerging parties must overcome significant institutional obstacles.

What kind of new parties were most likely to emerge during the period of brokerage politics? The electoral system rewards those parties whose support is concentrated in specific geographical areas and penalizes those with more dispersed support. In addition, the electoral weight of the two central provinces, with over 60 percent of seats in the Commons, ensures that these interests could not be ignored by brokerage parties. Therefore, one might expect that parties based in disaffected peripheral regions would most likely emerge. To the extent that the brokerage parties did not successfully incorporate the concerns of the growing numbers of the working class, one might also expect a working-class party to emerge.

The electoral data presented in Table 10.1 indicate that both types of parties emerged during the brokerage period, although neither was able to rise to a governing position. The two-party system was shattered in the 1921 election, which saw the election of 65 Progressive candidates, 15 more than the Conservatives. The Progressives won all but a handful of prairie seats, and almost one-third of the Ontario seats (most in northern or rural Ontario). As the second-place party, the Progressives were entitled to form the official opposition in the House of Commons. However, the Progressive caucus was dominated by populist members who were hostile to the existing system of disciplined party combat in the legislature, which they saw as placing inordinate power in the hands of party leaders. (Populism involves a suspicion of "the leaders" or "the politicians" and places greater faith in the goodness or common sense of the people—see Dossier 2.9.) Thus, instead of using their western regional base as a platform from which to challenge the central-Canadian orientation of the major parties, the Progressives refused the mantle of official Opposition and supported the minority Liberal government instead. Progressive leader C.A. Crerar was even co-opted into the government ministry. This strategy led the Progressives to lose much of their support over the next decade, and the party disappeared as a national force by the 1935 federal election.

Although the anti-party sentiment of the Progressives contributed to their political demise, it led to the name of the current Progressive Conservative Party. In 1943 John Bracken, premier of Manitoba from 1922 to 1943, was persuaded to move to federal politics and lead the Conservative party. Bracken had led the Manitoba Progressives, and his anti-party views had contributed to the formation of a "Liberal-Progressive" coalition, which won three successive provincial elections in the 1930s. In 1941 Bracken invited all parties in the Manitoba legislature to join in a coalition government, and all but a handful of members did so. In 1943 the same anti-party sentiment led Bracken to demand the addition of "Progressive" to the name of the Conservative Party as the price of agreeing to lead that party at the national level. Bracken never led his re-named party to victory, however, and thus never had the opportunity to attempt to replicate at the federal level his provincial success in promoting inter-party cooperation.

The Progressives left another, more significant, imprint on Canadian politics. Despite the brevity of their stint on the stage of national politics, they inaugurated a new era of regionally based third parties, including a new party of the left. The 1921 election witnessed the election not only of 65 Progressives but also of two independent labour candidates, J.S. Woodsworth and William Irvine. By the late 1920s there had emerged in Parliament a loose association of labour MPs and some of the more radical Progressive MPs, which became known as the **Ginger Group,** for the spice it added to parliamentary debate. At the instigation of the Ginger Group and the League for Social Reconstruction (LSR)—a university-based group of socialists modelled on the

British Fabian Society—a meeting of the Western Labour Conference in 1932 voted to create a new socialist political party.[42] The party held its founding convention in Regina the next year, calling itself the "Co-operative Commonwealth Federation—Farmer, Labour, Socialist." As its subtitle suggested, the CCF tried to appeal to regionally (western) based farmers, the working class, and intellectual socialists.

The farmer–labour alliance within the CCF was an uneasy one. The tendency of farmer votes to be tightly clustered geographically (particularly in the Prairies) and of labour votes to be more dispersed resulted in the CCF's winning more contests in rural western constituencies than in urban constituencies. Thus the parliamentary wing of the CCF had a distinctly western character. Its outward appearance as a party of western farmers made it more difficult for the party to appeal to the urban working class. That difficulty was compounded by divisions within the union movement, regarding both its organizational structure and its approach to political action. For most of the period of brokerage parties, the major central union organization, the Trades and Labour Congress (TLC), was dominated by American-based multinational unions that held to the Gompers approach of remaining politically independent and trying to influence governments of any partisan stripe. In the mid-1930s a more militant and politically active group of industrial unions was expelled from the TLC and formed the Canadian Congress of Labour (CCL). Beginning in 1942 the CCL declared at each convention that the CCF was the "political arm of labour" and urged its member unions to affiliate with the party.[43] Few did. Organized labour was not able to take a more unified and politically active position until the merger of the TLC and CCL into the Canadian Labour Congress (CLC) in 1956. As we shall see, that merger provided the impetus for the transformation of the CCF into the NDP in the early 1960s. Along with the Liberal and Conservative parties, the CCF–NDP is one of the five relatively stable components of the modern party system identified in Dossier 10.5.

In addition to contributing members to the Ginger Group, and thus influencing the creation of the CCF–NDP, the Progressive Party also demonstrated the tendency of the electoral system to generate regional third parties. Whereas some forms of regional discontent found voice in the leftist CCF, others were more at home in a populist party of the ideological right: Social Credit. Following the political ideas developed by British engineer Major Douglas and articulated in the Canadian West by fundamentalist minister and radio preacher William ("Bible Bill") Aberhart, the Social Credit Party emerged during the 1935 election, in the middle of the Great Depression, as an important voice for western farmers.[44] Ever since, right-wing populists from Western Canada, operating either through their own regional protest party or as a wing of one of the traditional parties, have been another of the five groups underpinning Canada's party system.

Social Credit's support (measured by the party's seats rather than votes) came almost exclusively from Alberta during this third period of party development, and from 1935 to 1957 it captured all but a handful of the Commons seats from that province. The party collapsed in 1958 when western populists—along with Quebec nationalists (yet another of the five long-term forces in Canadian politics)—migrated en masse into the Conservative party, led by the fiery westerner John Diefenbaker, contributing to a landslide Conservative victory.

Thus, protest parties, particularly those from the West, were an important feature of the period of brokerage politics from 1921 to 1957. The perception that the two old-line parties were more responsive to the concerns and interests of Ontario and Quebec was widely shared in the West, and parties emerged to articulate and advocate western interests. Unfortunately for westerners, these parties never gained more than a minority position within the legislature. The Liberals during this period continued to draw support from across the country, particularly from the electorally important provinces in central Canada. If they wanted a more effective say on the government benches, westerners did not achieve it by pursuing the third-party strategy. Similarly, the new working-class party (the CCF) found only limited success at the national level, its appeal hampered by a combination of three factors: the tensions and lack of representational clarity that resulted from the alliance of western farmers with the urban working class; the divisions in the union movement within English Canada; and the explicitly anti-CCF position of the religiously based unions in Quebec. The electoral system's distortions in translating votes into seats established a threshold for electoral success that the party was able to overcome only in regional pockets of strength.

Third Period: 1963–1988

The electoral realignment brought about by Diefenbaker's Conservatives integrated westerners once again into one of the two major parties and temporarily ended the Liberals' stranglehold under the brokerage model. Thereafter, the representation of third parties in Parliament gradually declined until only the NDP was left. In addition, given the focus on personality that characterizes the modern electronic media, parties became more closely identified with their leaders, and their success at the polls was increasingly determined by attitudes toward the leader. In short, the third period was an era of **electronic politics** and **personal parties**[45] dominated by a two-plus-one party system. All three parties, moreover, emphasized "national appeal" in their explicit electoral rhetoric; overtly regional appeals were eschewed.

The CCF–NDP provides a good example of the nationalization of political perspective. The CCF, which gained most of its support from western farmers, transformed itself (with the help of the newly formed Canadian Labour Congress) into the New Democratic Party in 1961. Whereas the CCF had attempted to unite the disparate groups that were opposed to the economic powers of central Canada—namely, farmers, industrial workers, and socialists—the NDP was created to pursue more vigorously the interests of the predominantly urban working class. The strategy was for the NDP to form stronger ties with organized labour and for unions and their members to play a more active role by supporting the party directly.[46] Despite the electoral system's tendency to reward regional voting strength, the NDP adopted an explicitly national approach to political competition, and downplayed the regional character of its appeal.[47]

Although the NDP survived this period of declining third parties, the regionally based Social Credit/Créditiste party did not. (The Raliement Créditiste, the Quebec wing of Social Credit, provided a federal outlet for Quebec nationalism.) In his landslide election of 1958, Diefenbaker won a majority of seats in each region of the country, not only capturing the traditional Liberal bastion of Quebec but also displacing third parties from the Prairies. Although the Conservatives were unable to hold Quebec, which briefly drifted to the Créditistes before throwing its support behind the Trudeau Liberals, they were able to retain the West.

Party development in this third period was influenced by profound changes in the nature of the society parties purported to represent. Canadian society was far more urbanized and industrialized in the 1960s and 1970s than it had been at the end of the Second World War. In the postwar period, urbanization and industrialization extended beyond the industrial core of Ontario and Quebec to become standard features of the western and Atlantic regions. As one illustration of this trend, the combined population of Calgary and Edmonton, 23.0 percent of Alberta's population in 1941, skyrocketed to 51.7 percent by 1971.[48] Thus, Canada's regions became less socially and economically differentiated. Similarly, there was a shift of economic power westward. The economic centre of the country moved from Montreal to Toronto and there was substantial growth in the economic clout of Vancouver and Calgary.

To these socio-demographic changes were added two important technological developments: (1) the availability and increased use of television as a source of political information and as a tool for campaigning, and (2) the development of public-opinion polling techniques to evaluate support for party policies and leaders. Television provided for a national flow of information on a scale that had never been possible through the print media, and it provided a medium for parties to appeal directly to a national electorate. It had the added effect of personalizing politics—making it a contest between individuals instead of between competing groups or ideas. The availability of public-opinion polling enabled the party leadership to bypass traditional sources of information and measure the attitudes and preferences of Canadians directly. No longer was it necessary to have a regional spokesperson represent the views of a section of the country. Such information could now be obtained more directly, and perhaps more accurately, through public-opinion polling.

Parties that were successful in the 1960s, 1970s, and 1980s—the Liberals and Conservatives, and, to a lesser extent, the New Democrats—were forced to adjust to the new environment of electronic politics or be shut out of power. Perhaps the most profound consequence of the third period was the increased importance of political leadership. With the personalization of electoral politics, a premium was placed on choosing a party leader who is able to appeal to a broad spectrum of the electorate. The party leader not only must sell the party's platform and approach to the electorate but must do so in both official languages. The slowness of the Conservative

Party to recognize the importance of leader images in Canadian politics helped keep it in opposition through most of the 1970s, though the party was handsomely rewarded in the 1980s with the selection of a leader more suited to the electronic age. Likewise, a failure to recognize the political realities of bilingualism probably kept John Crosbie out of the leadership of the Conservatives in 1983 and contributed to Dave Barrett's defeat in the NDP's leadership contest in 1989.

The institutional environment for political parties also changed in ways that were to have an important effect on party development. Foremost among these changes was the development of modern executive federalism. Substantial increases in education spending, the development of a provincially administered national health-care system, and increased demand for social-assistance expenditures placed the provincial governments in a position of rising importance. The increased salience and power of provincial governments was accompanied by a substantially expanded role for provincial premiers in national politics, with the result that federal–provincial relations were increasingly conducted in first ministers' meetings. This shifting of power to first ministers, and the mediation of federal–provincial conflict through agencies of interstate federalism, reduced the need for the intrastate federalism embodied in the regional spokespersons of brokerage parties. Consequently, the parties relied less on this intrastate mechanism.

A second major institutional change was the fundamental shift in the registration and financing of political parties brought about by the 1974 **Election Expenses Act.** As noted earlier in this chapter, the act provided for more public financing of parties through a system of tax credits for political donations, and for a more open and accountable funding system in which parties were required to publicly declare their revenue and expenditures. It also set limits on the amount of money parties and candidates could spend in election campaigns and on the amount of television exposure parties could purchase. The net effect of these changes was a substantial improvement in the financial stability of each of the major parties (albeit with significant fluctuation depending on the party's electoral performance) and a consequent expansion in their national headquarters. Parties responded to the new institutional environment by developing direct-mail campaigns and appealing for funds beyond the party membership, which remains small for each of the parties. It is paradoxical that as party organizations became stronger, more stable, and more financially secure, they also became increasingly dominated by the party leader and his or her key advisers. These contrasting trends have resulted in the increasing separation of the parliamentary and extraparliamentary wings of parties.

Both the institutional and societal changes in the political environment influenced the strategies adopted by parties. The nationalization and personalization of political campaigning, the increased importance of provincial premiers as representatives of their province's or region's interests at federal–provincial conferences, and the shifting economic base of the country worked against regional political appeals and strengthened the parties' national perspective.

The decline of overtly regional parties and the greater national orientation of the three surviving parties did not, however, mean the death of regionalism. Regionalism remained a central theme of public discussion, and no amount of nationalistic rhetoric could change the regional reality of partisan politics. Despite their attempts to appeal to the national electorate, the three major parties were often regionally fragmented in the House of Commons. For most of this period, the electoral system gave the Liberal Party a disproportionate share of the Quebec seats and shut out both the Conservatives and the NDP in the province. Likewise, the Conservatives (and to a lesser extent the NDP) were strong in the West, while the Liberals were also-rans in the region. Even the Liberal majority produced by the so-called Trudeaumania election in 1968—the biggest Liberal majority of this period—was based largely in Ontario and Quebec (120 of the Liberals' 155 seats came from those two provinces); Trudeau at his most popular was unable to improve his party's performance much in the prairie West or Atlantic Canada.

This kind of regional fragmentation in Commons seats persisted until 1984, when the leadership of the Conservative Party passed from Joe Clark, a westerner, to Brian Mulroney, a Quebec businessman with strong personal ties to such Quebec nationalists as Lucien Bouchard. In the 1980 election the Clark-led Conservatives won one of the 75 seats from Quebec; in 1984, with Mulroney at the helm, they won 58 Quebec seats. By adding Quebec to the Conservative Party's power base in the West, and turning in a strong performance in the rest of the country as well, Mulroney turned "national party" rhetoric into reality for the first time since Diefenbaker's 1958 electoral landslide.

As in Diefenbaker's case, however, Mulroney's national coalition turned out to be a temporary exception, though Mulroney did manage to hold it together for nine years. In 1993 regionalism in partisan politics would re-emerge with a vengeance, bringing the period of apparently "national" parties to an abrupt and dramatic end.

Fourth Period: 1993–Present

The 1993 election produced a remarkable partisan realignment of the House of Commons. With 41 percent of the national vote, the Liberal Party won 60 percent (177) of the 295 seats in the House of Commons, up from 83 seats in 1988. Perhaps more remarkable, the Liberals won 98 of 99 seats in Ontario with 53 percent of the votes from that province. Both the Conservatives and New Democrats fell short of the 12 seats needed for official party status in the House of Commons. The PC decline was unprecedented in Canadian federal politics—the party dropped from 169 seats in 1988 to two seats in 1993, although it retained 16 percent of the national vote. The NDP fared little better, falling from 43 seats in 1988 to nine seats in 1993 on the basis of 7 percent of the national vote. The Bloc Québécois, a separatist party running candidates for the first time, and only in the province of Quebec, won 54 of that province's 75 seats—nationally the largest number of seats behind the governing

Liberals. As a result, the Bloc, with only 13 percent of the national vote, became the official opposition in the Commons. Following closely behind the Bloc was the Reform Party, whose 19 percent of the national vote translated into 52 seats in the House of Commons, all but one of them from the four western provinces, including 22 of 26 in Alberta and 24 of 32 in British Columbia. The Reform Party's performance was notable because the party was formed in 1987 and had not won a single seat in the 1988 election, although it had won a by-election for a Commons seat in 1989. Only once previously in Canadian political history had the Liberals and Conservatives not locked up the top two positions, the exception being the 1921 second-place finish of the Progressives. The Conservatives' fifth-place finish, with only two seats in the House of Commons, was a startling development.

The trend toward increased regional fragmentation of the party system in 1993 continued through the 1997 election; indeed, the latter showed even greater regional trends. The Liberal Party remained the national government, although its proportion of the vote dropped from 41 to 38 percent. As a result, the Liberals won only 155, or just over 51 percent, of the 301 Commons seats, down significantly from the 60 percent of seats they secured in 1993, but still enough to form a majority government. Fully 82 percent of these Liberal seats were concentrated in central Canada. By far the largest number came from Ontario, where the Liberals won all but two of 103 seats on the strength of 49 percent of the vote. The Liberals also won 26 of the 75 Quebec seats, many of them in constituencies with significant non-francophone populations. The Liberals had enough electoral support across the country to come second in many ridings outside Ontario and Quebec but only enough to win 28 seats outside the Canadian heartland.

The Reform Party strengthened its western support, winning 60 seats on the basis of 19 percent of the national vote and displacing the BQ as the official opposition. But Reform failed to pick up any seats east of Manitoba. Although the BQ's support fell somewhat in Quebec, the party retained considerable support in the province and emerged as the third-largest party in the Commons with 44 of Quebec's 75 seats on the strength of 11 percent of the national vote. Both the NDP and the PCs surpassed the 12-seat threshold required to regain official party status in the House of Commons, but both placed well behind the parties with more regionally concentrated votes. The NDP, which tied the BQ in percentage of the national vote, won less than half as many seats (8 in the Maritimes and 13 in the West, for a total of 21). Similarly, the PCs, who gained as high a percentage of votes nationally as Reform, won only one-third as many seats (a total of 20 seats, all but two of them east of Ontario).

In sum, and in rough terms, the Liberals emerged from the 1997 election as the party of Ontario, Reform as the party of the West, the BQ as the party of Quebec, the PCs as the party of the Maritimes, and the NDP as the party of parts of the Maritimes and the West. Certainly this is how things look when one examines representation in the House of Commons. Popular vote figures tell a somewhat different story, with parties generally winning more votes in their areas of weakness than their seat totals in those areas might suggest; still, it is hard to deny that regional fragmentation of Canada's national party system has reached extreme levels.

What is the significance of this radical fragmentation of the party system? In one sense, it appears to be a startling new departure. In a deeper sense, it can be seen as the logical expression of long-term forces in Canadian politics. Consider the five stable partisan groupings identified in Dossier 10.5: Liberals, Conservatives, CCF–NDP, western right-wing populists, and Quebec nationalists. The first three are long-established political parties; the last two sometimes form their own political parties—Social Credit, Reform; Créditiste, Bloc Québécois—and at other times form wings within the Liberal or Conservative parties. The dramatic fragmentation of the party system in 1993 and 1997 occurred because western populists and Quebec nationalists voted simultaneously, and in large numbers, for their own federal parties.

The Conservative Party has been the big loser in this migration of western populists and Quebec nationalists into their own federal parties. In the context of Canada's first-past-the-post electoral system, the Liberal Party has a sufficient base of centrist support to form majority governments (or at least relatively stable minority governments) even when western populists or Quebec nationalists, or both, throw much of their support elsewhere. The Conservative Party, by contrast, has for many decades been unable to hold power without the support of both western populists and Quebec nationalists. Diefenbaker managed this coalition of unlikely bedfellows in his landslide victory of 1958. In that election, Diefenbaker's own populism attracted Social Credit voters into the fold, while in Quebec the conservative nationalist premier, Maurice Duplessis, threw the weight of his Union Nationale machine behind Diefenbaker. Mulroney achieved much the same kind of coalition in 1984 and 1988. He already had the support of westerners, whose long-term disenchantment with the Liberals had been deepened by the Trudeau government's National Energy Program. Mulroney added Quebec nationalists—most prominently, Lucien Bouchard—to his coalition by promising to address Quebec's constitutional concerns, a promise that led to the Meech Lake Accord.

If one discounts Joe Clark's short-lived minority government in 1979, the governments of R.B. Bennett (1930–35), John Diefenbaker (1957–63), and Brian Mulroney (1984–93) represent the only periods of Conservative rule since the Conservative-led Unionist government of 1917–21. All three of these Conservative "interludes" came after long periods of Liberal rule, when voters were anxious to "throw the rascals out." As Harper and Flanagan put it, "the same story has been replayed since 1917. For the Progressive Conservative party to come to power, the PCs' leader has had to attract support from western populists and Quebec nationalists in addition to core Tory support in Ontario and the Maritime provinces, and the public has had to be desperate to remove the Liberals."[49] Harper and Flanagan go on to point out that "such a 'throw them out' coalition can win an election but can't really govern, because its elements have different aspirations …"

FIGURE 10.1 **FIVE PARTIES, SIX DIMENSIONS**

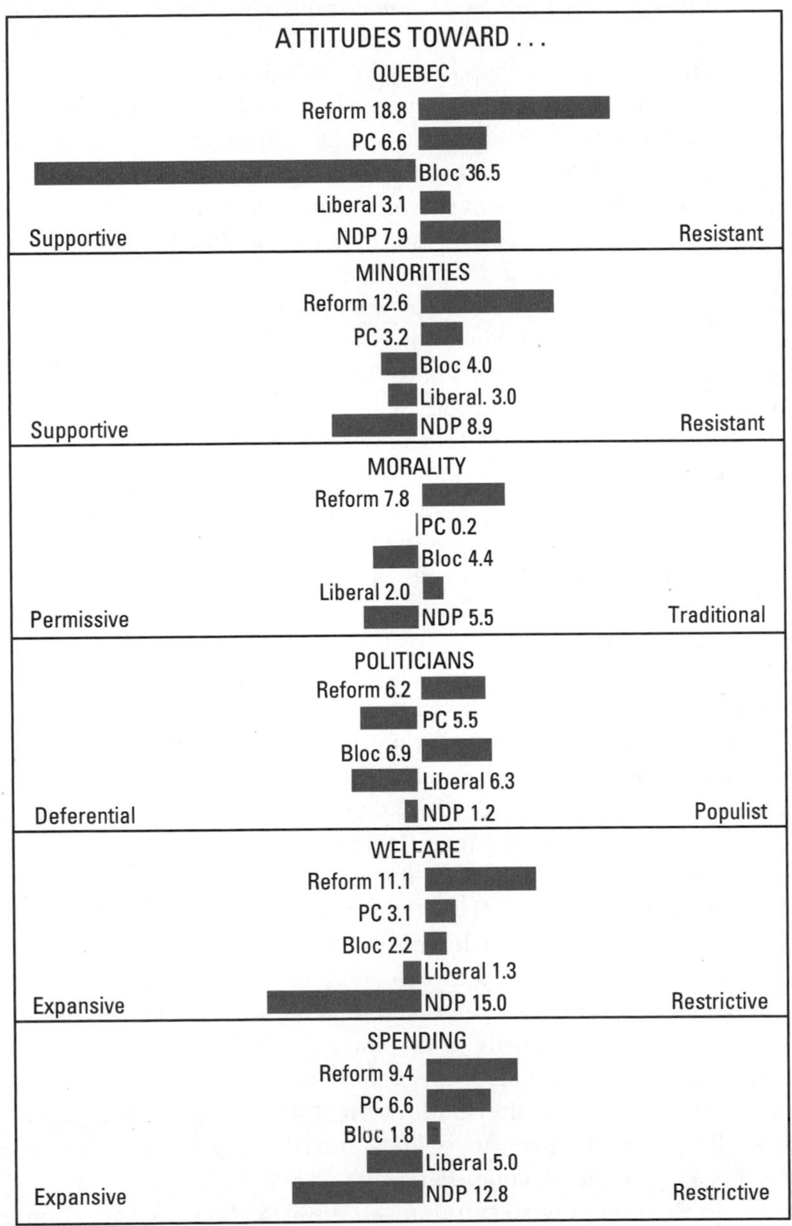

Source: Tom Flanagan and Stephen Harper, "Conservative Politics in Canada: Past, Present & Future," in William D. Gairdner, ed., *After Liberalism: Essays in Search of Freedom, Virtue and Order* (Toronto: Stoddart, 1988). Reprinted with the permission of Stoddart Publishing Co. Limited, Don Mills, Ontario.

Western populists, at least those of the right, want a smaller, more parsimonious government that treats all provinces equally. Quebec nationalists demand a federal government that offers Quebec special treatment by transferring to Quebec both revenue and powers. And eastern Tories generally want a traditional and centralist approach to government.[50]

The "core Tory" support tends to stick with the Conservative party, but sooner or later one of the other components of the coalition—either the western populists or the Quebec nationalists—defects, leaving the party without enough support to govern. In Diefenbaker's case, only Quebec voters abandoned the party, and, as noted above, these voters eventually drifted back into the Liberal fold. In the case of Mulroney's coalition, both western populists and Quebec nationalists defected simultaneously, leaving the PCs with only their core Tory support. Both defecting groups, moreover, emerged in their own regionally concentrated parties: Reform and the BQ. At this point the electoral system kicked in, over-rewarding the regionally concentrated strength of Reform and the BQ and drastically under-rewarding the more thinly spread support of the PCs and the NDP.

Why, more precisely, did the western and Quebec wings of the Conservative coalition defect? The Quebec nationalists did so over the Meech Lake Accord. In the late spring of 1990, when the federal government was pressing hard to secure the ratification of the accord, a parliamentary committee headed by then Conservative MP Jean Charest—later to become the federal Conservative leader and later still the leader of the Quebec Liberal Party—tabled a report that recommended a number of additions to the Meech Lake Accord. Four days later, minister of the Environment Lucien Bouchard, one of Prime Minister Mulroney's closest personal friends, quit the Conservative cabinet and caucus in protest over the government's handling of the constitutional issue. Bouchard was particularly incensed by the content of the committee report, which he saw as weakening the accord's commitments to Quebec. In late July 1990, a month after the failure of Meech, Bouchard was joined by five Conservative MPs and one Liberal MP in forming the Bloc Québécois, a Quebec-based political party committed to that province's separation from Canada. The Bloc thus became the first political party since Confederation to emerge from within the national Parliament, a fact rich with irony in view of the party's goal of making the Canadian Parliament irrelevant to Quebec. The following month the Bloc's numbers were increased by one when the fledgling party won a stunning by-election victory in Quebec, capturing two-thirds of the votes. Over time the Bloc forged stronger ties with the provincial Parti Québécois and more clearly articulated its vision of an independent Quebec. In the aftermath of the 1995 Quebec independence referendum, Lucien Bouchard left federal politics and the BQ to step into the shoes of the departing PQ premier, Jacques Parizeau.

In the case of western populists, the defection from the Conservatives to the Reform Party was under way in the mid- to late 1980s. The Reform Party was founded in Winnipeg, in the fall of 1987, under the banner "The West Wants In!" At first blush, the timing seemed curious. Throughout the period of Liberal dominance from the mid-1960s to the mid-1980s, westerners had consistently supported the Conservative Party. As a consequence, most western MPs during this period sat on the opposition benches in the House of Commons. In the 1984 election, in which Brian Mulroney succeeded in attracting much of the Quebec vote, the Conservative Party won a strong majority government. If one discounts the short-lived government of Joe Clark, this was the first time in a generation that westerners found themselves not only represented in significant numbers on the government side of the House but also holding some of the most senior portfolios. This new position of strength on the government benches led many westerners to have high expectations of the Conservative government. The government proved unwilling or unable to meet those expectations, however. For many westerners, the suspicion that no Canadian federal government responding to the population density of Ontario and Quebec would adequately address their regional concerns was confirmed in the spring of 1987, when the government awarded a contract to service Canada's fleet of CF-18 military jets. The competition was between Bristol Aerospace of Winnipeg and Canadair of Montreal. Although the bid by Bristol was technically superior and less costly, Canadair was awarded the contract—a decision widely interpreted as being politically motivated. The anger and frustration in Western Canada was palpable. Mulroney's attempt to keep Quebec nationalists and western populists within the party began to unravel. Within six months the Reform Party was formed to harness and direct western discontent.

The founding convention of the Reform Party chose as its leader Preston Manning, son of Ernest Manning, who was a former Social Credit premier of Alberta. The Reform Party's platform was based on populism, constitutional reform, and social and fiscal conservatism. A year after its founding, Reform contested the 1988 federal election in the four western provinces. Although the party had pockets of support in the election (it received over 15 percent of the vote in Alberta), it failed to win a single seat. However, in 1989 Reform's Deborah Gray won a by-election victory in Alberta and so became the party's first elected member of Parliament. Later that year the government of Alberta held an election for the appointment of a senator from the province, and Reform's Stan Waters won by a wide margin. In June 1990 Prime Minister Mulroney followed the advice of the Alberta government and appointed Waters to the Senate. Waters became known as Canada's first elected senator.

At its biennial assembly in 1991 the Reform Party passed a resolution supporting an eastward expansion from the four western provinces into Ontario and the Atlantic region. The party was attempting to broaden its appeal and to attract, in addition to the western protest vote, a more general protest vote against the political and economic status quo. Although Reform achieved a major electoral breakthrough in 1993 and gained the status of official Opposition in 1997, the party was unable to expand on the purely western stronghold that its Commons representation reflected.

Although five parties now hold seats in the House of Commons, Canadian elections are contested by a coterie of minor also-ran parties. In 1993, for example, 14 registered political parties ran candidates, the largest number of parties to do so in Canada's history. In addition to the five major parties, there was the Abolitionist

Party, the Christian Heritage Party, the Canada Party, the Green Party, the Libertarian Party, the Marxist-Leninist Party, the National Party, the Natural Law Party, and the Commonwealth Party. Parties like the Marxist-Leninists and the Libertarians have been contesting Canadian elections for years, but others, such as the National Party and the Natural Law Party, were formed just prior to the 1993 election. The list is always shifting. The National Party folded after the 1993 election.

One of the reasons for this proliferation of parties is that registered political party status provides tax advantages to groups interested in spreading a political, or even a non-political, message. For example, individuals and groups concerned about environmental preservation and enhancement could pursue their cause by making tax-creditable contributions to the Green Party. Antiabortion groups could contribute to the Christian Heritage Party, and devotees of the Transcendental Meditation movement could support the Natural Law Party. Most of these parties command little financial and organizational resources. They have few party members and no members of Parliament. However, success in electing members to the House of Commons may sometimes be secondary to the benefit of having an outlet for tax-creditable contributions in spreading the message of a group's cause. Because they are funded largely through tax-creditable contributions, such parties might exist as minor political organizations for long periods even without electoral success.

The Future of the Party System

Will Canada's current system of five parties in the House of Commons change? Almost certainly, if only because voters will eventually want to throw the Liberals out of office. Since the advent of the multiparty system in 1921, the pragmatic and centrist Liberal Party, with its particular strength in seat-rich central Canada, has governed about 75 percent of the time. (Over the course of the entire 20th century, the Liberals will have governed 70 percent of the time.) By themselves, none of the other four main political groups can knock off the Liberals. The voting power of social democrats has always been too thinly spread to bring the CCF–NDP to power. So has the core Tory support of the Progressive Conservative Party. Right-wing populists have shown that they can capture a substantial number of seats in Western Canada, just as Quebec nationalists have done in their province, but there aren't enough seats in either region to sustain a government. History shows that the Liberals can be defeated only by some kind of coalition among the other groups, such as the electorally successful but politically unstable coalitions of Tories, western populists, and Quebec nationalists put together by Diefenbaker and Mulroney. As long as all of the other four groups wage political war with one another as well as with the Liberals, as they have done since 1993, it is difficult to imagine how the Liberals can be toppled, though a Liberal minority government is not out of the question. However, neither the public nor opposition politicians will stand for the perpetual rule of one party. Government parties in Canada can and often do remain in place for long periods, but sooner or later voters demand, and politicians supply (however temporarily), an electorally viable alternative.

The NDP has tried to do its part by moving somewhat toward the centre. Modelling itself on the successful centre-left approaches of such parties as Britain's Labour Party, the NDP announced in the summer of 1998 that it would work more closely with business interests. Some union activists were unhappy with this strategy, but it was clearly designed to move the NDP in from the margins of Canadian federal politics and to create a viable alternative to the left of the Liberals.

On the right, the cause of an electorally viable alternative to the Liberals would be advanced if either Reform or the PCs won the so-called "fight for the right," consigning the other to political oblivion. But the PCs are so far behind in the West and Reform is so weak in Quebec and Atlantic Canada that neither party seems likely to displace its conservative opponent in these regions anytime soon. The crucial battleground is Ontario, where the PCs and Reform split the right-wing vote fairly evenly in 1993 and 1997, allowing the Liberals to "come up the middle" and win a vast majority of the province's ridings in both elections. If one of the two parties could win the "fight for the right" in this seat-rich province, it might create a favourable momentum in its areas of weakness.

Alternatively, some observers have proposed a "unite the right" approach under which Reform and the PCs would cooperate rather than each trying to become the only party of the right. For example, it has been suggested that the two parties refrain from running against each other in the same constituencies. Reform and the PCs would run without opposition by the other party in their areas of strength. The right-wing vote would thus not be split and the two parties together could win enough seats to form a coalition government, much as the Liberal and National parties do in Australia and the Christian Democratic Union and the Christian Social Union do in Germany.

In a variation on this strategy, some constituency associations from the two parties have considered holding joint candidate nomination meetings, so that a single candidate would run under both the PC and Reform banners in that riding. Again, this would avoid splitting the right-wing vote to the benefit of the Liberals or the NDP.

Yet another approach is the so-called United Alternative proposed by Preston Manning at the Reform Party's convention in May 1998. Declaring the traditional left–right continuum to be outmoded and irrelevant, Manning proposed a new party, one inclusive enough to appeal to individuals from all the other parties and thus large enough to be a viable alternative to the Liberals. The Reform Party itself would disband and merge into this larger entity. Naturally, Manning's opponents decried his proposed United Alternative as a cynical recruitment scheme for the Reform Party. However this may be, the fact is that some kind of alternative to the Liberals will eventually emerge, and that this alternative is likely to involve some "unification" of the current political parties. How much unification will occur, and how durable it will be, remains to be seen.

PARTIES AS ORGANIZATIONS

Political parties are essential features of democratic political systems. Most formal definitions of democracy include the existence of a competitive party system as a key characteristic that distinguishes democratic political systems from other kinds of political systems.[51] As representative political organizations, parties perform a number of important functions in democracies, including selecting candidates for political office, choosing party leaders, developing policy initiatives, running election campaigns, and of course raising money to enable the party to perform these functions. Since parties are largely unregulated in the way they pursue many of their functions, they have been relatively free to develop their own style of organization. The organizations adopted by Canada's major parties reflect the fact that they operate within a Westminster-style parliamentary system in a relatively loose federal system of government. Parliamentary government has led each party to adopt a fairly rigid form of party discipline for its caucus members. Even the Reform Party, which is in principle in favour of loosening discipline, has disciplined maverick MPs, sometimes expelling them from the caucus and party. Federalism has led the Liberals, Conservatives, and NDP to develop quite separate federal and provincial wings, although the parties differ in the degree of autonomy with which the two levels operate. Reform has rejected the formation of provincial wings, while in Quebec the federal BQ enjoys an informal alliance with the provincial PQ.

If party organizations were influenced only by these common institutional factors, all parties would look alike. They do not. Different ideologies and targeted bases of support have led to significant differences in the ways in which the parties try to represent the interests of their membership. Some parties are more democratic in organization than others. This section examines both the similarities and differences in how the major parties are organized and how they perform their various functions.

Organizational Structure

Figure 10.2 shows in schematic form the organizational structure of the five parties represented in the federal Parliament.[52] The structures of these parties bear a number of striking similarities, but the way in which authority flows within these structures varies. Each party is governed by its constitution and each constitution vests final authority in a party "convention," "assembly," "general meeting," or "congress," which convenes every two years. Generally, these biennial conventions are **policy conventions,** not **leadership conventions,** which select a party leader. In the New Democratic Party, however, a vote on the party leadership is held at each biennial policy convention, although to date no sitting NDP leader has faced a serious challenge in the leadership election at convention. We shall return to the subject of leadership selection below.

The status of the biennial general convention as a "policy convention" is especially marked in the case of the New Democratic Party. All policy resolutions passed by conventions since the party was founded, in 1961, are collected in a resolutions reference manual and are removed only when they have been "overtaken by events or superseded by subsequent resolutions."[53] The reference manual contains hundreds of resolutions, on everything from "The Structure of Economic Planning" and "Financing Child Care" to "Livelihood of Trappers." The resolutions reference is intended to provide for greater democratization in the lines of authority within the party, since the party leadership is bound by convention resolutions. These resolutions can be an albatross around the neck of the leader, since resolutions on matters such as the nationalization of banks are often used by the party's political opponents to portray the NDP as committed to wholesale nationalization of key sectors of the Canadian economy, even though the party leadership may be less committed to such a policy.

As befits the Reform Party's populism, policy development in that party can result not only from the votes of delegates at the assembly but also through referendums among the wider party membership. Referendums can be initiated by a motion passed at an assembly, by an executive council motion, or by an initiative supported by 5 percent of the membership.

One can get an indication of a party's targeted bases of support by noting the delegate status of those who attend conventions. Delegates from the parties' **constituency associations**—the base on which each organizational chart rests—are the most numerous at the party conventions but are not the only delegates there. The parties generally award delegate status to members of caucus as well as to those holding executive positions. In addition, the Liberals and Conservatives award delegate credentials in as many as 18 different categories, including members of provincial legislatures, campus clubs, senators, and candidates who were defeated in the previous federal election. The BQ gives delegate status to the presidents of the "commissions" depicted in the chart, including commissions representing the interests of cultural communities and the elderly. The NDP has six delegate categories: constituency, caucus, youth, federal council, central labour, and affiliated organizations (mainly trade unions). As with the Liberals and Conservatives, a majority of NDP delegates (usually about two-thirds) are from constituency associations. Unlike the Liberals and Progressive Conservatives, about 20–25 percent of NDP delegates come from trade unions. The Reform Party does not set out delegate categories.

Although constituency delegates are the most common delegate type at each party's convention, significant differences exist in the way the parties award delegate positions to constituencies. In the Liberal and Conservative parties, each constituency receives an equal number of delegate positions, regardless of the strength of the party in the constituency. In the NDP, by contrast, constituencies receive delegate positions based on the size of their membership—the larger the membership, the greater the number of delegates. This system of awarding delegate positions has resulted in a rather curious regional distribution of delegate positions at NDP conventions, with the vast majority of delegates being from Ontario and the West. Indeed, there are usually more NDP constituency delegates from Saskatchewan than from Quebec, a fact that is both cause and consequence of the party's historic weakness east of Ontario. Awarding

FIGURE 10.2 ORGANIZATION CHARTS, CANADIAN POLITICAL PARTIES

Schematic Organization Chart, Liberal Party of Canada (1990 constitution)

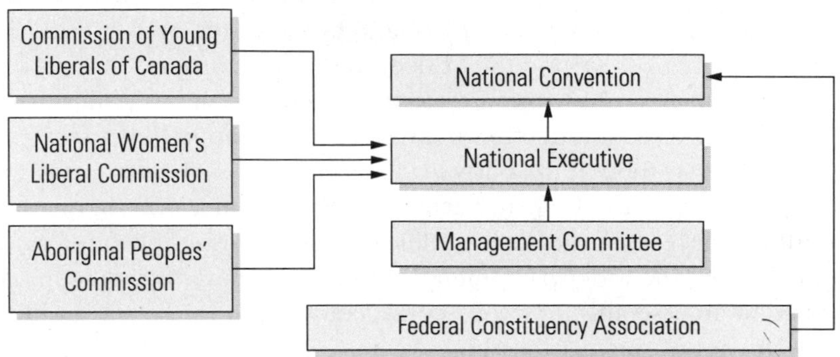

Schematic Organization Chart, Reform Party of Canada

Schematic Organization Chart, Bloc Québécois

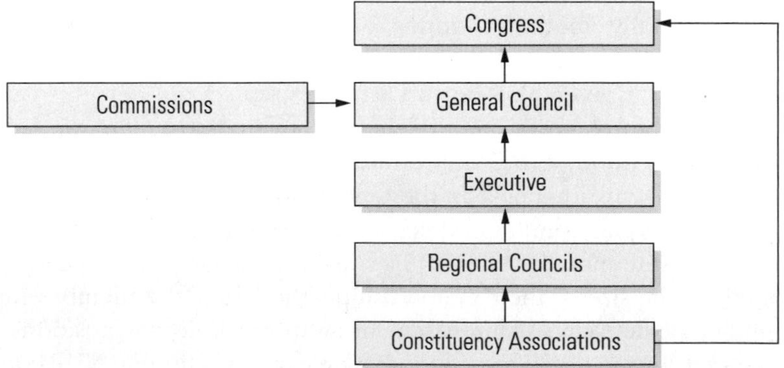

Schematic Organization Chart, New Democratic Party of Canada (1989 constitution)

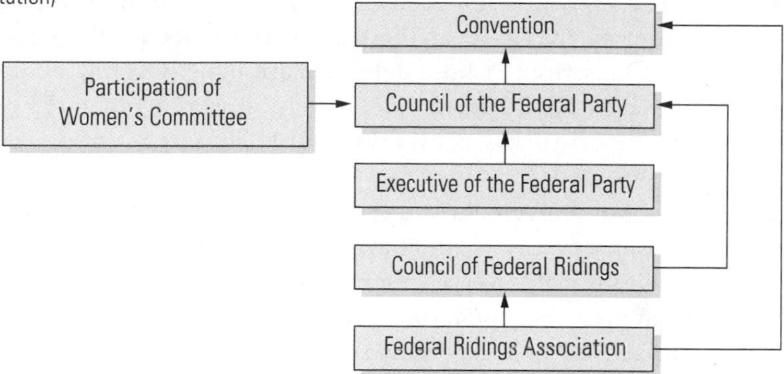

Schematic Organization Chart, Progressive Conservative Party of Canada (1989 constitution)

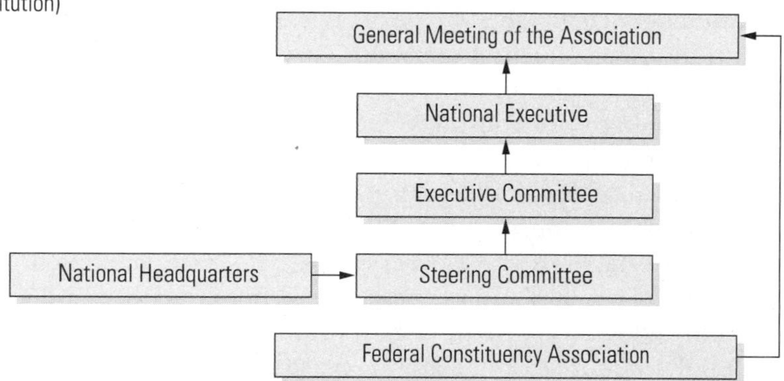

Source: Adapted from Herman Bakvis, ed. *Canadian Political Parties: Leaders, Candidates, and Organization* (Toronto: Dundurn Press, 1991), 273–277. Reproduced with the permission of the Minister of Supply and Services, 1994.

delegate positions based on the membership in a constituency is also the practice in the Reform Party, and may similarly minimize the role of Quebeckers in the party. The BQ too ties the size of constituency delegations to constituency size, though, like the Reform Party, it guarantees every constituency a minimum number of delegates.

Two groups that have received particular attention from parties in the awarding of convention delegate positions are women and youth. Historically, both groups have been underrepresented among party activists and insiders and they remain underrepresented in legislatures. More recently, most of the parties have tried to increase the representation of both groups at conventions. For example, both the Liberal and Conservative parties have quotas for female representation among the constituency and youth delegates to party conventions, with the result that 37 percent of delegates to the 1983 Conservative convention and 45 percent of delegates to the 1990 Liberal convention were women.[54] The BQ constitution calls for constituency associations to elect, as far as possible, equal numbers of male and female delegates. Among New Democrats, there is no across-the-board quota for female constituency delegates, apart from a single Participation of Women (POW) delegate from each constituency. Most constituency associations, however, attempt to elect delegates on the basis of gender parity. However, this trend has not been followed among affiliated unions, the great majority of whose delegates are male. Overall, about 36 percent of delegates to the 1989 NDP leadership convention were women. Even fewer women are delegates to Reform Party conventions; only 26 percent of delegates to its 1992 convention were women.

Whereas women remain somewhat underrepresented at conventions, both the Liberal and Conservative parties have gone in the other direction for youth members, who are significantly overrepresented at their conventions. The Liberals and Conservatives have relatively generous provisions for the representation of youth delegates through campus political clubs as well as through constituency associations. The number of delegates under 30 who attended Conservative conventions increased from 20 percent in 1967 to 40 percent in 1983; the comparable figures for the Liberal Party range from 20 percent in 1968 to 36 percent in 1990.[55] The BQ guarantees that each constituency delegation will contain at least three youth members and gives delegate status to the president of the Youth Forum, one of the party's "commissions." Perhaps surprisingly, the New Democratic Party has been less generous in awarding constituency delegate positions to young party members. For example, members of the New Democratic Youth (NDY) make up less than three percent of convention delegates, while as recently as 1989 delegates under 30 from both the NDY and constituency associations constituted only 10 percent of total convention delegates.[56] Thus, unlike the Liberals and Conservatives, who have attempted to target young voters as a base of support and as a reservoir of future activists and leaders, the NDP has made little effort to appeal directly to youth by encouraging their participation at conventions. Even more extreme in this regard is the Reform Party; only 3 percent of delegates to this party's 1992 convention were under 30 years of age.

Below the level of the general convention, each party has some kind of executive structure. The Liberal Party, for example, is governed between conventions by a national executive of approximately 50 voting members. In addition, the Liberals have committees in such areas as policy development, organization, constitutional and legal affairs, communications and publicity, multiculturalism, financial management, national platform, and national campaign.

The Reform Party is governed by an executive council consisting of the leader and up to three councillors from each province and one from each territory. Interim policies and objectives are determined by the leader or the caucus and approved by the executive council. A liaison committee exists to ensure harmony between the caucus and executive council.

The BQ chart shows a general council, which meets at least once a year and which includes the caucus, the presidents of all constituency associations, the presidents of regional councils, and representatives of some of the commissions, including the Youth Forum. The day-to-day affairs of the party are governed by the executive, in effect a subcommittee of the general council.

The Progressive Conservative Party is governed by a national executive of approximately 150 members, which in turn delegates most of its authority to an executive committee of about 40 members. Below the executive committee is a 15-member steering committee, which in turn is linked to the party's national headquarters.

Between conventions the NDP is governed by the federal council, which numbers approximately 150 members. It is similar in size and authority to the Progressive Conservatives' national executive and usually meets at least twice a year. Between meetings of the federal council the NDP is governed by the executive.

Of the three parties with provincial wings, the NDP's organizational structure is more federal than that of the Liberals and Conservatives. For example, one cannot directly buy a membership in the federal NDP but becomes a member by joining organizations that are themselves affiliated with the NDP, such as provincial sections of the party. All members of provincial sections of the NDP automatically become members of the federal party. This organizational structure encourages the affiliation of other groups, particularly trade unions, to the party. These organizations in turn receive representation on the party's decision-making bodies, such as the convention and the federal council. The organization chart also shows a committee devoted exclusively to the participation of women.

Like the NDP, the BQ has a series of commissions, including the aforementioned commissions on cultural communities, the elderly, and youth. The Liberals too build group identities and representation into their organizational structure. Thus the Liberal chart shows three commissions targeting groups based on age, sex, and race—the Commission of Young Liberals, the National Women's Liberal Commission, and the Aboriginal People's Commission. This relatively complex structure provides multiple avenues of access to the Liberal Party and can thus increase its representational capacity, although sometimes at the cost of organizational coherence. For example, one of the curious features of the 1990 Liberal Party leadership convention was that all of the forums for discussion among delegates were organized and run by one of the three commissions—youth, women, and Aboriginal peoples—each of which has a particular interest and agenda within the party. The convention was held on the weekend of June 23, 1990, the very weekend the Meech Lake Accord died. Although this convention might have provided a unique opportunity for the Liberal Party as a whole to debate the significance of the failure of Meech Lake, there was no forum for such a general debate to take place.

What immediately strikes one about the organization of the extraparliamentary wings of the major parties in Canada is how few Canadians are involved in directing party affairs. In terms of their organizational structure, Canadian political parties have been described as "squat, truncated pyramids"[57] in which small numbers of activists, organized hierarchically, engage in the largest portion of party decision-making. Furthermore, the higher up in the pyramid one goes, the less parties reflect the characteristics of the electorate they purport to represent. However, one of the key structures within all parties is their federal constituency associations, which disaggregate each party into relatively independent organizations of local activists scattered from one end of the country to another; the great majority of party activists are located in these organizations. Although the nationalization of Canadian electoral politics during the electronic age has decreased the role of local constituency organizations, they have remained important players in a number of party functions, as the following sections illustrate.

Selection of Candidates

Parties perform an important gatekeeping function in filling seats in the House of Commons. It is rare for a candidate to be elected to the House of Commons without first gaining the nomination of a political party. In the 1993 federal election, a total of 2155 candidates representing 14 parties, together with 51 independents and 100 candidates with no party affiliation,[58] contested the 295 seats in the House of Commons. Of these, 85.3 percent of party-nominated candidates and 99.3 percent of independents and those with no party affiliation were defeated. Obviously, winning a party's nomination is no guarantee of victory. However, without the endorsement of a political party a candidate has almost no chance of winning.

In general, the practice of Canada's major political parties has been to grant to local constituency associations a good deal of autonomy in selecting candidates to carry the party's banner in an election. Although a number of controversial candidate nomination meetings have been held during recent election periods, primarily because some candidates have resorted to widespread recruiting of "instant" party members to support their cause, the general trend is for nomination meetings to be attended by relatively few voters. A study of candidate nominations undertaken by Ken Carty and Lynda Erickson revealed that the typical constituency association has slightly over 500 members. Furthermore, only about one-third of the membership in constituency associations typically attends a nomination meeting, making these meetings particularly susceptible to takeover by "instant" party members.[59]

However, blatant manipulation of the candidate nomination process should not be overemphasized, for the obvious reason that most nominations are, quite literally, no contest. The majority of party nominations—approximately two-thirds—have only one candidate and are won by acclamation.[60] Incumbents enjoy an especially easy road to renomination; almost 90 percent of them are unopposed.

Although the prerogative for nomination generally is exercised by the local constituency association, the party leader has the right to veto a candidate's nomination. This veto is provided to all party leaders by the Canada Elections Act. The leader's veto has been used in several celebrated cases. It was first used by Conservative leader Robert Stanfield in 1974, when he refused to certify the candidacy of an anti-bilingualism candidate in New Brunswick, and later by Brian Mulroney, who vetoed the candidacy of Sinclair Stevens, a former minister found to have breached conflict-of-interest guidelines. Leading up to the 1993 election, the leader's veto was used by Reform leader Preston Manning, Conservative leader Kim

Campbell, and Liberal leader Jean Chrétien. Chrétien used the device to increase the number of female Liberal Party candidates.

Leadership Selection

For the first half-century following Confederation, party leaders were chosen by the caucus. Leaders headed the parliamentary wing of the party and it seemed natural that they would be chosen from among the MPs who would support their policies. The shift to selecting leaders during a party convention consisting mainly of representatives of constituency associations first occurred in the Liberal Party, more out of political necessity than a commitment to greater democratic representation. In the 1917 election the Liberal Party was divided between those who supported conscription and those who did not. Most of the supporters ran as Unionists in the election and supported Conservative leader Robert Borden's Union government. The Liberal Party was reduced to little more than a Quebec party in the House of Commons. Liberal leader Wilfrid Laurier's death in 1919 thus created a problem for the party. A caucus-chosen leader would be a Quebecker, which would only cement the party's image as a Quebec party. To lessen the likelihood of that outcome, the Liberal Party held a national convention to select a new leader. The convention was attended not only by caucus members but also by representatives from constituency associations across the country; they chose William Lyon Mackenzie King as leader. The Conservative Party followed suit and at its 1927 convention selected R.B. Bennett as leader. The CCF–NDP have used conventions to select leaders since the founding of the CCF in 1933.

We have noted the efforts of parties to increase the representation of women and youth at party conventions. This has affected the kinds of leaders chosen at leadership conventions. Until recently, leadership of the major political parties was an exclusively male domain. The gender barrier was finally broken in 1989 with the selection of Audrey McLaughlin as NDP leader. Four years later Kim Campbell was chosen to lead the Conservative Party, and because of the party's control of the House of Commons she became Canada's first female prime minister. It is no coincidence that as their role increased in political parties and as their numbers increased at party conventions, women became much more successful in competing for party leadership positions. Similarly, there was much commentary at the time of Kim Campbell's victory about her status as a self-proclaimed baby boomer, an obvious appeal to the large number of youth delegates at the convention. The runner-up to Campbell in the 1993 Conservative leadership, Jean Charest, was only 34 at the time of the contest, and if elected would have become the youngest prime minister in Canadian history. Charest came within 187 votes of winning the contest. These examples serve as reminders that the way in which parties choose their leaders—particularly the way in which they allocate convention delegates—can have a strong impact on political winners and losers.

The way in which parties choose their leaders is changing, however. Although conventions of party delegates have been the traditional way of selecting Canadian party leaders, they are rapidly being displaced by the direct election of the leader by all members of the party. After first being used by the Parti Québécois in 1985, the **direct election of leader** has been used at the provincial level in at least half the provinces, including by the Conservatives in Alberta, Ontario, and Prince Edward Island, and by the Liberals in Nova Scotia.

At the federal level the Conservatives in 1998 implemented a direct election process in which all party members voted in their constituencies to select a new leader. To give equal weight to the constituencies, the party assigned to each 100 points, to be distributed among the leadership candidates in proportion to their share of the vote in the constituency. Thus, a leadership candidate receiving 40 percent of the vote in a constituency would receive 40 of that riding's 100 points, a candidate receiving 30 percent of the vote would receive 30 of the riding's points, and so on. The points from all constituencies were totalled to determine the winner.

The constitution of the Reform Party also calls for the direct election of the leader. Although Preston Manning was selected the first leader of the Reform Party in a traditional leadership convention, future leaders are to be directly elected by party members. The BQ membership also elects their party leader directly, and the federal Liberals have amended their constitution to require the principle of direct election of leader in the next leadership contest.[61] As for the NDP, it still uses the convention method to choose its leader from a slate of candidates, but has implemented a system of direct election to establish that slate; in effect, a "primary" election is held among party members to choose the leadership candidates who will compete at the convention.

The impetus for this shift from party convention to direct election stems from various factors, including the perception that leadership conventions are expensive, controversial practices that have been used in delegate selection meetings, and the belief that Canadians want more direct and participatory involvement in political decision making.[62] On the other hand, leadership conventions present parties with a number of benefits. They are a prized reward to party activists for their faithful service and they provide an opportunity for activists from across the country to network with one another and rub elbows with party leaders and notables. Perhaps most important, leadership conventions are major events that receive an invaluable amount of media coverage.

Party Financing

Money has been referred to as the "mother's milk of politics." Parties are able to perform their functions only with sufficient money, and all parties expend considerable effort in raising funds. Prior to the passage of the Election Expenses Act in 1974, reliable information on parties' financial affairs was difficult to find. The act, however, sets limits on the amount of money parties can spend in election campaigns, establishes a procedure for the registration of parties, institutes a mechanism for partial public financing of parties, and requires registered parties to submit audited financial statements for each fiscal year. The financial report describes the total revenues and expenditures for the year and also requires the disclosure of the names of all those who made donations of $100 or more. Some aspects of party financing, such as regulating candidate expenditures on leadership campaigns, are left entirely to the discretion of the parties and do not require public disclosure. Nonetheless, tracking parties' finances is far easier today than it was before the implementation of the Election Expenses Act.

Table 10.2 presents the financial returns for all registered federal parties in 1995. Total revenues for registered federal parties ranged from a low of $4600 for the Abolitionist Party to highs of over $13 million for the Liberals and the NDP, with the NDP coming out slightly ahead. Total revenue for the NDP is not directly comparable to that for the other parties, however, because the NDP total includes funds receipted by the party's provincial sections. Excluding provincially receipted funds, the NDP raised between $7 million and $8 million in 1995. The Progressive Conservative and Reform parties each raised a little over $5 million. For the Conservatives, this represents a considerable decline from past financial glories. In 1992, for example, while they still formed a majority government, the Conservatives raised $11.5 million, more than any other federal party that year. Conversely, the Liberals who raised the most funds (over $13 million) in 1995, when they formed the government, raised only $7.6 million in 1992, when they were on the opposition benches. There are obvious financial benefits to being the party in government. At $1.7 million in 1995, the BQ falls far behind the other parties represented in the Commons, but of course it operates only in Quebec. None of the remaining parties raised much more than $100,000 in1995. Most raised considerably less.

A more detailed examination of the parties' fiscal returns reveals substantial differences in their sources of funding. The Bloc Québécois received all of its money from individuals. Among the four parties represented in the Commons, only the Reform Party relies predominantly (80 percent) on donations from individual Canadians. Both the Liberals and Conservatives receive substantial donations from corporations as well as from individuals, whereas the NDP receives significant funding from trade unions. However, the donations that trade unions make to the NDP are considerably more modest than corporate funding of the Liberals and Conservatives. For example, in 1995 the Liberals received $7.5 million in corporate contributions, while the Conservatives received $2.9 million (a reversal of their rank order in 1992, when the Conservatives were in power and the Liberals in opposition). By contrast, the NDP received only $1.2 million from trade unions. The Reform Party in 1995 received no financial contributions from unions and only $815,520 from corporations. Of course, money in politics does not guarantee electoral success, but it does enable parties to fulfill their functions as essential organizations within the political system.

TABLE 10.2 Federal Party Financial Contributions, 1994–1995

	INDIVIDUALS		BUSINESS ORGANIZATIONS		TRADE UNIONS		OTHER[1]		TOTAL
	$	%	$	%	$	%	$	%	$
Liberal Party of Canada	5,637,042	42.6	7,510,126	56.8	24,364	0.2	57,925	0.4	13,229,457
Contributors	39,019		7,539		25		98		46,681
Progressive Conservative Party of Canada	2,713,640	48.7	2,859,552	51.3	0	0.0	1,718	0.0	5,574,910
Contributors	15,870		2,227				4		18,101
New Democratic Party[2]	4,994,681	36.2	425,445	3.1	1,214,559	8.8	6,898,742	50.1	13,533,427
Contributors	55,438		567		1,007		53		57,065
Reform Party of Canada[3]	4,226,403	79.9	815,520	15.4	0	0.0	245,129	4.6	5,287,052
Contributors	32,982		925				0		33,907
Bloc Québécois	1,683,356	100.0	0	0.0	0	0.0	0	0.0	1,683,356
Contributors	25,848								25,848
Marxist-Leninist Party of Canada	15,500	100.0	0	0.0	0	0.0	0	0.0	15,500
Contributors	31								31
Natural Law Party of Canada	75,882	87.0	11,357	13.0	0	0.0	0	0.0	87,239
Contributors	230		7						237
Party for the Commonwealth of Canada	64,894	100.0	0	0.0	0	0.0	0	0.0	64,894
Contributors	112								112
Green Party of Canada	35,955	100.0	0	0.0	0	0.0	0	0.0	35,955
Contributors	282								282
Abolitionist Party of Canada	3,450	75.0	1,150	25.0	0	0.0	0	0.0	4,600
Contributors	3		1						4
Canada Party	24.910	99.6	100	0.0	0	0.0	0	0.0	25,010
Contributors	192		1						193
Christian Heritage Party of Canada	119,378	93.3	8,530	6.6	0	0.0	0	0.0	127,908
Contributors	1,602		21						1,623
Libertarian Party of Canada	49,746	98.9	575	1.1	0	0.0	0	0.0	50,321
Contributors	279		6						285

1. May include contributions from governments, other organizations, and other sources.
2. Includes sectionally receipted revenues under provincial legislation and miscellaneous fundraising functions.
3. Individual contributions include membership dues.

Source: Elections Canada. *Registered Political Parties' Fiscal Period Returns 1995*, vols. 1 and 2 (Ottawa, 1995).

CONCLUSION

Political parties are central to political representation in a democratic system. Various forces give parties their form and substance. The economy, the general characteristics of society and social relations, and the political attitudes of members of society play a role in shaping party development. People favour moderate or extremist parties, "catch-all" parties or single-interest parties, nationalist parties, clerical parties, agrarian parties, leftist or rightist parties, depending on such societal characteristics. Parties are not determined by society, however; they play an important role in developing their own mobilizational strategy. Parties may choose to appeal to particular groups in society, for example, by giving them special representation within the party and at party conventions, as most of the major parties in Canada have done. Parties may link themselves formally to economic groups, as the NDP has done with labour unions, or they may maintain strong informal links, as the Liberals and Conservatives have done with business groups. In addition, the leaders they choose and the policies they advocate are important aspects of a party's mobilizational strategy. Finally, the formal institutions of government, including in particular the electoral system, play a key role in determining the shape of the party system.

Parties are clearly a central component in the process of interest representation, but no party will satisfy all interests. People who feel inadequately represented by existing parties sometimes try to start new ones, but the organizational, financial, and personnel costs of operating a political party, the electoral barriers to new-party success (at least on a national scale), and the fact that parties must compete for power anew at least once every five years pose substantial obstacles to this strategy. Parties, in effect, may not be the optimal path for all individuals and groups seeking public influence. The next chapter examines an alternative form of political organization—interest groups.

KEY TERMS

political culture
class politics
civic culture
fragment theory
spatial model
cadre parties
extraparliamentary wings
brokerage party
ministerialist parties
Ginger Group
electronic politics
personal parties
Election Expenses Act
policy conventions
leadership conventions
constituency associations
direct election of leader

DISCUSSION QUESTIONS

1. What are the reasons for establishing a "united alternative" to the Liberal Party? What are the obstacles to such an alternative?
2. Is it better to have party leaders elected directly by party members or by delegates to a party convention?
3. What are the pros and cons of the Conservative Party's decision to award leadership selection points to each constituency, to be distributed in proportion to each leadership candidate's share of the vote in that constituency?
4. If you were advising the NDP or the Reform Party, would you advise them to try to broaden their base in order to achieve power or to satisfy themselves with their existing power bases and influence the government's agenda from the opposition benches?
5. There has been an ongoing debate within the Reform Party about whether to establish provincial wings. What would you advise the party to do?

SUGGESTED READINGS

Archer, Keith, and Alan Whitehorn. *Political Activists: The NDP in Convention.* Toronto: Oxford University Press, 1997.

Bakvis, Herman, ed. *Canadian Political Parties: Leaders, Candidates, and Organization.* Vol. 13 of the Research Studies of the Royal Commission on Electoral Reform and Party Financing. Toronto: Dundurn Press, 1991.

Blake, Donald E., R.K. Carty, and Lynda Erickson. *Grassroots Politicians: Party Activists in British Columbia.* Vancouver: University of British Columbia Press, 1991.

Brodie, Janine, and Jane Jenson. *Crisis, Challenge and Change: Party and Class in Canada Revisited.* Ottawa: Carleton University Press, 1988.

Canada. Royal Commission on Electoral Reform and Party Financing. *Reforming Electoral Democracy.* Vol. 1. Final Report. Ottawa: Supply and Services, 1991.

Carty, R.K. *Canadian Political Party Systems: A Reader.* Peterborough, Ont.: Broadview Press, 1992.

Courtney, John C. *Do Conventions Matter? Choosing National Party Leaders in Canada.* Montreal & Kingston: McGill-Queen's University Press.

Gagnon, Alain G., and A. Brian Tanguay, eds. *Canadian Parties in Transition: Discourse, Organization, Representation.* Scarborough: ITP Nelson, 1989.

Perlin, George, ed. *Party Democracy in Canada: The Politics of National Party Conventions.* Scarborough: Prentice Hall Canada, 1988.

Thorburn, Hugh G., ed. *Party Politics in Canada.* 6th ed. Scarborough: Prentice Hall Canada, 1991.

Wearing, Joseph. *Strained Relations: Canadian Parties and Voters.* Toronto: McClelland & Stewart, 1988.

Whitehorn, Alan. *Canadian Socialism: Essays on the CCF–NDP.* Toronto: Oxford University Press, 1992.

NOTES

1. Tom Flanagan, "The Alternative Vote: An Electoral System for Canada," *Inroads* 7 (1998), 73.
2. Canada, Royal Commission on Electoral Reform and Party Financing, *Reforming Electoral Democracy,* vol. 1 (Toronto: Dundurn Press, 1991), 207.
3. Joseph LaPalombara, *Democracy: Italian Style* (New Haven, Conn.: Yale University Press, 1987).
4. See, among others, Hugh G. Thorburn, ed., *Party Politics in Canada,* 6th ed. (Scarborough: Prentice-Hall Canada, 1991).
5. For a further discussion of these factors, see Herbert Kitschelt, *The Logics of Party Formation: Ecological Politics in Belgium and West Germany* (Ithaca, N.Y.: Cornell University Press, 1989); and Keith Archer and Faron Ellis, "Opinion Structure of Party Activists: The Reform Party of Canada," *Canadian Journal of Political Science* 27 (1994), 277–308.
6. Gabriel Almond and Sidney Verba, *The Civic Culture,* abridged ed. (Boston: Little Brown, 1965), 13.
7. Almond and Verba, *The Civic Culture.*
8. Alex Inkeles and Daniel Levinson, "National Character: The Study of Modal Personality and Socio-Cultural Systems," in Gardner Lindzey, ed., *Handbook of Social Psychology,* vol. 2 (Reading, Mass.: Addison-Wesley, 1954); Lucien Pye, *Politics, Personality and Nation Building* (New Haven, Conn.: Yale University Press, 1962).
9. Louis Hartz, *The Liberal Tradition in America* (New York: Harcourt, Brace and World, 1955).
10. Ibid.
11. Gad Horowitz, "Conservatism, Liberalism and Socialism in Canada: An Interpretation," *Canadian Journal of Economics and Political Science* 32 (1966), 143–171; Gad Horowitz, *Canadian Labour in Politics* (Toronto: University of Toronto Press, 1968). See also H. D. Forbes, "Hartz–Horowitz at Twenty: Nationalism, Toryism and Socialism in Canada and the United States," *Canadian Journal of Political Science* 20 (1987), 287–315.
12. See also Seymour Martin Lipset, *Revolution and Counter-Revolution: The United States and Canada* (New York: Basic Books, 1968).
13. Horowitz, "Conservatism, Liberalism and Socialism in Canada."
14. For a balanced view of some of the strengths and shortcomings of the Hartz–Horowitz approach, see Forbes, "Hartz–Horowitz at Twenty: Nationalism, Toryism and Socialism in Canada and the United States."
15. John Porter, *The Vertical Mosaic: An Analysis of Social Class and Power in Canada* (Toronto: University of Toronto Press, 1965).

16. Frank Underhill, *In Search of Canadian Liberalism* (Toronto: Macmillan, 1961), 168. Punch and Judy are marionettes.
17. Janine Brodie and Jane Jenson, "Piercing the Smokescreen: Brokerage Parties and Class Politics," in Alain G. Gagnon and A. Brian Tanguay, eds., *Canadian Parties in Transition: Discourse, Organization, Representation* (Scarborough: ITP Nelson, 1989), 24–44. See also Janine Brodie and Jane Jenson, *Crisis, Challenge and Change: Party and Class in Canada,* rev. ed. (Ottawa: Carleton University Press, 1988).
18. Brodie and Jenson, *Crisis, Challenge and Change.*
19. Business unionism refers to a union's emphasis on collective bargaining (particularly on increasing wage settlements and job security), in contrast to unions that undertake to develop a class consciousness among their members.
20. Brodie and Jenson, *Crisis, Challenge and Change.*
21. Claude Galipeau, "Political Parties, Interest Groups, and New Social Movements: Toward New Representation?" in Gagnon and Tanguay, eds., *Canadian Parties in Transition,* 404–426.
22. Anthony Downs, *An Economic Theory of Democracy* (New York: Harper and Row, 1957).
23. Harold Hotelling, "Stability in Competition," *Economic Journal* 39 (1929), 41–57.
24. Downs, *An Economic Theory of Democracy,* 114–141.
25. Allan Kornberg, William Mishler, and Joel Smith, "Political Elite and Mass Perceptions of Party Locations in Issue Space: Some Tests of Two Positions," *British Journal of Political Science* 5 (1975), 161–185.
26. Another critique of Downs can be found in Albert O. Hirschman, *Exit Voice and Loyalty: Responses to Decline in Firms, Organizations and States* (Cambridge, Mass.: Harvard University Press, 1970).
27. Donald Blake, *Two Political Worlds: Parties and Voting in British Columbia* (Vancouver: University of British Columbia Press, 1985).
28. Khayyam Z. Paltiel, "Political Marketing, Party Finance, and the Decline of Canadian Parties," in Gagnon and Tanguay, eds., *Canadian Parties in Transition,* 332–353.
29. Ibid., 345–347. In November 1992 an Alberta court overturned aspects of the Election Expenses Act that restricted broadcast time during election periods. The regulations that were struck down allocated broadcast time in proportion to a party's performance in the previous election. New regulations are being drafted by the broadcast arbitrator.
30. See, for example, Maurice Pinard, *The Rise of a Third Party,* enlarged ed. (Montreal and Kingston: McGill-Queen's University Press, 1975).
31. Here we are adapting R.K. Carty, "Three Canadian Party Systems: An Interpretation of the Development of National Politics," in George Perlin, ed., *Party Democracy in Canada: The Politics of National Party Conventions* (Scarborough: Prentice-Hall Canada, 1988), 15–30. Carty in turn follows David Smith, "Party Government, Representation, and National Integration in Canada," in Peter Aucoin, Research Coordinator, *Party Government and Regional Representation in Canada* (Toronto: University of Toronto Press, 1985).
32. Andre Siegfried, *The Race Question in Canada* (Toronto: McClelland & Stewart, 1966 [1906]), 114.
33. Maurice Duverger, *Political Parties* (New York: John Wiley and Sons, 1954). First published as *Les Partis Politiques* (Paris: Armand Colin, 1951).

34. Seymour Martin Lipset and Stein Rokkan, "Introduction," in Seymour Martin Lipset and Stein Rokkan, eds., *Party Systems and Voter Alignments* (New York: Free Press, 1967).
35. See Keith Archer, "The Failure of the New Democratic Party: Unions, Unionists and Politics in Canada," *Canadian Journal of Political Science* 18 (1985), 353–366.
36. Maureen Appel Molot and Glen Williams, "The Political Economy of Continentalism," in Michael S. Whittington and Glen Williams, eds., *Canadian Politics in the 1980s,* 2nd ed. (Toronto: Methuen, 1984), 81–104.
37. Keith Archer, *Political Choices and Electoral Consequences: A Study of Organized Labour and the New Democratic Party* (Montreal and Kingston: McGill-Queen's University Press, 1990).
38. Brodie and Jenson, *Crisis, Challenge and Change.*
39. Carty, "Three Canadian Party Systems," 20.
40. Ibid. See also Chapter 6.
41. Ibid.
42. Michiel Horn, "The LSR, the CCF, and the Regina Manifesto," in J. William Brennan, ed., *Building the Cooperative Commonwealth: Essays on the Democratic Socialist Tradition in Canada* (Regina: Canadian Plains Research Center, 1984), 25–41.
43. Horowitz, *Canadian Labour in Politics.*
44. C.B. MacPherson, *Democracy in Alberta: Social Credit and the Party System,* 2nd ed. (Toronto: University of Toronto Press, 1962); Alvin Finkel, *The Social Credit Phenomenon in Alberta* (Toronto: University of Toronto Press, 1989).
45. Carty, "Three Canadian Party Systems."
46. Desmond Morton, *The New Democrats 1961–1986: The Politics of Change* (Toronto: Copp Clark Pitman, 1986).
47. The NDP's strategy has not been entirely successful for a number of reasons. First, unions have not provided the level of support that was anticipated at the time of the party's founding. Second, the Canadian work force is not highly unionized. Less than 40 percent of those who are employed belong to a union. Of those who do, many belong to public-sector unions, which are prevented by law or convention from directly supporting a particular party. Third, many union members ignore the suggestions of their union leadership on political matters. There are countless reasons for voting for one party or another, and the wishes of one's union leadership do not always prevail. Finally, in many constituencies the NDP is not electorally competitive, and it has never formed the government nationally. For many voters, supporting a third party is viewed as a wasted vote. See Archer, *Political Choices and Electoral Consequences.*
48. Canada, Statistics Canada, *Census, 1986* (Ottawa: Minister of Supply and Services).
49. Stephen Harper and Tom Flanagan, "Our Benign Dictatorship," *The Next City,* Winter 1996–97, 39.
50. Ibid.
51. See, for example, Robert A. Dahl, *A Preface to Democratic Theory* (Chicago: University of Chicago Press, 1956).
52. This section borrows heavily from Réjean Pelletier, "The Structures of Canadian Political Parties: How They Operate," in Herman Bakvis, ed., *Canadian Political Parties: Leaders, Candidates, and Organization,* vol. 13 of the Research Studies of the Royal Commission on Electoral Reform and Party Financing (Toronto: Dundurn Press, 1991), 265–311.
53. New Democratic Party, *Resolutions Reference,* 1986.

54. George Perlin, "Attitudes of Liberal Convention Delegates toward Proposals for Reform of the Process of Leadership," in Bakvis, ed., *Canadian Political Parties,* 61.

55. Ibid., 62.

56. Alan Whitehorn and Keith Archer, "Party Activists and Political Leadership: A Case Study of the NDP," in Richard Price, Maureen Mancuso, and Ronald Wagenberg, eds., *Leaders and Leadership in Canadian Politics* (Toronto: Oxford University Press, 1994).

57. Allan Kornberg, Joel Smith, and Harold D. Clarke, *Citizen Politicians—Canada* (Durham, N.C.: Carolina Academic Press, 1979).

58. Independent candidates are those who have not been nominated by a political party. Candidates with no party affiliation were nominated by a party, but the party failed to fulfill the requirements for registered party status, one of which is to nominate candidates in at least 50 constituencies. If the party fails to fulfill the registration requirements, candidates nominated by that party are listed on the election ballot as having no affiliation.

59. R.K. Carty and Lynda Erickson, "Candidate Nomination in Canada's National Political Parties," in Bakvis, ed., *Canadian Political Parties,* 114.

60. Ibid., 120.

61. Peter Woolstencroft, " 'Tories Kick Machine to Bits': Leadership Selection and the Ontario Progressive Conservative Party," in R. Kenneth Carty, Lynda Erickson, and Donald E. Blake, eds., *Leaders and Parties in Canadian Politics: Experiences of the Provinces* (Toronto: Harcourt Brace Jovanovich, 1992), 203–204.

62. Ibid., 203.

INTEREST GROUPS AND REPRESENTATIONAL INSTITUTIONS

11

The fact that most citizens apparently no longer see the political party as a primary vehicle for communicating with government has led governments to find alternative means of communication and citizens to use other ways of influencing the decision-making process. For governments, public consultation, which is usually initiated by one of the administrative agencies rather than by the political arm, has become a widely used means of assessing individual and group views on policy issues. For individuals, there are four alternatives to the party system itself: individual petitions to agencies; individual petitions to MPs; the hiring of a lobbyist; and, finally, participation in an interest group.[1]

Societal interests can be politically represented in a variety of ways. The electoral system and legislatures organize representation on a spatial principle—MPs represent everyone in a geographically defined riding. But territory is increasingly less important in the way individuals view their interests and relevant political associations. Interest groups and the associational system of which they are part reflect a different representational principle, one that is often in tension with more traditional political institutions. But interest groups and the electoral system connect in various ways as well—interest groups do not seek political power directly but seek to influence political outcomes, often by changing public opinion, lobbying governments, or providing financial support to political parties. As Chapter 8 showed, groups can also launch litigation against government policy, increasingly on the grounds that it violates Charter rights. The relationship between groups and government is not always adversarial, since Canadian governments have sometimes supported groups whose activities seemed consistent with public-policy objectives. The nature of the relationship depends in large part on the nature of associational systems themselves in particular sectors (whether concentrated or dispersed, for example), which in the Canadian case are often relatively weak. This chapter explores the nature of groups, their relation to government, and their activities. It concludes that "group dynamics" in the political system are likely to increase in the future, posing substantial challenges to governments and the representational principles on which they are based.

■ ■ ■

In broadest terms, Canada is a liberal-democratic state, and, as previous chapters showed, the constitutional principle of popular representation lies at the heart of any such system. Every liberal democracy evolves its own representational institutions, but for most of the 19th and 20th centuries political parties and electoral systems have been the prime vehicles of popular participation in governance. Citizens can represent themselves more directly, however, through interest groups and **lobbying.** To a degree, these two institutional forms of representation can comfortably coexist as long as parties remain preeminent. However, once interest group representation begins to take on a greater role—and as parties consequently lose more of their legitimacy—the two logics of representation increasingly conflict.

Throughout this book, we have traced the tension between territorial and non-territorial imperatives in Canadian institutional politics. The same tension is evident in the competing logics underlying the electoral and party systems, on one hand, and the interest group system, on the other. The logic of electoral and party systems is one of territorial or spatial representation. That is to say, the electoral system is organized on a constituency basis across the country, so each legislator represents citizens who live in some specific territory. This system assumes that the territory within which a group of people live is an important basis for the interests that they share. But interests in a complex modern society are not necessarily organized along spatial or territorial lines. Space and territory are largely irrelevant to the women's movement, for example, or the environmental movement. Business associations and labour unions too draw members from across the country. The electoral systems and political parties, then, are institutions designed to represent interests that are organized spatially or territorially; interest associations, by contrast, tend to represent sectoral interests that cut across the lines on maps that define electoral constituencies. In a sense, forms of spatial representation assume that people who live in a given territory—Vancouver, Ottawa, or sections of Toronto—have more in common with one another than with people who live elsewhere. This is not always true, especially as society becomes more complex and people begin to define themselves in terms of identities that have little or no spatial reference. The recent growth of interest groups in the political process is therefore more than a matter of increased participation. It suggests a potential clash between representational principles (or institutional logics) based on space, territory, and function.[2]

No one knows exactly how many interest groups or associations there are in Canada. The 1997–98 *Directory of Canadian Associations* lists over 19,000 nonprofit business, professional, trade, and consumer organizations. The three largest categories are trade, industry, and commerce (6341); health (3309); and "special interest" (8722).[3] Among them are large, visible organizations such as the Canadian Labour Congress, the Canadian Bankers' Association, the National Action Committee on the Status of Women, and the Canadian Automobile Association. But there are many small, obscure, and even esoteric ones—Canadian balloonists, astrologers, and hide tanners all have their own associations. A large proportion of the Canadian adult population belongs to at least one and probably several groups, from ski clubs to charities and community associations. Many children belong to groups too: hockey associations, Cubs and Guides, zoo groups. OWL TV and YTV encourage viewership by enlisting their young audiences in clubs, by sending them magazines, and by sponsoring contests. Many of these groups and associations are formed solely to further the shared interests of their members outside of the political arena. But many are increasingly drawn into that arena or formed for that specific purpose.

The political significance and visibility of associations has grown steadily in the postwar years. For example, the number of associations listed in the *Canadian Almanac and Directory* tripled between 1945 and 1982,[4] and groups representing various **social movements** (e.g., students, women, Aboriginals, ethnic minorities, and environmentalists) have grown rapidly since the 1960s and 1970s to become routine participants in the policymaking process.[5] This expansion is paralleled by the rapid growth in the number of national business associations since 1945.[6] The appearance of hundreds of groups as witnesses before parliamentary committees, royal commissions, or task forces is now considered normal, whereas it would have been remarkable 25 years ago.

In Canadian political life, the role and visibility of interest groups has been heightened in three broad areas. The first is through self-representation in the policy process. As mentioned above, the key period of growth in the **associational system** occurred in the postwar period, principally in the late 1960s and early 1970s. Social movement groups as well as business and labour organizations multiplied, and they were not content to have their interests channelled through political parties. They lobbied, engaged in advocacy, demanded a voice in shaping public policy and implementing programs. Parliamentary consultations through committee hearings expanded, as did a host of other types of mechanisms, from special panels, roundtables, advisory boards, and conferences. This trend has been reinforced recently by theories of public administration that stress the importance of consulting "clients" and "customers" and developing partnerships for the delivery of programs. Consultation and citizen engagement are now the mantras of both elected and appointed officials.

The second area in which the role and visibility of groups has increased is constitutional issues. Previous chapters have sketched Canada's tortured history around the Meech Lake Accord and Charlottetown Accord debacles. The increasing importance of citizens' groups and the notion of the "citizens' constitution" arced across these events as ordinary Canadians became increasingly impatient with the traditional mode of intergovernmental bargaining behind closed doors. The Meech

Lake Accord was widely reviled because it had not been inclusive of societal interests such as the particular interests of women and Aboriginals, and once the Charlottetown Accord was hammered out, politicians felt compelled to submit it to a national referendum. Indeed, the process of creating the Charlottetown Accord was designed to engage citizens more directly, beginning with the Spicer Forum's role in 1991 in lancing the boil of Meech Lake by consulting 400,000 Canadians and 13,000 groups. More recently, the 1995 Quebec referendum saw thousands of Canadians travel to Montreal at the eleventh hour to participate in a show of support for the No side. Whatever its impact (and ironically it may have stimulated more Yes votes), it was an unprecedented display of "people power" in the constitutional arena.

The third area in which interest groups have become more directly engaged in the political process is in elections—not in running for election themselves but in working to sway public opinion on election issues. Millions of dollars were spent by third parties to support or oppose the Free Trade Agreement in the 1988 federal election. The problem here hinges on the clash between Canada's election laws and freedom of speech and association. The federal Referendum Act stipulates that any group or individual intending to spend more than $5000 during a campaign must register with the chief electoral officer. In October 1997 there was a successful constitutional challenge to Quebec's referendum law, which stipulates that all political parties and organizations must register with either the Yes or the No committees, and that only those committees can incur expenses related to the referendum campaign.[7] The Canada Elections Act has a section (successfully challenged by the National Citizens' Coalition in 1993 and again before the Alberta Court of Appeal in June 1995) that limits the campaign expenses of third parties to $1000. Canada's chief electoral officer, noting that political parties faced spending restrictions that third parties did not, called for new legislative provisions in his October 1997 report.

> *The present situation creates an anomaly, since registered political parties and candidates are subject to certain rules regarding their funding and the expenses they may incur to promote their candidacy or challenge that of their opponents, while third parties are not subject to any such constraints. In the long run, it can be expected that this situation, if not remedied, will erode the financial foundation of the electoral system. Both parties and candidates will feel at a disadvantage compared with third parties, who will be able to organize and fund their activities in the shadows without any limits on the expenses they may incur while pursuing their goals.*[8]

This increasing role of interest groups has posed important challenges to the Canadian political system. As mentioned, the electoral system is territorially based, so political parties tend to operate with a logic different from that of interest groups—one that emphasizes a broad platform that appeals across a wide area. The Westminster system concentrates power in the cabinet and encourages a bureaucratic culture of confidentiality and hierarchy. Our traditional form of government-centred federalism was clearly hostile to public input. On the other hand, several key institutions, principally the Charter of Rights and Freedoms, have encouraged interest group challenges to closed government. As previous chapters argued, the Charter is an important institutional innovation in the Canadian political system because it injects a new language of rights into traditional political discourse and because it emphasizes interests that are associated with specific categories of rights. Language, gender, and ethnicity, for example, are given a special prominence in the Charter and have stimulated interest groups to crystallize around "their" clauses and sections. From the perspective of this chapter, these interests are not organized territorially. The language of rights is neither spatial nor governmental. It is a language of identities that knows few territorial constraints, a language of claims posed against governments. Inevitably, the representational principles promoted in the Charter have clashed with those at the root of both federalism and the parliamentary system.

The **representation of interests** outside the party system is therefore more than a matter of counting groups and seeing how they influence government. The significance of interest groups and the rising demand for public consultation lie in the logic of representation they pose to the principles of Canada's political institutions—a logic that differs from that of the political parties. We need to understand this different representational logic, its internal coherence, and the challenge it poses to other institutions. Despite the rhetoric of politicians and officials on the importance of grassroots democracy, political engagement, and partnership, increasing the role of the associational system in Canadian governance is sometimes actively resisted. It is never easy.

This chapter first considers the nature of interest groups and parties. It then reviews some of the institutional tensions between the logic of the associational system and the principles of Parliament, federalism, and the Charter. It concludes with an analysis of the institutional features of the Canadian associational system and what interest groups do to exert pressure.

INTERESTS, GROUPS, AND POLITICS

Two important characteristics of groups are that they are voluntary and autonomous. This means, first, that groups arise from the free association of individuals who share interests and goals and who want to pursue those interests and goals with others. Second, group members decide how the group is organized and how it runs its internal affairs. This includes considerations such as how large the group will be, where its affiliates are located, how its meetings are conducted, and what powers and responsibilities its officers have. These rules form the group's "constitution." Third, members join voluntarily and thus may leave voluntarily, though some conditions may be attached to withdrawal. Finally, voluntary groups normally rely on their own resources, principally membership dues, but also perhaps the sale of services to members and even the general public. The Canadian Automobile Association is a good

Gun lobby rally on Parliament Hill, September 22, 1998. Several thousand opponents of the federal firearm registry gathered to protest against Bill C-68. (CP photo/Tom Hanson)

example. Members pay annual fees, in addition to which they may purchase special services such as insurance and airline tickets. Smaller groups usually have low membership fees that they supplement with everything from door-to-door canvassing to bake sales.

The **voluntary** and **autonomous** nature of associations will vary in the real world. As groups mature and grow, they often develop complex bureaucracies that develop an interest in organizational survival and development. The group's continued existence is therefore less a result of original members' interests than of organizational inertia. As well, many groups operate on shoestring budgets and welcome support from government agencies. Most of the prominent women's organizations in Canada, for example, such as the National Action Committee on the Status of Women, have received substantial funding from government in the past, though funding has been reduced yearly since 1991.[9] A reliance on public funding may compromise a group's autonomy, since its goals have to be compatible with those of the funding program, and often its internal procedures have to meet with government approval (e.g., annual elections, accounting procedures). REAL (Real, Equal, and Active for Life) Women was refused funding under the federal Women's Program in 1988 in part because its approach to women's equality was not compatible with the funding agency's guiding policy.[10] In other cases, such as unions and collective bargaining, government legislation permits the union to be the sole representative of workers in a business enterprise. These important exceptions to the principles of voluntarism and autonomy will be taken up later in the chapter.

Another important characteristic of voluntary associations is that they are interested in **influence** rather than political office. Political parties try to acquire power. Parties field candidates and contest elections in order to represent voters in the legislature. They too are voluntary associations, but the primary means for achieving their goals is the capture of office. Interest associations sometimes have broad agendas but pursue them by means other than contesting elections. The Council of Canadians lobbies on a variety of economic and social policy issues, as does the Business Council on National Issues (BCNI). While both these groups have made their (usually opposing) views known in various ways during election campaigns, they have not themselves tried to run candidates.[11] This distinction between interest associations and political parties suggests that interest groups, even the large national ones, are normally concerned with representing the views of a narrower group. In formal terms, parties in a democratic system seek office in order to manage the state in the broad public interest, whereas interest associations seek to influence the state (and political parties) on behalf of a narrower constituency. It is important, however, not to make too rigid a distinction between groups, parties, and political power. The members of groups are often members of political parties as well, and in this way groups may get closer to political power than is sometimes assumed. The New Democratic Party, for example, is strongly influenced by labour unions and social advocacy organizations. Indeed, as noted in Chapter 10, many labour unions have traditionally seen the NDP as their political arm. While the connections are murkier in the case of the Liberals, business interests seem to have **privileged access.**[12] Of course, interest groups can also constitute themselves as political parties for the marketing and financial advantages that doing so confers, even if they have no hope of winning power. The Natural Law Party, which ran for the first time in the 1993 election, is simply an arm of the Maharishi Mahesh Yogi's Transcendental Meditation movement.[13] The Green Party solicits political donations, which have tax advantages, for donors, in order to fund court cases and pay fines for environmental protesters.[14] Finally, interest groups based on broad social movements can claim a wide constituency indeed—environmentalists, for example, sometimes claim to speak for the entire human race, most other species, and Mother Earth herself.

While all voluntary associations represent interests, not all associations feel compelled to represent those interests in the political sphere. A local chess club, a baby-sitting co-op, a skiers' association, an organization devoted to hiking in the Rockies—examples of non-political groups are numerous. These groups exist to enable members to communicate with like-minded individuals, to pool resources, or to achieve ends that they might not be able to achieve singly. It is easy to go hiking by yourself, for example, but by joining a club you meet others with the same interest and perhaps find out about new trails. As a group, the hikers might be able to get discounts on transportation or equipment. None of this requires political action. It is certainly **collective action,** in that individuals are trying to act in concert, but it is not political. It is easy to imagine how this group's activities might become political, however. Hiking requires wilderness, and wilderness areas depend on government policy. Since it is in the interest of hikers to have a place to hike, it is also in their interest to persuade government to protect wilderness areas. This is the rationale behind the extensive political activities of groups like the Sierra Club. Their members may not be interested in politics per se, but their shared interests (e.g., wilderness recreation) often require extensive pressure on government.[15]

This chapter is concerned only with a subset of voluntary associations, namely, those that pursue their collective interests in the political arena by trying to influence government policy. We will call this subset of the associational universe **interest groups.** While it is impossible to determine the actual size of the subset, it must be large indeed. The growth and evolution of the Canadian state described in Chapter 7 suggests that most groups will at some point brush up against some law, policy, or program that affects their interests. More fundamentally, groups and the associational system to which they belong are profoundly affected by the nature of the political regime. The regime, in terms of the concepts developed in Chapter 1, sets the rules of the game and thereby shapes interests and the way they are expressed. Before looking at the different types of groups that dot the Canadian associational landscape, we need to have a better grasp of the relationship between the associational system and the larger regime.

INTEREST GROUPS AND POLITICAL INSTITUTIONS

As Paul Pross observes, the fact that interest groups seek to influence the political system means that they have to deal with the system of power as they find it. Interest groups are "adaptive instruments of political communication" that mould themselves to the prevailing distribution of power.[16] The "structure and behaviour of pressure groups are functions of the political systems in which they are located."[17] Groups obviously try to exercise some influence over the distribution of power (and, as we noted in Chapter 1, a great deal of their energy may be devoted to challenging any "rules of the game" that constrain their objectives), but at any given point the regime or institutional framework has more effect on them than they do on it.

A stark example of how dependent interest groups are on the institutional structure of the state can be seen in the practices of former communist countries. The official ideology and practice of those regimes was designed to suppress voluntary associations and instead harness all associational life to the Communist Party. In the case of churches and other religious associations, often the best the regime could do was limit their activities (though sometimes worship was also banned). Only trade unions approved by the state were allowed; youth organizations were linked to the party, and most professional associations were connected to the party and the government in some way. In formerly communist Poland, the Solidarity trade union was attacked and suppressed because it was a voluntary association in the sense described above: established by its members, committed to its own goals, and unconnected to the state. Under these conditions it took courage to establish organizations, even small and apparently innocuous ones, since the regime as a whole regarded voluntary associations with suspicion. All these conditions hold today in regimes like Cuba and China.

In liberal-democratic regimes like Canada, the United States, and members of the European Union, the political tradition of **freedom of association** encourages citizens to form groups to pursue their private interests through collective means. In a fundamental sense, then, the very existence of an associational system depends on the regime's acceptance of the principle of freedom of association. Along with this freedom, however, must go **freedom of speech** and **freedom of conscience,** since it would be meaningless to be part of a group that could not express itself. These freedoms are fundamental to liberal-democratic regimes, and since they are also fundamental to the development of a healthy associational system, liberal democracy has often been identified with the presence of a developed associational system. American political scientists, for example, have described their system, and indeed all liberal democracies, as **pluralist** systems, since they allow a plurality of interests to be pursued in civil society and politics to be pursued through a wide variety of associations.[18]

Canadian liberal democracy, we have argued, is characterized by three major organizational features: federalism, parliamentary democracy, and constitutionally entrenched rights. As readers of the book to this point will have learned to expect, each of these features has profound, and sometimes contradictory, effects on the associational system. Federalism affects the regime's **degree of centralization.** One way to conceptualize the effect of this institutional arrangement is to think in terms of "veto" or access points. Interest groups try to influence public policy by influencing governments. Other things being equal, if the number of relevant decision-making units increases—through a federal establishment of two orders of government, for example—the sheer number of points at which influence might be exercised will presumably increase as well. As Kent Weaver and Bert Rockman put it, "Where two levels of government share jurisdiction and must negotiate agreements in many policy areas (for example, in Canada), the result is to add to veto points and presumably to increase the difficulty of achieving policy innovation."[19] This observation makes most sense in cases where jurisdictions overlap and the two levels of government have roughly equal policy capacity. One of the best examples of this was interest group mobilization in opposition to the Meech Lake and Charlottetown accords—since both federal and provincial consent was required for a constitutional amendment, groups could lobby on two fronts. Provincially concentrated industries, such as forestry in British Columbia, oil and gas in Alberta, or car manufacturing in Ontario, can more effectively resist federal policies they dislike by lobbying their provincial governments to speak on their behalf. Two good recent examples of this were the Pacific salmon dispute and a proposed federal carbon tax. In the first case, British Columbia Premier Glen Clark went much further than Ottawa was prepared to go in resisting American overfishing in Canadian waters; in the second, Alberta Premier Ralph Klein sternly warned Ottawa against the imposition of a carbon tax because of the harm it would do to the oil and gas industry.

Another characteristic of Canadian federalism is the presence of Quebec. Any country with regional differences, especially one in which those differences are amplified through federal structures, will have an associational system that varies regionally and between regions and the national level. The special circumstances in Quebec, however, pose special problems for associational coordination. Language is one difficulty and is sometimes compounded by different social traditions. In the field of human rights, for example, Quebec has a rich tradition of Catholic overseas missionary work and social action that differs significantly from the English-Canadian pattern. Understandably, many human rights organizations are split between Quebec and "Canadian" offices. Amnesty International, for example, whose "Canadian section" was established in 1973 as one organization, now has two branches, one in Quebec and one in Ottawa.[20]

This brings us to another potential effect of federalism. Since interest groups are adaptive instruments of political communication, a federal system that is sufficiently decentralized may encourage the associational system to be decentralized as well. Groups will form at both the national and regional levels and may mirror the jurisdictional division of powers. Groups in a federal system, in short, may develop a federal structure. This structure has several implications for the efficacy of interest group lobbying. It usually means that the national organization is to some degree a creature of the local, provincial, or regional chapters. The Canadian labour movement is a case in point. The Canadian Labour Congress, for example, is a federal body in that it is made up of both national and provincially based labour organizations.[21] Its policy capability (i.e., the degree to which the national body can arrive at independent positions that it can then impose on its members) is constrained by a variety of factors, of which federal structure is one. According to Pross, this problem is "endemic" among Canadian groups: "Even organizations that concern themselves only with the work of a single provincial government must contend with the divisive influence of territorial or sectoral particularism."[22]

The fragmenting effect of federalism on associational life in Canada is widely accepted in the literature,[23] but recent work on Canadian business associations has thrown some doubt on the hypothesis. Even in economic policy areas that are either shared jurisdictions or primarily provincial, half of all business associations have a centralized structure.[24] As Stephen Brooks and Andrew Stritch point out, however, even if in this particular case federalism does not appear to have any special decentralizing effect, there still remain some important regional divisions that even centralized organizations find hard to bridge.[25] Nonetheless, our conclusions about the fragmenting effect of federalism do need to be accepted cautiously. Prominent national associations, for example, have sprung up in areas of virtually exclusive provincial jurisdiction, such as education.[26] Associations might consider it rational to establish themselves as national groups, even in areas of shared jurisdiction, because they can assume that the federal government has substantial power to affect their policy preferences.

Regimes also vary in the **degree of concentration** of power. If federalism disperses power, we have learned that parliamentary institutions concentrate it. From the point of view of the associational system, parliamentary government limits the points of access to either order of government. Such has been the traditional portrait of the Canadian system. The parliamentary system has meant that power in both orders of government is concentrated in the cabinet, that parties are highly disciplined (and therefore closed to external influences), and that decision making is tightly controlled and even secretive. Under these conditions, interest groups have traditionally had few points of access. Cabinet ministers and senior officials have been the key actors in the political system, and they are not easily pressured. What this amounts to is a closed system controlled largely by bureaucrats. Not surprisingly, bureaucrats like to deal with other bureaucrats, and access to power therefore has traditionally been the privilege of large, bureaucratized organizations. For other organizations—those with small constituencies, limited funds, and a focus on narrow and transitory issues—the system has largely been closed. Even the earliest studies of Canadian interest groups agreed on one thing: the most striking feature of the Canadian policy system was its lack of openness. The Westminster style of government forces parties to be disciplined and in any case concentrates power in the cabinet. The bureaucratic system associated with this is also hierarchical. The result is a political system that places a premium on access to authority because it is such a scarce commodity. The system places great impediments in the way of those who would raise issues from the outside, since those with power on the inside are relatively well insulated from pressures.[27] Success means access, and access requires the careful cultivation of communication, consultation, and information. Groups that are not ready to accommodate and reach consensus get frozen out of the system or ignored. This contrasts with the American congressional system, where parties are loosely organized and legislators are susceptible to pressure from groups and constituents. Legislative politics in the United States allows much greater flexibility and independence for elected members and so multiplies the points of access in the system for interest groups.

Pross has offered the most sophisticated analysis of the relationship of the parliamentary system to Canadian interest groups. He points to the growth of government in the 20th century, and its increasing importance in the management of complex industrial and economic policies, as crucial developments that dramatically altered patterns of interest group influence. Technical mastery of policy details, the importance of information and data as well as expertise, drove politicians (and hence Parliament) to the margins of political power. The 1930s to the 1960s was the "age of the mandarins" (and of the cooperative federalism described in Chapter 4) that encouraged behind-the-scenes negotiations and informational exchanges between government bureaucracies and interest group bureaucracies. As Pross describes it, the key to political success for groups in this age was information and bureaucratic influence:

The need for expert knowledge dictated the hiring of specialists, or dependence on elaborate committee structures capable of tapping the expertise of group members. Equally important was the need to employ group representatives who had both intimate knowledge of the bureaucracies they had to deal with and an ability to work at the various levels at which policy was made. Publicists and animateurs, on the other hand, were not needed; nor, in general, was a large staff. As long as the information resources of the membership could be tapped fairly efficiently, and as long as group representatives knew their way around Ottawa, or the provincial capital, groups could function effectively from a modest base. More important than the scale of resources was the extent of their institutionalization. An effective collective memory, a relationship of trust with officials, and an intimate acquaintance with process and issues were vital, and these could only be acquired with time. Hence, few groups could be effective unless they established an institutional presence.[28]

The cozy era of cooperative federalism gave certain types of interest groups privileged access to government. As we noted in Chapters 3 and 4, however, this era was gradually superseded from the 1960s to the 1980s by one of "executive federalism," which was dominated by first ministers' conferences (FMCs). Parliament continued to be irrelevant, as cabinets struck deals that they could then push through with their legislative majorities. The institutional logic of FMCs as a key instrument of Canadian federalism is highly centralized and executive-dominated—not a propitious environment for interest group pressure. Groups rarely have an idea of what is going on (indeed, even governments may be in the dark initially regarding the agenda of a meeting), and they have little information about the deals that are being made. Richard Simeon was among the first to identify the marginalization of interest groups as one of the effects of the growing reliance of Canadian federalism on FMCs. In his classic study of pensions, fiscal policy, and constitutional negotiations, he noted that in "no case did interest groups have a significant effect on the outcome, once the issue entered the federal–provincial arena."[29] The dynamics of the process, according to Simeon, tended to lead governments to sacrifice interest group demands in order to achieve other goals in intergovernmental bargaining. Regional or provincially based interest groups probably gain a voice they might not otherwise have if their governments make their case for them, but the point is that it is governments, not the groups themselves, that are engaged in the negotiations. As Carolyn Tuohy puts it, "The fragmentation of interests means, in general, that it is the federal–provincial template, often complicated by bureaucratic intricacies, that dominates policy-making. In the inevitable negotiations over the balance of federal and provincial power, interests seek to exert influence through one or another level of government (or both), depending on their strategic advantage."[30]

For the last generation, political power in Canada at the national level has been concentrated among bureaucrats and cabinet ministers, and Parliament has seemed little more than a raucous sideshow. Indeed, Canadian political culture was arguably marked by a willing deference to political and other institutional authorities. No more. As Peter C. Newman puts it: "Experience has made it impossible to believe any longer in responsible politicians, pious priests, sensible Royals, trustworthy lawyers, peaceloving peacekeepers, reliable bankers, principled businessmen or honest diplomats."[31] Pross noted some time ago that the "public has grown increasingly skeptical of the authority of professional expertise and of the disinterestedness of bureaucratic advice,"[32] arguing that this might lead to a resurgence of the legitimacy of Parliament as a forum for citizen participation.[33] It is undeniable that the scope of parliamentary consultations over major pieces of legislation has expanded dramatically. This is true of foreign and trade policy, where for example there are now annual consultations on broad policy and on human rights.[34] It is also true of fiscal policy, which now is shaped by cross-country consultations that take place almost the entire year.[35] A major exercise such as the Social Security Review in 1994 saw 1200 submissions from organizations and 40,000 completed "workbooks" from individual Canadians.[36] Numbers like these on major pieces of legislation are now routine, as often are rallies, demonstrations, marches, and other forms of citizen engagement. What is not clear is how much influence all this activity actually has on policymaking. We come back to this issue in the conclusion to this chapter.

In addition to federalism and parliamentary democracy, the Canadian regime is characterized by the Charter of Rights and Freedoms and by the resulting new role for courts and quasi-judicial agencies. All provinces as well as the federal government have human rights legislation and commissions to administer and enforce it. In addition, the Charter's adoption in 1982 has meant that all federal and provincial laws, as well as a good deal of administrative practice, must be consistent with the rights and freedoms listed therein. The courts have the predominant role in deciding what the Charter actually means. Previously, interest groups disgruntled with a particular piece of legislation or policy could only lobby government. Now, if they have the resources, they can pursue legal challenges based on the Charter in the hope of having the offending legislation declared unconstitutional. The tactic is expensive and not always successful. In 1983, for example, the National Citizens' Coalition (NCC) won a dramatic legal victory against the Canada Elections Act provisions that tried to limit election advertising by individuals and groups other than political parties.[37] Several years later, the NCC lost a court case it had sponsored against compulsory union dues.[38] Women's organizations have used the courts on several occasions to launch attacks on public policies that allegedly contravene the Charter. The vehicle for these attacks has been the federally funded Court Challenges Program, which was launched in 1985, briefly cancelled, and reinstated in altered form in 1993. The fund has also been important for gay and lesbian groups such as EGALE (Equality for Gays and Lesbians Everywhere) in various legal challenges that have led the courts to pronounce that sexual orientation, even though it is not mentioned in the Charter, is a prohibited ground of discrimination under section 15.[39]

The preceding should not be seen in static terms. Regimes change and in broad terms associational systems will change with them. The introduction of the Charter, for example, encouraged interest groups to take legal action as a means of influencing politics. As the pendulum swung from centralization to decentralization in Canadian federalism, the associational system tended to change in the same direction. In the 1960s and 1970s, as governments faced growing hostility and suspicion from citizens, they turned increasingly to interest groups as partners in order to enhance their own legitimacy. The advent of television and, more recently, the **Internet** has altered the means that groups have at their disposal to make their case known to a wider public. As well, the associational system has its own internal dynamics that lead it to evolve in new directions. New groups become institutionalized and bureaucratic, old ones die, others change focus and adopt new priorities. A clear understanding of the associational system demands that we focus on the state and associations simultaneously.

COMMUNITIES, NETWORKS, AND THE STATE

Early interest group theory tended to concentrate on the impact of groups on the state.[40] More recent work has focused on the relationship between groups and government. In other words, the state and state agencies are no longer assumed to be passive targets of interest group pressure. The state's institutional architecture (e.g., open versus closed, federal versus unitary) affects the way interest groups behave and organize. By the same token, if we think of state agencies as actors—that is, as bureaucrats and officials with mandates, interests, and resources of their own—it is important to take account of their role and influence in the processes of interest group or associational representation.

A promising way to capture this dynamic of state–interest group interaction is through the concepts of **policy community** and **policy network.**[41] Both of these concepts try to convey the interaction of state agencies and interest groups and associations at what is called the **meso-political** level. This is a middle level of political action, positioned between the **macro-political** level and the **micro-political** level. The macro level is the system level; it is what we mean when we describe Canada as a parliamentary regime of the Westminster type. Other macro-political descriptions of Canada would be that it is a federal, liberal-democratic, and capitalist state. We routinely categorize countries such as Singapore as authoritarian and Iraq as a dictatorship. The use of such macro-level terminology is endemic in part because it seems natural to conceive of politics as taking place within regimes or nation-states, so we want to describe those regimes in some sensible way. But in doing this, we obviously assume that the system-level characteristics make a difference to everyday political life, that is, to the micro-level. In comparing a federal state to a unitary one (e.g., Canada to Britain or France), we might assume that politics in the federal state is more decentralized and perhaps more regionalized. While this is true in some senses, it is obviously false in others. France is a unitary state, but the intensity of regionalism there easily rivals that in Canada. So, while macro-level characteristics of political systems are helpful, they have to be used carefully. On the other hand, a concentration on the micro level (i.e., on what single actors do in specific situations) is so detailed that it rarely yields insights of a broader nature. It is hard to find patterns in the forest when one is carefully studying each and every tree.

The notions of policy community and policy network seek to capture the middle level between the general and the specific. A policy community, as William Coleman and Grace Skogstad define it, includes "all actors or potential actors with a direct or indirect interest in a policy area or function who share a common 'policy focus,' and who, with varying degrees of influence, shape policy outcomes over the long run."[42] Several categories of actors can potentially play a part in a policy community: federal government agencies, provincial government agencies, municipalities, national associations, provincial and local groups, individuals, and even foreign governments. To some extent, the range and number of players will depend on the nature of the policy issue. Environmental groups will not lobby on the AIDS issue, and the gay and lesbian rights movement will not be visible in forestry management issues. While most interest groups specialize in a particular policy area, there are some broad coalitions, or **umbrella groups,** that act on behalf of a cluster of associations. Examples would include the Canadian Alliance of Student Associations (13 member associations), the Canadian Council for International Co-operation (90 member associations), and the Canadian Labour Congress (12 provincial and territorial federations and 125 district labour councils). Interestingly, modern communications technology may be encouraging the growth of "loose networks" that are bigger than a single association but less coordinated than a formal umbrella group. We discuss this phenomenon at greater length below, but a good example is Citizens for Local Democracy (C4LD), a broad coalition of groups and individuals based in Ontario that resisted (unsuccessfully) the creation of a Toronto "megacity" through amalgamation of nearby municipalities. Their effort was spearheaded with information distributed over the Internet.[43]

There are six points to keep in mind about policy communities. First, their boundaries are permeable and somewhat fuzzy. This is because the range of attentive actors is large, even if those actors are not necessarily full-fledged players in the process. Also, as the previous paragraph pointed out, the policy participants will vary depending on how one defines the issue. Second, while the notion of "community" should not be taken too far, it still connotes something shared among the participants. At minimum it is a language, discourse, or terminology that serves as the community's *lingua franca.* Members of the poverty policy community, for example, will know what the following terms mean: VER (the variable entrance requirement in employment insurance), CHST (the Canada Health and Social Transfer), income-tested benefits (social benefits that are calibrated to income), and double discrimination (discrimination against persons who are simultaneously members of two or more minority groups, such as women of colour). They will rarely agree on policy objectives and goals, but they will share a common set of terms of debate.

Third, the membership in the community will vary over time. New groups and agencies form and coalesce, and policy issues get redefined. With these changes come changes in the number and type of actors (we return to this point below). Fourth, membership in the community is purely informal; indeed, the very designation of a "policy community" may be largely in the mind of the analyst. This does not make the community any less real; it simply means that, from a subjective viewpoint the associations and agencies active in an area will view the community differently. Nonetheless it is remarkable how similar those visions are. Individuals who have been active in a

FIGURE 11.1 **THE POLICY COMMUNITY "BUBBLE DIAGRAM"**

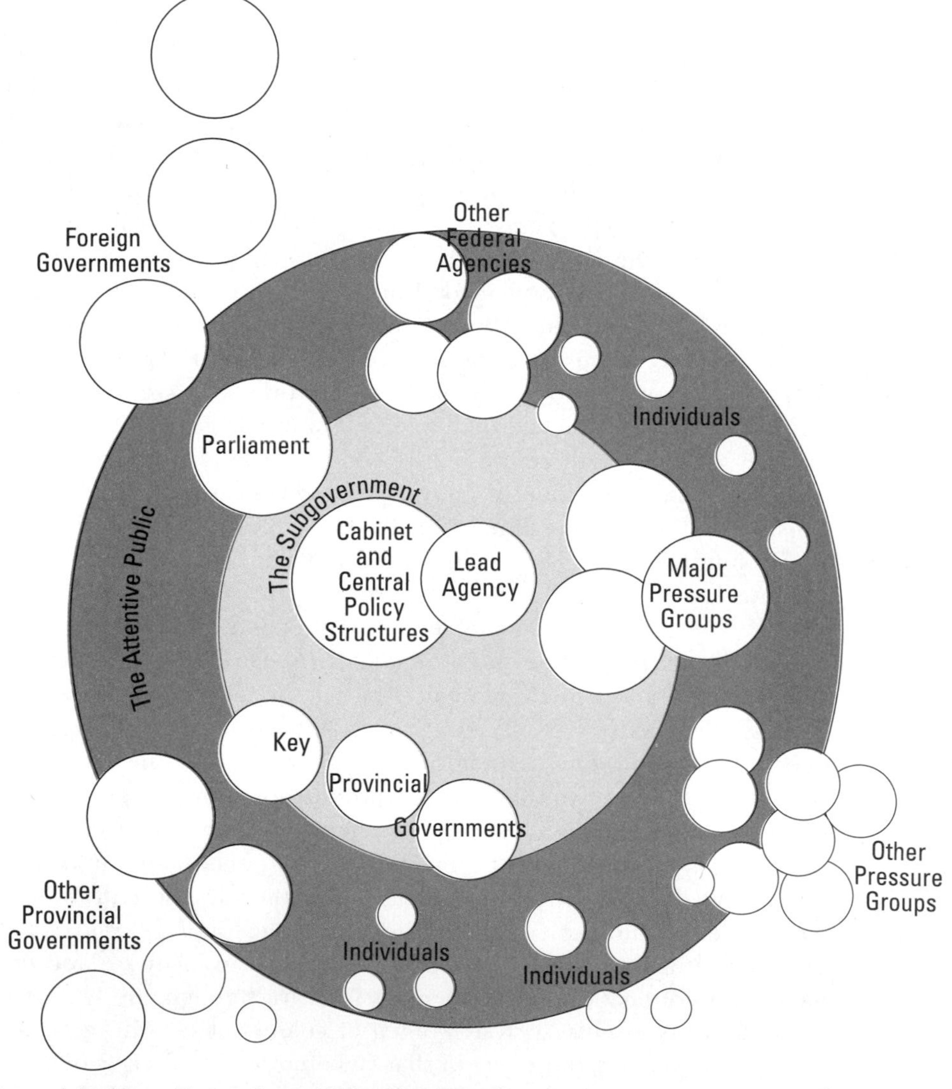

Source: A. Paul Pross, "Pressure Groups: Talking Chameleons," in Michael S. Whittington and Glen Williams, eds., *Canadian Politics in the 1990s* (Toronto: ITP Nelson, 1995), 267.

policy area for a long time get to know other actors and individuals, and there is usually strong consensus on who the key players are. Fifth, while a policy community is defined by its shared interest in a broad field of public policy, not every actor is interested in every issue that will arise in that area. In the poverty policy community, for example, pensioners' groups will tend to be less interested in support payments to single parents than they will be in pensions. At any given time there will be an agenda of issues dominating debate in the policy community. Finally, we must not forget about what Pross calls **issue-oriented groups.** These tend sometimes to fall between the cracks of policy community studies because they are so evanescent: their tactics are often bizarre and confrontational; they arise in the heat of an issue and sometimes rapidly melt away; they talk a different language and demand immediate results. They are rarely members of the mainstream policy "community," but they can influence the ways in which issues are defined and addressed within it. A good example is the environmental group Earth First!, which solicits members with this message:

> *Are you tired of namby-pamby environmental groups that are more worried about their image than saving wilderness? Is membership in some international organization not enough for you? Do you hate the smell of compromise? If you answered yes to any of these questions, then Earth First! is for you. Earth First! does not believe in compromise. We set forth the hard-line position of those who believe the Earth must come first.... Earth First! is different from other environmental groups. We believe in using all the tools in the tool box, ranging from grassroots organizing and litigation to civil disobedience and monkey-wrenching. Here are some things to keep in mind about Earth First! and some suggestions for being an active and effective Earth First!er: First of all, Earth First! is not an organization, but a movement. There are no members of Earth First!, only Earth First!ers. It is a belief in biocentrism, or Deep Ecology, and a practice of putting our beliefs into action.*[44]

This brings us directly to the notion of a policy network. The policy community concept concentrates on who is a member, without saying anything about how those members interact. But in terms of policymaking processes, the nature of the interaction is crucial. Two policy communities with an equal number of actors might have widely differing patterns of interaction among participants. State agencies might be strong in one but weak and disorganized in another. One would expect state interests to prevail in the first community, whereas associations might dominate in the second. Alternatively, one could conceive of a policy community wherein both state and associations are weak and disorganized. Presumably in this instance, policymaking would be confused and inconsistent. The policy network concept tries to capture the patterns in the relationships among state and associational actors in a policy community. To quote Coleman and Skogstad once more, a policy network describes "the properties that characterize the relationships among the particular set of actors that forms around an issue of importance to the policy community."[45] For them, the key relationships are between state agencies and organized interests or associations.[46]

Central variables in the relationship are the degree of autonomy and concentration of power among state agencies, and the degree of concentration or coordination of interests on the societal side. One could add the types of strategies used by the various associational and state actors, the discourse or language typical of the field, the ease of entry for interest groups, and a host of others. Scholars working in the field have discerned a variety of factors that seem to have some bearing on the nature of the relationship between the state and associations.[47] The key point is that the relationships do differ. In some cases, government agencies are well coordinated, with a clear idea of their policy goals. In other cases, they are disorganized and fragmented. Associational systems can be marked by a high degree of either concentration or dispersion. As well, relationships can vary over time as associations and government departments and agencies adapt to circumstances. When both government departments and the associational system are disorganized and fragmented, **policy capacity** (figuring out what needs to be done and then doing it) is likely to be low. Policy capacity is likely to be higher, however, if government agencies and associations are well coordinated and themselves capable.

One of the most ambitious attempts to map out a chunk of the Canadian associational system is William Coleman's study of business interest groups, entitled *Business and Politics: A Study of Collective Action* (1988). He examined nationally relevant economic interest associations in Canada. To qualify, organizations had to have (1) an established set of rules that specified leaders who could speak for the association as a whole, (2) a permanent staff, (3) a budgetary process for the acquisition and disbursement of funds, and (4) a set of criteria for defining eligible members.[48] According to Coleman, at least 660 nationally relevant business associations have existed since Confederation, along with 125 farmers' associations. Of those, 484 business associations and 95 farmers' associations remained active in 1980. Among the business groups, manufacturing associations were the largest single bloc, at 41 percent of the total. Within manufacturing, the dominant sectors were food processing, textiles and clothing, chemicals, and fabricated metals. Furthermore, Coleman found that the "most striking characteristic of the domains of business associations is their product specialization."[49] Canadian business associations, in other words, are for the most part highly specialized, representing sectors or parts of sectors.

What difference do these details about business associations make to our understanding of politics? Coleman reminds us that the "pressure" or advocacy model of interest group activity is only part of what is possible in business–state relations. Associations can also participate in policy formulation and policy implementation. They can work so closely with government that it is more appropriate to see theirs as an insider's relationship. As insiders they participate; as outsiders they advocate. While business associations in Canada certainly have not relinquished their advocacy role, it is an open question as to how much they participate. The international research on this question suggests that policy participation depends on two key factors. First, the association must be able to order and coordinate the range of information and positions among its members; it must speak with a clear voice at the policymaking table.

Second, the association must be autonomous from its members and the state; it must be able to rise above particularistic interests and perhaps even direct some if its members on certain issues. The evidence shows that Canadian business associations are rarely "policy capable" in this sense. According to Coleman, there is no single business community in Canada but "rather a series of autonomous communities, joined often only by the tenuous ties of large conglomerate firms. Fragmentation begins at the top, where we found no overarching peak [i.e., umbrella] associations but a series of competing, sometimes influential lobby groups."[50] This does not necessarily mean that business interests are weak in the political system, since other competing interests (e.g., labour) may be even weaker. But if contemporary policies such as industrial policy require coordination between business and government, Canada is in a weak position to pursue these policies, because policy networks in the business sector are themselves weak.

Business organizations are among the best examples of what Pross calls **institutional groups.** They are institutionalized in the sense of being stable, organizationally developed, in possession of significant resources and personnel, and focused on a broad agenda of issues. These groups are in for the "long haul" and consequently cultivate their relations with officials, often developing highly technical expertise in specific policy areas, which they then trade for policy influence. But groups addressing what Pross calls "conscience issues" or social justice and broad cultural questions, are increasingly evident today: gender equality, ethnic and cultural rights, environment, peace, human rights. Many are well organized, even if they do not approach the level of organization and stability characteristic of Canada's largest business associations. They may not be the most powerful organizations in Canada's various policy networks, but they are among the most visible, and for that reason alone deserve attention.

Issue-oriented groups are also interesting because their membership poses a problem for theories of politics and collective behaviour that are built on assumptions of rationality and self-interest. In *The Logic of Collective Action* (1965), Mancur Olson argued that in many situations it would be rational for people to refrain from joining or contributing to groups. This was because many groups serve a constituency even if all the potential members of that constituency are not group members. For example, any public benefit gained in an organization representing automobile owners would accrue to all auto owners, not just those who had joined the group. Under these conditions, which Olson developed into a formal model, individuals would have an incentive to be **free riders,** and the larger the group the more likely the presence of free riders (since visibility of contributions or abstentions is inversely related to group size).

Olson concluded that groups would have to develop various strategies in order to bind membership and cultivate support. Among these strategies were what he called **selective incentives,** that is, benefits that only members of the organization can receive (e.g., members of an automobile club get discounts at hotels and restaurants). Small constituencies of interest seeking relatively concentrated benefits, in Olson's analysis, were likely to be the most effective in overcoming collective-action problems. In practical terms, Olson identified business lobbies as among the most politically effective in the policy process. Their constituencies are small, often numbering at most only a few hundred firms, and the benefits they seek in the policy process are often highly concentrated (e.g., tariff protection), while their costs are widely spread (e.g., marginally higher prices for consumers). The corollary was that large constituencies, representing broad interests seeking diffuse benefits whose costs might be concentrated among other groups, would have a difficult time. Olson's theory of collective action seemed, paradoxically, to predict the rarity of broad collective action.

As logical a model as it was, it failed to account for precisely the type of group that was soon to figure prominently in the politics of the 1970s and 1980s: social movements and **public-interest groups.**[51] As Sidney Tarrow has noted, "It is ironic that Olson's work—which has been used to demonstrate the unlikelihood of collective action—was published just as the western world was erupting in a paroxysm of protest, riot, rebellion, and increased political involvement."[52] The pattern of interest group politics changed substantially in the late 1960s. New public interest groups suddenly began to crowd a field that had once been dominated by economically oriented producer associations. Jack Walker acknowledged that the very groups that have been reasonably successful in policy terms over the last 20 years—"citizen groups" that have only a cause or an idea and who represent the socially disadvantaged—are the ones that, according to traditional theory, should be moribund. In developing a database of American national voluntary associations, Walker concluded that "there are more interest groups operating in Washington today than in the years before World War II, and ... citizen groups make up a much larger proportion of the total than ever before."[53]

The surprising strength of interest groups, which Olson's analysis suggests should be weak, is explained by the fact that the state often supports such groups in ways that compensate for the free-rider problem. Thus, Walker found that a significant number of the citizen groups he studied had support from government agencies. In looking at groups in education, transport, and environmental protection, he argued that

> *the formation of new groups was one of the consequences of major new legislation, not one of the causes of its passage. A pressure model of the policymaking process in which an essentially passive legislature responds to petitions from groups of citizens who have spontaneously organized because of common social or economic concerns must yield to a model in which influences for change come as much from inside the government as from beyond its institutional boundaries.*[54]

Alan Cairns and Cynthia Williams, in discussing some Canadian social movements and the constitution, have noted how the collective action undertaken by language, ethnic, and gender movements has focused on rights claims and on demands centred on identity. They argue that the recent Canadian preoccupation with rights involves making political claims against the state. "The state becomes the major instrument to facilitate or block changes. The resultant group politics of competitive affirmation politicizes newly emergent cleavages. Drawing on the rhetoric of rights, citizen groups seek to employ the state for their own advancement."[55]

One of the most obvious ways in which the state can help client groups to overcome the free-rider problem is to fund them. At the federal level, almost all departments have been involved in the funding of client groups. The now defunct department of the Secretary of State of Canada (SSC) was perhaps the most active, providing millions in grants to over 3000 citizens' organizations. In the majority of cases, SSC grants were the primary source of funding for these organizations. In this way the SSC supported some of the most visible and active advocacy organizations in Canadian politics: Alliance Québec, provincial francophone organizations, the Canadian Ethnocultural Council, the Women's Legal Education and Action Fund, the Canadian Day Care Advocacy Association, the National Action Committee on the Status of Women, and various Aboriginal organizations like the Assembly of First Nations. As advocacy organizations these groups are active in areas that are vital to Canada's contemporary policy debates (e.g., linguistic rights, immigration and multiculturalism, and gender equality).

While government funding is important, it is only one state-sponsored resource available to citizen organizations attempting to overcome the free-rider problem. Another is law, including constitutional law. As we argued in previous chapters, the Charter of Rights provides certain interest groups with important non-monetary resources with which to bolster their public salience and pursue their policy agendas. When a constitution protects francophone rights, for example, francophone organizations suddenly acquire precious legitimacy. Sometimes legal and financial resources converge. The Court Challenges Program is a good example of the complementarity of advocacy funding and the constitution. The program funded Charter-based litigation on language- and equality-rights issues. Its creation encouraged women's groups (many of which depended on government grants in the first place) to form the Legal Education and Action Fund (LEAF) to litigate gender-equality cases. The Conservatives discontinued the program in 1993, but Kim Campbell reinstated it, in somewhat altered form, just before the federal election campaign that year.

Recent years have not been kind to public-interest groups engaged primarily in political advocacy for more activist government—the type of group discussed in the previous two paragraphs. (As we shall see at the end of this chapter, other types of groups are enjoying renewed legitimacy, though not necessarily the funding that goes with it.) Funding of interest groups engaged in both advocacy and service delivery in the social-policy, environmental, industrial, and defence sectors peaked in the early 1990s at about $1.5 billion annually.[56] Cuts began several years later, under the Mulroney government. Its key agenda was to cut government spending and it was annoyed to discover that its most vociferous critics were large groups like the National Action Committee on the Status of Women and the Canadian Council on Social

Development. The continuing drift of Canadian politics to the right, with the rise of the Reform Party and the more conservative tilt of the Liberals after 1993, created a more sceptical climate about the role of government in supporting "special interests." Liberal MP John Bryden expressed the critical mood of the times with a special maverick report he drafted on several large public-interest organizations.[57] In 1994 the Treasury Board announced guidelines and criteria for departments in funding interest groups, the principal point being that small, narrowly focused, financially dependent advocacy groups at odds with government policy should receive low priority.[58] These criteria fed into the Program Review exercise launched in 1995 and supported a wide range of often deep cuts in departmental support to various advocacy organizations. As Cardozo points out, however, not all funding was reduced equally: "The clear favourites for funding appear to be organizations that will undertake research and/or other services, which is new territory for many groups."[59]

WHAT DO GROUPS DO?

What groups do depends on what groups want. Returning to Pross's categories, institutional groups want stable, long-term relationships with government and so prefer to develop quiet, stable patterns of interaction with government agencies—patterns that usually hinge on the exchange of information. Issue-oriented groups want to win on their issue and are thus almost completely uninterested in long-term relationships. They want to apply pressure in almost the pure sense of the term: the more uncomfortable and cornered decision makers are, the better. Sometimes, however, even institutional groups can take the gloves off and fight openly for their interests. A dramatic example is the clash between public-sector unions and provincial governments over cutbacks and program reductions. In 1996–97, hundreds of thousands of workers (especially in Premier Mike Harris's Ontario) were called out for public demonstrations and illegal strikes to make their point.

In general, the continuum of interest group activity runs from *protest* to *participation.* At one extreme, groups and associations are outsiders in the policy process. They want to exercise pressure, and often try to do so through the mobilization of public opinion. At the other extreme, groups are insiders, almost partners, in the policy process. They provide information, analysis, advice, and even support. Between the two extremes lies a variety of strategies and tactics; a brief description follows.

Protest

- Outsiders to the policy process, groups are usually keyed to a single issue of overriding importance.
- Reliance on marches, demonstrations, visible actions of any sort that attract media attention; sometimes the more bizarre, the better.
- Suits groups with few resources. Examples: animal-rights activists, pro- and anti-abortion groups.

- Advantage: gets attention and, if cleverly done, can turn public opinion.
- Disadvantage: risks alienating policymakers and the public.

Public Information Campaigns

- Increasingly used by a wide variety of groups, both insiders and outsiders. Key is perception that decisions are being made on the basis of a certain view of public opinion. The imperative is therefore to change opinion, either quickly or over the life cycle of the issue. Can involve targeted information campaigns, broad-based advertising, personal appearances, interviews, and publications. Example: the advertising war between teachers' unions and the Ontario Conservative government during the 10-day illegal strike in fall 1997.
- Advantage: ultimately, politicians have to respond to the public mood, and getting opinion on your side can effect major reversals or concessions.
- Disadvantage: requires constant attention, sometimes can smack of propaganda, and success is usually long-term rather than immediate.

Presentations

- Outsiders and insiders make presentations to commissions, task forces, regulatory agencies, advisory bodies, and parliamentary committees. Influence sometimes depends on quality of information, but presentations can combine with protest tactics to capture media attention. Example: virtually all groups.
- Advantage: if policy alternative formulated in creative and persuasive way, can have impact.
- Disadvantage: wastes time and effort, since hearings often have little bearing on policy.

Litigation

- Has appearance of outsiders' strategy, since it hauls government in front of courts. Charter challenges are most common. Example: Women's Legal Education and Action Fund, Court Challenges Program.
- Advantage: to win can mean to win big, as in abortion cases.
- Disadvantage: expensive and time-consuming.

Lobbying Politicians

- More of an insiders' game, but MPs and MLAs are targets for most groups as they try to effect policy change or express their interests. Best results if you can lobby a cabinet minister, especially one with control over the portfolio you are interested in. Example: most associations mentioned in Coleman business study.
- Advantage: relatively cheap if done by the groups, expensive if you hire a firm.

- Disadvantage: lobbying sometimes has little effect, because most politicians are powerless.

Contacting Officials

- Insiders only. Officials in Canadian system like discretion. The currency of exchange is information, especially technical information. Most government departments lack strong analytical capabilities, so associations with their own special claim of expertise have an edge. Example: umbrella associations.
- Advantage: since bureaucrats have a lot of power, close relations can yield results.
- Disadvantage: takes time to build relations, and often difficult to figure out who has power among the bureaucratic tribes. Must remain discreet, even when decisions go against you.

Participation in Policy Decisionmaking

- Same as above, but relations are ongoing, almost permanent. Involved in policy design and, at times, implementation.

These strategies are applied in often fluid political circumstances and are best understood in terms of the specific issue at hand and the players on the field. A good example is Bill C-71, an act to regulate the manufacture, sale, labelling, and promotion of tobacco products, which received royal assent on April 25, 1997. The spark for the legislation was a case brought to the Supreme Court of Canada by the Canadian Tobacco Manufacturers' Council against the 1988 Tobacco Products Control Act. That act placed a total ban on tobacco ads and included various other restrictions that the council claimed were unconstitutional violations of free speech. The court ruled in favour of the council in September 1995, striking down provisions dealing with advertising and labelling. The battle was then joined in "one of the most intense lobbies ever waged by the health community on one side and by the tobacco companies on the other."[60] Health advocates were led by the Non-Smokers' Rights Association and the Canadian Cancer Society. The tobacco lobby, powerful but fighting an uphill battle against public opinion, included the Tobacco Council (its three members being the tobacco companies themselves—RJR-MacDonald, Imperial Tobacco, and Rothman's Benson and Hedges) and a strange alliance with the sports and arts communities, who depend on $60 million annually of tobacco advertising and sponsorship (half of it spent in Quebec). The Liberals announced their legislative plans in late 1996 and the lobbies swung into action—was it a health issue or a sponsorship issue? The legislation was eventually passed with strong provisions on labelling, marketing to youth, and sponsorship, though these would have to be fleshed out in regulations. The tobacco lobby lost the first round, but gained in the second as the Health minister announced that the regulations would permit cigarette logos on racing cars and some relaxation of advertising provisions. Notably, the

Canadian Grand Prix was to run in Montreal that coming summer and the Liberals wanted to avoid electoral trouble there.

On April 22, 1997, the tobacco companies launched another court case, arguing that the new provisions of Bill C-17 (which had not yet received royal assent) violated the Charter, and asked for a temporary stay. The court rejected the request, and the law went into effect just before the 1997 federal election. By July the question was whether Allan Rock, the new minister of Health, would honour the promise made in April to permit cigarette logos at car racing events. If he carried through, it was likely he'd be besieged by other arts and sports groups seeking a similar concession.[61] Health groups were mobilizing as well: the Coalition Québécoise pour le contrôle du Tabac (consisting of the Quebec division of the Canadian Cancer Society, health clinics, municipalities, students, and parents) sponsored a car and driver in the grand prix sporting an antismoking logo. "Indeed, our decision to sponsor a racing-car driver underlines our firm belief that this type of advertising is an effective means of convincing consumers.... We will use our new advertising vehicle to convey the message that tobacco is a deadly product."[62] By December 1997 Rock agreed to make amendments to the act to allow sponsorship for motor racing but refused to extend the exemption to other sporting or cultural activities. The Alliance for Sponsorship Freedom (which antismoking groups claimed was a front for the Tobacco Council) made a public plea to have the legislation phased in over seven years, while the tobacco companies began to inform various groups and organizations of millions of dollars of sponsorship cuts.[63] On February 14, 1998, Ottawa announced that cigarette taxes would be increased in Ontario, Quebec, Nova Scotia, Prince Edward Island, and New Brunswick to deter youth smoking. Allan Rock was preparing to introduce his amendments to the Tobacco Act to permit sponsorship of Formula One racing, but speculation was rife that he might extend that exemption to other groups.[64] Lobbying never ends.

It should be clear from the preceding lists and case that the range of activities is broad indeed. Some groups and associations combine strategies, though most tend to prefer one mode or another. "Insiders" typically rely on quiet lobbying tactics, while "outsider" groups tend to try to attract attention through protests or work at changing public opinion. Furthermore, businesses can choose to lobby on their own behalf or work with trade associations. Social-action groups tend to be weak to begin with and so place a higher premium on coalition building and collective action.

Since interest groups try to influence the policy process, a successful group is by definition one that influences that process in its preferred direction. Many factors determine success, from the nature of the issue to the organizational characteristics of the policy community and the stage of the policy process. But these factors can be capitalized on only with the proper resources, so the organizational characteristics of the groups themselves become a key variable in understanding group influence in politics. For this reason business groups and associations are often at the centre of fears that public policy is being unduly affected by special pressures. Business has several theoretical advantages in policymaking that are denied to other types of groups.

DOSSIER 11.1 TOBACCO LOBBYING AND THE SENATE

Friends and foes of the Liberals' tobacco legislation will face off in the Senate this week as C-71 goes before the Legal and Constitutional Affairs Committee. Anti-smoking activists may have cheered the bill's passage through the House two weeks ago, supported by all but the Bloc Québécois and a half dozen renegade Liberal and Reform MPs, but many were equally taken aback by the blatant, in-your-face lobby efforts of the tobacco industry.

Wine and cheese receptions serenaded by bluegrass bands in the Hall of Honour, not-so-friendly allusions to Quebec–Canada relations in the House of Commons, and plain old threats ("Amend this bill or we pull the plug on the broadcast of this weekend's Formula One race") may have characterized the tobacco lobby's sabre rattling so far. But now that the bill has moved on to the Senate, its enemies will likely move out of the spotlight and back into more traditional lobbyist territory.

"Senate lobbying is far more discreet," says Cynthia Callard, who represents Physicians for a Smoke-Free Canada. "It won't be as apparent as in the House of Commons, especially to those outside of the smoky backrooms of those who influence decision-making." Callard, a veteran of the tobacco wars, was unsurprised by the last-minute histrionics on behalf of the tobacco industry in the House, but she doesn't expect to see a reprise in the Senate.

"They exploited the fears of Montrealers, creating the idea that this bill was excessively strong, but I'm not sure if they can make people honk their horns twice." She looks forward to putting "stronger evidence" into the public record at the next round of committee hearings. "The 'sober second thought' should take the hysteria, and we'll be able to show that these measures are moderate, not extreme." Callard is optimistic that the bill will eventually pass. "The Senate chooses its battles with the government carefully. It has its own PR concerns, and most senators can't afford to champion the tobacco industry over the interests of children. They'd end up looking like the Republicans in the United States." But she is concerned about the potential for lobbying within the Chamber itself.

Three senators, Liberal Michael Kirby and Tories William Kelly and Roch Bolduc, sit on the boards of tobacco companies RJR-MacDonald and Rothmans, Inc., respectively. For his part, Kirby has disclosed his conflict of interest and has previously voiced his intention to withdraw from any debate and subsequent votes on the issue. As for Kelly and Bolduc, the Office of the Leader of the Opposition is a little more coy. "It's a non-issue," insists Fiona MacLeod, who says that the two have yet to disclose, because "it doesn't matter at this point." She says that if the matter comes to a vote, they would "very likely" abstain.

Callard is not alone in her fears that these senators could act as "in-house lobbyists" for the tobacco industry. Janice Forsythe of the Canadian Council on Smoking and Health, is also keeping a close eye on the possibility. "The tobacco lobby is incredibly well placed in the Senate, and its members may have had opportunities for access that the anti-tobacco lobbyists haven't." While she doesn't expect the senators to vote on the bill, having previously declared conflicts of interest on tobacco-related issues, she says there's no way to be sure about participation in formal discussions. "We're concerned about the access that the tobacco lobby has to these and other senators."

Garfield Mahood with the Non-Smokers' Rights Association is only half-joking when he suggests that "the lobby has been in the Senate for a long time—perhaps millennia." He thinks it's important that the public be fully aware that some senators could be working behind the scenes to encourage colleagues to support amendments agreeable to the industry. "The best outcome for a Michael Kirby would be amendments sufficient to delay the timetable so the bill would die on the Order Paper when the election is called." Some sources who have been keeping tabs on the inner chamber dynamics, however, suggest that the so-called "tobacco senators" have already been put on the hot seat by their respective caucuses. "If they make too much of a fuss, or are too visible, it could cause trouble for them, both personally and politically."

Whatever its plan of attack, Mahood believes the tobacco lobby will again concentrate most of its efforts on the sponsorship issue, especially a delay in the implementation of the law. "Sponsorship is now the marketing vehicle of choice for cigarette companies." Tobacco industry advocates opposed to the bill would argue with Mahood's assertion. The official line has always been that sponsorship and advertising is aimed at people who already smoke, not at recruiting youth, but the impassioned arguments against the bill's new restrictions on advertising at events resulted in little change at the House of Commons stage.

But Marie Josée Lapointe of the Canadian Tobacco Manufacturers Council says the industry still has faith in the system. "We hope to get a fair hearing, our brief is more substantial since we've had time to look at the bill and come up with amendments." She suggests that business and legal issues will take centre stage during this round of committee hearings. "We have jurists looking at the issue right now." And faith in the system notwithstanding, the industry has contingency plans. "If this bill becomes law, we'll take it right back to the courts."

Liberal Senator Philippe Gigantes may not be the answer to Lapointe's prayers, but as the only Quebec Liberal on the Legal and Constitutional Affairs Committee, he's likely to be a magnet for lobby efforts, a prospect with which he seems unfamiliar. "My two regrets in politics have been that I've never been lobbied, and I've never been offered a bribe. Do you think that makes me significant?" He says he has some tough questions for the tobacco companies. "I want to ask them, why do you advertise?" Gigantes wonders why, if recruiting young people is not a goal, tobacco companies don't target "old wheezers" who already smoke, rather than put logos on racing cars driven by heroic figures. He looks forward to grilling the cigarette companies, and says he expects at least two weeks of committee hearings.

He may not be in the eye of the hurricane anymore, but it's a good bet that Health Minister David Dingwall is paying close attention to events in the Senate.

Anti-smoking activists were quick to laud his efforts in getting the bill as far as he has done. "The minister did a fabulous job getting this legislation through Cabinet," says Forsythe, while even the self-described irascible Mahood agrees that Dingwall showed "remarkable commitment." But getting the bill through the House was only the start of his odyssey. Getting C-71 through the Senate, in one piece and with time to spare before a probable election call, could require him to flex a little political muscle—not to mention show off some of the lobby-wrangling tricks he's picked up over the last few months.

Source: *The Lobby Monitor* 8 (March 17, 1997) [on-line, World Wide Web; cited October 1, 1998]; available at http://www.arcpub.com/lmarchiv.htm.

For one thing, given the capitalist nature of the Canadian economy, prosperity and jobs still depend on private-sector decisions about investment and development. If business is unhappy with taxes or social policies, the argument runs, it will invest elsewhere. This assumption alone assures a more attentive hearing for groups like the Canadian Bankers' Association, the Business Council on National Issues, and the Canadian Chamber of Commerce. Business also enjoys financial resources well beyond the capacities of other groups. It can hire lobbyists (and deduct their cost as a business expense!) and make substantial political contributions to parties. Many politicians are either drawn from the business community or have extensive social connections with members of that community.

The evidence on business lobbying success supports the notion of privileged access to some degree but has to be treated cautiously. Ottawa and the provincial capitals have blossomed in recent years with companies and individuals who lobby government on behalf of others. For reasons of ideology and personal contacts, specific firms tend to be in favour with specific governments at any given time. The corollary is that when governments are replaced, lobbying firms tend to be too.[65] Concerns that cronyism and business influence were ruling the corridors of power in Ottawa finally led to the 1985 Lobbyists Registration Act. The original legislation had some huge holes—for example, it narrowly defined lobbyists as those who actually arrange meetings or communicate with public officials on behalf of clients—but nonetheless for the first time yielded some hard information on the scope of the lobbying industry at the federal level. The 1985 act distinguished between Tier I and Tier II lobbyists. A Tier I lobbyist "is an individual who, for payment and on behalf of a client, undertakes to arrange a meeting with a public office holder or to communicate with a public office holder in an attempt to influence the development, making or amendment of any federal law, regulation, policy or program or the award of any federal monetary grant or the award of any federal contract."[66] Tier II lobbyists act on behalf of their employer for the same ends (with the exception of awarding of contracts.)

Amendments to the act came into force on January 31, 1996, and were designed to elicit more comprehensive information about lobbyists and their activities. The act now provides for three categories of lobbyists. Consultant lobbyists "are individuals who, for payment and on behalf of a client, undertake to: arrange a meeting between their client and a public office holder; or to lobby for the making, developing or amending of any federal law, regulation, policy or program, or the awarding of any federal monetary grant, contribution or other financial benefit, or the awarding of any federal contract." In-house lobbyists (corporate) "are employees of corporations that carry on commercial activities for financial gain and who, as a significant part of their duties, communicate with federal public office holders in an attempt to influence the same activities as for consultant lobbyists, except the awarding of contracts. These employees are usually full-time officers of a corporation whose primary function is public affairs or government relations work." Finally, the senior executive officer of noncommercial organizations must register as in-house lobbyists (organizations) "when one or more employees communicate with federal public office holders in an attempt to influence government decisions and where the accumulated activity of all such employees would constitute a significant part of the duties of one employee."[67] Lobbyists were also required to provide more information: "the name or description of the specific legislative proposals, bills, regulations, policies, programs, grants, contributions or contracts sought; the names of the federal departments or other governmental institutions lobbied; the source and amount of any government funding; and the communication techniques used, such as grass-roots lobbying. Corporations and organizations must also provide a general description of their business or activities." Not all communication with government is considered lobbying, so the act excludes appearances before parliamentary committees, submissions to public officials on the enforcement of laws or regulations, and submissions that are a response to a request. Table 11.1 shows the top 20 subjects of lobbying at the federal level. By the end of March 1997, registrations showed that there were 485 consultant lobbyists, 349 in-house (corporate) lobbyists representing 177 firms, and 295 nonprofit societies.

Another vehicle of business representation in government is the industry or trade association. Some of the most prominent and visible trade associations are national in scope and broadly focused in terms of policy interests (e.g., the Business Council on National Issues and the Canadian Chamber of Commerce). Others represent major sectors of the economy, such as the Canadian Bankers' Association or the Canadian Manufacturers' Association. There are trade associations in the agricultural sector, such as the Canadian Federation of Agriculture, but also much more sectorally specific ones such as the Canadian Cattlemen's Association. For 1980 Coleman found a total of 484 national business groups and 95 farmers' associations, but despite their "national" character, their most striking feature was their product specialization. The associations were weakly integrated, and on the business side, with few exceptions, the groups tended to "be quite small, with one to two professional staff members and one to two clerical people."[68]

Given the resources and access of many business associations, business lobbying can be overpowering. During the negotiations over free trade with the United

DOSSIER 11.2 INTEREST-GROUP ADVOCACY ADVERTISING FOR THE 1988 FREE TRADE AGREEMENT

The Canada–U.S. Free Trade Agreement (FTA) was signed in January 1988, to go into effect on January 1, 1989. The deal became the central issue in the November 21, 1988, federal election, with both pro- and anti-FTA groups buying media advertising time to sway public opinion. The table and chart below show the extent of pro-FTA advertising paid for by business groups (Canadian Alliance for Trade and Job Opportunities) and the increasing intensity of those ads as election day approached.

COMPARISON OF PRO-FREE TRADE AND PC PARTY AND CANDIDATE ADVERTISING (DOLLARS)

Canadian Alliance for Trade and Job Opportunities	2,307,670
Government of Alberta	727,000
National Citizens' Coalition	150,000
Other pro-free trade	454,234
Total pro-free trade expenditures	3,638,904
PC Party advertising	4,716,737
PC candidate advertising	7,462,877
Total PC advertising	12,179,614
Amount of pro-free trade advertising for every $1.00 of PC Party and PC candidate advertising	0.30

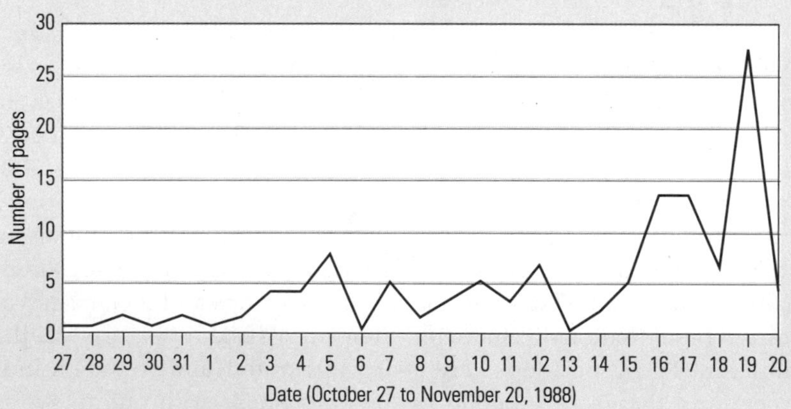

Source: Janet Hiebert, "Interest Groups and Canadian Federal Elections," in *Interest Groups and Elections in Canada,* vol. 2 of the Research Studies of the Royal Commission on Electoral Reform and Party Financing, ed. F. Leslie Seidle (Toronto: Dundurn Press, 1991), table 1.4 and figure 1.1 at pages 22 and 25. Reproduced with the permission of the Minister of Supply and Services Canada, 1994.

States in 1988 and the ensuing election of that fall, business associations led by the Business Council on National Issues (BCNI) spent millions of dollars to counter the lobbying and public-information campaigns that had been undertaken by social-movement organizations, trade unions, and others in an attempt to stop the free-trade accord. From March 1987 to April 1988, for example, the business umbrella organization of the Canadian Alliance for Trade and Job Opportunities spent almost $3 million defending the deal. Most of this money was raised through the membership of the BCNI. The bulk was spent on advertising and consultants. Once the election campaign got under way and public opinion seemed to be supporting opponents of the deal, the alliance raised another $2.3 million to spend on newspaper inserts to counter an anti-FTA cartoon book put out by the ProCanada Network. The Conservatives won the election and the FTA went ahead.[69] In October 1993, when the victorious Liberals under Jean Chrétien threatened to pull the plug on the multi-billion-dollar EH-101 helicopter deal signed by the previous Tory government, military contractors pulled out all the stops in lobbying for their contracts. Paul Manson, president of Paramax, a company with a significant stake in the deal, told *The Globe and Mail* that the "good of the nation is very much at stake in this decision." He said that he and other military contractors would talk to a "number of Liberals whose names are being mentioned as potential cabinet ministers" and that they would pressure newly elected Liberal MPs by warning of "massive layoffs" in their ridings.[70] In this case, however, the business lobby failed. The EH-101 contract was cancelled.[71]

Business can influence government in more subtle ways than direct lobbying. One of the most important vehicles for this more general type of influence—a type

TABLE 11.1 TOP 20 SUBJECTS OF LOBBYING

1. Industry	11. Government procurement
2. Taxation and finance	12. Energy
3. International trade	13. Agriculture
4. Environment	14. Financial institutions
5. Health	15. Intellectual property
6. Transportation	16. International relations
7. Science and technology	17. Regional development
8. Consumer issues	18. Telecommunications
9. Internal trade	19. Labour
10. Employment and training	20. Small business

Source: Lobbyists Registration Act, *Annual Report for Year Ended March 31, 1997* [on-line, World Wide Web; cited October 1, 1998]; available at http://strategis.ic.gc.ca.

TABLE 11.2 TOP 15 LOBBYING FIRMS (IN TERMS OF NUMBER OF CLIENTS)

	REGISTERED CLIENTS	
ORGANIZATION	APRIL 1997	AUGUST 1993
The Capital Hill Group	84	59
GPC Government Policy Consultants	64	81
SAMCI	50	48
Hill & Knowlton Canada	46	81
Government Business Consulting Group	38	63
Earnscliffe Strategy Group	35	25
IGRG-Industry-Government Relations	27	N/A
Association House	25	N/A
Osler, Hoskin & Harcourt	23	68
Grey, Clark, Shih & Associates	19	23
McMillan Binch	17	32
Public Perspectives Inc.	15	N/A
Tactix Government Consulting Inc.	14	N/A
Gowling, Strathy	14	N/A
Borden & Elliot	14	13

Source: *The Lobby Monitor* 8 (April 28, 1997), 3.

usually closed to smaller, non-economically based organizations—is the campaign donation. Until 1974, when Ottawa passed the new Election Expenses Act, the Liberals and Conservatives relied almost exclusively on corporate contributions.[72] As noted in Chapter 10, the act stipulated spending limits for the parties and candidates and reimbursed candidates for a portion of their election expenses as long as they received at least 15 percent of the vote. Although corporate donations declined as a proportion of total financial support for parties and candidates, they still account for half or more of total contributions to the Liberal and Conservative parties. In 1996 the Liberals received $7.8 million from 7421 businesses, or 55 percent of its total donations of $14.1 million. Whereas the Conservatives had collected $11.5 million in donations in 1992, by 1996 donations had dropped to $6.7 million, of which $3.1 million came from 2678 companies. The NDP receives virtually no corporate donations, but some of its donations came from trade unions (as much as a third of individual donations). The Reform Party received only $907,769 from 951 corporations, with the bulk of its revenues provided by the widest base of small individual contributions

(66,982 in all).[73] Any contribution over $100 must be publicly reported. Despite the constraints imposed by the act, corporations still give, and the actual number of corporate donations has actually increased. Both the Conservatives and Liberals receive one-half or more of their contributions from business and commercial organizations. Large contributions (defined as over $10,000) are not uncommon, and many companies give equal amounts to both the Liberals and the Conservatives. The central question behind all this corporate support to political parties is whether it enables business to exercise disproportionate influence over public policy. According to William Stanbury, despite the protestations by politicians that they neither know nor care who contributes to their campaigns or parties, the practice of political contributions keeps avenues of communication open and provides access that is clearly greater than that experienced by other interest groups and associations.

> *When a corporation makes a large donation, the following things occur: (1) its senior executives have a personal contact with a high party official, which in the future may be used as a point of access in making contacts with cabinet ministers; (2) senior party officials are made aware of the enterprise's generosity ... [These] two facts can hardly hurt the firm when it makes contact with those officials to obtain information or an introduction to the right people in the executive (both political and bureaucratic).*[74]

At the other end of the interest group spectrum are public-interest groups or social-movement groups. Jeremy Wilson reports, for example, that the Canadian environmental movement comprises at least 1800 organizations, from the small grassroots type (e.g., local recycling committee) to the large national organizations such as Greenpeace and the Canadian Wildlife Federation, which respectively claim to have over 300,000 and 620,000 members.[75] Despite a strong volunteer base, these membership numbers have not translated into the sort of financial capacity that seems typical of the corporate sector. As Wilson points out, "No environmental group is able to pay well-connected Ottawa lobby firms large monthly retainers, or to afford extensive television advocacy advertising campaigns."[76] Unlike corporations, which for the most part try to establish ongoing links with politicians and the bureaucracy, environmental groups try first to move public opinion through educational campaigns and protest strategies that capture media attention.

From a rational choice point of view, social-movement organizations are at a disadvantage because they pursue "public goods," that is, benefits that accrue to a wide constituency. Members of that constituency receive the benefit whether they support the group or free ride on its efforts; consequently, support tends to be wide but shallow.[77] An alternate explanation of their difficulties is that these groups often represent conscience communities interested in equality or justice issues. This can sometimes be an obvious advantage, but sometimes the support of "good causes" is not as powerful an incentive to mobilize as the desire for material gain. As well, the potential supporters for many of these groups are often large in numbers but spread out nationally or even internationally. This also poses a challenge for mobilization.

Finally, good lobbying often depends on good information, and most of these groups do not have the funds to do first-rate research.

This is where modern information technologies, particularly the convergence of telephone, computer, and TV, may be making a difference to groups in this sector. All of the problems listed above can be seen as challenges to communication, persuasion, coalition building, and information gathering. New information technologies, especially the Internet, are providing these groups with new, cheaper, and more efficient means of addressing all of these collective-action problems.

Most writers point to the Internet as being the crucial technology that has created the opportunity for networks and new communities to be created. Bill Gates, head of the Microsoft empire, argues that political organizing will be much easier because of Web. "It will become so easy to organize a political movement that no cause will be too small or scattered."[78] Ronfeldt notes the growing importance of multi-organizational networks: "Growing numbers and varieties of non-governmental organizations (NGOs—some of them also called private voluntary organizations, PVOs) are forming network-like coalitions, in many instances to strengthen their efforts to influence the behavior of governments and businesses. The examples include new networks among special interests, public interest, pressure, lobbying and/or advocacy groups."[79]

Interestingly, social-advocacy groups or public-interest groups—especially those with a global agenda—have appeared to gain the most from the Internet and the new possibilities of connectivity.[80] Other things being equal, the more geographically distributed an interest, and the more symbolic it is (rather than material), the more difficult it is to organize. The Internet is an obvious way to address this difficulty, and, not surprisingly, some of the earliest migrations (1982) onto the Net were by organizations dedicated to weaving together networks of social justice and activist groups around the world, such as the Association for Progressive Communications (APC) and the Institute for Global Communications (IGC).[81] As Spiro notes:

> *The explosion in nongovernmental activity reflects the dramatically heightened permeability of national borders and improvements in communications that have allowed territorially dispersed individuals to develop common agendas and objectives at the international level. Modern communication is much less dependent on location; increased*

DOSSIER 11.3 INTERNATIONAL INTEREST GROUP ACTIVITY IN THE ELECTRONIC AGE

OneWorld On-Line: http://www.oneworld.org/about/index.html

Canadian Web Networks Membership Site List:
http://forest.web.net/web/livelink?func=db.pubshow&htmlfile=pubmemsmall.html

travel, the fax, and perhaps most important the Internet have created the possibility of a cohesion that is not tied to territory. If national groupings are communities in the sense that the nation is always conceived as a deep, horizontal partnership, today's non-national affinities have at least the potential themselves to evolve into communities of similar marrow. By providing institutional homes in the same way that states have accommodated nationalism, NGOs are the inevitable beneficiaries of the emergence of the new global communities.[82]

But the Internet can also support the development of affinity groups—people who share an interest (not necessarily political), such as Malaysian cooking, but who would be hard-pressed to find others with that interest nearby. This is what Rheingold refers to when he discusses the rise of "virtual communities": "Nonprofit organizations on the neighborhood, city, and regional levels, and **non-governmental organizations (NGOs)** on the global level, can be seen as modern manifestations of what the enlightenment philosophers of democracy would have called 'civil society.'"[83] Nor is this only a global phenomenon. Schwartz argues that the Internet not only allows unprecedented levels of political mobilization but that it also permits community and neighbourhood building: "The Internet empowers us when it expands the range of partnerships available and enables us to work together on behalf of common goals. No other technology fulfills this mission quite so well. We watch television. We listen to the radio. We talk on the telephone. Yet, on the Internet, we can meet, get to know one another, and start to collaborate—several hundred of us at a time."[84]

In a rich if speculative paper, Stanbury and Vertinsky largely accept these conclusions but add some distinct hypotheses of their own on the impact of Internet technology on interest groups.[85] For example, they note some possible impacts on group size and recruitment. With the overhead costs of communication dramatically lowered, it is possible that the minimum economic size of a group might be smaller. Groups will be able to recruit and raise funds more efficiently. The increased ability to communicate with others about one's interests may encourage deeper commitment and willingness to organize to influence policy. By the same token, there may also be greater exit from as well as entry to groups. They anticipate a great deal of turbulence and competition, though this echoes the worries discussed above about fragmentation and instability. It is possible that with this greater fluidity in the creation and demise of groups will come greater emphasis on coalition building on an issue-by-issue basis (indeed, there may be more issue-specific organizations).[86] In terms of strategies and tactics, they see some clear advantages in the new information technology:

Electronically-linked members/supporters make body counts cheaper and more easily verifiable. Episodic recruitment and mobilization of action (from rallies to a flood of telephone calls or e-mail) may also be easier, since the effective use of triggers (e.g., the distribution of salient information) may help assemble a temporary coalition focusing on the specific issue and event, irrespective of the long-term organizational commitments. Because of the increased competition for people's attention, the result may be the creation of more intense issue politics.[87]

More people might be involved with groups but more episodically and without intense long-term commitments. In turn this might mean less pressure to become involved in the governance of these groups, leaving the field to professional staff. In a scenario far removed from that of Rheingold and Schwartz, Stanbury and Vertinsky suggest the possibility of an increase in the number of interest groups run by a small core of activists who seek to trigger action/support by a mass of people. This is not the creation of new virtual communities but raises the spectre of electronic mobs rallied by professional mobilizers as necessary.

It is too early to tell whether the Internet will be a democratic nirvana or populist hell, but the signs are that it is having an impact on the ways in which groups organize and share information, both among themselves and with government. Many issues have a global dimension, and groups now can mobilize globally. The international campaign to ban land mines, for example, started in 1992 with a mere handful of individuals and organizations based in the United States. By late 1997, when a treaty was signed in Ottawa, thousands of organizations around the world had worked together and lobbied their governments and international organizations. Another current example is the Multilateral Agreement on Investment. The Council of Canadians is fighting the agreement on home turf but is linked to a global network of groups opposed to the initiative. The same dynamic is at play with groups like Amnesty International, or the international women's movement. As Castells notes: "Humanitarian causes, such as the ones supported by Amnesty International, Medicins sans frontières, Greenpeace, Oxfam, Food First, and thousands and thousands of both local and global, activist groups and non-governmental organizations around the world, are the most powerful proactive, mobilizing factor in informational politics."[88]

CONCLUSION

Liberal democracy without interest groups is scarcely conceivable, but the role of interest groups in democratic policymaking is still both obscure and contested. The logic of our key representational institutions is a logic of aggregation—political parties, for example, try to pull together positions on a wide variety of issues. It is also a logic of territorial representation. Interest groups, particularly ones connected to broad social movements like women's equality or environmental viability, challenge these assumptions to some extent. Interest groups are primarily "sectoral," to use Pross's phrase, not spatial. The intensity of these interests can often be high, and the scope of interests can be so broad that issues that might traditionally be defined as economic or regional get redefined in terms of the organization's agenda. This intensity and fragmentation has led some observers to worry that the public interest is being drowned out by a chorus of special pleadings.[89] Politicians and the public have expressed concern about the influence of "special interests" (i.e., narrow or privileged interests) in politics. Parties gradually become less relevant as groups seek to exercise influence separately in the political system. The increase of third-party advertising in elections is a sign that interest groups no longer trust political parties to articulate positions for them.

The picture is more complex than it appears, of course. First, traditional political parties continue to be the main vehicles pursuing formal political power, so while their relations with groups may change and evolve, they will not be easily sidelined. Second, the variety and scope of the associational system in Canada have grown tremendously in the last 20 years. The "special interests" of the first half of the 20th century were corporate and business interests that exercised their influence through political contributions and through close relations with governments and political parties. That era is gone, though corporate influence continues to be felt in the form of donations, lobbyists, and direct attempts to shape public policy through pressure from firms and trade associations. The Canadian corporate sector is far from monolithic, and its internal divisions mean that business rarely speaks with a single voice, if it speaks coherently at all. The example of free trade and the 1988 election, where a clear business position was orchestrated by the Business Council on National Issues, is more of an exception than the rule. The degree of business unanimity on a host of economic issues in the last decade is a bit misleading—as the federal deficit came to be perceived as a major problem, the scope of disagreement among business narrowed considerably. Business lobbyists wanted expenditure cuts and a balanced budget, and there were no debates over new policies. With deficits a thing of the past, substantive policy debate will be revived, and the usual splits among business interests (i.e., sectoral, regional) will surface.

Even if business influence were more focused than it is, it would now have to compete with a plethora of other organizations, many of which represent the "new politics" of social movements.[90] The fastest-growing components of the Canadian associational system have been groups representing the interests of women, youth, ethnics, environmentalists, peace activists, and social-policy and human-rights advocates. In terms of financial resources, none of these groups can compete with corporations or national trade associations, but they wield influence nonetheless. What they lack in funds, they often make up in membership and volunteers and, with the Internet, communications capacity. While they may not have the same easy access to senior political personnel or officials, they have legitimacy that sometimes outweighs that of the corporate sector. Through the use of imaginative protest tactics, they can capture public attention and often public support in a way closed to corporations. Foreign governments are sometimes more sympathetic to social-movement groups than to either economic interests or government spokespersons. This helps explain the success of groups like Greenpeace in the campaign against the Newfoundland seal hunt, and the Cree in their fight against the Quebec government's Great Whale hydro project.

The role of interest groups and the associational system is likely to increase in the next few years, for four reasons. First, while there seems to be growing optimism and some return to trust among the electorate, politicians and political parties are still held in low regard by most Canadians. Many groups, on the other hand, enjoy high levels of legitimacy. Second, as noted in this chapter and in others in the book, the Charter of Rights and Freedoms has given many groups new leverage in challenging public policy. Litigation is expensive, and many business interests have been able to make successful Charter arguments (e.g., the tobacco lobby), but it is a new avenue that has been used successfully by women's groups, gays and lesbians, labour unions, and Aboriginal groups. Third, for the time being governments across the country are proclaiming the importance of consultation and partnership with "civil society." As we noted above, funding and support for advocacy organizations have in fact been in decline for the last decade, and even as social services get shifted to the voluntary and charitable sectors, the financial and logistical support needed to make program delivery work are not. Nonetheless, consultation is "in" and policymakers cannot avoid, even if they would wish to, connecting with a wide variety of organizations. A 1995 federal government guide to "partnering," for example, explicitly connected government downsizing, alternative service delivery, quality, and public consultation: "The necessity to provide affordable quality programs and services, combined with a renewed political will and the possibilities offered by emerging technologies, have made various forms of partnering more attractive to federal managers." The same document, however, noted the institutional tensions involved: "Such collaborative arrangements are not without their difficulties. When the Crown is involved, consideration must be given to its responsibilities concerning legal issues, problems of definition, management issues, financial and contracting issues, human resources issues, official languages issues, even political issues."[91] Finally, as mentioned above, groups may be developing a new capacity for mobilization and for building networked coalitions through the use of new information technologies.

For some, this burgeoning growth in the associational system will make our politics hostage to shifting coalitions of "special interests." For others, the opposite is true: a robust associational system is the foundation of the "social capital" required to support democratic institutions.[92] In either event, the balance of representation institutions will be a challenging one. The problem is that our political institutions—from Parliament and federalism to the amending formulas of the constitution itself—operate according to a logic that is relatively closed, hierarchical, and obviously representational. Referendums, consultations, and direct representation by groups and organizations of citizens assume, by contrast, that citizens want to act for themselves. As Stein, Cameron, and Simeon argue: "The critical task is the linking of the right kind of citizen processes to official processes under appropriate conditions and with appropriate goals. The efficacy of public participation depends on the purposes it seeks to achieve, the kinds of processes that are used, and the sequencing in a broader process of political discussion and negotiation."[93]

In everything from the constitution to public-policy formation, the public wants to be heard and heard directly. Political parties have lost a great deal of their legitimacy in the last decade, and their decline has been matched by a growth in the number and visibility of interest groups. The point this chapter has tried to make is that these developments signal more than a mere rebalancing of the elements of the Canadian political system. Given that our institutions are designed to represent interests in certain ways, the challenge of a richer and more active associational system is, in the present climate, a challenge to the system itself. In seeking new forms of representation and in developing new modes of exercising influence, Canadian interest groups have to some extent unwittingly posed the more fundamental issue of how far parliamentary institutions can go in absorbing an entirely new representational principle.

KEY TERMS

- lobbying
- social movements
- associational system
- representation of interests
- voluntary
- autonomous
- influence
- privileged access
- collective action
- interest groups
- freedom of association
- freedom of speech
- freedom of conscience
- pluralist
- degree of centralization
- degree of concentration
- Internet
- policy community
- policy network
- meso-political
- macro-political
- micro-political
- umbrella groups
- issue-oriented groups
- policy capacity
- institutional groups
- free riders
- selective incentives
- public-interest groups
- non-governmental organizations (NGOs)

DISCUSSION QUESTIONS

1. Discuss the impact of federalism on interest associations, both in terms of the way that groups organize and how they are likely to perceive issues.
2. In what ways has the Charter changed interest group politics in Canada?

3. Imagine that you are in charge of an environmental group opposed to a nearby development project that is sponsored by several large corporations. Develop a checklist of the strategies of opposition and representation you would use to halt the development.
4. Federal and provincial governments in Canada routinely provide financial support to NGOs and associations that engage in political advocacy. Examples include support to ethnic groups, women, linguistic minorities, and consumer associations. What are the arguments for and against such funding?
5. Governments at all levels are "consulting" more with individuals and associations as part of the policy process, and groups naturally expect to have more influence as a result. Often they do not, largely because of constraints in the rest of the legislative and political system. Consider the points made in previous chapters about cabinet secrecy, concentration of authority in the parliamentary system, and the subordinate role of officials. How might these factors limit the influence that interest groups are able to exercise over government departments that consult on proposed legislation or policies?

SUGGESTED READINGS

Atkinson, Michael M., and William D. Coleman. "Policy Networks, Policy Communities and the Problems of Governance," *Governance* 5 (April 1992), 154–180.

Cardozo, Andrew. "Lion Taming: Downsizing the Opponents of Downsizing." In Gene Swimmer, ed., *How Ottawa Spends 1996–97: Life under the Knife.* Ottawa: Carleton University Press, 1996, 303–336.

Coleman, William D. *Business and Politics: A Study of Collective Action.* Kingston and Montreal: McGill-Queen's University Press, 1988.

Coleman, William D., and Grace Skogstad, eds. *Policy Communities and Public Policy in Canada: A Structural Approach.* Toronto: Copp Clark Pitman, 1990.

Pal, Leslie A. *Interests of State: The Politics of Language, Multiculturalism and Feminism in Canada.* Kingston and Montreal: McGill-Queen's University Press, 1993.

Paltiel, Khayyam Z. "The Changing Environment and Role of Special Interest Groups," *Canadian Public Administration* 25 (1982), 198–210.

Phillips, Susan D. "How Ottawa Blends: Shifting Government Relationships with Interest Groups." In Frances Abele, ed., *How Ottawa Spends 1991–1992: The Politics of Fragmentation.* Ottawa: Carleton University Press, 1991, 183–227.

Pross, A. Paul. *Group Politics and Public Policy.* 2nd ed. Toronto: Oxford University Press, 1992.

Stein, Janice Gross, David R. Cameron, and Richard Simeon, with Alan Alexandroff. *Citizen Engagement in Conflict Resolution: Lessons for Canada in International Experience*. Toronto: C.D. Howe Institute, 1997.

Van Waarden, F. "Dimensions and Types of Policy Networks." *European Journal of Political Research* 21 (1992), 29–52.

NOTES

1. A. Paul Pross and Iain Stewart, "Lobbying, the Voluntary Sector, and the Public Purse," in Susan D. Phillips, ed., *How Ottawa Spends 1993–1994: A More Democratic Canada ...?* (Ottawa: Carleton University Press, 1993), 110.
2. A. Paul Pross has illuminated this issue in several works. See "Space, Function, and Interest: The Problem of Legitimacy in the Canadian State," in O.P. Dwivedi, ed., *The Administrative State in Canada* (Toronto: University of Toronto Press, 1982), 107–129; and *Group Politics and Public Policy*, 2nd ed. (Toronto: Oxford University Press, 1992), Chapter 10.
3. Canadian Associations Mailing List [on-line, World Wide Web; cited March 4, 1998]; available at http://world.mmltd.com/files/homepage.html.
4. Pross, *Group Politics and Public Policy*, 65.
5. Khayyam Z. Paltiel, "The Changing Environment and Role of Special Interest Groups," *Canadian Public Administration* 25 (1982), 198–210.
6. William D. Coleman, *Business and Politics: A Study of Collective Action* (Montreal and Kingston: McGill-Queen's University Press, 1988), 18–30.
7. *Libman v. Quebec (Attorney General)* [on-line, World Wide Web; cited October 29, 1998]; available at http://www.droit.umontreal.ca/doc/csc-scc/en/pub/1997/vol13/html/1997scr3_0569.html.
8. *Report of the Chief Electoral Officer of Canada on the 36th General Election* [on-line, World Wide Web; cited March 4, 1998]; available at http://www.elections.ca/election/ceo_rprt/recomm_e.htm#thirdparty.
9. See Janine Brodie, *Politics on the Margins: Restructuring and the Canadian Women's Movement* (Halifax: Fernwood Press, 1995); and Sandra Burt, "The Status of Women: Learning to Live without the State," in Andrew F. Johnson and Andrew Stritch, eds., *Canadian Public Policy: Globalization and Political Parties* (Toronto: Copp Clark, 1997), 251–274.
10. Leslie A. Pal, *Interests of State: The Politics of Language, Multiculturalism and Feminism in Canada* (Kingston and Montreal: McGill-Queen's University Press, 1993), 143–147.
11. A good recent example of the differing views of the two organizations concerns the ongoing negotiation over a Multilateral Agreement on Investment. The BCNI's support for the agreement, and the Council's rejection, were expressed in testimony before the Sub-Committee on International Trade, Trade Disputes and Investment of the Standing Committee on Foreign Affairs and International Trade, *Minutes and Proceedings*, November 25, 1997; and Standing Committee on Foreign Affairs and International Trade, *Minutes and Proceedings*, November 17, 1997.
12. Classic treatments of the alliances behind the CCF–NDP and the Liberals are Walter Young, *Anatomy of a Party: The National CCF—1932–1961* (Toronto: University of Toronto

Press, 1969); and Reginald Whitaker, *The Government Party* (Toronto: University of Toronto Press, 1977). For more analyses, see the essays in A.G. Gagnon and A.B. Tanguay, eds., *Canadian Parties in Transition: Discourse, Organization, and Representation*, 2nd ed. (Scarborough: ITP Nelson, 1996).

13. The party's leader, Neil Paterson, is a director of Maharishi Heaven on Earth Development Corporation and sits on the executive council of the Maharishi's Global Administration through Natural Law [on-line, World Wide Web; cited March 4, 1998]; available at http://www.natural-law.ca/paterson/NPBio.html.
14. See "Green Parties to Support Protesters," News Release, Green Party of Canada, September 27, 1996 [on-line, World Wide Web; cited March 4, 1998]; available at http://green.ca/english/news/nr960927.htm.
15. As the Sierra Club points out, it was "founded by naturalist and writer John Muir in 1892 to protect the wilderness of the Sierra Nevada. Over the years, the activities of the Sierra Club have expanded to include issues ranging from climate change and ozone depletion to toxic chemical contamination and loss of biological diversity." For a glimpse of the range of issues the Sierra Club concerns itself with, see Sierra Club of Canada Web site [on-line, World Wide Web; cited March 4, 1998]; available at http://www.sierraclub.ca/national/index.html.
16. Pross, *Group Politics and Public Policy*, 48.
17. A. Paul Pross, "Pressure Groups: Adaptive Instruments of Political Communication," in A. Paul Pross, ed., *Pressure Group Behaviour in Canadian Politics* (Toronto: McGraw-Hill Ryerson, 1975), 5.
18. The literature on pluralism is huge. See Robert R. Alford and Roger Friedland, *Powers of Theory: Capitalism, the State, and Democracy* (Cambridge: Cambridge University Press, 1985), part 1; Patrick Dunleavy and Brendan O'Leary, *Theories of the State: The Politics of Liberal Democracy* (London: Macmillan, 1987), Chapter 2.
19. R. Kent Weaver and Bert A. Rockman, "Assessing the Effects of Institutions," in R. Kent Weaver and Bert A. Rockman, eds., *Do Institutions Matter? Government Capabilities in the United States and Abroad* (Washington: Brookings Institution, 1993), 32.
20. A similar pattern occurs in Belgium. It should be noted that despite the division, the two branches there coordinate their information and lobbying activities.
21. David Kwavnick, *Organized Labour and Pressure Politics: The Canadian Labour Congress, 1956–1968* (Montreal and Kingston: McGill-Queen's University Press, 1972).
22. Pross, *Group Politics and Public Policy*, 212.
23. It is also a conclusion of some long standing. See Helen Jones Dawson, "National Pressure Groups and the Federal Government," in Pross, ed., *Pressure Group Behaviour in Canadian Politics*, 27–58.
24. Coleman, *Business and Politics*, 242.
25. Stephen Brooks and Andrew Stritch, *Business and Government in Canada* (Scarborough: Prentice-Hall Canada, 1991), 180.
26. Canadian Parents for French, for example, has almost 200 chapters across the country that champion bilingual immersion education; see Pal, *Interests of State.*
27. Pross, "Pressure Groups," 19.
28. Pross, *Group Politics and Public Policy*, 64–65.
29. Richard Simeon, *Federal–Provincial Diplomacy: The Making of Recent Policy in Canada* (Toronto: University of Toronto Press, 1972), 280–281.

30. Carolyn J. Tuohy, *Policy and Politics in Canada: Institutionalized Ambivalence* (Philadelphia: Temple University Press, 1992), 43.
31. Peter C. Newman, *The Canadian Revolution 1985–1995: From Deference to Defiance* (Toronto: Viking, 1995), 395. Also see Neil Nevitte, *The Decline of Deference: Canadian Value Change in Cross-National Perspective* (Peterborough, Ont.: Broadview Press, 1996).
32. Pross, *Group Politics and Public Policy*, 76.
33. Ibid., 79.
34. On human rights consultations, see Robert M. Campbell and Leslie A. Pal, eds., *The Real Worlds of Canadian Politics: Cases in Process and Policy*, 3rd ed. (Peterborough, Ont.: Broadview Press, 1994), Chapter 4.
35. Evert A. Lindquist, "Citizens, Experts and Budgets: Evaluating Ottawa's Emerging Budget Process," in Susan B. Phillips, ed., *How Ottawa Spends 1994–95: Making Change* (Ottawa: Carleton University Press, 1994), 91–128.
36. Herman Bakvis, "Shrinking the House of 'HRIF': Program Review and the Department of Human Resources Development," in Gene Swimmer, ed., *How Ottawa Spends 1996–97: Life under the Knife* (Ottawa: Carleton University Press), 142.
37. *National Citizens' Coalition Inc. and Brown v. Canada (A.-G.)* (1984) 5 W.W.R. 436.
38. See Christopher P. Manfredi, "Re Lavigne and Ontario Public Employees Union: Public Administration and Remedial Decree Litigation under the Charter of Rights and Freedoms," *Canadian Public Administration* 34 (1991), 395–416.
39. Miriam Smith, "The Liberal Government and Rights Claims: The Lesbian and Gay Case," in Leslie A. Pal, ed., *How Ottawa Spends 1998–99: The Challenge of a Second Mandate* (Toronto: Oxford University Press, 1998), 293–314.
40. Salisbury claimed that the "ultimate focus of nearly all political science discussion of interest groups is the effect of group activity on governmental decisions." Robert H. Salisbury, "Interest Groups," in Fred I. Greenstein and Nelson Polsby, eds., *Handbook of Political Science*, vol. 4 (Reading, Mass.: Addison-Wesley, 1975), 206.
41. For a general review of these concepts, see Grant Jordan and Klaus Schubert, "A Preliminary Ordering of Policy Network Labels," *European Journal of Political Research* 21 (1992), 7–27; and R.A.W. Rhodes and David Marsh, "New Directions in the Study of Policy Networks," *European Journal of Political Research* 21 (1992), 181–205. For a discussion that links them to the structure and behaviour of public bureaucracies, see Evert Lindquist, "Public Managers and Policy Communities: Learning to Meet New Challenges," *Canadian Public Administration* 35 (Summer 1992), 127–159.
42. William D. Coleman and Grace Skogstad, "Policy Communities and Policy Networks: A Structural Approach," in Coleman and Skogstad, eds., *Policy Communities and Public Policy in Canada*, 25.
43. Citizens for Local Democracy Web site is available from http://community.web.net/citizens.
44. Earth First! Web site is available from http://www.enviroweb.org/ef/primer/WhyEFI.html.
45. Coleman and Skogstad, "Policy Communities and Policy Networks," in ibid., 26.
46. For a critical analysis of how well the policy communities literature does this, see Evert A. Lindquist, "New Agendas for Research on Policy Communities: Policy Analysis, Administration, and Governance," in Laurent Dobuzinskis, Michael Howlett, and David Laycock, eds., *Policy Studies in Canada: The State of the Art* (Toronto: University of Toronto Press), 219–241.

47. See Michael M. Atkinson and William D. Coleman, "Strong States and Weak States: Sectoral Policy Networks in Advanced Capitalist Economies," *British Journal of Political Science* 19 (1989), 47–67; Rhodes and Marsh, "New Directions in the Study of Policy Networks"; Grant Jordan and Klaus Schubert, "A Preliminary Ordering of Policy Network Labels," *European Journal of Political Research* 21 (1992), 7–27; F. Van Waarden, "Dimensions and Types of Policy Networks," *European Journal of Political Research* 21 (1992), 29–52; Grant A. Jordan, "Iron Triangles, Woolly Corporatism and Elastic Nets: Images of the Policy Process," *Journal of Public Policy* 1 (1981), 95–123.
48. Coleman, *Business and Politics,* 14. National relevance was defined as acting to represent an interest on a national basis, and/or in a province or group of provinces accounting for 35 percent of national production or employment in the sector, and/or in Quebec as paralleling a national organization.
49. Ibid., 31.
50. Ibid., 219.
51. For overviews, see Sidney Tarrow, "Social Movements in Contentious Politics: A Review Article," *American Political Science Review* 90 (December 1996), 874–883; Doug McAdam, John D. McCarthy, and Mayer N. Zald, eds., *Comparative Perspectives on Social Movements: Political Opportunities, Mobilizing Structures, and Cultural Framings* (Cambridge: Cambridge University Press, 1996).
52. Sidney Tarrow, *Struggle, Politics, and Reform: Collective Action, Social Movements, and Cycles of Protest* (Center for International Relations, Cornell University, Western Societies Program, Occasional Paper No. 21, 1989), 12.
53. Jack L. Walker, "The Origins and Maintenance of Interest Groups in America," *American Political Science Review* 77 (June 1983), 395.
54. Ibid., 403.
55. Alan C. Cairns and Cynthia Williams, "Constitutionalism, Citizenship, and Society in Canada: An Overview," in Alan Cairns and Cynthia Williams, eds., *Constitutionalism, Citizenship, and Society in Canada,* vol. 33 of the Research Studies of the Royal Commission on the Economic Union and Development Prospects for Canada (Toronto: University of Toronto Press, 1985), 13.
56. Andrew Cardozo, "Lion Taming: Downsizing the Opponents of Downsizing," in Gene Swimmer, ed., *How Ottawa Spends 1996–97: Life under the Knife* (Ottawa: Carleton University Press, 1996), 311.
57. John Bryden, *Special Interest Group Funding* (Ottawa: n.p., 1994).
58. Treasury Board Secretariat, Program Branch, "The Review of Interest Group Funding," (Ottawa: Treasury Board of Canada, 1994). For the research behind this document, see Peter Finkle, Kernaghan Webb, William T. Stanbury, and A. Paul Pross, *Federal Government Relations with Interest Groups: A Reconsideration* (Ottawa: Consumer and Corporate Affairs Canada, 1994).
59. Cardozo, "Lion Taming," 325.
60. Terrance Wills, "Tobacco Bill Passes," *The Gazette* [Montreal], April 17, 1997, A12.
61. Susan Riley, "Tobacco Issue Will Be a Test for Rock," *The Gazette* [Montreal], July 22, 1997, B3.
62. Jeff Heinrich, "Coalition on Track against Tobacco," *The Gazette* [Montreal], July 25, 1997, A5.

63. Mark Kennedy, "Tobacco 'Blackmail' Won't Work, Rock Vows," *Ottawa Citizen*, December 9, 1997, A4.
64. Anne McIlroy and Shawn McCarthy, "Ottawa, 5 Provinces Hit Smokers with Tax Hike," *Globe and Mail*, February 14, 1998.
65. John Sawatsky, *The Insiders: Government, Business, and the Lobbyists* (Toronto: McClelland & Stewart, 1987).
66. Lobbyists Registration Act, *Annual Report for the Year Ended March 31, 1992* (Ottawa, 1992), 5.
67. Lobbyists Registration Act, *Annual Report for Year Ended March 31, 1996* [on-line, World Wide Web; cited October 1, 1998]; available at http://strategis.ic.gc.ca.
68. Coleman, *Business and Politics*, 40–46.
69. G. Bruce Doern and Brian W. Tomlin, *Faith and Fear: The Free Trade Story* (Toronto: Stoddart, 1991), 219.
70. *Globe and Mail* [Toronto], October 28, 1993, A3.
71. The government eventually placed an order for virtually the same type of helicopter in late 1997, however.
72. Khayyam Z. Paltiel, *Political Party Financing in Canada* (Toronto: McGraw-Hill, 1970).
73. *Registered Political Parties' Fiscal Period Returns for 1996*, vol. 1 (Ottawa: Chief Electoral Officer of Canada).
74. Stanbury, *Business–Government Relations in Canada*, 482. For a similar but more recent treatment, see William T. Stanbury, *Money in Politics: Financing Federal Parties and Candidates in Canada* (Ottawa: Royal Commission on Electoral Reform and Party Financing, 1991).
75. Jeremy Wilson, "Green Lobbies: Pressure Groups and Environmental Policy," in Robert Boardman, ed., *Canadian Environmental Policy: Ecosystems, Politics, and Process* (Toronto: Oxford University Press, 1992), 110–111.
76. Ibid., 113.
77. For a debate on the nature of social movement of public-interest groups, see W.T. Stanbury, "A Sceptic's Guide to the Claims of So-Called Public Interest Groups," *Canadian Public Administration* 36 (Winter 1993), 580–605; and Susan Phillips, "Of Public Interest Groups and Sceptics: A Realist's Reply to Professor Stanbury," *Canadian Public Administration* 36 (Winter 1993), 606–616.
78. Bill Gates, *The Road Ahead* (New York: Viking, 1995), 271.
79. David Ronfeldt, "Cyberocracy is Coming," *The Information Society* 8 (1992), 276.
80. Ronald J. Deibert, "Altered Worlds: Social Forces in the Hypermedia Environment," in Cynthia J. Alexander and Leslie A. Pal, eds., *Digital Democracy: Policy and Politics in the Wired World* (Toronto: Oxford University Press, 1998), 21–45; W.T. Stanbury and Ilan B. Vertinsky, "Assessing the Impact of New Information Technologies on Interest Group Behaviour and Policymaking," in Thomas J. Courchene, ed., *Technology, Information and Public Policy*, the Bell Canada Papers on Economic and Public Policy (Kingston: John Deutsch Institute for the Study of Economic Policy, 1995), 293–379; W.T. Stanbury and Ilan B. Vertinsky, "Information Technologies and Transnational Interest Groups: The Challenge for Diplomacy," *Canadian Foreign Policy* 2 (Winter 1994), 87–99.
81. IGC started in 1982 with EcoNet, established by several foundations and a donation from Apple Computer. Peacenet was started in 1984 by another group of foundations, then PeaceNet and EcoNet joined in 1987 as part of IGC. APC was formed in 1990 to

coordinate a global network of activist networks. During the Gulf War, APC networks were a valuable "backchannel" to a nightly managed event. Earlier, during an attempted coup in the Soviet Union in 1990, Russian APC partners were able to circumvent the phone system, patch links through Moscow, Leningrad, and the Baltic states to NordNet Sweden, and then to the London-based GreenNet, which conveyed to the rest of APC. See Howard Rheingold, *The Virtual Community: Homesteading on the Electronic Frontier* (New York: Harper Perennial, 1993), 266; Rory O'Brien, "The APC Computer Networks: Global Networking for Change," *Canadian Journal of Information Science* 17 (July 1992), 16–24; Susanne Sallin, *The Association for Progressive Communications: A Cooperative Effort to Meet the Information Needs of Non-Governmental Organizations*, a case study prepared for the Harvard-CIESIN Project on Global Environmental Change Information Policy (Boston: Harvard University, 1994) [on-line, World Wide Web; cited March 5, 1998]; available at http://www.ciesin.org/kiosk/publications/94-0010.txt.

82. Peter J. Spiro, "New Global Communities: Nongovernmental Organizations in International Decision-Making Institutions," *Washington Quarterly* 18, no. 1 (1994), 47–48.
83. Howard Rheingold, *The Virtual Community*, 261.
84. Edward Schwartz, *NetActivism: How Citizens Use the Net* (Sebastopol, Calif.: Songline Studios, 1996), 177. Schwartz has been involved with Neighborhoods Online [on-line, World Wide Web; cited October 1, 1998]; available at http://libertynet.org/nol/natl.html.
85. W.T. Stanbury and Ilan B. Vertinsky, "Assessing the Impact of New Information Technologies on Interest Group Behaviour and Policymaking," in Thomas J. Courchene, ed., *Technology, Information and Public Policy*, the Bell Canada Papers on Economic and Public Policy (Kingston: John Deutsch Institute for the Study of Economic Policy, 1995), 293–237. This summary is drawn from section IV of their paper.
86. Pal found some evidence for this in his study of human rights organizations. An analysis of these groups on the Net shows a strong core of organizations surrounded by a periphery of smaller, highly focused, single-issue or "single-service" sites (e.g., statistical information) and the de facto creation of broad electronic coalitions through "super-sites" such as OneWorld Online [on-line, World Wide Web; cited March 5, 1998]; available at http://www.oneworld.org. See Leslie A. Pal, "Bits of Justice: Human Rights on the Internet," in Evan Potter, ed., *Cyber-Diplomacy* (Ottawa: Carleton University Press, forthcoming).
87. W.T. Stanbury and Ilan B. Vertinsky, "Assessing the Impact of New Information Technologies on Interest Group Behaviour and Policymaking," in Thomas J. Courchene, ed., *Technology, Information and Public Policy*, the Bell Canada Papers on Economic and Public Policy (Kingston: John Deutsch Institute for the Study of Economic Policy, 1995), 328.
88. Manuel Castells, *The Power of Identity* (Oxford: Blackwell Publishers, 1997), 352.
89. Reginald W. Bibby, *Mosaic Madness: The Poverty and Potential of Life in Canada* (Don Mills, Ont.: Stoddart, 1990). For an American perspective, see Jonathan Rauch, *Demosclerosis: The Silent Killer of American Government* (New York: Times Books, 1994).
90. For essays on the larger themes implied by these developments, see Charles S. Maier, ed., *Changing Boundaries of the Political: Essays on the Evolving Balance between the State and Society, Public and Private in Europe* (Cambridge: Cambridge University Press, 1987).
91. Treasury Board Secretariat, *The Federal Government as 'Partner': Six Steps to Successful Collaboration* (Ottawa, 1995) [on-line, World Wide Web; cited October 1, 1998]; available at http://www.tbs-sct.gc.ca/pubs%5Fpol/opepubs/tb%5Fo3/fgpe%5Fe.html.

92. Robert Putnam, *Making Democracy Work: Civic Traditions in Modern Italy* (Princeton: Princeton University Press, 1993); also see Robert Putnam, "Bowling Alone," *Journal of Democracy* 6 (January 1995), 65–78 [on-line, World Wide Web; cited October 1, 1998]; available at http://muse.jhu.edu/demo/journal_of_democracy/v006/putnam.html.

93. Janice Gross Stein, David R. Cameron, and Richard Simeon, with Alan Alexandroff, *Citizen Engagement in Conflict Resolution: Lessons for Canada in International Experience* (Toronto: C.D. Howe Institute, 1997), 10 [on-line, World Wide Web; cited October 1, 1998]; available at http://www.cdhowe.org/eng/pub/frame.html.

APPENDIX

The Constitution Acts 1867 to 1982

THE CONSTITUTION ACT, 1867

30 & 31 Victoria, c. 3. (U.K.)
(Consolidated with amendments)

An Act for the Union of Canada, Nova Scotia, and New Brunswick, and the Government thereof; and for Purposes connected therewith

(29th March 1867.)

WHEREAS the Provinces of Canada, Nova Scotia, and New Brunswick have expressed their Desire to be federally united into One Dominion under the Crown of the United Kingdom of Great Britain and Ireland, with a Constitution similar in Principle to that of the United Kingdom:

And whereas such a Union would conduce to the Welfare of the Provinces and promote the Interests of the British Empire:

And whereas on the Establishment of the Union by Authority of Parliament it is expedient, not only that the Constitution of the Legislative Authority in the Dominion be provided for, but also that the Nature of the Executive Government therein be declared:

And whereas it is expedient that Provision be made for the eventual Admission into the Union of other Parts of British North America:[1]

---

(1) The enacting clause was repealed by the *Statute Law Revision Act, 1893*, 56-57 Vict., c. 14 (U.K.). It read as follows:

Be it therefore enacted and declared by the Queen's most Excellent Majesty, by and with the Advice and Consent of the Lords Spiritual and Temporal, and Commons, in this present Parliament assembled, and by the Authority of the same, as follows:

I. PRELIMINARY

Short title

1. This Act may be cited as the *Constitution Act, 1867*.[2]

2. Repealed[3]

II. UNION

Declaration of Union

3. It shall be lawful for the Queen, by and with the Advice of Her Majesty's Most Honourable Privy Council, to declare by Proclamation that, on and after a Day therein appointed, not being more than Six Months after the passing of this Act, the Provinces of Canada, Nova Scotia, and New Brunswick shall form and be One Dominion under the Name of Canada; and on and after that Day those Three Provinces shall form and be One Dominion under that Name accordingly.[4]

Construction of subsequent Provisions of Act

4. Unless it is otherwise expressed or implied, the Name Canada shall be taken to mean Canada as constituted under this Act.[5]

Four Provinces

5. Canada shall be divided into Four Provinces, named Ontario, Quebec, Nova Scotia, and New Brunswick.[6]

---

(2) As enacted by the *Constitution Act, 1982*, which came into force on April 17, 1982. The section, as originally enacted, read as follows:

> **1.** This Act may be cited as The British North America Act, 1867.

(3) Section 2, repealed by the *Statute Law Revision Act, 1893*, 56-57 Vict., c. 14 (U.K.), read as follows:

> **2.** The Provisions of this Act referring to Her Majesty the Queen extend also to the Heirs and Successors of Her Majesty, Kings and Queens of the United Kingdom of Great Britain and Ireland.

(4) The first day of July, 1867, was fixed by proclamation dated May 22, 1867.

(5) Partially repealed by the *Statute Law Revision Act, 1893*, 56-57 Vict., c. 14 (U.K.). As originally enacted the section read as follows:

> **4.** The subsequent Provisions of this Act shall, unless it is otherwise expressed or implied, commence and have effect on and after the Union, that is to say, on and after the Day appointed for the Union taking effect in the Queen's Proclamation; and in the same Provisions, unless it is otherwise expressed or implied, the Name Canada shall be taken to mean Canada as constituted under this Act.

(6) Canada now consists of ten provinces (Ontario, Quebec, Nova Scotia, New Brunswick, Manitoba, British Columbia, Prince Edward Island, Alberta, Saskatchewan and Newfoundland) and two territories (the Yukon Territory and the Northwest Territories).

The first territories added to the Union were Rupert's Land and the North-Western Territory, (subsequently designated the Northwest Territories), which were admitted pursuant to section 146 of the *Constitution Act, 1867* and the *Rupert's Land Act, 1868*, 31-32 Vict., c. 105 (U.K.), by the *Rupert's Land and North-Western Territory Order* of June 23, 1870, effective July 15, 1870. Prior to the admission of those territories the Parliament of Canada enacted *An Act for the temporary Government of Rupert's Land and the North-Western Territory when united with Canada* (32-33 Vict., c. 3), and the *Manitoba Act, 1870*, (33 Vict., c.3), which provided for the formation of the Province of Manitoba.

British Columbia was admitted into the Union pursuant to section 146 of the *Constitution Act, 1867*, by the *British Columbia Terms of Union*, being Order in Council of May 16, 1871, effective July 20, 1871.

Prince Edward Island was admitted pursuant to section 146 of the *Constitution Act, 1867*, by the *Prince Edward Island Terms of Union*, being Order in Council of June 26, 1873, effective July 1, 1873.

On June 29, 1871, the United Kingdom Parliament enacted the *Constitution Act, 1871* (34-35 Vict., c. 28) authorizing the creation of additional provinces out of territories not included in any province. Pursuant to this statute, the Parliament of Canada enacted the *Alberta Act*, (July 20, 1905, 4-5 Edw. VII c. 3) and the *Saskatchewan Act*, (July 20, 1905, 4-5 Edw. VII, c. 42), providing for the creation of the provinces of Alberta and Saskatchewan, respectively. Both these Acts came into force on Sept. 1, 1905.

6. The Parts of the Province of Canada (as it exists at the passing of this Act) which formerly constituted respectively the Provinces of Upper Canada and Lower Canada shall be deemed to be severed, and shall form Two separate Provinces. The Part which formerly constituted the Province of Upper Canada shall constitute the Province of Ontario; and the Part which formerly constituted the Province of Lower Canada shall constitute the Province of Quebec.

Provinces of Ontario and Quebec

7. The Provinces of Nova Scotia and New Brunswick shall have the same Limits as at the passing of this Act.

Provinces of Nova Scotia and New Brunswick

8. In the general Census of the Population of Canada which is hereby required to be taken in the Year One thousand eight hundred and seventy-one, and in every Tenth Year thereafter, the respective Populations of the Four Provinces shall be distinguished.

Decennial Census

III. EXECUTIVE POWER

9. The Executive Government and Authority of and over Canada is hereby declared to continue and be vested in the Queen.

Declaration of Executive Power in the Queen

10. The Provisions of this Act referring to the Governor General extend and apply to the Governor General for the Time being of Canada, or other the Chief Executive Officer or Administrator for the Time being carrying on the Government of Canada on behalf and in the Name of the Queen, by whatever Title he is designated.

Application of Provisions referring to Governor General

11. There shall be a Council to aid and advise in the Government of Canada, to be styled the Queen's Privy Council for Canada; and the Persons who are to be Members of that Council shall be from Time to Time chosen and summoned by the Governor General and sworn in as Privy Councillors, and Members thereof may be from Time to Time removed by the Governor General.

Constitution of Privy Council for Canada

Meanwhile, all remaining British possessions and territories in North America and the islands adjacent thereto, except the colony of Newfoundland and its dependencies, were admitted into the Canadian Confederation by the *Adjacent Territories Order*, dated July 31, 1880.

The Parliament of Canada added portions of the Northwest Territories to the adjoining provinces in 1912 by *The Ontario Boundaries Extension Act*, S.C. 1912, 2 Geo. V, c. 40. *The Quebec Boundaries Extension Act*, 1912, 2 Geo V, c. 45 and *The Manitoba Boundaries Extension Act, 1912*, 2 Geo. V, c. 32, and further additions were made to Manitoba by *The Manitoba Boundaries Extension Act, 1930*, 20-21 Geo. V, c. 28.

The Yukon Territory was created out of the Northwest Territories in 1898 by *The Yukon Territory Act*, 61 Vict., c. 6, (Canada).

Newfoundland was added on March 31, 1949, by the *Newfoundland Act*, (U.K.), 12-13 Geo. VI, c. 22, which ratified the Terms of Union of Newfoundland with Canada.

All Powers under Acts to be exercised by Governor General with Advice of Privy Council, or alone

12. All Powers, Authorities, and Functions which under any Act of the Parliament of Great Britain, or of the Parliament of the United Kingdom of Great Britain and Ireland, or of the Legislature of Upper Canada, Lower Canada, Canada, Nova Scotia, or New Brunswick, are at the Union vested in or exerciseable by the respective Governors or Lieutenant Governors of those Provinces, with the Advice, or with the Advice and Consent, of the respective Executive Councils thereof, or in conjunction with those Councils, or with any Number of Members thereof, or by those Governors or Lieutenant Governors individually, shall, as far as the same continue in existence and capable of being exercised after the Union in relation to the Government of Canada, be vested in and exerciseable by the Governor General, with the Advice or the Advice and Consent of or in conjunction with the Queen's Privy Council for Canada, or any Members thereof, or by the Governor General individually, as the Case requires, subject nevertheless (except with respect to such as exist under Acts of the Parliament of Great Britain or the Parliament of the United Kingdom of Great Britain and Ireland) to be abolished or altered by the Parliament of Canada.[7]

Application of Provisions referring to Governor General in Council

13. The Provisions of this Act referring to the Governor General in Council shall be construed as referring to the Governor General acting by and with the Advice of the Queen's Privy Council for Canada.

Power to Her Majesty to authorize Governor General to appoint Deputies

14. It shall be lawful for the Queen, if Her Majesty thinks fit, to authorize the Governor General from Time to Time to appoint any Person or any Persons jointly or severally to be his Deputy or Deputies within any Part or Parts of Canada, and in that Capacity to exercise during the Pleasure of the Governor General such of the Powers, Authorities, and Functions of the Governor General as the Governor General deems it necessary or expedient to assign to him or them, subject to any Limitations or Directions expressed or given by the Queen; but the Appointment of such a Deputy or Deputies shall not affect the Exercise by the Governor General himself of any Power, Authority, or Function.

Command of Armed Forces to continue to be vested in the Queen

15. The Command-in-Chief of the Land and Naval Militia, and of all Naval and Military Forces, of and in Canada, is hereby declared to continue and be vested in the Queen.

Seat of Government of Canada

16. Until the Queen otherwise directs, the Seat of Government of Canada shall be Ottawa.

(7) See the note to section 129, *infra.*

IV. LEGISLATIVE POWER

17. There shall be One Parliament for Canada, consisting of the Queen, an Upper House styled the Senate, and the House of Commons.

Constitution of Parliament of Canada

18. The privileges, immunities, and powers to be held, enjoyed, and exercised by the Senate and by the House of Commons, and by the members thereof respectively, shall be such as are from time to time defined by Act of the Parliament of Canada, but so that any Act of the Parliament of Canada defining such privileges, immunities, and powers shall not confer any privileges, immunities, or powers exceeding those at the passing of such Act held, enjoyed, and exercised by the Commons House of Parliament of the United Kingdom of Great Britain and Ireland, and by the members thereof.[8]

Privileges, etc., of Houses

19. The Parliament of Canada shall be called together not later than Six Months after the Union.[9]

First Session of the Parliament of Canada

20. Repealed.[10]

The Senate

21. The Senate shall, subject to the Provisions of this Act, consist of One Hundred and four Members, who shall be styled Senators.[11]

Number of Senators

22. In relation to the Constitution of the Senate Canada shall be deemed to consist of *Four* Divisions: ——

Representation of Provinces in Senate

---

(8) Repealed and re-enacted by the *Parliament of Canada Act*, 1875, 38-39 Vict., c. 38 (U.K.). The original section read as follows:

> **18.** The Privileges, Immunities, and Powers to be held, enjoyed, and exercised by the Senate and by the House of Commons and by the Members thereof respectively shall be such as are from Time to Time defined by Act of the Parliament of Canada, but so that the same shall never exceed those at the passing of this Act held, enjoyed, and exercised by the Commons House of Parliament of the United Kingdom of Great Britain and Ireland and by the Members thereof.

(9) Spent. The first session of the first Parliament began on November 6, 1867.

(10) Section 20, repealed by the *Constitution Act, 1982*, read as follows:

> **20.** There shall be a Session of the Parliament of Canada once at least in every Year, so that Twelve Months shall not intervene between the last Sitting of the Parliament in one Session and its first sitting in the next Session.

Section 20 has been replaced by section 5 of the *Constitution Act, 1982*, which provides that there shall be a sitting of Parliament at least once every twelve months.

(11) As amended by the *Constitution Act, 1915*, 5-6 Geo. V, c. 45 (U.K.) and modified by the *Newfoundland Act*, 12-13 Geo. VI, c. 22 (U.K.), and the *Constitution Act (No. 2), 1975*, S.C. 1974-75-76, c. 53.

1. Ontario;

2. Quebec;

3. The Maritime Provinces, Nova Scotia and New Brunswick, and Prince Edward Island;

4. The Western Provinces of Manitoba, British Columbia, Saskatchewan, and Alberta;

which Four Divisions shall (subject to the Provisions of this Act) be equally represented in the Senate as follows: Ontario by twenty-four senators; Quebec by twenty-four senators; the Maritime Provinces and Prince Edward Island by twenty-four senators, ten thereof representing Nova Scotia, ten thereof representing New Brunswick, and four thereof representing Prince Edward Island; the Western Provinces by twenty four senators, six thereof representing Manitoba, six thereof representing British Columbia, six thereof representing Saskatchewan, and six thereof representing Alberta; Newfoundland shall be entitled to be represented in the Senate by six members; the Yukon Territory and the Northwest Territories shall be entitled to be represented in the Senate by one member each.

In the Case of Quebec each of the Twenty-four Senators representing that Province shall be appointed for One of the Twenty-four Electoral Divisions of Lower Canada specified in Schedule A. to Chapter One of the Consolidated Statutes of Canada. [12]

The original section read as follows:

> **21.** The Senate shall, subject to the Provisions of this Act, consist of Seventy-two Members, who shall be styled Senators.

The *Manitoba Act, 1870,* added two for Manitoba; the *British Columbia Terms of Union* added three; upon admission of Prince Edward Island four more were provided by section 147 of the *Constitution Act, 1867*; the *Alberta Act* and the *Saskatchewan Act* each added four. The Senate was reconstituted at 96 by the *Constitution Act, 1915.* Six more Senators were added upon union with Newfoundland, and one Senator each was added for the Yukon Territory and the Northwest Territories by the *Constitution Act (No. 2), 1975.*

(12) As Amended by the *Constitution Act, 1915,* 5-6 Geo. V, c. 45 (U.K.), the *Newfoundland Act,* 12-13 Geo. VI, c. 22 (U.K.), and the *Constitution Act (No. 2),* 1975, S.C. 1974-75-76, c. 53. The original section read as follows:

> **22.** In relation to the Constitution of the Senate, Canada shall be deemed to consist of Three Divisions:
>
> 1. Ontario;
>
> 2. Quebec;
>
> 3. The Maritime Provinces, Nova Soctia and New Brunswick;

23. The Qualifications of a Senator shall be as follows:

Qualifications of Senator

(1) He shall be of the full age of Thirty Years:

(2) He shall be either a natural-born Subject of the Queen, or a Subject of the Queen naturalized by an Act of the Parliament of Great Britain, or of the Parliament of the United Kingdom of Great Britain and Ireland, or of the Legislature of One of the Provinces of Upper Canada, Lower Canada, Canada, Nova Scotia, or New Brunswick, before the Union, or of the Parliament of Canada after the Union:

(3) He shall be legally or equitably seised as of Freehold for his own Use and Benefit of Lands or Tenements held in Free and Common Socage, or seised or possessed for his own Use and Benefit of Lands or Tenements held in Franc-alleu or in Roture, within the Province for which he is appointed, of the Value of Four thousand Dollars, over and above all Rents, Dues, Debts, Charges, Mortgages, and Incumbrances due or payable out of or charged on or affecting the same:

(4) His Real and Personal Property shall be together worth Four thousand Dollars over and above his Debts and Liabilities:

(5) He shall be resident in the Province for which he is appointed:

(6) In the case of Quebec he shall have his Real Property Qualification in the Electoral Division for which he is appointed, or shall be resident in that Division.13

24. The Governor General shall from Time to Time, in the Queen's Name, by Instrument under the Great Seal of Canada, summon qualified Persons to the Senate; and, subject to the Provisions of this Act, every person so summoned shall become and be a Member of the Senate and a Senator.

Summons of Senator

---

which Three Divisions shall (subject to the Provisions of this Act) be equally represented in the Senate as follows: Ontario by Twenty-four Senators; Quebec by Twenty-four Senators; and the Maritime Provinces by Twenty-four Senators, Twelve thereof representing Nova Scotia, and Twelve thereof representing New Brunswick.

In the case of Quebec each of the Twenty-four Senators representing that Province shall be appointed for One of the Twenty-four Electoral Divisions of Lower Canada specified in Schedule A. to Chapter One of the Consolidated Statutes of Canada.

(13) Section 2 of the *Constitution Act (No. 2), 1975*, S.C. 1974-75-76, c. 53 provided that for the purposes of that Act (which added one Senator each for the Yukon Territory and the Northwest Territories) the term "Province" in section 23 of the *Constitution Act, 1867*, has the same meaning as is assigned to the term "province" by section 35 of the *Interpretation Act*, R.S.C. 1985, c. I-21, which provides that the term "province" means "a province of Canada, and includes the Yukon Territory and the Northwest Territories."

25. Repealed. [14]

Addition of Senators in certain cases

26. If at any Time on the Recommendation of the Governor General the Queen thinks fit to direct that Four or Eight Members be added to the Senate, the Governor General may by Summons to Four or Eight qualified Persons (as the Case may be), representing equally the Four Divisions of Canada, add to the Senate accordingly.[15]

Reduction of Senate to normal Number

27. In case of such Addition being at any Time made, the Governor General shall not summon any Person to the Senate, except on a further like Direction by the Queen on the like Recommendation, to represent one of the Four Divisions until such Division is represented by Twenty-Four Senators and no more.[16]

Maximum Number of Senators

28. The Number of Senators shall not at any Time exceed One Hundred and twelve.[17]

Tenure of Place in Senate

29. (1) Subject to subsection (2), a Senator shall, subject to the provisions of this Act, hold his place in the Senate for life.

Retirement upon attaining age of seventy-five years

(2) A Senator who is summoned to the Senate after the coming into force of this subsection shall, subject to this Act, hold his place in the Senate until he attains the age of seventy-five years.[18]

---

(14) Repealed by the *Statute Law Revision Act, 1893,* 56-57 Vict., c. 14 (U.K.). The section read as follows:

> **25.** Such persons shall be first summoned to the Senate as the Queen by Warrant under Her Majesty's Royal Sign Manual thinks fits to approve, and their Names shall be inserted in the Queen's Proclamation of Union.

(15) As amended by the *Constitution Act, 1915,* 5-6 Geo. V, c. 45 (U.K.). The original section read as follows:

> **26.** If at any time on the Recommendation of the Governor General the Queen thinks fit to direct that Three or Six Members be added to the Senate, the Governor General may by Summons to Three or Six qualified Persons (as the Case may be), representing equally the Three Divisions of Canada, add to the Senate accordingly.

(16) As amended by the *Constitution Act, 1915,* 5-6 Geo. V, c. 45 (U.K.). The original section read as follows:

> **27.** In case of such Addition being at any Time made the Governor General shall not summon any Person to the Senate except on a further like Direction by the Queen on the like Recommendation, until each of the Three Divisions of Canada is represented by Twenty-four Senators and no more.

(17) As amended by the *Constitution Act, 1915,* 5-6 Geo. V, c. 45 (U.K.), and the *Constitution Act (No. 2), 1975,* S.C. 1974-75-76, c. 53. The original section read as follows:

> **28.** The Number of Senators shall not at any Time exceed Seventy-eight.

(18) As enacted by the *Constitution Act, 1965,* S.C., 1965, c. 4, which came into force on June 1, 1965. The original section read as follows:

> **29.** A Senator shall , subject to the Provisions of this Act, hold his Place in the Senate for Life.

30. A Senator may by Writing under his Hand addressed to the Governor General resign his Place in the Senate, and thereupon the same shall be vacant.

Resignation of Place in Senate

31. The Place of a Senator shall become vacant in any of the following Cases:

Disqualification of Senators

(1) If for Two consecutive Sessions of the Parliament he fails to give his Attendance in the Senate:

(2) If he takes an Oath or makes a Declaration or Acknowledgment of Allegiance, Obedience, or Adherence to a Foreign Power, or does an Act whereby he becomes a Subject or Citizen, or entitled to the Rights or Privileges of a Subject or Citizen, of a Foreign Power:

(3) If he is adjudged Bankrupt or Insolvent, or applies for the Benefit of any Law relating to Insolvent Debtors, or becomes a public Defaulter:

(4) If he is attainted of Treason or convicted of Felony or of any infamous Crime:

(5) If he ceases to be qualified in respect of Property or of Residence; provided, that a Senator shall not be deemed to have ceased to be qualified in respect of Residence by reason only of his residing at the Seat of the Government of Canada while holding an Office under that Government requiring his Presence there.

32. When a Vacancy happens in the Senate by Resignation, Death, or otherwise, the Governor General shall by Summons to a fit and qualified Person fill the Vacancy.

Summons on Vacancy in Senate

33. If any Question arises respecting the Qualification of a Senator or a Vacancy in the Senate the same shall be heard and determined by the Senate.

Questions as to Qualifications and Vacancies in Senate

34. The Governor General may from Time to Time, by Instrument under the Great Seal of Canada, appoint a Senator to be Speaker of the Senate, and may remove him and appoint another in his Stead.[19]

Appointment of Speaker of Senate

(19) Provision for exercising the functions of Speaker during his absence is made by Part II of the *Parliament of Canada Act*, R.S.C. 1985, c. P-1 (formerly the *Speaker of the Senate Act*, R.S.C. 1970, c. S-14). Doubts as to the power of Parliament to enact the *Speaker of the Senate Act* were removed by the *Canadian Speaker (Appointment of Deputy) Act, 1895*, 2nd Sess., 59 Vict., c. 3 (U.K.), which was repealed by the *Constitution Act, 1982*.

Quorum of Senate

35. Until the Parliament of Canada otherwise provides, the Presence of at least Fifteen Senators, including the Speaker, shall be necessary to constitute a Meeting of the Senate for the Exercise of its Powers.

Voting in Senate

36. Questions arising in the Senate shall be decided by a Majority of Voices, and the Speaker shall in all Cases have a Vote, and when the Voices are equal the Decision shall be deemed to be in the Negative.

The House of Commons

Constitution of House of Commons in Canada

37. The House of Commons shall, subject to the Provisions of this Act, consist of two hundred and ninety-five members of whom ninety-nine shall be elected for Ontario, seventy-five for Quebec, eleven for Nova Scotia, ten for New Brunswick, fourteen for Manitoba, thirty-two for British Columbia, four for Prince Edward Island, twenty-six for Alberta, fourteen for Saskatchewan, seven for Newfoundland, one for the Yukon Territory and two for the Northwest Territories.[20]

Summoning of House of Commons

38. The Governor General shall from Time to Time, in the Queen's Name, by Instrument under the Great Seal of Canada, summon and call together the House of Commons.

Senators not to sit in House of Commons

39. A Senator shall not be capable of being elected or of sitting or voting as a Member of the House of Commons.

Electoral districts of the four Provinces

40. Until the Parliament of Canada otherwise provides, Ontario, Quebec, Nova Scotia, and New Brunswick shall, for the Purposes of the Election of Members to serve in the House of Commons, be divided into Electoral districts as follows:

1. — ONTARIO

Ontario shall be divided into the Counties, Ridings of Counties, Cities, Parts of Cities, and Towns enumerated in the First Schedule to this Act, each whereof shall be an Electoral District, each such District as numbered in that Schedule being entitled to return One Member.

---

(20) The figures given here result from the application of Section 51, as enacted by the *Constitution Act, 1985 (Representation)*, S. C., 1986, c. 8, Part 1, and readjusted pursuant to the *Electoral Boundaries Readjustment Act*, R.S.C., 1985, c. E-3. The original section (which was altered from time to time as the result of the addition of new provinces and changes in population) read as follows:

> **37.** The House of Commons shall, subject to the Provisions of this Act, consist of one hundred and eighty-one members, of whom Eighty-two shall be elected for Ontario, Sixty-five for Quebec, Nineteen for Nova Scotia, and Fifteen for New Brunswick.

2. — QUEBEC

Quebec shall be divided into Sixty-five Electoral Districts, composed of the Sixty-five Electoral Divisions into which Lower Canada is at the passing of this Act divided under Chapter Two of the Consolidated Statutes of Canada, Chapter Seventy-five of the Consolidated Statutes for Lower Canada, and the Act of the Province of Canada of the Twenty-third Year of the Queen, Chapter One, or any other Act amending the same in force at the Union, so that each such Electoral Division shall be for the Purposes of this Act an Electoral District entitled to return One Member.

3. — NOVA SCOTIA

Each of the Eighteen Counties of Nova Scotia shall be an Electoral District. The County of Halifax shall be entitled to return Two Members, and each of the other Counties One Member.

4. — NEW BRUNSWICK

Each of the Fourteen Counties into which New Brunswick is divided, including the City and County of St. John, shall be an Electoral District. The City of St. John shall also be a separate Electoral District. Each of those Fifteen Electoral Districts shall be entitled to return One Member.[21]

Continuance of existing Election Laws until Parliament of Canada otherwise provides

41. Until the Parliament of Canada otherwise provides, all Laws in force in the several Provinces at the Union relative to the following Matters or any of them, namely, — the Qualifications and Disqualifications of Persons to be elected or to sit or vote as Members of the House of Assembly or Legislative Assembly in the several Provinces, the Voters at Elections of such Members, the Oaths to be taken by Voters, the Returning Officers, their Powers and Duties, the Proceedings at Elections, the Periods during which Elections may be continued, the Trial of controverted Elections, and Proceedings incident thereto, the vacating of Seats of Members, and the Execution of new Writs in case of Seats vacated otherwise than by Dissolution, — shall respectively apply to Elections of Members to serve in the House of Commons for the same several Provinces.

(21) Spent. The electoral districts are now established by Proclamations issued from time to time under the *Electoral Boundaries Readjustment Act*, R.S.C. 1985, c. E-3, as amended for particular districts by Acts of Parliament, for which see the most recent Table of Public Statutes.

Provided that, until the Parliament of Canada otherwise provides, at any Election for a Member of the House of Commons for the District of Algoma, in addition to Persons qualified by the Law of the Province of Canada to vote, every Male British Subject, aged Twenty-one Years or upwards, being a Householder, shall have a Vote.[22]

42. Repealed.[23]

43. Repealed.[24]

As to Election of Speaker of House of Commons

44. The House of Commons on its first assembling after a General Election shall proceed with all practicable Speed to elect One of its Members to be Speaker.

As to filling up Vacancy in Office of Speaker

45. In case of a Vacancy happening in the Office of Speaker by Death, Resignation, or otherwise, the House of Commons shall with all practicable Speed proceed to elect another of its Members to be Speaker.

Speaker to preside

46. The Speaker shall preside at all Meetings of the House of Commons.

Provision in case of Absence of Speaker

47. Until the Parliament of Canada otherwise provides, in case of the Absence for any Reason of the Speaker from the Chair of the House of Commons for a Period of Forty-eight consecutive Hours, the House may elect another of its Members to act as Speaker, and the Member so elected shall during the Continuance of such Absence of the Speaker have and execute all the Powers, Privileges, and Duties of Speaker.[25]

---

(22) Spent. Elections are now provided for by the *Canada Elections Act,* R.S.C. 1985, c. E-2; controverted elections by the *Dominion Controverted Elections Act,* R.S.C. 1985, c. C-39; qualifications and disqualifications of members by the *Parliament of Canada Act,* R.S.C. 1985, c. P-1. The right of citizens to vote and hold office is provided for in section 3 of the *Constitution Act, 1982.*

(23) Repealed by the *Statute Law Revision Act, 1893,* 56-57 Vict., c. 14 (U.K.). The section read as follows:

> **42.** For the First Election of Members to serve in the House of Commons the Governor General shall cause Writs to be issued by such Person, in such Form, and addressed to such Returning Officers as he thinks fit.
>
> The Person issuing Writs under this Section shall have the like Powers as are possessed at the Union by the Officers charged with the issuing of Writs for the Election of Members to serve in the respective House of Assembly or Legislative Assembly of the Province of Canada, Nova Scotia, or New Brunswick; and the Returning Officers to whom Writs are directed under this Section shall have the like Powers as are possessed at the Union by the Officers charged with the returning of Writs for the Election of Members to serve in the same respective House of Assembly or Legislative Assembly.

(24) Repealed by the *Statute Law Revision Act, 1893,* 56-57 Vict. c. 14 (U.K..). The section read as follows:

> **43.** In case a Vacancy in the Representation in the House of Commons of any Electoral District happens before the Meeting of the Parliament, or after the Meeting of the Parliament before Provision is made by the Parliament in this Behalf, the Provisions of the last foregoing Section of this Act shall extend and apply to the issuing and returning of a Writ in respect of such Vacant District.

(25) Provision for exercising the functions of Speaker during his absence is now made by Part III of the *Parliament of Canada Act,* R.S.C. 1985, c. P-1.

48. The Presence of at least Twenty Members of the House of Commons shall be necessary to constitute a Meeting of the House for the Exercise of its Powers, and for that Purpose the Speaker shall be reckoned as a Member.

Quorum of House of Commons

49. Questions arising in the House of Commons shall be decided by a Majority of Voices other than that of the Speaker, and when the Voices are equal, but not otherwise, the Speaker shall have a Vote.

Voting in House of Commons

50. Every House of Commons shall continue for Five Years from the Day of the Return of the Writs for choosing the House (subject to be sooner dissolved by the Governor General), and no longer.[26]

Duration of House of Commons

51. (1) The number of members of the House of Commons and the representation of the provinces therein shall, on the coming into force of this subsection and thereafter on the completion of each decennial census, be readjusted by such authority, in such manner, and from such time as the Parliament of Canada from time to time provides, subject and according to the following rules:

Readjustment of representation in Commons

Rules

1. There shall be assigned to each of the provinces a number of members equal to the number obtained by dividing the total population of the provinces by two hundred and seventy-nine and by dividing the population of each province by the quotient so obtained, counting any remainder in excess of 0.50 as one after the said process of division.

2. If the total number of members that would be assigned to a province by the application of rule 1 is less than the total number assigned to that province on the date of coming into force of this subsection, there shall be added to the number of members so assigned such number of members as will result in the province having the same number of members as were assigned on that date.[27]

(26) The term of the twelfth Parliament was extended by the *British North America Act, 1916,* 6-7 Geo. V. c. 19 (U.K.), which Act was repealed by the *Statute Law Revision Act, 1927,* 17-18 Geo. V. c. 42 (U.K.). See also subsection 4(1) of the *Constitution Act, 1982,* which provides that no House of Commons shall continue for longer than five years from the date fixed for the return of the writs at a general election of its members, and subsection 4(2) thereof, which provides for continuation of the House of Commons in special circumstances.

(27) As enacted by the *Constitution Act, 1985 (Representation),* S.C. 1986, c. 8, Part I, which came into force on March 6, 1986 (See SI/86-49). The section, as originally enacted, read as follows:

51. On the Completion of the Census in the Year One Thousand eight hundred and seventy-one, and of each subsequent decennial Census, the Representation of the Four Provinces shall be readjusted by such Authority, in such Manner, and from such Time, as the Parliament of Canada from Time to Time provides, subject and according to the following Rules:

(1) Quebec shall have the fixed Number of Sixty-five Members:

(2) There shall be assigned to each of the other Provinces such a Number of Members as will bear the same Proportion to the Number of its Population (ascertained at such Census) as the Number Sixty-five bears to the Number of the Population of Quebec (so ascertained):

(3) In the Computation of the Number of Members for a Province a fractional Part not exceeding One Half of the whole Number requisite for entitling the Province to a Member shall be disregarded; but a fractional Part exceeding One Half of that Number shall be equivalent to the whole Number:

(4) On any such Re-adjustment the Number of Members for a Province shall not be reduced unless the Proportion which the Number of the Population of the Province bore to the Number of the aggregate Population of Canada at the then last preceding Re-adjustment of the Number of Members for the Province is ascertained at the then latest Census to be diminished by One Twentieth Part or upwards:

(5) Such Re-adjustment shall not take effect until the Termination of the then existing Parliament.

The section was amended by the *Statute Law Revision Act, 1893,* 56-57 Vict., c. 14 (U.K.) by repealing the words from "of the census" to "seventy-one and" and the word "subsequent".

By the *British North America Act, 1943,* 6-7 Geo. VI., c. 30 (U.K.), which Act was repealed by the *Constitution Act, 1982,* redistribution of seats following the 1941 census was postponed until the first session of Parliament after the war. The section was re-enacted by the *British North America Act, 1946,* 9-10 Geo. VI., c. 63 (U.K.), which Act was also repealed by the *Constitution Act, 1982,* to read as follows:

51. (1) The number of members of the House of Commons shall be two hundred and fifty-five and the representation of the provinces therein shall forthwith upon the coming into force of this section and thereafter on the completion of each decennial census be readjusted by such authority, in such manner, and from such time as the Parliament of Canada from time to time provides, subject and according to the following rules:

(1) Subject as hereinafter provided, there shall be assigned to each of the provinces a number of members computed by dividing the total population of the provinces by two hundred and fifty-four and by dividing the population of each province by the quotient so obtained, disregarding, except as hereinafter in this section provided, the remainder, if any, after the said process of division.

(2) If the total number of members assigned to all the provinces pursuant to rule one is less than two hundred and fifty-four, additional members shall be assigned to the provinces (one to a province) having remainders in the computation under rule one commencing with the province having the largest remainder and continuing with the other provinces in the order of the magnitude of their respective remainders until the total number of members assigned is two hundred and fifty-four.

(3) Notwithstanding anything in this section, if upon completion of a computation under rules one and two, the number of members to be assigned to a province is less than the number of senators representing the said province, rules one and two shall cease to apply in respect of the said province, and there shall be assigned to the said province a number of members equal to the said number of senators.

(4) In the event that rules one and two cease to apply in respect of a province then, for the purpose of computing the number of members to be assigned to the provinces in respect of which rules one and two continue to apply, the total population of the provinces shall be reduced by the number of the population of the province in respect of which rules one and two have ceased to apply and the number two hundred and fifty-four shall be reduced by the number of members assigned to such province pursuant to rule three.

(5) Such readjustment shall not take effect until the termination of the then existing Parliament.

(2) The Yukon Territory as constituted by Chapter forty-one of the Statutes of Canada, 1901, together with any Part of Canada not comprised within a province which may from time to time be included therein by the Parliament of Canada for the purposes of representation in Parliament, shall be entitled to one member.

The section was re-enacted by the *British North America Act, 1952,* S.C. 1952, c. 15, which Act was also repealed by the *Constitution Act, 1982,* as follows:

51. (1) Subject as hereinafter provided, the number of members of the House of Commons shall be two hundred and sixty-three and the representation of the provinces therein shall forthwith upon the coming into force of this section and thereafter on the completion of each decennial census be readjusted by such authority, in such manner, and from such time as the Parliament of Canada from time to time provides, subject and according to the following rules:

1. There shall be assigned to each of the provinces a number of members computed by dividing the total population of the provinces by two hundred and sixty-one and by dividing the population of each province by the quotient so obtained, disregarding, except as hereinafter in this section provided, the remainder, if any, after the said process of division.

2. If the total number of members assigned to all the provinces pursuant to rule one is less than two hundred and sixty-one, additional members shall be assigned to the provinces (one to a province) having remainders in the computation under rule one commencing with the province having the largest remainder and continuing with the other provinces in the order of the magnitude of their respective remainders until the total number of members assigned is two hundred and sixty-one.

3. Notwithstanding anything in this section, if upon completion of a computation under rules one and two the number of members to be assigned to a province is less than the number of senators representing the said province, rules one and two shall cease to apply in respect of the said province, and there shall be assigned to the said province a number of members equal to the said number of senators.

4. In the event that rules one and two cease to apply in respect of a province then, for the purposes of computing the number of members to be assigned to the provinces in respect of which rules one and two continue to apply, the total population of the provinces shall be reduced by the number of the population of the province in respect of which rules one and two have ceased to apply and the number two hundred and sixty-one shall be reduced by the number of members assigned to such province pursuant to rule three.

5. On any such readjustment the number of members for any province shall not be reduced by more than fifteen per cent below the representation to which such province was entitled under rules one to four of the subsection at the last preceding readjustment of the representation of that province, and there shall be no reduction in the representation of any province as a result of which that province would have a smaller number of members than any other province that according to the results of the then last decennial census did not have a larger population; but for the purposes of any subsequent readjustment of representation under this section any increase in the number of members of the House of Commons resulting from the application of this rule shall not be included in the divisor mentioned in rules one to four of this subsection.

6. Such readjustment shall not take effect until the termination of the then existing Parliament.

(2) The Yukon Territory as constituted by chapter forty-one of the statutes of Canada, 1901, shall be entitled to one member, and such other part of Canada not comprised within a province as may from time to time be defined by the Parliament of Canada shall be entitled to one member.

Subsection 51(1) was re-enacted by *Constitution Act, 1974,* S.C. 1974-75-76, c. 13 to read as follows:

51. (1) The number of members of the House of Commons and the representation of the provinces therein shall upon the coming into force of this subsection and thereafter on the completion of each decennial census be readjusted by such authority, in such manner, and from such time as the Parliament of Canada from time to time provides, subject and according to the following Rules:

1. There shall be assigned to Quebec seventy-five members in the readjustment following the completion of the decennial census taken in the year 1971, and thereafter four additional members in each subsequent readjustment.

2. Subject to Rules 5(2) and (3), there shall be assigned to a large province a number of members equal to the number obtained by dividing the population of the large province by the electoral quotient of Quebec.

3. Subject to Rules 5(2) and (3), there shall be assigned to a small province a number of members equal to the number obtained by dividing

(*a*) the sum of the populations, determined according to the results of the penultimate decennial census, of the provinces (other than Quebec) having populations of less than one and a half million, determined according to the results of that census, by the sum of the numbers of members assigned to those provinces in the readjustment following the completion of that census; and

(*b*) the population of the small province by the quotient obtained under paragraph (*a*).

4. Subject to Rules 5(1) (*a*), (2) and (3) there shall be assigned to an intermediate province a number of members equal to the number obtained

(*a*) by dividing the sum of the populations of the provinces (other than Quebec) having populations of less than one and a half million by the sum of the number of members assigned to those provinces under any of Rules 3,5 (1) (b), (2) and (3);

(*b*) by dividing the population of the intermediate province by the quotient obtained under paragraph (*a*); and

(*c*) by adding to the number of members assigned to the intermediate province in the readjustment following the completion of the penultimate decennial census one-half of the difference resulting from the subtraction of that number from the quotient obtained under paragraph (*b*).

5. (1) On any readjustment,

(*a*) if no province (other than Quebec) has a population of less than one and a half million, Rule 4 shall not be applied and, subject to Rules 5(2) and (3), there shall be assigned to an intermediate province a number of members equal to the number obtained by dividing

(i) the sum of the populations, determined according to the results of the penultimate decennial census, of the provinces, (other than Quebec) having populations of not less than one and a half million and not more than two and a half million, determined according to the results of that census, by the sum of the numbers of members assigned to those provinces in the readjustment following the completion of that census, and

(ii) the population of the intermediate province by the quotient obtained under subparagraph (i);

(*b*) if a province (other than Quebec) having a population of

(i) less than one and a half million, or

(ii) not less than one and a half million and not more than two and a half million

does not have a population greater than its population determined according to the results of the penultimate decennial census, it shall, subject to Rules 5 (2) and (3), be assigned the number of members assigned to it in the readjustment following the completion of that census.

(2) On any readjustment,

(*a*) if, under any of Rules 2 to 5 (1), the number of members to be assigned to a province (in this paragraph referred to as " the first province") is smaller than the number of members to be assigned to any other province not having a population greater than that of the first province, those Rules shall not be applied to the first province and it shall be assigned a number of members equal to the largest number of members to be assigned to any other province not having a population greater than that of the first province;

(*b*) if, under any of Rules 2 to 5 (1)(*a*), the number of members to be assigned to a province is smaller than the number of members assigned to it in the readjustment following the completion of the penultimate decennial census, those Rules shall not be applied to it and it shall be assigned the latter number of members;

(*c*) if both paragraphs (*a*) and (*b*) apply to a province, it shall be assigned a number of members equal to the greater of the numbers produced under those paragraphs.

(3) On any readjustment,

(*a*) if the electoral quotient of a province (in this paragraph referred to as "the first province") obtained by dividing its population by the number of members to be assigned to it under any of Rules 2 to 5 (2) is greater than the electoral quotient of Quebec, those Rules shall not be applied to the first province and it shall be assigned a number of members equal to the number obtained by dividing its population by the electoral quotient of Quebec;

(2) The Yukon Territory as bounded and described in the schedule to chapter Y-2 of the Revised Statutes of Canada, 1970, shall be entitled to one member, and the Northwest Territories as bounded and described in section 2 of the chapter N-22 of the Revised Statutes of Canada, 1970, shall be entitled to two members.[28]

Yukon Territory and Northwest Territories

51A. Notwithstanding anything in this Act a province shall always be entitled to a number of members in the House of Commons not less than the number of senators representing such province.[29]

Constitution of House of Commons

52. The Number of Members of the House of Commons may be from Time to Time increased by the Parliament of Canada, provided the proportionate Representation of the Provinces prescribed by this Act is not thereby disturbed.

(*b*) if, as a result of the application of Rule 6 (2) (*a*), the number of members assigned to a province under paragraph (*a*) equals the number of members to be assigned to it under any of Rules 2 to 5 (2), it shall be assigned that number of members and paragraph (*a*) shall cease to apply to that province.

6. (1) In these Rules,

"electoral quotient" means, in respect of a province, the quotient obtained by dividing its population, determined according to the results of the then most recent decennial census, by the number of members to be assigned to it under any of Rules 1 to 5 (3) in the readjustment following the completion of that census;

"intermediate province" means a province (other than Quebec) having a population greater than its population determined according to the results of the penultimate decennial census but not more than two and a half million and not less than one and a half million;

"large province" means a province (other than Quebec) having a population greater than two and a half million;

"penultimate decennial census" means the decennial census that preceded the then most recent decennial census;

"population" means, except where otherwise specified, the population determined according to the results of the then most recent decennial census;

"small province" means a province (other than Quebec) having a population greater than its population determined according to the results of the penultimate decennial census and less than one and half million.

(2) For the purposes of these Rules,

(*a*) if any fraction less than one remains upon completion of the final calculation that produces the number of members to be assigned to a province, that number of members shall equal the number so produced disregarding the fraction;

(*b*) if more than one readjustment follows the completion of a decennial census, the most recent of those readjustments shall, upon taking effect, be deemed to be the only readjustment following the completion of that census;

(*c*) a readjustment shall not take effect until the termination of the then existing Parliament.

(28) As enacted by the *Constitution Act (No. 1), 1975*, S.C. 1974-75-76, c. 28.

(29) As enacted by the *Constitution Act, 1915*, 5-6 Geo. V, c. 45 (U.K.)

Appropriation and Tax Bills

53. Bills for appropriating any Part of the Public Revenue, or for imposing any Tax or Impost, shall originate in the House of Commons.

Recommendation of Money Votes

54. It shall not be lawful for the House of Commons to adopt or pass any Vote, Resolution, Address, or Bill for the Appropriation of any Part of the Public Revenue, or of any Tax or Impost, to any Purpose that has not been first recommended to that House by Message of the Governor General in the Session in which such Vote, Resolution, Address, or Bill is proposed.

Royal Assent to Bills, etc.

55. Where a Bill passed by the Houses of the Parliament is presented to the Governor General for the Queen's Assent, he shall declare, according to his Discretion, but subject to the Provisions of this Act and to Her Majesty's Instructions, either that he assents thereto in the Queen's Name, or that he withholds the Queen's Assent, or that he reserves the Bill for the Signification of the Queen's Pleasure.

Disallowance by Order in Council of Act assented to by Governor General

56. Where the Governor General assents to a Bill in the Queen's Name, he shall by the first convenient Opportunity send an authentic Copy of the Act to One of Her Majesty's Principal Secretaries of State, and if the Queen in Council within Two Years after Receipt thereof by the Secretary of State thinks fit to disallow the Act, such Disallowance (with a Certificate of the Secretary of State of the Day on which the Act was received by him) being signified by the Governor General, by Speech or Message to each of the Houses of the Parliament or by Proclamation, shall annul the Act from and after the Day of such Signification.

Signification of Queen's Pleasure on Bill reserved

57. A Bill reserved for the Signification of the Queen's Pleasure shall not have any Force unless and until, within Two Years from the Day on which it was presented to the Governor General for the Queen's Assent, the Governor General signifies, by Speech or Message to each of the Houses of the Parliament or by Proclamation, that it has received the Assent of the Queen in Council.

An Entry of every such Speech, Message, or Proclamation shall be made in the Journal of each House, and a Duplicate thereof duly attested shall be delivered to the proper Officer to be kept among the Records of Canada.

V. PROVINCIAL CONSTITUTIONS

Executive Power

Appointment of Lieutenant Governors of Provinces

58. For each Province there shall be an Officer, styled the Lieutenant Governor, appointed by the Governor General in Council by Instrument under the Great Seal of Canada.

Tenure of Office of Lieutenant Governor

59. A Lieutenant Governor shall hold Office during the Pleasure of the Governor General; but any Lieutenant Governor appointed after the Commencement of the First Session of the Parliament of Canada shall not be removable within Five Years from his Appointment, except for Cause assigned, which shall be communicated to him in Writing within One Month after the Order for his Removal is made, and shall be communicated by Message to the Senate and to the House of Commons within One Week thereafter if the Parliament is then sitting, and if not then within One Week after the Commencement of the next Session of the Parliament.

Salaries of Lieutenant Governors

60. The Salaries of the Lieutenant Governors shall be fixed and provided by the Parliament of Canada.[30]

Oaths, etc., of Lieutenant Governor

61. Every Lieutenant Governor shall, before assuming the Duties of his Office, make and subscribe before the Governor General or some Person authorized by him Oaths of Allegiance and Office similar to those taken by the Governor General.

Application of Provisions referring to Lieutenant Governor

62. The Provisions of this Act referring to the Lieutenant Governor extend and apply to the Lieutenant Governor for the Time being of each Province, or other the Chief Executive Officer or Administrator for the Time being carrying on the Government of the Province, by whatever Title he is designated.

Appointment of Executive Officers for Ontario and Quebec

63. The Executive Council of Ontario and of Quebec shall be composed of such Persons as the Lieutenant Governor from Time to Time thinks fit, and in the first instance of the following Officers, namely, — the Attorney General, the Secretary and Registrar of the Province, the Treasurer of the Province, the Commissioner of Crown Lands, and the Commissioner of Agriculture and Public Works, with in Quebec the Speaker of the Legislative Council and the Solicitor General.[31]

(30) Provided for by the *Salaries Act*, R.S.C. 1985, c. S-3.

(31) Now provided for in Ontario by the *Executive Council Act*, R.S.C. 1980, c. 147, and in Quebec by the *Executive Power Act*, R.S.Q. 1977, c. E-18.

Executive Government of Nova Scotia and New Brunswick

64. The Constitution of the Executive Authority in each of the Provinces of Nova Scotia and New Brunswick shall, subject to the Provisions of this Act, continue as it exists at the Union until altered under the Authority of this Act.[32]

Powers to be exercised by Lieutenant Governor of Ontario or Quebec with Advice, or alone

65. All Powers, Authorities, and Functions which under any Act of the Parliament of Great Britain, or of the Parliament of the United Kingdom of Great Britain and Ireland, or of the Legislature of Upper Canada, Lower Canada, or Canada, were or are before or at the Union vested in or exerciseable by the respective Governors or Lieutenant Governors of those Provinces, with the Advice or with the Advise and Consent of the respective Executive Councils thereof, or in conjunction with those Councils, or with any Number of Members thereof, or by those Governors or Lieutenant Governors individually, shall, as far as the same are capable of being exercised after the Union in relation to the Government of Ontario and Quebec respectively, be vested in and shall or may be exercised by the Lieutenant Governor of Ontario and Quebec respectively, with the Advice or the Advice and Consent of or in conjunction with the respective Executive Councils, or any Members thereof, or by the Lieutenant Governor individually, as the Case requires, subject nevertheless (except with respect to such as exist under Acts of the Parliament of Great Britain, or of the Parliament of the United Kingdom of Great Britain and Ireland,) to be abolished or altered by the respective Legislatures of Ontario and Quebec.[33]

Application of Provisions referring to Lieutenant Governor in Council

66. The Provisions of this Act referring to the Lieutenant Governor in Council shall be construed as referring to the Lieutenant Governor of the Province acting by and with the Advice of the Executive Council thereof.

Administration in Absence, etc., of Lieutenant Governor

67. The Governor General in Council may from Time to Time appoint an Administrator to execute the Office and Functions of Lieutenant Governor during his Absence, Illness, or other Inability.

Seats of Provincial Governments

68. Unless and until the Executive Government of any Province otherwise directs with respect to that Province, the Seats of Government of the Provinces shall be as follows, namely, — of Ontario, the City of Toronto; of Quebec, the City of Quebec; of Nova Scotia, the City of Halifax; and of New Brunswick, the City of Fredericton.

---

(32) A similar provision was included in each of the instruments admitting British Columbia, Prince Edward Island, and Newfoundland. The Executive Authorities for Manitoba, Alberta and Saskatchewan were established by the statutes creating those provinces. See the notes to section 5, *supra.*

(33) See the notes to section 129, *infra.*

1. — ONTARIO

69. There shall be a Legislature for Ontario consisting of the Lieutenant Governor and of One House, styled the Legislative Assembly of Ontario. Legislature for Ontario

70. The Legislative Assembly of Ontario shall be composed of Eighty-two Members, to be elected to represent the Eighty-two Electoral Districts set forth in the First Schedule to this Act.[34] Electoral districts

2. — QUEBEC

71. There shall be a Legislature for Quebec consisting of the Lieutenant Governor and of Two Houses, styled the Legislative Council of Quebec and the Legislative Assembly of Quebec.[35] Legislature for Quebec

72. The Legislative Council of Quebec shall be composed of Twenty-four Members, to be appointed by the Lieutenant Governor, in the Queen's Name, by Instrument under the Great Seat of Quebec, one being appointed to represent each of the Twenty-four Electoral Divisions of Lower Canada in this Act referred to, and each holding Office for the Term of his Life, unless the Legislature of Quebec otherwise provides under the Provisions of this Act. Constitution of Legislative Council

73. The Qualifications of the Legislative Councillors of Quebec shall be the same as those of the Senators for Quebec. Qualification of Legislative Councillors

74. The Place of a Legislative Councillor of Quebec shall become vacant in the Cases, *mutatis mutandis*, in which the Place of Senator becomes vacant. Resignation, Disqualification, etc.

75. When a Vacancy happens in the Legislative Council of Quebec by Resignation, Death, or otherwise, the Lieutenant Governor, in the Queen's Name, by Instrument under the Great Seal of Quebec, shall appoint a fit and qualified Person to fill the Vacancy. Vacancies

(34) Spent. Now covered by the *Representation Act*, R.S.O. 1980, c. 450.

(35) The Act respecting the Legislative Council of Quebec, S.Q. 1968, c.9, provided that the Legislature for Quebec shall consist of the Lieutenant Governor and the National Assembly of Quebec, and repealed the provisions of the *Legislature Act*, R.S.Q. 1964, c. 6, relating to the Legislative Council of Quebec. Sections 72 to 79 following are therefore completely spent.

Questions as to Vacancies, etc.

76. If any Question arises respecting the Qualification of a Legislative Councillor of Quebec, or a Vacancy in the Legislative Council of Quebec, the same shall be heard and determined by the Legislative Council.

Speaker of Legislative Council

77. The Lieutenant Governor may from Time to Time, by Instrument under the Great Seal of Quebec, appoint a Member of the Legislative Council of Quebec to be Speaker thereof, and may remove him and appoint another in his Stead.

Quorum of Legislative Council

78. Until the Legislature of Quebec otherwise provides, the Presence of at least Ten Members of the Legislative Council, including the Speaker, shall be necessary to constitute a Meeting for the Exercise of its Powers.

Voting in Legislative Council

79. Questions arising in the Legislative Council of Quebec shall be decided by a Majority of Voices, and the Speaker shall in all Cases have a Vote, and when the Voices are equal the Decision shall be deemed to be in the Negative.

Constitution of Legislative Assembly of Quebec

80. The Legislative Assembly of Quebec shall be composed of Sixty-five Members, to be elected to represent the Sixty-five Electoral Divisions or Districts of Lower Canada in this Act referred to, subject to Alteration thereof by the Legislature of Quebec: Provided that it shall not be lawful to present to the Lieutenant Governor of Quebec for Assent any Bill for altering the Limits of any of the Electoral Divisions or Districts mentioned in the Second Schedule to this Act, unless the Second and Third Readings of such Bill have been passed in the Legislative Assembly with the Concurrence of the Majority of the Members representing all those Electoral Divisions or Districts, and the Assent shall not be given to such Bill unless an Address has been presented by the Legislative Assembly to the Lieutenant Governor stating that it has been so passed.[36]

3. — ONTARIO AND QUEBEC

81. Repealed.[37]

---

(36) The Act respecting electoral districts, S.Q. 1970, c. 7, s. 1, provides that this section no longer has effect.

(37) Repealed by the *Statute Law Revision Act, 1893*, 56-57 Vict. c. 14 (U.K.). The section read as follows:

> **81.** The Legislatures of Ontario and Quebec respectively shall be called together not later than Six Months after the Union.

82. The Lieutenant Governor of Ontario and of Quebec shall from Time to Time, in the Queen's Name, by Instrument under the Great Seal of the Province, summon and call together the Legislative Assembly of the Province.

Summoning of Legislative Assemblies

83. Until the Legislature of Ontario or of Quebec otherwise provides, a Person accepting or holding in Ontario or in Quebec any Office, Commission, or Employment, permanent or temporary, at the Nomination of the Lieutenant Governor, to which an annual Salary, or any Fee, Allowance, Emolument, or Profit of any Kind or Amount whatever from the Province is attached, shall not be eligible as a Member of the Legislative Assembly of the respective Province, nor shall he sit or vote as such; but nothing in this Section shall make ineligible any Person being a Member of the Executive Council of the respective Province, or holding any of the following Offices, that is to say, the Offices of Attorney General, Secretary and Registrar of the Province, Treasurer of the Province, Commissioner of Crown Lands, and Commissioner of Agriculture and Public Works, and in Quebec Solicitor General, or shall disqualify him to sit or vote in the House for which he is elected, provided he is elected while holding such Office.[38]

Restriction on election of Holders of offices

84. Until the legislatures of Ontario and Quebec respectively otherwise provide, all Laws which at the Union are in force in those Provinces respectively, relative to the following Matters, or any of them, namely, — the Qualifications and Disqualifications of Persons to be elected or to sit or vote as Members of the Assembly of Canada, the Qualifications or Disqualifications of Voters, the Oaths to be taken by Voters, the Returning Officers, their Powers and Duties, the Proceedings at Elections, the Periods during which such Elections may be continued, and the Trial of controverted Elections and the Proceedings incident thereto, the vacating of the Seats of Members and the issuing and execution of new Writs in case of Seats vacated otherwise than by Dissolution, — shall respectively apply to Elections of Members to serve in the respective Legislative Assemblies of Ontario and Quebec.

Continuance of existing Election Laws

(38) Probably spent. The subject-matter of this section is now covered in Ontario by the *Legislative Assembly Act*, R.S.O. 1980, c. 235, and in Quebec by the *National Assembly Act*, R.S.Q. c. A-23.1.

Provided that, until the Legislature of Ontario otherwise provides, at any Election for a Member of the Legislative Assembly of Ontario for the District of Algoma, in addition to Persons qualified by the Law of the Province of Canada to vote, every Male British Subject, aged Twenty-one Years or upwards, being a Householder, shall have a Vote.[39]

Duration of Legislative Assemblies

85. Every Legislative Assembly of Ontario and every Legislative Assembly of Quebec shall continue for Four Years from the Day of the Return of the Writs for choosing the same (subject nevertheless to either the Legislative Assembly of Ontario or the Legislative Assembly of Quebec being sooner dissolved by the Lieutenant Governor of the Province), and no longer.[40]

Yearly Session of Legislature

86. There shall be a Session of the Legislature of Ontario and of that of Quebec once at least in every Year, so that Twelve Months shall not intervene between the last Sitting of the Legislature in each Province in one Session and its first Sitting in the next Session.[41]

Speaker, Quorum, etc.

87. The following Provisions of this Act respecting the House of Commons of Canada shall extend and apply to the Legislative Assemblies of Ontario and Quebec, that is to say, — the Provisions relating to the Election of a Speaker originally and on Vacancies, the Duties of the Speaker, the Absence of the Speaker, the Quorum, and the Mode of voting, as if those Provisions were here re-enacted and made applicable in Terms to each such Legislative Assembly.

4. — NOVA SCOTIA AND NEW BRUNSWICK

Constitutions of Legislatures of Nova Scotia and New Brunswick

88. The Constitution of the Legislature of each of the Provinces of Nova Scotia and New Brunswick shall, subject to the Provisions of this Act, continue as it exists at the Union until altered under the Authority of this Act.[42]

---

(39) Probably spent. The subject-matter of this section is now covered in Ontario by the *Election Act*, R.S.O. 1980, c. 133, and the *Legislative Assembly Act*, R.S.O. 1980, c. 235, in Quebec by the *Elections Act*, S.Q. 1979, c. 56 and the *National Assembly Act*, R.S.Q. c. A-23.1.

(40) The maximum duration of the Legislative Assemblies of Ontario and Quebec has been changed to five years. See the *Legislative Assembly Act*, R.S.O. 1980. c. 235, and the *National Assembly Act*, R.S.Q. c. A-23.1, respectively. See also section 4 of the *Constitution Act, 1982*, which provides a maximum duration for a legislative assembly of five years but also authorizes continuation in special circumstances.

(41) See also section 5 of the *Constitution Act, 1982*, which provides that there shall be a sitting of each legislature at least once every twelve months.

5. — ONTARIO, QUEBEC, AND NOVA SCOTIA

89. Repealed.[43]

6. — THE FOUR PROVINCES

90. The following Provisions of this Act respecting the Parliament of Canada, namely, — the Provisions relating to Appropriation and Tax Bills, the Recommendation of Money Votes, the Assent to Bills, the Disallowance of Acts, and the Signification of Pleasure on Bills reserved, — shall extend and apply to the Legislatures of the several Provinces as if those Provisions were here re-enacted and made applicable in Terms to the respective Provinces and the Legislatures thereof, with the Substitution of the Lieutenant Governor of the Province for the Governor General, of the Governor General for the Queen and for a Secretary of State, of One Year for Two Years, and of the Province for Canada.

Application to Legislatures of Provisions respecting Money Votes, etc.

---

(42) Partially repealed by the *Statute Law Revision Act, 1893,* 56-57 Vict., c. 14 (U.K.), which deleted the following concluding words of the original enactment:

> and the House of Assembly of New Brunswick existing at the passing of this Act shall, unless sooner dissolved, continue for the Period for which it was elected.

A similar provision was included in each of the instruments admitting British Columbia, Prince Edward Island and Newfoundland. The Legislatures of Manitoba, Alberta and Saskatchewan were established by the statutes creating those provinces. See the footnotes to section 5, *supra.*

See also sections 3 to 5 of the *Constitution Act, 1982,* which prescribe democratic rights applicable to all provinces, and subitem 2(2) of the Schedule to that Act, which sets out the repeal of section 20 of the *Manitoba Act, 1870.* Section 20 of the *Manitoba Act, 1870,* has been replaced by section 5 of the *Constitution Act, 1982.*

Section 20 reads as follows:

> **20.** There shall be a Session of the Legislature once at least in every year, so that twelve months shall not intervene between the last sitting of the Legislature in one Session and its first sitting in the next Session.

(43) Repealed by the *Statute Law Revision Act, 1893,* 56-57 Vict. c. 14 (U.K.). The section read as follows:

> **5.** — Ontario, Quebec, and Nova Scotia.
>
> **89.** Each of the Lieutenant Governors of Ontario, Quebec and Nova Scotia shall cause Writs to be issued for the First Election of Members of the Legislative Assembly thereof in such Form and by such Person as he thinks fit, and at such Time and addressed to such Returning Officer as the Governor General directs, and so that the First Election of Member of Assembly for any Electoral District or any Subdivision thereof shall be held at the same Time and at the same Places as the Election for a Member to serve in the House of Commons of Canada for that Electoral District.

VI. DISTRIBUTION OF LEGISLATIVE POWERS

Powers of the Parliament

Legislative Authority of Parliament of Canada

91. It shall be lawful for the Queen, by and with the Advice and Consent of the Senate and House of Commons, to make Laws for the Peace, Order, and good Government of Canada, in relation to all Matters not coming within the Classes of Subjects by this Act assigned exclusively to the Legislatures of the Provinces; and for greater Certainty, but not so as to restrict the Generality of the foregoing Terms of this Section, it is hereby declared that (notwithstanding anything in this Act) the exclusive Legislative Authority of the Parliament of Canada extends to all Matters coming within the Classes of Subjects next hereinafter enumerated; that is to say,—

1. Repealed.[44]

1A. The Public Debt and Property.[45]

2. The Regulation of Trade and Commerce.

2A. Unemployment insurance.[46]

3. The raising of Money by any Mode or System of Taxation.

4. The borrowing of Money on the Public Credit.

5. Postal Service.

6. The Census and Statistics.

7. Militia, Military and Naval Service, and Defence.

---

(44) Class I was added by the *British North America (No. 2) Act, 1949,* 13 Geo. VI, c. 81 (U.K.). That Act and class I were repealed by the *Constitution Act, 1982.* The matters referred to in class I are provided for in subsection 4 (2) and Part V of the *Constitution Act, 1982.* As enacted, class I read as follows:

1. The amendment from time to time of the Constitution of Canada, except as regards matters coming within the classes of subjects by this Act assigned exclusively to the Legislatures of the provinces, or as regards rights or privileges by this or any other Constitutional Act granted or secured to the Legislature or the Government of a province, or to any class of persons with respect to schools or as regards the use of the English or the French language or as regards the requirements that there shall be a session of the Parliament of Canada at least once each year, and that no House of Commons shall continue for more than five years from the day of the return of the Writs for choosing the House: provided, however, that a House of Commons may in time of real or apprehended war, invasion or insurrection be continued by the Parliament of Canada if such continuation is not opposed by the votes of more than one-third of the members of such House.

(45) Re-numbered by the *British North America (No. 2) Act, 1949.*

(46) Added by the *Constitution Act, 1940,* 3-4 Geo. VI, c. 36 (U.K.).

8. The fixing of and providing for the Salaries and Allowances of Civil and other Officers of the Government of Canada.
9. Beacons, Buoys, Lighthouses, and Sable Island.
10. Navigation and Shipping.
11. Quarantine and the Establishment and Maintenance of Marine Hospitals.
12. Sea Coast and Inland Fisheries.
13. Ferries between a Province and any British or Foreign Country or between Two Provinces.
14. Currency and Coinage.
15. Banking, Incorporation of Banks, and the Issue of Paper Money.
16. Savings Banks.
17. Weights and Measures.
18. Bills of Exchange and Promissory Notes.
19. Interest.
20. Legal Tender.
21. Bankruptcy and Insolvency.
22. Patents of Invention and Discovery.
23. Copyrights.
24. Indians, and Lands reserved for Indians.
25. Naturalization and Aliens.
26. Marriage and Divorcc.
27. The Criminal Law, except the Constitution of Courts of Criminal Jurisdiction, but including the Procedure in Criminal Matters.
28. The Establishment, Maintenance, and Management of Penitentiaries.
29. Such Classes of Subjects as are expressly excepted in the Enumeration of the Classes of Subjects by this Act assigned exclusively to the Legislatures of the Provinces.

And any Matter coming within any of the Classes of Subjects enumerated in this Section shall not be deemed to come within the Class of Matters of a local or private Nature comprised in the Enumeration of the Classes of Subjects by this Act assigned exclusively to the Legislatures of the Provinces.[47]

---

(47) Legislative authority has been conferred on Parliament by other Acts as follows:

1. The *Constitution Act, 1871,* 34-35 Vict., c. 28 (U.K.).

> **2.** The Parliament of Canada may from time to time establish new Provinces in any territories forming for the time being part of the Dominion of Canada, but not included in any Province thereof, and may, at the time of such establishment, make provision for the constitution and administration of any such Province, and for the passing of laws for the peace, order, and good government of such Province, and for its representation in the said Parliament.
>
> **3.** The Parliament of Canada may from time to time, with the consent of the Legislature of any province of the said Dominion, increase, diminish, or otherwise alter the limits of such Province, upon such terms and conditions as may be agreed to by the said Legislature, and may, with the like consent, make provision respecting the effect and operation of any such increase or diminution or alteration of territory in relation to any Province affected thereby.
>
> **4.** The Parliament of Canada may from time to time make provision for the administration, peace, order, and good government of any territory not for the time being included in any Province.
>
> **5.** The following Acts passed by the said Parliament of Canada, and intituled respectively —"An Act for the temporary government of Rupert's Land and the North Western Territory when united with Canada"; and "An Act to amend and continue the Act thirty-two and thirty-three Victoria, chapter three, and to establish and provide for the government of "the Province of Manitoba", shall be and be deemed to have been valid and effectual for all purposes whatsoever from the date at which they respectively received the assent, in the Queen's name, of the Governor General of the said Dominion of Canada.
>
> **6.** Except as provided by the third section of this Act, it shall not be competent for the Parliament of Canada to alter the provisions of the last-mentioned Act of the said Parliament in so far as it relates to the Province of Manitoba, or of any other Act hereafter establishing new Provinces in the said Dominion, subject always to the right of the Legislature of the Province of Manitoba to alter from time to time the provisions of any law respecting the qualification of electors and members of the Legislative Assembly, and to make laws respecting elections in the said province.

The *Rupert's Land Act, 1868,* 31-32 Vict., c. 105 (U.K.) (repealed by the *Statute Law Revision Act, 1893,* 56-57 Vict., c. 14 (U.K.)) had previously conferred similar authority in relation to Rupert's Land and the North Western Territory upon admission of those areas.

2. The *Constitution Act, 1886,* 49-50 Vict., c. 35, (U.K.).

> **1.** The Parliament of Canada may from time to time make provision for the representation in the Senate and House of Commons of Canada, or in either of them, of any territories which for the time being form part of the Dominion of Canada, but are not included in any province thereof.

3. The *Statute of Westminster, 1931,* 22 Geo. V, c.4 (U.K.).

> **3.** It is hereby declared and enacted that the Parliament of a Dominion has full power to make laws having extra-territorial operation.

4. Under section 44 of the *Constitution Act, 1982,* Parliament has exclusive authority to amend the Constitution of Canada in relation to the executive government of Canada or the Senate and House of Commons. Sections 38, 41, 42, and 43 of that Act authorize the Senate and House of Commons to give their approval to certain other constitutional amendments by resolution.

Exclusive Powers of Provincial Legislatures

92. In each Province the Legislature may exclusively make Laws in relation to Matters coming within the Classes of Subjects next hereinafter enumerated; that is to say, —

Subjects of exclusive Provincial Legislation

1. Repealed.[48]
2. Direct Taxation within the Province in order to the raising of a Revenue for Provincial Purposes.
3. The borrowing of Money on the sole Credit of the Province.
4. The Establishment and Tenure of Provincial Offices and the Appointment and Payment of Provincial Officers.
5. The Management and Sale of the Public Lands belonging to the Province and of the Timber and Wood thereon.
6. The Establishment, Maintenance, and Management of Public and Reformatory Prisons in and for the Province.
7. The Establishment, Maintenance, and Management of Hospitals, Asylums, Charities, and Eleemosynary Institutions in and for the Province, other than Marine Hospitals.
8. Municipal Institutions in the Province.
9. Shop, Saloon, Tavern, Auctioneer, and other Licences in order to the raising of a Revenue for Provincial, Local, or Municipal Purposes.

---

(48) Class I was repealed by the *Constitution Act, 1982.* As enacted, it read as follows:

> 1. The Amendment from Time to Time, notwithstanding anything in this Act, of the Constitution of the Province, except as regards the Office of Lieutenant Governor.

Section 45 of the *Constitution Act, 1982* now authorizes legislatures to make laws amending the constitution of the province. Sections 38, 41, 42, and 43 of that Act authorize legislative assemblies to give their approval by resolution to certain other amendments to the Constitution of Canada.

10. Local Works and Undertakings other than such as are of the following Classes:—

(a) Lines of Steam or other Ships, Railways, Canals, Telegraphs, and other Works and Undertakings connecting the Province with any other or others of the Provinces, or extending beyond the Limits of the Province:

(b) Lines of Steam Ships between the Province and any British or Foreign Country:

(c) Such Works as, although wholly situate within the Province, are before or after their Execution declared by the Parliament of Canada to be for the general Advantage of Canada or for the Advantage of Two or more of the Provinces.

11. The Incorporation of Companies with Provincial Objects.

12. The Solemnization of Marriage in the Province.

13. Property and Civil Rights in the Province.

14. The Administration of Justice in the Province, including the Constitution, Maintenance, and Organization of Provincial Courts, both of Civil and of Criminal Jurisdiction, and including Procedure in Civil Matters in those Courts.

15. The Imposition of Punishment by Fine, Penalty, or Imprisonment for enforcing any Law of the Province made in relation to any Matter coming within any of the Classes of Subjects enumerated in this Section.

16. Generally all Matters of a merely local or private Nature in the Province.

Non-Renewable Natural Resources, Forestry Resources and Electrical Energy

Laws respecting non-renewable natural resources, forestry resources and electrical energy

92A. (1) In each province, the legislature may exclusively make laws in relation to

(*a*) exploration for non-renewable natural resources in the province;

(*b*) development, conservation and management of non-renewable natural resources and forestry resources in the province, including laws in relation to the rate of primary production therefrom; and

(*c*) development, conservation and management of sites and facilities in the province for the generation and production of electrical energy.

Export from provinces of resources

(2) In each province, the legislature may make laws in relation to the export from the province to another part of Canada of the primary production from non-renewable natural resources and forestry resources in the province and the production from facilities in the province for the generation of electrical energy, but such laws may not authorize or provide for discrimination in prices or in supplies exported to another part of Canada.

Authority of Parliament

(3) Nothing in subsection (2) derogates from the authority of Parliament to enact laws in relation to the matters referred to in that subsection and, where such a law of Parliament and a law of a province conflict, the law of Parliament prevails to the extent of the conflict.

Taxation of resources

(4) In each province, the legislature may make laws in relation to the raising of money by any mode or system of taxation in respect of

(*a*) non-renewable natural resources and forestry resources in the province and the primary production therefrom, and

(*b*) sites and facilities in the province for the generation of electrical energy and the production therefrom,

whether or not such production is exported in whole or in part from the province, but such laws may not authorize or provide for taxation that differentiates between production exported to another part of Canada and production not exported from the province.

"Primary production"

(5) The expression "primary production" has the meaning assigned by the Sixth Schedule.

Existing powers or rights

(6) Nothing in subsections (1) to (5) derogates from any powers or rights that a legislature or government of a province had immediately before the coming into force of this section.[49]

(49) Added by the *Constitution Act, 1982.*

Education

Legislation respecting Education

93. In and for each Province the Legislature may exclusively make Laws in relation to Education, subject and according to the following Provisions:—

(1) Nothing in any such Law shall prejudicially affect any Right or Privilege with respect to Denominational Schools which any Class of Persons have by Law in the Province at the Union:

(2) All the Powers, Privileges, and Duties at the Union by Law conferred and imposed in Upper Canada on the Separate Schools and School Trustees of the Queen's Roman Catholic Subjects shall be and the same are hereby extended to the Dissentient Schools of the Queen's Protestant and Roman Catholic Subjects in Quebec:

(3) Where in any Province a system of separate or Dissentient Schools exists by Law at the Union or is thereafter established by the Legislature of the Province, an Appeal shall lie to the Governor General in Council from any Act or Decision of any Provincial Authority affecting any Right or Privilege of the Protestant or Roman Catholic Minority of the Queen's Subjects in relation to Education:

(4) In case any such Provincial Law as from Time to Time seems to the Governor General in Council requisite for the due Execution of the Provisions of this Section is not made, or in case any Decision of the Governor General in Council on any appeal under this Section is not duly executed by the proper Provincial Authority in that Behalf, then and in every such Case, and as far only as the Circumstances of each Case require, the Parliament of Canada may make remedial Laws for the due Execution of the Provisions of this Section and of any Decision of the Governor General in Council under this Section.[50]

---

(50) Altered for Manitoba by section 22 of the *Manitoba Act, 1870,* 33 Vict., c.3 (Canada), (confirmed by the *Constitution Act, 1871*), which reads as follows:

> **22.** In and for the Province, the said Legislature may exclusively make Laws in relation to Education, subject and according to the following provisions: —
>
> (1) Nothing in any such Law shall prejudicially affect any right or privilege with respect to Denominational Schools which any class of persons have by Law or practice in the Province at the Union:

(2) An appeal shall lie to the Governor General in Council from any Act or decision of the Legislature of the Province, or of any Provincial Authority, affecting any right or privilege, of the Protestant or Roman Catholic minority of the Queen's subjects in relation to Education:

(3) In case any such Provincial Law, as from time to time seems to the Governor General in Council requisite for the due execution of the provisions of this section, is not made, or in case any decision of the Governor General in Council on any appeal under this section is not duly executed by the proper Provincial Authority in that behalf, then , and in every such case, and as far only as the circumstances of each case require, the Parliament of Canada may make remedial Laws for the due execution of the provisions of this section, and of any decision of the Governor General in Council under this section.

Altered for Alberta by section 17 of the *Alberta Act,* 4-5 Edw. VII, c. 3, 1905 (Canada), which reads as follows:

17. Section 93 of the *Constitution Act, 1867,* shall apply to the said province, with the substitution for paragraph (1) of the said section 93 of the following paragraph: —

(1) Nothing in any such law shall prejudicially affect any right or privilege with respect to separate schools which any class of persons have at the date of the passing of this Act, under the terms of chapters 29 and 30 of the Ordinances of the Northwest Territories, passed in the year 1901, or with respect to religious instruction in any public or separate school as provided for in the said ordinances.

2. In the appropriation by the Legislature or distribution by the Government of the province of any moneys for the support of schools organized and carried on in accordance with the said chapter 29 or any Act passed in amendment thereof, or in substitution therefor, there shall be no discrimination against schools of any class described in the said chapter 29.

3. Where the expression "by law" is employed in paragraph 3 of the said section 93, it shall be held to mean the law as set out in the said chapters 29 and 30, and where the expression "at the Union" is employed, in the said paragraph 3, it shall be held to mean the date at which this Act comes into force.

Altered for Saskatchewan by section 17 of the *Saskatchewan Act,* 4-5 Edw. VII, c. 42, 1905 (Canada), which reads as follows:

17. Section 93 of the *Constitution Act, 1867,* shall apply to the said province, with the substitution for paragraph (1) of the said section 93, of the following paragraph: -

(1) Nothing in any such law shall prejudicially affect any right or privilege with respect to separate schools which any class of persons have at the date of the passing of this Act, under the terms chapters 29 and 30 of the Ordinances of the Northwest Territories, passed in the year 1901, or with respect to religious instruction in any public or separate school as provided for in the said ordinances.

2. In the appropriation by the Legislature or distribution by the Government of the province of any moneys for the support of schools organized and carried on in accordance with the said chapter 29, or any Act passed in amendment thereof or in substitution therefor, there shall be no discrimination against schools of any class described in the said chapter 29.

3. Where the expression "by law" is employed in paragraph (3) of the said section 93, it shall be held to mean the law as set out in the said chapters 29 and 30; and where the expression "at the Union" is employed in the said paragraph (3), it shall be held to mean the date at which this Act comes into force.

Altered for Newfoundland by Term 17 of the Terms of Union of Newfoundland with Canada (confirmed by the *Newfoundland Act,* 12-13 Geo. VI, C. 22 (U.K)). Term 17 of the Terms of Union of Newfoundland with Canada set out in the Schedule to the *Newfoundland Act,* which was amended by the *Constitution Amendment, 1987 (Newfoundland Act),* (see SI/88-11) reads as follows:

17. (1) In lieu of section ninety-three of the *Constitution Act, 1867,* the following term shall apply in respect of the Province of Newfoundland.

In and for the Province of Newfoundland the Legislature shall have exclusive authority to make laws in relation to education, but the Legislature will not have authority to make laws prejudicially affecting any right or privilege with respect to denominational schools, common (amalgamated) schools, or denominational colleges, that any class or classes of persons have by law in Newfoundland at the date of Union, and out of public funds of the Province of Newfoundland, provided for education,

Uniformity of Laws in Ontario, Nova Scotia, and New Brunswick

Legislation for Uniformity of Laws in Three Provinces

94. Notwithstanding anything in this Act, the Parliament of Canada may make Provision for the Uniformity of all or any of the Laws relative to Property and Civil Rights in Ontario, Nova Scotia, and New Brunswick, and of the Procedure of all or any of the Courts in those Three Provinces, and from and after the passing of any Act in that Behalf the Power of the Parliament of Canada to make Laws in relation to any Matter comprised in any such Act shall, notwithstanding anything in this Act, be unrestricted; but any Act of the Parliament of Canada making Provision for such Uniformity shall not have effect in any Province unless and until it is adopted and enacted as Law by the Legislature thereof.

Old Age Pensions

Legislation respecting old age pensions and supplementary benefits

94A. The Parliament of Canada may make laws in relation to old age pensions and supplementary benefits, including survivors' and disability benefits irrespective of age, but no such law shall affect the operation of any law present or future of a provincial legislature in relation to any such matter.[51]

(a) all such schools shall receive their share of such funds in accordance with scales determined on a non-discriminatory basis from time to time by the Legislature for all schools then being conducted under authority of the Legislature; and

(b) all such colleges shall receive their share of any grant from time to time voted for all colleges then being conducted under authority of the Legislature, such grant being distributed on a non-discriminatory basis.

(2) For the purposes of paragraph one of this Term, the Pentecostal Assemblies of Newfoundland have in Newfoundland all the same rights and privileges with respect to denominational schools and denominational colleges as any other class or classes of persons had by law in Newfoundland at the date of Union, and the words "all such schools" in paragraph (a) of paragraph one of this Term and the words "all such colleges" in paragraph (b) of paragraph one of this Term include, respectively, the schools and the colleges of the Pentecostal Assemblies of Newfoundland.

See also sections 23, 29, and 59 of the *Constitution Act, 1982.* Section 23 provides for new minority language educational rights and section 59 permits a delay in respect of the coming into force in Quebec of one aspect of those rights. Section 29 provides that nothing in the *Canadian Charter of Rights and Freedoms* abrogates or derogates from any rights or privileges guaranteed by or under the Constitution of Canada in respect of denominational, separate or dissentient schools.

(51) Added by the *Constitution Act, 1964,* 12-13 Eliz. II, c. 73 (U.K.). As originally enacted by the *British North America Act, 1951,* 14-15 Geo. VI, c. 32 (U.K.), which was repealed by the *Constitution Act, 1982,* section 94A read as follows:

Agriculture and Immigration

95. In each Province the Legislature may make Laws in relation to Agriculture in the Province, and to Immigration into the Province; and it is hereby declared that the Parliament of Canada may from Time to Time make Laws in relation to Agriculture in all or any of the Provinces, and to Immigration into all or any of the Provinces; and any Law of the Legislature of a Province relative to Agriculture or to Immigration shall have effect in and for the Province as long and as far only as it is not repugnant to any Act of the Parliament of Canada.

Concurrent Powers of Legislation respecting Agriculture, etc.

VII. JUDICATURE

96. The Governor General shall appoint the Judges of the Superior, District, and County Courts in each Province, except those of the Courts of Probate in Nova Scotia and New Brunswick.

Appointment of Judges

97. Until the Laws relative to Property and Civil Rights in Ontario, Nova Scotia, and New Brunswick, and the Procedure of the Courts in those Provinces, are made uniform, the Judges of the Courts of those Provinces appointed by the Governor General shall be selected from the respective Bars of those Provinces.

Selection of Judges in Ontario, etc.

98. The Judges of the Courts of Quebec shall be selected from the Bar of that Province.

Selection of Judges in Quebec

99. (1) Subject to subsection two of this section, the Judges of the Superior Courts shall hold office during good behaviour, but shall be removable by the Governor General on Address of the Senate and House of Commons.

Tenure of office of Judges

(2) A Judge of a Superior Court, whether appointed before or after the coming into force of this section, shall cease to hold office upon attaining the age of seventy-five years, or upon the coming into force of this section if at that time he has already attained that age.[52]

Termination at age 75

94A. It is hereby declared that the Parliament of Canada may from time to time make laws in relation to old age pensions in Canada, but no law made by the Parliament of Canada in relation to old age pensions shall affect the operation of any law present or future of a Provincial Legislature in relation to old age pensions.

(52) Repealed and re-enacted by the *Constitution Act, 1960,* 9 Eliz. II, c. 2 (U.K.), which came into force on March 1, 1961. The original section read as follows:

99. The Judges of the Superior Courts shall hold Office during good Behaviour, but shall be removable by the Governor General on Address of the Senate and House of Commons.

Salaries, etc., of Judges

100. The Salaries, Allowances, and Pensions of the Judges of the Superior, District, and County Courts (except the Courts of Probate in Nova Scotia and New Brunswick), and of the Admiralty Courts in Cases where the Judges thereof are for the Time being paid by Salary, shall be fixed and provided by the Parliament of Canada.[53]

General Court of Appeal, etc.

101. The Parliament of Canada may, notwithstanding anything in this Act, from Time to Time provide for the Constitution, Maintenance, and Organization of a General Court of Appeal for Canada, and for the Establishment of any additional Courts for the better Administration of the Laws of Canada.[54]

VIII. REVENUES; DEBTS; ASSETS; TAXATION

Creation of Consolidated Revenue Fund

102. All Duties and Revenues over which the respective Legislatures of Canada, Nova Scotia, and New Brunswick before and at the Union had and have Power of Appropriation, except such Portions thereof as are by this Act reserved to the respective Legislatures of the Provinces, or are raised by them in accordance with the special Powers conferred on them by this Act, shall form One Consolidated Revenue Fund, to be appropriated for the Public Service of Canada in the Manner and subject to the Charges in this Act provided.

Expenses of Collection, etc.

103. The Consolidated Revenue Fund of Canada shall be permanently charged with the Costs, Charges, and Expenses incident to the Collection, Management, and Receipt thereof, and the same shall form the First Charge thereon, subject to be reviewed and audited in such Manner as shall be ordered by the Governor General in Council until the Parliament otherwise provides.

Interest of Provincial Public Debts

104. The annual Interest of the Public Debts of the several Provinces of Canada, Nova Scotia, and New Brunswick at the Union shall form the Second Charge on the Consolidated Revenue Fund of Canada.

Salary of Governor General

105. Unless altered by the Parliament of Canada, the Salary of the Governor General shall be Ten thousand Pounds Sterling Money of the United Kingdom of Great Britain and Ireland, payable out of the Consolidated Revenue Fund of Canada, and the same shall form the Third Charge thereon.[55]

---

(53) Now provided for in the *Judges Act,* R.S.C. 1985, c. J-1.

(54) See the *Supreme Court Act,* R.S.C. 1985, c. S-26, the *Federal Court Act,* R.S.C. 1985, c. F-7 and the *Tax Court of Canada Act,* R.S.C. 1985, c. T-2.

(55) Now covered by the *Governor General's Act,* R.S.C. 1985, c. G-9.

106. Subject to the several Payments by this Act charged on the Consolidated Revenue Fund of Canada, the same shall be appropriated by the Parliament of Canada for the Public Service.

Appropriation from Time to Time

107. All Stocks, Cash, Banker's Balances, and Securities for Money belonging to each Province at the Time of the Union, except as in this Act mentioned, shall be the Property of Canada, and shall be taken in Reduction of the Amount of the respective Debts of the Provinces at the Union.

Transfer of Stocks, etc.

108. The Public Works and Property of each Province, enumerated in the Third Schedule to this Act, shall be the Property of Canada.

Transfer of Property in Schedule

109. All Lands, Mines, Minerals, and Royalties belonging to the Several Provinces of Canada, Nova Scotia, and New Brunswick at the Union, and all Sums then due or payable for such Lands, Mines, Minerals, or Royalties, shall belong to the several Provinces of Ontario, Quebec, Nova Scotia, and New Brunswick in which the same are situate or arise, subject to any Trusts existing in respect thereof, and to any Interest other than that of the Province in the same.[56]

Property in Lands, Mines, etc.

110. All Assets connected with such Portions of the Public Debt of each Province as are assumed by that Province shall belong to that Province.

Assets connected with Provincial Debts

111. Canada shall be liable for the Debts and Liabilities of each Province existing at the Union.

Canada to be liable for Provincial Debts

112. Ontario and Quebec conjointly shall be liable to Canada for the Amount (if any) by which the Debt of the Province of Canada exceeds at the Union Sixty-two million five hundred thousand Dollars, and shall be charged with Interest at the Rate of Five per Centum per Annum thereon.

Debts of Ontario and Quebec

113. The Assets enumerated in the Fourth Schedule to this Act belonging at the Union to the Province of Canada shall be the property of Ontario and Quebec conjointly.

Assets of Ontario and Quebec

---

(56) Manitoba, Alberta and Saskatchewan were placed in the same position as the original provinces by the *Constitution Act, 1930,* 20-21 Geo. V, c. 26 (U.K.).

These matters were dealt with in respect of British Columbia by the *British Columbia Terms of Union* and also in part by the *Constitution Act, 1930.*

Newfoundland was also placed in the same position by the *Newfoundland Act,* 12-13 Geo. VI, c. 22 (U.K.).

With respect to Prince Edward Island, see the Schedule to the *Prince Edward Island Terms of Union.*

Debt of Nova Scotia

114. Nova Scotia shall be liable to Canada for the Amount (if any) by which its Public Debt exceeds at the Union Eight million Dollars, and shall be charged with Interest at the Rate of Five per Centum per Annum thereon.[57]

Debt of New Brunswick

115. New Brunswick shall be liable to Canada for the Amount (if any) by which its Public Debt exceeds at the Union Seven million Dollars, and shall be charged with Interest at the Rate of Five per Centum per Annum thereon.

Payment of interest to Nova Scotia and New Brunswick

116. In case the Public Debts of Nova Scotia and New Brunswick do not at the Union amount to Eight million and Seven million Dollars respectively, they shall respectively receive by half-yearly Payments in advance from the Government of Canada Interest at Five per Centum per Annum on the Difference between the actual Amounts of their respective Debts and such stipulated Amounts.

Provincial Public Property

117. The several Provinces shall retain all their respective Public Property not otherwise disposed of in this Act, subject to the Right of Canada to assume any Lands or Public Property required for Fortifications or for the Defence of the Country.

118. Repealed.[58]

---

(57) The obligations imposed by this section, sections 115 and 116, and similar obligations under the instruments creating or admitting other provinces, have been carried into legislation of the Parliament of Canada and are now to be found in the *Provincial Subsidies Act*, R.S.C. 1985, c. P-26.

(58) Repealed by the *Statute Law Revision Act, 1950*, 14 Geo. VI, c. 6 (U.K.). As originally enacted the section read as follows:

> **118.** The following Sums shall be paid yearly by Canada to the several Provinces for the Support of their Governments and Legislatures:

	Dollars.
Ontario	Eighty thousand.
Quebec	Seventy thousand.
Nova Scotia	Sixty thousand.
New Brunswick	Fifty thousand.
	Two hundred and sixty thousand;

> and an annual Grant in aid of each Province shall be made, equal to Eighty cents per Head of the Population as ascertained by the Census of One thousand eight hundred and sixty-one, and in the case of Nova Scotia and New Brunswick, by each subsequent Decennial Census until the Population of each of those two Provinces amounts to Four hundred thousand Souls, at which Rate such Grant shall thereafter remain. Such Grants shall be in full Settlement of all future Demands on Canada, and shall be paid half-yearly in advance to each Province; but the Government of Canada shall deduct from such Grants, as against any Province, all Sums chargeable as Interest on the Public Debt of that Province in excess of the several Amounts stipulated in this Act.

The section was made obsolete by the *Constitution Act, 1907*, 7 Edw. VII , c. 11 (U.K.) which provided:

1. (1) The following grants shall be made yearly by Canada to every province, which at the commencement of this Act is a province of the Dominion, for its local purposes and the support of its Government and Legislature: —

(a) A fixed grant —

where the population of the province is under one hundred and fifty thousand, of one hundred thousand dollars;

where the population of the province is one hundred and fifty thousand, but does not exceed two hundred thousand, of one hundred and fifty thousand dollars;

where the population of the province is two hundred thousand, but does not exceed four hundred thousand, of one hundred and eighty thousand dollars;

where the population of the province is four hundred thousand, but does not exceed eight hundred thousand, of one hundred and ninety thousand dollars;

where the population of the province is eight hundred thousand, but does no exceed one million five hundred thousand, of two hundred and twenty thousand dollars;

where the population of the province exceeds one million five hundred thousand, of two hundred and forty thousand dollars; and

(b) Subject to the special provisions of this Act as to the provinces of British Columbia and Prince Edward Island, a grant at the rate of eighty cents per head of the population of the province up to the number of two million five hundred thousand, and at the rate of sixty cents per head of so much of the population as exceeds that number.

(2) An additional grant of one hundred thousand dollars shall be made yearly to the province of British Columbia for a period of ten years from the commencement of this Act.

(3) The population of a province shall be ascertained from time to time in the case of the provinces of Manitoba, Saskatchewan, and Alberta respectively by the last quinquennial census or statutory estimate of population made under the Acts establishing those provinces or any other Act of the Parliament of Canada making provision for the purpose, and in the case of any other province by the last decennial census for the time being.

(4) The grants payable under this Act shall be paid half-yearly in advance to each province.

(5) The grants payable under this Act shall be substituted for the grants or subsidies (in this Act referred to as existing grants) payable for the like purposes at the commencement of this Act to the several provinces of the Dominion under the provisions of section one hundred and eighteen of the *Constitution Act, 1867*, or of any Order in Council establishing a province, or of any Act of the Parliament of Canada containing directions for the payment of any such grant or subsidy, and those provisions shall cease to have effect.

(6) The Government of Canada shall have the same power of deducting sums charged against a province on account of the interest on public debt in the case of the grant payable under this Act to the province as they have in the case of the existing grant.

(7) Nothing in this Act shall affect the obligation of the Government of Canada to pay to any province any grant which is payable to that province, other than the existing grant for which the grant under this Act is substituted.

(8) In the case of the provinces of British Columbia and Prince Edward Island, the amount paid on account of the grant payable per head of the population to the provinces under this Act shall not at any time be less than the amount of the corresponding grant payable at the commencement of this Act, and if it is found on any decennial census that the population of the province has decreased since the last decennial census, the amount paid on account of the grant shall not be decreased below the amount then payable, notwithstanding the decrease of the population.

Further Grant to New Brunswick

119. New Brunswick shall receive by half-yearly Payments in advance from Canada for the Period of Ten Years from the Union an additional Allowance of Sixty-three thousand Dollars per Annum; but as long as the Public Debt of that Province remains under Seven million Dollars, a Deduction equal to the Interest at Five per Centum per Annum on such Deficiency shall be made from that Allowance of Sixty three thousand Dollars.[59]

Form of Payments

120. All Payments to be made under this Act, or in discharge of Liabilities created under any Act of the Provinces of Canada, Nova Scotia, and New Brunswick respectively, and assumed by Canada, shall, until the Parliament of Canada otherwise directs, be made in such Form and Manner as may from Time to Time be ordered by the Governor General in Council.

Canadian Manufactures, etc.

121. All Articles of the Growth, Produce, or Manufacture of any one of the Provinces shall, from and after the Union, be admitted free into each of the other Provinces.

Continuance of Customs and Excise Laws

122. The Customs and Excise Laws of each Province shall, subject to the Provisions of this Act, continue in force until altered by the Parliament of Canada.[60]

Exportation and Importation as between Two Provinces

123. Where Customs Duties are, at the Union, leviable on any Goods, Wares, or Merchandises in any Two Provinces, those Goods, Wares, and Merchandises may, from and after the Union, be imported from one of those Provinces into the other of them on Proof of Payment of the Customs Duty leviable thereon in the Province of Exportation, and on Payment of such further Amount (if any) of Customs Duty as is leviable thereon in the Province of Importation.[61]

See the *Provincial Subsidies Act*, R.S.C. 1985, c. P-26 and the *Federal-Provincial Fiscal Arrangements and Federal Post-Secondary Education and Health Contributions Act*, R.S.C. 1985, c. F-8.

See also Part III of the *Constitution Act, 1982*, which sets out commitments by Parliament and the provincial legislatures respecting equal opportunities, economic development and the provision of essential public services and a commitment by Parliament and the government of Canada to the principle of making equalization payments.

(59) Spent.

(60) Spent. Now covered by the *Customs Act*, R.S.C. 1985, c. 1 (2nd Supp.), the *Customs Tariff*, R.S.C. 1985, c. 41 (3rd Supp.), the *Excise Act*, R.S.C. 1985, c. E-14 and the *Excise Tax Act*, R.S.C. 1985, c. E-15.

(61) Spent.

124. Nothing in this Act shall affect the Right of New Brunswick to levy the Lumber Dues provided in Chapter Fifteen of Title Three of the Revised Statutes of New Brunswick, or in any Act amending that Act before or after the Union, and not increasing the Amount of such Dues; but the Lumber of any of the Provinces other than New Brunswick shall not be subject to such Dues.[62]

Lumber Dues in New Brunswick

125. No Lands or Property belonging to Canada or any Province shall be liable to Taxation.

Exemption of Public Lands, etc.

126. Such Portions of the Duties and Revenues over which the respective Legislatures of Canada, Nova Scotia, and New Brunswick had before the Union Power of Appropriation as are by this Act reserved to the respective Governments or Legislatures of the Provinces, and all Duties and Revenues raised by them in accordance with the special Powers conferred upon them by this Act, shall in each Province form One Consolidated Revuenue Fund to be appropriated for the Public Service of the Province.

Provincial Consolidated Revenue Fund

IX. MISCELLANEOUS PROVISIONS

General

127. Repealed.[63]

(62) These dues were repealed in 1873 by 36 Vict., c. 16 (N.B). And see *An Act respecting the Export Duties imposed on Lumber*, etc. (1873) 36 Vict., c. 41 (Canada), and section 2 of the *Provincial Subsidies Act*, R.S.C. 1985, c. P-26.

(63) Repealed by the *Statute Law Revision Act, 1893*, 56-57 Vict., c. 14 (U.K.). The section read as follows.

> **127.** If any Person being at the passing of this Act a Member of the Legislative Council of Canada, Nova Scotia, or New Brunswick, to whom a Place in the Senate is offered, does not within Thirty Days thereafter, by Writing under his Hand addressed to the Governor General of the Province of Canada or to the Lieutenant Governor of Nova Scotia or New Brunswick (as the Case may be), accept the same, he shall be deemed to have declined the same; and any Person who, being at the passing of this Act a Member of the Legislative Council of Nova Scotia or New Brunswick, accepts a Place in the Senate shall thereby vacate his Seat in such Legislative Council.

Oath of Allegiance, etc.

128. Every Member of the Senate or House of Commons of Canada shall before taking his Seat therein take and subscribe before the Governor General or some Person authorized by him, and every Member of a Legislative Council or Legislative Assembly of any Province shall before taking his Seat therein take and subscribe before the Lieutenant Governor of the Province or some Person authorized by him, the Oath of Allegiance contained in the Fifth Schedule to this Act; and every Member of the Senate of Canada and every Member of the Legislative Council of Quebec shall also, before taking his Seat therein, take and subscribe before the Governor General, or some Person authorized by him, the Declaration of Qualification contained in the same Schedule.

Continuance of existing Laws, Courts, Officers, etc.

129. Except as otherwise provided by this Act, all Laws in force in Canada, Nova Scotia or New Brunswick at the Union, and all Courts of Civil and Criminal Jurisdiction, and all legal Commissions, Powers, and Authorities, and all Officers, Judicial, Administrative, and Ministerial, existing therein at the Union, shall continue in Ontario, Quebec, Nova Scotia, and New Brunswick respectively, as if the Union had not been made; subject nevertheless (except with respect to such as are enacted by or exist under Acts of the Parliament of Great Britain or of the Parliament of the United Kingdom of Great Britain and Ireland), to be repealed, abolished, or altered by the Parliament of Canada, or by the Legislature of the respective Province, according to the Authority of the Parliament or of that Legislature under this Act.[64]

Transfer of Officers to Canada

130. Until the Parliament of Canada otherwise provides, all Officers of the several Provinces having Duties to discharge in relation to Matters other than those coming within the Classes of Subjects by this Act assigned exclusively to the Legislatures of the Provinces shall be Officers of Canada, and shall continue to discharge the Duties of their respective Offices under the same Liabilities, Responsibilities, and Penalties as if the Union had not been made.[65]

Appointment of new Officers

131. Until the Parliament of Canada otherwise provides, the Governor General in Council may from Time to Time appoint such Officers as the Governor General in Council deems necessary or proper for the effectual Execution of this Act.

---

(64) The restriction against altering or repealing laws enacted by or existing under statutes of the United Kingdom was removed by the *Statute of Westminster, 1931*, 22 Geo. V. c. 4 (U.K,) except in respect of certain constitutional documents. Comprehensive procedures for amending enactments forming part of the Constitution of Canada were provided by Part V of the *Constitution Act, 1982*, (U.K.) 1982, c. 11.

(65) Spent.

132. The Parliament and Government of Canada shall have all Powers necessary or proper for performing the Obligations of Canada or of any Province thereof, as Part of the British Empire, towards Foreign Countries, arising under Treaties between the Empire and such Foreign Countries.

Treaty Obligations

133. Either the English or the French Language may be used by any Person in the Debates of the Houses of the Parliament of Canada and of the Houses of the Legislature of Quebec; and both those Languages shall be used in the respective Records and Journals of those Houses; and either of those Languages may be used by any Person or in any Pleading or Process in or issuing from any Court of Canada established under this Act, and in or from all or any of the Courts of Quebec.

Use of English and French Languages

The Acts of the Parliament of Canada and of the Legislature of Quebec shall be printed and published in both those Languages.[66]

Ontario and Quebec

134. Until the Legislature of Ontario or of Quebec otherwise provides, the Lieutenant Governors of Ontario and Quebec may each appoint under the Great Seal of the Province the following Officers, to hold Office during Pleasure, that is to say, — the Attorney General, the Secretary and Registrar of the Province, the Treasurer of the Province, the Commissioner of Crown Lands, and the Commissioner of Agriculture and Public Works, and in the Case of Quebec the Solicitor General, and may, by Order of the Lieutenant Governor in Council, from Time to Time prescribe the Duties of

Appointment of Executive Officers for Ontario and Quebec

(66) A similar provision was enacted for Manitoba by section 23 of the *Manitoba Act, 1870,* 33 Vict., c. 3 (Canada), (confirmed by the *Constitution Act, 1871*). Section 23 read as follows:

> **23.** Either the English or the French language may be used by any person in the debates of the Houses of the Legislature, and both these languages shall be used in the respective Records and Journals of those Houses; and either of those languages may be used by any person, or in any Pleading or Process, in or issuing from any Court of Canada established under the British North America Act, 1867, or in or from all or any of the Courts of the Province. The Acts of the Legislature shall be printed and published in both those languages.

Sections 17 to 19 of the *Constitution Act, 1982,* restate the language rights set out in section 133 in respect of Parliament and the courts established under the *Constitution Act, 1867,* and also guarantees those rights in respect of the legislature of New Brunswick and the courts of that province.

Section 16 and sections 20, 21 and 23 of the *Constitution Act, 1982* recognize additional language rights in respect of the English and French languages. Section 22 preserves language rights and privileges of languages other than English and French.

those Officers, and of the several Departments over which they shall preside or to which they shall belong, and of the Officers and Clerks thereof, and may also appoint other and additional Officers to hold Office during Pleasure, and may from Time to Time prescribe the Duties of those Officers, and of the several Departments over which they shall preside or to which they shall belong, and of the Officers and Clerks thereof.[67]

Powers, Duties, etc. of Executive Officers

135. Until the Legislature of Ontario or Quebec otherwise provides, all Rights, Powers, Duties, Functions, Responsibilities, or Authorities at the passing of this Act vested in or imposed on the Attorney General, Solicitor General, Secretary and Registrar of the Province of Canada, Minister of Finance, Commissioner of Crown Lands, Commissioner of Public Works, and Minister of Agriculture and Receiver General, by any Law, Statute, or Ordinance of Upper Canada, Lower Canada, or Canada, and not repugnant to this Act, shall be vested in or imposed on any Officer to be appointed by the Lieutenant Governor for the Discharge of the same or any of them; and the Commissioner of Agriculture and Public Works shall perform the Duties and Functions of the Office of Minister of Agriculture at the passing of this Act imposed by the Law of the Province of Canada, as well as those of the Commissioner of Public Works.[68]

Great Seals

136. Until altered by the Lieutenant Governor in Council, the Great Seals of Ontario and Quebec respectively shall be the same, or of the same Design, as those used in the Provinces of Upper Canada and Lower Canada respectively before their Union as the Province of Canada.

Construction of temporary Acts

137. The words "and from thence to the End of the then next ensuing Session of the Legislature," or Words to the same Effect, used in any temporary Act of the Province of Canada not expired before the Union, shall be construed to extend and apply to the next Session of the Parliament of Canada if the Subject Matter of the Act is within the Powers of the same as defined by this Act, or to the next Sessions of the Legislatures of Ontario and Quebec respectively if the Subject Matter of the Act is within the Powers of the same as defined by this Act.

---

(67) Spent. Now covered in Ontario by the *Executive Council Act*, R.S.O. 1980, c. 147 and in Quebec by the *Executive Power Act*, R.S.Q. 1977, c. E-18.

(68) Probably spent.

138. From and after the Union the Use of the Words "Upper Canada" instead of "Ontario," or "Lower Canada" instead of "Quebec," in any Deed, Writ, Process, Pleading, Document, Matter, or Thing shall not invalidate the same.

As to Errors in Names

139. Any Proclamation under the Great Seal of the Province of Canada issued before the Union to take effect at a Time which is subsequent to the Union, whether relating to that Province, or to Upper Canada, or to Lower Canada, and the several Matters and Things therein proclaimed, shall be and continue of like Force and Effect as if the Union had not been made.[69]

As to issue of Proclamations before Union, to commence after Union

140. Any Proclamation which is authorized by any Act of the Legislature of the Province of Canada to be issued under the Great Seal of the Province of Canada, whether relating to that Province, or to Upper Canada, or to Lower Canada, and which is not issued before the Union, may be issued by the Lieutenant Governor of Ontario or of Quebec, as its Subject Matter requires, under the Great Seal thereof; and from and after the Issue of such Proclamation the same and the several Matters and Things therein proclaimed shall be and continue of the like Force and Effect in Ontario or Quebec as if the Union had not been made.[70]

As to issue of Proclamations after Union

141. The Penitentiary of the Province of Canada shall, until the Parliament of Canada otherwise provides, be and continue the Penitentiary of Ontario and of Quebec.[71]

Penitentiary

142. The Division and Adjustment of the Debts, Credits, Liabilities, Properties, and Assets of Upper Canada and Lower Canada shall be referred to the Arbitrament of Three Arbitrators, One chosen by the Government of Ontario, One by the Government of Quebec, and One by the Government of Canada; and the Selection of the Arbitrators shall not be made until the Parliament of Canada and the Legislatures of Ontario and Quebec have met; and the Arbitrator chosen by the Government of Canada shall not be a Resident either in Ontario or in Quebec.[72]

Arbitration respecting Debts, etc.

(69) Probably spent.

(70) Probably spent.

(71) Spent. Penitentiaries are now provided for by the *Penitentiary Act*, R.S.C. 1985, c. P-5.

(72) Spent. See pages (xi) and (xii) of the Public Accounts, 1902-1903.

Division of Records

143. The Governor General in Council may from Time to Time order that such and so many of the Records, Books, and Documents of the Province of Canada as he thinks fit shall be appropriated and delivered either to Ontario or to Quebec, and the same shall thenceforth be the Property of that Province; and any Copy thereof or Extract therefrom, duly certified by the Officer having charge of the Original thereof, shall be admitted as Evidence.[73]

Constitution of Townships in Quebec

144. The Lieutenant Governor of Quebec may from Time to Time, by Proclamation under the Great Seal of the Province, to take effect from a Day to be appointed therein, constitute Townships in those Parts of the Province of Quebec in which Townships are not then already constituted, and fix the Metes and Bounds thereof.

X. INTERCOLONIAL RAILWAY

145. Repealed.[74]

XI. ADMISSION OF OTHER COLONIES

Power to admit Newfoundland, etc., into the Union

146. It shall be lawful for the Queen, by and with the Advice of Her Majesty's Most Honourable Privy Council, on Addresses from the Houses of the Parliament of Canada, and from the Houses of the respective Legislatures of the Colonies or Provinces of Newfoundland, Prince Edward Island, and British Columbia, to admit those Colonies or Provinces, or any of them, into the Union, and on Address from the Houses of the Parliament of Canada to admit Rupert's Land and the North-western Territory, or either of them, into the Union, on such Terms and Conditions in each Case as are in the Addresses expressed and as the Queen thinks fit to approve, subject to the Provisions of this Act; and the Provisions of any Order in Council in that Behalf shall have effect as if they had been enacted by the Parliament of the United Kingdom of Great Britain and Ireland.[75]

---

(73) Probably spent. Two orders were made under this section on January 24, 1868.

(74) Repealed by the *Statute Law Revision Act, 1893,* 56-57 Vict., c. 14 (U.K.). The section read as follows:

X. — Intercolonial Railway

145. Inasmuch as the Provinces of Canada, Nova Scotia, and New Brunswick have joined in a Declaration that the Construction of the Intercolonial Railway is essential to the Consolidation of the Union of British North America, and to the Assent thereto of Nova Scotia and New Brunswick, and have consequently agreed that Provision should be made for its immediate Construction by the Government of Canada; Therefore, in order to give effect to that Agreement, it shall be the Duty of the Government and Parliament of Canada to provide for the Commencement, within Six Months after the Union, of a Railway connecting the River St. Lawrence with the City of Halifax in Nova Scotia, and for the Construction thereof without Intermission, and the Completion thereof with all practicable Speed.

(75) All territories mentioned in this section are now part of Canada. See the notes to section 5, *supra.*

As to Representation of Newfoundland and Prince Edward Island in Senate

147. In case of the Admission of Newfoundland and Prince Edward Island, or either of them, each shall be entitled to a Representation in the Senate of Canada of Four Members, and (notwithstanding anything in this Act) in case of the Admission of Newfoundland the normal Number of Senators shall be Seventy-six and their maximum Number shall be Eighty-two; but Prince Edward Island when admitted shall be deemed to be comprised in the third of the Three Divisions into which Canada is, in relation to the Constitution of the Senate, divided by this Act, and accordingly, after the Admission of Prince Edward Island, whether Newfoundland is admitted or not, the Representation of Nova Scotia and New Brunswick in the Senate shall, as Vacancies occur, be reduced from Twelve to Ten Members respectively, and the Representation of each of those Provinces shall not be increased at any Time beyond Ten, except under the Provisions of this Act for the Appointment of Three or Six additional Senators under the Direction of the Queen.[76]

(76) Spent. See the notes to sections 21, 22, 26, 27 and 28, *supra*.

SCHEDULES

THE FIRST SCHEDULE[77]

Electoral Districts of Ontario

A.

EXISTING ELECTORAL DIVISIONS.

COUNTIES

1. Prescott.
2. Glengarry.
3. Stormont.
4. Dundas.
5. Russell.
6. Carleton.
7. Prince Edward.
8. Halton.
9. Essex.

RIDINGS OF COUNTIES

10. North Riding of Lanark.
11. South Riding of Lanark.
12. North Riding of Leeds and North Riding of Grenville.
13. South Riding of Leeds.
14. South Riding of Grenville.
15. East Riding of Northumberland.
16. West Riding of Northumberland (excepting therefrom the Township of South Monaghan).
17. East Riding of Durham.
18. West Riding of Durham.
19. North Riding of Ontario.
20. South Riding of Ontario.
21. East Riding of York.
22. West Riding of York.
23. North Riding of York.
24. North Riding of Wentworth.
25. South Riding of Wentworth.
26. East Riding of Elgin.

---

(77) Spent. *Representation Act*, R.S.O. 1970, c. 413.

27. West Riding of Elgin.
28. North Riding of Waterloo.
29. South Riding of Waterloo.
30. North Riding of Brant.
31. South Riding of Brant.
32. North Riding of Oxford.
33. South Riding of Oxford.
34. East Riding of Middlesex.

CITIES, PARTS OF CITIES, AND TOWNS

35. West Toronto.
36. East Toronto.
37. Hamilton.
38. Ottawa.
39. Kingston.
40. London.
41. Town of Brockville, with the Township of Elizabethtown thereto attached.
42. Town of Niagara, with the Township of Niagara thereto attached.
43. Town of Cornwall, with the Township of Cornwall thereto attached.

B.

NEW ELECTORAL DIVISIONS

44. The Provisional Judicial District of ALGOMA.

The County of BRUCE, divided into Two Ridings, to be called respectively the North and South Ridings: —

45. The North Riding of Bruce to consist of the Townships of Bury, Lindsay, Eastnor, Albermarle, Amable, Arran, Bruce, Elderslie, and Saugeen, and the Village of Southampton.

46. The South Riding of Bruce to consist of the Townships of Kincardine (including the Village of Kincardine), Greenock, Brant, Huron, Kinloss, Culross, and Carrick.

The County of HURON, divided into Two Ridings, to be called respectively the North and South Ridings: —

47. The North Riding to consist of the Townships of Ashfield, Wawanosh, Turnberry, Howick, Morris, Grey, Colborne, Hullett, including the Village of Clinton, and McKillop.

48. The South Riding to consist of the Town of Goderich and the Townships of Goderich, Tuckersmith, Stanley, Hay, Usborne, and Stephen.

The County of MIDDLESEX divided into three Ridings, to be called respectively the North, West, and East Ridings:—

49. The North Riding to consist of the Townships of McGillivary and Biddulph (taken from the County of Huron), and Williams East, Williams West, Adelaide, and Lobo.

50. The West Riding to consist of the Townships of Delaware, Carradoc, Metcalfe, Mosa and Ekfrid, and the Village of Strathroy.

[The East Riding to consist of the Townships now embraced therein, and be bounded as it is at present.]

51. The County of LAMBTON to consist of Townships of Bosanquet, Warwick, Plympton, Sarnia, Moore, Enniskillen, and Brooke, and the Town of Sarnia.

52. The County of KENT to consist of the Townships of Chatham, Dover, East Tilbury, Romney, Raleigh, and Harwich, and the Town of Chatham.

53. The County of BOTHWELL to consist of the Townships of Sombra, Dawn, and Euphemia (taken from the County of Lambton), and the Townships of Zone, Camden with the Gore thereof, Orford, and Howard (taken from the County of Kent).

The County of GREY divided into Two Ridings to be called respectively the South and North Ridings: —

54. The South Riding to consist of the Townships of Bentinck, Glenelg, Artemesia, Osprey, Normanby, Egremont, Proton, and Melancthon.

55. The North Riding to consist of the Townships of Collingwood, Euphrasia, Holland, Saint-Vincent, Sydenham, Sullivan, Derby, and Keppel, Sarawak and Brooke, and the Town of Owen Sound.

The County of PERTH divided into Two Ridings, to be called respectively the South and North Ridings: —

56. The North Riding to consist of the Townships of Wallace, Elma, Logan, Ellice, Mornington, and North Easthope, and the Town of Stratford.

57. The South Riding to consist of the Townships of Blanchard, Downie, South Easthope, Fullarton, Hibbert, and the Villages of Mitchell and Ste. Marys.

The County of WELLINGTON divided into Three Ridings to be called respectively North, South and Centre Ridings: —

58. The North Riding to consist of the Townships of Amaranth, Arthur, Luther, Minto, Maryborough, Peel, and the Village of Mount Forest.

59. The Centre Riding to consist of the Townships of Garafraxa, Erin, Eramosa, Nichol, and Pilkington, and the Villages of Fergus and Elora.

60. The South Riding to consist of the Town of Guelph, and the Townships of Guelph and Puslinch.

The County of NORFOLK, divided into Two Ridings, to be called respectively the South and North Ridings: —

61. The South Riding to consist of the Townships of Charlotteville, Houghton, Walsingham, and Woodhouse, and with the Gore thereof.

62. The North Riding to consist of the Townships of Middleton, Townsend, and Windham, and the Town of Simcoe.

63. The County of HALDIMAND to consist of the Townships of Oneida, Seneca, Cayuga North, Cayuga South, Raynham, Walpole, and Dunn.

64. The County of MONCK to consist of the Townships of Canborough and Moulton, and Sherbrooke, and the Village of Dunnville (taken from the County of Haldimand), the Townships of Caister and Gainsborough (taken from the County of Lincoln), and the Townships of Pelham and Wainfleet (taken from the County of Welland).

65. The County of LINCOLN to consist of the Townships of Clinton, Grantham, Grimsby, and Louth, and the Town of St. Catherines.

66. The County of WELLAND to consist of the Townships of Bertie, Crowland, Humberstone, Stamford, Thorold, and Willoughby, and the Villages of Chippewa, Clifton, Fort Erie, Thorold, and Welland.

67. The County of PEEL to consist of the Townships of Chinguacousy, Toronto, and the Gore of Toronto, and the Villages of Brampton and Streetsville.

68. The County of CARDWELL to consist of the Townships of Albion and Caledon (taken from the County of Peel), and the Townships of Adjala and Mono (taken from the County of Simcoe).

The County of SIMCOE, divided into Two Ridings, to be called respectively the South and North Ridings: —

69. The South Riding to consist of the Townships of West Gwillimbury, Tecumseth, Innisfil, Essa, Tosorontio, Mulmur, and the Village of Bradford.

70. The North Riding to consist of the Townships of Sunnidale, Vespra, Flos, Oro, Medonte, Orillia and Matchedash, Tiny and Tay, Balaklava and Robinson, and the Towns of Barrie and Collingwood.

The County of VICTORIA, divided into Two Ridings, to be called respectively the South and North Ridings: —

71. The South Riding to consist of the Townships of Ops, Mariposa, Emily, Verulam, and the Town of Lindsay.

72. The North Riding to consist of the Townships of Anson, Bexley, Carden, Dalton, Digby, Eldon, Fenelon, Hindon, Laxton, Lutterworth, Macaulay and Draper, Sommerville, and Morrison, Muskoka, Monck and Watt (taken from the County of Simcoe), and any other surveyed Townships lying to the North of the said North Riding.

The County of PETERBOROUGH, divided into Two Ridings, to be called respectively the West and East Ridings:—

73. The West Riding to consist of the Townships of South Monaghan (taken from the County of Northumberland),

North Monaghan, Smith, and Ennismore, and the Town of Peterborough.

74. The East Riding to consist of the Townships of Asphodel, Belmont and Methuen, Douro, Dummer, Galway, Harvey, Minden, Stanhope and Dysart, Otonabee, and Snowden, and the Village of Ashburnham, and any other surveyed Townships lying to the North of the said East Riding.

The County of HASTINGS , divided into Three Ridings, to be called respectively the West, East, and North Ridings: —

75. The West Riding to consist of the Town of Belleville, the Township of Sydney, and the Village of Trenton.

76. The East Riding to consist of the Townships of Thurlow, Tyendinaga, and Hungerford.

77. The North Riding to consist of the Townships of Rawdon, Huntingdon, Madoc, Elzevir, Tudor, Marmora, and Lake, and the Village of Stirling, and any other surveyed Townships lying to the North of the said North Riding.

78. The County of LENNOX to consist of the Townships of Richmond, Adolphustown, North Fredericksburg, South Fredericksburg, Ernest Town, and Amherst Island, and the Village of Napanee.

79. The County of ADDINGTON to consist of the Townships of Camden, Portland, Sheffield, Hinchinbrooke, Kaladar, Kennebec, Olden, Oso, Anglesea, Barrie, Clarendon, Palmerston, Effingham, Abinger, Miller, Canonto, Denbigh, Loughborough, and Bedford.

80. The County of FRONTENAC to consist of the Townships of Kingston, Wolfe Island, Pittsburg and Howe Island, and Storrington.

The County of RENFREW, divided into Two Ridings, to be called respectively the South and North Ridings: —

81. The South Riding to consist of the Townships of McNab, Bagot, Blithfield, Brougham, Horton, Admaston, Grattan, Matawatchan, Griffith, Lyndoch, Raglan, Radcliffe, Brudenell, Sebastopol, and the Villages of Arnprior and Renfrew.

82. The North Riding to consist of the Townships of Ross, Bromley, Westmeath, Stafford, Pembroke, Wilberforce, Alice, Petawawa, Buchanan, South Algona, North Algona, Fraser, McKay, Wylie, Rolph, Head, Maria, Clara, Haggerty, Sherwood, Burns, and Richards, and any other surveyed Townships lying North-westerly of the said North Riding.

Every Town and incorporated Village existing at the Union, not especially mentioned in this Schedule, is to be taken as Part of the County or Riding within which it is locally situate.

THE SECOND SCHEDULE

Electoral Districts of Quebec specially fixed

COUNTIES OF —

Pontiac.
Ottawa.
Argenteuil.
Huntingdon.
Missisquoi.
Brome.
Shefford.
Stanstead.
Compton.
Wolfe and Richmond.
Megantic.

Town of Sherbrooke.

THE THIRD SCHEDULE

Provincial Publics Works and Property to be the Property of Canada

1. Canals, with Lands and Water Power connected therewith.
2. Public Harbours.
3. Lighthouses and Piers, and Sable Island.
4. Steamboats, Dredges, and public Vessels.
5. Rivers and Lake Improvements.

6. Railways and Railway Stocks, Mortgages, and other Debts due by Railway Companies.
7. Military Roads.
8. Custom Houses, Post Offices, and all other Public Buildings, except such as the Government of Canada appropriate for the Use of the Provincial Legislatures and Governments
9. Property transferred by the Imperial Government, and known as Ordnance Property.
10. Armouries, Drill Sheds, Military Clothing, and Munitions of War, and Lands set apart for general Public Purposes.

THE FOURTH SCHEDULE

Assets to be the Property of Ontario and Quebec conjointly

Upper Canada Building Fund.
Lunatic Asylums.
Normal School.
Court Houses in Aylmer., Montreal., Kamouraska. } Lower Canada.
Law Society, Upper Canada.
Montreal Turnpike Trust.
University Permanent Fund.
Royal Institution.
Consolidated Municipal Loan Fund, Upper Canada.
Consolidated Municipal Loan Fund, Lower Canada.
Agricultural Society, Upper Canada.
Lower Canada Legislative Grant.
Quebec Fire Loan.
Temiscouata Advance Account.
Quebec Turnpike Trust.
Education — East.
Building and Jury Fund, Lower Canada.
Municipalities Fund.
Lower Canada Superior Education Income Fund.

THE FIFTH SCHEDULE

OATH OF ALLEGIANCE

I *A.B.* do swear, That I will be faithful and bear true Allegiance to Her Majesty Queen Victoria.

Note. — The Name of the King or Queen of the United Kingdom of Great Britain and Ireland for the Time being is to be substituted from Time to Time, with proper Terms of Reference thereto.

DECLARATION OF QUALIFICATION

I *A.B.* do declare and testify, That I am by Law duly qualified to be appointed a Member of the Senate of Canada [*or as the Case may be*], and that I am legally or equitably seised as of Freehold for my own Use and Benefit of Lands of Tenements held in Free and Common Socage [*or* seised or possessed for my own Use and Benefit of Lands or Tenements held in Franc-alleu or in Roture (*as the Case may be*),] in the Province of Nova Scotia [*or as the Case may be*] of the Value of Four thousand Dollars over and above all Rents, Dues, Debts, Mortgages, Charges, and Incumbrances due or payable out of or charged on or affecting the same, and that I have not collusively or colourably obtained a Title to or become possessed of the said Lands and Tenements or any Part thereof for the Purpose of enabling me to become a Member of the Senate of Canada [*or as the Case may be*], and that my Real and Personal Property are together worth Four thousand Dollars over and above my Debts and Liabilities.

THE SIXTH SCHEDULE[78]

Primary Production from Non-Renewable Natural Resources and Forestry Resources

1. For the purposes of Section 92A of this Act,

---

(78) As enacted by the *Constitution Act, 1982.*

(*a*) production from a non-renewable natural resource is primary production therefrom if

(i) it is in the form in which it exists upon its recovery or severance from its natural state, or

(ii) it is a product resulting from processing or refining the resource, and is not a manufactured product or a product resulting from refining crude oil, refining upgraded heavy crude oil, refining gases or liquids derived from coal or refining a synthetic equivalent of crude oil; and

(*b*) production from a forestry resource is primary production therefrom if it consists of sawlogs, poles, lumber, wood chips, sawdust or any other primary wood product, or wood pulp, and is not a product manufactured from wood.

CONSTITUTION ACT, 1982[79]

SCHEDULE B

CONSTITUTION ACT, 1982

PART I

CANADIAN CHARTER OF RIGHTS AND FREEDOMS

Whereas Canada is founded upon principles that recognize the supremacy of God and the rule of law:

Guarantee of Rights and Freedoms

Rights and freedoms in Canada

1. The *Canadian Charter of Rights and Freedoms* guarantees the rights and freedoms set out in it subject only to such reasonable limits prescribed by law as can be demonstrably justified in a free and democratic society.

Fundamental Freedoms

Fundamental freedoms

2. Everyone has the following fundamental freedoms:

(*a*) freedom of conscience and religion;
(*b*) freedom of thought, belief, opinion and expression, including freedom of the press and other media of communication;

---

(79) Enacted as Schedule B to the *Canada Act 1982,* (U.K.) 1982, c. 11, which came into force on April 17, 1982. *The Canada Act 1982,* other than Schedules A and B thereto, reads as follows:

An Act to give effect to a request by the Senate and House of Commons of Canada

Whereas Canada has requested and consented to the enactment of an Act of the Parliament of the United Kingdom to give effect to the provisions hereinafter set forth and the Senate and the House of Commons of Canada in Parliament assembled have submitted an address to Her Majesty requesting that Her Majesty may graciously be pleased to cause a Bill to be laid before the Parliament of the United Kingdom for that purpose.

Be it therefore enacted by the Queen's Most Excellent Majesty, by and with the advice and consent of the Lords Spiritual and Temporal, and Commons, in this present Parliament assembled, and by the authority of the same, as follows:

1. The *Constitution Act, 1982* set out in Schedule B to this Act is hereby enacted for and shall have the force of law in Canada and shall come into force as provided in that Act.

2. No Act of Parliament of the United Kingdom passed after the *Constitution Act, 1982* comes into force shall extend to Canada as part of its law.

3. So far as it is not contained in Schedule B, the French version of this Act is set out in Schedule A to this Act and has the same authority in Canada as the English version thereof.

4. This Act may be cited as the *Canada Act 1982.*

(*c*) freedom of peaceful assembly; and

(*d*) freedom of association.

Democratic Rights

3. Every citizen of Canada has the right to vote in an election of members of the House of Commons or of a legislative assembly and to be qualified for membership therein. Democratic rights of citizens

4. (1) No House of Commons and no legislative assembly shall continue for longer than five years from the date fixed for the return of the writs of a general election of its members.[80] Maximum duration of legislative bodies

(2) In time of real or apprehended war, invasion or insurrection, a House of Commons may be continued by Parliament and a legislative assembly may be continued by the legislature beyond five years if such continuation is not opposed by the votes of more than one-third of the members of the House of Commons or the legislative assembly, as the case may be.[81] Continuation in special circumstances

5. There shall be a sitting of Parliament and of each legislature at least once every twelve months.[82] Annual sitting of legislative bodies

Mobility Rights

6. (1) Every citizen of Canada has the right to enter, remain in and leave Canada. Mobility of citizens

(2) Every citizen of Canada and every person who has the status of a permanent resident of Canada has the right Rights to move and gain livelihood

(*a*) to move to and take up residence in any province; and

(*b*) to pursue the gaining of a livelihood in any province.

(3) The rights specified in subsection (2) are subject to Limitation

(*a*) any laws or practices of general application in force in a province other than those that discriminate among persons primarily on the basis of province of present or previous residence; and

(80) See section 50 and the footnotes to sections 85 and 88 of the *Constitution Act, 1867.*

(81) Replaces part of Class 1 of section 91 of the *Constitution Act, 1867,* which was repealed as set out in subitem 1(3) of the Schedule to this Act.

(82) See the footnotes to sections 20, 86 and 88 of the *Constitution Act, 1867.*

(*b*) any laws providing for reasonable residency requirements as a qualification for the receipt of publicly provided social services.

Affirmative action programs

(4) Subsections (2) and (3) do not preclude any law, program or activity that has as its object the amelioration in a province of conditions of individuals in that province who are socially or economically disadvantaged if the rate of employment in that province is below the rate of employment in Canada.

Legal Rights

Life, liberty and security of person

7. Everyone has the right to life, liberty and security of the person and the right not to be deprived thereof except in accordance with the principles of fundamental justice.

Search or seizure

8. Everyone has the right to be secure against unreasonable search or seizure.

Detention or imprisonment

9. Everyone has the right not to be arbitrarily detained or imprisoned.

Arrest or detention

10. Everyone has the right on arrest or detention

(*a*) to be informed promptly of the reasons therefor;

(*b*) to retain and instruct counsel without delay and to be informed of that right; and

(*c*) to have the validity of the detention determined by way of *habeas corpus* and to be released if the detention is not lawful.

Proceedings in criminal and penal matters

11. Any person charged with an offence has the right

(*a*) to be informed without unreasonable delay of the specific offence;

(*b*) to be tried within a reasonable time;

(*c*) not to be compelled to be a witness in proceedings against that person in respect of the offence;

(*d*) to be presumed innocent until proven guilty according to law in a fair and public hearing by an independent and impartial tribunal;

(*e*) not to be denied reasonable bail without just cause;

(*f*) except in the case of an offence under military law tried before a military tribunal, to the benefit of trial by jury where the maximum punishment for the offence is imprisonment for five years or a more severe punishment;

(*g*) not to be found guilty on account of any act or omission unless, at the time of the act or omission, it constituted an offence under Canadian or international law or was criminal according to the general principles of law recognized by the community of nations;

(*h*) if finally acquitted of the offence, not to be tried for it again and, if finally found guilty and punished for the offence, not to be tried or punished for it again; and

(*i*) if found guilty of the offence and if the punishment for the offence has been varied between the time of commission and the time of sentencing, to the benefit of the lesser punishment.

12. Everyone has the right not to be subjected to any cruel and unusual treatment or punishment. Treatment or punishment

13. A witness who testifies in any proceedings has the right not to have any incriminating evidence so given used to incriminate that witness in any other proceedings, except in a prosecution for perjury or for the giving of contradictory evidence. Self-crimination

14. A party or witness in any proceedings who does not understand or speak the language in which the proceedings are conducted or who is deaf has the right to the assistance of an interpreter. Interpreter

Equality Rights

15. (1) Every individual is equal before and under the law and has the right to the equal protection and equal benefit of the law without discrimination and, in particular, without discrimination based on race, national or ethnic origin, colour, religion, sex, age or mental or physical disability. Equality before and under law and equal protection and benefit of law

Affirmative action programs

2) Subsection (1) does not preclude any law, program or activity that has as its object the amelioration of conditions of disadvantaged individuals or groups including those that are disadvantaged because of race, national or ethnic origin, colour, religion, sex, age or mental or physical disability.[83]

Official Languages of Canada

Official languages of Canada

16. (1) English and French are the official languages of Canada and have equality of status and equal rights and privileges as to their use in all institutions of the Parliament and government of Canada.

Official languages of New Brunswick

(2) English and French are the official languages of New Brunswick and have equality of status and equal rights and privileges as to their use in all institutions of the legislature and government of New Brunswick.

Advancement of status and use

(3) Nothing in this Charter limits the authority of Parliament or a legislature to advance the equality of status or use of English and French.

Proceedings of Parliament

17. (1) Everyone has the right to use English or French in any debates and other proceedings of Parliament.[84]

Proceedings of New Brunswick legislature

(2) Everyone has the right to use English or French in any debates and other proceedings of the legislature of New Brunswick.[85]

Parliamentary statutes and records

18. (1) The statutes, records and journals of Parliament shall be printed and published in English and French and both language versions are equally authoritative.[86]

New Brunswick statutes and records

(2) The statutes, records and journals of the legislature of New Brunswick shall be printed and published in English and French and both language versions are equally authoritative.[87]

---

(83) Subsection 32(2) provides that section 15 shall not have effect until three years after section 32 comes into force.

Section 32 came into force on April 17, 1982; therefore, section 15 had effect on April 17, 1985.

(84) See section 133 of the *Constitution Act, 1867*, and the footnote thereto.

(85) Id.

(86) Id.

(87) Id.

19. (1) Either English or French may be used by any person in, or in any pleading in or process issuing from, any court established by Parliament.[88]

Proceedings in courts established by Parliament

(2) Either English or French may be used by any person in, or in any pleading in or process issuing from, any court of New Brunswick.[89]

Proceedings in New Brunswick courts

20. (1) Any member of the public in Canada has the right to communicate with, and to receive available services from, any head or central office of an institution of the Parliament or government of Canada in English or French, and has the same right with respect to any other office of any such institution where

Communications by public with federal institutions

(*a*) there is a significant demand for communications with and services from that office in such language; or

(*b*) due to the nature of the office, it is reasonable that communications with and services from that office be available in both English and French.

(2) Any member of the public in New Brunswick has the right to communicate with, and to receive available services from, any office of an institution of the legislature or government of New Brunswick in English or French.

Communications by public with New Brunswick institutions

21. Nothing in sections 16 to 20 abrogates or derogates from any right, privilege or obligation with respect to the English and French languages, or either of them, that exists or is continued by virtue of any other provision of the Constitution of Canada.[90]

Continuation of existing constitutional provisions

(88) Id.

(89) Id.

(90) See, for example, section 133 of the *Constitution Act, 1867*, and the reference to the *Manitoba Act, 1870*, in the footnote thereto.

Rights and privileges preserved

22. Nothing in sections 16 to 20 abrogates or derogates from any legal or customary right or privilege acquired or enjoyed either before or after the coming into force of this Charter with respect to any language that is not English or French.

Minority Language Educational Rights

Language of instruction

23. (1) Citizens of Canada

(*a*) whose first language learned and still understood is that of the English or French linguistic minority population of the province in which they reside, or

(*b*) who have received their primary school instruction in Canada in English or French and reside in a province where the language in which they received that instruction is the language of the English or French linguistic minority population of the province,

have the right to have their children receive primary and secondary school instruction in that language in that province.[91]

Continuity of language instruction

(2) Citizens of Canada of whom any child has received or is receiving primary or secondary school instruction in English or French in Canada, have the right to have all their children receive primary and secondary school instruction in the same language.

Application where numbers warrant

(3) The right of citizens of Canada under subsections (1) and (2) to have their children receive primary and secondary school instruction in the language of the English or French linguistic minority population of a province

(*a*) applies wherever in the province the number of children of citizens who have such a right is sufficient to warrant the provision to them out of public funds of minority language instruction; and

(*b*) includes, where the number of those children so warrants, the right to have them receive that instruction in minority language educational facilities provided out of public funds.

---

(91) Paragraph 23(1)(*a*) is not in force in respect of Quebec. See section 59 *infra*.

Enforcement

24. (1) Anyone whose rights or freedoms, as guaranteed by this Charter, have been infringed or denied may apply to a court of competent jurisdiction to obtain such remedy as the court considers appropriate and just in the circumstances.

Enforcement of guaranteed rights and freedoms

(2) Where, in proceedings under subsection (1), a court concludes that evidence was obtained in a manner that infringed or denied any rights or freedoms guaranteed by this Charter, the evidence shall be excluded if it is established that, having regard to all the circumstances, the admission of it in the proceedings would bring the administration of justice into disrepute.

Exclusion of evidence bringing administration of justice into disrepute

General

25. The guarantee in this Charter of certain rights and freedoms shall not be construed so as to abrogate or derogate from any aboriginal, treaty or other rights or freedoms that pertain to the aboriginal peoples of Canada including

Aboriginal rights and freedoms not affected by Charter

(*a*) any rights or freedoms that have been recognized by the Royal Proclamation of October 7, 1763; and

(*b*) any rights or freedoms that now exist by way of land claims agreements or may be so acquired.[92]

26. The guarantee in this Charter of certain rights and freedoms shall not be construed as denying the existence of any other rights or freedoms that exist in Canada.

Other rights and freedoms not affected by Charter

27. This Charter shall be interpreted in a manner consistent with the preservation and enhancement of the multicultural heritage of Canadians.

Multicultural heritage

28. Notwithstanding anything in this Charter, the rights and freedoms referred to in it are guaranteed equally to male and female persons.

Rights guaranteed equally to both sexes

29. Nothing in this Charter abrogates or derogates from any rights or privileges guaranteed by or under the Constitution of Canada in respect of denominational, separate or dissentient schools.[93]

Rights respecting certain schools preserved

(92) Paragraph 25(*b*) was repealed and re-enacted by the *Constitution Amendment Proclamation, 1983. See* SI/84-102.

Paragraph 25(*b*) as originally enacted read as follows:

"(*b*) any rights or freedoms that may be acquired by the aboriginal peoples of Canada by way of land claims settlement."

(93) See section 93 of the *Constitution Act, 1867,* and the footnote thereto.

Application to territories and territorial authorities

30. A reference in this Charter to a Province or to the legislative assembly or legislature of a province shall be deemed to include a reference to the Yukon Territory and the Northwest Territories, or to the appropriate legislative authority thereof, as the case may be.

Legislative powers not extended

31. Nothing in this Charter extends the legislative powers of any body or authority.

Application of Charter

Application of Charter

32. (1) This Charter applies

(*a*) to the Parliament and government of Canada in respect of all matters within the authority of Parliament including all matters relating to the Yukon Territory and Northwest Territories; and

(*b*) to the legislature and government of each province in respect of all matters within the authority of the legislature of each province.

Exception

(2) Notwithstanding subsection (1), section 15 shall not have effect until three years after this section comes into force.

Exception where express declaration

33. (1) Parliament or the legislature of a province may expressly declare in an Act of Parliament or of the legislature, as the case may be, that the Act or a provision thereof shall operate notwithstanding a provision included in section 2 or sections 7 to 15 of this Charter.

Operation of exception

(2) An Act or a provision of an Act in respect of which a declaration made under this section is in effect shall have such operation as it would have but for the provision of this Charter referred to in the declaration.

Five year limitation

(3) A declaration made under subsection (1) shall cease to have effect five years after it comes into force or on such earlier date as may be specified in the declaration.

Re-enactment

(4) Parliament or the legislature of a province may re-enact a declaration made under subsection (1).

Five year limitation

(5) Subsection (3) applies in respect of a re-enactment made under subsection (4).

Citation

Citation

34. This Part may be cited as the *Canadian Charter of Rights and Freedoms.*

PART II

RIGHTS OF THE ABORIGINAL PEOPLES OF CANADA

35. (1) The existing aboriginal and treaty rights of the aboriginal peoples of Canada are hereby recognized and affirmed.

Recognition of existing aboriginal and treaty rights

(2) In this Act, "aboriginal peoples of Canada" includes the Indian, Inuit and Métis peoples of Canada.

Definition of "aboriginal peoples of Canada"

(3) For greater certainty, in subsection (1) "treaty rights" includes rights that now exist by way of land claims agreements or may be so acquired.

Land claims agreements

(4) Notwithstanding any other provision of this Act, the aboriginal and treaty rights referred to in subsection (1) are guaranteed equally to male and female persons.[94]

Aboriginal and treaty rights are guaranteed equally to both sexes

35.1 The government of Canada and the provincial governments are committed to the principle that, before any amendment is made to Class 24 of section 91 of the "*Constitution Act, 1867*", to section 25 of this Act or to this Part,

Commitment to participation in constitutional conference.

(*a*) a constitutional conference that includes in its agenda an item relating to the proposed amendment, composed of the Prime Minister of Canada and the first ministers of the provinces, will be convened by the Prime Minister of Canada; and

(*b*) the Prime Minister of Canada will invite representatives of the aboriginal peoples of Canada to participate in the discussions on that item.[95]

(94) Subsections 35(3) and (4) were added by the *Constitution Amendment Proclamation, 1983. See* SI/84-102.

(95) Section 35.1 was added by the *Constitution Amendment Proclamation, 1983. See* SI/84-102.

PART III

EQUALIZATION AND REGIONAL DISPARITIES

Commitment to promote equal opportunities

36. (1) Without altering the legislative authority of Parliament or of the provincial legislatures, or the rights of any of them with respect to the exercise of their legislative authority, Parliament and the legislatures, together with the government of Canada and the provincial governments, are committed to

(*a*) promoting equal opportunities for the well-being of Canadians;

(*b*) furthering economic development to reduce disparity in opportunities; and

(*c*) providing essential public services of reasonable quality to all Canadians.

Commitment respecting public services

(2) Parliament and the government of Canada are committed to the principle of making equalization payments to ensure that provincial governments have sufficient revenues to provide reasonably comparable levels of public services at reasonably comparable levels of taxation.[96]

PART IV

CONSTITUTIONAL CONFERENCE

37.[97]

---

(96) See the footnotes to sections 114 and 118 of the *Constitution Act, 1867.*

(97) Section 54 provided for the repeal of Part IV one year after Part VII came into force. Part VII came into force on April 17, 1982 thereby repealing Part IV on April 17, 1983.

Part IV, as originally enacted, read as follows:

> **37.1** (1) A constitutional conference composed of the Prime Minister of Canada and the first ministers of the provinces shall be convened by the Prime Minister of Canada within one year after this Part comes into force.
>
> (2) The conference convened under subsection (1) shall have included in its agenda an item respecting constitutional matters that directly affect the aboriginal peoples of Canada, including the identification and definition of the rights of those peoples to be included in the Constituion of Canada, and the Prime Minister of Canada shall invite representatives of those peoples to participate in the discussions on that item.
>
> (3) The Prime Minister of Canada shall invite elected representatives of the governments of the Yukon Territory and the Northwest Territories to participate in the discussions on any item on the agenda of the conference convened under subsection (1) that, in the opinion of the Prime Minister, directly affects the Yukon Territory and the Northwest Territories.

PART IV.1

CONSTITUTIONAL CONFERENCES

37.1.[98]

PART V

PROCEDURE FOR AMENDING CONSTITUTION OF CANADA[99]

38. (1) An amendment to the Constitution of Canada may be made by proclamation issued by the Governor General under the Great Seal of Canada where so authorized by

General procedure for amending Constitution of Canada

---

(98) Part IV.1., which was added by the *Constitution Amendment Proclamation, 1983* (see SI/84-102), was repealed on April 18, 1987 by section 54.1.

Part IV.1, as originally enacted, read as follows:

> **37.1** (1) In addition to the conference convened in March 1983, at least two constitutional conferences composed of the Prime Minister of Canada and the first ministers of the provinces shall be convened by the Prime Minister of Canada, the first within three years after April 17, 1982 and the second within five years after that date.
>
> (2) Each conference convened under subsection (1) shall have included in its agenda constitutional matters that directly affect the aboriginal peoples of Canada, and the Prime Minister of Canada shall invite representatives of those peoples to participate in the discussions on those matters.
>
> (3) The Prime Minister of Canada shall invite elected representatives of the governments of the Yukon Territory and the Northwest Territories to participate in the discussions on any item on the agenda of a conference convened under subsection (1) that, in the opinion of the Prime Minister, directly affects the Yukon Territory and the Northwest Territories.
>
> (4) Nothing in this section shall be construed so as to derogate from subsection 35(1).

(99) Prior to the enactment of Part V certain provisions of the Constitution of Canada and the provincial constitutions could be amended pursuant to the *Constitution Act, 1867*. See the footnotes to section 91, Class 1 and section 92, Class 1 thereof, *supra*. Other amendments to the Constitution could only be made by enactment of the Parliament of the United Kingdom.

(*a*) resolutions of the Senate and House of Commons; and

(*b*) resolutions of the legislative assemblies of at least two-thirds of the provinces that have, in the aggregate, according to the then latest general census, at least fifty per cent of the population of all the provinces.

Majority of members

(2) An amendment made under subsection (1) that derogates from the legislative powers, the proprietary rights or any other rights or privileges of the legislature or government of a province shall require a resolution supported by a majority of the members of each of the Senate, the House of Commons and the legislative assemblies required under subsection (1).

Expression of dissent

(3) An amendment referred to in subsection (2) shall not have effect in a province the legislative assembly of which has expressed its dissent thereto by resolution supported by a majority of its members prior to the issue of the proclamation to which the amendment relates unless that legislative assembly, subsequently, by resolution supported by a majority of its members, revokes its dissent and authorizes the amendment.

Revocation of dissent

(4) A resolution of dissent made for the purposes of subsection (3) may be revoked at any time before or after the issue of the proclamation to which it relates.

Restriction on proclamation

39. (1) A proclamation shall not be issued under subsection 38 (1) before the expiration of one year from the adoption of the resolution initiating the amendment procedure thereunder, unless the legislative assembly of each province has previously adopted a resolution of assent of dissent.

Idem

(2) A proclamation shall not be issued under subsection 38 (1) after the expiration of three years from the adoption of the resolution initiating the amendment procedure thereunder.

Compensation

40. Where an amendment is made under subsection 38(1) that transfers provincial legislative powers relating to education or other cultural matters from provincial legislatures to Parliament, Canada shall provide reasonable compensation to any province to which the amendment does not apply.

Amendment by unanimous consent

41. An amendment to the Constitution of Canada in relation to the following matters may be made by proclamation issued by the Governor General under the Great Seal of Canada only where authorized by resolutions of the Senate and House of Commons and of the legislative assembly of each province:

(*a*) the office of the Queen, the Governor General and the Lieutenant Governor of a province;

(*b*) the right of a province to a number of members in the House of Commons not less than the number of Senators by which the province is entitled to be represented at the time this Part comes into force;

(*c*) subject to section 43, the use of the English or the French language;

(*d*) the composition of the Supreme Court of Canada; and

(*e*) an amendment to this Part.

42. (1) An amendment to the Constitution of Canada in relation to the following matters may be made only in accordance with subsection 38(1):

Amendment by general procedure

(*a*) the principle of proportionate representation of the provinces in the House of Commons prescribed by the Constitution of Canada;

(*b*) the powers of the Senate and the method of selecting Senators;

(*c*) the number of members by which a province is entitled to be represented in the Senate and the residence qualifications of Senators;

(*d*) subject to paragraph 41(*d*), the Supreme Court of Canada;

(*e*) the extension of existing provinces into the territories; and

(*f*) notwithstanding any other law or practice, the establishment of new provinces.

(2) Subsections 38(2) to (4) do not apply in respect of amendments in relation to matters referred to in subsection (1).

Exception

43. An amendment to the Constitution of Canada in relation to any provision that applies to one or more, but not all, provinces, including

Amendment of provisions relating to some but not all provinces

(*a*) any alteration to boundaries between provinces, and

(*b*) any amendment to any provision that relates to the use of the English or the French language within a province, may be made by proclamation issued by the Governor General under the Great Seal of Canada only where so authorized by resolutions of the Senate and House of Commons and of the legislative assembly of each province to which the amendment applies.

Amendments by Parliament

44. Subject to sections 41 and 42, Parliament may exclusively make laws amending the Constitution of Canada in relation to the executive government of Canada or the Senate and House of Commons.

Amendments by provincial legislatures

45. Subject to section 41, the legislature of each province may exclusively make laws amending the constitution of the province.

Initiation of amendment procedures

46. (1) The procedures for amendment under sections 38, 41, 42 and 43 may be initiated either by the Senate or the House of Commons or by the legislative assembly of a province.

Revocation of authorization

(2) A resolution of assent made for the purposes of this Part may be revoked at any time before the issue of a proclamation authorized by it.

Amendments without Senate resolution

47. (1) An amendment to the Constitution of Canada made by proclamation under section 38, 41, 42 or 43 may be made without a resolution of the Senate authorizing the issue of the proclamation if, within one hundred and eighty days after the adoption by the House of Commons of a resolution authorizing its issue, the Senate has not adopted such a resolution and if, at any time after the expiration of that period, the House of Commons again adopts the resolution.

Computation of period

(2) Any period when Parliament is prorogued or dissolved shall not be counted in computing the one hundred and eighty day period referred to in subsection (1).

Advice to issue proclamation

48. The Queen's Privy Council for Canada shall advise the Governor General to issue a proclamation under this Part forthwith on the adoption of the resolutions required for an amendment made by proclamation under this Part.

Constitutional conference

49. A constitutional conference composed of the Prime Minister of Canada and the first ministers of the provinces shall be convened by the Prime Minister of Canada within fifteen years after this Part comes into force to review the provisions of this Part.

PART VI

AMENDMENT TO THE CONSTITUTION ACT, 1867

50.[100]

51.[101]

PART VII

GENERAL

Primacy of Constitution of Canada

52. (1) The Constitution of Canada is the supreme law of Canada, and any law that is inconsistent with the provisions of the Constitution is, to the extent of the inconsistency, of no force or effect.

Constitution of Canada

(2) The Constitution of Canada includes

(*a*) the *Canada Act 1982*, including this Act;

(*b*) the Acts and orders referred to in the schedule; and

(*c*) any amendment to any Act or order referred to in paragraph (*a*) or (*b*).

Amendments to Constitution of Canada

(3) Amendments to the Constitution of Canada shall be made only in accordance with the authority contained in the Constitution of Canada.

Repeals and new names

53. (1) The enactments referred to in Column I of the schedule are hereby repealed or amended to the extent indicated in Column II thereof and, unless repealed, shall continue as law in Canada under the names set out in Column III thereof.

Consequential amendments

(2) Every enactment, except the *Canada Act 1982*, that refers to an enactment referred to in the schedule by the name in Column I thereof is hereby amended by substituting for that name the corresponding name in Column III thereof, and any British North America Act not referred to in the schedule may be cited as the *Constitution Act* followed by the year and number, if any, of its enactment.

(100) The amendment is set out in the Consolidation of the *Constitution Act, 1867,* as section 92A thereof.

(101) The amendment is set out in the Consolidation of the *Constitution Act, 1867,* as the Sixth Schedule thereof.

Repeal and consequential amendments

54. Part IV is repealed on the day that is one year after this Part comes into force and this section may be repealed and this Act renumbered, consequentially upon the repeal of Part IV and this section, by proclamation issued by the Governor General under the Great Seal of Canada. [102]

54.1. [103]

French version of Constitution of Canada

55. A French version of the portions of the Constitution of Canada referred to in the schedule shall be prepared by the Minister of Justice of Canada as expeditiously as possible and, when any portion thereof sufficient to warrant action being taken has been so prepared, it shall be put forward for enactment by proclamation issued by the Governor General under the Great Seal of Canada pursuant to the procedure then applicable to an amendment of the same provisions of the Constitution of Canada.

English and French versions of certain constitutional texts

56. Where any portion of the Constitution of Canada has been or is enacted in English and French or where a French version of any portion of the Constitution is enacted pursuant to section 55, the English and French versions of that portion of the Constitution are equally authoritative.

English and French versions of this Act

57. The English and French versions of this Act are equally authoritative.

Commencement

58. Subject to section 59, this Act shall come into force on a day to be fixed by proclamation issued by the Queen or the Governor General under the Great Seal of Canada.[104]

Commencement of paragraph 23(1)(*a*) in respect of Quebec

59. (1) Paragraph 23(1)(*a*) shall come into force in respect of Quebec on a day to be fixed by proclamation issued by the Queen or the Governor General under the Great Seal of Canada.

---

(102) Part VII came into force on April 17, 1982. *See* SI/82-97.

(103) Section 54.1, which was added by the *Constitution Amendment Proclamation, 1983* (see SI/84-102), provided for the repeal of Part IV.1 and section 54.1 on April 18, 1987.

Section 54.1, as originally enacted, read as follows:

"**54.1** Part IV.1 and this section are repealed on April 18, 1987."

(104) The Act, with the exception of paragraph 23(1)(*a*) in respect of Quebec, came into force on April 17, 1982 by proclamation issued by the Queen. *See* SI/82-97.

(2) A proclamation under subsection (1) shall be issued only where authorized by the legislative assembly or government of Quebec.[105]

Authorization of Quebec

(3) This section may be repealed on the day paragraph 23(1)(*a*) comes into force in respect of Quebec and this Act amended and renumbered, consequentially upon the repeal of this section, by proclamation issued by the Queen or the Governor General under the Great Seal of Canada.

Repeal of this section

60. This Act may be cited as the *Constitution Act, 1982,* and the Constitution Acts 1867 to 1975 (No.2) and this Act may be cited together as the *Constitution Acts, 1867 to 1982.*

Short title and citations

61. A reference to the *"Constitution Acts, 1867 to 1982"* shall be deemed to include a reference to the *"Constitution Amendment Proclamation, 1983."*[106]

References

(105) No proclamation has been issued under section 59.

(106) Section 61 was added by the *Constitution Amendment Proclamation, 1983. See* SI/84-102.

See also section 3 of the *Constitution Act, 1985* (*Representation*), S.C. 1986, c. 8, Part I and the *Constitution Amendment, 1987 (Newfoundland Act)* SI/88-11.

INDEX

To the owner of this book

We hope that you have enjoyed *Parameters of Power*, second edition, and we would like to know as much about your experiences with this text as you would care to offer. Only through your comments and those of others can we learn how to make this a better text for future readers.

School ________________ Your instructor's name ______________________

Course ___________ Was the text required? _______ Recommended? _____

1. What did you like the most about *Parameters of Power*, second edition?

____

____

____

2. How useful was this text for your course?

____

____

____

3. Do you have any recommendations for ways to improve the next edition of this text?

____

____

____

4. In the space below or in a separate letter, please write any other comments you have about the book. (For example, please feel free to comment on reading level, writing style, terminology, design features, and learning aids.)

____

____

____

____

Optional

Your name ____________________________ Date ________________

May ITP Nelson quote you, either in promotion for *Parameters of Power*, second edition, or in future publishing ventures?

Yes _______ No _______

Thanks!

You can also send your comments to us via e-mail at
college_arts_hum@nelson.com

PLEASE TAPE SHUT. DO NOT STAPLE.

TAPE SHUT

TAPE SHUT

FOLD HERE

MAIL POSTE

Canada Post Corporation
Société canadienne des postes

Postage paid / Port payé
if mailed in Canada / si posté au Canada
Business Reply / Réponse d'affaires

0066102399 01

0066102399-M1K5G4-BR01

TAPE SHUT

TAPE SHUT

ITP NELSON
MARKET AND PRODUCT DEVELOPMENT
PO BOX 60225 STN BRM B
TORONTO ON M7Y 2H1